Great are the works of the LORD,
studied by all who rejoice in them.

Psalm 111:2

Constructive Christian Theology in the Worldwide Church

Edited by

William R. Barr

WILLIAM B. EERDMANS PUBLISHING COMPANY
GRAND RAPIDS, MICHIGAN / CAMBRIDGE, U.K.

© 1997 Wm. B. Eerdmans Publishing Co.

255 Jefferson Ave. S.E., Grand Rapids, Michigan 49503 /

P.O. Box 163, Cambridge CB3 9PU U.K.

Printed in the United States of America

02 01 00 99 98 97   7 6 5 4 3 2 1

Library of Congress Cataloging-in-Publication Data

Constructive Christian theology in the worldwide church /
edited by William R. Barr.
p.   cm.
Includes bibliographical references and indexes.
ISBN 0-8028-4143-0 (pbk.: alk. paper)
1. Theology, Doctrinal. 2. Christianity and culture.
I. Barr, William R., 1934- .
BT80.C65   1997
230 — dc21   96-53630
CIP

Contents

v

Part IV: The Significance of Jesus Christ

Preface

Constructing — and reconstructing — Christian theology is a work of the whole church. Certainly, academically educated theologians can assist in this effort, but seeking a deeper and clearer articulation of Christian faith in the contemporary setting involves all Christians and the church as a whole. Too often, however, works on theology, and especially works on constructive or systematic theology, do not reflect this global quest for understanding in the church. This symposium/anthology is an attempt to give a more inclusive account of the contributions Christians from various parts of the world are making to theological understanding in our time. Not all these contributions take the form of scholarly essays; some are expressed in songs, dances, stories, and rituals of people in their native cultures as well as in living out their faith in their work, worship, and interactions with others within and outside the church.

Surely in the future the church's theology and works in theology will have to reflect this global quest more adequately than has been the case to date. Increasingly, with new technologies and almost instantaneous worldwide communication, we now have the capability of entering immediately into conversation with peoples throughout the world community. As this global conversation develops also within the church, and with those of other views outside the church, it will include theological understanding formed in many different situations, cultural contexts, and traditions; therefore it should not be surprising that there will be different points of view even among Christians. This cross-cultural conversation will require all of the participants to develop ways of communicating theological insights with integrity not only to people within their own cultural contexts but also to those in other situations and contexts than their own.

In this conversation and interaction of Christians around the world, their different perspectives as well as the common faith they share will inform this discussion. Hopefully what will occur will be something like the conversation

around the family table in which both individual differences and common
loyalty and family solidarity bind the members together. But of course this
conversation is not only an in-house discussion; it occurs also as Christians join
with others in the struggle for life in our conflictive world. This volume invites
you, the reader, also to share in this conversation. One of the aims of this
symposium is to stimulate your own thinking as part of the wider and ongoing
conversation on these matters.

To be sure, not all theological views current within the church today are
represented here. The present collection is at best only a "sampler," as it were,
of some of the views being articulated within the worldwide Christian community. The contributions included here were selected to indicate something of
the range of current theological reflection as well as some growing edges of
creative and conservative thinking among Christians around the world on the
central topics or doctrines of Christian faith. It should be clear that these
contributions are part of an ongoing conversation within the Christian community and in relations of Christians with those of other faiths and persuasions
concerning the meaning and implications of Christian faith today. That is always
an unfinished task; but it is a task that the gospel itself, and not only the needs
of the time, requires of Christians and the church.

Acknowledgments

Gratitude is expressed to the following journals for permission to reprint materials included in this collection: *African Theological Journal,* Orville W. Nyblade, editor (Lutheran Theological College, Makumira, Tanzania); *Chinese Theological Review,* Jancie Wickeri, editor (Foundation for Theological Education in Southeast Asia, Holland, MI); *Epiphany: A Journal of Faith and Insight,* Mother Marcia Corbett, editor (Christ the Savior Brotherhood, Indianapolis, IN); *The Ecumenical Review,* Konrad Raiser, editor (World Council of Churches, Geneva, Switzerland); *Evangelical Journal,* William S. Sailer, editor (Evangelical School of Theology, Myerstown, PA); *Evangelical Quarterly: An International Review of Bible and Theology,* I. Howard Marshall, editor (Paternoster Periodicals, Carlisle, Cumbria); *Evangelical Review of Theology,* Bruce J. Nicholls, editor (World Evangelical Fellowship, Paternoster Publications, Carlisle, Cumbria); *Greek Orthodox Theological Review,* The Rev. Dr. Nomikos Michael Vaporis et al., editors (Holy Cross Greek Orthodox School of Theology, Brookline, MA); *The International Review of Missions,* Christopher Duraising, editor (World Council of Churches, Geneva, Switzerland); *The Journal of the Interdenominational Theological Center* (The ITC Press, Atlanta, GA); *Journal of Ecumenical Studies,* Leonard Swidler, editor, Nancy E. Krody, managing editor (Temple University, Philadelphia, PA); *Journal of the Evangelical Theological Society,* Ronald Youngblood, editor (Bethel Seminary West, San Diego, CA); *Journal of Feminist Studies in Religion,* Elizabeth Pritchard, managing editor (Harvard Divinity School, Cambridge, MA); *The Nigerian Journal of Theology* (Catholic Theological Association of Nigeria, Imo State, Nigeria); *Modern Theology,* L. Gregory Jones and Stephen Fowl, editors (Blackwell Publishers, Oxford, England); *The Pacific Journal of Theology,* Carrie Walker-Jones, editor (The South Pacific Association of Theological Schools, Suva, Fiji); *Pacifica: Journal of the Melbourne College of Divinity,* John Honner, S.J., editor (Melbourne, Australia); *Sobornost, Incorporating Eastern Churches Review,* Sergei Hackel, editor (1 Canterbury Road, Oxford, England); *Sojourners,* Jim Wallis et al., editors (Washington, D.C.); *Themelios: An International Journal for Theological and Religious Studies Students* (Religious and Theological Studies Fellowship, Leicester, England); *Theology Today,* Thomas G. Long and Patrick D. Miller, editors (Princeton Theological Seminary, Princeton, NJ); *Toronto Journal of Theology,* Phyllis Airhart et al., editors (Toronto School of Theology, Toronto, Ontario, Canada); *Wesleyan Theological Journal,* Barry L. Callen, editor (Wesleyan Theological Society, Wilmore, KY); *Westminster Theological Journal,* Moisés Silva, editor (Westminster Theological Seminary, Philadelphia, PA).

In addition, I wish to express deep gratitude to Barbara Miller for her patient and diligent work in transcribing this manuscript and for helpful suggestions along the way.

Finally, I am grateful to my family — to Donna, Greg, and Jennifer — for their support in my work on this project.

WILLIAM R. BARR

Contributors

William R. Barr is Professor of Theology at Lexington Theological Seminary, Lexington, Kentucky, and is coeditor, with Rena Yocom, of *The Church in the Movement of the Spirit* (1994).

Frans Jozef van Beeck, S.J., teaches theology at Loyola University, Chicago. His major writing to date is a multivolume systematic theology, *God Encountered: A Contemporary Catholic Systematic Theology* (3 vols., 1989-1995).

Carol P. Christ is the author of *Diving Deep and Surfacing* (3rd ed., 1995), *Laughter of Aphrodite* (1987), *Odyssey with the Goddess* (1995), and the forthcoming *Goddess Emerging: A Theology*. With Judith Plaskow, she co-edited *Womanspirit Rising* (1978) and *Weaving the Visions* (1989).

John Y. May, B.A., Lehigh University, M.A., University of Pittsburgh, is a lay theologian and a member of the American Scientific Affiliation.

Verna E. F. Harrison is a Byzantinist teaching at the University of Berkeley, California. She is the author of *Grace and Human Freedom according to St. Gregory of Nyssa* (1992).

Romney M. Moseley is Associate Professor of Divinity at Trinity College, Toronto School of Theology.

Kan Baoping is a graduate of Nanjing Theological Seminary and now teaches on the faculty there.

Harvie M. Conn is Professor of Missions at Westminster Theological Seminary. He earlier served for twelve years as a missionary to Korea. He is the author of *Contemporary World Theology* (1974) and *Eternal Word and Changing Worlds: Theology, Anthropology, and Mission in Trialogue* (1992), among other works.

The Rev. Dr. Emmanuel Clapsis teaches theology at the Holy Cross Greek Orthodox School of Theology, Brookline, MA, USA. He is the author of numerous articles and chapters in books.

Susan B. Thistlethwaite teaches theology at Chicago Theological Seminary. She is the author of *Sex, Race and God: Christian Feminism in Black and White* (1989), and, with Mary Potter Engel, she edited *Lift Every Voice: Constructing Christian Theologies from the Underside* (1990) and *Beyond Theological Tourism: Mentoring as a Grassroots Approach to Theological Education* (1994).

Howard A. Snyder, formerly a pastor and missionary to Brazil, is presently Associate Professor of Church Renewal at United Theological Seminary in Dayton, Ohio. He is the author of *The Community of the King* (1977), *Liberating the Church* (1983), and *Models of the Kingdom* (1991), among other writings.

John Mbiti, a Kenyan theologian, and formerly director of the World Council of Churches Study Center, is now a pastor and lecturer in Burgdorf, Switzerland. He is author of *Bible and Theology in African Christianity* (1986), *Concepts of God in Africa* (1970), *New Testament Eschatology in an African Background* (1971), and *The Prayers of African Religion* (1975), among other works.

Michael Welker is currently Professor of Systematic Theology at the University of Heidelberg. His most recent work is *God the Spirit* (1994).

Sr. Macrina is chair of the editorial board of the Orthodox journal *Epiphany*, published in Indianapolis, Indiana.

Sr. Keiti Ann Kanongata'a was the keynote speaker at the South Pacific Association of Theological Schools' regionwide consultation on "Women and Ministry in the Pacific in the 1990s," held in Suva, Fiji.

Dr. George E. Tinker (Osage-Cherokee) is Assistant Professor of Cross-cultural Ministries at Iliff School of Theology, Denver, Colorado, USA. He is the author of *Missionary Conquest: The Gospel and Native American Genocide* (1993), among other writings.

Tiina Allik teaches in the Department of Religious Studies at Loyola University, New Orleans, Louisiana, USA.

David Parker is the Academic Dean of the Bible College of Queensland, Australia. He has written on the evangelical heritage of Australian Protestantism.

Stanley J. Samartha (Church of South India) is a visiting professor at the United Theological College in Bangalore, South India. He was the first director of the World Council of Churches' Programme on Dialogue with Other Living Faiths and Ideologies. He is the author of *Courage for Dialogue* (1981), *The Search for a New Hermeneutics in Asian Christian Theology* (1987), and *One Christ, Many Religions: Toward a Revised Christology* (1991), among other works.

Kwok Pui-lan is a lecturer in the religion department at the Chinese University of Hong Kong. She is the author of *Chinese Women and Christianity* (1992) and most recently *Discovering the Bible in the Nonbiblical World* (1995).

Evaristi Magoti, W.F., is a Roman Catholic priest presently serving in Portugal.

Gerald L. Bray lectures at Oak Hill College in London, U.K. He is the author of *Holiness and the Will of God* (1979) and *Creeds, Councils and Christ* (1984).

S. Mark Heim, a member of the American Baptist Churches in the U.S.A., has been an Assistant Professor of Christian Theology at the Andover Newton Theological School since 1982, following a pastorate at the Baptist church in Franklin, NH, and a teaching assistantship at Boston College. He is the author of *Is Christ the Only Way?* (1985) and coedited, with T. Stylianopoulos, *Spirit of Truth: Ecumenical Perspectives on the Holy Spirit* (1986). His articles and book reviews have appeared in a variety of denominational and ecumenical scholarly journals.

Ellen Leonard, C.S.J., is Associate Professor of Theology at St. Michael's College, Toronto School of Theology. She contributed a chapter to *Imaging Christ: Politics, Art, Spirituality,* published by Proceedings of the Theology Institute (1991).

Jacquelyn Grant is Assistant Professor of Systematic Theology at the Interdenominational Theological Center (ITC) in Atlanta, GA. She is the author of *White Women's Christ and Black Women's Jesus* (1984).

John Onaiyekan is a Nigerian theologian and Roman Catholic bishop of Ilọrin. He has participated in a number of ecumenical meetings and was a delegate to the Fifth World Conference on Faith and Order.

Denis Edwards teaches theology at Saint Francis Xavier Seminary in South Australia. He is the author of *What Are They Saying About Salvation?* (1986) and *Jesus the Wisdom of God: An Ecological Theology* (1995).

Joyce Hollyday is Associate Editor of *Sojourners* magazine. She has edited, with Jim Wallis, *Cloud of Witness* (1991). ·

Thor Halvor Hovland teaches at the Lutheran Theological Seminary, Mapumulo, Natal, Africa.

Gennadios Limouris is on the staff of the Faith and Order Department of the World Council of Churches, Geneva, Switzerland. He is the editor of *Church, Kingdom, World: The Church as Mystery and Prophetic Sign* (1986). He has also edited *Icons: Windows on Eternity* (1990), *Justice, Peace and the Integrity of Creation: Insights from Orthodoxy* (1990), *Orthodox Perspectives on Baptism, Eucharist, and Ministry* (1985), and *Orthodox Visions of Ecumenism* (1994).

C. René Padilla is chair of The International Fellowship of Evangelical Mission Theologians and general secretary of the Latin American Theological Fraternity in Buenos Aires, Argentina. He is the coeditor, with Mark Lau Branson, of *Conflict and Context: Hermeneutics in the Americas* (1986).

Julio de Santa Ana is director of the Ecumenical Centre for Evangelism and Popular Education, São Paulo, Brazil. He is the editor of *Good News to the Poor* (1977), *Protestantismo, cultura y sociedad* (1970), *Towards a Church of the Poor* (1979), and *Separation Without Hope?* (1978).

Nigel Biggar is Chaplain of Oriel College and librarian of Latimer House, the University of Oxford. He is the editor of *Cities of Gods: Faith, Politics, and Pluralism in Judaism, Christianity, and Islam* (1986) and the author of *The Hastening That Waits: Karl Barth's Ethics* (1993).

Jacques Goulet teaches at Mount Saint Vincent University in Halifax, Nova Scotia.

Aruna Gnanadason has served as the executive secretary of the All India Council of Christian Women/National Council of Churches in India. She now serves as director of the World Council of Churches' subunit on Women in Church and Society. She is the author of *No Longer a Secret: The Church and Violence against Women* (1993).

Paula M. Cooey is Professor of Religion at Trinity University in San Antonio. She is the author of *Jonathan Edwards on Nature and Destiny* (1985), and *Religious Imagination and the Body: A Feminist Analysis* (1994), and coeditor of *After Patriarchy: Feminist Transformations of the World Religions* (1991).

Kosuke Koyama has taught in Thailand and New Zealand, and now teaches at Union Theological Seminary in New York City. He is the author of a number of works, including *Waterbuffalo Theology* (1974), *Three Mile an Hour God* (1979), and *Mount Fuji and Mount Sinai: A Pilgrimage in Theology* (1984).

Ignatios IV is the Greek Orthodox Patriarch of Antioch and All the East and is a president of the World Council of Churches.

John R. Sachs, S.J., is Assistant Professor of Systematic Theology at Weston School of Theology. He is author of *The Christian View of Humanity: Basic Christian Anthropology* (1991).

William V. Crockett is Associate Professor of New Testament at Alliance Theological Seminary in Nyack, New York. He is editor and contributor to *Four Views on Hell* (1992).

INTRODUCTION

Re-forming Theology in the
Global Conversation

WILLIAM R. BARR

Today and in the years ahead Christian theology will need to be developed through interaction and conversation among Christians around the world in the worldwide church, and with those of other persuasions in the world community.[1] This is clear already from the fact that increasingly we are rubbing shoulders with persons of other cultures in our local communities through our work, through the products we use, through the news media, and via the global Internet, as well as in many other ways. Furthermore, the need for global conversation is evident from the fact that creative theological voices are speaking out today from many lands and cultures. The European-American hegemony in modern Christian theology is rapidly passing as we enter what some speak of as a "postmodern" era. Here we encounter a rich variety of perspectives and ways of understanding, including theological understanding, among the world's peoples. This need for interaction holds true as well in the church, for the church has become a worldwide community embracing peoples of many different languages, perspectives, customs, and ways of life, and these shape as well as are shaped by theological understanding.

I. Contextual Concreteness vs. Contextual Captivity

The concern to do theology concretely within particular cultural and social contexts has to be affirmed on the basis of the Christian proclamation of the Incarna-

---

1. Increased dialogue between Christians and those of other faiths is urgently needed. But to pursue such discussion in this volume would greatly expand its limits and perhaps take us far afield. However, several of the essays included here call for and offer suggestions for interreligious dialogue and make proposals for how such dialogue should be approached from a Christian perspective.

tion, God's self-presentation within a particular historical context in the history of Israel and in the person of Jesus Christ. Because theology has to do with the juncture of the divine and the historical, the intersection of human cries for help and the freely given gift of divine help and redemption, it must address the specific realities of its situation in terms that are understandable within that situation. The very nature of the Christian proclamation therefore requires that theological understanding be concretely contextual in relating the gospel and its redemptive significance to the life of every people to whom the gospel comes.

And, indeed, all theologies, whether they acknowledge it or not, are contextual in that they inevitably reflect the culture in which they emerge. Even if they are presented as universally valid, that is to say, applicable to all peoples, when those in other cultural contexts reflect critically on what they hear they recognize that such theologies are influenced by presuppositions, values, perceptions, images, and the language of their particular cultural and social origins. The increasing awareness of the cultural shaping of theological understanding is leading Christians in all parts of the world — in Asia, Africa, Latin America, and elsewhere — to develop intentionally contextual theologies addressed to their particular situations.

This development offers a number of advantages. First and most important, it implants the gospel more deeply in the life of the people, drawing upon resources from their particular cultural context — images, stories, and customs — to interpret and make understandable theological meaning. At the same time such implantation can show the prophetic power of the gospel to transform cultural assumptions and values. This process is sometimes called "inculturation," "contextualization," or "indigenization,"[2] and involves a creative and transformative transplanting of the gospel from one cultural context to another. As such, it is to be distinguished from "acculturation," merely accommodating or conforming the gospel to the worldview and values of a culture. Thus, in recent years we have seen the development of Black, Hispanic, African, Asian, Pacific Islands, Latin American, and Caribbean theologies in distinction from European and North American theologies.

To say this is not simply to endorse a currently faddish pluralism but rather to recognize that global pluralism can contribute to a fuller and more varied understanding of the gospel.

---

2. These terms exhibit different nuances and connotations, but all have to do with the implanting of the gospel in various cultural and social contexts. See further on this, Aylward Shorter, *Toward a Theology of Inculturation* (Maryknoll, NY: Orbis Books, 1988); Mercy Amba Oduyoye, *Hearing and Knowing: Theological Reflections on Christianity in Africa* (Maryknoll, NY: Orbis Books, 1986), esp. 53-55; Somen Das, ed., *Christian Faith and Multiform Culture in India* (Bangalore: United Theological College, 1987); and Rodrigo D. Tano, *Theology in the Philippine Setting: A Case Study in the Contextualization of Theology* (Quezon City, the Philippines: New Day Publishers, 1981). See also on this matter, Hilary Regan and Alan J. Torrance, eds., *Christ and Context: The Confrontation between Gospel and Culture* (Edinburgh: T & T Clark, 1993).

But such cultural contextualization can easily slip into cultural captivity or provincialism if it overlooks the fact that the gospel cannot be confined to any one cultural context but reaches across cultural boundaries. It can also obscure the fact that the understanding of the gospel in all our various contexts impinges upon and affects those in other contexts in our increasingly interdependent world society. As the Sri Lankan theologian Tissa Balasuriya points out, the influence of contextual theologies cannot be limited to their particular contexts, for they also have consequences for those in other contexts.[3] Because the gospel is the message and power of God's creative-redemptive work of justice and reconciliation breaking through and breaking down all humanly constructed divisions, it cannot be confined to any one context. Even though we may not be able to formulate a transcultural theology, this does not mean that the gospel is not itself universal nor that the God to which it witnesses is not the God of all peoples. Indeed, precisely in conversation across cultures there may come a clearer recognition both of the situationally concrete and the universal reach of the gospel. This leads Balasuriya to go on to contend that "rejection of the false universalisms of the past should not dissuade us from at least trying to evolve the general outlines of a truly universal theology grounded in the basic elements of the human condition and the overall world situation."[4] But whether a universal theology can be built on such a basis is nonetheless debatable since perception of the human condition and of the current world situation is also subject to a variety of readings across cultures (as a comparison of, say, African and Asian perspectives makes clear). In any case, what seems to be indisputable is that conversation across cultural boundaries might clarify not only the human condition but also other aspects of theological understanding. This is not to overlook the difficulties and problems in such conversations,[5] such as differences in language and ways of viewing the world; but addressing these difficulties can lead to greater understanding among those who continue in this conversation with goodwill.

II. The Gospel and Culture(s)

Engaging in cross-cultural theological discussion brings to the fore many issues, some more local and others more general in scope, and it brings to bear new

3. See Tissa Balasuriya, *Planetary Theology* (Maryknoll, NY: Orbis Books, 1984), 14.
4. Ibid.
5. See further on this, e.g., José M. de Mesa, *In Solidarity with Culture: Studies in Theological Re-rooting*, Maryhill Studies 4 (Quezon City, the Philippines: Maryhill School of Theology, 1987); Enoch H. Oglesby, *Born in the Fire: Case Studies in Christian Ethics and Globalization* (New York: Pilgrim Press, 1990); and Max Stackhouse, *Apologia: Contextualization, Globalization, and Mission in Theological Education* (Grand Rapids, MI: Wm. B. Eerdmans, 1987).

perspectives on perennial theological issues, such as hermeneutics, which has to do with different ways of understanding; the authority and interpretation of Scripture and the role of church traditions; the nature of God's activity and how it is to be discerned in today's world; and the interpretation in various cultures of the classical *loci* (doctrines) of Christian theology — namely, God, Christ, the church, and so on. As in all theological inquiry, the primary aim is to seek a clearer, deeper understanding of God in relation to the world and human life for the sake of more faithful and responsible participation in God's mission in and for the world. But cross-cultural discussion makes clear that there are many and various ways in which such understanding takes shape in different cultural contexts.

Furthermore, in cross-cultural conversation it should not be overlooked that in some cultures, and especially among the poor and oppressed in every culture, the experience of God is often expressed more in songs and stories, and sometimes in dance and customs, than in concepts and systems of doc-trine.[6] The wisdom expressed in such forms may articulate a depth and passion of theological understanding that goes beyond logically precise concepts and argumentation. Consequently, conversation across cultures must take into account a wide range of ways of communicating theological understanding. That is why this volume includes stories and poems as well as theological essays.

Yet in many and various ways Christians in their particular cultures and traditions (with a small "t") are trying more fully to understand and articulate their shared faith-Tradition (with a capital "T") as Christians, their unity in the one Christ and the one God that constitutes their basic and essential unity in the church. Just as it would be a mistake, therefore, to downplay the particular confessional, denominational, and cultural traditions in which the church exists, so it would be even more a mistake to allow a concentration on these to obscure the common Tradition in which Christians participate and in which they are joined in the body of Christ. As at Pentecost each one heard the gospel pro-claimed in her or his own language,[7] Christians must recognize that their varied theological understandings are guided by the one Spirit and are varied expres-sions of the one gospel that they are called to proclaim. Cross-cultural theolog-ical conversation is therefore not merely a pastime for scholars but a calling of the church and Christians. Theirs is the duty to proclaim and interpret the gospel not only in their different situations but also in their interactions and life together with others in the global community, "so that the world may believe" (John 17:21).

6. As pointed out, e.g., by Susan Brooks Thistlethwaite and Mary Potter Engel, eds., *Lift Every Voice: Constructing Christian Theologies from the Underside* (San Francisco: Harper & Row Publishers, 1990), 6.

7. "How is it that we hear, each of us, [the gospel] in our own native language?" (Acts 2:8).

III. Different Paths to Theological Understanding

However, not only do Christians in different cultures have different views concerning God, Christ, the church, and the other *loci*, but Christians in various cultures (and in minority cultures within a dominant culture) understand and express their understanding in distinctively different ways. For instance, consultations of women from various cultures bring to the fore not only that women's experience has often been ignored or minimized in male-dominated cultures but also that women's experiences are distinctive and extremely varied in African, Asian, Pacific Islands, and Latin American contexts. Not only does the experience of women give a new cast to traditional theological concepts — such as notions of God's power and rule in creation — but women often take different approaches to theology, weaving theological understanding not so much out of concepts as out of vibrant images, stories, memories and hopes.[8]

Somewhat similar is the approach to theological understanding characteristic of Pacific Islands peoples and those of other so-called "primitive" cultures. As Sevati Tuwere, a Fijian theologian, puts it, such theologies not only emphasize stories, songs, dance, and rituals but they also often have a strong sense of "place," that theology is or should be generated out of a "sacred place."[9] God is perceived not only in the course of historical events but also as dwelling in a special place in the midst of the people. In biblical imagery this is referred to as God's "tabernacling" among the people; in the imagery of the Islands, it is understood as the sacred mountain or grove in which the divine is encountered. Such perceptions have concrete physical, geographical, and symbolic locations — as well as important implications for God's care for and indwelling of creation.[10]

As the contributions in this volume make evident, there is no one way of seeking theological understanding. Rather, consideration needs to be given to a wide variety of ways of coming to deeper theological understanding. But this does not necessarily imply a relativism in which no critical judgments can be made; what it does demand is careful listening to and consideration of what has been found through ways of seeking theological wisdom that are

8. See on this, e.g., Virginia Fabella and Mercy Amba Oduyoye, *With Passion and Compassion: Third World Women Doing Theology* (Maryknoll, NY: Orbis Books, 1989); Elsa Tamez, ed., *Through Her Eyes: Women's Theology from Latin America* (Maryknoll, NY: Orbis Books, 1990); and Letty Russell et al., eds., *Inheriting Our Mothers' Gardens: Feminist Theology in Third World Perspective* (Philadelphia: The Westminster Press, 1988).

9. Sevati Tuwere, "Emerging Themes for a Pacific Theology," *Pacific Journal of Theology,* Series II, No. 7 (1992): esp. 52-53. There are similarities here also to Native American perspectives, as George Tinker points out in his essay "The Full Circle of Liberation: An American Indian Theology of Place," *Sojourners* 21 (Oct. 1992): 12-17. See also his essay "The Integrity of Creation: Restoring Trinitarian Balance" in Part III of this volume.

10. See, e.g., David Hallman, ed., *Ecotheology: Insights from South and North* (Maryknoll, NY: Orbis Books, 1994).

different from our own. It not only requires that we try to ascertain why and how the perspectives of others may be similar to or different from ours. It also asks that we try, as far as possible, to see things from others' points of view, through their eyes, before making judgments concerning their views. Such dialogue requires courage, patience, and empathetic understanding. But it also holds the promise and potential of helping its participants come to a better understanding not only of the views of others but of their own views as well.

IV. A Round-table Discussion

Clearly, then, a necessary presupposition of any serious cross-cultural theological discussion must be what is sometimes spoken of as a "level playing field," meaning that no view is from the outset more privileged than others. But a better image, I would suggest, may be that of a round-table discussion at which all participants have equal opportunity to present their views and enter into conversation with others. This is not to overlook that in the current world situation economic and social realities do not give all the participants in the discussion equal access to the table as far as education, possibilities of travel, and access to media of communication, publication, and dissemination of their views are concerned. Especially the poor and marginalized are disadvantaged in gaining access to such discussion; therefore, it is important to make sure that their voices are included and attended to.

Robert Schreiter asks pointedly whether arrangements for and practice of global conversation, even in the church, allow for such varied and divergent contributions to the discussion, and whether participants are willing to re-view theology not provincially but at the intersection of global and local concerns.[11] But such willingness may have to develop out of growing trust and openness among participants in the course of the conversation as they struggle to understand and respond to views different from their own.

Such cross-cultural conversation may open up to all the participants a new and larger vision of cooperative interaction among those of different views not only on global and regional levels but also in local communities and congregations, where there is also a wide range of theological perspectives among Christians and churches.

The round-table discussion modeled in this collection may (and hopefully will) serve to stimulate such discussions among Christians in local communities as well as in wider arenas within the global church.

---

11. Robert J. Schreiter, "Christian Theology between the Global and the Local," *Theological Education* 29 (Spring 1993): 113-26.

V. The Agenda of Christian Global Discussion

However, it cannot simply be assumed that all participants even in Christian theological discussion will be able to agree on an agenda for cross-cultural conversation. A number of voices today call for setting aside the classical theological agenda (which was developed through Western Christianity) in favor of what are perceived as more pressing present concerns, such as the ecological crisis, the population explosion, growing disparity between wealthy and economically poorer countries, the spread of AIDS, urban violence, and the like. Unquestionably, theology today and in the future must give careful attention to such issues. But if theology is not simply to echo current public discussion of such issues, it must bring to bear in consideration of them insights gained from the theological tradition, study of Scripture, and the gospel's proclamation of God's revelation. In this effort it is necessary to reflect on the basic components or themes of Christian faith. That is why this volume is structured around the classic themes of Christian theology and attempts to bring into conversation concerning them perspectives from different cultural, racial, confessional, and gender points of view around the world.

Yet, addressing the classic themes of Christian faith in cross-cultural discussion can be done responsibly only in awareness of and in relation to the urgent social and personal issues of our time. The pieces collected here reflect such concerns. They express creative and critical thinking on classical Christian themes in relation to the contemporary situation. All participants are concerned to understand more deeply and clearly the mystery of God as revealed in Christ and through the Spirit in relation to the contemporary situation. At the same time they recognize that, as David Wells puts it, the aim of theology is not to "master" the subject of this knowledge but rather to come to a greater realization and appreciation of its utter inexhaustibility.[12] But because in Christian perspective God is not a remote and totally hidden mystery but rather a God who wills to be known, theology must speak of the revelation of this God in the language and life of every culture to which the gospel comes. It is just this consideration that constitutes, as Wells notes, the "missionary nature of theology," its boundaries-transcending impulse. And certainly in our contemporary situation this task requires not only intracultural but also cross-cultural conversation.

12. See David Wells, "The Theologian's Craft," in John D. Woodbridge and Thomas Edward McComiskey, eds., *Doing Theology in Today's World* (Grand Rapids, MI: Zondervan Publishing House, 1991), 171. See also the elaboration of this view in Wells's recent work *God in the Wasteland: The Reality of Truth in a World of Fading Dreams* (Grand Rapids, MI: Wm. B. Eerdmans Publishing Co., 1994).

VI. Theology as an Always Unfinished Task

Cross-cultural theological discussion exposes the limits of every theological view and reminds those engaged in such discussion that theology is never, at least in this life, finished. This realization arises already from recognition of the transcendent mystery of God that our finite minds can never fully comprehend (for, as Isa. 55:8-9 reminds us, God's thoughts are "not your thoughts, nor are your ways my ways, says the LORD. For as the heavens are higher than the earth, so are my ways higher than your ways and my thoughts than your thoughts"). If Christians and theologians are sometimes prone to forget that this is so within their own cultural frameworks of understanding, the encounter with those from other cultural perspectives can jar them awake to the limits of all human attempts to articulate the awesome mystery of the God manifested in the gospel and known in the life and suffering of people.[13] Even those who believe that God has revealed a certain deposit of truths or propositions that are essential to Christian faith have to admit that there is still much more to be known of God than we presently know and understand, and that even our best knowledge of God is, as Paul suggests, as though seen in a mirror dimly.

But the recognition of the limits of theological understanding is not only an acknowledgment of the finite and historically conditioned character of all human knowledge; it is also, in the Christian perspective, an expectation and anticipation of a fuller theological understanding toward which and into which God through the power of the Holy Spirit promises to lead those who press on in faith and hope. As Wolfhart Pannenberg has said, theological knowledge is always "preliminary knowledge" (vorläufig Erkenntnis), a knowledge that anticipates the future fullness of God's revelation.[14] Because of this, theological understanding is always a venture in hope. Though in this life such understanding shares in the struggling and suffering creation and reflects that struggle in its own fallibility and limitations, it is a vision that can be continually enlarged through interaction with others on the way to the fullness of life in God's future.

One clear indication of this is that participation in cross-cultural interaction involves an encounter with the other(s) whose perspectives cannot be simply assimilated to our own, and therefore whose views expose the limits of our own understanding while also challenging us to further and fuller understanding.

13. See further on this, e.g., Juan G. Feliciano, "Suffering: A Hispanic Epistemology," Journal of Hispanic/Latino Theology 2 (August 1994): 41-50; also James H. Cone, "Black Theology and the Imperative and Dilemma of Solidarity," in Lorine M. Getz and Ruy O. Costa, eds., Struggles for Solidarity: Liberation Theologies (Minneapolis: Augsburg Fortress Press, 1992), 47-48.

14. Wolfhart Pannenberg, Systematic Theology, vol. 1, trans. Geoffrey W. Bromiley (Grand Rapids, MI: Wm. B. Eerdmans Publishing Co., 1991), 16 and 55-58.

As the British Quaker theologian Rex Ambler has pointed out, though we face many challenges and difficulties as we work with others to fashion a sustainable world community toward the twenty-first century, if these difficulties are not to overwhelm us they must be seen in the perspective of faith in God, who is with us in this struggle, empowering people with vision and courage to press on in solidarity with those who suffer in hope of the liberation, healing, and transformation of creation.[15]

The cross-cultural theological discussion contained in this volume manifests the promise as well as the struggle toward this aim. These contributions obviously display basic differences and even disagreements among Christians. But it may be that even such differences can help lead us into deeper theological understanding. And each step in such understanding opens even larger vistas that beckon us on. The more we know, or think we know, in this quest, the more it seems there is yet to know. That is why the conversation must be ongoing. It is also why we will never cease to learn from conversation with one another, both within and across cultures.

15. Rex Ambler, *Global Theology: The Meaning of Faith in the Present World Crisis* (London: SCM Press Ltd./Philadelphia: Trinity Press International, 1990), 37-41.

PART I

Constructing Theology
from Diverse Perspectives

INTRODUCING THE ISSUE

Speaking of God Today

How do we come to a true knowledge of God? And how should such knowledge be expressed, tested, and communicated in the contemporary situation? These are the basic questions of what is called theological method. Certainly these questions are framed and dealt with in quite different ways as Christians gather on a beach in Fiji, talk with others in working for justice, congregate in a rural village in India, gather around a fire on the African savannas, reflect together in a North American congregation or seminary, or listen to a renowned theologian in a European university lecture hall. But in one way or another, all who think about their faith have to deal with such questions in giving account of their knowledge of God.

The basic question of how to come to true knowledge of God also includes several other, related questions such as: Where should we turn in seeking knowledge of God (the question of the source or sources of theological understanding)? How should we proceed in developing theological understanding (the question of the stages and progression in theological reflection), and What is or should be normative in judging the truthfulness, adequacy, and fruitfulness of theological knowledge? Today theological method must also include consideration of biblical hermeneutics, contextual perception and articulation of faith, and its personal and social implications.

These questions are not as abstract as they might at first appear. For in seeking to live faithfully we have to be concerned about the basis and validity of our knowledge of God. Have we understood God aright? And are we really following in God's way rather than simply "going with the flow"?

In wrestling with such questions, Christians generally turn to Scripture in quest of divine revelation. As some Christians see it, Scripture itself is that revelation, either in the form of a body of ideas or doctrines or as a narrative or story in the development of which God and God's will are disclosed. But some other Christians consider such a view too limited, as does, for example, progressive Catholic theologian Frans Jozef van Beeck, who argues in his contribution in this section that revelation as God's personal self-communication to those who receive it is a relation in which content (ideas and propositions) and process (the dynamic encounter and interaction of God and human beings) are inseparably connected. Thus knowledge of God is more, he says, than merely grasping certain concepts; it involves also an affirmative response of one's whole life and the life of a people to God's self-communication.

Drawing on women's experience and a critical interpretation of Elisabeth Schüssler Fiorenza's views, Carol Christ speaks of theology as "embodied thinking," thinking that involves the whole person and that is perceptive and imaginative. She recognizes the historically conditioned character of theological views but argues, against a pragmatic reductionism, that such views make a revisable but definitive claim to truth.

John May, a lay theologian speaking out of an evangelical background, insists that in Scripture revelation signifies primarily the communication of God's word as conveying an objective and intelligible knowledge of God. This is not incompatible with faith as trust and commitment, he argues, but rather is the cognitive aspect of faith that undergirds its volitional and relational aspects.

That Eastern Orthodox Christianity brings distinctive insights to this discussion is exhibited in Verna Harrison's contribution, in which she compares the theologian to an iconographer who forms concepts and verbal pictures reflective of transcendent divine reality. She suggests that artistic and conceptual modes of expression can mutually balance and inform each other.

Yet, as Caribbean theologian Romney Moseley points out, theological understanding is always shaped in a particular social and cultural context. Furthermore, theology is not only what academic theologians say but is also the way the church expresses its faith in how it lives in the world. He points out that the church in the Caribbean and in other areas of what is called the Third World is struggling to overcome legacies of colonialism and domination and trying to forge its own witness to the gospel in the midst of rapidly changing economic and political forces.

The contextual formation of theological understanding is underscored by Kan Baoping, speaking from his Chinese background and experience. Pointing out that all theology reflects the particular social context in which it is done, Baoping urges theology to be more intentional about addressing its specific context. The theological task, he contends, is not only to show how God speaks to that context but also how God is at work within it to liberate and transform life.

Yet such attempts always run certain risks and dangers, Harvie Conn points out. Even the translation of Scripture into various languages and cultures runs the risk of accommodating its message to cultural presuppositions and biases. And this becomes even more risky when Christians attempt to reformulate Christian understanding drawing on images, ideas, and customs of various cultures. Conn argues that evangelicals have been more sensitive to such dangers than have more liberal liberationist proponents, although he reminds evangelicals that in the early church and up to the present effective evangelism has required the church to interpret the gospel meaningfully in various cultures.

The essays in this section show some of the different perspectives and issues in current global discussion of theological method. They also reveal some of the basic differences among Christians in this discussion. Here it becomes clear that issues of theological method cannot be resolved without attention to the central doctrines of Christian faith concerning God, Christ, the church, and so on. The tendency in some recent Western theology to become obsessed with theological method can obscure this and needs to recognize more clearly that theological method both shapes and is shaped by other components of Christian understanding.

Divine Revelation:
Intervention or Self-Communication?

FRANS JOZEF VAN BEECK, S.J.

This essay takes up a crux in systematic theology: the understanding of super-natural divine revelation — a doctrine whose credibility has been widely called into question at least since the mid-eighteenth century, especially in cultures where Christianity has encountered the challenge of Deism. Thus the problem can responsibly be regarded as one of the principal intellectual challenges, if not the principal, offered to Christianity by widespread (if often implicit) judg-ments characteristic of the modern era. It is a problem with multiple ramifica-tions as well. For further down the line, it involves the interpretation, philo-sophically as well as theologically, of a number of fundamental relationships in Christian doctrine and theology: those between grace and nature, positive rev-elation and natural human religiosity, historic Christianity and the universal possibility of faith. Ultimately, of course, what is involved is the truth of the Christian doctrine of God as triune, as well as its theological intelligibility.[1]

This essay is divided into three parts of unequal length. An introductory first part serves to define the issues and propose some dimensions of a fresh approach. This approach will be detailed in the second part, the body of the essay. Finally, a brief third section will offer some concluding reflections de-

---

1. This article is preparatory to a treatment of revelation that will mark the transition from fundamental theology to the doctrine of God in the projected second volume of the author's systematic theology. It also carries out a promise made in §23.3.b of the first volume of that work, which appeared as *God Encountered: A Contemporary Catholic Systematic Theology* 1: *Understand-ing the Christian Faith* (San Francisco: Harper & Row, 1989), henceforth quoted as *GE*. For the second part of this essay I am substantially indebted to sensitive and constructive criticism offered by two friends and colleagues at Loyola University, Chicago: Jill N. Reich and James J. Walter.

Reprinted with permission from the journal *Theological Studies* 52 (1991): 199-226.

signed to insert the ideas we have developed into the wider context of the contemporary, post–Vatican II understanding of divine revelation.

Revelation: Divine Intervention?

This introductory part will attempt to define the issue of divine revelation. It develops in four relatively short sections. The first of these will briefly orchestrate the issue itself; the second will offer a succinct analysis of a fairly representative, though unsatisfactory treatment by a contemporary English theologian of note; the third will venture a quick glance at a few patristic themes, in the interest of suggesting a correct placement of the issue. On this basis, the fourth will propose some dimensions of a fresh approach.

The Issue

At the heart of the issue lies a dilemma: the forced choice (or so it seems to many) between integralism (or fundamentalism) and modernism (or reductionism).[2] Must we theologians bow our reflective, critical heads before any scandalous facts, before what is often referred to as the "objectivity" of the Christian faith? In other words, are we to acknowledge that the substance of the Christian religion is a matter of true divine "intervention"? Or can we adequately account for Christianity if we reduce it to historic experiences that are immanently human, experiences that have yielded and continue to yield, Christianity's historic self-expression in worship, life, and teaching? The dilemma can be posed less abstractly in the form of oft-heard concrete questions, as follows:

Does the Creed mean to affirm that the living God has been, and is being actually encountered in the world? Or can this metaphor be reduced, ultimately, to a dramatic manner of giving symbolic expression to a particular set of human religious experiences? Does Israel's covenant refer to a reality of partnership, one that involves, not just historic Israel, but the living God as well? Or is this a naive picture, which simply conveys an intense experience of partnership on the part of Israel? Is Israel's experience essentially available naturally and universally to all nations (where, of course, it is liable to be expressed in different, but virtually equivalent, sets of symbols)? Or, to take an explicitly Christian theme, is it truly God who is known in the real, historic person of Jesus Christ, and, moreover, is God thus known in a wholly unique, definitive, unsurpassable manner? Or is it enough to understand Jesus Christ as the symbol of a new, definitive level in the immemorial development of human religious conscious-

2. Cf. *GE*, §§18-20.

ness; and hence, is Christianity reducible to the highest form of humanity's awareness of God? In other words, is the orthodox interpreter of the Creed forced to opt for the (naive?) acceptance of the order of Christian grace as a genuinely *new reality*, one that encompasses and perfects the natural order? Or is it legitimate to propose a critical reconception of the order of grace as a reinterpretation of the one, single natural reality that we know as "creation"?

Issues like these are explicitly raised (and usually answered in a reductionist spirit) by theologians with existentialist learnings.[3] In the Anglo-Saxon and North American world, somewhat less pervious to the mood of existentialism, the dilemmas just formulated often explicitly hinge on the neuralgic issue of divine "intervention." This is doubtlessly due to the influences that derive, not just from liberal Evangelicalism and Deism,[4] but specifically also from the atmosphere created by Newton's theological cosmology, in which the inner coherence and consistency of "the system of nature" bulks so large.[5] As long as the normative world-picture was "premodern," it is often suggested, there was relatively little questioning of the possibility of divine intervention ("inbreaking") in the natural order: this allegedly made it easy (or at least relatively easy) to accept supernatural intervention as well, specifically in the form of scriptural inspiration, miracles, and revelation. But we moderns (so the explanation continues) now live, if not in a closed natural order, then at least in an autonomous one. This predisposes us to regard grace and revelation as purely alternative, elective, not strictly demonstrable interpretations of a world order that is essentially stable (if evolutionary, and in that sense historical). Such a world order spontaneously suggests a single, consistent, *natural* divine plan. As a result there is, for many of us, a curious, arbitrary otherworldliness involved in conceiving of the world order as reflecting an integral divine plan of a *supernatural* kind — even if it is one in which grace is carefully coordinated with natural reality. For even in this coordinated scheme, revelation is liable to be experienced as opposed to nature. " Nature," after all, evokes a sense of autonomy: it sums up the (relatively) independent universe created by God, knowable by the human mind exercising its native independence. "Grace," on the other hand, evokes a sense of heteronomy: it sums up the universe of Christian faith, produced by a mysterious, saving divine intervention in history, to be acknowledged only by

3. Well-known examples are Rudolf Bultmann's essay "New Testament and Mythology," in *Kerygma and Myth*, ed. Hans Werner Bartsch (New York: Harper & Row, 1961), 1-44, with its rejection of all divine intervention as a throwback to mythology, and Willi Marxsen's *The Resurrection of Jesus of Nazareth* (Philadelphia: Fortress, 1970), with its reduction of Jesus' resurrection to a human, if Christian, *Inpretament*.

4. Cf. *GE* §20.2-4, §28.2.

5. On this whole complex of issues, and on its influence on the question of the very possibility of Christian faith, cf. Michael J. Buckley's delightful monographs *Motion and Motion's God: Thematic Variations in Aristotle, Cicero, Newton, and Hegel* (Princeton, NJ: Princeton University Press, 1971) and *At the Origins of Modern Atheism* (New Haven and London: Yale University Press, 1987).

a profession of utter dependence. Faced with this dilemma, we moderns are naturally reluctant to fall back upon a naive "interventionism"; as a result, we sometimes find ourselves (only slightly less reluctantly) settling for what really amounts to a form of Deism.

Maurice Wiles' Proposal

The dilemmas just stated are strikingly, as well as representatively, instanced in Maurice Wiles' elegant and stimulating *The Remaking of Christian Doctrine*.[6] In Wiles' view, God, being the creator of the universe, cannot but be committed, foundationally, to its independence. This axiom yields a fundamental criterion with which to test the credibility of all religious affirmations: we are to refrain from "claiming any effective causation on the part of God in relation to particular occurrences." In Wiles' proposed reconstruction of Christian theology, this becomes *the* criterion. Together with the two (formal) criteria of coherence and economy,[7] it determines the whole "pattern of belief" to be developed; but in doing so, it also determines the content of what can be credibly proposed as the true substance of mature belief. This criterion operates negatively: like Ockham's razor, it shaves away anything in the profession of faith not required by itself. The motive behind the operation is the classic — and valid! — concern of the apologist: to test the Christian faith by the standard of human intellectual integrity in believing. Many of our thinking contemporaries, Wiles implies, cannot be fairly compelled to give intellectual assent to more than what can survive the application of this principle. He admits that the operation does yield a form of deism, but one that is acceptable: it does not cut off all relatedness, on the part of God, to the world, even if it does restrict that relatedness to God's being "source of existence and giver of purpose to the whole."[8]

In keeping with the restrictions demanded by the principle, Wiles proceeds to whittle away at the doctrines of Christ's person and work, as well as the doctrine of the working of the Holy Spirit, till they have become mere instances of a single, *universal* proposition: God's "purposive concern" in regard to the world as a whole. Since this proposition is universal, it does not depend for its validity on any historic instances; for God's concern for the world, God's "care," is sufficiently ascertainable from creation.[9] That is also why the doctrines themselves can continue to be affirmed as having real meaning. Still, it is understood

---

6. London: SCM, 1975. For Wiles' dilemmatic approach to the issue and his proposal for a "middle way," cf. esp. 115ff.

7. *The Remaking of Christine Doctrine*, 17-19.

8. Ibid., 38, 17-19.

9. This is a truly rationalist conception, reminiscent of Lessing's dictum: "Accidental truths of history can never become the proof of necessary truths of reason." Quotation from Henry Chadwick, *Lessing's Theological Writings* (Stanford, Calif.: Stanford University Press, 1957), 53.

that any such meaning must be reductively understood: it derives, not from the doctrine claimed as true because revealed in history, but solely from the affirmer's judgment of what can possibly be meant by any affirmation concerning God in relation to the world. In this way, God having been reduced to the status of the provident, caring creator of all that is, the intractable particulars of Christianity's positive profession of faith have ceased to be an embarrassment.

From some of the examples Wiles gives, we may infer with a fair degree of probability just where that embarrassment lies. Wiles' rendition of some of the central Christian doctrinal claims is excessively "interventionist": claims made on behalf of direct biblical inspiration,[10] on behalf of Jesus' divine Sonship viewed as a hard historical fact that should be establishable apart from Christian faith,[11] on behalf of the universal, totally objective atoning efficacy of one particular historical event: Jesus' death on the cross. It must be granted, doctrines thus proposed *are* unbelievable to anyone who prizes, as Wiles does, human freedom, maturity, and responsibility.[12] But the question is whether Wiles' versions of these doctrines are not straw men. Is the crude interventionism Wiles finds implicit in these revealed doctrines really integral to them? Or, for that matter, does the great tradition require it? The main argument of the present essay will imply that the answer must be no on both counts, and that Wiles' proposal involves a reduced version of the Christian faith — specifically, a modernist one.

Placing the Issue

Before we attempt to develop a basic understanding of revelation (often misleadingly called "divine intervention") by means of systematic reflection and argument, let us suggest a broad historical and cultural placement of the issue, as well as a first philosophical analysis.

Let us start with a few witnesses from the second and third centuries. The apologists, Irenaeus, and Origen are obviously innocent, not only of the modern "turn to the subject," but also of the scientific mentality that objects to divine intervention in the chain of cosmic causation. Still, this does not mean that their view of divine self-revelation was naively "interventionist." Thus the *Letter to Diognetus* explicitly insists that God does not intrude by means of physical force of the kind that overcomes opposing forces; rather, God sends the Son in gentleness.[13] Irenaeus insists that God, being creator, is at home in the world, and therefore that God does not need to break to enter; being immanent (that

---

10. *The Remaking of Christian Doctrine,* 106, 116.
11. Ibid., 41-60.
12. Cf. ibid., 116ff.
13. *Letter to Diognetus* 7.2-5.

is, immanent in such a fundamental way as only a truly transcendent God can be), the Logos does not intervene in the world from outside.[14]

Origen draws a conclusion from this. He agrees with Celsus that God does respect the world's integrity as it develops toward its intended completion. But he reminds Celsus that the road to that completion runs through that particular repository of the Logos which is the human person, made in the divine image. Hence, if God guides the world, "God does not take care, as Celsus imagines, only of the universe as a whole, but in addition to that He takes particular care of every rational being."[15] One and a half century later, Gregory of Nyssa rounds out the argument. God is not remote, but close to the world, for "the divine is equally in all and it permeates the whole of creation in the same way, and nothing could remain in being apart from the One Who Is."[16] Hence, unlike the meddlesome gods of the ancient pantheons, God does not "intervene." But, Gregory implies, God does relate to each being in accordance with its nature; specifically, God intimately relates to the human person, capable, by virtue of the divine resemblance and the capacity for moral action, of making the perfection of God a matter of inner-worldly experience, by "being perfect as your heavenly Father is perfect" (Matt. 5:48).[17]

The conclusion is obvious. The Church Fathers' notion of God's activity in the world is not rooted in a naive (in Bultmann's language, "mythological") conception of "effective causation on the part of God in relation to particular occurrences." Instead, the Fathers place all divine action in the world in the context of an understanding of divine immanence, an understanding in which the human person plays a decisive role. This, it would seem, leads to a hermeneutical ground rule. In cases where patristic passages do seem to imply or express a naive understanding of the divine activity in the world, the realization that their thought is embedded in a deep sense of God's immanence should temper our modern eagerness to attribute mechanical, "interventionist" ideas to them.[18] In fact, could it not be argued that the Fathers could afford to sound naive precisely because the theological and cosmological metaphysics they were operating on were anything but naive?

Where, then, in the history of Western culture, are we to place the problematic idea that God "intervenes"? Not in the Middle Ages, which were familiar

14. *Adv. Haer.* 5.2.1.

15. *C. Celsum* 4.99 (*Contra Celsum,* trans. Henry Chadwick [3rd ed.; Cambridge: Cambridge University Press, 1980], 262-63). Cf. *GE* §27.4.c.

16. *What Does the Christian's Profession Mean? (De professione christiana), Gregorii Nysseni Opera,* ed. W. Jaeger et al. (Leiden, 1921-) 8.1, p. 138.

17. Ibid. 8.1, pp. 137.12–138.24.

18. Thus I must disagree on hermeneutical grounds with Maurice Wiles, who alleges that the patristic understanding of scriptural inspiration, with very few exceptions, looked upon the Spirit as a foreign, "additional" factor, and hence regarded the human author's role as purely instrumental and, consequently, as entirely passive (*The Remaking of Christian Doctrine,* 89-90, 106, 116).

with divine immanence and recognized the hand of God in the world, while at the same time enjoying a sophisticated philosophical understanding of the distinction between God as *causa prima* and the inner-worldly causality exercised by the whole range of secondary causes. These latter operated under the sustaining, immanent impulse of the *causa prima,* understood as the transcendent source, not just of efficient causality, but also, and especially, of formal and final causality.

The answer, therefore, must be: in the first half of the sixteenth century, which witnessed the rise of the cultivation of "objectivity" as never before. The world began more and more to look like an immense collection of discrete, relatively impenetrable objects, all of which offered themselves for description and definition by means of discrete truths capable of being spelled out objectively on the printed page. Mathematics and mechanics began to be the paradigm of both truth and reality, and even of art, as, among other things, the laws of optical perspective began to be rigorously enforced. And since all objects began to be thought of as affecting each other only extrinsically, efficient causality gained an almost absolute prominence.

The problem is, of course, that efficient causality best explains the mutual relations of solid bodies, inanimate objects. But lifeless things are inert; they are foreign to each other, or at best contiguous; if they affect each other at all, they do so only extrinsically (at least in the macroscopic world of everyday observation, on which the new cosmology was based). Living beings, by contrast, exist differently, though they share many of the properties of inanimate things. They actively transcend themselves so as to take on their physical environment; they are characterized by an immanent ability both to communicate with other beings like themselves and to seek self-actualization by means of growth and development, both in inner consistency and in interactiveness, that is, in an interplay of immanence and transcendence. Human persons are characterized by an immanence that gives rise to an even further transcendence. They transcend not only themselves but also their physical environment, and they do so self-consciously. Though part of the material order, they are *selves,* open to *otherness as such* — other persons and, ultimately, God. Efficient causality fails to account for all these forms of immanence and transcendence; to account for them, both Jewish and Christian philosophical traditions have appealed to formal and final causality, as David B. Burrell has recently explained once again.[19]

In this light, David Jenkins would seem to offer a skewed analysis of cultural developments when he writes: "Christianity, having settled down into its medieval moulds, was largely unable to 'take' the strictly neutral and secular

19. Cf. his "Divine Practical Knowing: How an Eternal God Acts in Time," in *Divine Action: Studies Inspired by the Philosophical Theology of Austin Farrer,* ed. Brian Hebblethwaite and Edward Henderson (Edinburgh: T. & T. Clark, 1990), 93-102.

approach to everything in the universe (including, eventually, man in so far as he is homogeneous with the rest of the universe), which is the essence of the scientific approach and which gives it its liberating and creative effect."[20] As a matter of historical fact, the separation of humanity from the universe is not the result of the scientific mentality at all, or at least not initially. It was an implicit assumption of that mentality's favorite method, which favored the reduction of all causality to efficient causality. The method was immensely successful, and hence persuasive. In time, however, the method helped drive the synthetic, interpretative spirit out of the world of objectivity; it had to take refuge in a different world.[21]

Thus the protest against "divine intervention" is part of scientific method as it arose in the sixteenth century. The mechanization of the Western world picture[22] and its aftermath created a theological problem. Curiously, Christians ended up joining the movement set afoot by the method; many of them became pious Cartesians, too, and withdrew from the world to save their purely spiritual souls. In light of all this, it would have been more correct, perhaps, for David Jenkins to write that, with few exceptions (Pascal being one of them), Christians failed not so much to "take" the undifferentiated scientific and secular approach to everything in the universe, as to take it *on*.

We can now go back to Maurice Wiles' *Remaking*. Wiles fully realizes that efficient causality fails to account for revelation; hence he rejects any notion of special divine presence associated with particular instances of "effective causation." The problem, however, is that he does not confront the defective anthropology implicit in modern culture's unawareness of the concepts of formal and final causality. The concept of revelation that Wiles rejects is neither supernatural nor attuned to humanity; hence, he is right to reject it. But he himself remains incapable of developing a concept of revelation that accommodates what he so obviously prizes in human beings: freedom, maturity, and responsi-

---

20. *The Glory of Man* (New York: Charles Scribner's, 1967), 62.

21. To take one eloquent example, the great anatomist Vesalius (1514-1564), whose anatomical atlases show that he was the first to *see* the body scientifically, clinically, dispassionately, with an eye as keen as his scalpel, is a Platonist as well as a Cartesian *avant la lettre*. He completely separates soul from body and spirit from matter, and names God, not creator, implying a coherent world, but *opifex* ("craftsman"), implying a world of mere things. Vesalius can write: "And thus we will render thanks, singing hymns to God the maker of all things, for having bestowed on us a reasonable soul, which we have in common with the angels (as Plato also suggested, not unmindful of the much-abused philosophers). On the strength of that [soul], if there is but faith, we shall enjoy that eternal happiness, when it will no longer be necessary to inquire into the seat and the substance of the soul by the anatomizing of bodies or by means of reason weighed down by bodily shackles" (trans. from J. H. van den Berg, *Het menselijk lichaam*, 2 [Nijkerk: G. F. Callenbach, 1965], 221 n. 5). On Vesalius, cf. *The Illustrations from the Works of Andreas Vesalius*, ed. J. B. de-C. M. Saunders and Charles D. O'Malley (New York: Dover, 1973); cf. also F. J. van Beeck, *Christ Proclaimed* (New York-Ramsey-Toronto: Paulist, 1979), 41, 45, 525-32.

22. Cf. E. J. Dijksterhuis, *The Mechanization of the World Picture* (Oxford: Clarendon, 1961).

bility — the very features that are the authentic human correlates of the self-revelation of God, as the second part of this essay will argue.[23]

Some Dimensions of a Fresh Approach

The realizations developed so far must give us our cues to a fresh approach to the problem of divine revelation, an approach that must respect both the tradition and the culture we live in. The patristic tradition suggests that the abiding immanence of the transcendent God in the natural order is an essential key to revelation, and that the presence of the specifically human element in the world is of crucial relevance to both the reality and the understanding of God's immanence in it. Our culture, for its part, insists that faith be wedded to human authenticity and integrity; consequently, it wishes to satisfy itself that Christian revelation is not predicated on a naively interventionist concept of divine activity in the world.

Other realizations will have to guide our analysis as well. If divine revelation is specifically connected with the presence of the specifically human in the cosmos, then our analysis is well advised to pay special attention to the distinctive ways in which the world of things functions in the world of persons. In the process of doing so, we are likely, incidentally, to discover remedies for some of the painful dichotomies typical of modernity. There is the Cartesian rift between matter and spirit, between the world and God, and hence, between human reason and divine revelation. Since Kant, there is the added dichotomy between (infrahuman) nature and (human) freedom. Nature, we must rediscover, is neither fixed nor a closed circle, but pliable — that is, amenable to historicity and consequently to freedom. And since nature is not an inert, purely material prison, reason is not its prisoner; hence, human understanding really does reach beyond the world of objects (even if Locke and Kant strongly suggest the opposite); reason is natively open to the presence of spirit in the world and hence to nature's attunement to the order of grace. And if this implies (as it does) that grace is not intrusive, then revelation cannot be narrowly historical; that is, it cannot occur purely adventitiously, in the shape of discrete, readily

---

23. The extent to which the sixteenth- and seventeenth-century mechanization of the world picture is an intellectual watershed in the understanding of the "effects" of God's saving action is well demonstrated by the fact that Aquinas has as yet no problems attributing efficient ("instrumental") causality to both the sacraments and Christ's Passion, even though he adds that formal ("exemplary") causality must play a part in explaining the effects of his Resurrection; see, e.g., *ST* 3, q.62, a.5, in c and ad 1; q.56, a.1, ad 3. By contrast, a modern theologian like Karl Rahner resolutely opts, both in an early essay and in his mature *Foundations of Christian Faith*, for formal causality as the central category to understand grace as *communication* of divine life. See "Some Implications of the Scholastic Concept of Uncreated Grace," in *Theological Investigations*, 1 (Baltimore: Helicon, 1966), 319-46; *Foundations of Christian Faith: An Introduction to the Idea of Christianity* (New York: Seabury, 1978), 120-22.

identifiable historical occurrences entirely wrought by God; rather it must in some real sense be the flower of nature's immanent aspiration towards transcendence.

It is with themes like these in mind that we must attempt a fresh theological understanding of divine revelation. We will do so by way of analysis of a specifically human phenomenon: communication between and among persons. Our expectation that human communication will prove to provide a useful analogy to divine revelation is based on two well-known claims. First, language about God cannot but avail itself of metaphors borrowed from human concerns and experiences in the world. Secondly, divine revelation is a form of communication.

Our analysis will discover that the reality of divine revelation is inseparable from the very processes that serve as analogies toward its understanding. Human communication, in other words, will prove to be the indispensable anthropological infrastructure of divine revelation.

Divine Revelation and Its Anthropological Infrastructure

We must now develop in detail the fresh approach which we have proposed. The body of our essay offers neither a new theology of revelation, nor a systematic account of its ramifications in specific areas, for example, in regard to scriptural inspiration. It offers rather a set of basic, primary steps which create room for a satisfactory contemporary understanding of the traditional doctrine of divine revelation. Specifically, our argument will develop, in five consecutive moves, an understanding of communication among human persons as the anthropological infrastructure of divine revelation.

Communication: Process and Content

Anyone whose experience has been shaped by encounters with other persons realizes that communication between persons involves more than the transmission of content, even though all communication does involve some kind of identifiable content.[24] Human communication involves more than things com-

---

24. The content of communication consists in the things we communicate *to* others. These things are "goods": material goods like merchandise, professional services, money, and gifts; "somatic" goods like handshakes and kisses; "mental" goods (usually conveyed verbally) like birthday wishes, promises, and (especially) ideas and concepts. With regard to the latter, it must be noted that there prevails a real analogy between the verbal communicating of ideas/concepts and the behavioral conveying of things in that both are interpersonal transactions. Of course, words (especially terms) are also cognitive; this gives them a capacity for "impersonalness" and abstraction that things and somatic goods do not have, at least not to the same extent. That capacity lies in

municated; communication is not a mere transfer of "matter" between and among people. For content to be communicated relatively undistorted from one person to another, what is required on the part of both is an interpersonal context — an awareness of mutual presence, of actively and receptively being with one another. Such a context, in fact, is not required only for the satisfactory conveying of content already possessed by one person involved in the encounter; in intellectual communication, we require a context of interpersonalness to succeed in satisfactorily articulating the content we are conveying.[25] Thus, to repeat Martin Buber's insight, communication as encounter ("I-Thou") is the matrix of communication as articulation and sharing of content ("I-It"). Or, *communication-with is the matrix of communication-to.* Or again, in communication, parts taken from the world of things are meaningfully integrated into an encounter between or among persons.

It follows that interpersonal encounter and content-sharing are not two discrete events related to each other in a merely occasional fashion — events that only happen to occur simultaneously. In actual communication, the personal encounter and the content conveyed are intrinsically correlated; if they were not, it would be impossible to tell the difference between appropriate and inappropriate communication.

Whenever human communication is experienced as appropriate, the content communicated is harmoniously integrated into the encounter. In appropriate communication, therefore, there is broad symbolic consonance between the quality of mutual presence and the content communicated, both at the giving and at the receiving end. That is, the content positively carries and conveys the encounter, while at the same time shaping, tempering, and regulating it. Thus appropriate communication ranges from the simple kindness that is fitting when, say, a travel agent gives a customer the required information about airline schedules, to the deep tenderness that suits the encounter between, say, two persons sharing their love of God.

Needless to say, there is a wide area of possibilities for inappropriate communication; human communication is essentially precarious; in most in-

---

the ability of words to signify, i.e., to represent things and ideas/concepts outside the context of particular situations. In that sense, words enable us to take our distance from interpersonal situations so as to transcend them intellectually; for that reason, verbal communication, being cognitive, often favors the content of communicative activity at the expense of its interpersonal elements. But we must remember that in using words we not only know things but also handle them, especially by using words to name them, i.e., verbally point to them; and in the interpersonal sphere, we use words (even abstract ones) performatively, as J. L. Austin has shown in his classic *How to Do Things with Words* (Cambridge: Harvard University Press, 1962). Consequently, all communication, including verbal communication that is chiefly cognitive, is a form of behavior; it is "gestural" (cf. F. J. van Beeck, *Christ Proclaimed*, 85-98). From this it follows that all content, including material and somatic goods, functions symbolically, as will be explained.

25. That context may be remote. Think, e.g., of the "audience" that any author imagines, whether implicitly or explicitly, while writing with a view to publication.

stances, communication involves a struggle with elements of inappropriateness. Inappropriate communication is characterized (not by integration but) by alienation — that is, by appreciable symbolic dissonance. Among countless possible instances, we can think of drastic ones, like the case of the frustrated lover angrily shouting, "But I love you!" or, at the other extreme, the case of the bank teller who, disconcertingly, seems to put his very soul into the cash he counts out to me.[26]

Interpersonal Self-Communication

Let us now begin gradually to take our distance from the element of content-sharing in communication, so as to focus mainly on the element of personal encounter. A first point to be made is that in every act of content-sharing, we always share more than *what* we share. In actual communication-situations, there is, inherent in all content, a surplus value, a reality that (mostly) remains unstated; for in whatever we do and say, we also express our own reality. Thus in communicating, we always do more than just exactly what we do, always say more than just exactly what we say; for in and beyond what we do and say we convey ourselves, albeit symbolically. This communication of self remains limited of course; nothing that we manifestly do or say ever succeeds in conveying the full, integral reality of our selves. That is, if symbolic communication reveals us, it also falls short of wholly giving us away; what we do and say manifests us, but something about us is bound to remain implicit in the manifesting. In fact, what is left implicit about us is often accentuated by the manifest: persons we have come to know really well are often more mysterious to us than others whom we know only superficially. All of this leaves the full reality of "*who* we really are" a perpetual mystery, never to be either expressed or captured in any particular act of communication.

This combination of self-manifestation and persistent hiddenness is carried ("symbolized") at the level of content. What we communicate is always necessarily limited. No matter how much content I communicate, it is never exhaustive: I could have thought of a different gift; to the handshake I could have added a kiss; I remember I left an important point of information to my partner's imagination. Thus the very limits of what we make manifest in com-

26. Here lie the experiential roots of Jean-Paul Sartre's thesis that interpersonal communication is nothing but a bitter illusion which illustrates the absurdity of human existence. Our struggle to communicate amidst the intractable world of things is perpetual; we humans find ourselves forever attracted to others, yet without ever being positively capable of reaching them as others. This shows we are ultimately doomed, as persons, to remain alienated; locked up inside ourselves, we are as isolated as things, but worse off, since, being self-conscious, we cannot help rebelling against it *(pour-soi)*. And with the weariness characteristic of *ressentiment*, Sartre suggests that the simple unselfconscious existence of things *(en-soi)* is a more appealing form of being than human life.

municating suggest the many goods not shared and the untold things that remain unstated; the content that I manifestly communicate also serves to symbolize the content that remains recessive.

But this means that I reveal and conceal myself not only in what I manifestly communicate, but also (and, in fact, often more eloquently) in the things I leave undone and unstated. And thus it is in the chiaroscuro created by what we do and do not do, say and do not say, that we most adequately communicate — that is, both reveal and conceal, both surrender and hold back — two realities, distinct yet integrated: our personal selves and what we mean to communicate.

This leads to one further, more radical step in communication, the interpersonal conveying of self is the active, originating element: it undergirds and sustains what occurs at the level of content. For even if I withhold content — that is, if I communicate "nothing in particular" — I cannot help conveying myself, somehow. That is, while we are physically with others, we are bound to convey something. Among other things, this accounts for the unpleasant fact that absent-minded persons can be ever so annoyingly present; it also explains why, in any encounter, those who are not involved, whether by design or out of impotence, have such a frustrating way of obstructing communication among those who are. As persons, therefore, we cannot not communicate; we cannot help "revealing," or "manifesting," ourselves, if always incompletely, and hence, never without at least some puzzlement. In any situation, we are players and participants, like it or not. This holds even when we absent ourselves physically: we cannot help suggesting some kind of message, even if we do not always articulate just what it is, in which case we leave it to others to second-guess what we might mean. Thus, whether by action or by default, we always communicate something, and in that "something" we also symbolically communicate ourselves. To exist as a person is to self-communicate, if always in particular, and hence partial, ways.

Now in communicating ourselves, both in what we manifest and in what we leave undone and unstated, we invite a response in kind. That response is the self-communication of others. Every act of self-communication is an appeal, a plea addressed to others to render themselves present to me in actuality. These moves, of course, involve sizeable risks on both sides, for full symbolic consonance between what I communicate and who I am is never insured in advance, neither in my offer of self-communication nor in others' response to it. Unintentionally, I may botch the way I come across; equally unintentionally, others may misinterpret me. Worse still, my invitations and appeals can meet with deliberate indifference and cold rejection on the part of others; and I myself have it in me to turn devious in addressing myself to others and seek to manipulate them.

Still, all these ominous realizations serve only to reinforce, rather than detract from, a fundamental truth: we can no more help appealing to others to communicate themselves to us than we can help communicating ourselves to them. To exist as a person is to invite the self-communication of others, if always in particular, and hence partial, ways.

Responsibility and Freedom

But this is where a fundamental human responsibility emerges, and inseparable from it, a fundamental human freedom. This can be explained in two successive moves, as follows:

The first move. At the interpersonal level, communication involves more than one bare personal existent acknowledging, in and through what he or she communicates, the bare existence of another person. Persons are valuable, not just derivatively, by reference to an extrinsic set of moral norms, but originally and inherently. The simple givenness of a person, therefore, is not a bare, neutral fact; it creates an ethical situation; each and every person intrinsically demands to be responded to, in a way each and every thing does not; among persons, factual availability for response establishes moral responsibility.[27]

In the self-communication by which I invite others to convey themselves to me I must acknowledge this responsibility. My self-communication should suggest an offer of positive regard and acceptance of the other as such. The self-revealing plea, "Be there for me," must imply the commitment, "I will be there for you." My offer of self-communication, no matter how implicit, must always intimate that, in the actuality of communicative behavior, I will encounter the other person, no matter how clumsily, in accordance with his or her intrinsic worth as a person.

This means that in every particular communication-situation, symbolic consonance in communication is not just a pragmatic issue that touches on the orderly transfer of content; it is a moral issue predicated on the abiding nature of personhood. Both my own integrity as a person and the integrity of the other demand that, in and through whatever we communicate, we do justice both to each other and to our own authentic selves.

27. Readers of Emmanuel Levinas will recognize in this proposition my deep indebtedness to his central thesis that the personal identity we bring to our encounters with others is not self-constituted, but responsive. That is, it is fundamentally beholden to the unconditional, essentially unilateral demand for justice that resides in the face, both utterly vulnerable and sovereignly authoritative, of the other, who precisely as other reveals God. The present treatment differs from Levinas' in that it places personal relatedness, and the responsive identity-experience that is inseparable from it (cf. *GE* §35.1), in the context of communication among fundamentally equal, and hence equally responsible partners. As a result, I understand the inescapable imperative inherent in personal encounter in terms of fundamental symmetry and mutuality. This implies an understanding of encounter (and the moral obligation inherent in it) as a matter of sympathy, and ultimately of God as compassionate love, demanding the active pursuit of justice without limits.

Needless to say, this justice is an elusive pursuit, since the personal integrity of both ourselves and others is beyond full comprehension or expression; the selfhood of persons, our own as well as others', and our mutual presence are indeed available to us, but only in symbol — that is, precariously and tentatively, in the ongoing experience of patient negotiation and interpretation. But it is precisely in thus seeking to do justice that we empower each other to overcome our inherent trepidation in the face both of what we are and of what we are meant to be more fully: persons responsively and responsibly present to one another.

Communicating our selves and inviting the self-communication of others, therefore, is not something we can suspend at will; it is inherent in our existence as persons. Hence, the demand for justice and integrity in interpretative communication is coextensive with human life itself; it is always with us, even though it surfaces only in particular communicative interactions, in the form of a demand for symbolic consonance. Thus personal integrity, our own and others', ceaselessly urges us to do justice to others, by sharing with them such things as we have at our disposal, and to do so in such a way as to share, in some fashion, our authentic selves with them as well. This sharing encompasses, on our part, a morally authoritative appeal extended to others to do justice in turn; thus we invite them to share with us such things as they have at their disposal, so as in some fashion to share themselves with us as well.[28]

The second move. Inseparably from the exercise of this fundamental responsibility between and among persons we become conscious of a fundamental freedom as well. As persons, we have seen, we are living gestures of responsible communication extended to others, as well as appeals for responsible communication in turn. Yet every time appropriate communication comes off, we are delighted and surprised — even thankful, so much so that we will want to talk about it, to the point of bearing witness to it. Much as appropriate communication is an obvious and natural thing to engage in, we apparently find it is not to be taken for granted. This begs for further reflection.

At the heart of the issue lies the following experience: in the presence of other persons, we never feel neutral. We feel either in touch or out of touch, basically connected or largely alienated. How to account for this?

---

28. The opposite of all this is disregard of others. This occurs in pardonable (if often culpable) ways when, to whatever extent, I treat another person inconsiderately, i.e., as subhuman, as a thing. But even things are entitled to an appropriate level of positive regard; between persons and things, true encounters (if subverbal ones) do occur; "mere things" do not exist. For this reason, inconsiderateness, however immoral, still involves that minimal form of positive regard that consists in the acknowledgment of the other's existence as part of the world. The ultimate immorality, and the true source of all violence against humanity as such, consists in actively ignoring human personalness as such — treating persons as nonpersons without value. This frightening possibility looms on the horizon of any worldview to the extent to which it is enslaved to things and desensitized to the whole range of the universe's spiritual ingredients. As a result, such a worldview is liable to recognize as really real only things, especially its own favorite ideas, ideologies, and idols.

To exist with other persons is to self-communicate and to invite self-communication. This is given; we cannot suspend it at will. Being with others is tantamount to being called to responsiveness; others call upon us willy-nilly; we are responsible to each other's personalness. No wonder factual inability or, worse, refusal to engage in appropriate communication strikes us as a moral failure, a failure of fundamental mutual justice. Not surprisingly, when, in a particular situation, we sense that communication is failing, we are liable to feel driven into some form of personal isolation; a curious self-consciousness (of a self-centered, nonliberating kind) may take hold of us; by way of cover, we may strike a pose or two, deliberately or instinctively; but the posturing only further checks the flow of encounter, or blocks it altogether. Symbolic dissonance has set in; inappropriate communication takes over; we become actors. Somehow the suspicion may come to us that we are being unpleasantly and unfairly judged, and found wanting. We only pretend we are communicating; we may even think this is the best we can do for now. Still, vaguely or keenly, we are conscious that we are betraying what we are, namely, persons responsibly present to persons. In failing to communicate appropriately, we are falling short of what is morally incumbent on us as persons, as well as being deprived of what is owed to us as persons.

But thank goodness, there is the other experience, too. Few things are so satisfying, exhilarating, or touching as "hitting it off," at any level of appropriateness, with other persons. Yet, curiously, whenever communication comes off, it will strike us as somehow unexpected — as a bounty we cannot wholly account for, let alone take credit for. We are satisfied, and in giving expression to our satisfaction, we are likely to recount, with gratitude, elements that contributed to the positive experience; but the elements never quite seem to explain fully why "it clicked." This drives home the realization that appropriate communication, while the most natural and pertinent thing in the world as well as a fundamental moral imperative, can never be compelled; it is a free interpersonal gift. How can this be?

In self-communicating, I freely extend to others what it is my deepest duty to extend to them as persons: my very self — that is, that which it is my sole as well as deepest privilege to extend. Others may jeopardize this freedom; they may succeed in tricking the gift of myself out of me by feigned love, or even in extorting it from me by violence; but it would be immoral for them even to try to do so. Others may also enhance this freedom. They can accept the gift of myself from me. They can even elicit it from me, by freely communicating themselves with me. In fact, it is precisely in response to acts of free self-communication that I find myself encouraged and empowered to communicate myself in turn. Without the inviting presence of others drawing me out of myself, and without myself agreeing to be drawn out, I might end up finding myself unmoved, habitually powerless to extend myself to anyone. That would be moral impotence indeed! Abandoned by others, or worse, having myself abandoned others,[29] I would find myself powerless freely to choose to be what I can neither deny I am nor help being: myself. Destined for an open identity cherished and developed by habits of relatedness, I would find myself mired in futile self-concern — my identity turned, perversely, into a prison.

Thus in the very act of appropriate communication we find ourselves personally exercising and enjoying, in constructive mutuality, a gracious, liberating inner freedom. This freedom is as fundamental to our life together as persons as the obligation to respond to each other; in appropriate communication, in other words, we freely agree to empower each other. Thus we freely endorse and enhance what we cannot help being: our selves — that most precious of things which we are also free to diminish and even reject, in self-defeating and ultimately unsuccessful self-contradiction.[30]

To sum up, to exist as persons is to communicate, and this communication consists in the actualization of ourselves and each other as persons dynamically present to each other; this actualization is successful to the extent that it is inspired by mutual empowerment freely given and accepted.

Self-Communication, Significant Others, and Tradition

This is where a twofold issue arises. We are impotent to communicate without at least some others to draw us out; our mutuality in communicating, in other words, is shot through with dependence, and what is more, dependence on the part of all. This dependence is at once ontic and actual, the former being foundational, the latter at least partial. It is *ontic* inasmuch as, for any communication to occur, all persons are dependent on the givenness of other persons — that is, on their factual availability for response; it is *actual* inasmuch as, in particular situations, at least *some* are at least partly dependent on the free initiative of particular others. We must explore the implications of both.

29. Note Martin Buber's observation that there is a decisive difference between these two forms of failure of relatedness: "the one who is abandoned by those to whom he uttered the true *Thou* is accepted by God, not the one who himself abandoned them" (*Ich und Du* [2nd ed.; Köln: Jakob Hegner, 1966], 123; *I and Thou*, trans. Walter Kaufmann [New York: Charles Scribner's Sons, 1970], 152).

30. Here we have laid bare the anthropological infrastructure of the experience of supernatural grace. Limiting communication to the conveying of content involves a neutral treatment of persons, as if they were mere agents designed only to manipulate the world of things by efficient causality. On account of their immanent authenticity, however, human persons are transcendent; they operate by formal and final causality as well. Hence, persons are owed gestures of communication, which involves a degree of benevolence; mere correctness is morally deficient; it amounts to a slight. Yet actually encountering others in keeping with their inherent nature as persons is an activity that can only be freely undertaken, and in that sense gracious — something which cannot be extorted as owed by right. In the interpersonal world, therefore, there is no such thing as "pure nature"; in dealing with each other, we either fail to meet the just demands of "nature," or we graciously and freely exceed them.

Appropriate communication constantly needs free initiative; it is neither self-originating nor self-sustaining. Whenever and wherever two or more persons are available to each other for encounter, all are indeed summoned to respond, but the question is who will grasp the opportunity. Or when an actual process of communication flags, the question is who will make the decisive move to revive it. Who will freely and creatively respond, and to whom, to actuate the process of mutual empowerment?

Many of us can name persons who have been personally significant to us. Not infrequently, they are people who have also been functionally significant to us; they gave us many things we are grateful for. More importantly, they had a way with things: the seemingly effortless way in which they did things suggested they were in control of what they had to give. Yet their real significance for us lies in the fact that they had a way with *us;* that suggested what kind of persons they were. Thus we have come to remember them, thankfully, as part of who we have become; they are integral to our autobiography, to the story of such enlightenment and self-awareness as has become ours. If they did train and model us, it was not in *their* favorite mold; in fact, they discouraged admiration and smiled at our self-conscious attempts at mimicry. Instead, they were creative, functionally and personally; thus they helped us find a shape of our own. Curiously, if they made problems for us (as quite often they did), they usually turned out not to be part of them. That is, they managed to identify with us without interfering with us; we sensed that they were concerned, but in such a way as to let us be; we felt free. They may have added to our self-knowledge by sharing with us (in a way we could accept) their informed judgments about us; yet they seemed less interested in *what* they understood *about* us than in understanding *us.* Apparently undaunted by the disparateness and incoherence of our experience of ourselves, of others, of our world, and of God, they succeeded in providing us with a welcoming, searching, illuminating presence. That presence felt like a pledge of acceptance. Thus we were enabled to let our philosophy of life and our self-knowledge, our judgments and our convictions take shape in our own minds; they were instrumental in revealing us to ourselves. And so, here we are, having grown into tolerably self-accepted and well-integrated persons, with a fairly comfortable sense of self-identity, and hence with a reasonable ability (as well as quiet courage) to reach out to others as scattered and confused now as we once were.

Invariably, we remember such persons as remarkably well-integrated and hence as quite self-sufficient. While they obviously enjoyed dealing with our immature or impotent selves, they did not seem to revel in helping us; if they were at all dependent on us, our dependence on them was far greater; we really needed them. Yet what seemed to matter to them was not so much our need as our selves, our inner potential for freedom and identity. In fact, what made them especially capable of enhancing us was that they clearly did not expect to be enhanced by us. Modest without self-abasement, engagingly unselfconscious, and clearly unimpressed by their own level of personal integration, they were carefree enough to be freely present to our struggling selves, penetratingly yet unobtrusively.

Persons like this illustrate a fundamental thesis. The actual event of appropriate interpersonal communication is always a matter of mutual presence and empowerment. But to initiate and sustain both the presence and the empowerment, what is needed is personal presence freely, that is, one-sidedly, undertaken, which is the fruit of personal identity come to maturity. The generous inner freedom of the mature is the soul of constructive communication.

This can also be formulated as follows: to the extent that persons acquire a habit of integrating the world of things, and thus a habit of transcending their immediate involvement in it, to that extent they will also be capable of personal presence to others, of freely identifying with them, and of communicating themselves to others in such a way as to enhance the latter's identity. Put more radically: the more transcendent persons are, the more immanent they are liable to be.

This has an important consequence: encounters in which significant others reveal themselves to us are appreciated by us only to the extent that in encountering them we find ourselves revealed to ourselves. This can be rephrased in the form of another crucial thesis: encounters in which we meet significant others as truly other are inseparable from authentic self-experience. Unlike the self-awareness predicated on various forms of self-analysis, self-examination, and introspection, authentic self-experience is responsive; in it we find, in ways inaccessible to our autonomous egos, self-enlightenment, self-recovery, self-correction and conversion, and growth. Even more pertinently, responsive self-experience guarantees and authenticates to us the reality of the significant other's presence. From the depth of our self-experience, therefore, we should never draw the conclusion that we are only experiencing ourselves. Rather, what we experience in our self-experience is the other precisely as other — that is, as one who encounters us without our ever being able to fully account for his or her identity.

Responsive self-experience becomes manifest in the phenomenon of witness. Most commonly, witness involves two levels of affirmation. First, we pay tribute, in both word and deed, to significant others on account of what they have given us. But secondly and more pertinently, we witness to significant others on account of who they have been for us; they are integral to ourselves inasmuch as we have become authentic, creative persons. Thus in "testimonial autobiography,"[31] we tend to place whatever things others have given us in the context of who they have been for us; what they did and said has come to symbolize who they are for us as persons. Grateful self-awareness rather than functional indebtedness prompts us to bear witness to significant others.

31. Cf. GE §41.2; §45.2; §46.2.

Not surprisingly, however, in testimonial autobiography we will also find ourselves attributing to significant others things which, as a matter of naked fact, they never did or said. But then, in giving a thankful account of ourselves we are not interested in naked facts; it is out of the fullness of our responsive self-experience that we make the attribution; there are certain things we cannot imagine we would do or understand here and now if we had not encountered them there and then.

All this can be put more theoretically. The self-revealing presence of significant others originally occurs in interpersonal encounters freely animated by initiators. Still, it is the recipients that will proceed to cherish the encounter as an abiding element of their self-awareness; they, therefore, are also the ones that will proceed to witness to it in the form of content — that is, by means of definitive actions and articulate statements. Typically, they will credit these doings and sayings not so much to themselves (even though they are authentically theirs) as to the significant others who continue to inspire them.

All of this serves to make a point crucial to our analysis: Significant (self-)communication that comes to us from others is never experienced as a mere intervention from outside. In interpersonal encounter, when the free (and in that sense transcendent) presence of another person communicates itself to us, it does so with an impact that is immanent. In interpersonal encounter, the inner testimony of self-experience matches the testimony of outward engagement with otherness. Our best touchstone of the significance of any encounter is immanent: it consists in the experience of finding our deeper, authentic selves engaged, actuated, restored, enhanced — surprisingly yet unmistakably.

So much for our analysis of the fact that all appropriate interpersonal communication is actually dependent on the mature freedom of significant others. Now we must explore the implications of the fact that we are ontically dependent on others for communication. It involves two levels of experience, of which the first is an experience of tradition.

Appropriate communication, we have said, is neither self-originating nor self-sustaining. This implies that whenever it occurs, not even the mature persons capable of authentically identifying with less mature others completely account for its occurrence. The reason for this is that mature persons that animate appropriate communication are not wholly self-made. Those to whose mature freedom and generosity we bear witness once encountered others to whom they came to bear witness; typically, significant others will acknowledge their dependence on the positive regard once freely extended to them by others significant to them, others not actually present. For mature persons, therefore, to engage in a communicative encounter is not the reinvention of the wheel every time they do it. Rather, the opposite is the case. As we encounter more and more persons as truly other, we discover that they become, in us, a quiet company of friends who equip us for encounters with yet others.[32] Significant others, in other words, are active participants in a tradition of freely undertaken benevolence to others.

However, there is something comparable on the receiving end as well. Those to whom significant others communicate themselves are not *tabulae rasae;* no matter how immature they may be, they are not without an identity of their own to start with. Interpersonal communication invariably builds on what is given; and we know from experience that this givenness includes an observable initial preparedness for interpersonal communication.

We conclude that authentic capacity for interpersonal communication is at least partly habitual, a matter of preexisting tradition. Our factual availability to each other for responsive and responsible encounter — the ground for our ontic dependence on each other for communication — is never completely formless.

Lest we make the mistake of casting the dynamic we are analyzing in narrowly (inter)personalist terms, an important point must be made here. Recipients of the mature presence of significant others, it was explained, will witness to that presence to others in word and deed, and they will do so also in the form of content — that is, by means of definite actions and articulate statements that convey the freshness of the experience. Typically, it was added, they will attribute these doings and sayings to the significant others that inspired them. Witness to the creative maturity of significant others, in other words, will breed new communication, not only of the live interpersonal variety, but also of the instrumental institutional kind, the kind that promises *stability.* Testimony borne by trustworthy witnesses founds reliable schools of action and thought; it tends toward the structuring of *traditions* (and eventually of a *culture*), in the twin forms of organized common life and traditional community wisdom.[33] Still, neither shared norms nor shared wisdom is a sure-fire device; they will function as means of appropriate communication only to the extent that they function *symbolically,* that is, as vehicles of a truly communicative, responsive life together. For such a meaningful life any community and any culture needs symbolic consonance; shared norms for action and the truths that enshrine shared wisdom must be experienced as meaningful and authentic. But

---

32. True encounter, in other words, enhances our disposition to engage in further encounters. It is enlightening to contrast this experience with the experience of accumulating things. As we collect things (i.e., whatever fits the category of content), we find that they tend to crowd each other out (not only in space and time, but also, say, in books, not to mention the memory, the mind, and especially the heart). It is to be noted that the category of things can include persons, to the extent that we collect them as if they were objects.

33. Note that the relationship between interpersonal encounter and witness to significant others in deed and word is analogous to the relationship between the worship of God and Christian witness in conduct and teaching (*GE* §47.5). Note, too, that any kind of norm for common life and any community wisdom must be learned in order to be understood, as George Lindbeck has well explained in *The Nature of Doctrine.*

all norms and wisdom depend for their meaningfulness on interpretation by authentic witnesses. All communities and cultures, therefore, need prophets, people who creatively shape the intractable here and now out of an affinity with the soul of the common tradition. In the long run, tradition is kept alive by authentic communicators, not by critics, and certainly not by taskmasters, letter-worshipers, and hacks.

Interpersonal Communication and Its Transcendent Precondition

Traditions, both of live interpersonal benevolence and of life-shaping structures of communication, go a long way to account for the actual occurrence of constructive interpersonal communication. Still, it would be rash to conclude that they adequately account for it. It is surely pointless to deny, at the strictly interpersonal level, that people do indeed grow in freedom and generosity from the benevolence shown to them by others. Still, it is primitive to think of sustained traditions of interpersonal communication solely in terms of a chain reaction of strictly personal empowerments; and in any case, we know from experience that any such imagined chains have weak links: we find ourselves also failing to live up to the positive regard extended to us by others and thus we interrupt the flow of constructive communication. At the level of institutions, it is true that people do indeed rely on stable traditions for appropriate communication; but we know that traditions can also harden and become a hindrance to communication rather than a help.

Thus we are faced with the fact that ultimately we find ourselves presented to each other for appropriate communication simply as we are, naked and without ado; just by being around each other, we mutually invite constructive ("creative") acceptance, and we discern each other's habitual capacity for it; in the final analysis, what we must respond to in communicating is our naked, unadorned selves, presented to each other in our irreducible otherness.

Yet the fact is that we do actually respond, and with a spontaneity that is never quite reducible to the merely appropriate. True encounters with others do occur, transcending the world of things; others get the best out of us, that is, the truly unexpected response we did not know we had inside us. When truly appropriate communication — the free mutual sharing of ourselves — does occur, it somehow reveals a spiritual wealth that surpasses the expectations prompted by the merely given. Living, immature as we are, in a precarious world, here we are, actually communicating; while not creating one another in any absolute sense, we do decisively affect each other as we grow as persons. Thus the fact that fruitful interpersonal communication animated by freedom and personal maturity does occur, even in the midst of chance and immaturity, is a marvel that eludes complete rationalization. There is something about the experience of interpersonal communication that suggests that, ultimately, it is simply a *gift* — *one* that will forever surprise the anticipations of even the most mature.

Not surprisingly, therefore, the free, mature, truly integrated, self-giving person is experienced, in some religious traditions, as a *witness* to a better world. Secure personal identity freely, unselfconsciously, and indeed unselfishly shared with others, we sense, must be somehow embedded in, and encompassed and supported by, a larger Presence that is ineffably free, eternal, generous, indefeasible, and mysteriously self-manifestingly,

> Ground of being, and granite of it: past all
> Grásp Gód, thronèd behind
> Death with sovereignty that heeds but hides, bodes but abides.[34]

Ultimately, that is, it must be a transcendent, gracious self-communicative Presence that inspires and guarantees the freedom with which the best among us communicate themselves to other persons. Only an unconditional, all-enabling Presence is transcendent enough to move our innermost immanence to open itself to others without anxiety about ourselves.[35]

But in that case that same Presence must also be so penetrating as to ground the deepest identity of all persons, in an acceptance so unconditional as to be wholly creative. There, at the core of each person, it establishes, not only the unconditional demand for positive regard that marks all persons as persons, but also their irresistible attractiveness. That is, God's everlasting offer of self-communication must be the transcendent precondition for the immanent appeal that invites us to touch and affect others so close to the core of their identities. By way of a variation on a theme played long ago by Aquinas, we might say, "All those who encounter others encounter God implicitly in whomever they encounter."[36] God's (self)-communication, therefore, could not

---

34. Gerard Manley Hopkins, *The Wreck of the Deutschland,* stanza 32.

35. We can think of persons of extraordinary maturity and commitment like Dag Hammarskjöld, whose reflections, collected in *Markings,* have led many to a renewed, truly responsible sense of God. Fictional characters may come to mind as well: Prince Leo Nikolayevich Myshkin in Dostoevsky's *The Idiot,* consciously modeled after Jesus Christ by its author; Tarrou in Albert Camus' *The Plague,* who has decided to identify with victims rather than join the cause of violence by fighting evil; and, in Iris Murdoch's novels, figures like Max LeJour in *The Unicorn* (1963), with his mature belief in the nonviolence of the Good, or, more recently, in *The Message to the Planet* (1989), the eccentric Marcus Vallar, who, after remarkable early careers as a mathematician and a painter, sets out on a tightrope search for the truth beyond the cosmic network, until at length he charms others by a wordless, enigmatic kindness, to which, however, he himself succumbs because it leads to "pure suffering," which is an attribute of God alone. On the truly adult person as a witness to the living God, cf. Thomas Merton's observations on "final integration" in *Contemplation in a World of Action,* 205-17; cf. also his *Faith and Violence,* 111-18. I am indebted to Walter E. Conn's anthology *Conversion* for the last two references.

36. Cf. *Quaestio disputata de veritate,* q.22, a.2, ad 1: Omnia cognoscentia cognoscunt implicite Deum in quolibet cognito ("All beings that know implicitly know God in whatever they know").

possibly be experienced as a mere intervention from outside; it graciously addresses us at the core of our identity, where we are made in the divine image and likeness, that is, in the image of Christ.

But in that case the divine Presence also encompasses our failures in communication; that is, it patiently and faithfully holds out hope for a renewal of encounter even when those involved in interpersonal communication prove inadequate, and when the traditions that support it languish and lapse. "God writes straight with crooked lines."

A well-known passage in Augustine's *Confessions* illustrates this insight. When at last he finds himself in communion with God in and through the community of the Church, Augustine is free, finally, to recall the implications of his experience of being, not so very long ago, the Prodigal Son. Completely at a loss, he recalls how he had wandered, first among the poets, then among the philosophers; none of them had connected and communicated with him in such a way as to nourish him and lead him to a mature sense of identity; he had been

> . . . barred from You as much as from the husks I gave to the swine to eat,
> . . . struggling and straining, short of truth.

Now a Christian, he has become a witness. With profound gratitude he recalls the significant others he has encountered on his slow, winding road to the Church: Monica, Alypius, Ambrose. They have been to him, not only reliable supporters of his authentic, long-lost self, but also faithful and effective witnesses to God's enduring presence. But that is not all. Participating in the community of faith has enabled Augustine also to discover what lay behind the communicative impasses and failures in his life. Ultimately, therefore, it is God, transcendent and immanent, who has led him to the truth, both by the banality of illusion and error and by the faithfulness of trustworthy friends. So he can conclude:

> Yet You were inside, deeper than my innermost self, and above, higher than my uppermost self.[37]

Here is the core of the catholic understanding of revelation. The divine self-communication comes from on high, yet it is inseparable from authentic human immanence. But far from simply becoming a matter of self-experience, the God who reveals the divine Self becomes more, not less, adorable and ungraspable for being so intimately manifest.[38] Thus divine self-communica-

---

37. *Confessions* 3.6.11 (CSEL 33.52-53): "longe peregrinabar abs te exclusus et a siliquis porcorum, quos de siliquis pascebam"; "laborans et aestuans inopia veri"; "tu autem eras interior intimo et superior summo meo."
38. Cf. *GE*, §34.2.

tion makes witnesses of human persons: God is "the God of Abraham, the God of Isaac, and the God of Jacob," and ultimately the "God of Jesus Christ." Yet while touching us as persons, God bids us reshape the world of both persons and things. In that world, we cannot hope ever to convey or understand God's self-revelation fully, whether in action or in speech, whether as a church community or as individual Christians. So we treasure such ways as the tradition has tried, while we keep on seeking inspiration to try new ways as we travel.

Concluding Reflections

Let us conclude with a few assorted reflections to establish linkage between the basic explorations spelled out in this essay and the understanding of divine revelation happily current today.

If our analyses are an attempt at broadening the basis of the Catholic understanding of revelation, they may also help remove some of its traditional rigidity. This rigidity is rooted in recent history. Explicit Catholic doctrine on divine revelation as such is a late development; it did not occur until the nineteenth century. Accordingly, the theological reflections associated with it took their cue, not from the great tradition, but almost exclusively from an eighteenth-century agenda: the deadlock between reason and Christian revelation. Practically speaking, therefore, "revelation" had come to be identified exclusively with the *mysteria proprie dicta* of the Incarnation and the mysteries directly connected with it (cf. DS 2779; 3015-20; 1341). This had led to two interconnected positions, misleading not only because of their unnecessary rigidity but also on account of their being out of touch with the great tradition.

The first position concerns both anthropology and Christian theology. The understanding of the "mysteries" of the faith, and of the way in which they had been delivered to the Church, had become far too content-oriented and rational. "Mystery" had long ceased to be understood as a matter both of God's ongoing self-communication to humanity and of the corresponding revelation in history of humanity's own authentic nature and destiny. Instead, it had come to be understood as a "deposit" of absolute truths, inaccessible to reason by definition, and hence acceptable only by God-given faith, upon the sole authority of the magisterium — an authority ultimately guaranteed by the revealing God. In response to this, the Second Vatican Council based its teaching about revelation on a broader, less rationalistic anthropology, enshrined in the *Pastoral Constitution on the Church in the Modern World* (cf. esp. *Gaudium et spes* 12). On a more strictly theological front, it described revelation in the salvation-historical terms proposed by the *Dogmatic Constitution on Divine Revelation* (*Dei verbum* 2-4). The explorations offered in this essay are substantially indebted to both of these moves.

The second position is likewise connected with salvation-history and aims at correcting a narrowly Christological understanding of revelation. In making the divinity of Jesus Christ into the sole determinative truth of revelation, Christian doctrine and theology had separated the historical Jesus from the mystery inherent in Israel's faith-tradition and in the "cloud of witnesses" (Heb 12:1) produced by it. The "pioneer and accomplisher of our faith" (Heb 12:2), the "faithful witness" (Rev 1:5; cf. 1 Tim 6:13), had almost entirely disappeared behind "the Word made flesh" (Jn 1:14). As a result, any Christology from below had become impossible, whether of the transcendental kind or of the kind that could take the historical life of Jesus the Jew seriously. Vatican II made essential corrections in this area. It recalled God's self-revelation to Abraham and to the People of Israel through Moses and through the Prophets (*Dei verbum* 14; cf. 4), and it insisted on salvation-historical revelation, by means of which "the deepest truth regarding both God and human salvation has shone forth to us in Christ, who is the mediator as well as the fulfillment of all of revelation" (*Dei verbum* 2). It will have escaped no one that the analysis of revelation proposed in this essay is fundamentally indebted to Israel's monotheism and the humanism that has been its fruit. In Israel's faith, it is precisely God's utter transcendence that guarantees the intimate divine presence to a humanity made in the divine image, and hence natively attuned to the privilege of hearing God's silent Word in the utterances of a succession of witnesses calling for responsiveness and responsibility.

In his important monograph *Models of Revelation*,[39] Avery Dulles has explained that revelation takes many forms, and hence that it allows for a variety of partial, yet convergent, theological approaches. Thus it can be viewed as doctrine, history, inner experience, dialectical presence, and new awareness. Readers familiar with Dulles' treatise will have noticed that the analysis proposed here attempts to do justice to the models proposed by Dulles in their organic interconnectedness. They will also have noticed that our treatment endorses Dulles' own constructive proposal: revelation is God's self-revealing presence mediated symbolically.[40]

Finally, our contention that significant (self)-communication that comes to us, both from others in their relative transcendence and from the

---

39. Garden City, N.Y.: Doubleday, 1983.

40. On the subject of symbolism and the usefulness of "dialogue" as a model of revelation, cf. also David Brown's "God and Symbolic Action," in *Divine Action: Studies Inspired by the Philosophical Theology of Austin Farrer*, ed. Brian Hebblethwaite and Edward Henderson (Edinburgh: T. & T. Clark, 1990), 103-22. The following proviso, however, is in order. Brown's appeal to telepathy and telekinesis (104) is an *argumentum ex ignoto*. It suggests (mistakenly, I think) that we are dealing with reliably established experiences and, what is more, with reliable insight into the structure of these experiences. More pertinently, however, the appeal to paranormal phenomena is not essential to Brown's argument; hence it could have been omitted.

utterly transcendent God, is never experienced as a mere intervention from outside involves an endorsement of an important thesis of Karl Rahner's: only those whose authenticity has been inwardly transformed by God's self-communication can interpret the historic symbols of revelation, that is, can understand divine revelation as it has taken shape in concrete, "categorical" forms.[41]

41. *Foundations of Christian Faith,* 149-50: "This transcendental knowledge . . . must be distinguished from verbal and propositional revelation as such. . . . [It] is a modification of our transcendental consciousness produced permanently by God in grace. . . . And as an element in our transcendentality which is produced by God's self-communication, it is already revelation in the proper sense. . . . Only when God is the subjective principle of the speaking and of man's hearing in faith can God in his own self express himself."

Embodied Thinking: Reflections on Feminist Theological Method

CAROL P. CHRIST

In a recently published essay entitled "Problems with Feminist Theory: Historicity and the Search for Sure Foundations,"[1] Sheila Greeve Davaney alleges that there is a fundamental contradiction in feminist theology which is a result of its failure to take the problematic character of knowledge seriously. Davaney states that the Enlightenment has bequeathed us two issues: (1) the quest for a certain and universal basis for thought rooted in the relation of the mind or thought to reality; and (2) the recognition of the historically situated and therefore relative character of thought. For Davaney, the second proposition negates the first, leaving us with the postmodern statement that there is "no such thing as objective, universally valid experience or knowledge. Human beings and our knowledge are irrevocably historical and hence conditioned by time and space." Davaney does not dispute the Nietzschean statement as mediated by Foucault that truth claims reflect a will to power. However, she asserts that "forms of discourse are *accepted* as truth, both by virtue of coercion and because of the possibilities such realms of discourse bring into being." In the second part of this statement, she introduces what she later calls a pragmatics of truth, in which truth claims, or, in weaker form, claims to the validity of discourse, are to be judged "upon the pragmatic grounds of what kind of existence these visions permitted or inhibited."[2]

According to Davaney, feminist theologians Elisabeth Schüssler Fiorenza,

1. *Embodied Love: Sensuality and Relationship as Feminist Values,* ed. Paula M. Cooey, Sharon Farmer, and Mary Ellen Ross (San Francisco: Harper & Row, 1987), 79-95.
2. "Problems with Feminist Theory," in *Embodied Love,* 82, 83, 93.

Published originally in the *Journal of Feminist Studies in Religion* 5 (Spring 1989): 7-15. Used with permission.

Rosemary Radford Ruether, and Mary Daly accept the modern and postmodern legacy when they assert that patriarchal thought reflects the will to power of men in given places and times. But Davaney argues that in different ways, each thinker has "rejected the full nihilistic [fully relativistic] implications of this line of thought."[3] Davaney argues that Schüssler Fiorenza and Ruether appeal in the end to a correspondence between feminist vision and divine nature or purpose, while Daly asserts the correspondence between feminist knowing and ultimate reality. Though Davaney's critique is limited to these three thinkers, the tenor of her rhetoric suggests that she does not believe that any feminist theologian has avoided this contradiction.

The issues Davaney raises are significant enough to warrant further consideration. In this essay, I will question her reading of the work of Elisabeth Schüssler Fiorenza, and then reflect in a more general way on whether feminist theology ought to accept the program of postmodernism, including what Davaney calls the nihilistic premises of thoroughgoing relativism.

Davaney admits that her case against Schüssler Fiorenza is the weakest because Schüssler Fiorenza as a historian has made the challenge of historical consciousness central in her work. While Davaney reads Schüssler Fiorenza as acknowledging the historical and relative character of all truth claims, she finds a contradictory set of assertions in Schüssler Fiorenza's work. Davaney asserts that despite her lip service to historical relativism, Schüssler Fiorenza "assumes the ontological reality of God and, further, that such divine reality is the source of the equalitarian possibilities she perceives in Christian tradition."[4]

I agree with Davaney that there is ambiguity in Schüssler Fiorenza's writing. I have read her work as embodying the contradiction which Davaney notes. However, in this essay I wish to suggest another reading. Davaney chooses a representative quotation from *In Memory of Her* to buttress her critique.

> Biblical revelation and truth are given only in those texts and interpretative models that transcend critically their patriarchal frameworks and allow for a vision of Christian women as historical actors and theological subjects.[5]

While this statement appears to support Davaney's contention that Schüssler Fiorenza makes universal claims for her reading of divine purposes, another reading is possible. Let me begin by noting the complexity of Schüssler Fiorenza's statement. (1) It grants some kind of status to "biblical revelation and truth." (I will return to this point below.) (2) It gives privileged status to "texts and models that critically transcend their patriarchal frameworks." While specifically feminist, this claim stands in the tradition of Marx and liberation

---

3. Ibid., 83.

4. Ibid., 88.

5. Ibid., 88; quoting *In Memory of Her: A Feminist Theological Reconstruction of Christian Origins* (New York: Crossroad, 1983), 30.

theology in granting privileged status to "the view from below." It seems to be applicable to texts and models which do not stand in biblical tradition or claim divine sanction. (3) It focuses on women as "historical actors and theological subjects," not on God as historical subject or object of ontological assertion. The focus on women as "historical actors" is consonant with the work of many feminist historians, especially Gerda Lerner, who is cited elsewhere by Schüssler Fiorenza. The notion of women as "theological subjects" appears to refer to the claims of women as historical actors to have been motivated by experience — either individual or (more likely, given Schüssler Fiorenza's focus on women-church) communal — of divine call. Women's subjective experience does not necessarily imply claims about the ontological or objective reality or nature of God or truth.

Davaney's interpretation of this passage focuses on Schüssler Fiorenza's apparent assertion that "biblical revelation and truth" exist, a notion that contradicts the historicist claim to the relativity of truth. But what if Schüssler Fiorenza is not so nakedly self-contradictory? Then we must assume the following implicit modifiers (noted in italics) to the quotation.

> *It is my experience and assertion that* biblical revelation and truth are given *to the community of womenchurch* only in those texts and interpretive models which transcend critically their patriarchal frameworks and allow for a vision of Christian women as historical actors and theological subjects.

As a statement about her own experience within the community of Christians struggling against patriarchal oppression, Schüssler Fiorenza's assertion can be accepted as being true for her and potentially for other members of the community of "womenchurch." We would then read the entire quotation not as a universal and objective statement about God, nor even about biblical revelation and truth, but as the subjective statement of one woman speaking for a larger group. If we were to ask this historical actor and theological subject why she chooses to identify herself and her interpretations of biblical revelation and truth within the community of womenchurch, she might reply by rehearsing historical and subjective reasons found in her published work: as a young woman in Germany in the 1950s and 1960s, she found more support for her struggles for equality in the Bible than in secular culture;[6] she continues to find a community of revelation and struggle in womenchurch; she feels responsibility to women in the churches; she believes she cannot abandon her history and identity as a Christian woman, but must work to transform Christianity through reclaiming the history of women.[7]

---

6. See "Feminist Spirituality, Christian Identity, and Catholic Vision," in *Womanspirit Rising: A Feminist Reader on Religion,* ed. Carol P. Christ and Judith Plaskow (San Francisco: Harper & Row, 1979), 137.

7. *In Memory of Her,* passim.

If this reading is correct, then the truth claims in Schüssler Fiorenza's work are not all on the same level. Insofar as she is writing as a feminist historian, her work relativizes predominant patriarchal paradigms — both religious and secular — used to interpret early Christian history. She is claiming to a wide audience that her reading of early Christian history is as plausible as other readings. Insofar as she argues that a model for historical interpretation which affirms women as historical actors is more plausible than one that does not, she argues that her reading is more accurate than standard patriarchal readings. Note, however, that even this stronger claim does not require theological justification; one could argue *mutatis mutandis* that women must have been historical actors in the creation of Sumerian religion, Hinduism, Communism, Nazism, etc. Moreover we are not required by the model of women as historical actors to accept that women played equal roles in shaping early Christian history — though Schüssler Fiorenza argues this as well.

Insofar, however, as Schüssler Fiorenza speaks as theological subject, as a Christian feminist, about the nature of women in the early Christian movement, her interpretative stance and claims are rooted in the contemporary experience of womenchurch. Unless she is making supposedly universal ontological and objective claims about the nature of God, then her claim that "biblical revelation and truth is found only in those texts and interpretative models that transcend critically their patriarchal frameworks" must be read as frankly historical and perspectival, intelligible to others, but persuasive only to those who already share or are willing to adopt her assumptions.

If this reading of Schüssler Fiorenza's work is plausible, then why did Davaney (and why do others) read her as making objective ontological statements, or as claiming to have uncovered the definitive truth about the early Christian movement and the Christian God? I believe there is an inherent ambiguity in the discourses — historical relativist, scholarly objective, Christian theological, feminist critical — which Schüssler Fiorenza combines in her work, that lends itself to such interpretations. The quotation cited by Davaney and much of Schüssler Fiorenza's rhetoric sound like traditional Christian theology and apologetics or like objective scholarly assertion. While we can hardly expect Schüssler Fiorenza (or any other feminist theologian) to preface every statement with "my view is," "it seems to me that," "from my perspective," we can note that given the history of absolute claims for truth in Christian theological traditions and in much scholarly writing, misunderstandings are likely to occur. Moreover, it is possible that Schüssler Fiorenza has not entirely freed herself from such habits of thought despite her stated intentions. Finally, it seems to me that the ambiguity in her discourse serves to make her work more acceptable to some Christians who are willing to accept Schüssler Fiorenza's conclusions about the roles of women in the early Christian movement, but not her radical relativizing of the nature of authority and of Christian truth claims.

Yet even this reading of Schüssler Fiorenza's historical and theological program would not satisfy Davaney. Davaney objects to all claims — including subjective and intersubjective or communal claims — about the referential nature of God language. Davaney would object to Schüssler Fiorenza's (on the reading I have offered here) retreat into perspectivalism in her justification of her vision of womenchurch as a present experience and historical reality. Davaney wishes feminist theology to subscribe not only to thoroughgoing historical relativism, but also to speak in a discourse which accepts the postmodernist view that since no correspondence between modes of thought and ontological reality can be proved, no claims about the nature of reality or of God should be made, unless such claims are acknowledged as being strictly pragmatic.

According to Davaney, whose position is influenced by that of her teacher Gordon Kaufman,[8] feminist theology should give up

> the appeal to ontological reality as a grounds [*sic*] of validation for our positions. First, feminist visions would be understood as thoroughly human constructions sharing the same *ontological* status as male perspectives. The validity of these competing "regimes of truth" would be judged not according to which was "closer to reality" but upon the pragmatic grounds of what kind of existence these visions permitted or inhibited. . . .
>
> Second, the status of religious symbols would undergo thorough reconsideration . . . feminist religious and theological language has implicitly been assumed to be referential in character . . . such a referential nature would be denied. Instead, religious symbols would be interpreted, along with the larger worldviews or visions that they center, as solely products of human imagination and the projection of human values and desire.[9]

Thus for Davaney it is not enough to acknowledge the perspectival nature of truth claims about feminism, about reality, or about God. Rather, we are asked not to make such claims at all. We are asked to adopt a distanced stance from all visions and truth claims — feminist and theological — because there is no neutral court in which such claims can be judged true or false. We are asked to treat all truth claims as hypotheses to be offered to another, but not fully explicated, neutral court in which they can be judged more or less conducive to producing a "kind of existence" that might be chosen or preferred. As Davaney notes, this solution does not resolve questions of value because it "raises the specter of nihilism in which all perspectives are equal and all differences are leveled."[10] She does not tell us how to resolve this problem, though she notes that it must be addressed.

Davaney's theological program, like Kaufman's, has definite attractiveness

8. Gordon D. Kaufman, *An Essay on Theological Method,* rev. ed. (Missoula, MT: Scholars Press, 1979).

9. Davaney, 93.

10. Ibid.

and merit. I agree with Kaufman and Davaney that religious symbols and theological assumptions ought not be uncritically passed on from generation to generation, but should be subjected to critical and pragmatic analysis concerning the kind of life they permit or inhibit. The feminist critique of God language (to which I have contributed) accepts this premise. And I appreciate the bold critiques of religious symbolism offered by Kaufman in *Theology for a Nuclear Age.*

I would like to suggest, however, that the position which Davaney champions is itself paradoxically yet deeply indebted to the Enlightenment search for universal truth. Davaney denies that universal truth can be found, as many Enlightenment thinkers hoped it could, in the correspondence of thought to reality. But she still hopes that there can be a universal forum in which questions of value can be adjudicated.

I am suspicious, on several grounds, of the broad and absolutist claims made for this method. First, Kaufman's method can be viewed as historically rooted in the isolation of theologians from the universe of discourse found in the academy and other intellectual circles of American life. Kaufman's "suspension of belief" in the referential character of theological symbols can be understood as an attempt to make theological discourse intelligible to those who do not believe in God or identify with the Christian faith and thus to restore to Christian theologians their onetime position as spokespersons for the moral values of the culture. This reading suggests that his hope (largely unfulfilled) was that philosophers and other intellectuals, including politicians, would take theological discourse seriously and enter into conversation with it, and conversely that theologians would enter into conversations with nontheological systems of value. Kaufman's desire that theologians reenter a public dialogue is commendable (though it could also be analyzed as reflecting a "will to power"). But will Kaufman's program in fact achieve its goal of enabling theologians to enter into American public discourse?

In an essay titled "Toward an American Public Theology," Ronald Thiemann makes the following comment:

> There has been a great deal of discussion in academic theology about "public theology." Most of that debate has focused on the question of whether theological arguments are available for public examination and whether theological arguments are intelligible beyond the confines of a particular religious community. While such issues are intellectually interesting and important within a rather small circle of academic theologians, they only begin to help us address what I consider the far more important question: will religious convictions and theological analyses have any real impact on the way our public lives are structured? Can a truly public theology have a salutary influence on the development of public policy within a pluralistic democratic nation?[11]

11. *Harvard Divinity Bulletin* 18, no. 1 (1987): 6.

Religious convictions — but not theological analyses of the liberal academic type — are having an obvious impact on American public life in the programs of the right, which have limited access to abortion, defeated the equal rights amendment, led publishers to be wary of offending fundamentalist sensibilities in school texts, fueled the arms race, supported the wars against "Godless Communism" in Latin America and elsewhere, etc. This type of religious influence, however, is not the type that more liberal intellectual theologians such as Kaufman, Thiemann, Davaney, Schüssler Fiorenza, and I find salutary. And certainly this influence is not fueled by a religious discourse that attempts to make itself intelligible to academics and intellectuals by denying the "referential character" of its truth claims, nor is it one that respects the plurality of value systems in American culture. Yet the impact of religious fundamentalism suggests that academic theology's criterion of public availability of discourse is not a necessary criterion for public influence.

While I find many admirable aspects in the Kaufmanian theological program, I suggest that its intellectual detachment, its sidestepping of the question of the referential nature of religious symbols in the lives of those for whom they have meaning, is its greatest weakness, and is a characteristic feminist theologians would do well *not* to emulate. Certainly I do not advocate that feminist theologians eschew the questions posed by the Enlightenment and create a feminist fundamentalism, though there are those who are pursuing this goal with greater and lesser degrees of clarity about their methods. I agree with modernism and postmodernism that we must be suspicious of all claims to universal truth, to a direct correspondence between our visions and ontological reality. I agree with Kaufman, Thiemann, and other liberal theologians that theology must be respectful of pluralism, and I share their hopes that nonfundamentalist forms of theology might once again have an impact upon American life. Like many other feminist thealogians, I believe that the symbol of Goddess could have a salutary effect not only on women's self-esteem and power, but on the ecological and nuclear crises. But I disagree with Davaney and Kaufman that the way to achieve this goal is to "embrace the full nihilistic implications" of thoroughgoing relativism. As I indicated above, I believe this theological move was rooted in a hope of making theology more "public" (implicitly understood as more accessible to modern intellectuals), a hope that has not been realized.

I find the theological method of Elisabeth Schüssler Fiorenza, as I have read it in this essay, a more viable model for theological reflection. I suggest that theology is more likely to be able to enter into conversation with other worldviews not from a stance of detachment, but from one of commitment. We should not present ourselves as detached critics of religious commitment, but, in Schüssler Fiorenza's words, as "theological subjects" who make truth claims in awareness of the perspectival and relative character of such claims. Truth may be relative, but we are relational beings, and in our lives, there are relative truths. In my life, and in the lives of most feminist theologians and thealogians, commitment to feminism does not have the same ontological status as commitment to patriarchalism. My passion for feminism is shaped by my felt experience, tempered by reflection, that it is more true to believe that women and men are equal and that women's contributions to the human community have been and are as important as men's, than to believe the opposite. While the experience of living as a feminist in interaction with feminists and others has led me [to] rethink many positions I once held, to be suspicious of labeling any particular program, lifestyle, or thealogical vision as the only valid way of achieving feminist goals, and to broaden and deepen my understanding of feminism, it has not shaken my conviction that women are fully human, nor that patriarchy (understood as a system of power relations including but not limited to the suppression of female power) has inhibited the possibilities of life on this earth. Similarly, in my life the symbol of Goddess has a referential character, pointing to women's creative powers and to human interdependence and connection with what patriarchal splitting has called "the natural world" (as if there were any other). I believe the symbol of Goddess has a particular power to evoke this and other realities and that other symbols are also necessary. But my belief that "we are nature," and that "this earth is my sister," as Susan Griffin expressed it,[12] are not merely intellectual hypotheses in my day-to-day life. Now as a cold wind blows outside my window on the almond blossoms and creates whitecaps on the sea, I feel deeply my connection to a fragile beauty and a power greater than my own. I am willing to submit these feelings and passions to pragmatic analysis, to ask whether the symbols that have meaning for me enhance human and all life on the planet, but I am not willing to act or write as if my commitment to feminism and my thealogical vision are not deeply and passionately held nor to pretend that I grant patriarchal or Christian views the same "ontological" status in my life.

As feminists then, I argue that we should not embrace the nihilism which Davaney, following Foucault and others, calls essential to postmodern consciousness. I argue that feminist theologians and thealogians must embrace the ambiguity of conditional but not absolute acceptance of the modern and postmodern frameworks. This ambiguity is necessary to feminism. We acknowledge the perspectival nature of all truth claims, but we are not thoroughgoing relativists, because our feminist experience contradicts that. We are not nihilists, because we believe that feminism has the potential to better the world. Similarly as theologians, we have religious experience and vision which ground our symbols and theological visions. While we ought not to assume that these experiences and visions can be objectively proved to all by rational argumentation, we nonetheless acknowledge that they function as grounding for our day-to-day lives. The Enlightenment program of universal truth available to

12. *Woman and Nature: The Roaring inside Her* (New York: Harper & Row, 1978), 219, 226.

every rational mind is not our program. We seek to speak a truth rooted in our experience, our time and place, our bodies. We can affirm the relativity of all universal truth claims, because we know that all truth claims are rooted in time and space, in experience and body. And there is no experience or body that is not perspectival. We can also be suspicious of universal feminist programs — because we are not all the same, especially not cross-culturally — while at the same time affirming with Mary Daly that as finite and limited individuals and within finite and limited communities, we do experience ourselves and our visions as rooted in being and truth. Because of the depth of our experience, we ought not adopt the detached abstractionism of the Enlightenment and postmodern programs, which in any case will appeal only to a limited segment of the intellectual elite. For feminists, the lessons of the Enlightenment and postmodernism should teach us to become more embodied, not more disembodied in our theologies. Purely pragmatic analyses of truth claims, while useful and necessary as a part of overall strategy, ought not to be the central principles of our theological program.

How then do we embrace what for us must be the ambiguous legacy of modern and postmodern consciousness? How do we present our views in the fullness of our embodied and perspectival commitment, without falling back into a premodern universalism that has rightly been criticized as expressing the will to power of those who have been able to express their views? I suggest it is not by pretending to an intellectual neutrality which in any case is only a pose, but rather by acknowledging and affirming the conditions of time and space, which limit our perspectives as well as giving them their distinctive perspectival power. This does not mean reducing feminist or theological claims to auto-biography, though frank acknowledgment of the autobiographical basis of our thinking is one of the ways we can positively affirm the relativity of our thought. But we can also scrutinize and argue for our positions, as Davaney suggests, both in terms of their pragmatic value and their ability to explain a broad range of experience beyond our own. We should be sensitive to the "will to power" of class, race, culture, or religious privilege which may be expressed in our work. We should expect our views to be challenged by those who hold other perspectives, and remain open to changing or modifying our views as our understanding grows. We should not hold our views so tightly that we cannot appreciate the perspectival truths embodied in the lives and works of others. We should think of our "truth claims" as a product of embodied *thinking*, not as eternally or universally valid *thought*.

I.3

Faith and Knowledge

JOHN Y. MAY

"So that you may *know* and *believe* me, and understand. . . ."[1]

Faith is multi-dimensional in nature. It is, among other things, a decision of the will in which the individual determines to follow God's guidelines. It is also assent to something viewed as being true.[2] While we exercise faith in its totality, it is this latter aspect of faith — its cognitive or conceptual quality — which will be the main focus of this essay.

What is the source or beginning point for faith? What serves as its basis? What is its object? In what way, if any, does faith relate to knowledge?

Faith as Response to Revelation

Faith, in distinctively biblical terms, is an intelligent response to revelation. It is receiving what God has revealed, relying on his testimony as true. Failure to grasp this aspect of faith can lead to a wholesale misunderstanding of Christian belief.

The Bible in its entirety sets forth this viewpoint of faith as a confident response to revelation. It is so important that we should briefly note several crucial passages on this subject (emphasis added):

Whoever hears my *word* and believes him who sent me has eternal life.[3]

---

1. Isaiah 43:10.
2. Bernard Ramm, commenting on this aspect of faith, observed that "if there is no sense of truth, no sense of meeting reality . . . [the] experience is worthless." *The God Who Makes a Difference* (Waco, Texas: Word Books, 1972), 107.
3. John 5:24.

Published originally in the *Evangelical Journal* 8 (1990): 83-90. Reprinted with permission.

How can they believe in the one of whom they have not heard? . . . faith comes from hearing the *message,* and the *message* is heard through the *word* of Christ.[4]

And you also were included in Christ when you heard the *word* of truth, the *gospel* of your salvation. Having believed, you were marked in him with a seal.[5]

When you received the *word* of God, which you heard from us, you accepted it . . . as it actually is, the *word* of God, which is at work in you who believe.[6]

Anyone who believes in the Son of God has this testimony. . . . Anyone who does not believe God has made him out to be a liar, because he has not believed the *testimony God has given* about his Son.[7]

What is unmistakably clear from these and other portions of Scripture is that Christian faith is always a response on the part of the individual to some revelation-based knowledge — the "word," the "message," the "gospel," the "testimony God has given." It is always a decisive, intelligible reaction to some piece of revealed information. Faith which does not meet this criterion may be credulity or wishful thinking, but it does not qualify as being biblical faith.

Faith Begins with Some Knowledge

Christian faith, as we have observed, starts with what God has revealed to us and has done for us. Authentic faith always begins with *some* knowledge. One person has commented that "a very little knowledge is often sufficient if a man is to believe, but some knowledge there must be."[8]

Faith, always starting with some knowledge, does not issue out of inward nothingness or a blind leap in the dark. It is not conceived in a cognitive vacuum. Alongside of the volitional and relational components of faith is the functioning of the intellect or mind. The intellect listens to or observes the content of some revelation-based knowledge (perhaps some portion of the gospel account, or some awareness of our need and Christ's provision for it)

4. Romans 10:14, 17.
5. Ephesians 1:13.
6. 1 Thessalonians 2:13.
7. 1 John 5:10.
8. J. Gresham Machen, *What Is Christianity?* (Grand Rapids: Eerdmans, 1951), 120-21. James I. Packer adds, "we need not wonder at instances of genuine faith and repentance resulting from amazingly little . . . formal instruction" ("The Means of Conversion," *Crux* 25.4 [Dec. 1989]: 19).

and then mentally consents to the information received. This process is a requisite part of the act of faith.[9]

One frequently cited example of supposed mindless belief is the irresponsible interpretation given by the Danish writer, Søren Kierkegaard, to Abraham's willingness to sacrifice his only son Isaac. That Abraham would be willing to actually follow through on a morally questionable command to kill his son seems, to Kierkegaard, a totally irrational yet essential basis for Abraham's commitment. But a cursory examination of the biblical text[10] and setting will yield a very different conclusion than that of Kierkegaard.

First, one must observe that at this point in Abraham's life he had built up a reservoir of faith-affirming experiences and confidence in both the person and promises of God. Secondly, Abraham had apparently been assured, somehow, that it was indeed this same trustworthy and faithful God (not the devil) who was demanding his willingness to carry out this act. Thirdly, the text specifically indicates that Abraham — even as he raised the knife in obedience — may have anticipated a substitution ("God himself will provide the lamb") or a restoration to life ("*we* will come back to you").[11] Indeed, Abraham's case is a classical example of faith as response to some knowledge-action in obedience to revelatory direction and a mental-spiritual wrestling with the meaning of the call to action with which he was confronted. In any event, there is no biblical justification whatsoever for Kierkegaard's absurd conclusion that Abraham's example demonstrated that "Faith begins precisely there where thinking leaves off."[12] On the contrary, Abraham's act of obedience — perplexing as it may be in many respects — is still another illustration of authentic faith as a response to revealed knowledge.

In view of the widespread misunderstanding of faith, we need to realize that one biblical writer, Paul, strongly denounced a believer's zeal or fervor which did not square with knowledge.[13] The continued growth of genuine faith too, Paul insisted, was dependent — among other things — on mental application: "be transformed by the renewing of your mind."[14] The key point here is that, for Christian faith, the whole process starts with at least some knowledge.

---

9. Edward J. Carnell insisted, "Surely, if faith is not related to knowledge . . . it is meaningless." *An Introduction to Christian Apologetics* (Grand Rapids: Eerdmans, 1950), 65.

10. Genesis 22.

11. See also Hebrews 11:17-19.

12. Søren Kierkegaard, *Fear and Trembling,* trans. Walter Lowrie (Princeton: Princeton University Press, 1941), 78.

13. Romans 10:2.

14. Romans 12:2.

Faith Focused in Christ

Christian faith ultimately is directed to the person of Christ. It is not interested in knowledgeless, pointless meditation. This is so because the focal point of God's revelation of himself and his revelatory acts centers in Christ. He becomes the primary representative and the culmination of the whole process of God's self-disclosure.

> In the past God Spoke . . . at many times and in various ways, but in these last days he has spoken to us by his Son.[15]

> No one has ever seen God, but God the only Son . . . has made him known.[16]

> If you really knew me [Jesus Christ], you would know my Father as well.[17]

> That they may know you, the only true God, and Jesus Christ, whom you have sent.[18]

What is the significance of all of this? Simply stated, the object of authentic faith is Christ. And what kind of person is he? He is not some flaky, mystical guru. He is described as the one in whom are personally embodied "all the treasures of wisdom and knowledge."[19]

Knowledge with Its Source in Revelation

With the role that knowledge plays in the act of believing, it is not surprising that knowledge is highly valued in the scriptural scheme of things.[20] After all, knowledge itself is one of the attributes of God, and as we have just observed, of the person of Christ as well. Following the initial exercise of faith, the believer is urged to seek additional knowledge through the study of the Bible under the guidance of God's Spirit.[21]

Some knowledge, we have observed, is revelation-based knowledge. Faith

---

15. Hebrews 1:1-2.
16. John 1:18.
17. John 14:7.
18. John 17:3.
19. Colossians 2:3.

20. Colossians 2:17. Instances of negative warning include those where a) the acquisition of knowledge results in either pride (1 Cor. 8:1) or an idolatrous obsession; and b) the acquired so-called "knowledge" clearly conflicts with revealed truth (1 Cor. 2:5-15; 2 Cor. 10:6).

21. The Spirit of God — instrumental in initial conversion to a right view and appropriation of the revealed information at one's disposal (John 16:8-9; Titus 3:5) — is also essential in the subsequent development of spiritual understanding and discovery as a believer grows in his commitment and Christian life (John 14:26; 16:12; 1 Cor. 2:10-14).

— that is, distinctively Christian faith — has its foundation in this kind of knowledge. By this, we mean that its source is primarily from revelation, the God-initiated disclosure of information in historical actions and verbal interpretations of their significance.[22] What are some of the characteristics of revelation?

1. It is Scriptural. The message or content of revelation is inscripturated, documented, recorded,[23] and specifically identified as God's word.[24] Christ often referred to, or prefaced his own remarks with the phrase "it is written";[25] he commended those who had searched the Scriptures[26] and reprimanded others for ignoring them.[27] This documentation gives revelation-based knowledge an objectivity of its own, independent of individual minds — an outside, objective frame of reference.[28]

The Scriptures, then, are the accredited medium by which we come into contact with God in Christ.[29] Christ's way to show us God was through the inscripturated revelation of him; he referred his listeners to a documented account of God's dealings with men in history and to his own personal fulfillment of its redemptive scheme.[30] The signposts to God were those things already recorded and then substantiated by further New Testament events and explanation. So, too, for us today; God reveals himself primarily through a written record, the Bible, and through Jesus Christ who is its central theme.

2. It is Interpretational. Revelation content often includes interpretation

22. Clark H. Pinnock says that in the biblical pattern of revelation, "event and interpretation are bound together in indivisible unity." *Biblical Revelation* (Chicago: Moody Press, 1971), 33.

23. Exodus 17:14; Jeremiah 30:2; Revelation 1:19.

24. 1 Thessalonians 2:13; 2 Peter 1:21, 2 Timothy 3:16; 1 Peter 1:23; 2 Chronicles 34:21.

25. Matthew 4:4, 7, 10.

26. John 5:39.

27. Matthew 22:29.

28. James I. Packer comments on the fact that "revelation is objectively and normatively presented in and by the Biblical witness to it." "Contemporary Views of Revelation," *Revelation and the Bible*, ed. Carl F. H. Henry (Grand Rapids: Baker Book House, 1958), 99. Carl Henry affirms that "God has objectively published his will in the . . . Scriptures, where it stands propositionally expressed for all to read and know." *Christian Personal Ethics* (Grand Rapids: Eerdmans, 1957), 341. Clark Pinnock also views "revelation as an objective and intelligible disclosure inscripturated in the Bible." *Biblical Revelation*, 12.

29. Thomas F. Torrance says, "God still comes to us clothed in the historical and biblical forms of his revelation which . . . directs us to Jesus Christ in the centre. . . ." *God and Rationality* (London: Oxford University Press, 1971), 184. Elsewhere he says, "Jesus Christ sends us back . . . to the Gospels and to their witness to the historical Jesus Christ. That is the appointed place in which nations and ages may meet God." *Space, Time and Resurrection* (Grand Rapids: Eerdmans, 1976), 147. James I. Packer explains, "the Bible is central and crucial to divine communication . . . because, first, it records, interprets, and shows the right response to God's revelation of Himself in history, and second, it is the means whereby God brings all subsequent believers to recognize, receive, and respond to that revelation for themselves." Chap. 10, *Evangelical Roots,* ed. Kenneth S. Kantzer (Nashville: Thomas Nelson Inc., 1978), 154.

30. Luke 24:27, 32, 44, 46.

of the facts, a statement of the meaning of revelatory events. Christ died, we are told, *for us*[31] and *for our sins*.[32] He rose from death, we are informed, *for our justification.*[33] While some facets of divine intention remain a mystery, we are not left in the dark as to God's primary purpose in redemptive action.

3. It is Reliable. With its origin in the word of God, revelation stems from a God who is consistent and cannot lie.[34] Perhaps of equal importance, it "fits" the realities of history. It is tied in with and founded upon facts verified by reliable human testimony — the credible product of what the writers describe as that "which we have *heard,* which we have *seen* with our eyes . . . and our hands have *touched*."[35] It maintains that Christ died, was buried, and rose again[36] — real happenings, events publicly attested in human history.[37] Revealed knowledge is repeatedly identified as, or related to, truth.[38]

4. It is Personal. While documented externally, the revelation-based knowledge is expressly provided for the reception and benefit of individuals. Redemptive revelation is intended to have a personal effect on one's life and has the power to bring salvation through Christ. Paul calls it the "power of God,"[39] "able to make us wise for salvation."[40]

These are just a few of the key characteristics of the revelation at our disposal and which serves as the sole source and foundation of authentic Christian faith. A recognition of this, however, does not call for the depreciation of reliable knowledge for other purposes and from other sources (e.g., scientific investigation[41] and historical research).

Knowledge, Faith and Evidence

Human knowledge — even that which refers to a source in revelation — is not always as complete as we might like it to be. Paul recognized that our understanding of moral-spiritual matters is oftentimes partial and incomplete.[42] Who

---

31. Romans 5:8.

32. 1 Corinthians 15:3.

33. Romans 4:25.

34. Hebrews 6:18; Titus 1:2; 2 Corinthians 1:18-19.

35. 1 John 1:1.

36. 1 Corinthians 15:1-8.

37. Referring to the historical dimension of God's self-revelation, Keith E. Yandell reminds us, "God has acted in history at real times and in real places to reveal himself to real persons and actually to act on their behalf." *Christianity and Philosophy* (Grand Rapids: Eerdmans, 1984), viii.

38. John 17:17; Ephesians 1:13; 2 Samuel 7:28.

39. Romans 1:16; 1 Thessalonians 1:5.

40. 2 Timothy 3:15.

41. See John Y. May, "Christianity and Science: A Reappraisal," *Evangelical Journal,* Fall 1987 and Spring 1988, Parts I and II, respectively.

42. 1 Corinthians 13:9,12.

is there who would not like additional insight, for example, on the role of suffering?

On the other hand, scriptural knowledge on some subjects is very abundant. The human intellect will never exhaust the depths of information of God's provision for redemptive forgiveness or on the meaning of the cross. Yet, the basics of God's plan of salvation are so clearly set forth in the Bible that a child can easily appropriate them in trustful acceptance.

Knowledge, then, plays a definite role in the act of faith. But is this revelation-based knowledge putting our faith on the right track? Is this knowledge really reliable as a foundation for life commitment?[43] Is there evidence to support its truth-claims?

Biblical knowledge has at least some evidential support. Obviously, this is not to imply that we have evidence (internal or external) to back up every propositional assertion of the Bible. Evidence is not always available or even necessary. Evidence, however, is desirable and sometimes important. For example, certain elements of biblical truth-claims (particularly the life, death and resurrection of Christ) have amazingly strong evidence for them. The New Testament writers, for example, report that they "did not follow cleverly invented stories" — or myths fabricated by human imagination — but were "eyewitnesses" of the events forming the basis for faith.[44]

Deeply imbedded in the terminology of New Testament narratives are frequently used terms such as "witness," "testimony," "trustworthy," and "eyewitness." These terms are there for a purpose.[45] They signal the compelling confirmation and support for the events on which Christian belief rests[46] — the firsthand authentication of "hard" historical facts, the raw data of empirical

43. Arthur Holmes points out that "this notion of 'reliability' is central to the biblical concept of truth. . . . To know the truth is to have reliable knowledge that should be followed." *Contours of a World View* (Grand Rapids: Eerdmans, 1983), 130. Carl F. H. Henry concurs: "The Scriptures are the . . . ongoing source of reliable objective knowledge concerning God's nature and ways." *God, Revelation and Authority,* II (Waco: Word Books, 1976), 13. John W. Montgomery indicates that "on the basis of accepted textual and historical analysis, the Gospel records are found to be trustworthy historical documents." *Where Is History Going?* (Minneapolis: Bethany House Publishers, 1972), 35.

44. 2 Peter 1:16.

45. John W. Montgomery notes that "the honest doubter will find compelling evidence in support of Christ's claims. This is why the New Testament makes so much of the eyewitness contact. . . ." *Faith Founded on Fact* (Nashville: Thomas Nelson Inc., 1978), 38. Ronald H. Nash claims, "The New Testament presents the resurrection of Jesus Christ as a historical event that is supported by the strongest possible eyewitness testimony." *Faith and Reason* (Grand Rapids: Zondervan, 1988), 266-67. Richard B. Gaffin contends that the correct understanding of the term "witness, then, is not merely personal testimony. Instead, it is . . . legally binding deposition, the kind that stands up in court." "The New Testament: How Do We Know for Sure?" *Christianity Today,* 32.2 (Feb. 5, 1988), 30.

46. Clark Pinnock insists that "to segregate Christian conviction from all empirical investigation is to make nonsense of it and to go against the precise claims of the gospel to be historical." *Biblical Revelation,* 46.

reality. They are there intentionally to form the solid foundation for faith, to urge appropriate individual response in reliance upon the biblical truth-claims, and to serve as an anchor for lifelong commitment to Christ.

In particular, it is no mere coincidence that Christianity puts such stress on the tremendous significance of the resurrection of Jesus Christ. The resurrection — including its historical and factual nature[47] — becomes the essential point for verification of the truth of revelation.[48] John W. Montgomery reminds us that Paul "presents Christ's resurrection as the capstone of his case for the truth of the gospel."[49]

In Summary

1. Authentic Christian faith is clearly related to some knowledge and cannot be divorced from it.[50] Reliable knowledge is a necessary ally of proper faith, providing both foundation and direction for it. That knowledge has some substantial evidentiary support.

2. A clear-headed knowledge of Christian truth is wholly compatible with a vibrant devotion to Christ. In fact, knowledge helps to produce conviction which can yield enthusiasm of the highest sort. Someone has observed, "The Gospel yields deep joy, and not the least of the reasons it does so is that it is true."[51] The cognitive aspect of faith is not in competition with its volitional and relational elements. Instead, it strengthens them, having the potential to make the commitment stronger and the personal relationship with Christ deeper.

47. For an excellent summary of evidence for the resurrection, see the talk given at Harvard by J. N. D. Anderson, University of London dean of law faculty, on "The Resurrection of Jesus Christ," *Christianity Today*, March 29, 1968, 4-9.

48. Clark Pinnock recalls that "the earliest believers . . . pressed boldly the claims of Jesus Christ as they had been dramatically verified in history by the fact of the Resurrection. Upon . . . this historical datum rested and continues to rest the truth of the Christian message." *Set Forth Your Case*, 1. Thomas F. Torrance maintains that "the resurrection is therefore our pledge that statements about God in Jesus Christ have an objective reference . . . and are not just projections out of the human heart and imagination." *Space, Time and Resurrection*, 72-73.

49. John W. Montgomery, *Faith Founded on Fact*, 78.

50. Faith, in biblical terms, does not require the depreciation of the intellect or of the knowledge it is capable of obtaining. At least for Christian faith, the act of believing is intelligible and the object of one's faith is clearly defined. In carefully assessing the nonbiblical distortion of faith as a "leap in the dark," Philip E. Hughes alertly reminds us that "the Spiritual invitation to trust in Christ is not an invitation to a game of chance." "Reason, History, and Biblical Authenticity," *Christianity Today*, Sept. 12, 1969, 6.

51. Clark Pinnock, *Set Forth Your Case*, 51.

Word as Icon in Greek Patristic Theology

VERNA E. F. HARRISON

The Seventh Ecumenical Council, whose 1200th anniversary we are celebrating this year (1987), establishes a direct parallel between the Gospel narrative and the painted representation of the icon. It says that these two things have their basis in the incarnation of Christ and that they presuppose each other and are mutually revelatory.[1] As is generally recognised, this teaching states clearly that the traditional icons of the Orthodox Church have a definite theological content and thus are much more than simply pictorial decorations.

What is less well-known is that this conciliar definition is saying something equally important about the words of Scripture and by extension about all other words which express the Church's faith, particularly in liturgical texts and patristic writings. It is saying that they are actually verbal icons. This means that, as far as possible, they seek to give concrete expression to the ineffable realities that are revealed and experienced within the Church's life. The theological writer and the iconographer are thus engaged in the same task, only they work in different media. This is why word and icon, as parallel expressions of the same experienced realities, presuppose each other and are mutually revelatory. As we seek to understand what they reveal, we can place them side by side and use them to interpret each other.

Fr. Florovsky writes in the spirit of the Seventh Council when he says that dogma is "a 'logical icon' of divine reality."[2] He means that when the Fathers use conceptual thought and language, they are not copying the philosophical

---

1. This statement comes from the council's doctrinal decision, found in Mansi 13:377-80. For an English translation see Leonid Ouspensky, *Theology of the Icon* (New York, 1978), 160-61.
2. Georges Florovsky, *Creation and Redemption* (*Collected Works*, vol. 3) (Belmont, Mass.: Norland Publishing Co., 1976), 29.

A paper given at the Fellowship Conference of 1987. Reprinted from *Sobornost* 10 (1988): 38-49. Used with permission.

systems current in their time, nor are they attempting to build another philo-sophical system of the same kind. That is, they are not employing logical inference to elaborate an intellectual construct as a kind of self-contained struc-ture. Instead they are utilising whatever conceptual materials are available to them from the surrounding philosophical culture as a means for expressing the truth revealed and experienced in the Church. They accept some concepts, reject others and substantially modify others according to how well they fulfill this iconic function.

The philosopher is like a secular artist. Conceptual structures are the medium he uses to create intellectual models expressing his own imaginative vision of reality. The Orthodox theologian, on the other hand, is like an iconog-rapher. He is gifted and trained in the use of concepts, just as the icon painter is skilled and educated in the techniques of his art. Yet in writing he uses these intellectual means to convey as much as possible of a Christian revelation that he knows and experiences in a manner surpassing conceptualisation.

It follows that in the visual representation of the icon, the narrative of the gospel, the pictorial language of liturgical poetry and the conceptualisation of dogma,[3] the Church is expressing the same things in different ways. Moreover, these diverse modes of expression are often joined together as well as occurring alongside each other. Thus icons frequently use visual means to depict dogmatic concepts as well as narrative scenes. In a similar way, as they attempt to convey an accurate understanding of doctrinal concepts, the Fathers often employ verbal pictures and other literary figures of language as well as logical argumen-tation. In the Orthodox world, artistic and conceptual modes of expression come together, coinhere in each other and are mutually revelatory. The same God is both Truth and Beauty, and all proper icons of him, whether verbal or visual, manifest both.

These principles have important implications for the correct interpreta-tion of patristic texts. At times literary scholars focus too narrowly on the aesthetic character of a document's style or figurative language while neglecting the ideas that these words are intended to convey. Meanwhile, philosophical and theological scholars tend to dismiss such literary forms as mere surface decorations and look beneath them for real conceptual content. Yet in many cases either of these approaches by itself will yield a seriously incomplete un-derstanding of the text. Although often figurative language has other functions, it is sometimes making as significant a theological statement as is made else-where through logical argumentation. So as we attempt to learn the Fathers' full theological teaching, we need to move beyond the academic division of labour that separates literature from philosophy and take account of both.

This is particularly true of the three great Cappadocian Fathers, who were

---

3. Liturgical music also belongs in this list, although its inclusion does not follow directly from the conciliar teaching.

gifted exponents of the classical literary tradition as well as profound thinkers. In order to show by example something of that which is involved in verbal iconography, I would like to explore two quite different ways in which literary form and conceptualisation converge in patristic texts. The first is St. Gregory of Nyssa's portrayal of the human person as a kind of receptacle; the second is St. Gregory Nazianzen's use of antithesis in Trinitarian theology.

Gregory of Nyssa: The Human Person as Receptacle

The bishop of Nyssa excels in rigorous logical reasoning, yet he also likes to use vivid pictorial language to express his ideas. As a result, the nuances of verbal imagery can serve to clarify the meanings of some of his key theological concepts.[4] In some instances, he uses the same images repeatedly with the same meanings so as to build up a rich and varied expression of an idea and its theological context.

Literary scholars call these word-pictures metaphors, but from a theological point of view it is more appropriate to call them verbal icons. The term "metaphor" points to the absence of the object to which a word literally refers; the term "icon" discloses the presence of a concrete spiritual reality depicted through pictorial language. Like painted icons, Gregory's verbal icons are windows or doors opening into the kingdom of God.

In one of his most philosophical works, the dialogue *On the Soul and the Resurrection,* the bishop of Nyssa describes human beings as "living receptacles with the faculty of choice" created by God to share in his own wealth of goodness.[5] In this key passage, the word "receptacle" functions primarily as an ontological concept. It certainly has a long philosophical pedigree. Plato understood the world's disorganised matter as a receptacle in which copies of the ideas came to be imprinted.[6]

With Gregory, however, the term's meaning has clearly shifted. The human person functions as a receptacle not as a material being but as an intellectual and spiritual being capable of participating in the divine life.[7]

4. For the parallel between picture language and philosophical reasoning in Gregory of Nyssa's writings, see Jean Laplace, ed., *Grégoire de Nysse. Le création de l'homme (Sources chrétiennes* 6) (Paris, 1943), 7-13. See my dissertation, "Grace and Human Freedom according to St. Gregory of Nyssa" (Graduate Theological Union, Berkeley, 1986), chs. 3 and 4, for an analysis of Gregory's concept of human participation in the divine and the ways in which he uses perfume, light and water imagery to clarify its meaning.

5. Gregory understands goodness very broadly to include all kinds of divine perfection, and especially all the virtues. See David L. Balas, *Metousia Theou: Man's Participation in God's Perfections according to St. Gregory of Nyssa (Studia Anselmiana* 55) (Rome, 1966), 68.

6. *Timaeus* 48E-49A.

7. Balas, *Metousia Theou,* provides an excellent analysis of Gregory's understanding of participation, which is a key concept in his theology.

> The intelligible nature [which in this context means primarily the human but also the angelic nature] came into being for this purpose, that the wealth of divine goods might not be idle. Living receptacles with the faculty of choice were constructed like vases by the wisdom that sustains all things in order that there would be some place capable of receiving these goods, a place that always becomes larger because of what is additionally poured into it. For participation in the divine good is such that it makes larger and more receptive that in which it exists.[8]

Thus the same divine goodness that fills up the human receptacle enlarges its capacity so that it can receive more. With the cooperation of human freedom, this in turn makes it even larger, so that it can receive still more, and so on. This picture of a continually expanding container, finite at every given point but always becoming larger with no limit to its increase in size, is one of the classic expressions of Gregory's doctrine of eternal growth.[9]

Already here there is a convergence of philosophical and literary modes of expression. The metaphysical concept of containment combines with the interface between divine infinity and human finitude to produce a vivid picture of a kind of jar getting bigger and bigger.

In a passage from the treatise *On Perfection*, Gregory uses receptacle imagery to clarify what he means by human participation in the divine. The text is speaking about freedom from passion and purity. For the bishop of Nyssa all human virtues are really participation in the divine life and activity.[10] That is, our passionlessness is actually Christ present in us as passionless. The text shows how this comes about:

> What is free from every passionate inclination looks to the source of passionlessness, who is Christ. Drawing from him as from a pure and incorruptible spring, a person will show in his thoughts such a likeness to the Prototype as exists between the water in the gushing spring and the water taken from there in a jar. For the purity in Christ and the purity seen in the person who participates in him are one in nature, though one is the flowing spring and the other draws from it.[11]

The water in the jar is the same as the water in the spring. This material continuity is an icon of the concrete ontological continuity between divine

---

8. *PG* 46:105A.

9. On eternal growth, see Jean Daniélou, *Platonisme et théologie mystique. Essai sur la doctrine spirituelle de Saint Grégoire de Nysse* (Paris, 1954), 291-307; Ekkehard Mühlenburg, *Die Unendlichkeit Gottes bei Gregor von Nyssa* (Göttingen, 1966), 152-58; and Everett Ferguson, "God's Infinity and Man's Mutability. Perpetual Progress according to Gregory of Nyssa," *Greek Orthodox Theological Review* 18 (1973): 59-78.

10. Gregory defines the image of God in the human person as a participation in all the divine attributes. See R. Leyes, *L'image de Dieu chez saint Grégoire de Nysse* (Paris, 1951).

11. Werner Jaeger, ed., *Gregorii Nysseni Opera* (Leiden, 1960-), 8.212.

virtue and the human virtue which is its presence, manifestation and activity. Thus, our participation in God is not only a causal dependence but also a shared possession of the same life. The imagery of spring, water and jar brings into focus what Gregory means by participation, a concept which can appear rather ambiguous from a purely philosophical point of view.

This pictorial language illustrates the difference between the divine and the human as well as their likeness. The spring gushes continually, and no boundary restricts the extent of its flow. This is an image of the infinity of divine life. The walls of the jar and the limited space inside it disclose creaturely and human finitude, which can only hold so much of the divine life given as grace. Even though the life itself is the same, the way it exists in us is radically different from the way it exists in God. The figurative language in *On Perfection* thus expresses the same idea as a more philosophical passage in *On the Making of Humanity*, where Gregory says that the divine and the human have the same attributes, but the substrata in which those attributes are present differ: one is uncreated while the other is created.[12]

The *Commentary on the Song of Songs* can perhaps be regarded as Gregory's masterpiece in the art of creating verbal icons out of figurative language. In his hands the poetic imagery of the Canticle becomes a vehicle for expressing many profound spiritual and theological insights. I would like to examine only one of the more striking of these images, the description of the bride as a well of living water (Cant. 4:15), which again utilises the concept of a receptacle to speak about the human person.

After quoting other passages from Scripture which depict the divine nature as a fountain of life, Gregory expresses wonder that the bride, who for him represents the Christian soul, is described in the same way:

> So too in our text the infallible Word declares that the bride is a well of living waters. Now here is a very strange paradox. All wells hold still water; only in the bride is there said to be running water. She has the depth of a well together with the constant flow of a river. Now how can we really do justice to the wonders revealed here in the symbol that is applied to the bride? It would seem that she has no further height to reach now that she has in all things been made like the archetypal Beauty. Very closely does she imitate his fountain in her own, his life in hers, that water by hers [. . .]. And this water flows from God [. . .]. The bride embraces and encompasses what flows into the well of her soul, and thus she becomes a storehouse of that living water that flows, or rather rushes, down from Libanus, as the Word tells us.[13]

In this passage, the human soul, like God, appears as a source of life flowing in all directions to the persons and things around it. Yet it is different from God

12. *PG* 44:184D.
13. Jaeger, *Opera* 6.293.

since its life originally comes not from itself but from outside, as water seeps into a well underground. The bride receives this life as grace from her divine Bridegroom. Thus her imitation of Christ results directly from her participation in him. The water flowing from her fountain is actually his life, though it has also become her own.

The image of the well of living water complements the image of the expanding container in the passage we considered earlier. There we saw that the human soul is enabled to receive more grace by continuing to be open toward God as he expands its capacity. Here we see that the well is replenished from underground as its water flows outward. That is, as the bride gives the life that fills her receptacle to others, she has space to receive more. In these texts, Gregory shows us two ways of opening ourselves to additional grace, love for God and love for our neighbour.

The receptacle idea plays a crucial role in expressing the bishop of Nyssa's understanding of how the human person comes to participate in the divine. The container functions both as an ontological concept and as a verbal picture. The richly nuanced images Gregory paints of it disclose how he sees the human interacting with the divine much more fully than would be possible without them.

Gregory Nazianzen: The Use of Antithesis

Let us now turn to the bishop of Nyssa's friend, the other Gregory from Nazianzus, called the Theologian. The Church remembers him above all for his work in seeking to articulate, as far as possible, the doctrine of the Trinity. He was a man steeped in the Hellenistic literary tradition, a poet and a master rhetorician as well as a deep thinker. He used all the resources available to him from his rhetorical training and talent as media through which to express his understanding of God.[14] He transformed the secular art of rhetoric, which was the central form of literary culture in his age, into a kind of Christian iconography. In his hands, the figures of speech so highly valued by the Second Sophistic at times come to express important doctrinal concepts as well as providing literary ornament.

From a theological point of view, the most important of these figures is antithesis, one of the basic building blocks of Greek rhetorical prose. An antithesis is basically a conjunction of two contrasting terms, expressing their unity as well as their opposition, as for example "the foolishness of the wise" or "life through death." These phrases gain their impact from the evident

---

14. On Nazianzen's rhetoric, see Marcel Guiget, *Saint Grégoire Nazianze et la rhétorique* (Paris, 1911), which remains a classic study; and Rosemary Radford Ruether, *Gregory of Nazianzus: Rhetor and Philosopher* (Oxford, 1969), esp. ch. 2.

contrast between folly and wisdom, death and life, yet they indicate ways in which these opposites genuinely occur together. Thus an antithesis is fundamentally a both/and statement. In literature there are innumerable variations on this theme.

One of Nazianzen's greatest achievements is his transformation of this standard literary form into a structure of thought which he uses to express some of his most important theological insights. He employs antithetical language to articulate a worldview in which unity in diversity and in unity are considered to be at the foundation of reality. This vision finds expression in his cosmology, anthropology and christology, but perhaps most essentially in his trinitarian doctrine.

Though scholars have noted the large role antithesis plays in his prose style, they have generally overlooked its place in his theology.[15] This may be an example of the tendency to overemphasise the separation between philosophical and literary modes of expression, which I mentioned earlier. In the light of this neglect, it would be illuminating to discuss antithesis in relation to several different aspects of Gregory's theology. But here I shall confine myself to two key texts which use antithetical language to speak of the Trinity.

Although Nazianzen uses several kinds of antitheses in his trinitarian discussions, the most fundamental consists in an affirmation of both oneness and threeness within God. This assertion finds one of its clearest expressions in his sermon on the Feast of Theophany, where he says:

> When I speak of God you must be illuminated by one light and also by three. Three in individualities, that is hypostases, if any prefer to call them that, or persons [. . .] but one in regard to the essence — that is, the Godhead. For they are divided undividedly, if I may so say; and they are united in division. For the Godhead is one in three, and the three are one, in whom the Godhead is, or (to speak more accurately) who are the Godhead.[16]

This passage exhibits the balanced phraseology that was prized by the Greek rhetoricians. Yet its purpose is theological as well as aesthetic. In other places, Gregory says that the correct understanding of the Trinity is a mean between two erroneous extremes, just as, according to the Hellenistic philosophical ideal, virtue is a mean between two extremes of vice.[17] He deliberately extends the

---

15. But there are some suggestive remarks pointing in this direction in Frederick W. Norris, "Gregory of Nazianzus' Doctrine of Jesus Christ" (Dissertation: Yale University, 1970); and Anna-Stina Ellverson, *The Dual Nature of Man: A Study in the Theological Anthropology of Gregory of Nazianzus* (Uppsala, 1981), 83-86.

16. Or. 39.11, *PG* 36:345C-D.

17. See especially Or. 42.16, *PG* 36:476C, and Or. 20.5-6, Justin Mossay, ed., *Grégoire de Nazianze, Discours 20-23 (Sources chrétiennes* 270) (Paris, 1980), 66-70. On the importance of the golden mean in Gregory's theology and spirituality, see Jean Plagnieux, *Saint Grégoire de Nazianze théologien* (Paris, 1951), 213-60.

aesthetic and ethical concept of balance into the realm of Christian doctrine. Over and over, he rejects the imposed imbalances of Sabellianism, which affirms oneness in God by denying authentic threeness, and Arianism, which affirms threeness by denying genuine unity. He regards the truth as a mean between these two extremes.

Antithetical thought is closely connected with the concept of balance, in which aesthetics and ontology coincide. Yet what is involved is clearly not a compromise, not an indistinct *tertium quid* situated somewhere between unity and diversity. Gregory says that the three persons are divided undividedly and united in division, that the Godhead is one in three and the three are one. These antitheses express a double affirmation of unity and diversity as occurring together in such a way that each retains its full integrity. The division between the three persons is undivided because it does not in any way compromise their complete unity of essence. Similarly, the divine unity and simplicity exist without interfering in the distinctness of each of the hypostases, which are thus united in division. Unity and diversity do not conflict or contradict each other; instead, they coexist and even coinhere. God is one in three in one.

It is sometimes said that the Greek Fathers emphasise the three hypostases in God over their common nature, while the Latin Fathers emphasise the one essence over the distinct persons.[18] This statement is an oversimplification, and it does not really apply to Gregory Nazianzen, central as he is to the Greek tradition. In stressing balance and antithesis, he takes great care to affirm divine unity and diversity equally and reject formulae that undercut either of these realities for the sake of the other. Thus he can be seen bypassing that which is sometimes considered a cause of friction between East and West.

Gregory begins his discussion by saying, "When I speak of God you must be illumined by one light and also by three." This statement is a key to understanding his antithetical thought. He shows us one light and three lights simultaneously and asks us to hold both perceptions in the mind together. This involves a definite mental discipline, an effort to accept the equality and harmony between two seemingly contrasting perceptions. We must avoid the tendency to derive one from the other or subordinate one to the other, as is the habit in Western logic, which begins with one proposition and then proceeds to infer a second one. The very starting point of reflection is an immediate apprehension of one light and three lights together. Both are original and both are primary.

It is at this point that the iconic character of Nazianzen's antithetical

---

18. For an expression of this point of view, see T. R. Martland, "A Study of Cappadocian and Augustinian Trinitarian Methodology," *Anglican Theological Review* 47 (1965): 252-63. Note that this Anglican is probably more harsh toward Augustine than many of the latter's Orthodox critics would want to be.

language about the Trinity becomes most evident. The verbal image of one light
and three lights contemplated simultaneously can perhaps be seen as paralleling
Rublev's icon of the Trinity, which shows three angelic figures, each unique, yet
all truly alike, joined inseparably in an eternal circle, a unity in which no part
can be pictured apart from the whole.

It is particularly important not to overlook the apophatic dimension of
antithetical thought. Between the contrasting affirmations there is always an
unspoken middle which holds the two poles together. In trinitarian theology,
this mysterious centre corresponds to the actual way in which oneness of essence
and threeness of persons are combined in God, something that is completely
unknowable, whatever it is. Antithetical language expresses strong dogmatic
affirmations which may even be reinforced by their contrast. Yes, there are
oneness and simplicity in God, and, yes, there is also irreducible diversity. Yet
between and around these affirmations there is also ample room for mystery,
for what is unrevealed and unknown about the divine nature.

In exhorting his hearers to be illumined by one light and three lights,
Gregory invites them to receive God's self-disclosure and make the appropriate response of adoration. He speaks as much about spirituality as about
doctrine; for him the two are indeed inseparable. His antithetical descriptions
of the Trinity are as much vehicles for meditation as for conceptual thought.
The silence between and around the affirmations of oneness and threeness,
like the space between and around the three figures in Rublev's painting, is
of great significance. St. Gregory's words and St. Andrei's colours are parallel
gateways into the ineffable and the invisible. Both are true icons of the Holy
Trinity.

The day after Gregory delivered the Theophany sermon we have been
considering, he went on to preach about holy baptism. As he exhorted his
hearers to receive the mystery of illumination and offer themselves entirely to
God, he also urged them to confess their faith in Father, Son and Holy Spirit.
This exhortation about the Trinity is worth quoting at length.

> This I give you to share, and to defend all your life, the one Godhead and
> power, found in the three in unity, and comprising the three separately, not
> unequal in substances or natures, neither increased nor diminished by supe-
> riorities or inferiorities; in every respect equal, in every respect the same; just
> as the beauty and the greatness of the heavens is one; the infinite conjunction
> of three infinite ones, each God when considered in himself; as the Father,
> so the Son, as the Son, so the Holy Spirit, each preserving his properties; the
> three-one God when contemplated together; each God because consubstan-
> tial; one God because of the monarchy. No sooner do I conceive the one than
> I am illumined by the three; no sooner do I distinguish the three than I am
> carried back to the one. When I picture one of the three I consider him as
> the whole, and my eyes are filled, and the greater part escapes me. I cannot
> grasp the greatness of that one so as to attribute a greater greatness to the

rest. When I contemplate the three together, I see but one torch, and cannot divide or measure the united light.[19]

The first part of this passage speaks primarily about trinitarian theology. It says that Father, Son and Spirit are each infinite and all perfectly equal to each other. Each person considered alone is the whole of God, yet taken together they are one God. This last point brings Gregory back to the antithetical relationship between oneness and threeness, which he develops by describing his mind moving back and forth as it contemplates God as Unity and Trinity.

So a text which begins as a rather technical theological discussion turns out to be saying some important things about trinitarian spirituality. In the fourth century, the Fathers were faced with the task of seeking to articulate conceptually how God is revealed to the Church as Father, Son and Spirit, three distinct persons, yet still one essence and divinity. This doctrinal articulation led them to the further task of explaining how the faithful can approach such a seemingly complicated God in worship. Suppose we think of the Father, the Son, the Spirit, each one separately, all three together, the Godhead as one. The question is, when we want to pray, where do we begin? And where do we proceed from there?

Nazianzen addresses these issues here. He says that as soon as he conceives the one he is illumined by the three, and the moment he distinguishes the three he is carried back to the one. He contemplates each of the Persons separately as an infinite light, all three together as a conjunction of three suns with a single combined radiance,[20] and the divine nature as one blazing torch. He does not find it necessary to hold all these images in his mind at once but discovers that wherever he starts, he is drawn from one aspect of the trinitarian revelation to the others. What emerges is a vast richness and wonder in worship, not a confusion.

The Theophany sermon showed us a still point in antithetical thought, where the mind contemplates one light and three lights together, contrasting but harmoniously coexisting and cohering in each other. The sermon on baptism shows us the dynamism of antithetical thinking, as the mind moves back and forth between the one essence and the three persons, and between each hypostasis in turn and the three together. The awareness of unity in God does not conflict with an awareness of diversity but instead lead[s] into it. Gregory is illuminated by the three as soon as he conceives of the one. Then his apprehension of the Three as distinct carries him back to the contemplation of the one. Thus he moves back

---

19. Or. 40.41, *PG* 36:417B-C.

20. For a fuller discussion of the image of three conjoined suns with a single light, see Or. 31.14, in Paul Gallay, ed., *Grégoire de Nazianze. Discours 27-31 (Sources chrétiennes 250)* (Paris, 1978), 302-4.

and forth between different aspects of the Godhead. His meditations on the Trinity disclose a picture of motion and rest ineffably combined.

Here again it may make sense to compare Nazianzen's description of God in antithetical language with Rublev's visual portrayal. In the painting, the three figures turn toward each other in such a way that the eye cannot rest on any one of them but is drawn back and forth from one to another. This dynamism as well as the dynamism we saw in Gregory's sermon on baptism may give us a glimpse of an eternal movement of love among the three persons of the Trinity. Both Nazianzen and Rublev indicate that any such movement must be understood as eternally joined with perfect rest, and it can never involve any alteration in the divine persons or their common essence.

Although it is rather more abstract than Gregory of Nyssa's picture language, Nazianzen's use of the literary figure of antithesis to speak of the Trinity is another significant kind of verbal iconography. The juxtaposition of contrasting words and the implicit silences between and around them, like the juxtaposition of three angelic figures and the spaces surrounding them in Rublev's painting, convey on many levels the mystery of oneness and threeness in God.

The Virtues of a Multidimensional Approach

The examples we have given of verbal iconography in the writings of Gregory of Nyssa and Gregory Nazianzen are sufficient to indicate its great richness and complexity. The language of patristic texts such as these expresses multiple levels of meaning which we need to consider in our quest to understand the teaching they convey. They are at once literary and conceptual, and they speak of both doctrine and spirituality.

In conclusion, I would like to suggest that the practice of viewing biblical and patristic texts as well as paintings, mosaics and liturgical words, music and actions as icons, in accordance with the spirit of the Seventh Ecumenical Council, has vast and far-reaching implications. It is important to remember that all these forms of iconography are multidimensional and may contain hidden levels of meaning that we have not yet discovered. The Byzantines were aware of this multiplicity, and their understanding of image, in the broadest sense, is appropriately subtle and nuanced. One good example of this is St. Maximus' discernment of several levels of meaning in the plan of the church building, a matter he discusses toward the beginning of the *Mystagogy*.[21]

This approach has many possible applications, but two in particular may be worth mentioning here. It could help us gain a better understanding of the Orthodox theology of the priesthood and patristic exegesis of Scripture.

It is generally recognised that as he serves the divine Liturgy, the priest

---

21. *PG* 91:664D-684A.

functions as an icon of Christ. Thus one often hears the argument that women cannot be priests because Christ is a man, so only a man can serve as his icon. Stated in this simple way, such a claim is in obvious conflict with Orthodox doctrine, which teaches that every human person bears the image of God and every Christian is called to embody the image of Christ. Such a statement is also particularly offensive to women because it implies that they are not fully human and cannot be fully Christian.

However, it is still true that the priest fulfills certain specific iconic functions as he serves, and it is safe to assume that his part in the liturgical action, like the structure of the church building itself, is probably iconic in a subtle and complex way. Moreover, the precise manner in which the priest is an icon needs to be clearly distinguished from all the other ways in which human beings can be images of God or Christ. The analysis of this aspect of priesthood is a matter that belongs within the domain of liturgical theology and has not yet been studied sufficiently in that context. The priest's maleness may in fact become a kind of icon within the liturgical action. It could actually prove to be an image of some spiritual reality which does not itself involve gender. So it is important not to make direct inferences from the maleness of the priesthood regarding the status or spiritual character of men and women in general. But it is impossible to draw any conclusions about these issues without a good deal of further cautious investigation.

In regard to Scripture, it is well known that the Greek Fathers often found several levels of meaning in each biblical text, and different ones approached it in different ways. If the inspired words are considered to be verbal icons, just such a multidimensional approach to their interpretation will appear as natural and appropriate. My suggestion is that over a period of centuries, the Fathers characteristically regarded many things as icons, from the words of Scripture to paintings and mosaics, and from the human person to the layout of the church building. The Seventh Council gave a definitive expression to this habit of thought at a crucial juncture in history, but the outlook itself existed throughout the earlier patristic period as well as continuing into later periods.

Modern scholars like to distinguish between typology and allegory in patristic biblical exegesis, and they claim that typology is historical and therefore legitimate, while allegory is ahistorical and illegitimate.[22] Yet they cannot entirely agree about the definitions of these two categories and sometimes have difficulty drawing the boundary line between them. This has tended to cast doubt on the value of patristic exegesis in general.

Perhaps some of these difficulties could be avoided if, instead of defining the various kinds of spiritual interpretation of Scripture through categories

---

22. For a recent statement of this view from an Orthodox perspective, see J. Breck, *The Power of the Word in the Worshiping Church* (Crestwood, 1986), 49-92.

invented by modern scholars, we would follow an approach suggested by the Seventh Council and think of the Fathers as looking for ways in which the biblical text functions as icon. Then the key question becomes, of what spiritual reality is this text an image, and how well does it manifest that reality? It would be worth trying this approach to see whether it can help us identify when patristic exegesis has lasting value and when it only expresses a fanciful personal opinion.[23]

23. At the Tenth International Conference on Patristic Studies in Oxford (1987) Frances M. Young presented a major address on "Exegetical Method and Scriptural Proof: The Bible in Doctrinal Debate." This highly suggestive lecture challenged the standard way of understanding patristic exegesis in terms of a distinction between historical, typological and allegorical levels of meaning, though from a perspective other than the one indicated here. One hopes that this paper will soon be published.

Decolonizing Theology in the Caribbean: Prospects for Hermeneutical Reconstruction

ROMNEY M. MOSELEY

For the past two decades Caribbean theologians have been trying to "decolonize" theology in order to lend theological support to the subversion of colonial domination.[1] Given the thoroughness of colonization in church and state by the British, French, Dutch and Spanish, decolonization requires a radical transformation in religious and political consciousness. In the political domain, decolonization is the forming of national and regional identities to complement the development of new structures of self-governance, independence and interdependence. In the theological domain, decolonization entails hermeneutical reconstruction — "critical discrimination as to what is primary and what is secondary, what is accidental, what is authentic and what is distortion"[2] in the meaning and praxis of Christianity.

It goes without saying that the political and ecclesiastical priorities established by the colonial powers were intended to perpetuate their domination. Anglican, Methodist, Baptist and Moravian missionaries played a significant role in the religious and educational colonization of the Caribbean. As the established ecclesiastical arm of the colonial government in the British West Indies, the Anglican church enjoyed a privileged status and

---

1. See, e.g., Kortright Davis, ed., *Moving Into Freedom* (Bridgetown, Barbados: Cedar Press, 1977); Noel L. Erskine, *Decolonizing Theology: A Caribbean Perspective* (Maryknoll, NY: Orbis Books, 1991); William Watty, *From Shore to Shore: Soundings in Caribbean Theology* (Kingston, Jamaica: Cedar Press, 1981).

2. Francis Schüssler Fiorenza, *Foundational Theology: Jesus and the Church* (New York: Crossroad, 1986), 304.

This article is a revised version of a paper presented at the Ecumenical Institute, Bossey, Switzerland, in July 1988, and later published in the *Toronto Journal of Theology* 6 (1990): 235-46. Used with permission of the journal.

exerted considerable political and economic power through the linkage of agricultural plantations and ecclesiastical glebes. After its disestablishment, the Anglican church became more actively involved in developing ecumenism in the Caribbean.

After almost four centuries of European domination, it is difficult to formulate a precise programme of decolonization for the Caribbean. In the church, there is no question that decolonization can only be accomplished as an ecumenical project. The colonial elitist distinctions between the Anglicans and nonconformists have exhausted their usefulness. However, vestiges of colonial dependence persist in the autocratic structure of the Anglican church, in governmental politics and in education. The University of the West Indies is yet to relinquish its dependence on the authority of external examiners. In short, the institutional mechanisms for perpetuating colonialism as a form of consciousness are so firmly established that it is difficult to separate the process of decolonization into discrete segments of Caribbean society. In the religious sphere this is especially troublesome.

> Traditionally, the Caribbean church, coming as it does out of a wholly colonial history, did not pay much attention to political issues on the one hand and supported the established powers on the other.
>
> At various times, however, individual church people — both clergy and laity — have stood up and fought the political authorities on matters of principle. This goes back, notably to the time of slavery. The institutional church, however, has always cooperated with and supported the "legal" authorities and has never questioned the fundamentals of the political system — even under colonialism. The exceptions to this have been a few nonconformist churches, especially in Jamaica and Guyana, which were characterized by their sense of cultural identity with the masses, e.g., the Baptist churches.[3]

In other words, the post-colonial church persists under the view that the critique of domination is not a constitutive element in theological reflection. The normative view is that theology is the history of doctrine or the profession of faith. Changing this perspective in the seminaries and churches is a primary step in the decolonization of theology.

The proposition that the decolonization of theology involves hermeneutical reconstruction calls for an examination of the relation of Christ and culture in the Caribbean and of the status of political ethics. Typologies are always limited in their ability to incorporate all aspects of the phenomenon. Nevertheless, the relation between Christianity and colonialism in the Caribbean resonates with H. Richard Niebuhr's typology, the "Christ above culture."[4] The

---

3. Neville Linton, "Some Aspects of Political Morality in the Caribbean," in *Perspectives on Political Ethics: An Ecumenical Inquiry* (Geneva, Switzerland: WCC Publications, 1983), 80.

4. H. Richard Niebuhr, *Christ and Culture* (New York: Harper and Row, 1951), 83.

Europeans were quite successful in implanting their models of Christianity within every aspect of Caribbean culture.

> That European churches did, in varying ways and times, play political roles was not a consciousness transferred to the colonies. . . . The "non-political" role of the church was accepted by the people particularly as its welfare and educational work were meeting felt needs, especially for neglected sectors of the society. At best in terms of politics the church was a watchdog against "abuse" but even that posture was from a conservative point of reference.[5]

Linton also points to the otherworldly dimension to this religiosity, as evidenced by the strong emphasis on personal salvation. In his judgment, the colonial church gave rise to "a post-colonial elite which was not oriented to transformation and liberation."[6]

Clearly, the decolonization of theology requires a re-visioning of the relation of Christ and culture. Niebuhr's view of Christ as transformer of culture centers on humanity being brought into a new covenantal relationship with God in Christ. It seems to me that with the decolonization of theology comes not only a new social ethic of justice and freedom, but also a new covenantal ethic.

Regrettably, the contemporary interest in decolonizing theology does not revolve around a central moral issue such as slavery. The moral consciousness which drove the anti-slavery crusades and eventually brought about the emancipation of slaves in the Caribbean in 1834 is not the driving force behind decolonization. Obviously, slavery and colonialism coexisted very well. While maintaining their slaves, the colonialists cultivated Caribbean models of European culture. With emancipation came land rights and education and financial opportunities. By 1845, the former slaves were replaced on the plantations by "indentured servants" from India. From the freedmen came a critical mass of civic leaders who would eventually lead the fight for self-government, independence and interdependence. Unfortunately, the atmosphere of regional solidarity which led to the formation of the Federation of the West Indies was subverted when Jamaica withdrew from the Federation and became independent in 1962. Trinidad and Tobago followed later the same year, and Barbados in 1966. But the drive for ecumemism in the churches did not vanish. By 1971, the Caribbean Conference of Churches (CCC) was formed.

Ecumenism, nation-building and regional cooperation in all areas of political life are all parts of the development of a distinctive post-colonial Caribbean identity. In response to these venturers, Clifford Payne, one of the early leaders in the Caribbean Conference of Churches, warns there is no distinctive non-Europeanized Caribbean identity.

5. Linton, "Some Aspects," 81.
6. Ibid.

The social, political and cultural dominance of Europe over Africa in the Caribbean has been so massive that no one with a sense of history should be surprised to find that the Caribbean person is still quite confused about who he [sic] really is. And it is not going to eliminate that confusion if, in our deep anger over "what Europe did to us," we take up the untenable position that the Caribbean owes little or nothing to Europe, and that all our roots are either in Africa or Asia. The simple fact is that the Caribbean reality can no more be explained if we leave Europe out of the account, than if we leave out Africa.[7]

Unfortunately, only vestiges of African religious life in the Caribbean remain. These are most visible in the Shango cults of Trinidad and Tobago, Vodun in Haiti, and Santeria in Cuba. In Jamaica, Rastafarianism, a relatively modern quasi-African religious movement founded in Jamaica in the 1930s, claims followers throughout the Caribbean but is hardly a vestige of African religious life. To this multicultural spectrum belong the religions of Judaism, Hinduism and Islam.

How then do we decolonize theology in the Caribbean? It seems to me that the decolonization of theology is both a retrieval of tradition and a hermeneutics of suspicion regarding the moral principles, values and truth claims of the tradition. Clearly, decolonization in the Caribbean does not entail the retrieval of its African, Asian or Carib religious heritage. There is certainly no attempt to formulate an African, Asian or native Carib Indian theology of liberation in the Caribbean. The Caribbean Conference of Churches stands out as the most significant agent of hermeneutical reconstruction.

Ecclesial Praxis in the Caribbean

Through its programme agencies, Christian Action for Development in the Caribbean (CADEC) and Action for Renewal (ARC), leaders of the Caribbean Conference of Churches joined forces with social scientists and educators to formulate an emancipatory vision of the Church. These agencies represented two vectors of ecclesial praxis. CADEC embraced the root metaphor of *development* on the assumption that the Caribbean was a "developing" region on the verge of "moving into freedom." Accordingly, social action in the areas of education, regional communication, public health and economic planning were incorporated into the identity of the ecumenical church. Whereas the colonialists preserved their power by the traditional strategy of *dividere et imperare,* the Caribbean Conference of Churches emphasized regional communication. They

7. Clifford Payne, "What Will a Caribbean Christ Look Like? A Preface to Caribbean Christology," in Idris Hamid (ed.), *Out of the Depths* (San Fernando, Trinidad: St. Andrew's Theological College, 1977), 3.

published *Caribbean Contact,* the first and only regional newspaper. Through the Agency for the Renewal of the Church, the CCC published tracts and held seminars to stimulate theological reflection. Altogether, the CCC attracted a wide spectrum of religious denominations, including the Roman Catholic Church. For the first time, the Caribbean has produced a truly ecumenical church. However, there is a notable absence of any systematic reflection on what constitutes a theology of decolonization. In a plethora of small pamphlets and monographs, theologians proclaimed the formation of the Caribbean Conference of Churches as a kairotic event in the salvation history of the region.[8] Among the leading thinkers on the subject is Professor Kortright Davis. A strong proponent of developmentalism, Davis stresses the qualities of progress and persistence and the belief that God will bring about the triumph of personal fulfillment over poverty and adversity.[9] In addition, he views regional cooperation and ecumenism as evidence that God is providing opportunities for Caribbean people to move out of the depths of colonial isolation and into full freedom.

Ironically, while Caribbean church leaders were pressing on with courses on "The Church and Development" in the theological seminaries in Barbados, Trinidad and Jamaica, liberation theologians in Latin America were advocating the end of developmentalism. Míguez Bonino challenged its paternalistic and antirevolutionary posture.[10] Gustavo Gutiérrez viewed developmentalism as an ally of bourgeois, progressive theology that concentrated on the profession of faith while ignoring the political and economic conditions that robbed the poor of their humanity.[11]

Caribbean theologians insisted that their historical context required an approach different from that of Latin American liberation theologians. Davis and others maintained that the metaphor of development captured the transition from dependence to independence and interdependence. Unlike liberation theologians in Latin America, Caribbean theologians did not see theology as a consciousness-raising tool. For the most part, they were content to craft ecclesiastically sanctioned statements in support of progress in the social and political arenas, but failed to adopt the conscientization undertaken by their counterparts in Latin America.

Both colonization and decolonization are products of particular class interests: colonization the tool of the ruling class; decolonization the musings of middle-class intellectuals. A major obstacle to the decolonization of theology in the Caribbean is class stratification. Whereas Latin American liberation the-

8. See Robert Cuthbert, *Ecumenism and Development: A Socio-Historical Analysis,* The Caribbean Conference of Churches (Ann Arbor, MI: University Microfilms, 1984).

9. Kortright Davis, *Mission for Caribbean Change* (New York: Peter Lang, 1982).

10. José Míguez Bonino, *Doing Theology in a Revolutionary Situation* (Philadelphia: Fortress Press, 1975).

11. Gustavo Gutiérrez, *A Theology of Liberation* (Maryknoll, NY: Orbis Books, 1973).

ologians insisted on forging bonds of solidarity between the uneducated peasants and middle-class academicians and church leaders through "base communities," no such efforts were undertaken in the colonial Caribbean. Accordingly, the claim cannot be made that decolonization of theology is in any way a grassroots movement of theology from the underside of history. The question is, then, who is decolonizing theology and for whom is it being decolonized?

Latin American liberation theologians are quick to align their emancipatory praxis with Marxist social theory so that the goal of liberation calls for an analysis of class interests and a "preferential option for the poor." Caribbean theologians, on the other hand, are obsessed with the artifacts of political independence — disestablishment of the colonial Church, and repatriation of colonial properties and bequests. These signs of empowerment stand in radical contrast to the context of powerlessness that liberation theologians regard as a priority in critical theological reflection. The Roman Catholics in the former colonies are no exception. There is no challenge to the *magisterium*. The Anglicans have made modest steps in separating from the Church of England through liturgical renewal. The Diocese of Jamaica approved the ordination of women in the seventies, but other dioceses in the Province of the West Indies are still resisting the ordination of women.

Meanwhile, the message of personal salvation and triumphal Christianity is beamed by American televangelists throughout the region and is becoming increasingly attractive to members of the mainline denominations. Indeed, the Americanization of religious life in the Caribbean has compounded the task of decolonization by defining Christian praxis as triumph over adversity. This teleological view of God's action in moving persons to higher levels of achievement and fulfillment is also found in Kortright Davis' exposition of human development in the Caribbean. Davis views the divine-human relationship in evolutionary terms. First, persons are viewed as co-creators with God, working towards the "realization of the image of God in his [*sic*] social and historical dimensions."[12] Secondly, this cooperative relationship is affirmed in the incarnation — God's reconciliation with humanity in the person of Jesus Christ. Thirdly, it is established in the Church — a community of faith shaped by the interdependence of the divine and the human. The thrust of this argument is that the history of salvation is the history of God's omnipotent presence in human history. Believers can count on God to empower them to overcome adversity and achieve their goals in life.

This emphasis on God's omnipotence encourages complacent, uncritical, bourgeois Christians to affirm absolute dependence on God while minimizing or ignoring the oppressive conditions of existence. For example, labour is identified with creative self-formation and the faithful are assured that work mediates divine activity in the world. There is no critical analysis of alienated labour

---

12. Davis, *Mission*, 165.

in light of structures of injustice and domination. In placing the burden of social transformation on upward economic and social mobility, these progressivists assume there is a natural ethical ordering of the universe that transmutes the egoistic corruption of justice into a harmonious, utilitarian higher order. Moreover, the Church is seen as an agent of divine cooperation in this venture.

Re-visioning Power and Liberation

The decolonization of theology in the Caribbean cannot proceed simply on the basis of cultural progress. Political independence, disestablishment of the Anglican Church, upward social mobility and economic power are strategic actions that are *preconditions* of freedom and justice, not their *realization*. If decolonization of theology has anything to do with the realization of freedom and justice, it must address the emancipatory actions of God in Christ Jesus and the identity of the Christ. The question of which comes first, soteriology or Christology, is irrelevant. The question is whether Christology should be done from "above" or from "below." Christology from above begins with Christ as the eternal Son of God, and moves from there to his incarnation and earthly life, and finally to his death, resurrection, and exaltation. Christology from below begins with the history of Jesus and then moves back to the question of his preexistence and incarnation.[13]

Fuller and Perkins suggest that among the disadvantages of a Christology from above are docetism, Apollinarianism, and monophysitism. In other words, the humanity of Jesus is violated in order to preserve his divinity. They argue that Christology from below "is the only acceptable way of doing New Testament Christology."[14] Their fundamental argument is that Christology is really "a theology of Jesus."[15]

What then are the salient features of this theology that are relevant to the Caribbean Church?

In focusing on the need for political and economic empowerment, Caribbean theologians have avoided the paradox of power and powerlessness found in the *kenosis* of Jesus Christ. They have adopted a Christology "from above" and ignored the radical irruption of history brought by the crucifixion. The crucified God embodies the paradox of power and powerlessness that subverts the triumphal religion. This is dramatically expressed by Paul in his letter to the church at Philippi.

> For the divine nature was his from the first; yet he did not think to snatch at equality with God, but made himself nothing, assuming the nature of a slave.

13. Reginald Fuller and Pheme Perkins, *Who Is This Christ?* (Philadelphia: Fortress Press, 1983), 5.
14. Ibid.
15. Fuller and Perkins, *Who Is This Christ?*, 8.

Bearing the human likeness, revealed in human shape, he humbled himself, and in obedience accepted even death — death on a cross.

Therefore God raised him to the heights and bestowed on him the name above all names, that at the name of Jesus every knee should bow — in heaven, on earth, and in the depths — and every tongue confess, "Jesus Christ is Lord," to the glory of God the Father. (Philippians 2:6-11)

This hymn takes us from creation through the incarnation to the *kenosis* on the cross, and finally to the universal glorification of Jesus Christ as Lord. We are struck by the paradox of God's presence in the world in the form of a slave or servant, and the lordship of Christ which "remains hidden and incomplete until all is handed over to the Father."[16] In the doctrine of the Trinity, Christology from below and from above are brought together.

In an age of developmentalism and triumphal religion, kenotic Christology might appear anachronistic. After years of colonialism and dependence, the people of the Caribbean deserve to be political and economic partners with the modern industrialized nations. But this does not mean that a theology of decolonization must incorporate the triumphal myths and metaphors of modernity. Maggie Ross astutely observes that "one of the greatest perils the culture and the churches face today is a growing unwillingness, a fear even, to live within the continuum, in the tension of paradox."[17] One of the ways that the paradoxical core of Christianity is eviscerated is by divorcing the glorified Christ from the crucified Christ. The most pressing challenge for Caribbean theologians today is to preserve the paradox of power and powerlessness of the gospel in an ethos of ecclesiastical and technological triumphalism. The tendency is to become embedded in false polarities such as the religious and the secular, church and state. In the *kenosis* of Jesus, God's identification with the weakness, incompleteness, and powerlessness of humanity is reaffirmed as it was in creation.

Given the historical significance of slavery and colonial domination, the methodological starting point of a theology of decolonization should be the experience of the most disadvantaged. Some liberation theologians have interpreted the most disadvantaged in Latin America as the poor, and have concluded that the gospel maintains an unequivocal preferential option for the poor.

The exact meaning of this option is to recognize the privileged status of the poor as the new and emerging historical subject which will carry on the Christian project in the world. The poor, here, are not understood simply as those in need, they are also the group with the historical strength, a capacity for change and a potential for evangelization. . . . The church is directed to

---

16. Fuller and Perkins, *Who Is This Christ?*, 142.
17. Maggie Ross, *Pillars of Flame: Power, Priesthood and Spiritual Maturity* (San Francisco: Harper and Row, 1988), xxxix.

all but begins with the poor, from their desires and struggles. Thus arise the essential themes of the church: social change creating a more just society; human rights interpreted as the rights of the poor majority; social justice and integral liberation, achieved primarily through sociohistorical freedom and concrete services on behalf of the disinherited of this world and so on.[18]

Delwin Brown takes issue with the idea of the "preferential option for the poor." He argues that this is not an epistemological privilege but an "epistemological priority."

This doctrine of the epistemological priority of the poor means that claims to truth must be tested, first, and foremost, in the situation of oppression, in relation to those who are oppressed and their experiences of suffering. Every claim about God must be examined in the scathing light of experienced oppression, there, if anywhere, to be stipulated as adequate and acceptable.[19]

The epistemological priority of the oppressed is an invitation to solidarity with victims. For Christians, God's solidarity with human suffering is to be met with our participation in the suffering of Jesus Christ ("For as we share abundantly in Christ's sufferings, so through Christ we share abundantly in comfort too"; II Cor. 1:5). We do so knowing that no amount of sacrificial suffering on our part can expiate the endless and senseless suffering that humans inflict on each other.

In short, the epistemological priority of the oppressed is a necessary methodological component of a theology of decolonization. What constitutes oppression in the Caribbean remains a question. Unlike the Latin American context, colonialism was not replaced by totalitarianism and dictatorships. With the exception of Grenada and Guyana, the former British territories were not subjected to totalitarianism and dictatorial rule. Poverty remains the most insidious form of oppression throughout the Caribbean. There is no doubt that the colonial powers created an economic system to serve their own interests — for example, sugar, cotton and rum. When the global markets ceased to support these ventures, the plantations in the Caribbean essentially exhausted their usefulness to the European industrialists. Faced with the few industries that are competitive on the world market, the Caribbean region suffers from perennial unemployment, underemployment and poverty. These are the most visible vestiges of the alienating effects of the economic structure created by colonialism. The harsh reality of economic oppression is perhaps mollified by the general climate of political stability and by a phenomenally high rate of literacy. The priority given to education by the colonialists ensured that the majority of

18. Leonardo Boff, *Church, Charisma and Power* (London, SCM Press, 1985), 9-10.
19. Delwin Brown, "Thinking about the God of the Poor: Questions for Liberation Theology from Process Thought," *Journal of the American Academy of Religion* 47.2 (Summer 1989): 276.

the population would be among the most literate in the world. Barbados, often referred to as "Little England," maintains a ninety-eight percent literacy rate. To these factors I would add the efforts to consolidate the political, economic and cultural identity of the Caribbean region. In this enterprise, the Caribbean Conference of Churches plays a significant role by providing an ecumenical context for theological and ethical reflection of the epistemological priority of the poor and on the use of power in the formation of communities of faith and moral action. It seems to me that a coherent methodological perspective on this process might be formulated from a kenotic Christology and a covenantal ethic of responsibility. To the latter I now turn.

Covenantal Ethics and Political Theology

According to H. Richard Niebuhr, the essential components of a covenantal ethic of responsibility are response, interpretation, and social solidarity.[20] Moral action is always in response to action upon us. The underlying social psychology is the capacity to engage in mutual social perspective-taking. For Niebuhr, this is the crux of the meaning of suffering — the bearing of each other's pain. The decolonization of theology in the Caribbean is meaningless if it does not heighten our commitment to bear each other's suffering. Moral response therefore requires continuous interpretation of the structure of moral action and clarification of issues such as who is included in the community of moral discourse, the dynamics of power and authority, and the language by which our interaction with each other is mediated.

The significance of interpretation stems from Niebuhr's coherence theory of value. Influenced by pragmatism, Niebuhr defines value in terms of its coherence with other claims of the good. He resists attempts to define the good on the basis of its correspondence to an absolute principle. In contrast to deontological ethics, Niebuhr does not subordinate the good to the right. He offers no absolute principle of right action. Neither does he adopt a teleological definition of the good in terms of the consequence and goals of moral action. Rather, he defines the good in terms of how it fits into a coherent set of relationships. What counts is the dynamic process of social interaction from which truth and value emerge.

The challenge of responsible action is to discern how it fits into a larger whole. The moral agent is not only an interpreter of the social situation but is also accountable to others and not an ultimate center of value and power. For Niebuhr, the "kingdom of God" is a metaphor of the overarching Whole into which human action ultimately fits. This metaphor bears with itself the eschato-

20. H. Richard Niebuhr, *The Responsible Self: An Essay in Moral Philosophy* (New York: Harper and Row, 1963), 61-65.

logical proviso that existence is not yet what it is intended to be. God, the Creator, Sovereign and Redeemer, is the ultimate Whole in relation to whom meaning and value are derived. Niebuhr considers Christ the exemplar of radically monotheistic faith.

This concept of radical monotheistic faith brings us to the matter of social solidarity. Niebuhr warns against the dangers of henotheism and polytheism.[21] Henotheism occurs when the ideologies of the nation or state become the ultimate center of value and power to which we owe trust and loyalty. Polytheism refers to multiple centers of ultimate value. Social solidarity has to do with the values underlying the ethic of responsibility. In the process of nation-building, political systems can become idolatrous centres of value and power. Niebuhr reminds us that the covenantal ethic is not to be confused with contractual agreements which serve the interests of specific persons and are made to accomplish limited objectives. A covenantal ethic embraces values that are ends in themselves — such as justice, freedom and truth. Covenant and vocation work together when persons understand themselves as being called to serve God and each other as trustworthy and loyal citizens.

The decolonization of theology in the Caribbean involves a paradigmatic transformation from the insidiousness of colonialism to a covenantal ethic of responsibility. The fact that this reconstructed vision of a community of faith is ecumenically grounded augurs well for the widening of the horizons of theological and ethical reflection on decolonization.

Finally, there can be no authentic decolonization as long as the oppressed fail to acknowledge their oppression. In a very practical way, the covenantal ethic has to do with the process of conscientization — the unmasking of symbols of oppression. Foremost among these in the Caribbean is the Europeanized Christ. Until there is a concerted effort to inject into the religious consciousness of the people their own history and aesthetic representations of faith, suffering and freedom, the decolonization of theology remains a thought experiment for speculative theologians.

The principal impediment to such indigenization is the increasing influence of North American culture on the Caribbean. It is not surprising therefore that the "semantic axis"[22] of decolonization is mediated by metaphors of development, achievement and fulfillment. From the time of the European colonizers we in the Caribbean have been persuaded that the better world is to be found beyond the horizons of our island homes. Though poor, we have not perceived our poverty as unchangeable and hopeless. Since the ownership of property was mostly settled at the time of emancipation from slavery, distribu-

---

21. Richard Niebuhr, *Radical Monotheism and Western Culture* (New York: Harper and Row, 1970).

22. J. Severino Croatto, "Biblical Hermeneutics in the Theologies of Liberation," in Virginia Fabella and Sergio Torres, eds., *Irruption of the Third World: Challenge to Theology* (Maryknoll, NY: Orbis Books, 1983), 140-67.

tive justice is not a salient feature of decolonization. Furthermore, we have not experienced a systematic abuse of human rights (except in Haiti and Guyana). In short, the Caribbean is a fertile field for theologies of progress and development.

What disturbs me is the theology of history mediated by these metaphors. God's action in the crucified Christ and participation in the suffering of the poor are subsumed under cultural progress and personal achievement. Against this linear developmentalism, I see the poor in the Caribbean preserving a paradoxical view of power and powerlessness.[23] They have transmitted the emancipatory faith of their enslaved ancestors from generation to generation as the mysterious paradox of fulfillment and emptiness found in the *kenosis* of Christ. This faith is essential to the struggle against territorial defensiveness and neo-colonialist elitism. It will enable the church to work as an ecumenical and covenantal community of faith. Indeed, the future of decolonization lies with the hope of the poor.

---

23. See John S. Pobee, *Who Are the Poor? The Beatitudes As a Call to Community* (Geneva, Switzerland: WCC Publications, 1987).

On Theological Contextualization

KAN BAOPING

The contextualization of theology has been a subject of debate for some time. Today especially, as more and more Chinese church personnel realize the importance of theological development for the Chinese church, the question of theological contextualization inevitably becomes a focus for discussion. From the entrance of Christianity into China until the establishment of new China in 1949, the Chinese Protestant church was under the supervision of foreign missionaries. She was like an infant who had not yet learned to walk, nor was she given the chance to learn. Under the foreign missionaries' exacting supervision, the maturation of the Chinese church was fraught with difficulty and was painstakingly slow. Each step in that maturing process had to follow in the missionaries' footsteps. Only after the establishment of new China, when the missionaries had to leave, did people realize how weak the Chinese church really was. Of course, in the past some farsighted Chinese church leaders had raised the issue of independence. But at that time China was subject to the foreign powers, so how could the church speak of independence? This historical background is the reason Chinese theology has essentially been a direct reflection of western theology. As Professor Chen Zemin, Vice-Principal of Nanjing Theological Seminary and Professor of Systematic Theology, has pointed out in his essay "The Task of Theological Construction in the Chinese Church," many people in the Chinese church conformed indiscriminately with whatever theological trend was fashionable in the West. Although foreign missionaries have been gone for over forty years, for some people in the Chinese church, that outmoded theological thinking still represents orthodoxy.

Today, as people consider how to establish a Christian theology with Chinese church characteristics, the issue of contextual theology has been put on the agenda. Just what is contextual theology? Why must theology be con-

Translated by Peter Barry, M.M. Published originally in the *Chinese Theological Review* (1991): 103-11. Reprinted with permission.

textualized? The issue must be conscientiously studied because such research will help us to find our own way in developing a Christian theology which fits the revelation that God is giving to Chinese Christians today, and which has both Chinese Christian characteristics and a close relationship to the context of the Chinese church. Our theology should not be an unexamined clone of western theology.

What Is Contextual Theology?

Before we can define contextual theology we must first understand what theology itself is. Paul Tillich considered theology to be an explanation of the content of the Christian faith (God's revelation). Professor Chen Zemin defines theology as: "the theory of the spiritual experience of the church; it is a summation of the religious experience of the church in a given historical period. As a system of thought, it begins with traditional doctrines and beliefs, but then takes fresh and distinctive spiritual experiences, systematizes them and elevates them to the level of theory which is then used to guide the work of the church and to point out the direction in which it should move." This is a broad definition of theology because it can generally be applied to all specific theologies. Or to put it another way, we can say that it includes all the explanations of the content of Christian faith. Furthermore, each specific theology is fixed by its specific historical and social conditions, cultural background, theological task, purpose and method. Let us take apologetics as an example. According to Tillich's definition, the theological task of apologetic is to answer all questions the context asks of God's message. Systematic theology, for instance, is a systematic explanation of the content of Christian faith. J. C. Wenger has said that systematic theology is "the content of the revealed Word of God. . . . Systematic theology then takes the Biblical teaching which has been derived from exegesis and from Biblical theology and combines the fruit of these studies into one comprehensive statement of the truth" (*Introduction to Theology*, 1954) Here, Wenger determines the method of systematic theology. Different theologies are concerned with different theological tasks and purposes, and therefore they choose different theological methods.

In the whole history of theology there has never been, nor can there ever be, a so-called "normative theology," which could be used at all times and under all circumstances to effectively guide the establishment of the Chinese church or Christians' spiritual life and practice of faith. And it is highly unlikely that there would be a theology that could act as a norm for or pass judgment on the effectiveness of other theologies. As was mentioned above, the reason for this is that each theology is limited by its own special context, theological task and purpose. There is no one suit of clothes which will fit every person. Clothes must be measured and tailored. Likewise in doing theology, it is the concrete context which determines the theological task, purpose and method.

Contextual theology cannot be identified with any other theology; however, it is not unlike other theologies. Professor Douglas John Hall has perceptively pointed out: "From its definition, Christian theology is basically interrelated with context. Christian theology is contextual by definition" (*Thinking the Faith*, 1989). This is to say that theology itself is already contextualized because any theology is interrelated with the concrete context in which it finds itself. No theology is produced in a historical or social vacuum. This is so because theology is a human activity. Humans live in time and space, and human thinking inevitably reflects the time and space in which those humans live. Therefore, no theology can avoid reflecting the context which produces it.

Since theology itself is already contextualized, why emphasize theological contextualization? In reality this emphasis is a reaction to the trend toward theological norms in traditional theology. Some people feel that certain old theological views should be considered "genuine" theology. In their view this "genuine" theology is not limited by time or space; it can be used to expound God's revelation in the same way to different churches and believers, regardless of social, cultural and historical conditions. It is, they feel, as universal and effective as the word of God. The idea of creating an "almighty" theology unrelated to a concrete context is sheer fantasy because theology in and of itself is interrelated with context. If someone can make this fantasy become a reality, the product is no longer theology, but a kind of religious ideology. The rationale for contextualizing theology deals with this problem.

It is worth noting that contextualization is not the same as situationalization. Context takes a historical view of social conditions of a given time. It emphasizes the link between past, present and future. Its concepts are two-dimensional. Situation on the other hand points to those things which happen around a given moment in time, including cultural, political and economic matters; it does not touch upon historical development. Its concepts are one-dimensional. Contextual theology, however, is produced in the two-dimensional plane of context. Contextual theology is the result of the contextualization of theology. The contextualization of theology allows for the expounding of God's revelation to the church and to believers at a certain moment in time while taking into account the historical, social, cultural and political environment and the background of that church and of those believers. Therefore, theological contextualization is not emphasized solely in order to raise past theologies to a new theoretical plane, nor simply to form a theological theory with context as the medium. The purpose of the contextualization of theology is to listen to how God speaks to the context, and to see how our faith is closely interrelated with God's revelation, and indeed with our very existence. During the process of contextualizing theology, we must be clearly aware, at each moment, of who is doing theology, of the cultural, social and political factors, and of the historical conditions under which it is being done. Without these few premises theology cannot be contextualized.

The Importance of Theological Contextualization

Why do we emphasize the importance of theological contextualization and why do we say theology in and of itself is already contextualized? First, because theology is a human activity, and all human activities are restricted by the social, cultural and historical conditions in which humans act. Doing theology is no exception. Humans are limited, and they are subject to the above-mentioned limitations. Therefore it is impossible for us to completely penetrate and comprehend God's revelation to us. We can only grasp the revelation God gives us at a specific historical period and under specific social conditions in a limited way. "For we know only in part; but when the complete comes, the partial will come to an end. When I was a child, I spoke like a child, I thought like a child, I reasoned like a child; when I became an adult, I put an end to childish ways. For now we see in a mirror, dimly, but then we will see face to face. Now I know only in part; then I will know fully, even as I have been fully known" (1 Cor. 13:9-12). Humankind's understanding of God's revelation is subject to the limitations of human nature as well as to the limitations of the context. At the same time, God gives his revelation to human beings in accordance with the context in which they find themselves. It is not certain that the understanding of God's revelation under one set of historical and social conditions can be used to explain God's revelation under another set of historical and social conditions. If we recognize this fact, we must of necessity deny the possibility of establishing a non-contextualized theology or a theology which is suitable to all historical periods and to all social environments. Therefore, we cannot merely duplicate a former theology with its understanding of God's revelation under the specific historical conditions of that time. Rather, we must understand the revelation God gives us today under the conditions of our own time. Moreover, we cannot merely copy modern western theology. Rather, based on our own concrete context, we must establish a theology which expresses our faith in accordance with our own special characteristics. Actually, we can use much of the content and theological method of western theology for reference, but using something for reference is not the same as borrowing it.

Human limitation is not the most important reason for the contextualization of theology. That is to say, it is not only because human beings are limited that we must have a limited understanding of God's revelation to us based on our context. The most important reason for contextualizing theology is because our God is a living and true God. The Christians of the first century believed that God was with them. We also believe that God is with us today. This proves that we believe that God is a living God. As Professor Hall pointed out, every time we say that God is with us, we at the same time acknowledge one fact: our theology has our context as its background. Our experience of God's presence among us explains the interrelationship between God's revelation and our specific context. If God did not reveal himself to us in accordance with a concrete context, how would we be able to experience God's presence among us?

The contextualization of theology has also to do with the guiding role of theology in the practice of faith. Theology is not just abstract theory. It should both arise out of the practice of faith and guide it. The Christian practices his or her faith within a concrete context. Since theology comes from the practice of faith, it must be interrelated with the context of faith practice. It is only because theology is interrelated with the context that it can turn and guide the practice of faith. Christians who live in different contexts have different faith needs, different comprehensions of Christian doctrine, and different understandings of God's revelation, and they will choose different expressions of faith or different ways of putting their faith into practice. If theology is not interrelated with a concrete context, then it would be impossible for it to be interrelated to faith needs, and therefore it could not be an effective guide for the practice of the faith.

To sum up, theology must be contextualized, and the key to the contextualization of theology is engagement. For theology to be contextualized, it must interrelate with context, and this interrelationship can only come about through engagement. Only through engagement with the concrete context can theology establish a relationship with the context, and thus become contextualized. Only because the Latin American theologians became engaged themselves in their struggle for liberation, only because they themselves accompanied the masses in their struggles for political and economic liberation, could they establish the liberation theology which so well expresses the faith of the mass of Latin American Christians. Therefore these theologians are able to impart the grassroots church's message of liberation theology in a systematic way and on a higher theoretical level, and use it to guide the faith practice of Latin American Christians. The major content of their faith practice is the message that God is just, and that he enters into the struggle against political and economic oppressors. The same holds true for Black theology. Professor James H. Cone, a theologian from New York's Union Theological Seminary, is himself a black person. Living in the United States, he has personally experienced the prejudice that a black person meets with in that society. Therefore the first line of the first page of his book *A Black Theology of Liberation* emphatically states: "Christian theology is a theology of liberation" (*A Black Theology of Liberation*, 1991). This represents the call for equality on the part of the great majority of black Christians living in the United States. God speaks to the context. Only if we become engaged with the context and establish a relationship with the context can we really receive the revelation God is giving to us.

Of course, there is the possibility that the contextualization process might get dangerously sidelined and a theology fail to become genuinely contextualized, in which case it could not be an accurate guide for the faith practice of the church and of Christians. In order to avoid this, we must be aware of several problems:

1. God speaks to the context, but he is not bound by the context. Although he is in the midst of the context, he is above the context. This is the meaning of the text: "one God and Father of all, who is above all and through all and in all" (Eph. 4:6). We must not, by emphasizing the transcendence of God, ignore the important fact that he speaks to the context. But at the same time because of the importance of context, we cannot disregard the universality of God's truth. Otherwise, God's truth would be reduced to relative truth, because its efficacy would only be felt in a specific context. Therefore we must treat the relationship between God's truth and context very carefully. Although contextual theology emphasizes the context and not the environment or the situation, it is necessary to deal carefully with the relationship between the context and the tradition of the church (this tradition does not refer to some customs or characteristics of the local church, but to the tradition handed down to us from the apostles). Contextual theology cannot simply repeat tradition, nor can it completely abandon it. Context is the situation of the interrelationship between the past and the future. If completely cut off from tradition, it becomes situation and it is no longer context. If theology enters into context without tradition and seeks to listen to God's word in that context, it will become bound by the surrounding environment. In this way, when we try to understand God's revelation in the environment in which we find ourselves, we will be readily controlled by social trends. Society's ideological trends and prevalent customs continually change, and we could only drift with the tide and lose our purpose and our prophetic character. When that happens, theology will become "trendy." Strictly speaking, such a theology is not [really] theology at all. It is only a religiously colored viewpoint regarding the ideological trends and problems in society. The movement to establish a "normative theology" is a reaction to this kind of "theological trendiness."

2. Context is not a norm for examining God's revelation, nor is it a tool for interpreting God's revelation. That is to say, contextual theology does not use context to explain God's word. Rather, within the context it observes how God speaks to that context. This is a crucial distinction. If we make context the norm, we are guilty of the error mentioned above, namely that theology becomes secularized. However, if we make tradition the norm, theology would not be interrelated with the concrete social existence of Christians, nor would it be interrelated with their concrete faith needs. Observing how God speaks to a context from within that context prevents us from making the two errors mentioned above.

3. Contextualizing theology is not the same as localizing it. Here we touch upon the question of indigenization. Indigenization or signification as it refers to the church, means that the church in China should sink roots in the soil of traditional Chinese culture. The church should not be the product of a foreign culture, but rather have a Chinese existence. The Chinese church ought to identify with Chinese culture. This will lead to mutual enrichment of both Chinese and Christian cultures. The purpose of the indigenization of the church is not only to cause more people to be baptized, but more importantly, to make the Christian gospel more meaningful. Contextualization, on the other hand, refers only to theology, indicating that Chinese Christians ought to develop a theology which is based on their own specific context, and not just appropriate western theology. Chinese Christians ought to identify with the Chinese people, and Chinese Christian theology ought to be closely interrelated with the Chinese context. A contextualized theology can provide a theoretical base for the indigenization of the church.

Theology must interrelate with a concrete context. Only in this way can theology on the one hand correctly understand the message God is giving to the context, and on the other hand accurately express the faith of Christians and satisfy the concrete needs of the church and of Christians. But it is important to note that contextualization is not the same as localization. When we relate theology with our concrete context, which is different from other contexts, we must remind ourselves that we are part of the universal church. This is so because no matter what context a church is in, that church springs from "one Lord, one faith, one baptism" (Eph. 4:5). From another angle, when we are doing theology, although we must consider any new meaning in the revelation which God gives us because this revelation occurs in accordance with our concrete context, we must also consider the meaning of this revelation in the tradition of the church and of faith because God's truth is everlasting and universal. Only in this way will the message of God recounted in our theology be in accordance with God's will, and appropriate to the needs of the church and of Christians.

The context in which today's Chinese church finds itself is that China is in the midst of carrying out a reform the likes of which she has never seen before. Through this reform we want to make our socialist motherland more strong and prosperous. During the process of this reform western ideas are flowing thick and fast. The Chinese church is no exception, but is on the receiving end of all kinds of theological opinions. In 1991, the China Christian Council was accepted as a full member of the World Council of Churches. This strengthens the link between the Chinese church and the universal church. In such a context, how can we run our church well in accordance with the Three-Self principle? How can we be compatible with socialism, and at the same time function as light and salt in society? How can we have our own special characteristics, and at the same time share together with the brothers and sisters of the universal church each one's spiritual experiences? First we must correctly know ourselves and know the concrete context in which we are placed. We must listen attentively to what God is saying to our context.

To produce a theology with Chinese Christian characteristics will be a slow and arduous process. But like a boat returning from a long journey, we can already see its mast cutting through the wind and waves on the far horizon.

Contextual Theologies:
The Problem of Agendas

HARVIE M. CONN

Mention the word "contextualization" in Reformed and evangelical circles and sooner or later another word pops up — syncretism. Why?

There are many answers to that question. Most certainly a basic one is our legitimate concern that the authority of the Bible will become lost in the plethora of localized theologies. If we start with our particular, historical situation, what will happen to the once-for-all character of the Bible as norm? In constantly taking account of the receptor cultures, isn't hermeneutic in danger of letting the medium become the message and the message become a massage? Will the "sameness" of the Bible get lost in a diversity of human cultures?

There are plenty of illustrations to confirm these fears. Liberation theologies often reduce the Bible from canon to paradigm. Korea's Minjung theology often sounds, through the voices of some of its advocates, to be more Korean than biblical.

My purpose in this paper, however, moves in another direction. I wish to suggest that there is still another cause for fears, and this among those committed to the full inerrancy of Scripture. It is not as obvious to us as is the expression of doubts regarding the authority of the Bible. In fact, we are only beginning to recognize its potential for creating trouble. I speak of our lack of sophistication about the circumstantial issues which all theologies, including evangelical and Reformed ones, address.

To put it positively, I wish to underline the place of the historical context in rightly doing theology. I shall use several key figures from the early church to point out the liabilities of misjudging context and indicate how that misjudgment has affected our understanding of theology. And, finally, I shall make

---

Reprinted by permission from the *Westminster Theological Journal* 52 (1990): 51-63.

a few comments about how evangelicals in the two-thirds world are attempting to be more aware of this issue of context.

I. Shifts in Perspective

The basic purpose of theological reflection has never changed — "the reflection of Christians upon the gospel in the light of their own circumstances."[1] John V. Taylor, the missionary statesman of the Church of England, remembers the heartbreaking moment when his son decided to give up on the church. "Father," he said on one occasion as the two left church together, "the preacher is saying all of the right things, but he isn't saying them *to* anybody. He doesn't know where I am and it would never occur to him to ask!"

Relevance and irrelevance are the words we have used in the past to justify the dilemma placed before us by Taylor's son. Are our sermons and our theology scratching where the world does not itch? How can we live out and share the gospel in such a way that the cultures of the world will respond, "God speaks my language!"? "If Jesus is the answer, what are the questions?"

In recent years, however, that question of relevance and what we have called "application" has become more dominant. Much more attention is being paid now to how our context, our setting, is related to gospel response. Recent discussions in hermeneutics have underlined these questions in terms of "the two horizons."[2] The global agendas of missionary Christianity are reminding us that our Anglo-Saxon applications don't always fit in Uganda or Uruguay or Bedford-Stuyvestant. Evangelical cultural anthropologists are exploring this cultural terrain and questioning the ease with which we used to talk. Now, we speak not of application but of inculturation, not of relevance but of indigenization and/or contextualization.

Are John Taylor's remarks about Africa true of Asia and North America and the Latin world as well?

> Christ has been presented as the answer to the questions a white man would ask, the solution to the needs that Western man would feel, the Savior of the world of the European world-view, the object of the adoration and prayer of historic Christendom. But if Christ were to appear as the answer to the questions that the Africans are asking, what would he look like? If he came into the world of African cosmology to redeem Man as Africans understand him, would he be recognizable to the rest of the Church Universal.[3]

In Japan, for example, the problem can be illustrated another way. The

---

1. Robert J. Schreiter, *Constructing Local Theologies* (Maryknoll, NY: Orbis Books, 1985), 1.
2. Harvie M. Conn, ed., *Inerrancy and Hermeneutic* (Grand Rapids: Baker, 1988), 189-94.
3. John V. Taylor, *The Primal Vision* (London: SCM Press, 1963), 24.

word *tsumi* is used to translate the Christian worldview built into the word *sin*. But in a shame-oriented culture like Japan, *tsumi* comes closer to the English word *imprudent*. To the non-Christian Japanese it does not convey the idea of moral right or wrong or of sinning against God or even against duty. "The fearful thing about *tsumi* is rather the inherent potential of being discovered in the act and therefore shamed for being imprudent."[4] To the Christian, *tsumi* speaks of rebellion against God, lawlessness. To the non-Christian, *tsumi* points to the fear of being out of harmony with society and nature, of acts disapproved by humanity. How will the Christian cross this "culture gap" and still hold the gospel in his or her hands after passing over?

The average evangelical listening to this kind of example and this kind of question might easily respond, "This is a question of application." And, in a sense, this answer is still a useful one. On the simplest understanding of communication, this kind of response is good enough — if communication is understood simply as the strategic skill needed for gift-wrapping packages of information materials. But there is more to see and more to say than that.

Making the gospel relevant to the Japanese or a disillusioned young Englishman requires more than a "gift of words." It requires a "gift for cultural understanding." You can't fool a cultural Archie Bunker by changing words like "this" to "dis" and "moron" to "meathead." Behind Archie's judgments on Poles and Blacks and Jews and Jesus is a cultural world that informs him, a cultural agenda that must be seen, "dark glasses" worn by Archie that tell him what God and his nextdoor neighbor are supposed to look like.

Biblically oriented theologizing is the work of a gospel optician who must assist the reluctant patient in trying on a new set of glasses. Words like *tsumi* are more than crossword-puzzle answers for the right number of squares in a verbal game. They are suitcases in which the user packs all his or her cultural luggage. They are glimpses through a window into someone else's cultural house. They are furniture arrangements that make the owner feel "comfortable" and "at home." They are cultural fences around a piece of property that say, "This belongs to me."

For theology to become theology, it must, at some time or other, rummage through those suitcases and be a Peeping Tom, looking through those windows. Reflecting biblically on what we find, on what we see, is called theology. It is what Bengt Sundkler called "an ever-renewed re-interpretation to the new generations and peoples of the given Gospel, a re-presentation of the will and the way of the one Christ in a dialogue with new thought-forms and culture patterns."[5]

---

4. David Hesselgrave, *Communicating Christ Cross-Culturally* (Grand Rapids: Zondervan, 1978), 268.

5. Bengt Sundkler, *The Christian Ministry in Africa* (Uppsala: Swedish Institute of Missionary Research, 1960), 281.

Theology, by this definition, is not a gentleman's hobby. Nor is it ever exclusively a Western, white gentleman's hobby. It is not simply the mental exercise of persons sitting on the high front balcony of a Spanish house watching travelers go by on the road beneath them.

> The 'balconeers' can overhear the travellers' talk and chat with them; they may comment critically on the way that the travellers walk; or they may discuss questions about the road, how it can exist at all or lead anywhere, what might be seen from different points along it, and so forth; but they are onlookers and their problems are theoretical only.[6]

A biblically oriented theology is done by the travelers whose questions come from their involvement in the trip. They are questions that call not only for comprehension but for decision and action. They ask not only, Why is this so? but also, Which way to go?

Theology is always theology-on-the-road. And, in this sense, it is not simply a question of relevance or of application. It is not a twofold question of, first, theological interpretation, and then, practical application. Interpretation and application are not two questions but one. As John Frame says, "We do not know what Scripture says until we know how it relates to our world."[7] Theology must always ask what Scripture says. But it always asks in terms of the questions and answers our cultures raise. And to ask what Scripture says, or what it means, is always to ask a question about application.

Evangelical theologians in the two-thirds world seem more sensitive to all this than we do in the white, Western world. A 1982 gathering in Bangkok expressed their concern "that our hermeneutic should both be loyal to historic Christianity and arise out of our engagement with our respective situations."[8] The same conference report says with concern, "Churches of the Two Thirds world are in danger of bondage to alien categories. These do not permit them to meet adequately the problems and challenges of proclaiming Christ in our contexts."[9]

Later in the same year (1982) appeared the Seoul Declaration, sponsored by the Asia Theological Association and bringing together Asia's evangelical theologians. Again, in even more explicit language, Western theology, "whether liberal or conservative, conservative or progressive," was criticized for an agenda obsessed with problems of "faith and reason," for abstractionism from life. It was said to have capitulated to the secularistic worldview associated with the Enlightenment. The report charged that "sometimes it has been utilized as a

---

6. James I. Packer, *Knowing God* (Downers Grove, IL: InterVarsity, 1973), 5.

7. John Frame, *Van Til the Theologian* (Phillipsburg, NJ: Pilgrim, 1976), 25.

8. Vinay Samuel and Chris Sugden, eds., *Sharing Jesus in the Two-Thirds World* (Grand Rapids: Eerdmans, 1983), 277.

9. Ibid.

means to justify colonialism, exploitation, and oppression, or it has done little or nothing to change these situations."[10] Orlando Costas comments that "this statement may lack precision. However, it does articulate a well-known criticism of western theologies."[11]

Where can we trace the origins of these alleged problems? And how does the agenda of the two-thirds world differ from ours? These are the questions we seek to answer now.

II. The Roots and Fruits of the Western Agenda

Melba Maggay, a Filipino Christian, suggests where to begin.

> Christians in Asia and Africa are taught to answer questions raised by Greek sophists in the fourth century. While we live in a culture still very much awed by the Power that can be clearly perceived in things that have been made, we start from the supposition that we are talking to post-Christian men long past the age of the mythical and therefore must belabour the existence of a supernatural God. We defend the Scriptures as if we speak to the scientific rationalist, and not to men who have yet to see nature 'demythologised,' stripped of the wondrous and the magical.[12]

History also reminds us that the two-thirds world's struggles with "translating" the gospel into their own cultural setting is not unique. The church did not begin with a prepackaged gospel kit and do its theologizing through a kind of cultural circumcision. Against the challenge of accretions and distortions brought about by tradition and cultural consensus, the message of the gospel was shaped. Even in the early years of the church evangelism was never proclamation in a vacuum and theology was not what was done by someone talking in someone else's sleep. Situations have always shaped our confessions of faith.

The early church was not afraid of letting the culture set its gospel agenda, though it recognized the risks. Origen (c. 185-254) advocated what he called "spoiling the Egyptians," taking from pagan thought and culture all that is good and true, and using it in the interests of Christian thought. He was not the first to make these demands. A new cultural context was forcing new questions on the church. The physical persecution of the church was shifting to more subtle levels of attack. Intellectual assaults were being mounted. Legal charges demanded answering. The church was increasingly isolating itself from any

---

10. Bong-rin Ro and Ruth Eshenaur, eds., *The Bible and Theology in Asian Contexts* (Taichung, Taiwan: Asia Theological Association, 1984), 23.

11. Orlando Costas, "Evangelical Theology in the Two Thirds World," *TSF Bulletin* 9/1 (Sept.-Oct. 1985): 7-13.

12. Melba Maggay, "The Indigenization of Theology," *Patmos* 1/1 (1979): 1.

earlier identification as a Jewish sect. What was its relation to the world Jewish community?

A pioneer and innovator in answering these questions was Justin Martyr (c. 100-165). To the urbane Hellenistic world, he heralded Christianity as "the only philosophy which I have found certain and adequate." The gospel and the best elements in Plato and the Stoics were seen as almost identical ways of apprehending the same truth. Between Christianity and Platonism "there is no gulf fixed so great that the passage from the one to the other is impossible or unnatural."[13]

The center of harmonization for Justin lay in his concept of the *Logos*. Using the Johannine vocabulary, Justin saw Jesus as the Logos inherent in all things and especially in the rational creation. All who have thought and acted rationally and rightly have done so because of their participation in Christ and universal Logos (*Apologia* 2.10.13). So both Abraham and Socrates were "Christians before Christ." Each rational being shares in the universal Logos. We possess a piece of this Logos, like a seed sown by the Divine Sower. Each philosopher speaks the truth according to one's share of this seed, and according to one's ability to perceive its implications.

Without being critical at this stage in the argument, at least we must recognize now Justin's effort to communitate Christ according to the agenda of his hearers. His ultimate intention was not to carry out a kind of philosophical penetration of the Christian message and blend Plato with Jesus. It was to remove the impression that Christianity was just another religion. In view of its universality, it was able to embrace them all. His goal was evangelistic, that of presenting Christianity as the fulfillment of a longing and desire in paganism.

Others followed Justin, speaking also to a context that drove them to underline some of Justin's earlier emphases. The so-called Alexandrian school of the third century faced new antagonists who sought to push the church further into their Greek corner. Fifteen or twenty years after Justin, the Platonist Celsus wrote a blistering attack on Christianity. Celsus' arguments were an exact reversal of Justin's. He may in fact have been answering them directly.[14] The Greeks, he contended, did not borrow from the Hebrews. It was, in fact, the reverse. Jesus had read Plato, and Paul had studied Heraclitus. Christianity is a corruption from the primordial truths enshrined in the ancient polytheistic tradition. How does one explain so many Christian deviations then? Replies Celsus, "The majority of Christians are stupid!" The dull-wittedness of the majority of Christians is no accidental fault to him and certainly not a virtue. It is symptomatic of the inherently irrational and anti-intellectual character of Christianity. Adding to this assault was the growing strength of Gnosticism, "a

---

13. Henry Chadwick, *Early Christian Thought and the Classical Tradition* (New York: Oxford University Press, 1966), 11-12.

14. Ibid., 132-33.

stepping stone from Plato to Plotinus." Obsessed with evil, it consisted essentially in a radical rejection of this world as being at best a disastrous accident and at the least a malevolent plot.[15]

Against this context, men like Origen and Clement of Alexandria (c. 150-215) shaped their presentation of the gospel. Philosophy for the Hellenistic world was *paideia,* the education of rational man. Greek culture was the pedagogue that prepared us for a new world culture. Clement, using Gal 3:23 and its reference to the law as "the pedagogue," presents Christianity as fulfilling "this paideutic mission of mankind to a higher degree than has been achieved before."[16] Before the coming of Christ, he proposed, philosophy was necessary for the Greeks to obtain righteousness. Philosophy was their schoolmaster to bring them to Christ, just as the law was the schoolmaster for the Hebrews. In the philosophies of the ancient Greeks, the Logos revealed himself, though dimly and vaguely. In those philosophies, he prepared that world for the gospel which would be preached to it.

For Clement, there is only one true philosophy, "the philosophy according to the Hebrews." And since the Greeks have drawn from it, so we do also. This "true philosophy" has two streams, Holy Scripture and Greek philosophy. They are like two rivers, at whose confluence Christianity springs forth (*Miscellanies* 6.8).

It was Clement's successor, Origen, who systematized even further this effort at communicating. And like his predecessors, his purposes were evangelistic. Eusebius, the church historian, notes that "a great many heretics, and not a few of the most distinguished philosophers, studied under him diligently . . . he became celebrated as a great philosopher even among the Greeks themselves." Origen asserts that he does not intend to deviate by a hairsbreadth from the teaching of the church. "We confess that we do want to educate all men with the Word of God, even if Celsus does not wish to believe it" (*Contra Celsum* 3.54).

How will we judge these early "borrowings from the Egyptians"? J. K. S. Reid, for example, sees Clement as roaming "round the rich intellectual world of his day with a far greater sense of mastery than Christian theologians had hitherto shown, fearlessly rebutting such elements as are incongruous with the Christian faith, and just as eagerly putting others to apologetic use."[17] Henry Chadwick sees Clement seeking "to make the Church safe for philosophy and the acceptance of classical literature."[18] Before we dismiss Origen's work as

---

15. Henry Chadwick, "Philo and the Beginnings of Christian Thought," in *The Cambridge History of Later Greek and Early Medieval Philosophy,* ed. A. H. Armstrong (New York: Cambridge University Press, 1967), 166.

16. Werner Jaeger, *Early Christianity and Greek Paideia* (London: Oxford University Press, 1961), 60.

17. J. K. S. Reid, *Christian Apologetics* (Grand Rapids: Eerdmans, 1969), 53.

18. Chadwick, "Philo," 180-81.

"biblical alchemy," we need to remember that nothing for Origen was true simply because Plato said it. In *Contra Celsum* and elsewhere he is occasionally prickly to the point of rudeness towards the classical tradition. For all these men, natural religion and natural ethics are not enough. There is salvation only in Christ, and good works done before justification are useless. The soul of man is so weakened and distracted that it cannot be redeemed apart from the power and grace of God in Christ (*Contra Celsum* 4.19). Behind all of these formulations is the heart of the evangelist seeking to share Christ with his cultural world.

In short, the intentions of these men could not have been better. In the language of Michael Green, they sought

> to embody biblical doctrine in cultural forms which would be acceptable in their society. Not to remove the scandal of the gospel, but so to present their message in terms acceptable to their hearers, that the real scandal of the gospel could be perceived and its challenge faced. . . . If Christ is for all men, then evangelists must run the risk of being misunderstood, of misunderstanding elements in the gospel themselves, of losing out on the transposition of parts of the message so long as they bear witness to him. Christians are called to live dangerously.[19]

Many of their mistakes, and many of ours, we can find understandable. What were they to say to pagan writers who charged that Christians promoted impiety to the gods, that they engaged in immoral practices, that their rejection of emperor worship was treasonable to the state? They answered by focusing on Christian ethics.

What gospel encouragement could they offer to a world fearfully aware of demonic activity and power? Celsus saw such demons as inferior subordinates of the great god. The Christians like Justin answered by focusing on Jesus' redemption as one that destroys the demons. "The power of exorcism lies in the name of Jesus," testified Origen (*Contra Celsum* 1.6). What answers could they give their critics who charged them with making blind assertions and giving no proof? They turned to an exposition of Christianity as "the true philosophy."[20]

At the same time, there were wrong turns taken and lessons to be learned of a negative sort also for us and for the two-thirds world. I suggest that at least one part of their mistake may have been made in perceiving their context. They shifted the attention of the church to a new target or receptor audience. About the middle of the second century, a large body of literature was aiming at the pagan majority of the population masses. But as the decades wore on, Christian writers spoke less and less to the illiterate masses. The Alexandrian School

---

19. Michael Green, *Evangelism in the Early Church* (Grand Rapids: Eerdmans, 1970), 142.
20. Adolf von Harnack, *History of Dogma* (7 vols.; repr. New York: Dover, 1961), 2.209-24.

addressed people who read for the purpose of obtaining better information. "They speak to the educated few, including the rulers of the Roman Empire. They address them individually as men of higher culture *(paideia),* who will approach such a problem in a philosophical spirit."[21] Thus the presentation of the gospel was drawn deeper into the pull of a rationalistic orbit. Holistic balance was distorted by the magnetic attraction of a philosophical outlook that cuts up reality into an intricate series of related philosophical problems.

A second related problem was their failure to deal with their own preunderstandings in evaluating the gospel agenda. Their predispositions, the presuppositions they brought to the theological task of hermeneutic, were themselves captive to the same charms of rational speculation. Clement of Alexandria came to Christianity by way of philosophy. Could one expect such a man to see easily the Christian as anyone other than the "true Gnostic"? Origen was a professional philosopher. Like a dentist who looks at faces and sees mouths, he looked at Christianity and saw the *paideia* of humanity, Greek wisdom at the bottom line of divine providence.

And finally a third problem remained. The cultural agenda they chose to address showed sin's cracks and dents but no serious injury. Sin's side effects could be treated in an emergency room on an out-patient basis. There was no need for intensive care units. Culture was good "and not an evil," commented Origen. "In fact, it is a road to virtue. It is no hindrance to the knowledge of God." Rather, it favors it (*Contra Celsum* 3.47, 49).

What of an antithesis between darkness and light? What of sin? Sin was the result of ignorance, not an inherited evil nature, argued Justin. With a highly optimistic confidence in human reasoning and free will, he fully expected that if the barriers of ignorance and misinformation were removed, the truth of Christ would shine in its own light. And if not, you could always blame the deceptions of demons. "The devils made me do it." Sin's darkness was no more apparent in the Alexandrian School. Clement was interested in free will, not inherited bondage or corruption of nature. And Origen reduced the fall to the state of preexistence, before the beginning of earthly life. Original sin became preoriginal sin.

Given these perspectives, accommodation became an easier way to deal with the cultural agenda issue than antithesis. But searching in good will for points of contact can become like falling on pitchforks in haystacks. Borrowing too many things from a neighbor, no matter how well intended, left the Western world with a very cluttered theological attic.[22]

Out of this came eventually a new understanding of how theology was formed. Theology saw itself as more and more an abstractionist task, a searching

21. Jaeger, *Early Christianity,* 27.

22. For amplification of this criticism, consult C. Van Til, *A Christian Theory of Knowledge* (Nutley, NJ: Presbyterian and Reformed, 1969), 109-18.

for essences untouched by the realities of the cultural context. The goal of theology became a rational display of the Platonic ideal. The Latin Fathers, with their legal training, reinforced this perception. The Cappadocian Fathers, Basil of Caesarea and the two Gregorys, in the second half of the fourth century, carry it on. In the language of Werner Jaeger:

> Even in their high appreciation of Origen, to whom they often refer, they show that they, like him, think of theology as a great science based on supreme scholarship and as a philosophical pursuit of the mind. And this science is part of the entire civilization that is theirs and in which they feel at home.[23]

Out of this, we suggest, comes a confusion of the Bible as norm with theology as a neutral search for the rationally ideal, the "heavenly principles." True theology is seen as *sui generis,* the liberating search of the mind for essence, core, unhindered by any kind of historical, geographical, or social qualifier. Theological pursuits are freed to become the Platonic search for abstract, rational principles.

Anglo-Saxon evangelicals are today properly concerned over current attitudes to biblical authority. Is the history we have just sketched also part of the reason why they become more fearful that any thinking which explores the tentative nature of theology will lead to a downward slide to syncretism? Do they see the rational core "ideal" of theology being threatened? How much of that fear is biblically proper? And how much is controlled by a hidden agenda that assumes theology, wherever it originates, is a rational given ontologized out of reality? Has the evangelical in the two-thirds world seen this history better than we have?

III. The Agenda of Evangelical Two-Thirds World Theologies

The emerging theologies in the two-thirds world share many things in common with Western models. (1) They are intentionally contextual and occasional, as is all theological effort. One will not always find great theological systems. But these systems have come late to the Anglo-Saxon world as well. The first centuries of church history did not produce a systematician like Calvin or Luther until there had been an Augustine writing on soteriology or an Anselm on the atonement to feed into the larger stream. In fact, there may be those who do not want to build such systems in the church of the two-thirds world. On the part of some, this could very well be a part of the criticism of the Anglo-Saxon world of theology. Some apparently might fear any theological system that appears to be timeless and culturally universal.

---

23. Jaeger, *Early Christianity,* 74.

(2) There is also a sense that this occasional, local character of theology is crucial if Christianity is to survive in its particular settings. And this too is a feeling shared with Justin and the Alexandrian School. We are aware, for example, that we must Christianize Africa. The African theologian shares that commitment with us. But with it, there is another question. How will we Africanize Christianity? How will we move from Christianity for Africa to Christianity in Africa. If Christianity is to survive in Africa, it must be seen as more than a relic of the colonial period. It must be truly African: it must speak to actual African concerns with an authentically African voice. The authenticity of all theology, argues one evangelical, depends on two factors; its Christian integrity and its cultural integrity.[24]

(3) We share together as well an inability to break ourselves free from our cultural preunderstandings. The same weakened view of sin that encouraged accommodation to our Greek and Latin cultures often inhibits theology in the two-thirds world. Is this not a major flaw, for example, in liberation theology? In its necessary protest against a reduction of sin to the merely private, is liberation theology still encumbered with too shallow a view of sin? Are some of the richest descriptions of sin in the Bible blurred? Is liberation theology willing to see sin as such a state of corruption that the elimination of poverty, oppression, racism, classism, and capitalism cannot alter the human condition of sinfulness in any radical way?[25]

But, after we have admitted the similarities, we are still left with differences that may be pointing to more hopeful learning signs for the future of theology. It is to a few of these signs that I point now in closing.

1. There appears to be a more conscious awareness among two-thirds world theologies of the human, cultural context and contextuality as a key in the process of theologizing. These evangelicals appear to find it easier to admit that all theology has always been situational. It has always been a case of theology in context. At the same time, these evangelicals also distance themselves from those who argue that context takes precedence over text. Old doubts concerning the authority of the Bible can emerge again, they warn, under the cloak of an enculturated hermeneutics.[26]

But even admitting this, there is still a lesson for us to learn, whether it be from Korean Minjung theology or American Black theologies of a liberal orientation. Theology cannot be done in an ontological vacuum. Theology speaks out of the historical context; and theology must speak to that context.

2. There also appears to be in two-thirds world theologies a deeper appreciation of the social and cultural dimensions of the historical context than one

24. Dick France, "Christianity on the March," *Third Way* 1/21 (November 3, 1977): 3-5.
25. For a fuller exposition of these problems, consult Harvie M. Conn, "Theologies of Liberation," in *Tensions in Contemporary Theology,* ed. S. Gundry and A. Johnson (Grand Rapids: Baker, 1986), 404-18.
26. Ro and Eshenaur, *Bible and Theology,* 9-12, 23-24.

finds elsewhere. These theologies have not made the mistake of the Alexandrian School and focused on the purely ontological and epistemological. Their setting does not seem to have allowed them that luxury. They have done their theologizing in a world of vast poverty, a world of oppressor and oppressed, a world of dependence and marginalization.

Where was theology to turn to respond to these issues? The agenda of inherited Anglo-Saxon theology did not speak to these issues. If theology was to speak to two-thirds world needs, it would need a new agenda. It would have to search for new answers. What does the Bible say about poverty and oppression? about nation-building and torture, racism and, dare I say it, sexism? The indexes of Anglo-Saxon theological texts yield little fruit for these kinds of questions.

3. There also appears to be in two-thirds world theologies a deeper interfacing with non-Christian religions. The churches of Asia especially have found it necessary to make the growth of the great traditions of Islam, Hinduism, and Buddhism a central emphasis in their theological development. Again, there seems to be little help in meeting this challenge from contemporary Anglo-Saxon theologies. Our world has left behind the interest in pagan religions shown by Justin and the Alexandrian School. We live in a post-Enlightenment world where we must spend our energies on Anglo-Saxon secularization and antisupernaturalism. There are some who fear an escalating self-preoccupation even of evangelical theology with its own welfare.

In the Buddhist context of Sri Lanka and Thailand, by contrast, theology finds itself oriented to questions of the nature of suffering, of impermanence and the non-self, of enlightenment. In Africa the dialogue is with Africa's traditional religions. What is the connection, if any, between Christian theology and African religions? Can Africa's religions become bridges, points of contact, for the development of a distinctly African sound to Christianity?

Anglo-Saxon theology will have much to learn from these studies. As our countries become increasingly pluralistic in religions, we will have to ask the same questions. We are already doing it with Judaism. Now our study of Hinduism, Islam, and Buddhism must begin.

4. Finally, there is a new recovery in two-thirds world evangelical theologies of the missiological nature of theology. That missiological dimension was present in the classical theologians we paid attention to at the beginning of this paper. But the results of their encounter led theology further away from that dimension. By contrast, this missiological dimension is being recovered in the two-thirds world theologies. In some settings, such as Asia or most of Africa, theology is forced to do its work without the benefit of the *corpus christianum*. In this setting theologizing has a more "missiological" sound to it. It is done with more consciousness that the non-Christian world is eavesdropping.

In settings like Latin America and among blacks in South Africa and North America, the church also sees itself as a marginalized minority. But in this instance their world is the world of institutionalized Christendom. But, either because of oppression or racism, they are forced to do their reflective work "from the underside." In these contexts, they carry on their efforts in spite of the *corpus christianum* or directly to it. In both of these contexts, theology then sees itself as a witness of a prophetic sort. The theological tone is more "missiological." Theologians sound more like evangelists.

IV. The Reaffirmation of "Situational" Theologizing

The lessons from the early church and from the two-thirds world converge. Contextualization is not a new discovery; it has always been a characteristic of theology as such. Paul's "task theology" is a biblical pattern for our own theologizing. Adrio König puts it this way:

> All theology, all reflection about the Bible should be done contextually, i.e., taking into consideration the context or situation of the theologian and the church. Everyone who thinks systematically about the meaning and implications of the biblical message should deliberately take up his own situation in his thinking. Theology is practiced in and from within a specific situation, but also in terms of and with a view to a specific situation.[27]

This is just saying that theology must be biblical but it need not be borrowed. Even evangelical theology will have a different look when it is shaped in a context where Confucius, not Kant, is king.

So a different twist to theology seems to be developing in the two-thirds world. It is addressing questions not usually dealt with by evangelical mainstream theologians in the northern hemisphere — ancestor practices in East Asia and Africa, Buddhist worldviews oriented to suffering, Muslim misunderstandings of Jesus, political and economic issues. "It offers critical evaluations of western theology and affirms at the same time its shared commitment to the authority and integrity of the Bible. It fears bondage to alien categories and confesses its loyalty to historic Christianity. It does not ask for approval but for affirmation."[28] One will hear sounds from the evangelical of the two-thirds world that may appear strange at first to Anglo-Saxon ears tuned to a Reformation creedal history through which the two-thirds world has not passed. Why will it sound different?

After a lengthy study of the 1982 Bangkok and Seoul statements referred to earlier, Orlando Costas answers our question this way:

---

27. Adrio König, "Contextual Theology," *Theologia evangelica* 14/3 (Dec. 1981): 37-43, p. 37.
28. Harvie M. Conn, "Looking to the Future: Evangelical Missions from North America in the Years Ahead," *Urban Mission* 5/3 (Jan. 1988): 28.

Evangelical theologians in these parts of the world are appropriating the best of their spiritual tradition and are putting it to use in a constructive critical dialogue with their interlocutors in and outside of their historical space. For them the evangelical tradition is not locked into the socio-cultural experience of the West. They insist that they have the right to articulate theologically the evangelical tradition in their own terms and in light of their own issues.[29]

Is not that our common calling in every age and in every cultural setting? And from it will there not come ultimately perhaps the richest contribution of all to the task of theology — the reminder to us all of what theology truly rooted in biblical revelation and addressing our real contexts can offer us? The ultimate test of any theological discourse, after all, is not only erudite precision but also transformative power. "It is a question of whether or not theology can articulate the faith in a way that is not only intellectually sound but spiritually energizing, and, therefore, capable of leading the people of God to be transformed in their way of life and to commit themselves to God's mission in the world."[30]

29. Costas, "Evangelical Theology," 10.
30. Ibid., 12.

Some Further Contributions to the Discussion

Kofi Appiah-Kubi and Sergio Torres, *African Theology en Route*. Maryknoll, NY: Orbis Books, 1979.

Arturo J. Bakuelas, *Mestizo Christianity: Theology from the Latin Perspective*. Maryknoll, NY: Orbis Books, 1995.

Karl Barth, *Evangelical Theology: An Introduction*. New York: Holt, Reinhart and Winston, 1963.

————, *Church Dogmatics*, Vol. 1: *The Doctrine of the Word of God*. Translated by G. T. Thomson. Edinburgh: T & T Clark, 1936.

Clodovis Boff, *Theology and Praxis: Epistemological Foundations*. Maryknoll, NY: Orbis Books, 1987.

Rebecca Chopp and Mark L. Taylor, *Reconstructing Christian Theology*. Minneapolis: Fortress Press, 1994.

Hyun Kyung Chung, *Struggle to be the Sun Again: Introducing Asian Women's Theology*. Maryknoll, NY: Orbis Books, 1990.

Martin Cook, *The Open Circle: Confessional Method in Theology*. Minneapolis: Fortress Press, 1991.

Somen Das, *Christian Faith and Multiform Culture in India*. Bangalore: United Theological College, 1987.

Kwesi A. Dickson, *Theology in Africa*. Maryknoll, NY: Orbis Books, 1984.

Virginia Fabella and Sergio Torres, eds., *Doing Theology in a Divided World*. Maryknoll, NY: Orbis Books, 1985.

———— and Mercy Amba Oduyoye, eds., *With Passion and Compassion: Third World Women Doing Theology*. Maryknoll, NY: Orbis Books, 1988.

Thomas N. Finger, *Christian Theology: An Eschatological Approach*. Scottdale, PA: Herald Press, 1985.

James Leo Garrett, *Systematic Theology: Biblical, Historical, and Evangelical*. 2 vols. Grand Rapids, MI: Wm. B. Eerdmans Publishing Co., 1990 and 1995.

Jerry Gill, *On Knowing God*. Philadelphia: Westminster Press, 1981.

Garrett Green, *Imaging God: Theology and the Religious Imagination.* San Francisco: Harper & Row, 1989.

Douglas John Hall, *Thinking the Faith.* Minneapolis: Augsburg, 1989.

Carl F. H. Henry, *God, Revelation and Authority,* Vols. 1 and 2. Waco, TX: Word Books Publisher, 1976.

Dwight N. Hopkins, *Shoes That Fit Our Feet: Sources for a Constructive Black Theology.* Maryknoll, NY: Orbis Books, 1993.

George Lindbeck, *The Nature of Doctrine: Religion and Theology in a Postliberal Age.* Philadelphia: Westminster Press, 1984.

Kosuke Koyama, *Mount Fuji and Mount Sinai.* London: SCM Press Ltd., 1984.

Vladimir Lossky, *The Mystical Theology of the Eastern Church.* Crestwood, NY: St. Vladimir's Seminary Press, 1976.

H. D. McDonald, *Theories of Revelation.* London: G. Allen & Unwin, 1963.

Sallie McFague, *Metaphorical Theology.* Philadelphia: Fortress Press, 1982.

Emmanuel Martey, *African Theology: Inculturation and Liberation.* Maryknoll, NY: Orbis Books, 1995.

H. Richard Niebuhr, *The Meaning of Revelation.* New York: Macmillan, 1941.

Schubert Ogden, *On Theology.* San Francisco: Harper & Row Publishers, 1986.

Wolfhart Pannenberg et al., *Revelation as History.* New York: Macmillan, 1968.

————, *Systematic Theology,* Vol. 1. Translated by Geoffrey W. Bromiley. Grand Rapids, MI: William B. Eerdmans Publishing Co., 1991.

Clark H. Pinnock, *Tracking the Maze.* San Francisco: Harper & Row, 1990.

Carl Raschke, *Theological Thinking: An Inquiry.* Atlanta, GA: Scholars Press, 1988.

Dietrich Ritschl, *The Logic of Theology.* Philadelphia: Fortress Press, 1987.

Robert Schreiter, *Constructing Local Theologies.* Maryknoll, NY: Orbis Books, 1985.

C. S. Song, *Theology from the Womb of Asia.* Maryknoll, NY: Orbis Books, 1986.

Elsa Tamez, ed., *Through Her Eyes: Women's Theology from Latin America.* Maryknoll, NY: Orbis Books, 1989.

David Tracy, *The Analogical Imagination.* New York: Crossroad, 1981.

G. W. Trompf, ed., *The Gospel Is Not Western: Black Theologies from the Southwest Pacific.* Maryknoll, NY: Orbis Books, 1987.

David Wells, *God in the Wasteland: The Reality of Truth in a World of Fading Dreams.* Grand Rapids, MI: Wm. B. Eerdmans Publishing Co., 1994.

Delores S. Williams, *Sisters in the Wilderness: The Challenge of Womanist God-Talk.* Maryknoll, NY: Orbis Books, 1994.

Charles M. Wood, *The Formation of Christian Understanding.* Philadelphia: Westminster Press, 1981.

Pamela Dickey Young, *Feminist Theology/Christian Theology: In Search of Method.* Minneapolis: Fortress Press, 1990.

PART II

Enlarging Our Understanding of God

INTRODUCING THE ISSUE

God Is More Than You Think

To speak of God is always a bold and risky undertaking. For what words and thoughts can adequately express the majesty, glory, and awesome reality of God? And as if this were not daunting enough, it is clear that today all thinking and speaking of God must be done in the midst of and in relation to a world in which there is massive suffering and terrible acts of cruelty. At the same time it is a world in which there are amazing acts of compassion, self-giving, and persistence in the struggle for justice and life. Furthermore, in recent years we have witnessed the unexpected and astonishing breaking through of barriers in such places as Haiti and South Africa, and the peace process in the Middle East and in Northern Ireland, although it is also true that such processes are not without problems and in other areas forces of repression have reasserted themselves.

Christian understanding of God seeks to discern the activity and disclosure of God in this complex situation in the light of the biblical witness to God's redemptive activity focused centrally in Jesus Christ. Here Christians see God presented most concretely and clearly, while recognizing that this revelation is grounded in Israel's witness to God and pours out into the Holy Spirit's activity in the church and in the world, opening eyes to the revelation of God in Christ and implementing its transforming power. But it is also true that Christians in different parts of the world and in different cultures perceive God in distinctively different ways. Yet these various perceptions do not have to lead to divisiveness; they can help those in all cultures to new insights and deeper understanding of the one God who, though conceived in different ways, gives life to all creatures.

The essays in this section have to do with expanding and deepening our understanding of God from a number of different perspectives. Writing from an Eastern Orthodox perspective, Emmanuel Clapsis suggests that we need to recover the Cappadocian theologians' insight that God, who is ultimately beyond all knowledge and comprehension, becomes known through many names.

Clapsis contends that these names are not so much theoretical definitions of the divine nature as they are expressions of adoration to God on the basis of God's relations to us. He points out that the early church writers were keenly aware of the provisional and relative nature of theological images and metaphors, and felt free to use feminine along with masculine images of God. From them we can learn the value of a rich variety of theological conceptions, "each of which acts as a corrective against the tendency of any particular one to become reified and literal."

But would acceptance of such pluralism actually serve to endorse the predominantly male language and imagery of God in Christian tradition and in many sectors of the church today? Susan Thistlethwaite contends that the root of the problem is a dualism of mind/body and spirit/nature that persists in liberal as well as in conservative theology. In her critique of Gordon Kaufman's concept of God as the ultimate point of reference of human constructive imagination, Thistlethwaite draws on feminine experience and images in arguing for a new model of divine/human relationship woven through the struggle of the oppressed for survival and life. Poets and novelists, she suggests, are sometimes more perceptive than theologians in calling attention to God's work in the world giving birth to and nurturing life in the face of forces of death and destruction.

Is this also in line with Scripture's witness to God? Writing from a Wesleyan perspective, Howard Snyder points to the emphasis on the holiness of God in Scripture. This is linked in the Holiness Movement with God's sanctifying power at work in the believer and the community of faith, rooting sin out of the heart and preparing for the coming of the reign of God in its fullness. Though premillennialists and postmillennialists describe this reign in different ways, both envision God as one who brings in a radical transformation of the world. This reign of God, Snyder argues, is at once experiential, social, present, and future, and requires a new pattern and quality of life.

Speaking out of an African context, John Mbiti, an internationally renowned biblical scholar and theologian, relates biblical concepts of God to images in traditional African religions. He suggests that God is known in various ways through the many African languages and stories. In these traditions God is not separated from nature but all of existence is viewed as sacred, as indwelt by God. He asks: Might it be that there is not such a sharp conflict between the transcendent creator God of Judeo-Christian faith and traditional African visions as earlier missionaries supposed? Can not the same God be encountered through the imagery of both cultural contexts: that of the West and that of the stories, songs, and dances of African peoples?

In his contribution to the discussion, Michael Welker, one of the rising younger European theologians, focuses on the work and manifestation of God as Spirit. Building on biblical images, Welker contends that an understanding of God's presence in the world as Spirit is directly relevant to contemporary scientific and social understanding and our increasing awareness of the inter-dependence of all of creation. Such a vision perceives God as working to unify, reconcile, transform, and mend the torn creation.

Still, perhaps parables and stories are finally the most effective way of communicating a deeper understanding of God. Sr. Macrina's narrative "Guarding God" shows God's power to give strength to the weak and suffering and to sustain the faith of those burdened with grief who must walk through darkness.

Naming God: An Orthodox View

EMMANUEL CLAPSIS

Today certain fundamental concepts of traditional Christian faith have been challenged and language, including the use of names, has become one of the most controversial issues in Christian theology. Particularly, feminist theology conceives its task as a "new naming" of self and world and, consequently, of the whole Christian tradition. The following quotation by Carol Christ and Judith Plaskow is an excellent summary of the feminist critique of language and emphasis on the importance of naming:

> It is through naming that humans progress from childhood to adulthood and learn to understand and shape the world about them. Under patriarchy, men have reserved to themselves the right to name, keeping women in a state of intellectual and spiritual dependency. . . . As women begin to name the world for themselves, they will upset the order that has been taken for granted throughout history. They will call themselves and the world into new being. Naming women's experience thus becomes the model not only for personal liberation and growth, but for the feminist transformation of culture and religion.[1]

Feminist theologians passionately raise the question of language and how it has been used in Christian tradition. They strongly criticize the image of God as Father, which, in their opinion, has been both absolutized by some and, in recent times, found meaningless by others.[2]

Orthodox theologians do not yet speak with one mind when they attempt

---

1. Carol Christ and Judith Plaskow, eds., *Womanspirit Rising: A Feminist Reader in Religion* (New York: Harper & Row, 1979), 7.
2. Sallie McFague, *Metaphorical Theology — Models of God in Religious Language* (Philadelphia: Fortress Press, 1982), 145.

From the *Ecumenical Review* 44/1 (Jan. 1992): 100-112. Used with permission of the journal.

to respond to such claims. For example, the Orthodox participants from the United States in the study of the WCC Faith and Order Commission on "The Community of Women and Men in the Church," in their responses to questions about language and imagery of God, stated: "We would never think of questioning that God was the Father, and could not conceive of God as Mother. Christ named God the Father: if we believe Christ, we cannot compromise."[3] Yet the Orthodox from France have stated: "The true meeting with God takes place beyond all images and all words, in the silence that is not speechlessness. This 'apophaticism' permeating Orthodox belief avoids the trap of a unilaterally masculine image of God. Orthodox iconography never represents God the Father. The divine paternity would not be represented by sexual image. The Heavenly Father should not be imagined as a bearded patriarch."[4] Such challenges compel us to study carefully the nature, the function and the significance of religious language and names in patristic literature, hoping that this will help us to shape paradigmatically the contemporary Orthodox attitude and response to this important issue.[5]

The Nature of Language

Human language, according to the Cappadocian Fathers, is the invention of human intellect. They emphasized that God created the world and humanity, then gave names to the objects of the world, reflecting the relationship that human beings established with them.[6] Human nature, having received from God the power of speech and utterance, and of expressing the will by the voice, gives things distinctive names by varying inflections of sound: and these sounds are the verbs and nouns which we use, and through which we signify the "meaning" of things. Thus while God has created the substance of all things, human beings have given names to them which reflect the kinds of relationships they have developed with God's creation. The naming of the world, through human reasoning and speech, structures in the memory of every human person the experience, understanding and information they acquire in life and which is constitutive of their understanding of reality. Names provide us with a description of things that exist so that we can distinguish them from each other, relate to them and "know" their existence.

3. Melanie A. May, "Conversations on Language and Imagery of God — Occasioned by the Community of Women and Men in the Church Study," *Union Seminary Quarterly Review* 40 (1985): 15.

4. *Ibid.*

5. Stylianos G. Papadopoulos, *Theologia kai Glossa* (Katerini, 1988); Konstantinos Papapetros, *He Ousia tes Theologias* (Athens, 1970), 43-64; Georgios Martzelos, *Hai Ousiai kai hoi Energeiai tou Theou: kata ton Megan Basileion* (Thessaloniki, 1984), 147-89.

6. Gregory of Nyssa, "Answer to Eunomius II," in *Nicene and Post-Nicene Fathers II* (Grand Rapids, 1954), Vol. 5, 275 (*PG* 45, 992-93).

The intellectual faculty, made as it was originally by God, acts . . . by itself when it looks out upon realities and that there be no confusion in its knowledge, affixes some verbal note to each several thing as a stamp to indicate its meaning.[7]

Names help people communicate their ideas and perception of the world to each other. For example, whenever someone speaks of "heaven" he or she directs the notion of the hearer to the object indicated by this name. Thus objects are depicted in the intellect of those who hear the appellation or name imposed upon them. But the nature of most things is not simple, and therefore cannot be connoted or comprehended in one word. Such objects are named according to their multiple qualities and our best possible understanding of them is derived from the totality of these qualities.[8]

However, this becomes more difficult when we try to name the realities of the intelligible world that our human senses cannot grasp. In such situations, according to St. Gregory of Nyssa, we develop relative ideas about the intelligible realities, hoping that the way we name them may be the most precise expression of the intelligible reality in itself. The ultimate goal is to perceive or understand the object of the intelligible world correctly and to express its "idea" with the most appropriate words and in the most precise manner. Thus whenever we try to understand and name realities of the intelligible world we must always prefer expressions which reveal "mental exactitude and correct verbal utterance." But this ideal situation is not always possible, especially with theological language, and therefore it is acceptable to acquire the right conception of the divine, and possibly express it with words which may happen to be inadequate to the thought.

Whenever, then, our thought is intent upon those high and unseen things which sense cannot reach (I mean, upon that divine and unspeakable world with regard to which it is an audacious thing to grasp in thought anything in it at random, and more audacious still to trust to any chance word the representing of the conception arising from it), then, I say, turning from the mere sound of phrases, uttered well or ill according to the mental faculty of the speaker, we search for the thought, and that alone, which is found within the phrases, to see whether that itself be sound, or otherwise; and we leave the minutiae of phrases and names to be dealt with by the artificialities of grammarians.[9]

Thus Gregory of Nyssa concludes that it is possible for us to describe or name adequately whatever our senses can grasp. But it is impossible to find any

7. Ibid., 290 (*PG* 45.1045).
8. Ibid., 278 (*PG* 45.1001ff.).
9. Ibid., 308 (*PG* 45.1104).

appropriate human term to describe divine realities, and therefore we are compelled to use many and different names in order [to] "divulge our surmises as they arise within us with regard to the Deity."[10]

Are names merely arbitrary signifiers of things that exist? St. Gregory of Nyssa seems to believe that names are words indicative of the actual nature of things, as this nature is conceived by humanity. However the human perception of the "actual nature of things," and its expression through names, does not constitute the nature of things as they actually are. Thus the human words signifying our conception of a subject are not to be substantially identified with that thing itself. Therefore names can be changed without altering the nature of that which they signify:

> For the things remain in themselves as they naturally are, while the mind, touching on existing things, reveals its thoughts by such words as are available. And just as the essence of Peter was not changed with the change of his name, so neither is any other of the things we contemplate changed in the process of mutation of names.[11]

It is plain to everyone that there is no single name that has in itself any substantial reality, but that every name is but a recognizing mark placed on some reality or some idea, having of itself no existence either as a fact or a thought.[12] This does not mean, however, that names can be changed or given arbitrarily without any regard for the nature or the qualities of the thing but, on the contrary, names should reflect as far as possible the nature of the qualities of things. And since language and names have been invented by their knowledge, understanding and interpretation of the world, the vernacular languages should be an instrument by which the world is named by the various human races.

> We assert, that He who brought all creation into being out of nothing is the Creator of things seen in substantial existence, not of unsubstantial words having no existence but in the sound of the voice and the lisp of the tongue. But things are named by the indication of the voice in conformity with the nature and qualities inherent in each, the names being adapted to the things according to the vernacular language of each several race.[13]

St. Gregory of Nyssa declared that God does not use or sanctify one particular form of language. In fact, even the biblical language which is attributed to God in the book of Genesis is not literally God's talk but that of Moses, who uses the language in which he had been educated and which people could understand, in order to communicate realities of "profound and divine

10. Ibid.
11. Ibid., 196 (*PG* 45.760).
12. Ibid., 278 (*PG* 45.1001).
13. Ibid., 276 (*PG* 45.996-97).

significance." St. Paul also knew how to adapt his speech to the capacity, habits and dispositions of his hearers so they would feel God's love for all people.[14] Taking into account the historicity of human understanding and the multiplicity of particular things and situations, the names by which people describe their experiences of the world and their life in it will vary at different occasions and parts of the world, although these names may still convey the same meaning or understanding of what exists.[15] This diversity accurately manifests the human condition since our words do not constitute the subject itself but only signify it by the name we give to it. Thus people of different language do not disagree from others in their knowledge of things, but only differ in names which they give them: "While the nature of things as constituted by God remains the same, the names which denote them are divided by so many differences of language, that it is no easy task even to calculate their number."[16]

Naming the Divine

The Fathers of the church reflected on the issue of naming God. They believed that human wisdom, apart from divine revelation and without the guidance of the Holy Spirit, is incapable of understanding (and therefore of naming) the divine Being. St. Gregory of Nazianzus in his *Second Theological Oration* recognizes the problem of religious knowledge and language. Asserting both the indescribability and the incomprehensibility of God, Gregory summarizes his position as follows:

> To know God is difficult, to speak of him impossible, as one of the Greek theologians taught — quite cleverly it seems to me; for in saying it is difficult, he appears to have comprehended him and yet escapes examination because of his unexpressibility; but in my opinion, to speak of God is impossible and to know him even more impossible. For what is known, some word can perhaps make plain, if not adequately at least obscurely, to anyone who has not completely lost his hearing or is mentally slow. But it is altogether impossible and impracticable mentally *(te dianoia)* to encompass so great a subject, not merely for the indolent with lowly inclinations, but even for those who aim high and love God — indeed for all created nature, in that this darkness and this thick fleshiness gets in the way of perceiving the Truth.[17]

14. Ibid.
15. Ibid.
16. Ibid., 275 (*PG* 45.996).
17. *The Second Theological Oration — On God* (Discourse 28.4). The Greek theologian to whom he refers is Plato, and the text to which he alludes is Plato's much quoted remark in the *Timaeus* (28e): "But it is an effort to discover the Father and Maker of all this universe; and it is impossible for the discoverer to speak of him to all men."

The Christian understanding of God, influenced by Judaism and Hellenistic philosophy, asserted the otherness of God through the use of apophatic language that primarily states not what God is, but what he is not as compared with created realities. Such language was and continues to be an important corrective to the highly anthropomorphic language that one finds in Scripture and Tradition. It heightens the sense of God's mystery. Gregory of Nyssa in his *Contra Eunomium* asserts that because of the utter unlikeness of the infinite Creator to finite creatures, no intuition of God's being is possible through human faculties alone. He insists that no rational discourse can give an account of God, and that no analysis or definition of an infinite being is possible. Therefore the complete knowledge of God is logically impossible. This is not simply due to any disability of human reasoning, but is a feature of God's very Being.

> The simplicity of true faith assumes God to be what He is, namely incapable of being grasped by any term or any idea or any other device of our apprehensions remaining beyond the reach not only of the human but of the angelic and of all supramundane intelligence, unthinkable, unutterable, above all expression in words, having but one name that can represent his proper nature, the single name of being "above every name."[18]

Here apophatic language denies the possibility of religious language and knowledge. This denial is partly philosophical: there is no logic common to ordinary language and to language used for the divine. But it is also partly religious: a God worthy of worship is beyond comparison with anything derivative from him.[19]

Despite their affirmation of God's indescribability and incomprehensibility, the Fathers of the church found religious language to describe what they suggested to be indescribable. St. Gregory of Nazianzus provides us with a clue by which we can understand this. He asserts:

> The divine cannot be named. . . . For no-one has ever breathed the whole air, nor has any mind located or language contained the being of God completely. But sketching his inward self from his outward characteristics, we may assemble an inadequate, weak and partial picture. And the one who makes the best theologian is not the one who knows the whole truth, but the one who creates the best picture, who assembles more of truth's image or shadow, or whatever we should call it.[20]

Divine revelation and grace make religious knowledge and language possible. This consequently makes the scriptural names of God foundational

---

18. Gregory of Nyssa, "Answer to Eunomius II," in *Nicene and Post-Nicene Fathers II*, Vol. 5, 309 (*PG* 45.1108).

19. Ibid., Gregory of Nazianzus, *Second Theological Oration*, 28.7.

20. Ibid., 30.17.

for the way that Christians have named the divine. Dionysius the Areopagite in his treatise on *Divine Names* states:

> Let us hold on to the scriptural rule that when we say anything about God, we should set down the truth not in the plausible words of human wisdom but in demonstration of the power granted by the Spirit to the scripture writers, a power by which, in a manner surpassing speech and knowledge, we reach a union superior to anything available to us by way of our own abilities or activities in the realm of discourse or of intellect. This is why we must not dare to resort to words or conceptions concerning that hidden divinity which transcends being, apart from what the sacred scriptures have divinely revealed . . . as cause of all existence, and therefore itself transcending existence, it alone could give an authoritative account of what it really is.[21]

What does Scripture tell us about the Deity? Dionysius the Areopagite states:

> Many scripture writers will tell you that the divinity is not only invisible and incomprehensible, but also "unsearchable and inscrutable," since there is no trace for anyone who would reach through into the hidden depths of this infinity. And yet, on the other hand, the Good is not absolutely incommunicable to everything. By itself it generously reveals a firm, transcendent beam, granting enlightenments proportionate to each being, and thereby draws sacred minds upward to its permitted contemplation, to participation and to the state of becoming like it.[22]

The Deity is self-revealed, and the writers of Scripture through the divine names refer "in revealing praises, to the processions of God."[23] According to St. Gregory of Nyssa this reflects the economy of the Holy Spirit, who "has delivered to us divine mysteries and teaches the realities that are beyond discourse by means of those that are accessible . . . we are raised in an analogous way, through each one of the things said on the subject of God, towards a higher conception of him."[24] Origen, while he points out that the question of names is simultaneously profound and obscure, thinks that:

> Certain sounds and syllables which are pronounced with or without aspiration, with either long or short sound-vowel, control those who are invoked probably by some natural power imperceptible to us. If this is so and names are not a matter of arbitrary convention, the Supreme God ought not to be invoked by any name except those used by Moses and the prophets and our Savior and Lord himself.[25]

---

21. Dionysius the Areopagite, *The Divine Names Book*, I, 1:1.
22. Ibid., Book I, 1:2.
23. *Divine Names*, 1.4.
24. *Nicene and Post-Nicene Fathers II*, Vol. 5, 197 (*PG* 45.761).
25. Origen, *Exhortation to Martyrdom*, 46; cf. *Contra Celsum*, 1.24; 5.45.

The way that the authors of Scripture named God signifies their own life of communion with God in their particular historical situation, and their illumination by God's grace which makes their human words about God the vehicle of God's self-revelation. This life of communion with God is presupposed as a basis for the proper appreciation of theological reflection. St. Gregory of Nazianzus suggests that attaining knowledge of God is not a matter for philosophers, but for those who have purified themselves:

> Not to everyone, my friends, does it belong to philosophize about God . . . but (only) on certain occasions, and before certain persons, and within certain limits. Not to all men, because it is permitted only to those who have been examined and are past masters in meditation, and who have been previously purified in soul and body, or at the very least are being purified. For the impure to touch the pure is not safe just as it is unsafe to fix weak eyes upon the sun's rays. And what is the permitted occasion? It is when we are free from all external defilement or disturbance, and when that which rules within us is not confused with vexations or erring images.[26]

Thus we must seriously consider in our theological endeavors the scriptural and patristic witness to God's relation with the world. We recognize in them a life of communion with God, and therefore they become foundational for the understanding and explication of the Christian faith. Recognizing also that the language of Christian tradition is historically conditioned in its expression (but not in its message), we must ask whether it is possible to express an understanding of God in a language other than that of Scripture and of the Fathers, and continue to be in communication with the uninterrupted Christian tradition. If this is permissible, then we must struggle to develop criteria by which we can tolerate or even accept new language that leads people to a new understanding and appreciation of God's presence in the world, without trivializing God's reality.

God's Many Names

Plato in *Cratylus* suggests that the true names of God are those which he calls himself, and since we cannot know these we must be content with the names with which we invoke God in prayer. Therefore an etymological investigation of the divine names can, at best, give us information only on the thoughts by which men were led when they gave names to God.[27] God who is beyond knowledge and comprehension becomes known through his self-limitations.

---

26. *The First Theological Oration* (Discourse 27).
27. *Cratylus* 400d-401a.

And so it is that the Transcendent is clothed in the terms of being, with shape and form on things which have neither, and numerous symbols are employed to convey the varied attributes of what is an imageless and supra-natural simplicity.[28]

Because of divine revelation God can be conceived only in personal terms; but all the anthropomorphic images by which we name his relationship with us must not be taken literally. They are figures of speech and not really facts: "For we have given names according to our own comprehension from our own attributes to those of God."[29] Gregory of Nyssa states that persons who argue that we can comprehend the nature of God through the significance of names are similar to those who think that they can enclose the whole sea in their own hands. "For as the hollow of one's hand is the whole deep, so is all the power of language in comparison with that Nature which is unspeakable and incomprehensible."[30]

In the Christian tradition God, who is above every name in regard to his nature, has also many names that refer to his gracious dealings with creation and reflect his manifold graces and love towards the world.[31] Each of these manifold graces is distinguished from the others by the name that it receives. Thus his providential care and working in creation is communicated into a name so that we may think of him in the aspect so named.[32] Consequently the names of God are not arbitrary, but signify God's relation to the world as this has been experienced and understood by those anointed with God's grace. "We do not signify things said of God before having conceived them and we conceive them according to what his energies teach us about him."[33] Yet the name itself cannot and does not contain the essence of God.

For God is not an expression, neither hath he his essence in voice or utterance. But God is of himself what also he is believed to be, but He is named, by those who call upon him, not what He is essentially, but He received his appellations from what are believed to be his operations in regard to our life.[34]

---

28. *Divine Names*, I,1.

29. *Theological Orations*, 5,22.

30. *Nicene and Post-Nicene Fathers II*, Vol. 5, 197 (*PG* 45.761).

31. Ibid., 10.1 (*PG* 45.852): "But, as I am so taught by the inspired scripture, I boldly affirm that he who is above every name has for us many names, receiving them in accordance with the variety of his gracious dealings with us, being called the Light when He disperses the gloom of ignorance, and the Life when He grants the boon on [of] immortality, and the way when He guides us from error to the truth . . . and a physician and resurrection, and all the like, with reference to us, imparting himself under various aspects by virtue of his benefits to us-ward."

32. Ibid., 280 (*PG* 45.1009-12).

33. Ibid., 269.

34. Ibid., 265 (*PG* 45.960).

The totality of the many names by which we address God provides, through their own specificity, some glimmerings of God's glory. Thus, despite the fact that the nature of God cannot be apprehended by human sense or reason it is possible for human thought, aided by God's self-revelation, to know God, "to catch some faint glimpse of what it seeks to know."[35] As we experience the love of God we struggle to express linguistically our understanding of the divine through the mould of a corresponding name. For this reason God's names reveal mostly our human understanding of his presence in the world. St. Gregory of Nyssa would state:

> Even by the word God *(theos)* we understand to have come into usage from the activity of his seeing; for our faith tells us that the Deity is every-where, and sees *(theasthai)* all things, and penetrates all things, and then we stamp this thought with this name *(theos)*, guided to it by the Holy Voice. . . . We are taught, then, by this word one sectional operation of the Divine Being, though we do not grasp in thought by means of his substance itself, believing nevertheless that the Divine glory suffers no loss because of our being at a loss for a naturally appropriate name. For this inability to give expression to such unutterable things, while it reflects upon the poverty of our own nature, affords an evidence of God's glory. . . . That he transcends every effort of thought, and is far beyond any circumscribing by a name, constitutes a proof to man of his ineffable majesty.[36]

The theological language of the Fathers does not provide us with theoretical definitions of the being of God, in the sense of knowing the unknown through the known. Rather, their language is doxological in its basic structure. It expresses adoration of God on the basis of his works. In the adoring glorification of God the worshipper focusses his or her attention entirely upon God, and that affects the use of language, which in being used to praise God loses its ordinary sense. In the act of adoration, human words are transferred to the sublime infinity of God and thus are set in contrast to their ordinary meaning. For example, when in doxological statements we speak about God's righteousness we release this word from the manipulation of our thoughts and become receptive to a new under-standing of "righteousness" based on the reality of God.[37] In the same manner and condition the image of God as Father does not confine the being of God within the limits of this human image, but iconoclastically bursts that image and compels us to learn anew from him the truth about his fatherhood. St. Gregory of Nazianzus very clearly states that the analogy of human generations points to, but does not identify, the mystery of the Son's generation from the Father.

35. Ibid.
36. Ibid., 309 (*PG* 45.1108).
37. Edmund Schlink, *The Coming Christ and the Coming Church* (Philadelphia: Fortress, 1968), 16-84.

I marvel that you do not venture so far as to conceive of marriages and times of pregnancy, and dangers of miscarriages, as if the Father could not have begotten at all if He had not begotten thus; or again, that you did not count up the modes of generation of birds and beasts and fishes, and bring under some one of them the divine and the ineffable generation, or even eliminate the Son out of your new hypothesis. And you cannot even see this, that as his generation according to the flesh differs from all other (for where among men do you know of a virgin mother?), so does He differ also in his spiritual generation.[38]

God is above all earthly conditions, and this reality needs to be expressed through ideas and phrases.

It is a sacred duty to use of him names privative of the things abhorrent to his nature, and to say all that we have so often enumerated already, viz. He is imperishable, and unending, and ungenerate, and the other terms of that class, where the sense inherent in each only informs us of the privation of that which is obvious to our perception, but does not interpret the actual nature of that which is thus removed from those abhorrent conditions. What the Deity is not, the signification of these names does point out, but what further thing, which is not these things, is essentially, remains undivulged. Moreover, even the rest of these names, the sense of which does indicate some position or some state, do not afford that indication of the Divine nature itself, but only of the results of our reverent speculations about it.[39]

Thus St. Gregory of Nyssa advocates struggling to work out an orthodox formula of thought, one whereby a worthy conception of God may be ensured. In this task we must always remember that Orthodoxy is not a thing of sounds and syllables but of the mind, and that therefore particular notions and ideas (and consequently *names*) can be expressed by different words which convey to us the same signification. For example, for the naming of "God as the First Cause who is without cause" we may substitute other names, such as Ungenerate, Eternal Subsistence, the Cause of all, the Principle of all, the First Cause or the One alone without cause. This is possible because they signify in like manner and force the same notion.[40]

In reference to the names Christians have given to Jesus Christ, St. Gregory of Nyssa suggests distinguishing two categories. One contains the names referring to his lofty and unspeakable glory in itself, apart from the created objects of his love; the other contains the names that indicate the variety of God's providential dispensations towards creation. He explains this distinction and its consequences by studying some of the major names of Christ. He notes that

38. *Theological Orations*, 3:3-4 (Discourse 29).
39. *Nicene and Post-Nicene Fathers II*, Vol. 5, 307 (*PG* 45.1100-1101).
40. Ibid., 7,4 (*PG* 45.760-61).

"the Lord would not have been called a vine, save for the planting of those who are rooted in him, nor a shepherd, had not the sheep of the House of Israel been lost, nor a physician, save for the sake of them that were sick. . . ." Christ is called "Son," and "Right Hand," and "Only-begotten," and "Word," and "Wisdom," and "Power," and other such names in relation to the Father, for example, he is called the "Power of God," the "Right Hand of God," the "Wisdom of God," the "Son and Only begotten of the Father," the "Word with God," and so on. St. Gregory affirms that all human images and names by which we describe our understanding of God are metaphorical in nature, expressing our understandings of God's benevolent relation with his creation:

> It follows from what we have stated, that in each of the names we are to contemplate some suitable sense appropriate to the subject, so that we may not miss the right understanding of them, and go astray from the doctrine of godliness. As, then, we transfer each of the other terms to that sense in which they may be applied to God, and reject in their case the immediate sense, so as not to understand material light, or a trodden way, or the bread which is produced by husbandry, or the word that is expressed by speech, but, instead of these, all those thoughts which present to us the magnitude of the power of the Word of God.[41]

Gregory states that if someone were to reject the ordinary and natural sense of the word "Son," by which we learn that he is of the same essence as him that begat him, then he must transfer the name to some more divine interpretation.[42] We are not concerned whether this has actually been done or whether Gregory is simply making an oratorical refutation of Eunomius's ideas about the origins of language. But it is worth noting that Gregory does not exclude such a possibility.

In reference to the name of God as Father, Gregory indicates that by calling God "the Father" we name not what the unknown God *is* but how he relates to his incarnate Logos, Jesus Christ.[43] Furthermore, the title "Father" indicates the personal character of the first person of the Trinity, who must be always related to the second person of the Trinity, his Logos. From a Christological perspective, the fatherhood of God and the sonship of his incarnate Logos indicate that the Son, Jesus Christ, is of the same nature as his Father. Thus St. Gregory believes that Jesus Christ passes over all those names by which the Deity is indicated in the historical books of the Old Testament, in the Prophets and in the Law and delivers to us as part of our profession of faith the title of "Father" as, being inherently relational, this is better suited to indicate the truth about the Son.[44]

41. Ibid., 3,7 (*PG* 45.612-13).
42. Ibid.
43. Ibid., 2,3 (*PG* 45.473).
44. Ibid., 2,2 (*PG* 45.468-69).

Yet Gregory of Nyssa would agree with Gregory of Nazianzus that God is beyond gender, since he transcends the order of human generation which, being corporeal, includes gender:

> For it does not follow that because the Son is the Son in some higher relation (inasmuch as we could not in any other way than this point out that he is of God and consubstantial), it would also be necessary to think that all the names of this lower world and of our kindred should be transferred to the Godhead. Or maybe you would consider our God to be male, according to the same argument, because He is called God the Father, and that deity is feminine, from the gender of the word, and Spirit neuter, because it has nothing to do with generation; but if you would be silly enough to say, with the old myths and fables, that God begot the Son by a marriage with his own will, we should be introduced to the hermaphrodite god of Marcion and Valentinus, who imagined these newfangled Aeons.[45]

Gregory of Nazianzus has struggled to name God with images and concepts other than the classic name of God as Father, Son and Holy Spirit. But, as he confesses, all these attempts have failed to find new images or illustrations to describe the Trinitarian nature of God:

> I have very carefully considered this matter in my own mind, and have looked at it in every point of view, in order to find some illustration of this most important subject, but I have been unable to discover anything on earth with which to compare the nature of Godhead. . . . For even if I did happen upon some tiny likeness, it escaped me for the most part, and left me down below with my example. . . . Finally, then, it seems best to me to let the images and the shadows go, as being deceitful and very far short of the truth; and clinging myself to the more reverent conception, and resting upon few words using the guidance of the Holy Spirit, keeping to the end as my genuine comrade and companion the enlightenment which I have received from him, and passing through this world to persuade all others also to the best of my powers to worship Father, Son and Holy Spirit, the one Godhead and power. To him belongs all glory and honour and might forever and ever.[46]

The fact that he could not find new images and names to describe the Godhead does not destroy the legitimacy of his efforts. The doctrinal activity of the first three centuries of the church had already brought into prominence several scriptural and nonscriptural images to illustrate the relation of the Son to the Father, the most important being that of the Father, Son and Logos. The next most important scriptural images were that of the icon (image or reflection, 2 Cor. 4:4 and Col. 1:15); apaugasma (brightness, ray or reflection, Heb. 1:3);

---

45. *The Fifth Theological Oration — On the Spirit* (Discourse 31), ibid., 198.
46. Gregory of Nazianzus, *Fifth Theological Oration*, 33.

and character (impression or stamp, also taken from Heb. 1:3). At least three other images had been added by Justin, Tertullian and others; the stream descending from its source, the branch coming from the trunk or from the root, and the fire being lit from fire.

Tertullian indeed had elaborated these into a kind of analogy for the Three Persons, using the images of source-stream-river, and of sun-sunbeam-point of light, to illustrate his doctrine of the Trinity. Gregory of Nyssa provides the following Trinitarian analogies: (1) two or three different disciplines in the mind of a single man, e.g., medicine, philosophy, and similar arts; (2) the smell of myrrh mingling with the air in a room so that they seem identical but are in fact distinct; (3) the light of the sun, the air and the wind mingling with each other but still remaining separate;[47] (4) the analogy of two lamps being lit from a third.[48] If we attribute to him the 38th in the collection of Basil's *Letters* we can add the image of the colours of the rainbow melting together yet distinct.

The Cappadocians generally were uneasy with all images designed to illustrate the relations of the Persons of the Trinity to each other, whether those images were scriptural, traditional or contemporary. They were much more aware than their predecessors of the weakness of virtually all images, implying as they do a lapse of time or "space" between the persons, and they repeatedly emphasized the inadequacy of all images to describe the deity. Basil of Caesarea wrote in one of his letters: "All theological utterance is less than the thought of him who speaks it, and less than the intention of him who is conducting the discussion, because language is somehow inadequate to represent our thoughts."[49] Elsewhere he reminds his readers that the divine writers only speak of God in metaphors and symbolic language, and in images which are often contradictory when taken literally,[50] and that if we believe only in that which can be fully expressed in words then the Christian faith and the Christian hope have vanished.[51]

It is evident that the Cappadocians had an undoctrinaire and flexible attitude to verbal formulae; aware of the inadequacy and limitations of language in expressing propositions about God, they were more concerned with the doctrine expressed by the language than with the language itself. This flexibility of the Cappadocians is explicitly declared by St. Gregory of Nyssa in the following passage:

> Since then it is orthodox to believe that He who is the cause of everything does not himself have any underlying cause, once this has been firmly fixed in the mind, what further controversy about words does there remain for

47. *Adversus Arium et Sabellium: de Patre et Filio,* 83.
48. *Adversus Maced,* PG 45.1307.
49. Basil, *Letters,* VII.44.
50. *Nicene and Post-Nicene Fathers II, op. cit.,* 1.14 (*PG* 45.300-301).
51. Ibid., 2.24.

sensible men, because every word by which such a concept is expressed comes to the same thing? Whether you say he is beginning and origin of everything or declare that he is unoriginate or that he exists ingenerately or subsists from eternity or is the cause of everything or alone has no cause, all these expressions are virtually equivalent to each other as far as the force of the things signified goes and the words have the same value, and it is futile to dispute subtly about one kind of vocal utterance or another, as if orthodoxy consisted in syllables and sounds and not in meaning.[52]

Feminine Images of God

Is it possible to describe or refer to God's relationship to the world through feminine images and names? We have noted that the Fathers of the church built their theological reflection on the nature of God on the basis of God's total incomprehensibility and indescribability. Based on God's revelation, his manifold graces and the guidance of the Holy Spirit, they then reach a relative understanding of his energies, leading them to doxology. Those who had an immediate experience of God's love in their lives summarized and codified their perception in names. Since the experience of God's presence in history varies according to circumstances and times, God has been named with many names that reflect his manifold graces. This was necessary to communicate the faith event to others. Yet, it is important to remember that whether we speak about God, in theology, or to God, in praise and prayer, the tools at our disposal are unequal to the task. All the images, concepts and statements are inescapably human, finite and creaturely.

The scriptural names of God are authoritative and indispensable for Christians because the church has recognized that these names reflect the life of communion that the scriptural authors had with God through the guidance and inspiration of the Holy Spirit. In Scripture Jesus of Nazareth refers to his unity with God through the concept of fatherhood, but already in the New Testament other images are also used; and many names which are not necessarily scriptural have been used in Christian tradition to refer to God's actions or ways of relating to the world.[53] In fact in some instances feminine metaphors were used to describe aspects of God's being and action. Jesus in the following passage adopts a provocatively maternal image for himself and his own feelings:

52. Ibid., 263 (*PG* 45.956).

53. Recent research has been surfacing the overlooked scriptural and extra-biblical female images of God; see esp. Phyllis Trible, *God and the Rhetoric of Sexuality* (Philadelphia: Fortress, 1978); Virginia Ramey Mollenkott, *The Divine Feminine: Biblical Imagery of God as Female* (New York: Crossroad, 1983). For patristic references on the same subject see Kari Elizabeth Borressen, "L'usage patristique de métaphores féminines dans le discours sur Dieu," *Revue théologique de Louvain* 13 (1982): 205-20.

"O Jerusalem, Jerusalem . . . how often would I have gathered your children together as a hen gathers her brood under her wings and you would not!" (Matt. 23:37; Luke 13:34). Clement urges the Christian to probe more deeply into the mysteries of divine love where he will discover the intriguing fact that God is at once Father, Mother and Lover:

> In his unspeakable greatness lies his fatherhood. In his fellowship with our experience is his motherhood. The Father takes a woman's nature in his love. It is in token of this that he begot the Son from his own being. The fruit born from love was love.[54]

St. Gregory of Palamas in his mystical understanding of God's salvific work in Jesus Christ writes: "Christ has become our brother by union to our flesh and our blood . . . he has also become our father through the holy baptism which makes us like him, and he nurses us from his own breast as a mother, filled with tenderness. . . ."[55] St. John of Kronstadt, reflecting upon the beauty of nature as an expression of God's love, writes: "In how many ways does not God rejoice us, his creatures, even by flowers? Like a tender mother, in his eternal power and wisdom, He every summer creates for us, out of nothing, these most beautiful plants."[56] In these references the Fathers use feminine images and refer to God as mother not in a literal but in a metaphorical sense. To say that "God is mother" is not to identify "God and mother," but to understand God in light of some of the characteristics associated with mothering — and simultaneously to affirm that God, in some significant and essential manner, is *not* a mother. The image of God as Mother may be seen as a partial, but perhaps illuminating way of speaking of certain aspects of God's relationship to the world. In a similar manner to call God Father means that the unknown God becomes known and related to us as father of Jesus Christ and, by adoption, as our father; but any effort to take the concept of his "fatherhood" literally and to define it from the ordinary understanding of fatherhood leads to Arianism and idolatry. Against Arianism the Fathers of the church, especially Athanasius and the Cappadocians, developed their theology of language, which is primarily apophatic and doxo-logical, expressing the ecclesial experience of God's presence in the world and more specifically in the lives of the saints and of his church.

While the Fathers prefer to refer to God with the many names used by the scriptural writers, and especially to use the way that Jesus referred to him, they are open to other non-scriptural and philosophical names to the extent that these refer to, represent and express scriptural truths about God. If God has many names that do not describe comprehensively or essentially his nature

---

54. *Quis Dives Salvetur?*, trans. in R. B. Tollinton, *Clement of Alexandria: A Study in Christian Liberalism* (London: 1914), 319-20.

55. Jean Meyendorff, *Introduction á l'étude de Grégoire Palama* (Paris: Seuil, 1959), 247-48.

56. *My Life in Christ* (New York: Jordanville, 1976), 27.

but refer to his personal way of being and to his manifold graces towards his creation, are there any feminine qualities or attributes in the Godhead that justify calling God mother without abandoning the names that he has assumed and has been called in the formative Christian tradition? From this study I have concluded that no human concept, word or image — each of which originates in the experience of created reality — can circumscribe the divine reality; nor can any human construct express, with any measure of adequacy, the mystery of God, who is ineffable. The very incomprehensibility of God demands a proliferation of images, and a variety of names, each of which acts as a corrective against the tendency of any particular one to become reified and literal.

God and Her Survival in a Nuclear Age

SUSAN B. THISTLETHWAITE

As director of the Los Alamos laboratory which developed the bomb, J. Robert Oppenheimer had the honor of naming its first test. He chose "Trinity" after one of John Donne's *Holy Sonnets*. Oppenheimer was merely the first though possibly one of the more erudite of modern interpreters of the bomb as "the Second Coming in Wrath" (Winston Churchill). Modern fundamentalists such as Hal Lindsey, Pat Robertson, and John Wesley White have specifically identified the bomb with God's judgment and the end of the world in a nuclear war as the salvation of the righteous.[1]

To whom can we turn for help in countering the threat of these theologies of salvation by nuclear destruction? The threat itself is very real. Some have argued that nuclear apocalypticism is the view of Ronald Reagan himself.[2] Certainly in the cultural trend that began in the late seventies, what used to be regarded as the aberration of the far right has now become the center, and what used to be the center is regarded as the left. A true left is currently out in left field. What is true of the general culture is also becoming true in theology. Rightist theologies are increasingly portrayed as the moderate option.[3]

It is my contention, however, that these theologies of salvation by the

1. See, e.g., Hal Lindsey, *The Late Great Planet Earth* (Grand Rapids, Mich.: Zondervan, 1970), and Lindsey's other widely selling books.

2. See Yehezkel Landau, "The President and the Prophets," in the special issue "Doomsday Religion," *Sojourners*, June-July 1984, 24-25.

3. A particularly instructive way of tracking this development is to observe which views dominate current mergers of Lutherans or Presbyterians. Data on the direction of the Lutheran discussion are available in the "Merger Watch" section of *Dialog*, a Lutheran journal. See particularly vol. 25 (Winter 1986): 58ff. and vol. 25 (Summer 1986): 214ff.

Reprinted from the *Journal of Feminist Studies* 4/1 (Spring 1988): 73-88. Used with permission of the journal.

bomb are, in fact, an evisceration of the doctrine of God.[4] My concern here is with the alternatives to these rightist theologies. What alternatives are there?

Protestant liberalism, as represented by the work of Gordon Kaufman and Paul Tillich, offers criticism of and a specific alternative to nuclearism. Mary Daly, a feminist theologian, provides a different critique and a very different alternative. I will argue in this essay that the Kaufman/Tillich route is not, in fact, a genuine alternative. Daly's work provides significant gains, but she, and other white feminists such as myself, need to attend to the work of black women writers who know firsthand about survival. The work of these black women challenges the white-dominated West, the particular location of the nuclear threat, to find ways of talking about God that both affirm the goodness and value of the world and mandate justice in history.

Liberals and the Bomb

It would seem at first glance that liberals of both Protestant and Catholic stripe would be the logical candidates to provide an alternative to nuclearism, since they are also the targets of fundamentalists. And it is true that a consistent theological statement condemning nuclearism has come from a liberal perspective. Gordon Kaufman's *Theology for a Nuclear Age* addresses nuclearism directly.[5]

Kaufman's work is self-described as "constructive theology." His well-known book *An Essay on Theological Method* defines the task of theology as construction:

> The distinctive and proper business of theology is neither interpretation of the vagaries of religious experience nor exposition of the particularities of scripture or of church doctrine but analysis, interpretation and reconstruction of the concept, and images of *God,* as found in the common language and traditions of the West.[6]

Constructive theology is the ongoing work of each generation of Christians to construct a world of meaningful discourse about God.

Constructive theology is a recent variant upon the basic themes of liberalism. One definition of "liberalism" in theology is that it is a trend in Protestant theology in the nineteenth and twentieth centuries "which aims to show that Christianity is rational and expedient and reconcilable with the human desire

---

4. "I am Become Death: God in the Nuclear Age" (Johnson Foundation Lectures, 1987), 1-7, 9, 27-28. In preparation for publication.

5. Gordon Kaufman, *Theology for a Nuclear Age* (Philadelphia: Westminster Press, 1985).

6. Gordon Kaufman, *An Essay on Theological Method* (Missoula, MT: Scholars Press, 1978), 41.

for autonomy."[7] While Kaufman's theological perspective takes issue with the classic starting point of liberalism (à la Friedrich Schleiermacher) that experience (God-consciousness) is the primary theological datum, his views are consistent with the later development of liberal theology.[8] The difficulties of defining liberalism preclude more than a definition in process. Suffice it to say that Kaufman's theology is liberal in that he adheres to the notion that theology is rational discourse, is possible discourse, and is necessary to a humanity that finds itself in history and must deal with that fact.

Why is it, asks Kaufman, that only the apocalyptic fundamentalists are asking the meaning of this "momentous religious fact right before our eyes"? Kaufman sets it as one of his tasks to pursue the logic of the "fundamentalists on the far religious right who follow out the implications of the biblical apocalyptic imagery of an earthy holocaust as the ultimate expression of God's sovereignty over history," and who "are apparently willing to go so far as to suggest that a nuclear disaster, if it ever comes, could only be an expression of the purposes of God." These fundamentalists further believe that those who work to prevent such a climax to human history are in fact guilty of opposing God's will. Kaufman's conclusion is that it is the notion of the sovereignty of God itself as "the central traditional claim" of Christian theology that is "way 'out of sync'" with the nuclear age.[9]

As a constructive theologian, rather than a deductive theologian who treats God as the only subject and human beings as the passive objects of God's action, Kaufman proposes a project of the human imagination to reconceive the relation of God, the world, and human beings. If one of the constructive tasks of theology is to make a meaningful world, one way to accomplish the task is to excite the human imagination to find a place in that world. The key point is that a "God conceived in terms of the metaphor of creativity or constructive power . . . will be of a very different sort from a God conceived in terms of violent destructiveness."[10] In the logic of Kaufman's argument, these different images will either excite human actions to transform creatively the institutions of the world toward construction, or find divine justification for destruction or passivity.

One experiences a strong sense of déjà vu in reading Kaufman's work. One reviewer even remarked on the similarity between the themes raised by Kaufman and "the passionate theological treatises of Bernard E. Meland and Henry Nelson Wieman as they explored the themes of elementalism and theistic

7. Karl Rahner and Herbert Vorgrimler, *Dictionary of Theology* (New York: Crossroad, 1985), 275-76.

8. Compare, e.g., Kaufman, *God the Problem* (Cambridge, Mass.: Harvard University Press, 1972), 68ff. with Friedrich Schleiermacher, *The Christian Faith* (Edinburgh: T and T Clark, 1976), 142ff.

9. Kaufman, *Nuclear Age*, 5-8.

10. Ibid., 25-26.

naturalism respectively."[11] There are strong echoes of the work of Paul Tillich in Kaufman's theology as well. Tillich, often painted as one who in the mid-twentieth century reacted against liberalism, in fact worked from basic liberal premises.[12]

The genius of Protestant liberalism is its embrace of the immanence of God in the world. The immanence of God, however, is the point most often cited as the weakness of liberalism. Its doctrine of God is said to be too sub-jective, so that revelation becomes synonymous with human experience, and there is no judgment on evil.[13] But in fact the weakness of liberalism resides not in its embrace of immanence, but in its half-hearted immanence, colored by romanticism and confined to a particular class and race experience.

Conservative critics of liberalism fault its accommodation to modern culture, charging that liberalism makes "man" the measure of all things and dethrones God. They also charge that liberalism fails to deal with the sinfulness of human nature and society's innate fallenness.[14] Liberalism has faults cer-tainly, but not these. Its failure has been rather that it has never repudiated the philosophy of Cartesianism or modern philosophical idealism and that it holds to a myth of the individual (usually a white male) who is the locus of an independently functioning objective reason. From this independent reason lib-erals generalize to "humanity," with an Anglo-Saxon male face.[15]

This means, however, that the embodied character of existence is never embraced, and hence a mind-body dualism remains in liberalism's commitment to immanence. The liberal thus repudiates the flesh of common human experience and extends that repudiation into communal life. As the solitary individual, the liberal is essentially alone, despairing of any genuine sociability. Robert Bellah, a prominent liberal, and coauthors Richard Madsen, William M. Sullivan, Ann Swidler and Steven M. Tipton, in their celebrated book decrying individualism, *Habits of the Heart*, focused on middle-class white churches, predominantly in California, not studying in any explicit way the women's movement or the black church.[16] But the latter two groups surely know something about solidarity. Bellah, et al., however, start from select premises, discover their own alienated individual-ism, and then project that onto the whole of American society, subtitling their work *Individualism and Commitment in American Life*. A more accurate subtitle, how-ever, would be *Dominant White Male Values and Alienation in American Life*.

11. Edgar Towne, review of *Theology for a Nuclear Age*, in *Encounter* (Spring 1986): 175-76.

12. Hannah Tillich, *From Time to Time* (New York: Stein and Day, 1973), 15.

13. See Karl Barth, "The Word of God and Experience," in *Church Dogmatics*, I, 1 (Edin-burgh: T. and T. Clark, 1936), 226-60.

14. Karl Barth, *Church Dogmatics*, III, 3 (1960), 312-49.

15. See Thistlethwaite, *Metaphors for the Contemporary Church* (New York: Pilgrim, 1984), for a review of this aspect of modern liberalism.

16. Robert Bellah et al., *Habits of the Heart: Individualism and Commitment in American Life* (Berkeley: University of California Press, 1985).

Such views have produced a doctrine of God both immanentalist and essentialist. While God is the basis of Existence (the ground of being), God (as the human consciousness) is alienated from the material, physical world.

This is itself a theology of nonbeing. Insofar as liberals have been unable to free themselves from the legacy of Platonism in Western philosophical thought, they have inherited a distaste (often a revulsion) for the body and its works.

In 1972 Kaufman wrote with some confidence that "though the cultural crisis that helped give neo-orthodoxy its hearing is by no means past, we have learned to live with it [the bomb] pretty well and are beginning to hope once again that man [*sic*] can sufficiently control his destiny to manage both the bomb and the population explosion."[17] Kaufman wrote these words in the second age of the bomb, the period in which images of nuclear destruction were pushed from the public mind by the Vietnam War. This second period of the bomb (according to Ira Chernus) was marked by a naive faith in human rationality — embodied strategically in the concept of deterrence.[18] Even though the acronym MAD (Mutually Assured Destruction) should easily have revealed that this was an unstable situation and anything but rational, it did not.

Faith in human rationality is a hallmark of liberalism. In 1972 Kaufman's problem with God is the term "God" itself. God is not feeling, not word, not ethics, not ecclesiastical structures, but "ultimate loyalty or faith." But as that which transcends any finite reference by definition (i.e., the ultimate), what meaning can the term have "to our modern empirical, secular, and pragmatic temper?" There is no clear empirical evidence for the existence of God, and evidence is the criterion sine qua non of reality in "the way we have come to conceive natural and historical order under the influences of modern scientific philosophical and historical studies."[19]

Kaufman's answer to this "problem" is that "God is a symbol for God," in the words of Paul Tillich whom he quotes.[20] And Kaufman does more than quote Tillich. He constructs a definition of God which depends on Tillich's "God above God" in *The Courage to Be*.[21] Kaufman writes, "God is a symbol — an imaginative construct — that enables men [*sic*] to view the world and themselves in such a way as to make action and morality ultimately (metaphysically) meaningful."[22]

---

17. Kaufman, *God the Problem*, 5.

18. Ira Chernus, "War and Myth: The Show Must Go On," *Journal of the American Academy of Religion* 53 (Sept. 1985): 456-57.

19. Kaufman, *God the Problem*, 5, 7, 8.

20. Ibid., 82, quoting Paul Tillich, *Dynamics of Faith* (New York: Harper and Brothers, 1957), 46.

21. Tillich, *The Courage to Be* (New Haven, Conn.: Yale University Press, 1952), 15, 182, 186-90.

22. Kaufman, *God the Problem*, 109.

Kaufman in his 1985 writings has not varied significantly from this definition of God. God as symbol is "the ultimate point of reference."[23] This lack of change may be regarded as surprising, since clearly his assessment of the capacity of human beings to "live with [the bomb] pretty well" has undergone a drastic reassessment.[24] But this reassessment has not included a weakening of the commitment to rationality. Kaufman continues to believe that disembodied reason will enable us to think our way to a concept of God that can "relativize" and "humanize" our situation. "We are attempting to find a contemporary way to think of God, to conceive that reality which grounds our existence, and devotion to which can provide us with significant orientation as we face the frightening pass to which human history today has come."[25]

Yet Kaufman's God "as point of reference" actually pulls his doctrine of God away from that which "grounds our being," namely our material, embodied life. In this sense the liberal God is wholly unaffected by what happens to us in this frightening nuclear age. Kaufman should be frightened. Kaufman is alone in facing this looming catastrophe.

The sense of being alone is the companion anthropology to the liberal doctrine of God. It is well to remember that the "God above God" of Paul Tillich is Tillich's answer to his assessment of the fundamental existential dilemma of "man" — estrangement.[26] Kaufman in his 1981 work *The Theological Imagination* describes the human need for the "social interdependence" experienced in childhood and then remarks that "the strong undercurrent of anxiety which most of us experience much of the time appears to be directly correlated with the absence, or potential absence, of such supporting figures."[27]

Kaufman is expressing two of the hallmarks of liberalism: both his own sense of alienation, and his projection of that experience onto the whole of humanity. He writes, "[A]s we mature to adulthood, we become aware that no human being can be absolutely relied on." "In this respect, as Paul Tillich has argued, human anxiety is 'ontological'; it belongs to our human existence as such."[28] From his own experience of existence as alienated, and from the conformation of this alienation he finds in Tillich, Kaufman projects this alienation into his definition of the human situation. But this alienation is interpreted wholly in abstract essentialist categories such as "ontological," or our "human existence as such," and never in concrete social and material terms.

The inability of liberals to actually deal with theologies of nuclearism of the religious right is based in the fact that the liberal God, as Carter Heyward

---

23. Kaufman, *Nuclear Age*, 33.
24. Kaufman now speaks of God as "web of all existence," and identifies nature as evolutionary process as well as human pursuit of progress. See *Nuclear Age*, chap. 3
25. Ibid., 34, 41.
26. Tillich, *Courage to Be*, 48, 52, 54, 75-77, 87, 90, 125-27, 132, 138, 169.
27. Kaufman, *The Theological Imagination* (Philadelphia: Westminster Press, 1981), 59.
28. Ibid., 60 and 62, quoting Paul Tillich, *The Courage to Be.*

put it, is "a noncontroversial gentleman."[29] That is, the God of liberalism is above the hassle of human history. The liberal's God does not care whether we rule the world and hence has nothing at stake. This limited God will not harm us — or help us either. The God of nuclearism has everything at stake.

God, the Goddess, and the Bomb

A radically different analysis of nuclearism emerges in the work of Mary Daly. In *Pure Lust*, she discusses Robert Oppenheimer and the bomb to illustrate the parameters of the "sadosociety." The sadosociety depends on the abstractionist, nature- and female-despising works of sadoasceticism. Her point is that sado-spirituality as the denial of the basis in nature of all life prepares society to accept as "rational" the notion that destruction is a form of saving. As in the Vietman War American troops "saved" Vietnamese villages by destroying them, so nuclearists will save the world from "Godless communism" by destroying it.

Oppenheimer is a classic example of "phallic asceticism," in Daly's terms. In 1932 he wrote to his brother Frank:

> Therefore I think that all things which evoke discipline: study and our duties to men and to the commonwealth, *war,* and personal hardship, and even the need for subsistence, ought to be greeted by us with profound gratitude; for only through them can we attain to the least detachment, and only so can we know *peace.*[30]

Oppenheimer's alienation is so complete that he does not recognize that he is in fact saying that the only way he can attain the detachment he equates with peace is to pursue war. Daly compares this view with George Orwell's *1984* in which the logic of the society he satirizes is summed up in the slogan "War is Peace." In an interview, Oppenheimer replies to a question about why the bomb was developed:

> It is my judgment in these things that when you see something that is tech-nically sweet, you go ahead and do it, and you argue about what to do about it only after you have had your technical success. That is the way it was with the atomic bomb. I don't think anybody opposed making it; there was some doubt about what to do with it after it was made.[31]

29. Carter Heyward, "Heterosexist Theology: Being Above It All," *Journal of Feminist Studies in Religion,* vol. III, no. 1 (Spring 1987): 38.

30. *Robert Oppenheimer: Letters and Recollections,* eds. Alice Kimball Smith and Charles Wiener (Cambridge, Mass.: Harvard University Press, 1980), 156, quoted in Mary Daly, *Pure Lust: Elemental Feminist Philosophy* (Boston: Beacon Press, 1984), 47.

31. Daly, 48, quoting Oppenheimer as cited in Robert J. Lipton, *The Broken Connection: On Death and the Continuity of Life* (New York: Simon and Schuster, Touchstone Books, 1979), 425.

In order to understand Daly's opposition to Oppenheimer's perspective on the bomb, it is necessary to grasp her underlying conviction in *Pure Lust* that patriarchy is another word for *biocide,* degenerative and life-violating tendencies which are becoming more aggressive in the "aging and deterioration of patriarchy itself."[32]

Biophilia, or love of life, is the opposite of the biocidal system of patriarchy. Women are intrinsically biophilic, but only when they are in touch with what Daly describes at length as the elements of the cosmos. Much of *Pure Lust* describes patriarchy's transformation of the "elements" into the elementary. Elements could be described as the interconnections of spirit and matter in all of nature. "Elemental Feminist Philosophy," the subtitle of *Pure Lust,* is the effort to name "the philosophy of being concerned with ontological potency, knowledge, passion, virtue, creation, transformation."[33] Daly's agenda is to find a way through the morass of mind/body dualism to a philosophy of being that reunites spirit and matter and does not make a radical disjunction of the physical and the metaphysical.

It is possible to describe one who would see research into the death of all life as "technically sweet" as in a mental state analogous to physical disease; "we might describe it as something like *telic decentralization* — a phrase used to describe the condition of an organism that has been turned against its own purposes, becoming unhealthy, disordered, autoallergic." But even this is inadequate, because *telos* implies that there has been a sense of "biophilic purposes," and decentralization implies that there had once been a center. But "sadospiritual asceticism is the ideology and behavior of those who show no evidence of ever having experienced biophilic Elemental purpose or center."[34]

When Oppenheimer named the first nuclear test "Trinity," he chose this name as the "sadospiritual legitimation of this lust and its technological ejaculations." The opening verse of the poem, "Batter my heart, three person'd God," is well chosen, according to Daly, because it reveals that "the battering of the Earth and of her creatures is the consequence of this disordered sentiment." Daly quotes the response of Winston Churchill to the report of the successful first test of the new weapon. Churchill, who was relaxing in his zippered siren suit, read the report, then waved his cigar with a flourish. "Stimson," he rumbled, "what was gunpowder? Trivial. What was electricity? Meaningless. This atomic bomb is the Second Coming in Wrath."[35]

God, as Kaufman put it in another context, is the problem for Daly. "The earthy/unearthly males have vaporized and then condensed/reified their self-images into the sublime product, god,"[36] in the process of projecting all that is

---

32. Daly, 102.

33. Ibid., 28.

34. Ibid., 48.

35. Ibid., 48; Churchill, as quoted in Lansing Lamont, *Day of Trinity* (New York: Atheneum Press, 1965), 261, in Daly, 49.

36. Daly, 73.

most holy and sacred onto the cosmos where it cannot undergo natural processes such as death. This theology must be wrathful because it must murder and dismember the Goddess. Unable to do away with nature per se, the underlying reality of which the Goddess is a symbol, Christian theologians have previously been content to murder her through ritual and preserve a certain carved remnant in Mary. The advent of nuclear technology, however, makes the complete murder of the Goddess (nature) possible, and has exposed this fault line at the heart of Christian theology — the ofttimes barely concealed contempt for the earth and its symbol, the Goddess.

Debates about God-language illustrate this well. The liberal male repudiates mother-language for God and exhibits low-grade hostility to abstract forms of address for the divinity (for example, Creator). The publication of the three-year lectionary cycle of the *Inclusive Language Lectionary* elicited violent responses to the experimental use of Mother as an optional form of address to God.[37]

"Women," however, "need the Goddess," as Carol Christ explicitly says in her now famous article. In identifying four reasons why women need the Goddess, Christ returns again and again to the symbolism of the female divinity as an affirmation of the bodily, material aspects of human existence. For Daly, the Goddess is the symbol of reintegration of the radical disconnections between mind and body, spirit and matter, transcendence and immanence whose symptom patriarchy is.[38]

Daly's work can be read as a corrective to the problem of liberalism, a fact she herself discusses at some length in considering the theology of Paul Tillich. Daly's reading of intellectual history in the West finds that the separation of philosophy and theology in the "Enlightenment" occurred alongside the ritual murder of the Goddess in the European witch hunts. "For dismemberment of wisdom logically correlates with the dismemberment of the Goddess." The separation of philosophy and theology has had several pernicious effects. One was the decrease in the "personal intensity of concern which motivated the medieval philosopher-theologians." Intimately connected to the emergence of the "disinterested" scholar is the "fact that philosophy was denuded of interest in final causality — a violation compared to lobotomy." Further, philosophers ceased having any interest in "separate intelligence" or angels. While Daly acknowledges that today such speculation is the stuff of science fiction, the "philosophy of angels has had power to inspire the philosophical imagination,

37. *Inclusive Language Lectionary,* 3 vols. (Philadelphia: Westminster, 1983-85). See Susan Brooks Thistlethwaite, "Opening the Mail that Did Not Tick," *Review of Books and Religion* 12 (May 1984), and, more recently, the excellent article on female language for God, Pamela Payne Allen, "Taking the Next Step in Inclusive Language," *The Christian Century* (April 23, 1986): 410-13.

38. Carol P. Christ, "Why Women Need the Goddess: Phenomenological, Psychological and Political Reflections," in *Womanspirit Rising: A Feminist Reader in Religion,* eds. Carol P. Christ and Judith Plaskow (San Francisco: Harper and Row, 1979), 273-87. Daly, 73.

raising questions about the nature of knowledge, will, change, being in time and space, and intuitive communication."[39]

When the spiritual/philosophical imagination is thus bifurcated, genuine creativity, which is rooted in the theological "spirit-force" of life, "becomes inaccessible" or "deeply buried." We are told it doesn't exist.

The greatness of Paul Tillich, in Daly's view, is that he of all recent theologians did not lose sight of final causality. He "noticed the materialization/fragmentation that prevails in modern philosophy, attributing this to a split between ontological and technical reason." Tillich's analysis of this split between ontological and technical reason is where the problems begin. From the insight that reason has been bifurcated, Tillich goes on to recommend that while reason in the sense of *Logos* determines the ends, and only in the second place the means, reason in the technical sense determines the means while accepting the ends from "somewhere else." There is no danger in this situation as long as technical reason is the *companion* of ontological reason, and "reasoning" is used to *fulfill the demands* of reason. This situation prevailed in most prephilosophical as well as philosophical periods of human history, although there always was the threat that "reasoning" might *separate* itself from reason. Since the middle of the nineteenth century this threat has become a dominating reality. The consequence is "that the ends are provided by *nonrational forces,* either by positive traditions, or by arbitrary decisions serving the *will to power*"[40] (Daly's emphasis).

In her choice of the phrases to emphasize, Daly uses Tillich's own vocabulary to illumine the flaw in his analysis. "Referring to technical reason as the 'companion' of ontological reason, he is appalled that the former has separated itself (herself?) from the latter, rather than fulfilling 'its' (his?) demands." Tillich thus pictures technical reason as a "sort of wayward wife who refused to meet the demands of her lord and master and finally not only threatened but actually obtained a divorce — in the middle of the nineteenth century." It is wholly unsurprising, Daly notes, that this is the period of separation. It is also the period of the first wave of feminism, in which female independence, represented by "technical reason," first emerged. Liberal feminism claimed "technical reason" for its own and opted for the body half of the mind/body split. The tension for liberal feminists has always been that "technical reason" is seen as a threat by liberals themselves, for liberals, including Tillich, are always afraid that the "subservient half will break away and become the servant of 'non-rational' forces."[41] The fact that liberal males accept this "bifurcated vision" is consistent with the other distortions of Western culture.

---

39. Daly, *Pure Lust,* 54, 154, 155.
40. Ibid., 155-56.
41. Ibid., 155, 156, 157.

Science, in the vision of Oppenheimer, is the result of this radical disjunc-
ture which sees nature as the object of scientific inquiry with no ends (final
causality) of its own. Tillich can see the problem with this view, but subverts
the remedy. Tillich was fascinated by the topic of being, as is well known. How
the mind comes to terms with the structure of reality (the ground of being)
preoccupied him for much of his career. Tillich proposes that "ontological
reason can be defined as the structure of the mind which enables it to *grasp*
and to *shape* reality" (emphasis Daly's).[42] Daly calls this the "'hairy claw' view
of ontological reason." Her point is that reality itself is reduced to that which
can be grasped. It is rendered a passive recipient of "'reason's' unsolicited
attentions."[43] But this actually makes reality into nothing for itself, and, in fact,
nothing for the would-be philosopher-theologian. Tillich writes:

> Mythology, cosmogony, and metaphysics have asked the question of being
> both implicitly and explicitly and have tried to answer it. It is the ultimate
> question, although fundamentally it is the expression of a state of existence
> rather than a formulated question. Whenever this state is experienced and
> this question is asked, everything disappears in the abyss of possible nonbeing;
> even a god would disappear if he were not being-itself.[44]

In identifying this flaw of liberal theology, Daly has touched bottom. The
God of liberalism is nothing, a vacuum left by the splitting of reality into two
halves, one of which presumes to dominate the other, but in fact is characterized
primarily by its own alienation. For liberalism, God is not death, God is nothing.

For Daly, Goddess is definitely not nothing. She is not limited even to the
Great Mother.

> . . . Fixation upon the "Great Mother" to the exclusion of the myriad other
> possibilities for Naming transcendence, can fix women into foreground cate-
> gories that block encounters with the inexhaustible Other, stopping the
> Metamorphic process.[45]

That is to say, the divine in Daly's work is not a substitution of female terms
for a male transcendent deity, nor is the divine reduced to Nature per se. The
entire model for divine/human relationship has changed. Limiting the divine
to a label instead of understanding the spiraling of metaphoric encounter
with shifting images of radical otherness is a symptom, in Daly's view, of "the
Standstill Society, the Stag-nation."[46] She gives a profound glimpse into what

42. Ibid., 158.
43. Ibid., 158-59.
44. Paul Tillich *Systematic Theology,* 3 vols. (Chicago: University of Chicago Press, 1951-63),
1:164, quoted in Daly, 159.
45. Daly, 403.
46. Ibid., 405.

it would mean to actually live in the physical world and in the imagination and not abandon the physical world for an abstractionist human consciousness.

Yet Daly also shares some characteristics with Kaufman and Tillich that undermine her commitment to the reintegration of nature and history. A clue to this is her use of the term "pure" in the title *Pure Lust*. The journey of *Pure Lust* is a movement, a spiral, through "Metamorphospheres" of Wild Weird women who are purified in the Realm of Fire from the Plastic and Potted Passions and Virtues and are able to break out of these spheres and get in touch with Natural Grace. It is a movement of purification.

It is significant to me that Daly has drawn on Alice Walker's novel *The Color Purple* to illustrate the movement toward the inexhaustible other. The philosopher (Daly) reads to a student from Walker's book:

> Don't look like nothing, she [Shug] say. It ain't a picture show. It ain't something you can look at apart from anything else, including yourself. I believe God is everything, say Shug. . . . She say, My first step away from the old white man was trees. Then air. Then birds. Then other people. But one day when I was sitting quiet and feeling like a motherless child, which I was, it came to me: that feeling of being part of everything, not separate at all.[47]

Daly continues, "Hearing these words, our Nag-Gnostic philosopher [Daly] and Novice Nag [her student] must feel essentially in accord with Shug and Celie."[48] I read Daly as saying that in the realm of purity all differences dissolve.

Kaufman has his own movement of purification. In his *Essay on Theological Method*, Kaufman presents a scheme (also operative in *Theology for a Nuclear Age*) of theological analysis that proceeds in three moments. The first moment is "pure phenomenological description," an "attempt to put the varieties of contemporary experience together into a concept of the world as a whole." The second moment is the imposition of the God concept constructed as "the human significance of the ultimate reality." Then comes the third moment in which "the works of artists, and physicists, social workers and philosophers, historians and economists, urban experts and students of the 'third world,' spokespersons for the problems of blacks, women, and other groups, must all be taken into account." After the entire scheme is constructed as "pure," then the messy masses are fit in. Granted Kaufman claims that these moments cannot "be taken up in simple, serial order."[49] But in his next paragraph he imagines a theologian embarking on moment three who is "grounded" in moments one

47. Ibid., 400, quoting Alice Walker, *The Color Purple* (New York: Harcourt Brace Jovanovich, 1982), 167.
48. Ibid., 400.
49. Kaufman, *An Essay on Theological Method*, 59-61.

and two. If these are not serial, their presentation and subsequent function certainly appear that way.

Both Daly and Kaufman regard the concrete, material alienation of women, blacks "and other groups" to be of import in theological construction, but only in a tertiary sense.

The Survival of the Ancestors, Self, and God

Audre Lorde commented at a panel on "The Personal and the Political" at the Second Sex Conference, October 29, 1979, that

> Black panelists' observation about the effects of relative powerlessness and the differences of relationships between black women and men from white women and men illustrates some of our unique problems as black feminists. If white American feminist theory need not deal with the differences between us, and the resulting difference in aspects of our oppression, then what do you do with the fact that the women who clean your houses and tend your children while you attend conferences on feminist theory are, for the most part, poor and third world women? What is the theory behind racist feminism?[50]

Simply put, there are women who, because of their economic, social and racial location, have no access to any of the spheres Daly describes. There can be no reintegration of nature and history without confronting the vast differences in women's historical conditions and making a *methodological* shift in light of those differences. We cannot "Leap with Wanderlust"[51] over poverty, over racism, over real history.

Our survival and that of God depend on knowing this. "Survival," as Audre Lorde has written, "is not an academic skill."[52] Academics, and here I speak for myself, don't know what we need to know about surviving. The irony of presenting a paper on this lack of knowledge is not lost on me. But this I do know: contact with the voices of historical difference and a confrontation with them *as* different is as crucial to our survival and God's as is the reintegration with nature.

In one of her early novels, *Meridian,* Alice Walker explores the spiritual truth that it is the connections to the heritage of black women that are the source of creativity in life and the wellspring of change. Meridian, the central character, seeks her identity through the legacy left her by other southern black

50. Audre Lorde, "The Master's Tools Will Never Dismantle the Master's House," in *This Bridge Called My Back: Writings by Radical Women of Color,* eds. Cherrie Moraga and Gloria Anzaldua (Watertown, Mass.: Persephone Press, 1981), 100.

51. Daly, 411.

52. Lorde, 99.

women. Meridian believes in the sacredness and continuity of life, the African spirituality of animism, "the spirit that inhabits all life."[53] Meridian discovers, against impossible odds, the societal forces in a perverted and distorted racist society which inhibit the natural growth of the living organism toward freedom. She learns that

> the respect she owed her life was to continue, against whatever obstacles, to live it, and not to give up any particle of it without a fight to the death, preferably not her own. And that this existence extended beyond herself to those around her because, in fact, the years in America had created them One Life.[54]

The Color Purple can be seen as not only encompassing the themes of Walker's earlier works, but also taking them to a resolution. This is the story of one Southern black family, and the oppression black women experience in their relationships with black men. Walker also examines incest and lesbian relationships. In loving Shug, Celie, the main character, who has been sexually abused by her father and physically abused by her husband, comes to value herself and life. Celie has managed not only to survive but to prevail against all odds. The strength she finds is in the solidarity of women who, in choosing freedom for themselves, also permit those around them, both female and male, to find the freedom that is the natural state of human life.

While many black women, including Walker, Zora Neale Hurston, and Toni Morrison, have used religious imagery and specifically Christian biblical imagery to frame their literary works, the answer to the question of who God is for the black woman writer permits no simple contrast between modes of Christian belief and African spiritualities. What was said of Emily Dickinson can be said of these writers as well: they use the Christian idiom much more than they permit it to use them. It is closer to the major theme of these writers to say that God becomes the black woman protagonist in both suffering and healing. Early in *Meridian* another character says of the protagonist, "she thinks *she's* God."[55]

Meridian is based not only on the conviction of life itself as sacred, but also on the dilemma of suffering and death giving birth to life. This novel explores nonviolent resistance after it has become unfashionable, pursuing the notion that unless those who wish to change society take on the struggle — even to the death — they will defeat their own revolution. That which they seek to destroy in society will resurrect itself in their own psyches. And simarily that which they defeat in themselves can become liberating for the community. It may be more accurate to say that it is life that is divine and

---

53. Walker, *Meridian* (New York: Washington Square Press, 1976), 5.
54. Ibid., 204.
55. Ibid., 22.

the self-conscious, self-loving black woman who allies herself with life can embody its divinity.

The Salt Eaters, a novel by Toni Cade Bambara, opens with the question, "Are you sure, sweetheart, that you want to be well?" The questioner is Minnie Ransom, faith healer cum therapist in the Southwest Community Infirmary of Claybourne, Georgia, where Velma Henry — the one being questioned — has been taken.[56] Velma, the tireless worker on good causes of the neighborhood, has just attempted suicide.

As Minnie's voice drones on, Velma's fractured consciousness allows scenes to drift in and out. Her "soul goes gathering,"[57] remembering what it's been like

> being called in on five-minute notice after all the interesting decisions had been made, called in out of personal loyalty and expected to break her hump pulling off what the men had decided was crucial for community good . . . be snatched at by childish, unmannish hands. . . . Like taking on entirely too much: drugs, prisons, alcohol, the schools, rape, battered women, abused children . . . the nuclear power issue. . . .[58]

Velma's healing takes place when she remembers/enters in spirit a place where time fuses the dead, the living and the unborn, and where "Isis lifted the veil." The spirits of African religions reign: Shango presides over the rites of transformation, and Ogun challenges chaos and forges transition; Obatala shapes creation, and Damballah ensures continuity and renewal; Anancy becomes a medium for the shapes of Brer Rabbit, Brer Bear, Brer Fox, Brer Terrapin, the Signifyin' Monkey. This is the place where the griot member of all humankind is reincarnated as the conjure woman, High John, John Henry, the Flying African, Stagolee, the Preacher, the blues singer, the jazz makers; where the sorcerers of African-American literary heritage from the eighteenth century until the present assemble as the Master Minds of global experience. For Bambara, time is a fusion of the ancestors and the future. When the community forgets that, and enters into the linear progressions of Western society with its crisis upon crisis: drugs, prisons, alcohol, the schools, rape, battered women, abused children, nuclear war . . . they are broken and can no longer heal either themselves or their world.[59]

For these black women writers, survival depends both on claiming the earth as divine and on claiming a non-Western understanding of history. Mary Daly has pointed out the vacuum at the heart of white, Protestant liberal

56. Toni Cade Bambara, *The Salt Eaters* (New York: Vintage Books, 1981), 3.

57. Ibid., 152.

58. Ibid., 25ff.

59. *Black Women Writers (1950-1980): A Critical Evaluation*, ed. Mari Evans (Garden City, NY: Doubleday, 1984), 64-65.

theology. Yet, she and other white feminists who understand the significance of claiming the earth and bodily process in divinity need to hear the difference race makes. From black women writers, I hear that history is to be taken as the location of struggle, of survival, of life and death.

Yes, the survival of God is the survival of nature: the earth and all its splendors, including but not limited to human beings. Surely the wanton destruction of the basis of life would be an irreparable rendering of the worship relationship that is the content of religion's use of the term God. But survival is not mere persistence in being nor is it the idea of progressive material success as defined in the West. God and her survival are threatened both by the otherworldly spirituality of nuclear fundamentalists that makes this earth of penultimate concern *and* by their companion capitalist materiality that measures all life for its monetary values. Survival is the fullness of life, the solidarity between the ancestry of the planet and the race to come. And you cannot find that vision in Plato or his heirs.

The Holy Reign of God

HOWARD A. SNYDER

Psalm 96 says: "Worship the Lord in the splendor of his holiness; tremble before him, all the earth. Say among the nations, 'The Lord reigns'" (96:9-10).

This whole psalm is a call for all the earth to praise God as Saviour and Ruler over all. "Declare his glory among the nations, his marvelous deeds among all peoples" (v. 3). God reigns; He has created all things; and "he will judge the world in righteousness and the peoples in his truth" (v. 13).

A number of the psalms sound the same theme:

The Lord reigns,
    let the nations tremble;
he sits enthroned between the cherubim,
    let the earth shake.
Great is the Lord in Zion;
    he is exalted over all the nations.
Let them praise your great and awesome name —
    he is holy.
The King is mighty, he loves justice —
    you have established equity;
    in Jacob you have done what is just and right.
Exalt the Lord our God and worship at his footstool;
    he is holy. (Ps. 99:1-5)

Psalm 47:8 says, "God reigns over the nations; God is seated on his holy throne." Psalm 29 also speaks of the holiness and the kingship of God (Ps. 29:2, 10). And we read in the Song of Moses and Miriam in Exodus 15 that God, who is "majestic in holiness," will "reign for ever and ever" (Ex. 15:11, 18).

Though other examples might be given, these are enough to lift up what

---

Reprinted with permission from the *Wesleyan Theological Journal* 24 (1989): 74-90.

I believe is a significant Biblical theme: the holy reign of God. These passages in fact tie together two themes I would like to address in this essay: the *holiness* of God and the *kingdom* or *reign* of God.

Both these themes are important for us in the Wesleyan tradition. Most of us are, first of all, in some way part of or heirs to the Holiness Movement. Also, we stand in a tradition which has stressed the sovereignty of God — though a tradition which, with a few exceptions, has not given much attention specifically to the theme of the Kingdom of God. . . .

My purpose in this paper is fairly simple: to explore the relationship between two Biblical themes which I believe are of concern and interest to all of us: the *holiness* of God and the *Kingdom* of God. My central thesis is this: Taking these two themes together leads us to a fuller apprehension of our faith and what it means to be faithful Christian disciples in the present age.

The principal problematic of this study can be posed as a series of questions: What is the relationship between the Biblical themes of the *holiness* and the *kingdom* or *reign* of God? In what ways does each truth help us to understand, and respond appropriately to, the other? And particularly, how might posing these questions illuminate our own Wesleyan tradition?

I. The Holy Reign of God in Scripture

As we have seen from the references just cited, the holiness and the reign of God are intimately linked in Scripture. The Old Testament reveals a holy God who is the sovereign Ruler over all He has made. Much more could be said about this theme in the Old Testament; suffice it to say that this perspective is assumed by the New Testament writers.

Jesus and the Kingdom

It has become increasingly recognized that the kingdom of God is a key theme in the New Testament, and especially in Jesus' own life and teachings. Jesus' initial announcement was, "Repent, for the kingdom of heaven is near" (Mt. 4:17; cf. Mk. 1:15), the same message John the Baptist had proclaimed (Mt. 3:2). We read that as Jesus began His public ministry He "went throughout Galilee, teaching in their synagogues, preaching the good news of the kingdom, and healing every disease and sickness among the people" (Mt. 4:23; cf. Mt. 9:35; Lk. 8:1).

The Sermon on the Mount is full of kingdom themes and kingdom imagery. The Beatitudes begin and end with references to the kingdom. The sermon includes the key injunction not to be preoccupied with food and clothing but to "seek first [God's] kingdom and his righteousness," or justice (Mt. 6:33).

Jesus sent out His disciples to proclaim, "The kingdom of heaven is near" and to heal and drive out demons (Mt. 10:7; cf. Lk. 9:1-2; 10:9-11). He spoke of the kingdom of God "forcefully advancing" (Mt. 11:12), and said the exorcisms He performed were evidence that "The kingdom of God has come upon you" (Mt. 12:28; Lk. 11:20). Jesus' parables of the kingdom speak of its small, seemingly insignificant beginnings, its supreme value, and its growth (Mt. 13; Mk. 4; Lk. 13). Jesus said, "Anyone who will not receive the kingdom of God like a little child will never enter it" (Mk. 10:15); in fact, it is next to impossible "for the rich to enter the kingdom of God"! (Mk. 10:23). To those who followed Him Jesus said, "Fear not, little flock, for your Father delights to give you the kingdom" (Lk. 12:32). Jesus said the kingdom of God is "within you" or "among you" (Lk. 17:21). He told Nicodemus, "No one can enter the kingdom of God unless he is born of water and the Spirit" (Jn. 3:5).

Even during the forty days following His resurrection, Jesus' theme with His disciples was the kingdom of God (Acts 1:3). Yet He linked the kingdom, not with times and dates but with the powerful filling with the Holy Spirit which would make them effective witnesses of the Gospel throughout the earth.

Simply looking at the Biblical references, one would have to say that Jesus spoke much more about the kingdom of God than He did about the holiness of God. He didn't come proclaiming God's *holiness* but God's *reign*.

This assertion must be qualified, however, in two or three ways. First, Jesus explicitly links the holiness and the reign of God in the Lord's Prayer: "Hallowed be your name, your kingdom come, your will be done on earth as it is in heaven" (Mt. 6:9-10). Christians are to pray that God's name be held holy, that His holiness be recognized and honored, and that God's reign be manifested fully on earth. Here, certainly, is a glimpse of the holy reign of God — and it comes in the setting of prayer.

We may note also Matthew 6:33, where seeking the kingdom of God is linked to God's righteousness and justice, thus pointing to the ethical character of God's reign and at least indirectly to God's holiness.

The Lord's Prayer seems clearly to be modeled on King David's prayer in 1 Chronicles 29:10-13. Here David, near the end of his reign, praises God for his greatness and his provision for the temple to be built under Solomon. David prays,

> Yours, O Lord, is the greatness and the power
> and the glory and the majesty and the splendor,
> for everything in heaven and earth is yours.
> Yours, O Lord, is the kingdom;
> you are exalted as head over all.
> Wealth and honor come from you,
> you are the ruler of all things. (1 Chron. 29:11-12)

David goes on to speak of the temple to be built for God's "Holy Name" (v. 16). Clearly this passage, so symbolic of the Messianic reign of Christ, is a picture of the holy reign of God — and thus adds significance to the Lord's Prayer, and the Sermon on the Mount generally, as grounded in the holy reign of God.

We might also note that the Lord's Prayer (especially the phrase, "Forgive us our debts") and the Beatitudes can be linked with the Jubilee passages of Isaiah 61:1-2 and Leviticus 25:8-55 (cf. Psalm 146:7-10). This relates to our theme at several levels. The Jubilee is a recognition and manifestation of God's sovereign reign and, as a sabbath of sabbaths, recalls the commandment to keep the sabbath day holy (Ex. 20:8-11; Dt. 5:12-15). Here the holiness and reign of God have specific ethical content: justice for the poor, release for the oppressed.

Jesus does then, in the Sermon on the Mount, connect holiness with the kingdom of God.

A *second* qualification to my earlier statement that Jesus speaks little about the holiness of God is this: In a real sense, Jesus' whole life and teaching were an explication of God's holiness. As R. Newton Flew says, "For the early Christian the Kingdom was indissolubly bound up with the person of Jesus Himself. . . . The Kingdom was perfection because He was at the center of it. *Ubi Christus, ibi Regnum Dei.*" He adds, ". . . the proclamation by Jesus of the Reign of God carried with it a doctrine of the ideal life which might be lived out in the present world."[1]

Jesus demonstrates what it means to say that God is holy. He himself is the Holy One (Lk. 1:35). When Jesus said, "Be perfect, . . . as your Father is perfect" (Mt. 5:48), or "Be merciful just as your Father is merciful" (Lk. 6:36), He was showing what holiness means. And His life was a demonstration of that meaning. Perhaps most importantly, Jesus says the greatest commandment is, " 'Love the Lord your God with all your heart and with all your soul and with all your mind.' This is the first and greatest commandment. And the second is like it: 'Love your neighbor as yourself' " (Mt. 22:37-40). This certainly is a preaching of what it means for "the children of the kingdom" to reflect God's holiness in their lives.

Jesus, then, came proclaiming the kingdom of God and embodying God's holiness. He demonstrated both the power and the ethical meaning of the kingdom in His own life, death, and resurrection. He empowers us with the Holy Spirit that we may live the life of the kingdom now, serving as kingdom witnesses throughout the earth.

Other New Testament References

The Apostle Paul, in his several references to the kingdom of God, links God's reign with righteousness and holiness. In our tradition, perhaps the most fa-

---

1. R. Newton Flew, *The Idea of Perfection in Christian Theology: An Historical Study of the Christian Ideal for the Present Life* (New York: Humanities Press, 1968), 5, 3.

miliar of these texts is Romans 14:17, "For the kingdom of God is not a matter of eating and drinking, but of righteousness, peace, and joy in the Holy Spirit." Wesleyans no doubt have gravitated to this text when they speak of the kingdom especially because of its reference to the Holy Spirit.

In 1 Corinthians 6, Paul says, "Do you not know that the wicked will not inherit the kingdom of God? . . . But you were washed, you were sanctified, you were justified in the name of the Lord Jesus Christ and by the Spirit of our God" (I Cor. 6:9, 11). In I Thessalonians Paul refers to the "holy, righteous and blameless" life he lived among the people, and says he urged the believers "to live lives worthy of God, who calls you into his kingdom and glory" (I Thess. 2:10, 12). While these may be considered somewhat incidental references, they show that in Paul's mind the kingdom of God was certainly linked with holiness — in these passages, not so much with God's holiness as with holiness as the Christian's quality of life, but a life which is a reflection, of course, of God's holiness.

Two other New Testament references may be noted in passing. Hebrews 12:28 tells us: "Therefore, since we are receiving a kingdom that cannot be shaken, let us be thankful, and so worship God acceptably with reverence and awe, for 'our God is a consuming fire'" (Heb. 12:28; cf. Dt. 4:24). Here the holy character of God our King is pictured.

The final reference is from the book of Revelation. In a real sense, the holy reign of God is the fundamental theme of the whole of the Apocalypse. God's holiness and sovereignty are graphically pictured here as the key to understanding history and the present meaning of Christian discipleship. In many ways the key verse is Revelation 11:15 — "The kingdom of the world has become the kingdom of our Lord and of his Christ, and he will reign for ever and ever." The passage goes on to picture a scene of reverent worship of the holy God. The victory of the kingdom of God is proclaimed in a setting of worship.

Summary

From the perspective of the holy reign of God, the Biblical revelation may be summarized as follows: God is holy and is sovereign over all He has made. The alienation of sin constitutes a fall from God's holiness and a rebellion against His reign. Yet God continues to exercise His sovereignty over His people and among the nations. He reveals His holy character through the law, the sacrificial system, and the prophets; He exercises His sovereignty both through and in spite of Israel's kings. Jesus comes as the messianic king, embodying in himself the holy character of God. As holy God and yet finite human, Jesus offers himself as an atonement and rises in triumph over all principalities and powers. He reigns now both as head of all creation and head of the church, His body, called to live now the holy character of God. Christians are called to serve Jesus Christ as their sovereign Lord and their example for life, empowered by Jesus' Spirit among them. They are called to continue the liberating works of the kingdom which Jesus began, living in the certain hope of the final manifestation of God's reign over all things, a reign in which the holiness of God will be reflected in a new heaven and new earth of universal *shalom*.

II. The Kingdom of God in the Wesleyan Tradition

We turn now to examine the ways the kingdom of God theme has been handled in the Wesleyan-Holiness tradition, beginning with Wesley and running on through to the present.

John Wesley

For John Wesley, the key Biblical text on the kingdom of God was Romans 14:17 — "For the kingdom of God is not a matter of eating and drinking, but of righteousness, peace, and joy in the Holy Spirit." The reason for Wesley's preference for this text is clear: He interpreted the kingdom of God, at least in its present dimensions, primarily in terms of the experience of sanctification in believers and especially in the community of believers. One can see this by noting the comments in his *Explanatory Notes upon the New Testament* regarding the kingdom of God. Almost always the meaning of the kingdom is associated with holiness or sanctification (in contrast to Bengel's comments in the *Gnomon*).

For example, regarding Jesus' initial proclamation of the kingdom (Mt. 4:17), Wesley says, "It is the peculiar business of Christ to establish the kingdom of heaven in the hearts of men."[2] Commenting on Matthew 13:24, Wesley says that the kingdom of heaven "sometimes signifies eternal glory; sometimes the way to it, inward religion; sometimes, as here, the gospel dispensation."[3] To say the kingdom of God is within or among you means the kingdom "is present in the soul of every true believer: it is a spiritual kingdom, an internal principle."[4] The kingdom of God mentioned in Romans 14:17 is "true religion"; its righteousness is "the image of God stamped on the heart; the love of God and man,

2. John Wesley, *Explanatory Notes upon the New Testament* (London: Epworth Press, 1958), 27.

3. Ibid., 70. Note the general sense of "gospel dispensation" here, in contrast to Fletcher's concept of the dispensation of the Spirit. See John Fletcher, "The Portrait of St. Paul or, The True Model for Christians and Pastors," *The Works of the Reverend John Fletcher*, 4 vols. (New York: Lane and Scott, 1851), 3:7-241, esp. pp. 116-67; Donald W. Dayton, *Theological Roots of Pentecostalism* (Grand Rapids: Francis Asbury Press/Zondervan, 1987), 51-54.

4. Ibid., 269.

accompanied with the *peace* that passeth all understanding, *and joy in the Holy Ghost.*"[5]

The Sermon on the Mount is the way to the kingdom.[6] This is so primarily because it teaches the meaning of true Christianity, what it means to be holy and happy; to live a life of all inward and outward holiness. The kingdom of God referred to in the first Beatitude is "the present, inward kingdom; righteousness and peace and joy in the Holy Ghost; as well as the eternal kingdom, if they endure to the end."[7] To seek first God's kingdom means: "Simply aim at this, that God, reigning in your heart, may fill it with the righteousness above described."[8] Wesley gives perhaps his fullest explication in his comment on the Lord's Prayer. "Thy kingdom come" means, "May Thy kingdom of grace come quickly, and swallow up all the kingdoms of earth! May all mankind, receiving Thee, O Christ, for their King, truly believing in Thy name, be filled with righteousness and peace and joy, with holiness and happiness, till they are removed hence into Thy kingdom of glory, to reign with Thee for ever and ever."[9]

Wesley saw the kingdom of God in terms of the present operation of God's grace in believers' lives, especially, but also in society. A progressive, dynamic understanding of salvation underlies all of Wesley's thought. Nevertheless, one detects a tension between the static and dynamic elements in Wesley. Even though he saw sanctification as dynamic and progressive, he was not entirely free of the classical Greek notion of perfection as changelessness, and salvation as the attainment of an eternal blessedness which is essentially static. This is seen also in his view of the kingdom. The kingdom is fundamentally the direct experience of God through Jesus Christ (the "kingdom of grace").

Wesley was quick to stress the present implications of the gospel and the requirement of the obedience of good works. But underlying this seems to be the suspicion that the only ultimate significance of good works and of the present life is their function in preparing us for eternity, conceived in somewhat static terms. Yet one must remember here Wesley's imaginative descriptions of what the new heaven and new earth might be like, for instance in his sermons "The General Deliverance," "The General Spread of the Gospel," and "The New Creation."

I think Donald Dayton is right in this regard when he says Wesley's "perfectionist soteriology tended . . . to an optimistic social vision. The result [eschatologically] was an ambiguous position that could easily move in the direction of postmillennialism. . . .

5. Ibid., 57.

6. John Wesley, "Upon our Lord's Sermon on the Mount, Discourse the First," *The Works of John Wesley,* ed. Frank Baker, vol. 1 (Nashville: Abingdon Press, 1984), 470.

7. Wesley, *Explanatory Notes,* 25.

8. Ibid., 41.

9. Ibid., 37. Cf. Wesley's sixth sermon on the Sermon on the Mount, which contains virtually the same wording.

"Wesley was so oriented to soteriology," Dayton continues, "that his followers could combine a basically Wesleyan scheme of salvation with a variety of eschatologies without an obvious sense of betrayal. But the basic thrust of Wesley's thought was probably better captured by the less apocalyptic and more postmillennial schemes of thought. Thus, while Wesley himself did not self-consciously adopt a millennial scheme, he helped to unleash forces that could and would move in that direction."[10]

Wesley did, of course, pass on much of Bengel's postmillennial scheme in the Revelation portion of his *Explanatory Notes upon the New Testament*.

In terms of our two themes here — the holiness and reign of God — Wesley clearly interpreted the latter in terms of the former. That is, holiness and sanctification were Wesley's chief concern, and became his paradigm for understanding the kingdom of God. One must remember, however, that for Wesley holiness named both the character of God as perfect love and the whole way of salvation *(via salutis)*, embracing, in effect, a whole theology of history, or history of salvation. In this sense there is perhaps a more fundamental, historical kingdom theology in Wesley than is generally recognized.

From Wesley to the Holiness Movement

A number of people, including several Wesleyan Theological Society members, have investigated the question of the transition from John Wesley to the theology of the nineteenth-century Holiness Movement in North America. In general, a certain narrowing of focus specifically to the doctrine of entire sanctification, and an increasingly individualizing tendency, have been noted, with at times an almost exclusive focus on the second crisis experience, in contrast to the wider sweep of Wesley's soteriological framework. And of course the question of the appropriateness or inappropriateness of Spirit-baptism language has received considerable attention.

Without retracing those discussions, I would like simply to state in summary form what I see as the meaning of this transition for the themes of the holiness and the reign of God, and then cite a few examples.

1. The kingdom of God played a smaller role in nineteenth-century Methodist and Holiness theology than it did in Wesley's thought. This was part of both a theological systematization (in the case of Methodism generally) and a theological narrowing (in the case of the Holiness Movement) evident in this period of transition.

2. Where the kingdom of God *was* treated, it was interpreted almost always in terms of holiness and the experience of entire sanctification, as was true with Wesley.

10. Dayton, 152-53.

3. The question of the kingdom of God inevitably arose to some degree in Holiness circles toward the end of the century with the upsurge of interest in premillennialism. Discussion of the kingdom here is almost totally limited to the millennial question.

By and large, the kingdom of God was simply not a theme of nineteenth-century Methodist and Holiness theology. It is intriguing, for instance, to find virtually no discussion of the kingdom of God in such books as Richard Watson's *Theological Institutes* (1823-29), Thomas Ralston's *Elements of Divinity* (1847), Benjamin Field's *Student's Handbook of Christian Theology* (1869) and Amos Binney's *Theological Compend* (1858). Daniel Steele's "Improved" edition of his father-in-law's *Compend* (1875) devotes merely two pages to "Messiah's Kingdom — Its Progress and Ultimate Triumph" in the general section "Last Things"; clearly the kingdom of God played no formative theological role.[11]

Watson's *Theological Institutes,* which had great impact in North American Methodism and was described in 1877 as "the standard of Methodist theology for a full half century,"[12] seems to have largely set the pattern here. Watson has no chapter or section on eschatology, or on the kingdom of God. The only reference to the kingdom I could find was an incidental one in the discussion of infant baptism, where Watson says Jesus more frequently used the phrase "kingdom of God" "to denote the Church in this present world, than in its state of glory."[13]

It appears, then, that whatever stress on the kingdom of God was present in Wesley's theology largely dropped out in nineteenth-century North American Methodism. An exception would be those Wesleyans around the time of Finney's revivalism who, like Finney, saw social reform as in some sense part of the firstfruits of the coming kingdom. Significant discussions of the kingdom emerged toward the end of the century as the theological climate was shifting. On the more conservative Holiness Movement side, the precipitating issue was millennialism. On the more "liberal" side within Methodism, the precipitating cause was the influence of German theology and the rise of the Social Gospel around the turn of the century. Robert Chiles in *Theological Transition in American Methodism: 1790-1935* notes,

> Study abroad brought back not only German Biblical research but also the philosophies of Schleiermacher, Lotze, and Ritschl. Ritschlianism in particular penetrated the English-speaking world. Commenting on the time, a Methodist wrote, "theological seminaries in America are filled with professors

11. Amos Binney and Daniel Steele, *Binney's Theological Compend Improved* . . . (New York: Methodist Book Concern, 1875, 1902), 139-41.

12. Robert E. Chiles, *Theological Transition in American Methodism: 1790-1935* (New York: Abingdon, 1965), 47.

13. Richard Watson, *Theological Institutes: Or a View of the Evidences, Doctrines, Morals, and Institutions of Christianity,* new ed., 2 vols. (New York: Lane and Scott, 1851), 2:637.

who have either sat in the Ritschlian lecture rooms in Berlin, Marburg, Göttingen, etc., and have come back devotees of the faith, or have imbibed at Ritschlian springs nearer home." [This influence] encouraged the further moralization of theological categories and also gave support to the emphasis on the Kingdom of God in the Social Gospel movement which helped polarize growing liberal conviction, inherited from revival and perfectionist traditions, that the whole of life must be brought under God's rule.[14]

Millennialism and the Kingdom

It is instructive in this connection to look at two figures in the Holiness Movement just one hundred or so years ago as they dealt with the upsurge of premillennialism but came out at opposite points. Here we see kingdom theologies being articulated within the Wesleyan Holiness milieu — emerging, however, not from the *internal* dynamic of the Wesleyan message but rather due to *external* pressures of prophetic and millennial discussions and, more broadly, pressures from the socio-cultural climate of the times.

The first of these is Daniel Steele, who had written the holiness classic, *Love Enthroned,* in 1877. In 1887 he published his *Antinomianism Revived, or, the Theology of the So-called Plymouth Brethren Examined and Refuted.*[15] The book is in large measure an attack on dispensational premillennialism as promoted at the Prophecy Conference in New York City in 1878.

Steele criticizes premillennialism for its extreme literalism and particularly for its pessimism, "the hopelessness of the world under the dispensation of the Holy Spirit."[16] He believes such pessimism dishonors and undercuts the role of the Holy Spirit and is incompatible with Scripture. Premillennialism, he says, "gives a Jewish and highly materialistic turn to the kingdom of Christ, and leads to a depreciation of the spiritual manifestation of Christ by the Comforter in this life."[17] He adds, "I believe that the general prevalence of pre-millennialism would be disastrous to the best interests of the Kingdom of Christ, now being spread over the earth by the joint agency of the Holy Spirit and consecrated believers."[18]

In this connection Steele has some sharp criticism of the evangelist D. L. Moody:

> Several years ago, D. L. Moody learned his method of Bible-study and Bible-readings from the English Plymouth Brethren. . . . He adopts their millen-

14. Chiles, 63.

15. Daniel Steele, *Antinomianism Revived, or, the Theology of the So-called Plymouth Brethren Examined and Refuted* (Boston: McDonald, Gill & Co., 1887).

16. Ibid., 169.

17. Ibid., 168.

18. Ibid., 265.

narianism, and preaches the personal reign of Christ on the earth as a substitute for the present agency of the Spirit and of preaching, which are regarded as inadequate for the successful evangelization of the world, and the
reconstruction of society on a Christian basis. His declaration that the world
is like a ship so hopelessly wrecked that it cannot be gotten off the rocks, but
must be left to perish, while Christians rescue as many of the passengers as
possible, is a pessimistic Plymouth idea.[19]

In this book and in some passages in *Milestone Papers*, published the next
year (1888), Steele goes beyond mere critique to sketch a positive Holiness
kingdom theology which is moderately dispensational and is postmillennial,
maintaining Wesley's optimism of grace. As Donald Dayton and others have
shown, Steele here is consciously reaching back to John Fletcher's terminology
and doctrine of three dispensations. Dayton notes, "Steele showed signs of the
shift that would take place in Holiness thought late in the nineteenth century.
Fletcher's doctrine of dispensations was regularly analyzed in Steele's works,
and these expositions were widely reprinted in various Holiness periodicals. We
have already noted Steele's call for an adoption of the vocabulary of Pentecost."[20]

Steele wrote, "We object to the pre-millenarian theory because its definition of the kingdom of Christ makes it an institution altogether different from
the Church, and entirely in the future. . . . The Chiliast represents the kingdom
as coming only at the descent of the King in person, and as then set up suddenly
by almightiness without the aid of human agency. But when we look into the
New Testament, we find no such difference in the use of the terms 'Church' and
'kingdom.' They seem to be used interchangeably. The kingdom is to be established by preaching, and it is to develop gradually till its ultimate triumph."[21]
Thus, "The Church is the kingdom begun."[22]

Steele thus affirms the growth and gradual progress of God's kingdom.
He criticizes a negative interpretation of the meaning of "leaven" in Jesus'
parable, noting, "Christ himself spoke of the kingdom of God as within, or
among, His hearers. The disciples were taught to pray for its complete triumph
on the earth. Parables illustrative of its slow progress, but ultimate universality,
were spoken. . . . The astonishing development of Christ's kingdom from small
beginnings through long ages is here plainly taught."[23] Steele adds, "In Christ's
comparison of the kingdom to leaven deposited in the meal, He intended to
teach the gradual diffusion, the pervasive and assimilative power, and the universal prevalence of the kingdom of heaven."[24]

19. Ibid., 55-56.
20. Dayton, 164.
21. Steele, 246.
22. Ibid., 250.
23. Ibid., 247.
24. Ibid., 248.

It is evident that, in reaction to premillennialism, Steele closely associates the kingdom of God with the church and sees it in highly spiritual terms. He speaks of Christ's "present spiritual reign in the Church."[25] There is, he says, "but one kingdom of Christ on earth, and that is spiritual, . . . the Church is the spiritual kingdom of Christ, and the only kingdom which He will establish on earth."[26] We are now in the Dispensation of the Spirit, the time in which the Holy Spirit by Pentecostal power builds the church:

> That was not a mere dash of rhetoric which fell from the pen of John Fletcher, when he spoke of the Pentecost as the opening of "the kingdom of the Holy Ghost." He has the signet ring of our glorified King Jesus, and reigns over the family on earth as the Son of man reigns over the family above. He has not shut himself up as an impersonal force in the tomb of uniform law, but he walks through the earth, a glorious personality, with the keys of divine power attached to his girdle, and with the rod of empire in his right hand. He works miracles in the realm of spirit, as did Immanuel in the realm of matter.[27]

Steele foresaw a sort of new Pentecost, perhaps the dawning of the authentic, Biblical millennium, through the heightened interest in the sanctifying and empowering work of the Holy Spirit. He saw "indications of the dawn of that returning day of Pentecost, when the Spirit shall be poured out in his fullness upon all who 'know the exceeding greatness of Christ's power to us-ward who believe.' The eastern sky has streaks of light betokening the sunrise of a day of power. Christians of every name, lone watchers on the mountain-tops, now see the edge of the ascending disk, and are shouting to the inhabitants of the dark valleys below to awake and arise, and behold the splendors of the King of Day."[28]

It is clear that Steele's view of the kingdom does maintain Wesley's optimism of grace and his "evangelical synergism." But it seems to me that, Biblically, it is open to three criticisms: (1) it is overly spiritualized; (2) it too closely identifies the kingdom with the Church; and (3) it distinguishes too sharply between the agency of Jesus Christ and that of the Holy Spirit. Here Steele is tripped up by the very kind of dispensationalism he criticizes. At all these points, it seems to me, Wesley is more balanced and more Biblical. Steele is also much closer to Pentecostalism at these points than was Wesley.

Other people in the Holiness Movement went the opposite direction of Steele, adopting premillennialism, and not all of these became Pentecostals after 1900 or 1906. I have chosen a somewhat obscure but intriguing example, Thomas H. Nelson, who until 1894 was a Free Methodist. In 1896 he published

25. Ibid., 251.

26. Ibid., 252.

27. Daniel Steele, *Milestone Papers, Doctrinal, Ethical, and Experimental, on Christian Progress* (New York: Eaton & Mains, 1878), 146.

28. Ibid., 148-49.

a book entitled *The Midnight Cry or the Consummation of All Things as Shown by Fulfilled Prophecies and the "Signs of the Times,"* in which he fully adopted the premillennial viewpoint.

Nelson had been an associate of Vivian A. Dake in the work of the Pentecost Bands, an aggressively evangelistic youth movement within Free Methodism which in the late 1880s and early 1890s started dozens of new churches and turned them over to the denomination (eleven in one year alone, according to Dake).[29] The Pentecost Bands were teams of young men or young women committed to a radical holiness discipleship, and the movement became controversial within the Free Methodist Church. Nelson succeeded Dake as leader of the Pentecost Bands when Dake died in Africa in 1892.

Following the Free Methodist General Conference of 1894 the Pentecost Bands left the Free Methodist Church, becoming an independent organization. Nelson served as their superintendent and apparently immediately founded the Pentecost Training School in St. Louis that same year.[30] The Bands eventually united with the Wesleyan Methodist Church.

In his book *The Midnight Cry,* Nelson called postmillennialism a "heresy" and said, "we fail to find any scripture for the dogma that is becoming so popular these days that the 'world is rapidly growing better,' and that the prevailing principles and influences will be successful in converting it and bringing about the millennium."[31] In Nelson's view, Christ's millennial reign will be literal and physical on a "renewed and glorified earth":

> We see no reason why this earth, when purged from sin, should not be the seat of Him who thus redeemed it? [*sic*] There is nothing essentially vile in physical substance. With sin and all its effects destroyed, this earth would be an Eden, and in a very literal sense the meek could inherit the earth.... thank God that sin is to be expunged and all its train of concomitant evils to be destroyed and righteousness, peace and plenty to be enjoyed, a universal Eden, presided over by [Jesus Christ].[32]

29. Thomas H. Nelson, *Life and Labors of Rev. Vivian A. Dake, Organizer and Leader of Pentecost Bands* (Chicago: T. B. Arnold, 1894), 470. Dake wrote in 1891, "During the past year we have given the Illinois conference one new society, the Central Illinois, five new societies, with one church dedicated and three under process of erection; the Wabash conference, five new societies with three churches dedicated and one under way, in addition to lots for two more churches. These are all dedicated to the church and the societies handed over to the respective conferences" (ibid., 470).

30. Byron S. Lamson, *Venture! The Frontiers of Free Methodism* (Winona Lake, IN: Light and Life Press, 1960), 129-38.

31. Thomas H. Nelson, *The Midnight Cry or The Consummation of All Things Shown by Fulfilled Prophecies and the "Signs of the Times"* (Indianapolis: Pentecost Band Publishing Company, 1896), 16, 18.

32. Ibid., 24.

With only four years remaining until the year 1900, Nelson calculated that the world was then over 5,990 years old. "The seventh thousand year day, the Lord's millennial sabbath, . . . is at hand. We are living in the Saturday evening of this world's history."[33] "All orthodox Christians, especially believers in the premillennial doctrine, expect that the kingdom of Christ is to come upon the earth and exist under His personal reign for 1,000 years," he said.[34]

Such views were not eccentric or unusual in the context of the times. The *Christian Herald and Signs of Our Times,* published in New York, with a circulation of 250,000, regularly carried articles supporting premillennial views during this period. A dozen years or so before the publication of Nelson's book the Reverend Michael Baxter in an article in the *Christian Herald* (which he edited) proved through a series of calculations that 1893 was the latest possible date for Christ's return and the beginning of the millennium.[35] It now appears he made some error in his calculations.

Significantly, Nelson's millenarianism fit well with a movement which named itself after Pentecost and was engaged in front-line battle with the forces of darkness. The missionary spirit of Nelson and the Pentecost Bands is well captured in the most popular of Vivian Dake's many hymns, which articulates a kind of radical holiness view of the reign of God:

> We'll girdle the globe with salvation,
>   With holiness unto the Lord;
> And light shall illumine each nation,
>   The light from the lamp of His Word.

The last verse:

> The watch fires kindle far and near,
> In every land let them appear,
> Till burning lines of gospel fire,
> Shall gird the world and mount up higher.[36]

In some ways Nelson's view of the kingdom of God is the reverse image of Steele's, and yet both considered their views Wesleyan and Biblical. One might argue that Nelson's views are more christocentric and less pneumatocentric, though more apocalyptic, than are Steele's in that his focus was more on the return and reign of Jesus Christ than on the present work of the Holy Spirit in believers. In fact, Dake's hymns are highly christological, with few references to

33. Ibid., 163.

34. Ibid., 164.

35. M. Baxter, "The Focus Year of Prophetic Chronology," *The Christian Herald and Signs of Our Times,* 17:18, New Series (May 3, 1883), 278.

36. *Free Methodist Hymnal,* 1910, No. 650.

the Holy Spirit. The emphasis is on radical Christlikeness for the sake of evangelism and missions.

Yet over all, it seems to me that the premillennial eschatology of Nelson and people like him moves even further away from the breadth and depth of Wesley. There is a kind of apocalypticism in this mentality that is foreign to the sense of growth and process one finds in Wesley. To a large degree, Wesley takes his cue from the *life* of Christ; Steele, from Christ's gift of the Spirit at Pentecost; and Nelson, from the Second Coming of Christ.

From 1900 to Today

I would argue that in general the Holiness Movement put major stress on the holiness of God to the neglect of the kingdom of God as a central organizing theme of theology and ethics. "Holiness or Christian perfection is the central idea of Christianity," argued Jesse T. Peck in his 1856 book *The Central Idea of Christianity*. The key fact about "the kingdom of grace" is holiness: "God . . . reigns in holiness, immaculate and infinite."[37] Very little else need be said about the kingdom of God.

Yet as Holiness churches and associations moved into the twentieth century, they found themselves affected in various ways by the Modernist-Fundamentalist controversy, in which two radically divergent views of God's kingdom were advocated. Almost to the same degree that the Social Gospel argued that the kingdom of God was a present, this-worldly, social reality to be achieved largely by human effort, the Fundamentalists insisted that the kingdom was a future reality totally dependent upon God's sovereignty. Though it would be literal and earthly in the future, its only present relevance was spiritual, other-worldly, and largely individual.

The various Holiness bodies were affected by these currents in differing degrees, some of the newer Holiness denominations officially adopting premillennial positions. Virtually no one in the Holiness Movement, however, made the kingdom of God a central theological theme or attempted to articulate a theology of the holy reign of God.

A major exception to this was E. Stanley Jones, the noted Methodist missionary to India whose book on Mahatma Gandhi influenced the young Martin Luther King Jr. In many ways Jones was a man much like Wesley: an evangelist at heart; a folk theologian; a man with a world parish; a popularizer and yet profound; interested in all of life, including health and psychology; a radical who stayed in the mainstream.

The unique thing about Jones (at least from the perspective of this paper)

37. Jesse T. Peck, *The Central Idea of Christianity*, abridged (Kansas City, MO: Beacon Hill Press, 1951), 7, 12.

is that his central theological paradigm shifted from holiness to the kingdom of God, and yet he remained fundamentally within the Holiness ethos. He is perhaps the only twentieth-century figure to articulate what might properly be called a theology of the *holy reign of God*. I would argue that some of the most appealing and dynamic aspects of Jones' kingdom theology are grounded precisely in his Wesleyanism. Conversely, Jones' teaching regarding discipleship and the Christian life escape much of the narrowness, parochialism, and compromising enculturation of most North American Holiness teaching precisely because of its grounding in a Biblical theology of the kingdom.

It is clear that the kingdom of God became the central organizing principle of Jones' theology, especially after his experiences in the Soviet Union and in India in the 1930s.

Jones wrote, "The Kingdom of God is the master-conception, the master-plan, the master-purpose, the master-will that gathers everything up into itself and gives it redemption, coherence, purpose, goal."[38] For him it is God's kingdom, not holiness, that is the central idea — or, rather, the central fact — of Christianity. Jesus is the meaning and embodiment of the kingdom: "As He is the Incarnation of God, so He is the Incarnation of the Reign of God. . . . to have relationship with Christ is to have relationship with the new Order embodied in Christ."[39]

Jones insisted that the kingdom of God "is redemption for the individual and for the whole of society."[40] Jesus, said Jones, "was so interested in the individual that those who are impressed with this fact have often forgotten the framework of a world-kingdom in which this interest was manifest. To be able to hold a world-vision with detailed interest in the individual — this is a realism that extends from the macrocosm to the microcosm — the whole range of life."[41] Jones especially insisted that the kingdom "is not an idea — it is a fact, a present, pressing, all demanding Fact"; it is "the ultimate environment."[42] People and nations may or may not acknowledge God's kingdom, but the kingdom *is*. It is built into the fabric of the universe.

The church has lost sight of the kingdom of God, Jones said, but is ripe for a rediscovery. "If the Christian Church should become a disciple of the Kingdom of God there would be a new burst of creative activity that would set herself and the world ablaze."[43]

Jones applied his understanding of the kingdom to all areas of life — economics, psychology, medicine, international relations, the environment, and

38. E. Stanley Jones, *Is the Kingdom of God Realism?* (New York: Abingdon-Cokesbury, 1940), 53.

39. Ibid., 54.

40. Ibid., 56.

41. Ibid., 24.

42. Ibid., 72, 77.

43. Ibid., 262-63.

the life of the church. "The kingdom of God is Christlikeness universalized," he said.[44] Jones carefully distinguished between the kingdom and the church; yet he said the church must exist for the kingdom. He sounds like Wesley when he applies the meaning of the kingdom to church life: "The Kingdom was to be given to a little flock and not merely to individuals. The Kingdom would come through group action. If these Kingdom-of-God groups are to be effective, they must be unreservedly committed to Christ and unbreakably committed to each other. They must enter a conspiracy of love to keep each other up to the highest."[45]

While one might point to certain limitations in Jones' theology, I find it at once the most creative, relevant, and Biblically based kingdom theology to emerge so far in this century. I would like to suggest it as a key paradigm — though not the only one — for understanding in our age the meaning of the holy reign of God.

III. Interpreting the Holy Reign of God

This brings us to my final section. What do we learn from the interplay of these two themes, the *holiness* and the *reign* of God? What are some of the practical implications for life and theology today? I would like to make several concluding comments.

Models of the Holy Reign of God

First of all, it seems to me that there are four possible models for understanding the relationship between the *holiness* of God and the *reign* of God:

1. *The experience of holiness IS the kingdom of God.* Here the kingdom is viewed as essentially spiritual and historical; the primary meaning of the kingdom is the personal experience of God's sanctifying presence in one's life. It is very easy for this view to make little or no distinction between the church and the kingdom.

This is, fundamentally, the model of John Wesley and of the Holiness Movement generally. It is perhaps best represented in the views of Daniel Steele, as presented above. While I would identify this as Wesley's primary model, his conception of the kingdom was broader than this, as we have seen.

2. *The kingdom of God IS holiness,* understood as justice, wholeness, *shalom.* This is, in effect the opposite of the first model: the kingdom is the key

---

44. E. Stanley Jones, *The Unshakable Kingdom and the Unchanging Person* (Nashville: Abingdon Press, 1972), 34.

45. Ibid., 272.

to understanding holiness, rather than the other way around. This might be seen as the Social Gospel understanding, where the primary focus is on society and the social meaning of holiness and the kingdom. Clearly there are elements of this view in Wesley and in E. Stanley Jones.

3. *Holiness is now; the kingdom is future.* Here there is a sharp dichotomy between the present and the future. The kingdom has to do with "last things," and so is of little concern in the present. Our present focus should be on holy living, and on the life of the church. We might see this as the Holiness variant of premillennial dispensationalism; one certainly sees this in people like Thomas H. Nelson, or in Seth Cook Rees' book *The Ideal Pentecostal Church.*[46]

4. *Holiness is the ethic of the kingdom.* The kingdom is God's reign, both present and future, and we are called to live a life that reflects the character of the King. Jesus Christ is the key to understanding the meaning of both holiness and the kingdom. Thus holiness is Christlikeness, empowered by the Holy Spirit, and the kingdom of God is the "grand design" for personal life and for society which shows us what God is doing in the world through Jesus Christ. I think E. Stanley Jones best represents this model, though elements of it are found also in Wesley. It perhaps is the closest to the revival-and-reform vision of mid-nineteenth-century figures like Charles Finney.

These four models are not necessarily mutually exclusive; yet they do represent distinctly different ways of understanding the reign of God.

Implications for Christian Discipleship

Finally, I believe this whole discussion of the holy reign of God suggests several implications for the meaning of Christian discipleship today. Here I am attempting to be both Biblically faithful and relevant to the world in which we must live out our daily Christian commitment.

1. *Christian discipleship must be understood in terms of BOTH the holiness and the reign of God.* Both themes point to fundamental and mutually supportive Biblical truths which are needed in our world today. As Christians, and as the Christian community, we need to experience both Christ *in* us and Christ *over* and *ahead* of us.

I think it is important in this connection to maintain a *trinitarian* understanding of holiness and the reign of God — particularly as a safeguard against subtle dispensational tendencies which may over-emphasize one person of the Trinity at the expense of the others or of the unity of the Three.

2. *The holiness theme accents the elements of ethics, personal experience, and Christian character* in one's conception of the kingdom of God. Holiness stresses

46. Seth Cook Rees, *The Ideal Pentecostal Church* (Cincinnati: M. W. Knapp, The Revivalist Office, 1897).

the *character* of God who is King, not just His power or sovereignty. Holy, personal love becomes the controlling center, not mere power, authority, or order. This is one point where the Wesleyan Holiness tradition ought to be making a key contribution to contemporary discussions of the kingdom of God.

The Wesleyan and Pietist traditions have stressed the moral change brought about by regeneration and sanctification — Christ *in* us as well as Christ *for* us; the renewed image of God as well as the Word of God. This is important if the contemporary church is really to embody the character of Jesus Christ and build kingdom communities which witness authentically to both the love and the power of Jesus Christ.

3. *The kingdom of God theme accents the broader historical, cultural, and social dimensions of holiness.* The theme of the kingdom of God brings in the global, cosmic perspective in ways that the theme of holiness too often does not. Wesley's understanding of "social holiness" makes more sense and can be more solidly grounded when interwoven with Biblical kingdom themes. Here is the basis for an ethic of liberation and social transformation.

4. *Both holiness and the kingdom of God embody the already/not yet character of God's redemptive action.* Christians already are "saints," are being sanctified, and yet have not fully attained perfection or maturity. The kingdom of God is here, is coming, and will come. God has acted decisively in Jesus Christ, and yet continues to act through Christ [and] the Spirit, and will act finally in the Second Coming of Christ. The already/not yet tension is similarly present in both themes precisely because both reflect the truth about God's saving, liberating action. Practically, this is a caution against pride and triumphalism and also our source of hope and confidence as we face the future.

5. Finally, when Biblically grounded, *both themes reflect a powerful optimism of grace* which can be a vital motive force for evangelism, social reform, and the building of authentic church life. The dynamism which Timothy Smith points to in his *Revivalism and Social Reform*[47] can become a key mechanism when the holiness and kingdom themes are combined with Biblical integrity. Part of the challenge before us today is to build communities of faith where the hope of the Gospel is soundly grounded in God's holiness and God's reign.

Much more could be said about these themes and about their interaction, but I think this overview identifies the major issues involved and the fruitfulness of accenting and combining these two strands of truth. May God help the church today truly to seek first His reign and righteousness, and to pray in faith, "May Your kingdom come, may Your will be done on earth as it is in heaven." This is the meaning of the holy reign of God.

---

47. Timothy L. Smith, *Revivalism and Social Reform: American Protestantism on the Eve of the Civil War* (New York: Abingdon Press, 1957).

God, Sin, and Salvation in African Religion

JOHN MBITI

There can be no balanced discussion of Christianity or the church in Africa without taking into serious consideration African religion, the religious heritage of the continent. African religion sprouted spontaneously without a founder. In the course of time it provided working answers to the mysteries and problems of life and has been passed down from generation to generation through oral tradition, ritual, ceremonies, dance and a common memory. It colors all aspects of life.

In Christian history, this century could well be described as Africa's mass entry into Christianity. Of course Christianity is not a foreign religion in our continent, having arrived shortly after the death and resurrection of our Lord Jesus Christ. In 1900 there were only 10 million Christians, accounting for 9.2% of the total population in Africa (which in this paper includes Madagascar and other islands). Today in 1988, we estimate a Christian population of about 270 million, or 46% of the population. The southern two-thirds of Africa has become predominantly Christian, while the northern two-thirds is predominantly Muslim. One of the immediate questions which poses itself is: What are the reasons for this rapid expansion of the Christian faith in Africa today? African religion is one of the main contributors to its rapid expansion. Others include the work of foreign missionaries, the work of African Christians themselves, and the use of the Bible in local languages. It was as if African religion had prepared the spiritual ground for the planting of Christianity. It was as if African religion said a big YES to the Gospel of Jesus Christ. It was as if the people heard Jesus saying to them: "I have not come to abolish . . . but to fulfill" (Matt. 5:17).

Statistically, African religion has been on the decrease, as people convert to Christianity (and less so to Islam). In 1900 there were 63 million adherents

---

From *The Journal of the Interdenominational Theological Center* (ITC) 16 (Fall 1988): 59-68. Used by permission of the journal.

of African religion, accounting for 58% of the total population. In 1988 there were about 68 million, or 10% of the population. What statistics do not and cannot show is the strength of African religion. Conversion to Christianity does not mean that the people shed their traditional religiosity and go naked into their new religion. They take their world view, their culture, and their spiritual needs with them into Christianity. Translations of the Bible into African languages use a vocabulary which is loaded with traditional African religion. Furthermore, for African Christians the world of the Bible is not a world of two to three thousand years ago, but a world of yesterday, today and tomorrow.

The impact of African religion is very great, and the statistics tell only a small part of it. It does not require much effort to find plenty of African religiosity in the churches. We can see parallels from the life of the African peoples who were cast into the diaspora in the New World by the rough and inhuman practice of slavery. In spite of their uprooting, in spite of the loss of their languages and the loss of their traditional setting, African religion has remained in their blood. How much more will this be the case for Africans who live in their own setting?

The Concept of God

Every book that sets out to describe African religion says something or other about God. Here I wish to take up the first question of how missionaries and African theologians have considered the relationship between the concepts of God in Christianity and in African religion. As the new wave of missionary activity spread in Africa in the nineteenth and twentieth centuries, the question arose as to whether the God whom the Bible describes, and who is the Father of our Lord and Savior Jesus Christ, is the same God who is acknowledged in African religion. Many of the earlier missionaries were of the opinion that it could not be the same God, and that there should be no mixing of Christianity and heathenism (as many regarded African religion to be). Fortunately this attitude has largely evaporated, apart from some extreme evangelical missionaries who deny that African religion has a concept of the living God.

However, there are serious missionary writers who have admitted or acknowledged that African religion is talking about the same God as the Bible. For example, John V. Taylor, in his *The Primal Vision* (London, 1963), acknowledges that Africa has known God all these millennia. Another major missionary contributor to this debate was Edwin W. Smith, who held the opinion that the same God is at work in the Judeo-Christian tradition and African religion. But while sympathizing with African religion, he sees it on a evolutionary ladder on which Christianity is at the top.

African theologians themselves are more or less agreed that the God whom African religion acknowledges is the same God as in the Bible. At the first conference of African theologians in Ibadan, January 1966, on the theme of "Biblical Revelation and African Beliefs," our final statement expresses clearly that:

> We believe that the God and Father of our Lord and Savior Jesus Christ . . . has been dealing with humankind at all times and in all parts of the world. It is with this conviction that we study the rich heritage of our African people and we have evidence that they know God and worship God. We recognize the radical quality of God's self-revelation in Jesus Christ. . . . This knowledge of God is not totally discontinuous with our people's previous traditional knowledge of God.

One African theologian, Gabriel Setiloane, however, has the opinion that what the missionaries have taught was not the God of the Bible but of Europeans. So he presents this argument in his book *The Image of God among the Sotho-Tswana* (Rotterdam, 1976). Among other things, he argues that by using the name of God, *Midomo,* in the Sotho-Tswana languages, the missionaries "devalued" the traditional Tswana concept of God.

What shall we say to all this?

(a) God is keen to reveal God's self. God is turning to make God's self known to African peoples. They know God, according to their languages. Their names of God reveal a deep set of visions and insights about God as Creator, Father/Mother of all, Giver of Children, Giver of Rain, the Glorious (Shining) one, the one [he/she] who is there now as from ancient of times (Tetekwaframua), the First, the Architect and Originator (Bore-Bore), the Wise One, Watcher of Everything, the Great Eye (Liisoddene), the Deliverer of those in trouble (Luvhunabaumba), the Besetting One (Shikakunamo), etc.

(b) God's revelation does not have boundaries. This knowledge and acknowledgment of God is the foundation of African religion. Within this traditional religiosity there is no atheist. Indeed, this knowledge is so fundamental that the Akan say in a proverb: "No one shows the child God" — that is, even children know God.

(c) Naturally we cannot expect all African people to have identical ideas about God. Each people (tribe) has evolved its own concepts within the framework of its own life. The geographical environment, for example, plays an important role in shaping people's concepts. The Ngombe, who live in the thick equatorial forest, speak of God as *Bilikonda* ("The Everlasting One of the Forest"). For African peoples, nature itself is an open witness to the being of God. So they see and depict God as the One behind the world of nature in all its wonders, mysteries and complexities. The social-political structure also has an influence on concepts of God. Human relationships to God are expressed through prayer, offerings, sacrifices, and spontaneous invocations.

(d) When it comes to the encounter between Christianity and African religion, we affirm that there is only one God who is acknowledged and worshipped in both. The encounter results in a two-way mixing of concepts for the enrichment of the people's religious life. As one African proverb says, "The river is made bigger by the small streams that flow into it." We acknowledge that because of Jesus Christ, Christianity has received a fuller picture of God than is otherwise possible outside.

(e) African Christians who are direct converts from African religion cannot understand the Christian teaching about God without the help of their traditional knowledge of God.

(f) There are gaps in the concepts of God in African religion which emerge in the light of Biblical faith. For example, in African religion there is virtually no notion of the eschatological concepts which are part and parcel of the Christian faith, and there is no talk about the Kingdom of God.

Sin in African Religion

This is another important theme, when we consider the presence of Christianity in Africa. There are practically no sermons which do not mention sin in one form or another. So the question arises, What does this term mean in the context of African religion, since people start from their understanding of this concept within their traditional setting? We shall handle this question briefly.

(a) Many scholars of African religion recognize that what we call sin has first and foremost to do with relationships in the community. In the African framework the community consists of the departed, the living, and those yet to be born. Any breach which punctuates this communal relationship amounts to sin, whatever words may be used for this concept.

(b) While *sin* is a breach of the individual against the corporate community, the community itself cannot commit a breach against God.

(c) In African myths of creation it is told how in one way or another, the paradisal relationship between God and humans was lost. There are many explanations of how this happened, the result of which was humankind's loss of three important gifts: immortality, resurrection (in case death occurred) and rejuvenation upon becoming old. The separation between God and humankind was an ontological and not a moral separation. Humankind did not become a sinner by nature through these acts which brought about the loss of the primeval paradise. There is no *original sin* in African religion, nor is a person born a sinner. A person is a sinner by deed in the context of the community of which the person is a member. *Sinning* is that which injures the philosophical principle of: *I am because we are, and since we are, therefore, I am.*

(e) The breaches of the moral, traditional and spiritual fabric of society have different weights and consequences. One of the most serious levels of relations is in the area of covenants. Breaches of covenants are the most serious form of sin. We can only enumerate some of the many covenants which

permeate African (and/or other) societies. Blood brotherhood and blood sisterhood covenants bind two people and their relatives into ties which are as
strong as the blood ties between biological brothers and sisters. There is an
exchange of blood from both sides, of which some drops may be sucked or
drunk or rubbed into each other's body. This is done in the presence of the
community, at which normally an animal is also slaughtered and communally
eaten.

There are adoption covenants which create child and parent relationships,
the child being already grown up or old enough to know what he is doing; land
covenants, marriage covenants, and covenants which bind people together into
the so-called "secret societies."

(f) *What happens when someone commits what amounts to a sin?* This is a
big question, which we cannot answer in detail. A number of measures are taken
by the community when someone commits an injury to the community.
"Cleansing" ceremonies or rituals are performed by ritual elders, medicine-men,
priests, or diviners. These usually involve the slaughtering of animals (like
chickens, sheep, goats or wild animals) and the use of blood. Thereby the
offender is re-accepted, reconciled, brought close to the other party and to the
wider community.

If the community itself experienced misfortunes like epidemics, locust
invasion, drought, disastrous flooding or famine, it was customary in most
societies to seek help from God. The commonest method was through communal sacrifices and offerings.

To my knowledge there is no concept in which ill-doings (sins) are dealt
with in the hereafter. Just as sin is committed in the present life, so must it be
removed during the present life.

Some Concluding Observations on the Concept of Sin

(a) This is an area which has received very little attention among scholars of
African religion.

(b) It seems that sin in African religion refers almost exclusively to the
area of relations between human beings, with spiritual realities and with nature.

(c) The question of language is extremely important. The English term
"sin" does not always translate precisely into African languages. It is necessary
to analyze these terms in order to penetrate their cultural and social meaning.
For example, in my language, Kikamba, spoken by about 4 million people in
Kenya, the term used by the Protestants is *nai*. The word actually means fever,
malaria, flu. The Roman Catholics use another term, *thavu*, which refers to the
state of being ritually unclean, as for example when a woman has menstruation.
So, when Christians use these two words, are they talking about malaria, fever,
menstruation or *sin*?

Salvation

(a) A certain measure of attention has been given to the theme of salvation in African religion. Among other things, African words which designate salvation receive an analysis which helps to open up the meaning of this term within the African religio-cultural setting. Linguistically considered, the terms for salvation seem to indicate that the concept is intimately related to the physical welfare of life.

(b) Prayers of African religion concentrate on various aspects of *salvation*. The majority of them are petitions, requests, intercessions and invocations for health or healing from disease and barrenness, success (hence salvation from failure) in undertakings, and protection from harm, danger or death. Others are in quest of peace and blessings; there are prayers of thanksgiving for saving acts, such as harvest, childbirth, recovery from danger or sickness. Blessings are often invoked in African societies, generally appealing to God to actualize the contents of blessings.

(c) Sacrifices of domestic and wild animals, as well as offerings, are made in probably all African societies. The basic idea behind this practice is to acknowledge the saving activities of God. In some desperate situations human beings were (and still are) sacrificed, or offered themselves voluntarily to be sacrificed, in order that others may be saved.

(d) In many areas of Africa there are shrines, sacred mountains, woods or forests, rocks or caves which people set apart as places for safekeeping, of refuge, of salvation. People or animals found in such places may not be molested or killed; also nature itself in such places is safe and protected.

(e) God and Salvation: Ultimately, God is the savior of people and all things, since God is their creator. There are many names or titles of God as well as sayings which portray God in saving or salvific activities. For example: God is the Giver of Life, the Giver of Rain or Water, the Protector of the poor (Tutungaboro, as the Barundi call God); the Deliver of those in trouble (Luvhunabaumba, as the Ila of Zambia call God), the Father religion. It absorbs the changes that come upon it, for better or for worse. Some of its concepts and practices become more and more obsolete or out of place. Others get changed to accommodate the changing situation. Some even become universalized through academic studies of African religion outside of Africa. Some of its values have been integrated into modern life and thought, and thus continue to serve a purpose in the lives of individuals and communities. To a great extent, contemporary African Christianity in the southern two-thirds of the continent is benefiting from the religious foundation already laid down through the ages by African religion. It is one of the main sources of doing theology in the African context.

The Holy Spirit

MICHAEL WELKER

"The one upon whom Yahweh's spirit rests is described as one who executes justice and righteousness in favor of the lowly and the poor, and who precisely in that manner acquires great power, who precisely in that manner builds strong loyal attachments."

The Holy Spirit is perhaps the most difficult person of the Trinity to conceive. It is hard even to say what one is talking about when one speaks of the Holy Spirit. The identity of the Holy Spirit is elusive, to say the least. Is it even comprehensible?

The Nicene Creed, setting the standard for many other confessional writings, calls the Holy Spirit "the Lord . . . who with the Father and the Son together is worshipped and glorified." But what are the Creed and the doctrinal traditions which follow it referring to when they speak of the Holy Spirit as *personal?* How can we understand the Holy Spirit as personal if, in accordance with the leading contemporary doctrinal traditions, the Spirit is regarded as the bond of peace or the bond of love between the Father and the Son? How can we understand the Spirit as personal if we regard the Spirit, still more abstractly, as relation — relation between the other two persons of the Trinity and, likewise, between God and human beings?

The difficult question concerning the sense in which the Holy Spirit could be understood as personal becomes considerably more complicated when we recognize that insights into the identity of the Holy Spirit must at the same time give insights into the *realism* of God's presence. In the Holy Spirit, God becomes present to human beings. In the Holy Spirit, the communication of human beings with God becomes reality. Consequently, any doctrine of the Holy Spirit has the responsibility of comprehending the "effective presence of the triune God in the life of the congregation as well as in the life of the

---

Reprinted from *Theology Today* 46/1 (April 1989): 5-20. Used with permission of the journal.

individual members."[1] Still more striking is Karl Barth's formulation in *Church Dogmatics* that "God's Spirit, the Holy Spirit, . . . is God Himself, so far as He cannot only come to human beings, but be in them, and so open up human beings for Himself, make them ready and capable."[2] Oepke Noordmans has spoken explicitly of the "realism of the Spirit."[3]

How can we simultaneously comprehend the Holy Spirit as personal, as a relation or even a network of relations, *and* as condition and fulfillment of the realistic presence of God? This complex of problems poses considerable difficulties to our understanding. Once the challenge is made clear, it is no wonder if, in the end, the only determinate claim made about the Holy Spirit is that the Spirit is indeterminate. Who can complain if we simply fall back on John 3:8: "The wind blows where it wills, and you hear the sound of it, but you do not know whence it comes or whither it goes; so it is with everyone who is born of the Spirit."

But we shall not take refuge in such vagueness. Instead, we shall chart a path that enables us to recognize the increasing determinacy of the statements by which biblical traditions witness to the Holy Spirit. Moveover, we shall provide a way of *conceiving* the impossibility of stereotyping those who have been born of the Spirit. We shall not content ourselves with the sigh: "God is nigh/And hard to grasp."

New insights for systematic theology frequently arise from the traditions of both the New and the Old Testaments. Systematic homogeneity and un-broken continuity need not be attributed to the complex of biblical traditions, but there are systems of connections — even to the very boundaries of canon formation — that make it possible to understand the contents of faith in accord with their many-faceted richness. This approach also proves itself with regard to the task of comprehending the identity of the Holy Spirit.

We shall begin by unfolding Old Testament presuppositions, in whose perspectives the basic traits of the activity of the Spirit can be illuminated. On the basis of these insights, we turn to the forgiveness of sins, showing why this is one of the central themes of the doctrine of the Holy Spirit. Next, we shall seek to clarify the difficult phenomenon of the descent and outpouring of the Spirit. Finally, we will be ready to consider the personhood of the Spirit.

---

1. Thus Paul Jacobs, *Theologie reformierter Bekenntnisschriften in Grundzügen* (Neukirchen: Neukirchener Verlag, 1959), 99.

2. *Church Dogmatics* I/1, 5f. (Retranslated to provide the inclusive language in the original.)

3. *Das Evangelium des Geistes* (Zürich: EVZ-Verlag, 1960), 46ff. Cf. also Eduard Schweizer, *Heiliger Geist* (Stuttgart: Kreuz-Verlag, 1978), 16f. [*The Holy Spirit* (Philadelphia: Fortress Press, 1980)].

I

Claus Westermann pointed out that we first encounter a "fixed, clearly defined, and abundantly attested use" of the word *ruaḥ,* "spirit," in the Old Testament "in the time of Judges in the context of charismatic leadership."[4] Two texts clearly present the dynamic of the working of the spirit.

Judges 3:7ff. reports that Israel, after it has fallen away from Yahweh, comes under foreign domination. Judges 3:9f. says: "The Israelites cried out to the LORD, and the LORD raised a champion for the Israelites to deliver them: Othniel the Kenizzite, a younger kinsman of Caleb. The spirit of the LORD descended upon him, and he became Israel's chieftain. He went out to war. . . ."[5] Yahweh gives the foreign king into Othniel's hands, and Israel has, as it says, "peace for forty years."

The report in I Samuel 11 likewise takes as its starting point a situation of collective powerlessness. The Ammonites are laying siege to the East Jordanian city of Jabesh-Gilead. Its inhabitants are ready to undergo subjection to Ammon: "Make a pact with us, and we will serve you." In response, the king of the Ammonites informs them: "I will make a pact with you on this condition, that everyone's right eye be gouged out; I will make this a humiliation for all Israel." Horrified, the city sends out messengers in search of a deliverer. They come to Saul and tell him of their distress and of the threatening danger. At that point, I Sam. 11:6f. says: "When he heard these things, the spirit of God gripped Saul and his anger blazed up. He took a yoke of oxen and cut them into pieces, which he sent by messengers throughout the territory of Israel with the warning, 'Thus shall be done to the cattle of anyone who does not follow Saul . . . into battle!' Terror from the LORD fell upon the people, and they came out as one man." It seems almost unnecessary to call attention to the fact that Saul routs the Ammonites (I Sam. 11:11).

Both these as well as similar stories (cf. Judges 6:34 and 11:29) report the *descent of God's spirit,* which enables the people of Israel to regain its capacity for action in emergency situations. In dire straits, which are recognized but appear to be unavoidable, a particular person successfully *restores solidarity, loyalty, and capacity for common action* among the people. It is said of this person that the spirit of God came over him or fell upon him, or that he was clothed with the spirit of God. The bearer of the spirit leads Israel out of the situation of fear, lament, and despairing paralysis. The atmosphere is one of "run for your lives," but "they came out as one."

At the same time, the accounts insist that the person upon whom the spirit has come is and remains a human being, not some supernatural being.

---

4. C. Westermann, "Geist im Alten Testament," *EvTh* 41 (1981): 223ff., 225.

5. Except where otherwise noted, Old Testament citations are from the Tanakh, while New Testament citations are from the RSV.

Mention is made of ancestral lineage and family relations, as well as of subsequent death. The process of securing loyalty may well involve a blatant threat ("Thus shall be done to the cattle of anyone who does not follow Saul into battle"). And the entire event which is bound up with the descent of the spirit can have personally painful consequences for the one upon whom the spirit comes. The spirit of God comes upon Jephthah, and he leads the Israelites to victory over the Ammonites. Connected with this event, however, he loses his only daughter (cf. Judges 11:30ff.).

Those upon whom the spirit comes restore public unity and the capacity to act in a situation of acute or chronic need among the people. In I Sam. 11, this restoration takes place by means of an armed contest, but it need not. The securing of public loyalty is effected more subtly in other stories. The most difficult of these are the Samson stories (Judges 13–16). They repeatedly emphasize that "the spirit of God fell upon Samson." What is the spirit of God doing? It comes upon the hero of a series of fabulous stories — a hero who at one moment is presented as a strong and crafty escape artist and lion-tamer; at another, as an unsavory he-man and fomenter of unrest. The stories make no effort to present Samson as an attractive hero. He is a braggart and a provocateur. He alienates his parents by marrying a Philistine, who adheres to her own people rather than to him. He is apparently incapable of learning how to stay out of various scrapes, competitions, and deceitful tricks involving the Philistines, who, according to Judges 14:4b, are ruling over Israel at the time. Yet this very Samson, it is repeatedly said, was driven about by the spirit of Yahweh. The spirit of God came down upon him.

The Samson stories are reactions to the chronic danger posed to Israel by the Philistines. Siegfried Herrmann has provided a striking description. The taking of land by the Philistines

> had preceded that of the Israelites. . . . On the west side of the Israelite territory, in its entire extension coming from the coastal plain, an organized power was gradually built up which pushed its outposts eastward all the way to the mountains. There they necessarily clashed with the Israelites. . . . The charismatic leadership was no longer equal to such a powerful and ongoing danger.[6]

Yet, how are we to understand the "fabulous" reaction of the Samson tradition, which arose "in the immediate environs of . . . Zora (today sar à, 23 km. west of Jerusalem)?"[7]

A military contest is not an option against the superior Philistines,[8] nor

---

6. *Geschichte Israels in alttestamentlicher Zeit*, 2. Aufl. (München: Kaiser Verlag, 1973), 169f. [*A History of Israel in Old Testament Times*, 2nd ed. (Philadelphia: Fortress Press, 1981)].

7. H. Gese, "Samson," *RGG*, 3. Aufl., Bd. 6, 41ff., 42.

8. Cf. ibid.

is a laissez-faire policy of assimilation. In this situation, the Samson stories present the *difficult dialectic of accommodation and distantiation.* Samson's life and his deeds become the official expression of Israel's preservation of its identity until a time comes that would be more conducive to liberation. Samson mediates a double lesson: On the one hand, stay with your own people; do not get mixed up with the Philistines, who are devious and brutal. On the other hand, remember that the Philistine may be strong, but the Israelite is stronger; the Philistine is clever, but the Israelite is more so. The change of identity from Samson the simple-minded dupe to Samson the possessor of superior strength and cleverness goes along with the formation of a differentiated position of public distantiation over against the Philistines: Steer clear of the Philistines; they are dangerous and cunning and are liable to kill. But if an encounter is unavoidable, do not be afraid of them. We are superior to them, if the spirit of God be with us. The ropes of their snares are but strings; one of us can take on a thousand of them.

Without getting into the fantastic exaggerations of the Samson stories, the complex double identity of Samson as the spirit comes upon him provokes the recognition that the early testimonies to the activity of God's spirit are unclear and open to misunderstanding. Ambiguities persist even where a pattern of the spirit's activity can be distinguished. Thus, several texts simply reflect the fact that the witnesses are at a loss in the face of the bizarre transformations that affect a person clearly in the grasp of God's spirit (e.g., I Sam. 19).

The lack of clarity and the ambivalence in the accounts of the spirit's activity are, however, eventually removed. The activity attributed to the bearer of the spirit attains to clearer determinacy, and the spirit of God appears in a way that is definitive. The three most important texts that document this development are found in the Isaianic traditions.

> But a shoot shall grow out of the stump of Jesse,
> A twig shall sprout from his stock.
> The spirit of the LORD shall alight upon him. . . .
> He shall not judge by what his eyes behold,
> Nor decide by what his ears perceive.
> Thus he shall judge the poor with equity
> And decide with justice for the lowly of the land. (Isa. 11:1ff.)

The earliest of Israel's legal codes available to us today already perceived this preferential option for the poor and the lowly in the land as an element of the law. Along with regulations that serve the settlement of legal conflicts, and along with provisions concerning cultic practice, we also find in the law stipulations that have as their content a renunciation of claims for the sake of the poor and the weak. What comes into play here are those stipulations of the law that concern the practice of mercy.

Stipulations that concern legal practice, cultic life, and the practice of mercy together form the functional complex of God's law.[9] To practice mercy is to renounce, in favor of the weak and the disadvantaged, direct maximization of one's own concrete prosperity. As an element of the law, the practice of mercy is supposed to be withdrawn from the domain of merely individual and contingent attitudes. Mercy is to become routine. The result is to be the same as legal regulation is intended to accomplish for judicial process and cultic life.

The early writing prophets make clear that where mercy is lacking, the other elements of the law (the judicial and cultic elements) also degenerate. When Israel does not maintain its sensitivity with regard to the poor and the weak in its midst, it begins to misuse cultic life and to twist the judicial process. That leads to the disruption, collapse, and destruction of the entire society. By contrast, *that society grows stronger in all its functional aspects which allows its poor and its outsiders, with the help of the law of mercy, to reach the general level of the economic, social, and judicial processes of communication and exchange.*

The charismatic leaders, upon whom the spirit of God came, gathered Israel in a situation of *external danger.* They restored Israel's capacity for externally directed solidarity and action. The bearer of the spirit who figures in the accounts given by the texts that now concern us, the bearer of the spirit upon whom the spirit of Yahweh is supposed to rest, overcomes a situation of *internal danger* for Israel.

The danger consists in the open or creeping erosion of an order that does not continually regenerate itself with regard to the weak and the outsiders, and that does not continually procure fresh loyalty. The one upon whom Yahweh's spirit rests is described as one who executes justice and righteousness in favor of the lowly and the poor, and who precisely in that manner acquires great power, who precisely in that manner builds strong, loyal attachments.

We find this same connection in Second and Third Isaiah. The spirit of Yahweh remains upon the one who powerfully extends and executes the justice of the law in favor of the poor and the weak.

> This is My servant, whom I uphold.
> My chosen one, in whom I delight.
> I have put My spirit upon him. . . .
> He shall teach the true way to the nations.
> He shall not break even a bruised reed,
> Or snuff out even a dim wick.
> He shall bring forth the true way. (Isa. 42:1, 3)

The text is explicit that the bearer of the spirit does not choose the usual strategies for obtaining political power and loyalty: "He shall not cry out or

9. See M. Welker, "Security of Expectations: Reformulating the Theology of Law and Gospel," *Journal of Religion* 66 (1986): 237ff.

shout aloud,/Or make his voice heard in the streets" (Isa. 42:2).[10] The servant preserves the endangered and the vulnerable. For that very reason, his judgment is sought out and yearned for. Indeed, he attains universal attention; there is a universal readiness to accept him. He shall extend his judgment to the peoples and into the most remote corners of the world: "And the coastlands shall await his teaching" (Isa. 42:4).

In Isa. 61:1ff., we encounter for the third time talk of the spirit of Yahweh resting upon the one who is sent to bring good news to the poor and to proclaim a year of liberation from slavery.[11] Compared with the other texts, this one contains a more explicit description of the great power of the people in whom justice is established by the bearer of the spirit. This *justice receives its dynamic power from the practice of mercy,* and in turn empowers the people in a way that both radiates outward and attracts others to them. This people will be called "'terebinths of saving justice,'/planted by Yahweh for the divine glory" (Isa. 61:3).[12] The social order of this people attracts foreign peoples, who, without compulsion, turn to the God of Israel (see Isa. 61:6). That leads to politically and even economically positive repercussions for that people which demonstrates exemplary justice, mediating judicial right and the practice of mercy.

By demonstrating a judicial order compatible with the practice of mercy — an order which, in fact, receives its dynamic power from the practice of mercy — a people enjoys more than just internal stability of great vitality and integrative capacity. It also radiates the glory of God externally. It wins the foreign peoples for itself and for its God. In this light, it is important to notice that this text, Isa. 61, is one that Jesus applies to himself in Lk. 4:16ff. And Mt. 12:18ff. explicitly connects Isa. 42 to Jesus and his activity. Jesus is the bearer of the spirit who, in the so-called messianic texts of the Isaianic traditions, still remains individually indeterminate. He is the one on whom the spirit of Yahweh rests and remains. What does that mean? Does Jesus prove to be a symbolic figure around which crystallize political or quasi-political programs that have undertaken to connect judicial right and morality and to build an exemplary social order? And is the bringing to life and carrying out of such a program — worthy of all honor, sympathetic support, and committed involvement — the work of the Holy Spirit?

---

10. I owe this most important insight to Patrick D. Miller, Jr., namely that the text does not talk at all about the usual way of achieving public loyalty by a victim. The servant achieves universal loyalty without any reinforcement by any public as such (that is, without any support by a political or moral power-structure). This has far-reaching consequences for the emergence of the universal public that is centered on the servant and characterized by the freedom and sensitivity of its individual participants.

11. This would be the place to look for the first biblical foundations of a way of talking about the Holy Spirit in terms of liberation theology.

12. *The New Jerusalem Bible,* trans. altered.

II

The way the early charismatic leaders restored loyalty, solidarity, and capacity for action among the people could in fact hardly be distinguished from the usual political and military strategies for procuring loyalty. The bearer of the spirit, on whom God's spirit rests, explicitly distances himself from the traditional, accustomed forms for generating public attention and procuring political loyalty. Isa. 11:1ff. uses the picture of a chopped-down tree to describe the annihilation of the Davidic dynasty and the radical destruction of the previous constitution of political life. The text describes, that is, the historical and political break in the continuity of the life of the people. The bearer of the spirit must start anew, from the ground up, like the sprout which grows out of a stump after a forest has been leveled.

In explicit opposition to the expected political forms for procuring public attention and loyalty, Isa. 42 also specifies the power that radiates from the bearer of the spirit. A slave — not a king — brings judicial right to the peoples. In doing so, he explicitly renounces the customary ways of arousing and binding public attention. He does not "make his voice heard in the streets." Mt. 12:18ff. makes clear reference to Isa. 42 in formulating Jesus' repeated prohibition against making his identity publicly known. Measured by all standards of political success, Jesus fails. Only after his failure, only after even the last of those faithful to him have abandoned him, shall there be no boundaries to his identity becoming public. Only then shall his identity be known without limit throughout the public sphere.

What is behind this emphatic separation from strategies for procuring political and public loyalty? Why does the bearer of the spirit so sharply reject the implementation strategies of all movements of political and moral renewal? How are we to understand the presuppositions and the patterns of behavior that are defined in opposition to political success? What can we make of conceptions that seem to call into question the realistic quality of the activity of the spirit? The answer is that the activity of Jesus Christ, on whom God's spirit rests, is directed toward the forgiveness of sins, redemption from the power of sin.

From the start, Jesus' activity moves on a level and in a situation in which the requisite private and public conditions for establishing justice in all its glory are simply not given. It is a situation in which one cannot even presuppose an effective will for improvement. There is no solidarity, no readiness to demonstrate loyalty, no legal sensitivity.

A powerful sign of the great crisis of our culture and of Christian faith and Christian theology, is the fact that we are no longer capable of understanding the phenomena of sin and the forgiveness of sin. We seem to live in a thoroughly moralized culture, which lumps all types of erroneous behavior together by making them the object of a process of universal moral perception and communication. Deeds are measured on a scale that runs from "evil" to "more evil," from "bad" to "worse." Those who do not wish to accept the limitations of that scale, who insist on specifying particular deeds and patterns of behavior as "sin," cannot hold out against a public opinion formed and continually reformed in our universally moralized culture. Whoever talks about "sin" is suspected of being either a religious functionary who compulsively insists on denying that the world has come of age, or a self-proclaimed super-moralist. However, the battles with those parties have already been fought. As a rule, the expression "sinful" is used today mainly for the slightly excessive consumption of sweets or alcoholic beverages, which, on the basis of either general reasonableness or a doctor's advice, one actually should have left off. That is, talk about sin has become incomprehensible and lost its function.

According to the Biblical traditions, however, sin is not just any instance of an evil deed, and certainly not one which is as easy to regulate or to leave off as a piece of cream torte or a second glass of liqueur. *Sin is, rather, any action or any spreading infection of the sinner's environment which, beyond any immediate wrong that it does, destroys the foundations for positive behavior and prospects for changes in behavior and in the way influence is exercised.* Sin perverts and destroys the forces that render possible a renewal of orientation, not only for the agent but also for the agent's environment.

This is why, according to the Bible, the fundamental form of sin is idolatry, which nullifies the relation with the living God. That means nothing other than that, through sin, human beings are cut off from the source of the renewal of the relations of human life. Through sin, human beings close themselves off to that source; and they block the access of others to it as well. Sin issues in *the destruction of the foundations of regeneration.* Thus, it is a deceitful power, from whose web one cannot be freed by one's own efforts. Because of this, it is senseless simply to bombard sinful human beings with moral appeals and sanctions. Sinful human beings must be seen in their situation of desperate need, a situation which each of us has admittedly helped to bring about, but which has gone out of control. The sinner is a human being who is suffering or threatened by suffering; if not subjectively, then at least objectively.

It may be that we can again become more sensitive to the phenomenon of sin. In ever more pressing and oppressing ways, we experience the fact that we have produced and continue to produce natural and cultural environments that have eminently negative repercussions.[13] Witness the destruction of the global climate by the clearing of the rain forests and the long-term destruction of the social climate by unemployment, especially among black youth. Everyone

13. Cf. N. Luhmann, *Ökologische Kommunikation. Kann die moderne Gesellschaft sich auf ökologische Gefährdungen einstellen?* (Opladen: Westdeutscher Verlag, 1986); M. Welker, "The Self-Jeopardizing of Human Societies and Whitehead's Conception of Peace," *Soundings* 70 (1987): 309ff.; *Kirche ohne Kurs? Aus Anlass der EKD-Studie "Christsein gestalten"* (Neukirchen: Neukirchener Verlag, 1987), esp. 29ff. and 72ff.

shares responsibility for such developments, yet no one wants them; everyone laments them, yet no one thinks he or she can change them. Accordingly, they give us occasion to pose anew the question of the destructive logic of sin.

Liberation from sin is brought by the bearer of the spirit, Jesus Christ, who intercedes prior to the level of our capacity for betterment, be it moral or whatever. That liberation intercedes *before* the forces of public capacity for renewal can be put to the test — and fail. Concretely, Jesus acts to forgive sin by, in the first instance, healing the sick and driving out demons (that is, forces that impair a human being in individually and socially living out his or her life; forces that harm a human being and his or her comrades, endanger them and destroy them, but which neither the one possessed nor those nearby can avert). When Jesus cures the sick or drives out demons, he intercedes in situations in which we see ourselves condemned to helplessness and feel ourselves paralyzed; where patience is of no avail and time does not heal; where the empty phrases by which we seek to assuage and encourage stick in our throat; where one lives between a sense of powerlessness and apathy and outbreaks of anxiety and despair.

Yet, how can the actions of Jesus of Nazareth be more today than illustrations, at best, of the concreteness in which the forgiveness of sins would have to operate? And as for the provision and restoration of freedom and the capacity for action, do we not today most effectively call upon our systems of health care and education? Moreover, do we not still hold in readiness for the intellectually demanding a few utopian schemes and philosophies of "human freedom"? What concrete use do we have for the activity of the bearer of the spirit and for the activity of the Holy Spirit? To answer this question, we must reflect upon what it means for the spirit to be poured out and to descend "from on high."

III

The statement that God's spirit is poured out from heaven upon all flesh seems to set the doctrine of the Holy Spirit worlds apart from contemporary notions of reality and from today's consciousness of truth.

The astrodome-model of the world, in which heaven is the dome that covers the earth, is for us one of the clearest pieces of evidence for the foolishness of the ancients and for the wonderful progress we have made since their time. We are so busy patting ourselves on the back that we easily overlook the fact that from antiquity onward, through all sorts of cultures, and most assuredly in the biblical traditions, the notion of heaven both distinguishes between and binds together several conceptual domains and several systems of reference.[14]

---

14. See M. Welker, *Universalität Gottes und Relativität der Welt. Theologische Kosmologie im Dialog mit dem amerikanischen Prozessdenken nach Whitehead*, 2., um ein Sachregister erw. Aufl. (Neukirchen: Neukirchener Verlag, 1988), 203ff.; J. Moltmann, *God in Creation: A New Theology*

One does, indeed, find conceptions of the material constitution of heaven and earth in the theological tradition that cosmology and scientific research have in fact surpassed Yet, heaven is not only characterized as that space which, from a human perspective, lies "over the earth," or as that which marks off or secures that space. Heaven is also conceived as a complex of powers and un-controllable forces, as the realm that is not amenable to human measurement or arbitrary manipulation, but that at the same time decisively determines life on this earth. Heaven, for instance, supplies and withdraws light and water. Thus, heaven and earth stand in a nonreciprocal relation. The fact that we are dependent upon an incoming supply of light, air, warmth, and water is only one sign and expression of that relation and its lack of reciprocity. Once one abandons the prejudice that ancient cultures were naive or even foolish, one recognizes that even so-called archaic thought makes use of procedures that merit the name of "scientific" in the best sense. Ancient cultures often take complex relations, which they have understood reasonably well, and reinvest them in contexts which they have not yet grasped, but which appear to be analogous. By so doing, they seek to gain insights into reality.

Specifically, knowledge about helpless dependencies upon natural forces and about ways of dealing with those dependencies is employed in order to unlock experiences with social forces to which one sees oneself delivered up. The advent of a windstorm, for example, is uncontrollable and its course and duration are unpredictable. Yet, it can be experienced with the senses. The situation is very similar with the social movements unleashed by the charismatic leaders upon whom God's spirit comes. As in the case of the wind, one wonders in vain why the movement could not be predicted. Why could not the people have been led together previously? How long will the solidarity last? Why does the unity of spirit dissolve again? Yet, the working of the combined social forces is as evident as the force of the wind: Israel goes out as one and defeats its enemies.

To look for analogous structures in these two sets of powers and to ascribe them to one reality shows penetrating systematic consistency. On the one hand, social and historically determinative powers are not subject to arbitrary control; on the other hand, neither are the physical powers of the forces of nature. The one reality to which both sets of powers are ascribed is heaven — which in this view is, of course, not to be understood in a merely naturalistic manner. Heaven is conceived as the location of natural and social powers. Very much in line with this conception, heaven is understood not only spatially, but also tem-porally, as well as in structures we are still far from being able rightly to decipher.

On the one hand, the biblical traditions can overcome a merely naturalistic

---

of Creation and the Spirit of God (San Francisco: Harper and Row, 1985), 158ff.; P. Miller, "Cosmology and World Order in the Old Testament: The Divine Council as Cosmic-Political Symbol," Horizons in Biblical Theology 9 (1987): 2, 53ff.

understanding of heaven. On the other hand, they resist the typically religious divinization of heaven and its powers. This combination is a great theological and scientific achievement. Although heaven is the location from which issue great natural and social powers, heaven is created. And, we must emphasize, it is a natural and cultural creature. Heaven, too, is subject to passing away — though it is relatively permanent and invariant compared to the fleeting, transitory conditions of the natural and political world on earth. Heaven is a creature and no god. Yet, in an inconceivable way, it brings and maintains together forces which on earth are dispersed in space and time. That is, when improbable, inconceivable concentrations of powers and forces come about on earth, the biblical traditions regard what is going on as an activity "from heaven." In many cases, that does no more than give a code name to what is happening. In other cases, however, it opens the way to understanding. The story of the event of Pentecost in Acts and the promise from Joel which is taken up there make this clear, each in its own way.

Joel 3 describes the pouring out of the spirit upon all flesh as the bestowal upon the whole people of the power to unlock the future, which is otherwise inaccessible to human beings.[15] Prophetic powers shall be given to all members of the people, not just to those to whom society normally listens and who determine what is normal, reasonable, and to be realistically expected. The spirit enables men and women, old and young, even slaves of both sexes, to unlock the future which God intends — and to do so with each other and for each other. Likewise, the event of Pentecost gives expression to the phenomenon of God's intentions and actions being made accessible to all human beings. Those who are filled with the Holy Spirit become capable of speaking in a way that can be understood in all the languages of that day. Without an abolishment of the difference of the languages, everybody is able to understand — as Acts puts it — "the mighty works of God."

On earth, human beings are distinguished and separated by languages, races, differences of sex and age, and social stratification. That the spirit is poured out "from heaven" means that such human beings, with each other and for each other, generate a trusting familiarity with God's will, and thus a trusting familiarity with the world, that they never achieve in their normal, finite, concrete perspectives. Although the Pentecost-event leads to a very complex aware-

---

15. "After that,
    I will pour out My spirit on all flesh;
    Your sons and daughters shall prophesy;
    Your old men shall dream dreams,
    And your young men shall see visions.
    I will even pour out my spirit
    Upon male and female slaves in those days." (Joel 3:1ff.)

W. Beyerlin, *We are Like Dreamers: Studies in Psalm 126* (Edinburgh: T & T Clark, 1982), is very illuminating on the difficult expression "Your old men shall dream dreams."

ness and understanding of the world, that does not mean that an indeterminate "fullness of the powers of heaven" has in some numinous way a numinous effect in human beings. Instead, human beings who are laid hold of and filled by the spirit are drawn into that trusting relation which Jesus Christ had to "God in heaven" (cf. Lk. 10f.; John 14f.). They gain that trust in themselves and the world that is given by God, which the New Testament calls being God's "children." The condition of being God's children brings with it the advent of an "inheritance" which includes "earth and heaven." Thus, what is unthinkable in the concrete earthly perspectives of individual human beings, and of societies and cultural circles which are marked off against each other, actually happens here with regard to "the mighty works of God." Successful universal understanding and enrichment, with simultaneous preservation of the multiplicity and variegated nature of life as it is really lived in its concreteness and as it takes on culturally diverse character, is achieved.

Especially in the Pauline writings, we find a striking description of the way in which those who have been given the spirit work together in their poly-concreteness. The spirit apportions to each person his or her particular gift for the general benefit (cf. I Cor. 12). That initiates a plurality of processes of communication that is conducive to the good of the participants in many and various ways. In this process, participants both give and receive benefit. The process transcends all individual and socially objectified conceptions of what would be the optimal situation. For the individual human being, however, the pouring out of the spirit means that he or she stands in a force field, that he or she belongs and contributes to a force field, in which he or she is more and more filled with "the fullness of God" (Eph. 3:19). This is so whether or not it is clear to the person involved. In both manifest and hidden ways, "all things work together for good" for the person, and must do so. From the power of the forgiveness of sin, a continually revitalized life grows in the spirit.

This life is resistant to all experiences of failure, hindrance, and futility. It is supported and strengthened from all sides. It itself works benefits on all sides. And it is itself strengthened in return. From our concrete perspectives, experiences, and scope of expectations, we cannot adequately grasp the multifaceted, reciprocally strengthened and strengthening process of cooperation. Abstractions and the reduction to general principles cannot do justice to the pluralistic concreteness. What can we do in order to come up with equivalents for that to which theological discourse about "heaven" and powers "from on high" seeks to give conceptual expression? One would have to develop in the human sciences the ability to think in terms of field structures, and one would have to render that kind of thinking plausible. Alternatively, one would have to resort to artistic means of representation.

But what speaks against the suspicion that this force field of the spirit, instituted "from heaven," is nothing more than a striking, collective sort of Paul Bunyan story? How does the working of the spirit attain and maintain a weight and a dignity independent of our participation? We shall respond to these questions by turning to the problem of the personhood of the spirit.

IV

Whoever is capable of thinking and of conceiving of a person only as an individual-human center of action will have to come to terms with the fact that the personhood of the Holy Spirit will simply remain impenetrable. If one starts with that representational model, one must stick to those statements of the New Testament that identify the Holy Spirit as the spirit of Christ (e.g., Rom. 8). For if what is at issue is the Holy Spirit as a clearly determinable, individual center of action, if that is what personhood must mean, then one will not be able to point to anything but Jesus Christ. He is the individual-human center of action of the spirit. Supported by the Johannine texts, one will even have to speak of a selflessness of the spirit, for the Holy Spirit does nothing other than give witness to Jesus Christ and direct attention to him: "the Holy Spirit . . . will teach you all things, and bring to your remembrance all that I have said to you" (John 14:26). The spirit of truth "will not speak on the spirit's own authority, but whatever the spirit hears the spirit will speak, and the spirit will declare to you the things that are to come. The spirit will glorify me, for the spirit will take what is mine and declare it to you" (John 16:13-14, trans. altered; cf. 15:26). A consideration of the Holy Spirit of that scope is, of course, not in itself mistaken. However, it offers only a reductionist presentation of the spirit. The reason for this reductionist presentation lies in the orientation on a conception of the person that is one-sided and simplistic.

Specifically, concentration on an autonomous agent who functions as a center of reference in no way provides a sufficient understanding of "person." An individual center of action, even when it is self-referentially regulated and develops self-consciousness, does not yet form a person. Only through a constituted social environment and in exchange with that environment does an individual, self-conscious center of action become a person. One can go so far as to say that it is the unity of that constituted social sphere that makes a person out of a self-relational, autonomously active center of reference,

Following a suggestion of Niklas Luhmann, I should like to use the concept of *resonance* to characterize the social sphere.[16] Only through a domain of

---

16. *Ökologische Kommunikation*, esp. 40ff. By "domain of resonance," I understand a centered plurality of relations of resonance which, beyond their common centering, can be independent of one another and not necessarily in harmony with each other. Nor are they necessarily in harmony with their "center of resonance." The same person can be simultaneously loved and hated, can in the same situation be understood, unintentionally misunderstood, and intentionally misunderstood. Moreover, the harmonized, objective picture of a person can differ from how she or he understands herself or himself or would like to be understood.

resonance does a center of action become a person. This idea calls for a brief explanation. If one does not let oneself be deceived by the ease of representation which is proper to the model of a center of action, one recognizes that a self-referentially regulated center of action can be a completely erratic or a robot-like phenomenon, which does not merit the designation "person." Rather, human beings or autonomously acting centers of social reference acquire traits of personhood only by being formed in multiple webs of relationships, which they center on themselves. Persons, as a rule, to some extent shape these webs, but they are not merely fruits of their own activity. We are, for example, persons by being children of our parents, friends of our friends, colleagues of our colleagues, and contemporaries of our contemporaries. We are persons by standing in interwoven patterns of resonance which we have a hand in shaping, just as we are marked by them. These patterns of resonance are only partially dependent upon our activity. Thus, we remain the child of our parents, regardless of how our attitude toward our family changes. We may, through our development, disappoint our friends, and they may even be totally of one mind in their estimation of our person as it has disappointed them — even when we see things very differently and make every effort to change the external perspectives on us in our favor.

The domain of resonance which constitutes our person is thus only partially under our control, even though it is centered upon us. This domain of resonance is only partially clear to us, even though we are the ones whom the whole thing is centrally about. We cannot fully assimilate the unity of perspectives on us that constitutes our "public" person, as that person is for our environment. On the other hand, we also repeatedly have the feeling that our person has been unjustly treated in this or that remark or demand.

If one wishes to understand the personhood of the Holy Spirit and the otherwise inexplicable biblical statements about the Spirit and the relation of the Spirit and Christ, one must observe the difference between a self-conscious center of action and that personal unity which we are in the *external perspectives* on us (that personal unity which we are in the unity of the domain of resonance which is centered upon us).[17]

The Holy Spirit is to be understood as the multiform unity of perspectives on Jesus Christ, a unity in which we participate and which we help to constitute. The Holy Spirit is thus *Christ's domain of resonance*. The Spirit is the public person who corresponds to the individual Jesus Christ.[18] Nevertheless, one

---

17. Cf. the instructive discussion of the use of the concept of "person" in Alaisdair Heron, *The Holy Spirit: The Holy Spirit in the Bible, the History of Christian Thought, and Recent Theology* (Philadelphia: Fortress Press, 1983), esp. 167ff.

18. See the comparative listing of New Testament expressions in Yves Congar, *I Believe in the Holy Spirit* (New York: Seabury Press, 1983); also the reflections on the "ecclesiological 'we'" in Heribert Mühlen, *Der Heilige Geist als Person. In der Trinität bei der Inkarnation und im Gnadenbund: Ich-Du-Wir.* 3 Aufl. (Münster: Aschendorff, 1966), 190ff.

cannot treat the person of Christ and the person of the Spirit as an indissoluble unity.[19] If one fixes upon the crucified Christ, abandoned by all the world and parted with all resonance, one will have to emphasize the *difference* between the person of Christ and the person of the Spirit. With regard to the crucified Christ, it thus becomes clear that there is no access to God that we can produce and make happen. *God* gives God's Spirit; *God* builds God's church, without the requisite conditions, where the requisite conditions are beyond our control (cf. Rom. 8:27). Indeed, God seeks out our destruction and perversion of all the requisite conditions as the precise location in which to build the church.

The forgiveness of sins is the process that creates the requisite conditions for the unity of human beings with God where those conditions do not exist. On the basis of the forgiveness of sins, the unity of Christ which Calvin so strikingly described comes into effect.[20] Human beings who are freed from sin and the self-destruction to which it leads do not merely passively participate through the Spirit in that event which brings fullness of life to this earth. In the Spirit, they are members and bearers of this event. In the truest sense of the word, they are full of God's power.

These human beings, mutually strengthening each other, constitute the field of Christ's power in the most diverse contexts and situations of life. This power is twofold: it both radiates outward and attracts others to its source. To be one with Christ, to be of Christ's spirit, to be in Christ, to bear Christ's spirit in us — these expressions from the Bible each illuminate one aspect of this differentiated, creative relation of unity. What one sees here is a relation of trusting intimacy with God — indeed, a participation in God — which, at the same time, takes seriously our concreteness and finitude, our frailty and fragility.

The Holy Spirit does not work in a way that bypasses finite human beings, but rather in and with our earthly existence. Precisely because the Spirit works in and through life as it is really lived in its concrete multiformity, it is difficult to distinguish those who are born of the Spirit. They live from the forgiveness of sins. They know that they depend continually upon preservation from the injury and disorientation that they themselves cause. But they are heterogeneous, with a multiformity which characterizes life as it is really lived. They reflect the powers of the heavenly fullness in a way that must appear simply incomprehensible, indeed, seems bizarre. But precisely in this condition, they become the vital force field that the third article of the Apostles' Creed sketches in just a few words. They present that force field for which the promise is intended: "and they will be called 'terebinths of saving justice,' planted by Yahweh for the divine glory."

19. Cf. H. Berkhof, *The Doctrine of the Holy Spirit* (Atlanta: John Knox Press, 1982), 19, 28ff.

20. See W. Krusche, *Das Wirken des Heiligen Geistes nach Calvin* (Göttingen: Vandenhoeck, 1957), 365ff.

Guarding God

SR. MACRINA

(adapted from a story told about Archbishop Andrew of New Diveyevo by one of his spiritual sons)

> It could have been the world's last winter —
> the cold sank its claws into the earth,
> into the bones and heart of the Russian land.
> At the priest's hearth, no room for warmth —
> a flame fought fitfully over the few
> low logs, green and damp at the core.
> The dim lampada hung in the corner
> to light the saints' faces in the darkening room.
> The priest labored with a pen by the lantern,
> forcing his fingers, cramped and numb.
> A knock cracked at the door and in came
> Vera crinkled with snow. The cold within
> her heart, more bitter than what the gale had brought.
> She stamped off snow and then she groaned,
> her low voice cutting deeper than the wolf's hungry moan.
> "Priest, my sister is dead. God did not spare her!
> All of these years we served Him with you.
> We baked your prosphoras, sewed your vestments.
> We served and fed the poor, with less than enough
> left for ourselves. So, God allows her
> this miserable and slow, this painful passing.
> Where is this God, you incense swinger!
> Are the Soviets right? Stalin now works

Reprinted from *Epiphany* 12/2 (Winter 1992): 23-26. Used with permission of the journal and Sr. Macrina.

to build a world based on His absence.
It makes more sense to me than your chants,
you stumbling, smokey, incense swinging *pop*."

When she finally paused for breath he spoke
quietly as if he were the voice of winter's
deep silence resonating in the dark room:
"Calm down, my dear."
   Her fury continued.
"Don't calm me down, priest! Contend with me!
Where is your God? Why has he left us?"
Here she stopped, fighting tears with despair.
"He took my sister when I needed her most.
What can you do with that but swing your censor?
Where is your religion, priest?"

"I serve the one all-powerful God . . ."
"And you are His helpless servant?"
   "Yes."
"When you bury my sister, you should know,
you bury my faith! Try and resurrect it!"

"I am sorry for your sister. I have three dead
to bury tonight in the dark. Prepare her.
Meet me by the forest path an hour before matins.
I will bring this very censor you now curse
and I will swing it and pray for her."

By government decree it was illegal
to bury a body or serve a *pannikhida*.
Vera came dragging the body in a blanket
in a drizzle of rain and freezing sleet.
"Swing your censor, priest!" She shrieked.
"We will see if your God will listen tonight.
We'll see which is stronger, your God or my grief."

"Calm yourself now." He sang in the grave tone,
"Holy God, holy Mighty, holy Immortal
have mercy on us."
   "Where is your God!
On a pink cloud?" She stumbled and sobbed,
dragging the corpse behind the priest,
a procession of two, oblivious to the blizzard.

"Holy God, holy Mighty, holy Immortal
have mercy on us."
      "It's pointless, you fool!
I cannot go further. She's too heavy —
this muck is too deep."
      "Try not to think about it."

"Is that your answer to pain, priest? Where is God?
Tonight we war against society," and she wept.
"We oppose the world, by dragging this body!
This must be Orthodoxy, this stinking corpse."

They made a slow march through mud and ice.
He chanted, she cursed. It seemed to him
she was no human woman pursuing him thus.
Rain and sleet fell and froze on those two.
Ice snapped in his beard and the rope they pulled.
She fell silent at last. He scarcely noticed.
Her words stung stillness from his heart.
What had happened to his faithful old Vera?
Terrible to think that God's presence could vanish
from the human heart; could be snuffed out
like a candle's flame in a drafty room.

"She's emotional, she grieves, she can't rob you,"
he told himself, and tried to pray — no words would come.
"I am a priest! God give me strength and silence."
He fell. "God," he prayed, "don't take my faith!
Leave at least a little so I can continue!"
The bloodiest battle, he knew, is unseen.
Better to be persecuted by the godless state
than by the faithful who've become faithless.
More bitter still the inner battle
when the Lord withdraws leaving darkness and shadow.
"Christ, let them scourge me, but do not leave me."

"I've let her rob me, give me Thy strength.
I must guard myself, and I must defend Thee."

The deep night folded around these two.
No star of hope, no heavenly help
penetrated that pall of poisonous doubt.
One thought came to him: chant the psalm.

Behind him the woman tugged, more fearful in silence.
Weariness was the weight that finally calmed her.
Grief and anger had beaten her and strove now
to master one another. Both fell limp at last.
But she, who'd been ravaged by them, continued.
What else could she do? She dragged and pulled
her sister's dead body, united now in silence
with the priest who chanted so calmly
in the face of rage, grief and silence —
united now, even with night and something beyond weariness.
She did not understand how her very weakness outlived
the devastation of grief. In the pit of wintry hell
her desolate heart began to lighten,
it wept gently, it burned. With what? With peace?

But the priest still swayed, uncertain in the night.
Holiness must be guarded, lest it evaporate.
He had failed to fight for the grace of God,
and she, poor creature, could not help herself.

"Blessed are the undefiled." In the wilderness
his words echoed with accusation, with
a heavenly weight on them. "I am defiled," he thought.
"She defiled me." "Blessed are the undefiled."
"O would that my ways were directed
to keep thy law" and he quietly wept.
"Then would I not be ashamed." He said to himself,
"I am not blessed." "Forsake me not. . . ."
The psalm continued, providing the path
through his trackless night, shaping the unseen
though still he thought, "I am not blessed."
Arriving at last at a shallow grave,
they lowered their load, "earth to earth."
He poured from his censor "ash to ash."
"Blessed are the undefiled." "I am defiled."
He muttered aloud. "I am not blessed."

"But Father," she said, "we are blessed."

Dedicated to the independent Orthodox workers who guard God's presence in
Australia.

Some Further Contributions to the Discussion

Leonardo Boff, *Trinity and Society.* Maryknoll, NY: Orbis Books, 1988.

James Montgomery Boice, *The Sovereign God.* Downers Grove, IL: InterVarsity Press, 1978.

————, *God and History.* Downers Grove, IL: InterVarsity Press, 1981.

Anna Case-Winters, *God's Power: Traditional Understandings and Contemporary Challenges.* Louisville, KY: Westminster/John Knox Press, 1990.

John B. Cobb, Jr., *God and the World.* Philadelphia: The Westminster Press, 1969.

James H. Cone, *God of the Oppressed.* New York: The Seabury Press, A Crossroads Book, 1975.

Kwesi Dickson and Paul Ellingworth, eds., *Biblical Revelation and African Beliefs.* London: Oxford University Press, 1969.

Jean-Marc Ela, *My Faith as an African.* Maryknoll, NY: Orbis Books, 1982.

David Ray Griffin, *God, Power, and Evil: A Process Theodicy.* Philadelphia: Westminster Press, 1976.

————, *God and Religion in the Postmodern World.* Albany, NY: State University of New York Press, 1989.

Gustavo Gutiérrez, *The God of Life.* Maryknoll, NY: Orbis Books, 1991.

Carl F. H. Henry, *God, Revelation and Authority,* Vol. II: *God Who Speaks and Shows.* Waco, TX: Word Books, 1976.

Rosemary Houghton, *The Passionate God.* New York: Paulist Press, 1981.

Peter C. Hodgson, *God in History.* Nashville: Abingdon Press, 1989.

Elizabeth A. Johnson, *She Who Is: The Mystery of God in Feminist Theological Discourse.* New York: Crossroad, 1992.

Major J. Jones, *The Color of God: The Concept of God in Afro-American Thought.* Macon, GA: Mercer, 1987.

Eberhard Jüngel, *God as the Mystery of the World.* Grand Rapids, MI: Wm. B. Eerdmans Publishing Co., 1983.

Walter Kasper, *The God of Jesus Christ.* New York: Crossroad, 1989.

Kazoh Kitamori, *Theology of the Pain of God.* Richmond, VA: John Knox Press, 1965.

Kosuke Koyama, *Three Mile an Hour God.* Maryknoll, NY: Orbis Books, 1979.

Hans Küng, *Does God Exist?: An Answer for Today.* Garden City, NY: Doubleday, 1980.

Catherine M. LaCugna, *God for Us.* San Francisco: HarperCollins, 1991.

Jung Young Lee, *The Theology of Change: A Christian Concept of God in an Eastern Perspective.* Maryknoll, NY: Orbis Books, 1979.

Vladimir Lossky, *The Vision of God.* London: Faith Press, 1963.

John S. Mbiti, *Concepts of God in Africa.* London: S.P.C.K., 1970.

Sallie McFague, *Models of God.* Philadelphia: Fortress Press, 1987.

Jürgen Moltmann, *The Crucified God.* San Francisco: Harper & Row, 1974.

————, *God in Creation.* San Francisco: Harper & Row, 1985.

————, *The Trinity and the Kingdom of God.* San Francisco: Harper & Row, 1981.

Thomas Oden, *The Living God.* San Francisco: Harper & Row Publishers, 1987.

Wolfhart Pannenberg, *The Idea of God and Human Freedom.* Philadelphia: Westminster Press.

————, *Systematic Theology,* Vol. I. Grand Rapids, MI: Wm. B. Eerdmans Publishing Co., 1991.

C. S. Song, *The Compassionate God.* Maryknoll, NY: Orbis Books, 1982.

Justin S. Ukpong, *African Theologies Now: A Profile.* Eldoret, Kenya: Gaba Publications, 1984.

PART III

Humanity within the Fabric of Creation

INTRODUCING THE ISSUE

Human Being in Relation to God

On the television screen flash scenes of ethnic slaughters, an abused child, a battered spouse, a polluted river. Borrowing the words of the psalmist, but in a mood of desperation rather than of praise, we might be tempted to cry out, "What are humans, O God, that you are mindful of them?!"

More broadly we might wonder who we human beings of so many varied ways of life are on this small planet in this vast universe? Or, to put the question in more explicit theological terms, who are we human beings within God's total creation? It is becoming ever clearer that a theological understanding of human beings today must be developed in the context of the growing interdependence of the world's peoples and the interdependence of humanity with its natural environment. Which is to say that humanity must be understood within the context of the whole of creation (not isolated from it), both in terms of human connectedness with this larger social and natural environment and in terms of the distinctiveness of human being in these relationships. Such a view is undergirded by the biblical creation narratives and the nature Psalms (such as Pss. 8, 19, and 104), which focus on human being within the larger picture of creation, as well as by eschatological visions that picture humans transformed within a new or renewed creation, a "new heaven and earth" (such as in Isa. 11, Jer. 32–33, and Rev. 21–22). As perceived in African cultures, it is only in my relations with others that I exist.[1]

In biblical perspective the relation of human beings to the rest of creation is defined in terms of God's love for all creatures and the calling of a people to bear witness to God's care for all of creation. In other words, humans are called to a life of wholeness, which includes care for the creation and participating with others in God's work of mending the torn creation. In this vocation, humans are said to be created in the "image of God." And yet it is all too evident

---

1. See further on this, John S. Pobee, *Toward an African Theology* (Nashville: Abingdon, 1979), 49-51.

that all persons in various ways resist God's calling (in other words, they "sin" and are "fallen," in classical theological terms). Yet the gospel proclaims that in Christ human beings are redeemed, renewed, sanctified, and called to share in God's work of transforming creation. But these themes must be understood concretely, and not just in abstract, general affirmations. More specifically, today they must be understood in relation to the protection and nurture of creation, the liberation and fulfillment of life, and the struggle to overcome violence and protect human dignity.[2] In addressing these issues, a theological understanding of humanity must be developed in relation to insights gained from the human sciences and philosophical anthropology as well as from wisdom traditions of native peoples.

Because Christians see in Christ what human beings are meant to be and are formed to be in God's grace, a Christian perception of human being and becoming is essentially christologically oriented, even when it must take account of the distortion that occurs through sin and acts of inhumanity and self-destruction. But in view of Christ, there can be no giving up on humanity nor resigning ourselves to attitudes of fatalism, despair, and hopelessness.

The contributions in this section weave various strands of a developing theological vision of human life in relation to the wider creation. From the Pacific Islands, theologian Keiti Ann Kanongata'a draws from women's experience and stories a vision of "birthing," of giving birth to new life that resists violence and oppression. She urges women to take more of a leadership role in the home and in church and society. She calls for women to acquire more education, to promote self-development, and to make a creative contribution to changing life in the Pacific region. She grounds this vision in Jesus' aim to liberate all people, including women, to share in the transformation of life in the power of God.

The native American Christian theologian George Tinker integrates insights from wisdom traditions of native American peoples with the biblical witness in developing a vision of the integral interrelation of humanity with the larger creation and the calling of humanity to help maintain balance and harmony in creation. He contends that a more holistic understanding of creation does not diminish human beings but provides a theological basis for understanding how human health and wholeness are tied to healing the wounded creation.

Tiina Allik points to the foundations of transformation in the biblical accounts of God's creation and blessing of humanity and the calling of both women and men to share in realizing their full potential as human beings. It is

2. See e.g., Janet Crawford and Michael Kinnamon, eds., *In God's Image* (Geneva: World Council of Churches, 1983); Mary Amba Oduyoye and Macimbi B. Z. Kanyoro, eds., *The Will to Arise* (Maryknoll, NY: Orbis Books, 1992); and José Comblin, *Retrieving the Human* (Maryknoll, NY: Orbis Books, 1990).

particularly in the human capacity for self-transcendence that she sees the creative possibility of human beings to shape their biological and social instincts and drives into a mutually supportive life together. But often, she notes, the creative contribution women can make to the development of such life has been denied or hampered. Yet feminists disagree among themselves about how to forge a more creative role for women in society and in the church. Allik contends that the dependence of human beings on cultural systems and social environments and their ability to creatively shape and reshape these underscore human finitude, but at the same time provide women and men a more realistic awareness of their creaturely limitations and their capacity for working together in expressing the image of God.

Evangelicals believe that such a hope is optimistic and is bound to be disappointed if it does not take seriously that human nature has been radically distorted through the fall. In their view Scripture clearly teaches a doctrine of original sin, transmitted and inherited from generation to generation, which vitiates even the best and highest of human intentions and actions. Though evangelicals differ over precisely how the transmission of original sin occurs, whether more biologically or historically and socially, and how it is related to divine providence and human freedom, they believe not only that the doctrine is firmly grounded biblically but also that the reality of original sin is all too evident in daily life. The undeniable fact of the universality of sin seems to them to lead to such a doctrine. From a Wesleyan perspective David Parker undertakes a careful critical examination of Calvinist, Arminian, and some contemporary evangelical interpretations of original sin and guilt and concludes by proposing a revision of the doctrine that he believes is more in line with biblical teaching concerning the universality and contagion of sin and yet preserves human responsibility and the possibility of redemption.

Stanley J. Samartha of the Church of South India broadens the discussion of a theological understanding of human being to include the plurality of religions and cultures and the shared struggles of peoples across cultures for justice and peace. He focuses the discussion in terms of the relations of the northern and south hemispheres, suggesting that this is not only a geographical concept but has to do even more with attitudes and ways of exercising economic and political power within the world community. At the same time he recognizes that new alignments of peoples and nations across this division are emerging, and he contends that what is ultimately at issue is not a contest between northern and southern hemispheres but the well-being of all the peoples of the earth. Christian theology, he argues, must enter into interreligious dialogues if humanity is to survive. He believes that Christian theology can bring to such dialogue out of its Jewish roots a concern for peace envisioned as just relations among humanity, nature, and God, as this is focused in Jesus' ministry and enactment of *shalom*. Such peace not only has inner, personal but also social and even cosmic dimensions.

This peace also has important implications for greater ecological responsibility, emphasizes Dr. Kwok Pui-lan, a Chinese theologian teaching in Hong Kong. She sees the ecological crisis and the mistreatment of women and children as linked with the increasing industrialization of the Third World. Women and nature are exploited and subjected to experimentation and exhaustion. To counter this, she suggests moving from a hierarchical model to an ecological model in which God, humans, and nature are seen as interrelated and are treated with respect and honor.

From an African context Evaristi Magoti urges that an understanding of human beings must not overlook how we face death. Unlike Western views in which death is marginalized or seen as but the transition of the individual soul to the afterlife, African customs emphasize the interconnectedness of all created reality, the plenitude of life, and God as the giver of life. Death signifies not simply an individual event but rather entering in a new way into the life of the larger community of creation, as an ancestor, and thus into its ongoing life. Is this not also, Magoti asks, what occurred with Jesus? His death signified God's decisive struggle with and overcoming of the powers of evil and the giving of life in and through the larger community of creation that derives from him. Jesus dies both the death of the blessed and the death of the sinner; thus he is able to be with those who die and to give them hope even in their dying.

A Pacific Women's Theology
of Birthing and Liberation

KEITI ANN KANONGATA'A

Women's Stories

In the past three years I have been involved as a facilitator and resource person in a number of workshops and consultations with women in the Pacific. In these meetings the main input was stories of women themselves. These meetings were an opportune forum for the women to tell their stories . . . their stories of "days gone by," of today, and their dream-stories for the future. I have been privileged to be a listener to these stories told by women from practically all the islands in the Pacific. It has been a moving picture of life experiences — of their happiness, their sorrows, their land, their relationships, their food, their clans, their cultures, and so forth. Our stories are ourselves!

Now there is a need for us to try to read more into our stories and to discover how they become the raw material for a women's theology in the Pacific. Collectively, the image that our stories project is that of *birthing. The Pacific woman is emerging from a life of confinement in a womb to a new world of complex realities.*

Our stories tell of our traditional life in the past, which is still part of our present. It is likened to a life in the womb. There is life and potential for growth, as well as security and warmth. But life in the womb is also characterized by confinement and limitation. Our world has been a small one, a village on an island. The traditional practices, the cultural taboos, the technical know-how, the social bondings and social activities or responsibilities — all of these have

Reprinted with permission from the *Pacific Journal of Theology* 7 (1992): 3-11. *The Pacific Journal of Theology* is published by the South Pacific Association of Theological Schools, based in Suva, Fiji.

been part of the "womb" experience. Women have had well-defined roles as homemakers and homecarers. Women have always been under the leadership of men.

Today we are in a process of birthing. To stay forever in the womb would be fatal. For growth toward respect for women as persons, birthing needs to happen. As the island Pacific expands its horizons and opens its doors to the outside world, many changes and challenges are arising. The Western way of life, the monetary economy, advanced technologies, the impact of world events, new religious beliefs and cultural norms, the push to expand one's horizons — all these opportunities are faced by the emerging Pacific woman in an emerging Pacific society.

Birthing is a time of excitement as well as tension. To meet the challenges of our "new world" we begin to plan and envision. We begin to dream dreams, and to hope. However, our dreams must be based on the realities faced at the time of the birthing process. We have to reach for the stars with our feet planted well on the earth.

As women of the Pacific have reflected on their present status in recent regional gatherings, this is in essence what they have said:

- The pace of growth for and by women in the Pacific is but a *crawl* for the majority of women. A good number are dragging their feet coming out, or trying to hold onto the walls of their "mothers' wombs," and only a handful of women are coming out boldly amidst great challenges. Among the challenges facing women are domestic violence, breakdown of family life, unemployment, child neglect, alcohol abuse, sexual abuse and even malnutrition. The handful of birthing women need to extend helping hands to those behind, while those behind need to exert more effort to come out into the world.
- Concerns about lack of assertiveness or need for affirmation need to be addressed before women can seek employment outside the home, or be able to publicly lead the community.
- There is a need for education at home, to understand cultural values and norms, the reasons behind traditional taboos, and communication mis-understandings between members of their families and clans. Gathering strength through working together, as well as talking about problems and not hiding from them would certainly enhance the resolution of conflicts and free women from constraints. Women need to understand that God has granted them the ability to learn.
- The cited abuses are impacting negatively on family and community relationships and the quality of life. The root causes of the abuse of women may be the weakening of the feeling of closeness between husband and wife, the husband being unemployed, inadequate family life education, no role models or known guidelines for young families to follow, and lack

of understanding on the part of family members about their roles as spouses, parents and community members.

Women's Identity

To be able to proceed with the birthing process it is necessary to take a closer look at the woman-person in this journey of life. The women of the Pacific are not just "women." They are "persons" as well. Traditionally, however, our women have been regarded as derivative. They have been considered "natural followers" rather than leaders, supporters rather than administrators, dependents rather than providers. Even when they are praised, it is usually in terms of achievement in an ancillary role. This anthropological point of view frequently is justified by turning to a literal reading of the creation account in Genesis 2 (the rib narrative), never the account in Genesis 1, where equality in creation is undeniable. The woman is referred to as the "weaker sex" in need of protection or direction. She is the man's helper, his "right hand," merely an extension of himself, enjoying little identity apart from him.

Women's lives, then, are defined by relationships. More often than not, women are first identified as daughter of, sister of, wife of, mother of, widow of, etc. Only secondarily are women identified by what they do — homemaker, weaver, teacher, nurse, etc. In contrast, men are defined primarily by their titles and what they do. Only secondarily are men defined by their relationships — father, husband, son. Neither of these approaches is adequate to express the fullness of a person's life. Women are workers as well as relational beings. So are men. Yet, stripped of the husband's name and title, stripped of the parents' names and titles, naked, Pacific women are considered leftovers, even though they are unique individuals.

To value the personhood of women is to see them in all their potential and uniqueness and not in terms of their functional usefulness only. Within the churches this means we should be encouraging men and women to find concrete ways of valuing each other for what they are and not just for what they do biologically or socially.

Today Pacific women are beginning to take a new look at themselves. We are acquiring insights into our authentic ability to do things and decide things as *women*. But this approach has been lacking in both society and church. It is in these settings where we feel most confined, where we feel most restricted, that we are beginning to question the appropriateness — even the justice — first of the situation itself and then of its underlying presuppositions. This explains why those who suffer oppression or who are relegated to marginality or invisibility within a society are sometimes better critics of that society than those who are privileged. This latter group, the privileged group, frequently takes its privilege for granted and does not question its appropriateness. We as restricted, confined Pacific women now have to develop truly women's insights that are expressed in values of wholeness, positiveness and non-violence. We must own our womanhood.

Doing Women's Theology

The prerequisite for doing theology is to have faith and a reflective mind. Theology is within the reach of ordinary Christian women, and they must be encouraged to do it — to think theologically about the new and old questions which arise from our special situation of birthing from the womb. Out of these questions are emerging new images and themes for a Pacific women's theology, including the image of the Womb and the theme of liberation.

The Womb of God

Women theologians are seeking to recover the word *rehem (womb)* to express the relationship between the womb and God's mercy.[1] God's maternal womb enables our birthing to come about with force and firmness but also with creativity and gentleness, without violence.

Once God is experienced not only as father, Lord, or strong warrior but also as mother, protecting and loving, struggle is tempered with festivity. God's compassion as flowing from a female, maternal source takes into itself the hurt and wounds of all the oppressed. God as Mother sides with those unfairly excluded from society and church. The tendency to exclude women from certain societal and church circles is not a male monopoly. Women, too, discriminate against their own. Thus we must be cautioned. God's preference is not for women as such but for the oppressed, regardless of who is oppressed and by whom. *A woman who does theology is called to bear witness to this compassionate, inclusive God with her body, her actions, her life.*

Women for Liberation

As Pacific women do theology they become more sensitive to the crucial issues in their present situation. Both women and men are called to be partners in establishing communion among all people in the Kingdom, whose structures foster justice, peace and love. The church is the community of all who are one in Christ. Therefore all its members are supposed to be one as Jesus and God

---

1. The Hebrew word *rehem* (womb) resembles another word, *rahmim* (bowels), which is often employed to express the mercy shown by God.

are one, a unity primarily of personal relationships and not merely an administrative unity, a hierarchical and structural unity. Today the structures of most churches in the Pacific deprive women of equal participation.

But the liberation struggle of women in the Pacific is not a struggle for supremacy. For there are neither superiors nor inferiors. All are equal. It is a struggle for the liberation and growth of all humanity, to bring about communion amongst all forms of life.

Turning to Luke 10:41-42, we learn that Jesus lived in a society whose culture prescribed a subservient role for women. But Jesus goes beyond the superficiality of the norms set by human beings. He breaks the barrier of gender. His coming is a call to women to enter into communion with him, to be his disciples and to be fully liberated. He loves and respects Mary and discourses with her. Jesus and Mary had the courage to break the shackles which bound women to an inferior position in society.

Today we need to hear more the call for inner liberation, both as rebirth of selfhood and as an organization of women's relationships with other women, men and the socio-cultural systems in which they live. The realization of self and the experience of God within lead to an internal transformation which in turn generates a new relationship with others beyond the current socio-cultural patterns of thought, feelings, attitudes and behaviour.

It was a woman who had the courage, sensitivity and love to honour Jesus with expensive ointment. This woman was not supposed to appear in public in her male-dominated world and speak to Jesus. But she dared. She honoured him in public. This woman challenged the structures of society which kept people in a relationship of domination/subordination. And Jesus supported her. Women are called by Jesus to take the initiative in challenging values and transforming exploitative structures.

It is not only women with special education or abilities, or religious women only, who are called by Jesus to liberate themselves and bring about liberating communion in the church and society, but all women without distinction, especially the most ordinary. The untouchables of society, illiterate women from the slums and the rural areas, the destitute, the raped and the prostitute, all are called by Jesus for the great task of communion.

Our hope for liberation lies in the fact that Pacific women have, to a greater extent, become sensitive to their local realities. Hence they are no longer silent, but are becoming aware of their personhood and rights and are organising themselves and protesting against the increasing violence meted out to them on account of their gender. Our civil and church authorities, who are generally men, are beginning to realise that women can no longer be overlooked but are a force which has to be reckoned with. Not only are women becoming more concerned with issues specific to themselves, but also with problems of wider significance, such as inadequate education, poverty, exploitation of the poorer classes in society, nuclear proliferation, militarism and ecological concerns.

While these are some of the issues actively addressed by the secular women's movement, Christian women in the Pacific are only now just beginning to make efforts to work along with secular women's groups and women of other faiths, and to recognise the above concerns as their own. Christian Pacific women *still need to realise that their identity as Christian women will have meaning only when they are able to go beyond narrow loyalties to participate totally in God's liberating action in the world today.*

In the religious sphere, women of the Pacific must address urgently two prominent religious issues: (1) the development of a theology of humanhood which recognises all individuals as equal with equal access to freedom, justice and peace; and (2) the struggle for the ordination of women, which is not possible at present in most Pacific churches.

An Emerging Women's Spirituality

Our personal and social experiences as Pacific women have shaped a particular form of spirituality which is emerging among us. This spirituality is nourished by our growing understanding of our self-image as birthing people. It is a spirituality that is joyful rather than austere, active rather than passive, expansive rather than limiting. It celebrates rather than fasts, it cooperates rather than controls, it is creative rather than conservative. Our spirituality is a process. It is not achieved once and for all, and we are always working on it.

The emerging spirituality of Pacific women promises to be vibrant, liberating and colourful. Its direction and tendencies seem to open up to greater possibilities of life and freedom and therefore to more and more opportunities to be truly, intensely and wholly alive!

Journey toward the Future

We are telling and hearing our stories, and they are beginning to make their vibrations felt in groups and individuals around the Pacific. At present we are beginning to be conscious of ourselves, but we also have to assess ourselves and work more intentionally toward inner and outer liberation. It is up to us now to recognise both our blessings and our brokenness, and to identify ourselves with our sisters living on the bottom of the "hierarchy pyramid." We are the "woman bent double" in the Gospel who was freed from her bondage and empowered to stand upright. We can break through the power of slavery, domination, exploitation, misunderstanding, and so on by identifying ourselves as women deformed by society and church. Only when we recognise the "woman bent double" in our midst will we be able to articulate theologically a vision of God's salvation and community that allows all women to become free from dehumanization.

In the quest for liberation, all — men and women — have a role to play. Women need liberation not to become like men — oh, no! — but to participate in the life and the work of the community, bringing to it a distinctive contribution. We have a special prophetic role, not only of creating a new awareness but also of promoting a people's movement. The real force for change must come from such a movement, particularly from women and others who are oppressed. Just as true liberation from economic and political oppression comes from the poor, liberation from the male domination of culture will come from oppressed women.

The whole of humanity is being challenged at the core of its existence. The modern materialistic society seems to necessitate a new radical alternative. Humanity needs more of the feminine intuitiveness, compassion and gentleness. There is also a need for dialogue. Dialogue in this sense means not just a verbal exchange of words, not a discussion or debate, but a process of entering into the world of the other.

To theologise our life in the Pacific, in a visionary way, means to fashion an alternative way of living in the world. This is a way of covenantal responsibility, a way of living known as the Reign of God. This way of living involves transformation of our minds, our hearts, our patterns of behaviour and our social systems. It calls for a total *metanoia.* This task before us is monumental.

Our churches need not be afraid of us. We are not an object of fear, but a bearer of hope and prophecy. We see in Mary, the mother of Jesus, a model of this new type of woman for the Pacific. Not only Mary in Nazareth or Bethlehem, but Mary on Calvary, Mary at the resurrection, Mary who not only hears the Word of God and treasures it in her heart, but Mary who also does it!

III.2

The Integrity of Creation: Restoring Trinitarian Balance

GEORGE E. TINKER

We live in a crazy and dangerous time. We are destroying God's creation at such an alarming rate, polluting the earth's waters and air, and at the same time inventing ever new and ever more brutal ways to oppress greater and greater portions of the earth's human population, ways more devastating than ever known before. We are told that ten percent of the world's rain forest is being destroyed, cut, cleared every year. Within fifteen years this regenerative source of the earth's oxygen supply will be completely destroyed. And even as this craziness continues, it has precipitated a new oppression of Indian tribal people in the jungles of Brazil and elsewhere, from whence come today a stream of reports of massacres and genocide. As if that were not enough, we live with the constant terror of violence and war, under the nuclear threat of total annihilation. It is in this context that we must consider the "integrity of creation" and the World Council of Churches' programme on Justice, Peace and the Integrity of Creation.

In times of crisis, the church has always been constructive and vital in its theology, and not protective or defensive. The modern crisis calls upon all of us as the church to respond with all our gifts of creativity, to think through theological issues in ways that will enable us all to image ourselves in new ways of being together as the church; new ways of experiencing God's salvific grace that is ours in Christ Jesus; new ways of proclaiming God's cry for justice; and ever new ways of implementing God's reign of peace in our threatened world. A reassessment of our theological reflections on creation is vital for our response.

The argument of this essay is that an adequate theology of creation becomes the indispensable foundation for the pursuit of justice and peace, that the resto-

Reprinted with permission from *The Ecumenical Review* 41 (Oct. 1989): 527-36.

ration of Trinitarian balance requires a strong and well-articulated affirmation of the first articles of the ecumenical creeds. Moreover, we will argue that an adequate theology of creation must include a theology of nature, that is, it must address the sacredness of all in the world and our relation as human beings to that all. If we can affirm the sacredness of the natural world, if we can begin to live our affirmation, if we begin to experience the world, including one another, as sacred, then God's demand for justice must become a vital and consuming concern. And God's desire for peace built on justice will then become our passion as well.

Integrity of Creation and Intercultural Dialogue

The death culture swarms
over the land bringing
honeysuckle eucalyptus palm
ivy brick and unfinished wood
torn from the forests to satisfy organic
craving. The death society walks
hypnotized by its silent knowledge
nor does it hear the drum quiet
to the core.
The trees know.
Look.
They are dying.[1]

As we in the World Council of Churches address this modern crisis of all of creation, it is most important that we be more open than ever before to one another in our cultural and denominational diversity. The West has much to learn from the East; just as the North has much to learn from the experiences and theological reflections of sisters and brothers in the South. In particular, if we are to be most creative, the voices of those who have not usually been heard, those who have usually been excluded from a share in the power of decision-making at policy and theological levels, those who have been regularly marginalized, their voices must be heard, lest anything be overlooked. The voices of indigenous peoples, tribal peoples, what we must call the fourth world, may have the most precious contribution to offer first- and second- and third-world people in this discussion.[2] As an American Indian, this author writes from the

---

1. The opening lines of Paula Gunn Allen's poem "Los Angeles, 1980," from her book of poetry *Shadow Country* (UCLA: American Indian Studies Center, 1982), 39.
2. In another context I have argued that indigenous peoples ought to be called first-world. Logically and morally this would begin to acknowledge their claims of priority in the lands where they have been violently subdued and shoved aside. "Does All People Include Native People?" in *God, Goods and the Common Good*, ed. Charles Lutz (Minneapolis: Augsburg, 1986), 125-36.

fourth-world perspective, the perspective of the poorest and most oppressed peoples of North America and indeed of all the Americas. This essay, then, must also be understood as a contribution from the indigenization of theology.

The particular gift of Native American peoples (and of other indigenous peoples) is an immediate awareness and experience of the sacredness and interdependence of all creation. American Indian cultures are rooted in the earth and particularly in tribally specific lands that have always been the foundation of Indian religious experience. Tribes suffer even today from the trauma of forced separation from their land base — the injustice, the dislocation, the resultant disruption of health and well-being, both spiritual and social. Yet, Native Americans still experience the world as sacred and still sense their own interrelatedness with all in the world. Whether traditional or Christian, this is their Native spirituality; and Native people are convinced that their spiritual insights may contribute much to the understanding, theologies, health and well-being of others in the world, especially to those who symbolize the source of their oppression.

In the JPIC process that will lead to the WCC convocation in Seoul in 1990, as we open ourselves to this dialogue, we may even find ourselves in our creativity returning to some very ancient and traditional ways of imaging the gospel that take us back to the origins of Christianity.

The First Shall Be the Last: Christomonism and the Loss of Creation

Christomonism, in the respectable form of the varieties of "fall/redemption" theologies of our different communions, appears to be the dominant heresy of our age, if I may be permitted a less pejorative and more neutrally descriptive use of the word *heresy*.[3] It certainly is the dominant theology, in practice at least, of many mainline denominations in the United States, and it provides us with a metaphoric language of salvation with which we have become most comfortable. My own denomination is a case in point.

The Evangelical Lutheran Church in America began its life on 1 January 1988, as the culmination of a several-year process. The merging churches formed a joint commission in 1980 to draft a proposed constitution for the new church body. Meeting two or three times a year, the commission generated several drafts of the constitutional document, each one with an ever-longer

---

3. From the Greek word *haeresis,* which Liddell and Scott define broadly as: taking choice, election, purpose, condition and more narrowly as a "system of philosophical principles, or those who profess such principles, sect, school." This in distinction from Webster's definition of the English word: "an opinion contrary to the orthodox opinion." In light of the work of Walter Bauer (*Rechtglaubigkeit und Ketzerei im ältesten Christentum*, 1934), and the rise of the ecumenical movement in the last one hundred years, we might be well advised to recover this more ancient use of the word as "school of thought."

"Statement of Purpose." That purpose statement became a wonderful laundry list directing the church's concern for advocacy for justice and peace for the poor and oppressed; spiritual nurturing of one another; and for evangelical outreach to all those around us in the world. It is, however, the first item on that list to which I wish to draw attention. No matter how good or long or inclusive the list becomes, it is always the first item that implicitly predicates the foundation for the rest of the list. It becomes the starting point for understanding the whole mission of the church, the starting point for the church's theological understanding.

From the first draft until the next to the last, the top of the list always began: "The purpose of this church shall be: A. To proclaim God's reconciling act in Christ Jesus." Now we may quibble from church to church over the wording of this affirmation. But surely few of us would question the importance of this proclamation of the self-identity of Christianity as the unique contribution of Christianity to the salvation of the world. At least in some degree it begins to articulate what is perhaps the central doctrine of Christianity for most of our churches and certainly for Lutheran churches. In one way or another it is the centrality of Christ's reconciling death and resurrection that marks each of our churches as Christian and binds us together in ecumenical dialogue and ministry in the World Council of Churches.[4]

Yet it is still appropriate, at both theological and sociological levels, to challenge the propriety of even so central a doctrine, and especially so when we are challenging not so much the doctrine itself but its relationship to other teachings and the systematic framework into which we have placed it. For even so central a doctrine does not live a life of its own, but necessarily functions in a variety of ways depending on the larger structure of which it is a part.

The immediate question before us is *not* whether we will affirm such a proclamation or its centrality to our Christian faith. The question is whether this is the appropriate *starting place* for a church's theological reflection. And concomitant questions will ask how the proclamation thus functions, and how it might otherwise function. The argument put forth here for discussion is: any structuring of theology that *begins* with "God's reconciling act in Christ Jesus" violates the traditional Trinitarian confession of Christianity and hence tones down the significance of doctrines of creation.

At an obvious level, to make the Christ event the starting point is to circumvent the First Article of the ancient ecumenical creeds and to begin with

4. For a structurally similar prioritizing of Second Article proclamation see the Preamble (paragraph 2) of "The Constitution of the United Church of Christ," 1984 edition. It begins: "The United Church of Christ acknowledges as its sole Head, Jesus Christ, Son of God and Saviour." So much for Trinitarian confession or the priority of First Article/creation proclamation. The U.S. Presbyterian constitution likewise begins with a section proclaiming the headship of Jesus Christ: "The Head of the Church," *The Constitution: Presbyterian Church (USA). Part II: Book of Order, 1983-1985* (New York, Offices of the General Assembly, 1981), ch. I:1, 13.

the Second Article. To some extent it could be argued that Creation/First Article concerns are not necessarily ignored but merely delayed in their consideration in favour of emphasizing the more central and more unique aspect of Christian faith. Certainly all our churches voice theological assent to the First Article of the creeds and give theological support to the doctrines of Creation embedded there. The point here is how we address those concerns and with what priority. It should become clear that first Article/Creation concerns are indeed devalued when their priority is deferred in favour of more immediate, first-place consideration of a "fall-redemption" category.

In quite a different way we can argue that the reaffirmation of Creation/First Article as the appropriate starting point for theological reflection becomes a much more affirming and constructive way to begin the proclamation of the gospel in the context of many indigenous cultures. My Native American ancestors had a relationship with God as Creator that was healthy and responsible long before they heard of God's reconciling act in Christ Jesus. To make fall/redemption the beginning point in theological proclamation generates traumatic experiences of spiritual and emotional dislocation for American Indians which some people survive and many do not. To the contrary, when that proclamation is put in the context of affirming what Native American peoples already know about God as Creator and all of creation as sacred and good, it can generate a genuinely healing and life-giving response. Moreover, from a Native American perspective, the affirmation of God's act of creation and the sacredness of all that has been created necessarily results in respect for all that is, in particular respect for one another in relationships marked first of all by justice and ultimately in relationships of harmony and balance that are a true experience of peace.

Moreover, at a functional level this devaluing of Creation/First Article concerns can have some striking consequences, consequences that are evidently little understood in middle-class, first-world churches, and perhaps in many others as well. But among Native Americans, and I suppose other fourth-world indigenous peoples, Christomonism can function in ways that heighten the inherent oppression and desperation and contribute to the process of internalization.

American Indians continue to suffer from the effects of conquest by European immigrants over the past five centuries. We live with the ongoing stigma of defeated peoples who have endured genocide; the intentional dismantling of cultural values; forced confinement on less desirable lands called "reservations"; intentionally nurtured dependency on the federal government; and conversion by missionaries who imposed a new culture on us. All this has resulted in a current situation marked by a dreadful poverty not usually associated with the United States in the minds of the international community. More to the point, its pervasive result is a depreciated level of self-esteem which all too readily internalizes any missionary preaching which intends first to convict people of their sin. Unfortunately, by the time the preacher gets to the "good news" of the gospel, people are so bogged down in their experience and internalization of brokenness and lack of self-worth that too often they never quite hear the proclamation of Good News in any actualized, existential sense. Both in terms of intrinsic Native American values, then, and in terms of Native American sociological and psychological realities a fall/redemption starting point is singularly unhelpful, while a First Article/Creation starting point would form a natural bond with indigenous cultural roots.

So the argument to this point is perhaps twofold. On the one hand a proper prioritizing of First Article/Creation concerns will enable the churches to appreciate and value the inherent spiritual gifts that many cultures, especially indigenous, tribal, fourth-world cultures, bring with them to Christianity, to their acceptance of the gospel of Jesus Christ. More than that, it would re-establish our own spiritual base for pursuing justice and peace. Secondly, this new appreciation for the spiritual insights of indigenous peoples can both lead us back to a stronger affirmation of the priority of creation in our oldest confessions and on to a new understanding of how that confession can function for healing and reintegration in a modern, disintegrating world. We will discover that respect for creation can become the spiritual and theological basis for justice and peace just as it is the spiritual and theological basis for God's reconciling act in Christ Jesus and the ongoing life of sanctification in the Holy Spirit. The World Council of Churches' programme on Justice, Peace and the Integrity of Creation represents one attempt to raise up once again Creation/First Article concerns in the consciousness of our churches.

Creation and Justice: The Spiritual Gift of Indigenous Peoples

> It has been a great many years since our white brothers came across the big waters and a great many of them have not got civilized yet; therefore we wish to be indulged in our savage state of life until we can have the same time to get civilized. . . . There is some of our white brothers as much savage as the Indian; for that reason we think we might as well enjoy our right as well as our white brothers.[5]

More often than not these days it is the role of indigenous people to voice perspectives that stir up the pot once again from the bottom in discussions with so-called first-, second- or third-world peoples. If this essay also performs such a function it will achieve this author's goal of contributing to constructive and creative theological dialogue. Yet it should be clearly understandable to all that

5. From a letter written by Shullushoma, a Chickasaw chief, to John C. Calhoun, U.S. Secretary of War, in 1824. Cited from Virginia Irving Armstrong, *I Have Spoken* (Swallow Press, 1971), xxiii.

deconstruction often is part of the constructive process. Sometimes we must unlearn what we know in order to learn what is genuinely new.

The Indian understanding of a universal harmony is well known, I think — that Indians understand themselves as a part of nature and not apart from it, somehow over it and possessing a special privilege to use it up. That harmony with nature is the beginning of all Native American spirituality — whether Christian or traditional. Hence, life as a gift is more than just my life or even human life in general, but every rock and every tree and every stream is a part of life and has life in itself. And all these things participate, along with human beings, in a spiritual harmony — a perception of the world which is much closer to Paul, where he talks of the whole of creation groaning as in the pains of childbirth (Rom. 8:22), than anything represented by modern industrial Christianity.

Perhaps the most precious gift that American Indians have to share with other peoples is our perspective on the interrelatedness of all of creation and our deep sense of relationship to the land in particular. We are all relatives: from buffaloes and eagles to trees and rocks, mountains and lakes. Just as there is no category of the inanimate, there can be no conception of anything in the created world that does not share in the sacredness infused in God's act of creation. Traditional stories relate dialogue and interaction between different animal relatives quite as if they were like us human beings, which, indeed, they may have been in some earlier age. Many tribal traditions then include stories that try to account for the necessity, for the sake of the survival of one species, of violent acts, perpetuated in hunting. In many of these stories, the four-legged and winged engage in long debate which concludes with a consensus to permit hunting by two-leggeds — for their good, that is, survival — but establishes certain parameters which will always ensure respect for the sacredness of all life.

Yet, the Indian understanding of creation as sacred, of Mother Earth as the source of all life, goes far beyond the notion of such Western counter-institutions as the Sierra Club or Greenpeace. It embraces far more than concern for harp seals, snail darters, Mono Lake or even a pair of hopelessly trapped whales. It embraces all of life from trees and animals to international relations. And this knowledge informs all of the community's activity, from hunting to dancing and even to writing grant proposals or administering government agencies. It especially concerns itself with the way we all live together. Perforce, it has to do with issues of justice and fairness.

Commitment to the harmony of nature results in love, nurture and acceptance. That is the witness indigenous Americans can give to the civilized world, if the world will accept that witness *and* if Indian life survives. (And the pressures of racism, individual and institutional in both state and church, are nearly overwhelming.) Indian life as a gift from God will survive only if Indian peoples are free to choose Indian lives, that is, to be *uncivilized*. And Indian

Christianity will survive only if it is free to develop quite independently of the dominant culture church.

Respect for creation and the recognition of the sacredness of all in creation is a deeply rooted spiritual base for American Indians, rooted in the soil of the tribal cultures of North America. That spiritual base is much more than words spoken in prayer, more than the stories that are told and the songs that are sung. It involves the whole identity of Indian peoples as tribal peoples. It has to do with how we image ourselves in the world. As a result, respect for creation and Indian spirituality must involve all of life — the individual's and the community's. It begins with the relationship American Indians of all tribes recognize, experience, sense and/or image with the earth. It is a matter of relatedness and interdependence that finally results in a necessary relationship of interdependence with all of nature.

In the story of Corn Woman told by tribes all along the eastern seaboard of North America, the sacrificial death and burial of First Mother results in abundant food and survival for all her starving children. Her voice, now as Corn Mother, comes to her children at that dramatic first harvest. From her dead body dragged around the clearing, her flesh and blood have given birth to tall, tassled green stalks of corn. This, she says, is her flesh given out of love to satisfy their hunger. Her bones buried in the middle of the clearing are reborn in beans, squash and other staples. And her voice directs their attention to a leafy plant. This, she says, is to help them with their prayers. Dried and smoked, it becomes Corn Mother's breath and carries their prayers upward to the sky. From these beginnings all those who have remembered this story and passed it on to new generations have recognized the gift of Corn Mother in the food they harvest from the earth and have recognized their dependence on and kinship with the earth. Earth itself becomes identified with First Mother, now Corn Mother.

So too Iatiku, the Creatrix in the Keresan Pueblo tradition, is identified with the Place of Emergence from the world below and finally with the earth. So too in ceremonies such as the sweat lodge purification rite, the functional relationship with the land, with earth as generative mother, becomes apparent. The sweat lodge is the womb, is the earth. We who are children of the earth return to the womb in this ceremony. Living relatives give of themselves to complete the ceremony. The rocks, the wood, the fire and the water are all expent in the process. The human participants also offer their suffering — for one who is sick, one who needs help, for all of creation. The rebirth with which the ceremony concludes is most dramatic in the old Osage form of the ceremony. At the end the participants emerge from the total darkness with a shout as they lift up the whole lodge and throw it over backwards.[6]

For our purposes the point in relating this much of the ceremony is to

6. Francis La Flesche, *War Ceremony and Peace Ceremony of the Osage Indians*, Bulletin No. 101, Bureau of American Ethnology (Washington, D.C.: U.S. Government Printing Office, 1939).

begin to demonstrate the relatedness of Indian people with the land, the earth. Hence one hears in the sweat lodge prayers and songs for the earth as well as prayers of respect for those relatives who give themselves for the sake of the ceremony. As the oldest of all relatives for the Sioux, especially the rocks receive such attention. But more than this, the balance and harmony of all things, the sacredness of all our relatives, respect for the purposeness of all relatives, and our interrelatedness also become a focus of songs and prayers.

The need for humans to be participants in the maintaining of balance and harmony then dominates all of life. Acts of violence against any relative disrupt the balance and are inexcusable — even those that become necessary. But balance can be restored if we stay within established boundaries. Animal relatives can be killed for food, shelter, tools and the like, but only if balance is ensured by performing the appropriate rituals and ceremonies. Quite often prayers need to be spoken or sung and even words of respect spoken to the animal itself, perhaps words explaining the purpose of this act of hunting and apologizing for it. Likewise most tribes engaged in elaborate rituals before going to war with another tribe. Even one's enemies must be respected. No killing was to be random. A tribe's survival or territorial integrity might be at risk. Nevertheless, maintaining balance, respect for all one's relatives, meant that four days of ceremony might be necessary before battle could be engaged.[7]

In the same way, people must show their respect before they cut down a tree for a Sun Dance ceremony. On the fourth day of preparation, a ritual procession will make its way to the chosen tree. Words are said to the tree explaining the necessity of the ensuing act of violence. The tree, which becomes the focus of devotion during the next four days of ceremony, is formally declared to be an enemy — and, hence, now due all the respect one gives one's enemy. Only then can balance be maintained when the tree is cut down, always in a ritual, sacred way. Paradoxically, this tree will serve as central to what is a ceremony of cosmic renewal.[8] Yet cutting down the tree necessarily risks creating imbalance and disintegration. But this paradoxical disjunction is part and parcel of the structures of existence: the causing of disharmony for the sake of harmony. The key here is respect for all creation. Precipitous action, even violence, cannot always be avoided. But respect for the sacredness of all and acknowledgment of our interrelatedness with all creation demand some sort of reciprocation in order to maintain harmony in the face of disharmony.

As we face the modern crisis of disintegration with new theological reflections, perhaps we need to ask: What reciprocal action is provided by the modern industrial-military complexes as they dig uranium out of the earth and

---

7. Such was the custom in my tribe, for instance. See La Flesche, *War Ceremony.*
8. See Arthur Amiotte, "The Lakota Sun Dance: Historical and Contemporary Perspectives," in *Sioux Indian Religion,* eds. Raymond J. DeMallie and Douglas R. Parks (Norman, OK: University of Oklahoma Press, 1987), 75-89.

pile up irreducible stockpiles of nuclear waste? What reciprocal act restores the earth as the rain forests are cleared? As factories spew their filth into the air or into rivers where fish no longer live? As we take from the earth to build bombs or create new luxuries, what do we return to the earth — besides the residual waste and the bodies of those who are killed by our sacrilegious indulgence?

American Indian people look back on a painful history of destruction which has plagued our peoples since the European invasion; we continue to suffer from ongoing oppression and the compound effects of oppression; we are still experiencing the continual disintegration of our tribal land bases; we painfully watch the ever-increasing attack on the earth and the things of the earth; and daily now we are hearing reports of the even greater suffering of tribal sisters and brothers in Latin America, Africa and other places. We cannot help but think that all these things, including our own suffering and experience of oppression, are intrinsically linked to the ways our oppressors pray. The spirituality of a people is always apparent in how a people lives with others, that is, in the respect we show for all our relatives. If we rape the earth, then we will rape each other as well. There can be no justice and no peace without respect for all that lives and a spiritual ideal of justice and peace that extends to all the world, even to the earth itself. This is an American Indian perception of reality and a contribution to the thinking of other peoples.

We need today a realignment of our theological thinking — and especially of our theological priorities. The most creative call for such a realignment may indeed come from the voices of indigenous peoples. If tribal perspectives can get a hearing in circles of first-, second-, and third-world theological discourse, they may well provide a strong impetus for a spiritual reimaging of ourselves as part of creation along with a consequential revitalizing of our concerns for justice and peace.

Harmony and Balance: Reimaging Creation

Standing again
within and among all things,
Standing with each other
as sisters and brothers, mothers and fathers,
daughters and sons, grandmothers and grandfathers —
the past and present generations of our people,
Standing again
with and among all items of life,
the land, rivers, mountains, plants, animals,
all life that is around us
that we are included with . . . ,

we acknowledge ourselves
to be in relationship that is responsible
and proper, that is loving and compassionate,
for the sake of the land and all people. . . .[9]

If we are to recover an appropriate prioritizing of Creation/First Article theological emphases and to respond to the modern crisis of disintegration of creation, then our theology must begin to lend itself to a new imaging of ourselves as human beings and our relationship to creation. We must become creative and articulate in our theological reflection in ways that will facilitate a new imaging of the tensive connection between self and creation on the part of individual members of our churches, and between whole communities and creation, meaning, of course, especially the bodies ecclesia. Only then will we be in a position to speak creatively and forcefully to the other social institutions of our world.

Creation must be understood as a whole, as more than that which is apart from us and around us. A holistic understanding of creation begins with a self-understanding of each individual and each community as an integral part of creation and not as artificially separate from it. Thus a theology of creation is not merely a justice (ecology) concern to be set alongside other justice concerns. But it is a foundational theology of self-understanding out of which justice, and then peace, will flow naturally and necessarily.

To treat creation as something which can be simply attached to other concerns, as "the integrity of creation" has been added to justice and peace in the theme of JPIC, allows us to think too easily of creation as a separate, if complementary, concern to justice and peace. The result, too often, has been to separate the concerns, much as the ecology movement in North America and Europe has effectively deflected much attention away from issues of justice and racism. We have also seen this same distraction from real issues of justice and human suffering at work in the peace movement, i.e., especially in the white, suburban anti-nuclear movement in North America.

It may be necessary at this late date for a healthy Christian creation theology to look to indigenous peoples around the world who are more firmly and self-consciously rooted in a creation-related self-understanding. Christian theology and Christian life may now have to learn from American Indian, tribal African, Pacific Island, tribal Asian and other indigenous peoples.

A theology of creation must begin with a self-understanding of individuals and communities as part of creation. We must understand that all things are related to one another and that human beings participate as one aspect of creation alongside the rest of creation. Our own health and welfare are inti-

9. From a Simon J. Ortiz (Acoma Pueblo) poem titled "Mid-America Prayer," in his book of poetry, *Fight Back: for the Sake of the People, for the Sake of the Land,* Institute for Native American Development (University of New Mexico, 1980), 1.

mately linked to the health and welfare of the whole of creation. The balance and harmony of creation must include human communities as part of that balance and harmony.

If our theology — and hence our human communities — can begin to wrestle seriously with the necessity of balance and harmony in all of creation, then our self-image as part of creation must also be deeply affected. As our self-perception and self-understanding begin to be self-consciously centered in respect for all creation, we will begin to participate actively not in the exploitation of the earth but in the establishment of balance and harmony. Our participation in the balance and harmony of all creation will then most naturally include other individuals and communities of human beings. And justice and then genuine peace will flow out of our concern for one another and all creation.

Our active participation on behalf of the peoples of Southern Africa, Tamils of Sri Lanka, the oppressed of Central and South America, American Indians and many others must be a spiritual struggle for the good — the genuine good — of all people and all creation. It is a struggle for balance and harmony. We dare not relegate a status to creation as just another concern among others — lest it distract us from all concerns.

III.3

Human Finitude and the Concept of Women's Experience

TIINA ALLIK

Many feminist thinkers, both outside and inside the Christian tradition, criticize what they see as a prevalent tendency in the Western philosophical and theological traditions to devalue human finitude.[1] Feminists both outside and inside the Christian tradition have good reasons for objecting to the devaluation of human finitude. Insofar as women have been linked to human finitude more closely than men, the devaluation of finitude is also a devaluation of women. The devaluation of finitude, insofar as it is based in a denial of the material

1. By finitude I mean the limitedness of human beings. In philosophical and theological discussions, human finitude is usually seen as a function of human participation in the physical and biological, spatial and temporal world. Human finitude has often been used to refer to the way in which human powers (such as, e.g., knowledge, physical strength, or the ability to impose order) never attain perfection but are always limited. Another way to look at human finitude is to think of it as human openness to the world, the ability to be affected by things in the world which one has not willed, including one's own unwilled and unconscious aspects. If one thinks of the goal of human existence as a state of complete control and mastery over oneself and one's environment, then this openness (which is one way of describing human finitude) is undesirable. It is a vulnerability to influences that will inevitably detract from one's ability to achieve the goal of complete mastery over oneself and one's environment. If, however, one values the spontaneity, the richness and the creativity that come from a mix of contingencies, one's emotional reactions and spontaneous impulses and one's ability to make decisions and carry them out, then one will also value the openness and vulnerability that is human finitude. In addition, if one values experiences in which one reacts to and receptively appreciates or appropriates what one has not willed — other people, unwilled aspects of oneself, and one's environment, then one would never want to do away with the vulnerability which is also the sensitivity which makes possible these experiences and interactions. In other words, human finitude is not only human limitedness, but also an openness and receptivity to the world, a basis for the creativity and spontaneity of human existence.

Reprinted with permission from the journal *Modern Theology* 9/1 (January 1993): 67-85.

roots of human life, has also impoverished our conceptions of the possibilities of human life, and has thus harmed both women and men.

Feminists within the Christian tradition have additional reasons for affirming the scope and goodness of human finitude.[2] The goodness of God's creation is a basic premise of traditional Christian theology. One premise of the biblical creation story is that God did not create a sinful world. According to traditional interpretations of the story, Adam and Eve, who lived in a sinless world, chose to disobey God's command and brought sin into the world. The central Christian teaching that God became incarnate in fully human form in the person of Jesus is also an affirmation of the redeemability and of the basic goodness of human beings. The teachings of the bodily resurrection of Christ and the promise of resurrection to all believers both affirm the basic goodness of human creatureliness in its bodiliness and finitude.

Nevertheless much of Christian theology has had an ambivalent attitude towards human finitude. There seems to be an internal conflict in much of Christian theology between the desire to affirm the basic goodness of human beings as created by God, and a tendency to denigrate life in the spatial, temporal, material world. The history of Christian theology exhibits a pervasive tendency to label certain features of human creaturely existence as inherently sinful, the result of sin, or at least something that needs to be overcome. Thus much of Christian theology has tended to confuse sin and human finitude, either by identifying finitude with sinfulness, by identifying finitude as the source or cause of the fall into sin, or by claiming that some of the implications of human finitude will be eliminated in the final, glorified human state.[3] Since in Christian theology the devaluation of human finitude, insofar as it is a devaluation of God's creation, ultimately casts aspersions on God's goodness, feminist theologians within the Christian tradition have

---

2. Carol Christ, a feminist theologian who has left the Christian tradition, criticizes Christian theology for its denial of finitude and death in "Reverence for Life: The Need for a Sense of Finitude," in *Embodied Love: Sensuality and Relationship as Feminist Values,* ed. Paula M. Cooey, Sharon A. Farmer and Mary Ellen Ross (San Francisco: Harper & Row, 1987), 51-64. Although I agree with Christ's claim that the teachings of the divinity of Christ, the resurrection, and original sin are often used by Christian theologians in ways that compromise the goodness of finite, bodily existence, she does not discuss how the tendency to denigrate created human existence can be criticized from within Christianity as a betrayal of basic Christian principles and as an internal inconsistency. The same goes for Christ's insight that the aseity and impassibility of God, insofar as they are held up as models for human existence, set an impossible, inhuman goal for human beings and thereby denigrate human finitude. Her perception of this use of teachings about the being of God is accurate, but she does not show how this use is also problematic from the standpoint of other Christian claims.

3. For discussions of how this internal conflict manifests itself in two twentieth-century Christian theologians, Karl Rahner and Stanley Hauerwas, see Tiina Allik, "Nature and Spirit: Agency and Concupiscence in Hauerwas and Rahner," *The Journal of Religious Ethics* 15/1 (Spring, 1987): 14-32 and "Karl Rahner on Materiality and Human Knowledge," *The Thomist* 49/3 (July, 1985): 367-86.

good reasons for unmasking and criticizing ambivalent attitudes toward human finitude.

I am in agreement with the primary aim of feminist criticisms of traditional conceptualizations of human personhood for their devaluation of finitude. However, I think that feminist theorists are sometimes unaware of how their own conceptualizations of what it means to be human conflict with their desire to affirm the value and full scope of human finitude.

All feminists have claimed that women have been denied equality with men and have thereby been excluded from male-dominated realms of human activity. The additional claim, that the perspective of women differs from that of men, that women's experience has been ignored by male-dominated fields, and that therefore the descriptive and explanatory work that has been done in those fields is at best incomplete, and most probably distorted, is now nearly ubiquitous in feminist writing. This additional claim leads to the attempt to reformulate and rework disciplines so that they will include women's experience. Often when feminists use the concept of women's experience, they refer to women's direct awareness of some aspect of reality. The object of women's direct awareness is often seen to be their participation in the material, biological realm. Thus the claim is made by some feminists that women's experience includes a direct awareness of the natural, as opposed to the cultural, realm.

In this essay I will argue that the use of the concept of women's experience to refer to women's direct awareness of some aspect of reality, without the mediation of concepts provided by linguistic and cultural communities, implies a view of human persons that does not acknowledge the full scope of human finitude and thereby also devalues it.[4] I will also argue that the motivations for this use of the concept of women's experience have to do with a search for

---

4. To put this criticism in a positive form: I am recommending to feminists that they take what George Lindbeck has described as the cultural-linguistic rather than the more popular experiential-expressivist approach to women's experience [*The Nature of Doctrine: Religion and Theology in a Postliberal Age* (Philadelphia: The Westminster Press, 1984)].

Most reviewers of Lindbeck's book seem to share David Tracy's opinion: "The hands may be the hands of Wittgenstein and Geertz but the voice is the voice of Karl Barth" ["Lindbeck's New Program for Theology," *The Thomist* 49/3 (July, 1985): 465]. Tracy is not persuaded by Lindbeck's formal proposal of the cultural-linguistic model as the best approach to religion because he thinks it is motivated by the Barthian-confessional nature of Lindbeck's substantive theological concerns. Gordon Kaufman, however, believes that Lindbeck's cultural-linguistic approach can be put in the service of theological concerns other than Lindbeck's own [review of *The Nature of Doctrine, Theology Today* 42 (July, 1985): 240-41].

I share Kaufman's view. There seems to me to be no good reason that feminist theologians both outside and inside the Christian tradition could not adopt an approach to religious truth (and to other kinds of truth) such as the one that Lindbeck describes, regardless of their theological predilections. They might adopt the cultural-linguistic approach for reasons diverging widely from Lindbeck's conservative theological proposals. Among their reasons might be the desire to maintain consistently the effects of human finitude on their anthropology and epistemology, a desire that Lindbeck and most other Christian theologians would share.

epistemological certainty. On the constructive side, I will argue that explanations of the differences between women's experience and men's experience that see these differences in terms of the sensitivity of human beings to their social environment acknowledge human· finitude more fully than explanations in terms of women's direct, unmediated awareness of some aspect of reality.

I. Two Feminist Views of Human Nature

The use of the concept of women's experience to refer to an unmediated experience of the natural realm can be seen as a response to traditional philosophical and theological views about human nature and also as a response to other feminist views. Various schemes for the classification of types of feminism have been discussed in the literature on feminism.[5] For the purposes of this essay I will make use of a distinction between two types of feminist approaches to human nature: single-anthropology and dual-anthropology feminism.[6] Single-anthropology feminism holds that there is one human nature which is the same for both men and women. The essence of this human nature is seen as the ability to function on the level of culture, to transcend human life on the biological level, to rise above the natural realm. Dual-anthropology feminism holds that there are two human natures, women's nature and men's nature. Women's nature includes a distinctive closeness to the natural realm, the body, and the emotions. Women's experience is an immediate experience of the natural realm, which is available to women in a way that it is not to men.

Feminists generally agree that traditional theories about human nature have been used to thwart women and to prevent them from realizing their full potential as human beings.[7] Although theories of human nature have varied greatly in Western philosophical and theological traditions, full humanity has often been seen as the fulfillment of certain capacities which are considered distinctive to the human species and which are also valued more highly than capacities that humans share with other species. These distinctively human capacities have been given content in various terms: rationality, memory, the capacity for the imaginative

---

5. See, e.g., Alison M. Jaggar, *Feminist Politics and Human Nature* (Sussex: The Harvester Press, 1983), and John Charvet, *Feminism* (London: J. M. Dent & Sons Ltd., 1982).

6. My main source for the distinction between these two types of feminist approaches to human nature is philosopher Jean Grimshaw's book *Philosophy and Feminist Thinking* (Minneapolis: University of Minnesota Press, 1986). See especially Chapter 4, "Human Nature and Women's Nature," 104-38.

The terms 'single anthropology' and 'dual anthropology' are used by Roman Catholic theologian Anne Carr in the chapter "Theological Anthropology and the Experience of Women" in her book *Transforming Grace: Christian Tradition and Women's Experience* (San Francisco: Harper & Row, 1988), 117-33. Carr's description of feminist views of human nature in terms of this distinction corresponds roughly to the distinction made by Grimshaw.

7. See Grimshaw, 111.

construction of projects that will transform present realities into a yet unseen future shape, control and manipulation of one's environment, free choice, moral responsibility, and the awareness of one's relationship to God. Despite variations in content, these distinctively human capacities have been seen as nonmaterial: as mental or spiritual capacities that are distinguishable from and sometimes opposed to bodily, biological, or physical capacities. Because these distinctively human capacities enable humans to rise above the biological, material realm that they share with other creatures, some modern thinkers have referred to them as the capacity for self-transcendence or as the capacity for transforming nature into culture.[8] In the language of Christian theology, these distinctively human capacities have usually been subsumed under the concept of the image of God in humans.

The dominant strands of Western philosophy and theology have seen women as less capable than men of exercising the most valued human capacities. Women have been considered either as part of a single humanity, but flawed in comparison to men and thus incapable of achieving full humanity, or they have been seen as a separate and unequal form of life. In either case, the claim has usually been (and often still is) that women are constrained by their bodies, by their participation in the material and biological realm, in a way that men are not.[9] The biological fact that women bear children and lactate has been seen as binding women to the material world and to their bodies and thus making it difficult for them to exercise the distinctively human, mental and spiritual capacities. The biological constraints on women have thus also been seen as dictating certain social roles and psychological characteristics for women which

---

8. In providing a schematic description of how more highly valued human capacities have been defined in opposition to the less highly valued aspects of human life that ensue from human participation in the material, biological world, I am bypassing the variety of senses that have historically been given to terms like "nature," "spirit," "matter," and "transcendence" and the multiple purposes for which these terms have been used. Nevertheless I think that this pattern of opposition exists and is worth describing in this schematized way. For more detailed studies of how thinkers in the Western tradition have defined highly valued human qualities in contrast to aspects of human life that ensue from human participation in the material, biological world and also in opposition to femininity see the following:

- Susan R. Bordo, *The Flight to Objectivity: Essay on Cartesianism and Culture* (Albany: State University of New York Press, 1987);
- Judith Van Herik, *Freud on Femininity and Faith* (Berkeley: University of California Press, 1982);
- Genevieve Lloyd, *The Man of Reason: "Male" and "Female" in Western Philosophy* (Minneapolis: University of Minnesota Press, 1984); and
- Robin May Schott, *Cognition and Eros: A Critique of the Kantian Paradigm* (Boston: Beacon Press, 1988).

9. Thomas Laqueur in *Making Sex: Body and Gender from the Greeks to Freud* (Cambridge: Harvard University Press, 1991) documents how, in the eighteenth century, views on the differences between the biology of men and women shifted from a one-sex to a two-sex model and that both models were used to argue against granting women rights equal to those of men.

are subordinate to and less valued than the social roles and psychological characteristics of men.[10]

Not only have women been seen as incapable of full humanity, but the achievement of full humanity has itself been defined in opposition to what has been considered feminine. Human rationality in particular has been defined in terms of the purification of the mind by the removal of contaminating elements associated with femininity, including the effects of bodiliness.[11]

Single-anthropology and dual-anthropology feminists disagree about how to respond to the devaluation of women. Nevertheless, both types of feminism are reactions to two features of traditional views of human nature:

1. the definition of full humanity as the exercise of highly valued capacities that involve a transcendence of the material, biological realm, implying that human participation in the material, biological realm is less valued, and
2. the claim that women are less capable than men of exercising the more highly valued capacities and are more completely dominated by human participation in the material, biological realm.

Single-anthropology feminism agrees with the traditional view that the most valuable human capacities are nonmaterial, mental or spiritual capacities which are distinctively human, and that these capacities consist of a transcendence of the material, biological aspect of human existence. However, single-anthropology feminism disagrees with the identification of women with the material, biological aspect of human existence. Proponents of single-anthropology feminism argue that women, as well as men, are capable of achieving full humanity as it has been defined in traditional views of human nature. That is, women, as well as men, are capable of transcending their embeddedness in the material, biological realm, of thinking clearly, rationally, objectively, and purposefully, of making moral decisions, of participating in the distinctively human realm of culture, and, in Christian theological terms, of fully imaging God. Thus the argument of the single-anthropology view is the following: because there is one human nature common to both men and women, women should be given rights and opportunities equal to those given to men.

Dual-anthropology feminism agrees with the traditional identification of women with the material, biological aspect of human existence. Because of women's distinctive closeness to the natural world and the material, biological aspect of human existence, women's perspectives and women's experiences differ from those of men. However, dual-anthropology feminism disagrees with the traditional devaluation of the material, biological aspect of human existence.

10. See Grimshaw, 111-13.
11. See references in n. 8.

Proponents of this view claim that women's closeness to nature, far from implying a devaluation of women, is the source for women's special strengths.
Because women have easier access to the natural world and to their bodies and
emotions, they define themselves in relationship to their environment and to
other people in ways that men do not. Therefore women are in a unique position
to develop new, ecologically and socially beneficial values for all of society.
Proponents of this view urge women to discover their essentially female nature,
to experience it to the fullest, and to develop the positive values that inhere in
women's distinctive closeness to nature and the material, biological aspect of
human existence.

The dual-anthropology claim, that women's experience differs significantly from men's experience, is a response to traditional views of human
nature, which posit a single human nature but devalue both human participation in the material, biological realm and also women. This claim is also a
response to single-anthropology feminism, which accepts uncritically the traditional view of human nature and continues the devaluation of the material,
biological aspect of human existence and of women. The aim of the dual-
anthropology view is to affirm both the value of characteristics which have
traditionally been associated with women and also the scope and goodness of
human participation in the material, biological realm.

II. The Nature/Culture Distinction

The problem with the dual-anthropology view is that in its challenge of single-
anthropology feminism and of traditional views it continues one of their assumptions. This assumption is that nature and culture are clearly distinguishable and separable realms of human existence. Single-anthropology feminism,
continuing traditional views of human nature, assumes that there are some
human capacities that are not conditioned by human participation in the material, biological realm and some capacities that are not conditioned by the human
capacity for culture-making. In other words, single-anthropology feminism
assumes that the natural and the cultural are, at least in some instances, clearly
distinguishable and separable realms of human experience. Dual-anthropology
feminism, while denying that there are any human capacities that are not
conditioned by human participation in the material, biological realm, assumes
that women have access to an experience of nature that is not mediated by
cultural categories. This is a way of affirming a purely natural aspect of human
experience that is not mediated by the individual's own culture-making capacities and the dependence of the individual's own culture-making capacities on
the cultural and social environment.

Philosopher Jean Grimshaw, in her book *Philosophy and Feminist Thinking*, shows how several single-anthropology feminists, including Kate Millett,

Betty Friedan, and Simone de Beauvoir, assume the separability of natural and cultural levels of human experience. She shows how all three devalue what have been traditional activities and preoccupations of women — domestic work and childrearing — by claiming that these activities fail to transcend the natural or biological level of human life. All three seem to assume both that typical women's work is purely material or biological and that the cultural level consists of rising above the constraints of the material or biological realm.

According to Millett, having been assigned the role of childrearing and domestic work, women have been arrested "at the level of biological experience," at the level of the animal rather than the level of the distinctively human.[12] According to Friedan, women have adjusted themselves to dealing mostly with food, things, and childrearing. By doing so they have "been blocked at the physiological level" of human life, the level which human animals have in common with other animals. At this level, humans, as other animals, are dependent on the material environment and not free and self-determining.[13] For Simone de Beauvoir, the achievement of full humanity consists of being a subject, as opposed to an object. Subjectivity puts one into the realm of human culture, the realm in which humans transcend nature. Women have not been allowed to become subjects, to achieve transcendence, to participate in the realm of culture, to be fully human. For example, although women are in a sense creative in giving birth, de Beauvoir sees this as a passive, rather than an active kind of creation. The child growing in the mother's body is not the object of a genuinely creative act, because the act of producing a child does not occur on the level of human subjectivity; "it is still only a gratuitous cellular growth, a brute fact of nature."[14]

Dual-anthropology feminists, on the other hand, attempt to provide a corrective for single-anthropology feminism's devaluation of the natural level — the material, biological aspect of human existence. Adrienne Rich, for example, sympathizes with single-anthropology feminists: "the body has been made so problematic for women that it has often seemed easier to shrug it off and travel as a disembodied spirit."[15] But she herself believes that the real task for feminists is not to deny the body but to show how true knowledge arises from one's experience of the body. For Rich, women's experience of the body is distinctively female: "female biology — the diffuse, intense sensuality radiating out from clitoris, breasts, uterus, vagina; the lunar cycles of menstruation; the gestation and fruition of life which can take place in the female body — has

12. Kate Millett, *Sexual Politics* (London: Virago, 1977), 26. Cited by Grimshaw, 114.

13. Betty Friedan, *The Feminine Mystique* (New York: W. W. Norton, 1963), 272-73, 266. Cited by Grimshaw, 115.

14. Simone de Beauvoir, *The Second Sex* (Penguin, 1972; 1st edn., 1949), 514. Cited by Grimshaw, 116.

15. Adrienne Rich, *Of Woman Born: Motherhood as Experience and Institution* (New York: W. W. Norton & Company, 1986, 1987), 40.

far more radical implications than we have yet come to appreciate."[16] This is an affirmation of the concreteness and particularity of the human experience of bodiliness. But women's experience of their bodiliness, for Rich, also seems to be unmediated and direct. This is evident when Rich focuses on women's experiences of motherhood. Most people would want to say that women's experiences of motherhood can be in conflict with what women have been taught to feel about motherhood, but Rich goes further than that. She claims that there is an experience of the body available to women that is "actual — as opposed to . . . culturally warped."[17] Thus, according to Rich, women's biology, if women do not deny their experience of it, provides women with a kind of direct and unmediated awareness of the material, biological realm.

Susan Griffin also centers much of her writing on women's experience of what is natural, as opposed to experience that has been distorted by cultural influence. As Grimshaw notes, Griffin denies the necessity for the opposition between culture and nature but also reaffirms the distinction. Griffin criticizes our culture, which "opposes spirit to the flesh and which uses culture as a way to deny the power of the natural."[18] She claims that in the ideologies that she opposes (sexism, racism, and the anti-nature bias of our culture) what is denied in the self is projected onto "the other," whether "the other" is nature or people of another sex or race. Yet when Griffin speaks of the persistent power of the natural in the face of ideologies that attempt to repress it or to deny its existence, she seems to assume the possibility of a direct experience of nature — an experience of the natural that is not mediated by any culturally constructed categories. Thus Griffin turns around and reaffirms nature and culture as clearly distinguishable and separable.

My argument here is that *both* single- and dual-anthropology feminism, because they both see the natural and the cultural as two clearly distinguishable and separable levels of human existence, deny the full scope of human finitude. It is easier to see this in the case of single-anthropology feminism. Single-anthropology feminism thinks of full humanity as the development of capacities which escape the conditioning of human bodiliness and finitude. Dual-anthropology feminism, on the other hand, explicitly affirms that even the so-called "higher" spiritual capacities are conditioned by human finitude and bodiliness and that this state of affairs is something that should be welcomed and celebrated. What dual-anthropology feminism implicitly denies, however, is that all experiences of human finitude and bodiliness are themselves mediated through cultural systems and social environments.

The openness, sensitivity, and dependence of human beings on cultural

---

16. Adrienne Rich, 39-40.

17. *Idem.*

18. Susan Griffin, *Made from This Earth: An Anthology of Writings by Susan Griffin* (New York: Harper & Row, 1982), 166.

systems and social environments are important aspects of human finitude. Most dual-anthropology feminists are aware that the concepts of human nature that have been used to oppress women have been constructed and internalized by human beings in cultural, social groups. However, many dual-anthropology feminists seem unaware that the experiences of the body and of human participation in the material, biological realm that they recommend are also mediated by concepts that are culturally constructed and socially internalized.

I believe that the reasons for this unawareness of how human finitude affects human experience of the material, biological world and of human bodiliness and finitude arise from the desire of dual-anthropology feminists to establish an epistemological foundation for their constructive claims. Dual-anthropology feminists want to transform male-dominated cultural systems, rather than merely make a place for women in these systems. They sometimes assume that the transformation of male-dominated systems is not possible unless feminists have established for themselves an area of experience and knowledge that will serve as a sure foundation for their criticisms of male-dominated cultural systems. They also assume that this foundation must be free of the influence of male-dominated cultural systems.

The feminist quest for autonomy from prevailing linguistic-cultural frameworks in order to establish a sure foundation from which to criticize and transform male-dominated cultural systems involves feminists in a dilemma. On the one hand, dual-anthropology feminists want to affirm the historicity and time- and place-bound nature of male-dominated systems. The dual-anthropology feminist challenge to claims of inevitability, timelessness, and universal applicability from the proponents of male-dominated cultural systems usually includes an affirmation of the contingency and conditioned nature of all human cultural systems. This is a way of affirming that all aspects of human existence and activity are finite. On the other hand, dual-anthropology feminists, in their attempts to establish a foundation for their criticisms of male-dominated cultural systems, sometimes appeal to a kind of 'pure experience' that is not mediated by the categories and conceptual frameworks provided by cultural environments and that is therefore also immune to criticism.[19]

---

19. There are interesting parallels between the feminist quest for autonomy and epistemological justification and other post-Enlightenment epistemological quests. Cf. Jeffrey Stout's *The Flight from Authority: Religion, Morality, and the Quest for Autonomy* (Notre Dame: University of Notre Dame Press, 1981) and Wayne Proudfoot's *Religious Experience* (Berkeley: University of California Press, 1985). Stout discusses how traditional philosophy after the Enlightenment, in order to maintain the certainty of knowledge based on authority while gaining autonomy from the authority of Church and Scripture, attempted to deny its own historical character and the conditions placed upon it by human finitude. Proudfoot argues that the claim of modern theology since Schleiermacher — that theology is founded on a kind of personal experience which is independent of public, culturally mediated conceptual categories — has the function of establishing religious experience as epistemologically autonomous and of protecting religious claims from outside criticism and challenge. My argument in the present essay is that some feminists, in

The feminist claim to a kind of 'pure experience' is a denial of an aspect of human finitude — the vulnerability and dependence of human beings on their social and cultural environments.[20] The use of women's experience in the sense of an unmediated experience and knowledge of reality that will provide a sure foundation for the validity of feminist claims shows that feminists are not always consistent with their avowed desire to challenge the prevailing attitudes of our culture on what it means to be human. These feminists are still assuming a conception of a kind of human experience which transcends the uncertainty, vulnerability, and historicity of human finitude.

III. Women's Experience as Culturally Constructed and Socially Mediated

Despite my criticisms of the use of the concept of women's experience to refer to an unmediated experience of the natural realm, I also think that differences between masculine and feminine experiences of what it means to be human are significant and worthy of examination. The notion of an experience of self and the world which is more common among women than men does not need to be used in a way that denies the culturally constructed nature of human experience. Feminist thinkers who observe significant differences between men and women do not need to explain those differences

their quest for epistemological autonomy and justification, are also implicitly denying the finitude of human experience and human knowing.

Sheila Davaney presents a similar argument about the epistemological assumptions of three feminist theologians in "Problems with Feminist Theory: Historicity and the Search for Sure Foundations," in *Embodied Love: Sensuality and Relationship as Feminist Values,* ed. Paula M. Cooey, Sharon A. Farmer and Mary Ellen Ross (San Francisco: Harper & Row, 1987), 79-95. Davaney points out that feminist thinkers, along with men, have inherited the peculiarly modern conflict between "the Enlightenment-inspired quest for certain truth and the countermodern recognition of the historical and, hence, relative character of all claims to truth." She shows persuasively that Rosemary Radford Ruether, Mary Daly, and Elisabeth Schüssler Fiorenza all display a tension between their acknowledgment of the historical character of all thought on the one hand and their apparent assumption that the truth of feminist claims consists of a correspondence to ultimate reality on the other hand. Although Davaney focuses on the epistemological dilemma, she is certainly aware of the anthropological implications of her discussion. For example, she points out, through a citation from philosopher Steve Doty, that modern historical consciousness is a corollary of a recognition of the finitude of human reason (81).

20. This vulnerability and dependence means that even revolutionary transformations of human perception and experience are mediated by the conceptual means at one's disposal. I do not mean to deny that radical changes in the experiences of individuals and groups take place. I do mean to say that these experiences are made possible by conceptual systems which provide adequate categories to identify, describe and interpret these experiences. This means that experience, whether of women or of other groups in a position to challenge the status quo because of their long history of suppression and oppression, cannot function conceptually as an Archimedean point.

in a way that assumes women's experience as an unmediated experience of the natural realm.

For example, Valerie Saiving's essay, "The Human Situation: A Feminine View,"[21] and Judith Plaskow's book, *Sex, Sin and Grace: Women's Experience and The Theologies of Reinhold Niebuhr and Paul Tillich,*[22] are similar as to the substantive challenges they present to theology, yet they have different approaches to the concept of women's experience. Both Saiving and Plaskow describe what they see as "significant differences between masculine and feminine experience."[23] Both claim that Christian theologians have conceptualized sin and grace on the assumption that male experience is equivalent to human experience. They argue that the introduction of women's experience into the theological picture would require changes in the content of Christian theology, not just the inclusion of women into previously male-dominated areas of activity.

Both Saiving and Plaskow analyze sin and grace in the theology of Reinhold Niebuhr, a representative twentieth-century theologian, as one example of how the assumption that male experience is equivalent to human experience has influenced theology. They see Niebuhr's analysis of the human situation and of sin as slanted in the direction of the experience of men. For Niebuhr, the human situation consists of a tension between finitude and self-transcendence. He defines two categories of sin: pride, which consists of denying one's creaturely limitations or one's finitude, and sensuality, which consists of denying one's capacity for self-transcendence and for fulfilling the image of God. Despite his schema of two categories for sin, Niebuhr sees pride as the basic sin. He analyzes sensuality as rooted in the basic sin of self-assertion, so that sensuality, the attempt to lose oneself in a particular part of one's own self or of the created world, is still basically a prideful assertion of one's self-will. Thus for Niebuhr, the primary human temptation is to resolve the anxiety inherent in the human situation by denying the limitations of human creatureliness. If the human situation and sin are seen in this way, salvation consists of a breaking apart of the pride of a self that thinks itself equal to God and able to resolve the anxiety that is basic to the human situation. Correspondingly, the content of salvation is a resigned humility and a self-sacrificing love which are the opposite of a self-absorbed and self-serving pride.

Women's temptation, on the other hand, according to both Saiving and Plaskow, is towards self-abnegation and the underdevelopment of the self. The problem for women has not been that they have pursued self-transcendence or

---

21. Reprinted in *Womanspirit Rising: A Feminist Reader in Religion,* ed. Carol P. Christ and Judith Plaskow (San Francisco: Harper & Row, 1979), 25-41. First printed in *The Journal of Religion* (April, 1960).

22. Judith Plaskow, *Sex, Sin and Grace: Women's Experience and the Theologies of Reinhold Niebuhr and Paul Tillich* (Lanham: University Press of America, 1980).

23. Saiving, 27.

the fulfillment of the image of God in an excessive and prideful way, so as to usurp the prerogatives of God himself. Rather, most women have been prone to the temptations of passivity, a resigned acceptance of the concrete contingencies which limit their lives, distractibility, and to losing themselves by defining their own identities in terms of others. Resigned humility, the acceptance of finitude as a necessary but unpleasant condition, and self-sacrificial love reinforce the primary temptations of women. The traditional goals of salvation are thus irrelevant or positively harmful for women (and also incidentally for other marginalized social groups).

One implication of Saiving's and Plaskow's discussions of women's experience of sin as different from that of men is that women need a concept of salvation that encourages them to develop a healthy striving towards self-assertion and the development of their capacities for transcendence. Another implication is that Niebuhr overestimates the universality of the temptation to deny one's finitude and creatureliness. Niebuhr's emphasis on sin as pride assumes a negative view of human finitude.[24] For Niebuhr, sin is the attempt to become like God, an attempt which is mistaken and doomed to failure, but also a natural way in which humans go wrong. Niebuhr assumes that human beings will naturally chafe at the limitations set upon them because of their creaturely status. Plaskow's claim is that this negative attitude towards finitude is not the only possible one and that many women, especially, do not share this attitude.

On the surface, both Plaskow and Saiving seem to take the dual-anthropology approach. As is typical in dual-anthropology approaches, one of their claims is that women's distinctive experience includes a friendlier attitude towards human finitude than that of men. But Saiving bases her description of differences between men and women on biological facts, which she thinks provide "a substratum or core of masculine and feminine orientations,"[25] whereas Plaskow does not do this. Plaskow makes no universal claims for her descriptions of the differences between women's experiences and men's experiences. She says that her view of women's experience is particular and concrete: it is "one view of modern, white, western, middle-class 'women's experience.' "[26] She defines women's experience as the interrelation between "male definitions of women and the lived experiences of women within, in relation and in opposition to these definitions."[27] Thus the concept of women's experience for her is not based on a foundational and universal feminine nature which is unaffected by social circumstances. She rejects the idea of a basic women's experience and nature that underlies indoctrination by male culture and education and that will appear once the distorted layers have been stripped away.[28]

24. Plaskow, 69-70.
25. Saiving, 29.
26. Plaskow, 6.
27. Plaskow, 10-11.
28. Plaskow, 11.

The result is that Plaskow preserves the primary claims of the dual-anthropology use of the concept of women's experience — that who you are (including your gender) determines how you see yourself, the world, and your relationship to the world, and that many women seem to have a less antagonistic attitude towards human finitude than do men. She thereby affirms one feature of human finitude — the particularity of human experience, including that of women. By rejecting the concept of women's experience as a direct, unmediated experience of the natural realm she avoids the implicit denial of another aspect of human finitude — the culturally constructed and socially mediated nature of the individual's particular experiences.

I will now turn to the works of two feminists in the social sciences whose work provides a way to conceptualize the distinctiveness of women's experience without denying its culturally constructed and socially mediated nature.

According to psychologist Carol Gilligan, women's experience differs in significant ways from men's experience, not because women are closer to nature by virtue of a distinctive female nature that provides an unmediated, direct awareness of the natural realm, but because women develop characteristic patterns and concepts for interpreting their experience from the social relationships that they experience as children and as adults. Gilligan is well known for her description of two different perspectives on morality — the justice perspective and the care perspective.[29] She and her colleagues have also shown that these moral perspectives correlate with two different ways of looking at self and others.

In the justice perspective, moral problems are seen as decisions about how to adjudicate conflicts between one's own claims and the claims of others. These conflicts are resolved by means of impartial standards, which consist of universal rules that are applied to all alike. Someone who looks at moral issues in terms of this perspective focuses on issues of injustice, such as oppression and inequality. The Golden Rule epitomizes this perspective: You should do to others as you would like them to do to you. The warrant for this is the claim that individuals are equivalent units with equal rights. This ethical perspective correlates with a view of the human self in which individuals are seen as independent and separate in relation to others. It is important to see that the justice perspective considers relationship as an important part of being human; nevertheless, it does not see relationships as constitutive of individuals, but rather as based on reciprocity between separate, independent individuals.

In the care perspective, moral problems are seen as issues of relationship or response. A solution of an ethical problem from the care perspective aims to

---

29. Carol Gilligan, *In a Different Voice: Psychological Theory and Women's Development* (Cambridge: Harvard University Press, 1982) and *Mapping the Moral Domain: A Contribution of Women's Thinking to Psychological Theory and Education*, ed. Carol Gilligan, Jartie Victoria Ward, Jill McLean Taylor, with Betty Bardige (Cambridge: Center for the Study of Gender, Education and Human Development, 1988).

maintain relationship, to promote the welfare of all the people involved insofar as possible, and to prevent harm. The ethical concerns of someone in the care perspective would focus on how to respond to the needs of others, particularly where someone is detached and disconnected from others, or vulnerable to abandonment and the indifference of others. This ethical perspective correlates with a view of the human self in which individuals are seen as connected in relation to others. The individual is, to some extent, seen as constituted by means of his/her relationships to others. Relationships are based, not necessarily on reciprocity, but on responsiveness to the other in his/her own terms. Others are seen as unique individuals with their own needs, situations and contexts.[30]

Gilligan and her colleagues, using Gilligan's theoretical framework of two perspectives, have discovered that most people are capable of using both perspectives, but that a phenomenon of focus appears. That is, given a particular moral dilemma or asked to discuss spontaneously a real-life moral dilemma, most people will use predominantly one perspective. Gilligan and her colleagues have shown that the use of these two perspectives is gender-related though not gender-specific. Not all men have a justice focus and not all women have a care focus; however, in most instances, more women than men will have a care focus and more men than women will have a justice focus.[31]

Gilligan's discovery of "the different voice" of the care perspective in women's moral narratives correlates with Saiving's and Plaskow's descriptions of the distinctiveness of women's experience. The positive side of women's temptation towards an underdevelopment of the self is the care perspective — the tendency to think of solutions to dilemmas in terms of satisfying the needs of other individuals in their own terms. For women who have matured in the use of the care perspective, the self is included in the consideration of how needs can best be fulfilled.

Gilligan explains the differences between the two moral perspectives in terms of their origins in early childhood relationships. Children of both sexes have experiences of inequality and experiences of attachment. According to Gilligan, the justice perspective is based on transformations of the child's experiences of inequality and the care perspective is based on transformations of the child's experiences of attachment.

---

30. My summaries of Gilligan's two perspectives on morality and self are based on Nona Plessner Lyons' "Two Perspectives: On Self, Relationships, and Morality," in *Mapping the Moral Domain*, 21-48 (see esp. Tables 1 and 2, 33, 35).

31. When Gilligan began her work, psychologists saw moral development in terms of the individual's development towards an understanding of the idea of justice. When this model of moral development was applied to girls and women, they were seen to have less sense of justice than boys and men.

In Gilligan's schema of two moral perspectives, neither is seen as an immature stage on the way to the other perspective. The two perspectives are two ways of seeing and organizing reality. Both perspectives are based on life-long concerns of human individuals and also have a developmental history in the life of the individual (Carol Gilligan and Grant Wiggins, "The Origins of Morality in Early Childhood Relationships," in *Mapping the Moral Domain*, 111).

The child's experiences of inequality are based on the child's awareness that he/she is not equal to adults and is relatively weak and dependent. The child usually looks forward to his/her growth towards equality and independence. In the process of growth, the child discovers that justice offers protection to the unequal in the face of oppression. The child learns to say, "That's not fair" or, "You have no right" when he or someone else faces oppression or injustice. These experiences are the basis of the justice perspective.

The child's experiences of attachment consist of the child's awareness that he or she is capable of caring for and hurting others and that others are capable of caring for and hurting him/her. The child loves those who care for him/her and discovers that love and attachment offer protection in the face of abandonment. The child learns to say, "You don't care" when faced with abandonment or indifference and also learns to say, "Don't turn away from others in need."[32] These experiences are the basis of the care perspective.

Gilligan proposes that differences between the use of the two moral perspectives by men and women are based on differences in the transformations of these basic childhood experiences. In the very young child, feelings of inequality in relation to the parent "who otherwise seems unmovable and all-powerful" may be mitigated by the experience of attachment to the parent. Girls usually continue to identify with and are attached to their mothers throughout childhood. The girl's feelings of inequality in relation to the mother "may be less overwhelming" than they would be without this identification and attachment. Girls, because of this typically positive experience in connection to attachment, may focus most of their attention on their connections with others and be less concerned about inequality in their relationships. Boys usually remain attached to their mothers throughout childhood but begin to identify with their fathers at an early age. The difference between the experience of girls and boys is that the boy is less likely to experience the kind of attachment to the father that the girl is able to feel towards the mother. In the boy, an experience of attachment to the father would mitigate the feelings of inequality with respect to the father. Instead, a concern for equaling or bettering the father's physical strength and position of authority may overtake the boy's concerns about attachment. Because of the lack of experiences of attachment that might mitigate feelings of inequality, boys may come to focus mostly on issues of equality with less concern about issues related to disconnection with others.[33]

The work of sociologist and psychoanalytic theorist Nancy Chodorow further explains the origins of the differences between women's experience and men's experience in terms of social relationships in childhood.[34] Chodorow

32. *Ibid.*, 114-15.
33. *Ibid.*, 116.
34. Nancy Chodorow, *The Reproduction of Mothering: Psychoanalysis and the Sociology of Gender* (Berkeley: University of California Press, 1978) and *Feminism and Psychoanalytic Theory* (New Haven: Yale University Press, 1989).

explains the origins of these differences in terms of psychoanalytic object relations theory. An assumption of this theory is that the development of personality is not only the result of the parents' or the child's conscious intentions. The child also forms his or her personality by internalizing features of social relationships, a process which is largely unconscious.

Chodorow proposes that differences between feminine and masculine personality can be accounted for by considering the effects of the fact that "women, universally, are largely responsible for early child care and for (at least) later female socialization."[35] Because women mother and because one of the social purposes of families is to produce heterosexually marrying offspring, both gender identity and sexual object choice must be established differently for girls than for boys, resulting in differences between feminine and masculine personality.

I will focus here on Chodorow's account of the differences in the development of gender identity in boys and girls. In some respects, the process of developing a gender identity is easier for girls than for boys.[36] For both boys and girls, the mother is the first person with whom the child identifies. Thus girls do not need to give up their primary identification with the mother in order to take on their adult role. Also, the mother is usually more often present and also more accessible to the children emotionally than is the father. Thus girls can more easily develop into what they see as their mother's role. The ease with which girls can adopt a feminine gender identity is reinforced by the fact that in our culture feminine gender identity is not seen as something that requires effort to be achieved or proved. All a girl needs to do is wait for her body to mature.

Boys, in contrast, need to actively reject their primary identification with the mother in order to establish their gender identity as masculine. Since the father is usually more distant than the mother, emotionally if not physically, and since the father's masculine role is not as visible, it is more difficult for boys to achieve masculine gender identity by identification with the father than for girls to achieve feminine gender identity by means of identification with the mother. Because of the relative unavailability of the father, masculine identity is seen largely as a negation of femininity. Boys may feel the need to vehemently reject or control what they perceive as feminine traits in themselves. Also, masculinity is seen in our culture as something which needs to be proven continually. Because of the difficulties of achieving a masculine gender identity, boys may reactively deny their own feminine traits, which are the result of their early identification with the mother, and also denigrate women and femininity in general.

35. Nancy Chodorow, "Family Structure and Feminine Personality," in *Feminism and Psychoanalytic Theory*, 45.

36. Nancy Chodorow, "Being and Doing: A Cross-Cultural Examination of the Socialization of Males and Females," in *Feminism and Psychoanalytic Theory*, 23-44.

The development of a feminine gender identity does not require a rejection of the girl's bond with the mother but rather promotes the feelings of attachment, relationship, and emotionality which are associated with the bond to the mother. Because the development of gender identity is easier for girls, a feminine sexual identity includes a sense of security. On the other hand, a girl who has achieved a feminine sexual identity may have doubts about whether or not she wants this identity. Western middle-class women learn that feminine qualities are not valued in school and in the public realm. Therefore a girl may question the value of her feminine gender identity, which is "reliant on her ability to inhibit herself and to respond to the demands of others" and which leads "eventually to an adult fate where her role and her dependence upon it doom her to bring up sons and daughters resentful of her and the femininity she represents."[37]

The basis of Gilligan's and Chodorow's suggestions as to reasons for the differences between women's experience and men's experience is the sensitivity of the human person to his/her social environment. Women and men experience themselves and the world differently because their development as children differs. The differences in the development of girl children and boy children are not based on an unmediated experience of sexual biology or any other feature of reality, but are shaped by the social structures of families.

Gilligan's and Chodorow's work supports the substance of the claims of dual-anthropology feminists as to significant differences between women's experience and men's experience. However, the advantage of approaches such as Gilligan's and Chodorow's is that they take account of and elaborate an important aspect of human finitude — the openness and vulnerability of human beings to their environment. Thus Gilligan's and Chodorow's work gives content to the concept of women's experience as distinctive yet also culturally constructed and socially mediated.

IV. Conclusion

In this essay I have argued that the claim of dual-anthropology feminists — that women have access to an unmediated experience of some aspect of reality — is misguided, given their desire to affirm the scope and value of human finitude. I have also suggested that the resistance of dual-anthropology feminists to the notion that women's experience is socially constructed and therefore always mediated by cultural concepts is due to their desire to establish a solid foundation for feminist claims, a foundation that is uncorrupted by sexist culture and invulnerable to challenge.

The denial of the culturally constructed nature of women's experience

37. *Ibid.*, 42.

implicitly denies an important feature of human finitude — the openness and vulnerability of human beings to their environment. Consequently, feminists' use of the concept of women's experience, if it is to be true to the feminist aim of affirming the scope and value of human finitude, needs to acknowledge the cultural construction of human personhood. I have suggested that work such as that of Carol Gilligan and Nancy Chodorow explains differences in masculine and feminine personality traits and women's and men's experience in terms of differing formative social relationships and thus takes account of this feature of human finitude.

For most of this essay, I have focused on the aspect of human finitude that is implicitly denied by many dual-anthropology feminists — the ways in which human experiences of bodiliness and participation in the material, biological realm are culturally constructed and socially mediated. However, I also want to emphasize that taking account of the cultural construction of human experience affirms the finitude of human culture-making activities as much as it affirms the mediated nature of human experiences of participation in the material, biological realm.

If one accepts the culturally constructed nature of women's and men's experiences, one also accepts that culture, which is usually associated with the so-called higher aspects of human beings, is an arena in which human beings display the thoroughgoing scope of human finitude. The capacities that have usually been seen as higher or as transcending the material, biological realm are not simple givens, nor are they unaffected by human embeddedness in the biological and social realms. Rather, these capacities are themselves formed and shaped by the contingencies of the individual's concrete and embodied relationships.

An important implication of Gilligan's work is that social relationships affect the development of cognitional abilities, such as moral reasoning.[38] This is an example of how the development of a so-called higher human capacity, namely moral reasoning, is conditioned by a person's social relationships and emotional experiences, especially in childhood. This conditioning is a mark of human finitude; yet it is still the cognitional ability, moral thinking, that bears the imprint of the environment's effects on the individual.

Human culture-making can be seen in terms of both the activity and the receptivity of human beings, activity corresponding to the more highly valued transcendent capacities and receptivity to human finitude. If one focuses on the aspects of culture that consist of active human self-construction, then culture is a manifestation of the so-called higher human capacities. If, however, culture is seen from the perspective of the individual who is born into a cultural setting, then it is clear that, to a large extent, the individual receives what is presented

38. Carol Gilligan, "Prologue: Adolescent Development Reconsidered," in *Mapping the Moral Domain*, xx.

externally by the culture and appropriates and internalizes it. The individual's vulnerability to the influence of his/her cultural setting can be seen as a manifestation of human finitude. In other words, culture is usually seen as the exercise of human capacities for transcending human embeddedness in the natural, biological realm. But the fact that culture-making capacities are gradually appropriated in concrete and particular settings is a manifestation of human bodiliness and finitude.

To conclude, I would recommend that feminists who are committed to elaborating the scope and value of human finitude, as well as significant differences in women's and men's experience, consider the usefulness of a view of human experience as culturally constructed and socially mediated.

Original Sin: A Study in Evangelical Theory

DAVID PARKER

Introduction

The doctrine of original sin, which refers to the "morally vitiated condition in which we find ourselves at birth as members of a sinful race,"[1] is commonly regarded as one of the most difficult parts of Christian theology. With talk of such matters as imputing Adam's sin to the race and our real incorporation in Adam, the doctrine seems to many to be a good example of some of the worst features of scholastic speculation.

Some theologians would go further and regard it as "offensive" or "a perversion of the Biblical doctrine of sin" and quite "untenable in its traditional forms." However, they would also generally concede that it does witness to a vital element in Christian truth, viz., that sin is "a dominant force, and the fact that all men are connected in the solidarity of sin."[2]

This makes it crucial for evangelicals who usually uphold it in a straightforward way because they believe it conserves a basic biblical teaching in a particularly emphatic manner. Thus, in an essay in *The Fundamentals* Thomas Whitelaw lists a number of key Scriptural passages in support of the doctrine, and then concludes:

> If these passages do not show that the Bible teaches the doctrine of original, or transmitted and inherited sin, it is difficult to see in what clearer or more

---

1. E. L. Mascall, "Sin," *Encyclopaedia Britannica* (1968), XX, 556.
2. Reinhold Niebuhr, "Sin," in M. Halverson and A. Cohen, eds., *A Handbook of Christian Theology* (London: Fontana, 1960), 352; E. Brunner, *The Christian Doctrine of Creation and Redemption* (London: Lutterworth, 1952), 103; H. Berkhof, *Christian Faith* (Grand Rapids: Eerdmans, 1979), 203.

Reprinted with permission from the *Evangelical Quarterly* 61/1 (1989): 51-69.

emphatic language the doctrine could have been taught. The truth of the doctrine may be challenged by those who repudiate the authority of Scripture; that it is a doctrine of Scripture can hardly be denied.[3]

But the importance of the doctrine for evangelicals lies not only in its specifically biblical content, but also in the fact that it is integrally related with other doctrines which are of primary theological and practical importance. These include the ideas of grace and salvation, the atonement, the nature of mankind, the function of baptism and evangelism. It also has implications for sanctification and ethics, and, moreover, the methodology used to derive the doctrine is dependent upon vital hermeneutical decisions and philosophical presuppositions.

History

The doctrine is not stated in its traditional form in the Bible. It is generally agreed that Augustine (building upon the work of some of his Western predecessors) was the first to formulate it in the context of his controversy with Pelagius, whose views provoked a turning point in the history [of] discussion of the subject.[4]

Pelagius taught that individuals are born with the same nature as Adam before the fall and that their subsequent sinning was a consequence only of their imitation of the sins of Adam. Hence Pelagius did not hold to a doctrine of original sin, largely because he felt that it had no scriptural basis and because he believed that the strongly deterministic emphasis of Augustine's teaching undercut a Christian's sense of moral responsibility.

In reaction, Augustine refined his teaching and spoke of the idea of generic sin by which "human nature, existing in its totality in Adam, was corrupted in the first act of transgression, and as such is transmitted to his descendants," the instrument of which is "the sexual appetite."[5] Basing his views on Romans 5:12, where the Vulgate translation of the Greek *eph ho* is *in quo* (in whom), which, according to Augustine, can only refer to Adam, he wrote,

> Nothing remains but to conclude that in the first man all are understood to have sinned, because all were in him when he sinned; whereby sin is brought in with birth and not removed save by the new birth. . . . It is manifest that

---

3. "The Biblical conception of sin" in *The Fundamentals*, XI, 7-22, cited from 15. See also Charles B. Williams, "Paul's Testimony to the Doctrine of Sin," VII, 49-63. The more recently published *Baker's Dictionary of Theology* and *Evangelical Dictionary of Theology* do not contain separate articles on original sin.

4. G. C. Berkouwer, *Sin* (Grand Rapids: Eerdmans, 1971), 430.

5. G. P. Fisher, *History of Christian Doctrine* (Edinburgh, T. & T. Clark, 1896), 185. Augustine's position is not always entirely clear (Fisher, 186; Berkouwer, *Sin*, 434).

in Adam all sin, so to speak, en masse. Hence, by that sin we become a corrupt mass — massa perditionis.[6]

Although Pelagianism was officially condemned at Carthage in A.D. 418 and at later councils, it reappeared in the modified form of Semi-Pelagianism, which taught that the first steps towards salvation could be taken by man although divine grace was needed for salvation. Both views were found during subsequent centuries with semi-Pelagianism often in the ascendancy.

The Augustinian view was revived by the Protestant reformers, with Calvin, for example, defining original sin as

> an hereditary depravity and corruption of our nature, diffused into all parts of the soul, which first makes us liable to God's wrath, then also brings forth in us those works which Scripture calls "works of the flesh." (Gal. 5:19) . . . since we through his (Adam's) transgression have become entangled in the curse, he is said to have made us guilty.[7]

With the development of biblical criticism, the historicity of the Genesis record was discredited and with it the idea of a literal period of innocence in the Garden followed by a fall through sin. Accordingly, the basis for the traditional doctrine was undermined. Contemporary philosophical and social developments produced a range of views about original sin, most of which tended strongly to contradict the traditional view by appealing to such notions as justice and personal responsibility.

Even amongst contemporary evangelicals there is a wide variety of views. At one end of the scale, there is a popular level statement such as the one from *The Fundamentals*, quoted above, and this from Paul Little,

> Because Adam's original sin is charged to us, we inherit a corrupt nature. . . . From Adam we received sin and guilt . . . sin is our corrupt nature.[8]

Yet, despite these clear affirmations, Donald G. Bloesch has suggested that the evangelical practice of revivalism may be guilty of a *de facto* denial of the doctrine through too great an optimism about man's freedom to "decide for salvation on his own" without the aid of divine grace.[9] There may well be considerable validity to such a claim, but as most will admit, human experience and the Bible point to a serious problem of sin, so the doctrine can hardly be dropped altogether despite its problems.

---

6. Fisher, 186. See also p. 190: "Persona corrumpit naturam; natura corrumpit personam; so the doctrine was summarily stated."

7. *The Institutes*, II, i, 8.

8. Paul Little, *Know What You Believe* (Homebush West: Anzea Books, 1973), 59f. See also Robert P. Lightner, *Evangelical Theology* (Grand Rapids: Baker, 1986), 174.

9. Donald G. Bloesch, *Essentials of Evangelical Theology* (New York: Harper and Row, 1978), I, 113.

Accordingly, at the other end of the scale there are lengthy treatments, such as those by Orton Wiley, Charles Hodge and G. C. Berkouwer, which develop complex statements on questions of imputation, divine justice and the impact of [the] doctrine on the scheme of theology. All of this suggests that there is a good deal of truth in Berkouwer's point that it is easier to spot and condemn the error of Pelagius than to provide a satisfactory positive alternative.[10]

Such a confusing state of affairs might be tolerable in the case of a peripheral doctrine or for systems of theology that do not lay claim to an absolute authority. But it clearly raises serious questions for evangelical theology which not only affirms the crucial importance of this doctrine in its own right and in relation to other doctrines, but which also bases itself on a belief in the authority, clarity and sufficiency of Scripture for all matters of faith and practice.

Issues

Because the form and the terminology of the traditional doctrine are not to be found as such in Scripture, it is desirable to identify some of the major general issues before considering particular doctrinal expressions.

To begin with, it must be noted that the term "original sin" itself is somewhat "misleading," as E. L. Mascall concedes, since it does not refer primarily to the original sin of Adam, or to the first sin of an individual, but only to the state in which we find ourselves at birth as members of the race.[11] Hence, to avoid misunderstanding, the terms "birth sin," "innate sin," "inherited sin," or "race sin" are sometimes preferred. But as Hendrikus Berkhof points out, it would appear that to the extent to which it is something which is "original" or innate, it can hardly be described as "sin," if sin is connected with personal responsibility for rejection of God's will.[12]

There is little dispute over the fact that the human race exists in a vitiated state; while this is certainly "asserted, assumed, and proved" in Scripture,[13] experience alone is necessary to demonstrate it, and even those who reject the traditional form of the doctrine readily agree that this is the case. This corrupt state involves a bias or proneness to sin which leads inevitably, but not necessarily, to actual sinning in the case of each individual.

Therefore, the simplest way of thinking of this doctrine is to regard it as the theoretical explanation (of whatever cogency) for the patently obvious

---

10. Berkouwer, 433, 435.
11. Mascall, "Sin," 556.
12. Hendrikus Berkhof, 204.
13. Charles Hodge, *Systematic Theology* (London: James Clarke, 1960), 231.

phenomenon of the universality of sin amongst humans. Thus E. J. Bicknell states that original sin is "at bottom the attempt to express the fact that all men fall into sin."[14]

From a biblical point of view, the universality of sin cannot be attributed to some external or physical characteristic (as some beliefs of gnostic or Manichean origin have it), for this would deny the doctrine of the creation of mankind in the divine image by suggesting that mankind is evil or defective *per se*. Rather, the fault must be a moral one, involving personal responsibility whereby each individual willingly consents to the inborn corruption and bias to sin and thereby actually sins.

The traditional formulation of the doctrine of original sin is intended to preserve this idea of personal involvement, for, as Berkouwer notes, the church has always agreed that it "may not function and cannot function as a means of excusing ourselves or hiding behind another man's guilt."[15] Therefore, even in its simplest form, it differs from the Pelagian view, yet in so doing it becomes little more than an alternative term for the state of depravity.[16]

However, because of ethical and metaphysical uncertainties surrounding the notion of an inborn tendency to sin and the links between this tendency and actual sins, it may be doubted if this way of understanding the doctrine has even succeeded in satisfactorily protecting the idea of sin. Yet it is not certain that support for a stronger view can be found in Scripture. Apart from a few notoriously controversial texts (viz., Ps. 51; Rom. 5; Eph. 2:3), all passages usually cited speak simply of the universality and inevitability of actual sins as a phenomenon, without offering any further metaphysical or theological explanation.

Nevertheless, formulating the doctrine of original sin as merely an explanation for the universality of sin does not satisfy a number of theologians because it does not seem to provide a strong enough explanation for the occurrence of sins.

To overcome this weakness, some theologians go further and speak of original sin and also of original guilt. The latter is defined as our judicial involvement with Adam's sin.[17] This is a stricter view for it refers to the inherited corruption of the human race as sin for which people are culpable and not merely as a vitiated state and a tendency to commit actual sins.

14. E. J. Bicknell, *A Theological Introduction to the Thirty Nine Articles* (London: Longmans, Green, 1955), 177. W. H. Griffith Thomas, *The Principles of Christian Theology* (Grand Rapids: Baker, 1979), 159. See also John Stacey, *Groundwork of Theology* (London: Epworth, 1977), 257: "The fall tells us the way things are."

15. Berkouwer, 435.

16. See especially Arminians such as H. Orton Wiley, *Christian Theology* (Kansas City: Beacon Hill, 1952), II, 125; and Ernest S. Williams, *Systematic Theology* (Springfield: Gospel Pub. House, 1953), II, 136.

17. Hodge, 227; J. Oliver Buswell, *A Systematic Theology of the Christian Religion* (Grand Rapids: Zondervan, 1962-63), II, 285.

This way of looking at original sin certainly succeeds in guarding against Pelagianism. However, to sustain such a view, it is necessary to show how it is feasible to think of mankind as a whole existing in a state which may be called "sinful" in any biblical sense, and also how individuals can be associated with each other and with Adam in such a way as to be genuinely responsible for Adam's sin.[18] It is in dealing with these issues that more problematic or even speculative elements make their appearance in the doctrinal formulations.

Thus to account for the universality of sin or "race-sin," reference is made to the concept of generic human nature. Then sin itself is defined as not only an act of rebellion or rejection of God's will, but as a "disposition or state" which "lacks conformity to the moral will of God."[19] Finally, various mechanisms are proposed to account for the link between Adam and mankind in regard to sin. The most common of these are the *physical,* by which Adam's descendants are born in a corrupt state by the laws of generation and consequently sin; the *organic,* by which Adam's descendants are regarded as literally (seminally) within him an undifferentiated or unindividualised state; and the *judicial,* by which Adam is regarded as the representative of all mankind in a legal sense so that he acts on their behalf in a covenantal (federal) relationship with God and they suffer the consequences of his fall, which includes death, depravity and guilt.

Some systems of theology make the process of imputing or reckoning sin and guilt to an individual (whether his own or Adam's) the entire problematic of original sin.[20] But this tends to distort the focus of the discussion by highlighting theories of imputation and ethical questions associated with guilt and the justice of God rather than seeing original sin as a call to the confession of our personal guilt and the grasping of the greater grace of God.[21] Such a distortion exacerbates the apparently scholastic nature of the doctrine, but at least it does serve to emphasise the racial or generic aspects of the doctrine and so distinguish it clearly from the separate ideas of depravity and actual sin.[22]

Therefore if the doctrine is to be retained at all, it needs to be stated in terms which deal with these more advanced issues. A review of some major evangelical schools of interpretation now follows.

---

18. Buswell, II, 286.

19. A. H. Strong, *Systematic Theology* (Valley Forge: Judson, 1907), 549, 577; L. Berkhof, *Systematic Theology* (Edinburgh: Banner of Truth, 1939), 246. H. Orton Wiley, *Christian Theology,* II.

20. Strong, 593f.

21. Berkouwer, 466.

22. Hodge, 227.

Reformed Theology

Reformed theology with its Augustinian roots is the most rigorous in its approach to original sin. A number of different examples may be found in readily accessible publications. They are similar but by no means identical in every detail.[23]

The view that sin is not only an act but also a state which is out of the will of God is usually found as a basic tenet of the conservative tradition of Reformed theology, as is the belief that the Genesis record of Adam is historically reliable. Reformed theologians usually reach similar conclusions about the nature of Adam's sin and its immediate impact upon him. More significantly for the present topic, they also see Adam's sin affecting mankind as the cause or origin of sinfulness and the ground for a judicial sentence of guilt which is levelled against all people.[24]

However, Reformed theologians differ among themselves over the modes of transmission of sin or the theories of imputation because of differing hermeneutical and theological schemes. Thus, J. Murray, L. Berkhof, J. O. Buswell and C. Hodge adopt the representative or federal mode, while A. H. Strong follows the organic or Augustinian mode. Strong also effectively restricts the idea of original sin to imputation, although he defines his terms carefully, assigning imputation to the divine treatment of sin and original sin itself to the abnormal human condition.[25]

Therefore, although there may be significant differences in theories of imputation between these theologians, the net effect is similar in that they all affirm a concept of race-sin derived from and dependent upon Adam. Furthermore, the theories of imputation are all constructed so that the link with Adam still leaves all people personally responsible for sin even if not individually involved.

In their treatment of the "abnormal human condition" they are more consistent. The starting point is the universality of sin as an empirical reality, the most obvious aspect of which is the "conscious violation of law" or actual sin. There is no difficulty in proving this notion by referring to Scripture and experience. However, it is a different situation when Reformed theology wishes to progress beyond this level and so distinguish itself from Pelagianism by

---

23. The four popular theologies examined here are those of L. Berkhof, J. O. Buswell, Charles Hodge and A. H. Strong. John Murray has also published a monograph on the topic (*The Imputation of Adam's Sin;* Grand Rapids: Eerdmans, 1959) adopting the representative view, and treating the topic from an exegetical perspective. This work expands on his observations in his commentary *The Epistle to the Romans* (Grand Rapids: Eerdmans, 1967). Because of the logic of Romans 5:12 and 5:15-19, where the sin of Adam is accounted to be the sin of all, Murray speaks of "solidaric sin" (*Imputation*, 95).

24. Hodge, 227.

25. Strong, 594.

proving that there is a link with Adam and also that sin is more than personal acts of sin. This is where it is necessary to call upon the notion of a corrupted human nature, which is the basis for a doctrine of original sin.

The clear statements of Scripture are not sufficient here, for as Buswell concedes, "The imputation of Adam's sin to his posterity is not explicitly developed in the Old Testament."[26] As far as the New Testament is concerned, he can only appeal to Romans 5 for an unequivocal statement on the topic. But even this is far from convincing when it is realised that interpreters from rather different schools of thought find the same passage supportive of their positions also! To demonstrate their case, Reformed theologians typically resort to a process of deduction that proposes a general law or common human nature to account for the universality of actual sins amongst human beings. Thus Strong writes,

> Reason seeks an underlying principle which will reduce these multitudinous phenomena to unity . . . we are compelled to refer these common moral phenomena to a common moral nature, and to find in it the cause of this universal, spontaneous, and all-controlling opposition to God and his law. The only possible solution of the problem is this, that the common nature of mankind is corrupt. . . . This unconscious and fundamental direction of the will, as the source of actual sin, must itself be sin; and of this sin all mankind are partakers.[27]

According to Reformed theology, then, it is this common human nature now tainted by corruption which the Bible means when it speaks of "the flesh" and the "carnal mind."

Buswell is one of the few to acknowledge in any detail the philosophical presuppositions involved in this process,[28] but even then, he does not allow this concession to affect his certainty about the racial dimension of sin. But this is a serious weakness because it is clear that only a doctrinal system presupposing the real existence of universals like "human nature" could include the notion of "race sin" or a generic human nature liable to be corrupted by the fall of its founder and head. If belief in the existence of universals is not part of one's theological or philosophical system, then the fact that all people do in fact sin may be accepted as an undoubted empirical and historical fact but one which requires no further explanation as to its cause or origin. In this case, there can be no doctrine of original sin and guilt except in the most elementary manner. The latter is a more popular philosophical position in the contemporary world, at least at the popular level.

The Augustinian or realist theory of imputation seems best suited to the

---

26. Buswell, 286.
27. Strong, 580.
28. Buswell, 300. See also Fisher, 185, on Augustine.

idea of a corrupted human nature, but it is notable that only Strong adopts it. The others reject this theory because it seems to be *too* materialistic, thus tending to obscure the personal or moral element in original sin. But it is impossible to avoid such a position if the idea of a generic human nature is to be held. It is this factor in Augustine's original presentation that ensured the church would retain infant baptism as the sacramental remedy for original sin. It also led in time to the idea of the immaculate conception of the Blessed Virgin Mary as a safeguard for the Virgin Birth in order to prevent Christ and Mary from being affected by original sin.

Similarly, in Reformed theology, the realist theory accounts for the belief that original sin is still present in the regenerate believer, although not imputed.[29] This has a practical effect by its impact on the doctrine of sanctification by ruling out the possibility of entire sanctification until original sin is removed at the glorification of the believer at death.

The notion of a common human nature which is tainted or corrupted by the fall also leads Reformed theology to assert a strict doctrine of original guilt, whereby Adam's descendants are judicially involved with his sin. They are therefore justly liable to its consequences in terms of both blameworthiness *(reatus culpae)* and liability to punishment *(reatus poenae)*. But according to the Reformed doctrine of sin, this corruption or depravity is itself sinful because it is a state which is contrary to God's will and wholly inclined to evil. As Hodge puts it, original sin or the corruption of nature derived from Adam is "truly and properly of the nature of sin, involving both guilt and pollution."[30] However, it must be observed that this is a special interpretation of the idea of sin, as Buswell implies when he refers to "sin, *in the form of corruption*" as dwelling in our nature.[31]

This idea of an original guilt is closely associated with the doctrine of total depravity which leaves mankind without hope of salvation apart from divine election. In its purest form, this is a harsh doctrine. Strong relieves it somewhat by stating that "actual sin, in which the personal agent reaffirms the underlying determination of his will, is *more guilty* than original sin alone" and that "no human being is finally condemned solely on account of original sin; but that all who, like infants, do not commit personal transgressions, are saved through the application of Christ's atonement."[32]

But even this does not seriously negate the idea of original sin, for Strong writes:

29. Hodge, 230; Griffith Thomas, 171f.
30. Hodge, 230. Note that Protestant theologians at the Reformation and later strongly rejected the distinction between *reatus culpae* and *reatus poenae* as "papistical," pointing out that "*reatus* is nothing else than obligation to *poenae*, which springs from *culpa*" (Turretine). (J. Murray, *Imputation*, 37, 79-85).
31. Buswell, 286.
32. Strong, 596.

There is a race-sin, therefore, as well as a personal sin; and that race-sin was committed by the first father of the race, when he comprised the whole race in himself. All mankind since that time have been born in the state into which he fell — a state of depravity, guilt, and condemnation.[33]

According to the Reformed theologians, nothing less than this can account for facts of life and the teaching of Scripture. Arminian theology, however, has a different view.

Arminian Theology

Some contemporary theologies in the broader Arminian tradition reject the traditional doctrine of original sin as having no explicit biblical warrant and as creating insoluble problems over the idea of original guilt.[34] But there are other, more conservative examples which assert the doctrine in no uncertain terms. Thus W. T. Purkiser writes,

> That there is a profound and permanent perversity in the heart of man is the fundamental, uncompromising assertion of Christianity about human nature. To this perversity Christian theology has given the name "original sin." The doctrine of original sin is not a mere appendage to Christian thought, but is one of the foundation stones of the building. For only in the light of man's enslavement to sin does the plan of redemption become intelligible. If man can solve his problems without divine assistance, then the incarnation of God in Christ is largely meaningless.[35]

Classical versions of Arminian theology (especially of the Wesleyan tradition), therefore, like Reformed theology, accept the reliability of the Genesis account and see sin as a rebellion against God, the consequences of which include the penalty of death. Furthermore, Arminian theology accepts a moderate expression of the natural and federal headship of Adam so that all mankind become involved in the results of his sin. Thus Arminian theology, in contrast with Pelagianism, does support a doctrine of original sin which it has defined as "the transmission of heredity guilt and depravity to all the natural progeny of the first sinning pair."[36] It is in discussion of these two elements of original sin that the distinctive elements of the Arminian position begin to emerge.

33. Strong, 596.

34. E.g., John Stacey, *Groundwork of Theology* (London: Epworth, 1977); H. Maldwyn Hughes, *Christian Foundations* (London: Epworth, 1927); Gordon S. Dicker, *Faith with Understanding* (Sydney: Unichurch Pub., 1981).

35. W. T. Purkiser, ed., *Exploring Our Faith* (Kansas City: Beacon Hill, 1960), 237.

36. Benjamin Field, *The Student's Handbook of Christian Theology* (London: Hodder and Stoughton, 1883), 122, quoting Hannah.

First of all, depravity, which is defined as the morally tainted nature inherited from Adam,[37] is not an evil infused by God as a judgment upon man but the result of the loss by Adam of original righteousness of God's life-giving presence and power, with the consequent state of spiritual death or depravity. Adam as head of the race passed on to his posterity that state or condition. That is to say, it is a case of "depravation" arising from "deprivation."[38] Arminianism affirms that mankind's morally depraved condition is the consistent teaching of Scripture and is assumed by it throughout.

Such a view of depravity calls for a particular view of inherited or original guilt. Arminian theology places great emphasis upon the distinction between guilt as personal blameworthiness and guilt as liability to penalty.[39] Both are true for actual sin and in the case of Adam's sin, but only the liability to penalty (reatus poenae) applies to race-sin, since it is argued that, on any moral principle, the posterity of Adam could not be personally responsible for his sin.

For biblical support, Field and Wiley both note the importance of a particular interpretation of the clause, "whose sins were not like the transgression of Adam" in Romans 5:14.[40] Here a distinction is made between Adam's sin and that of his posterity in that he sinned personally (incurring both kinds of guilt) but his posterity did not sin personally. Yet by empirical evidence, his posterity suffered death, which is stated to be the penal consequence of Adam's sin in his role as representative head of the race. This means that the posterity were dealt with as sinners because of their connection with Adam and not because of personal sins.

Such an arrangement is defended as being in harmony with God's justice, for it is not unnatural for one to suffer the results of another's actions, although in such a case one is not blamed for them.

Thus all mankind is born in a state of separation from God as a result of Adam's fall and therefore under the curse of the law and in need of restoration through Christ, as Galatians 3:14 and Ephesians 2:3 make plain. Accordingly, "heredity depravity (or original sin), then, is not only the law of natural heredity, but that law operating under the penal consequences of Adam's sin."[41] So, for Arminianism (in contrast to Reformed theology), "original sin [is] a depravity that results from deprivation . . . a loss of original righteousness and involves guilt only in the sense of culpable liability to punishment."[42]

To understand fully this apparently weaker view of Original Guilt, it is necessary to see the link with other theological themes, especially the fine balance in Romans 5 between Adam and the Fall on the one hand and Christ

37. This is similar to Reformed theology (Wiley, II, 119).

38. Wiley, II, 123; Field, 126.

39. I.e., reatus culpae and reatus poenae. Wiley, II, 126; Field, 124.

40. Field, 125; Wiley, II, 97.

41. Wiley, II, 125.

42. Charles W. Carter, ed., A Contemporary Wesleyan Theology (Grand Rapids: Zondervan, 1983), I, 263.

and righteousness on the other. This leads on to what Wiley calls the "distinctive doctrine" of Arminianism, viz., "the free gift of righteousness, or the unconditional diffusion of grace to all men, as a first benefit of the universal atonement made by Jesus Christ."[43] It is by this gift of prevenient grace "that the condemnation that rested on the race through Adam's sin is removed" and that accordingly "no child of Adam is condemned eternally, either from the original offense, or its consequences" or for the "depravity of his own nature."[44] So there is no need for a concept of election and reprobation as in Calvinism, or for the weaker view of Pelagianism which denies the penal consequences of Adam's sin altogether. There is also no role for sacramental infant baptism.

The Arminian view of Christ's atonement and prevenient grace, which mitigates the "culpability of original sin,"[45] is a much neater and stronger solution than others that have been offered, yet one that does not deny the "exceeding sinfulness of sin." It is also more positive because it leads on to the assurance of being able to deal with depravity in the life of the believer by the power of the gospel. Accordingly, Arminian theology teaches the "eradication" or purification of inherited corruption by the work of the Holy Spirit.[46]

Traditional Arminianism may offer a neater solution, but whether it has done so by merely re-defining terms is another matter. Some of its own advocates have their reservations, especially in regard to the meaning of the biblical texts and the ethical problems of the imputation of Adam's guilt.[47] This continuing difference illustrates the notorious "difficulty" of this doctrine, at least in its classical formulations. It is not surprising, then, that some contemporary theologians have attempted to find a more radical path to resolving it.[48]

Contemporary Solutions

Donald G. Bloesch

Donald Bloesch, who has attempted to "resolve past conflicts" by use of a radical biblical approach in his *Essentials of Evangelical Theology*,[49] recognizes the vital

43. Wiley, II, 130.

44. Wiley, II, 135.

45. Wiley, II, 136.

46. *Contemporary Wesleyan Theology*, 268.

47. *Contemporary Wesleyan Theology*, 268; Richard S. Taylor, *Beacon Dictionary of Theology* (Kansas City: Beacon Hill, n.d.), 378.

48. Not all contemporary theologians adopt a radical approach. See, e.g., Carl F. H. Henry, *God, Revelation and Authority* (Waco: Word, 1983), VI, 248, who takes a traditional Augustinian position. The works of G. C. Berkouwer and Hendrikus Berkhof could also be consulted.

49. Bloesch, *Essentials of Evangelical Theology* (2 vols.) (New York: Harper & Row, 1978), I, 5, "Total Depravity."

role of hermeneutics in dealing with the biblical material. He agrees with the view of Niebuhr that the Genesis record must be taken seriously if not literally. This can be done easily, he argues, if it is regarded as "symbolic or mythopoetic rather than univocal."[50] Using this principle, he concludes there was a real fall, but not necessarily an historical one, by which is evidently meant not one that can be confined to our present historical continuum but one that is prehistorical and universal.[51] The first man and the first fall are not only historical but also universal and representative.

Thus, by taking a wider view of Scripture, Bloesch is able to argue for a racial concept of sin. However, he is obliged to concede that no rational explanation can be offered for the relationship between primal sin and individual sin — it is, as Brunner noted, "sui generis." Hence Bloesch can only conclude, "original sin is not a biological taint but a spiritual contagion which is nevertheless, *in some inexplicable way,* passed on through biological generation," and accordingly, it is "not a natural necessity but a historical inevitability."[52] Yet despite this, Bloesch, in common with others, effectively denies a concept of Original Guilt *(reatus culpae)* when he states that original sin "does not become rooted in man until he assents to it and allows it to dominate his whole being."[53]

Millard J. Erickson

A similar position is taken in one of the most recently published evangelical statements — *Christian Theology* by Millard Erickson. After having reviewed the various issues and options, Erickson finds the starting point for his distinctive position by recognizing that a loose interpretation of the balance between Adam and Christ found in Romans chapter 5 may permit belief in an "unconscious faith" on the part of unbelievers. However, because such a concept is not sanctioned anywhere else in Scripture, he concludes that this must be a false interpretation of the passage.

But this line of thinking also rules out the possibility of the related idea of unconscious sin on the part of mankind. There is some basis for accepting that "we all were involved in Adam's sin and thus receive both the corrupted nature that was his after the fall, and the guilt and condemnation that attach to his sin." However, when it comes to the question of inherited guilt, the

50. Bloesch, 104. This is a view which Henry condemns when he finds it expressed by Dale Moody (Henry, 248).

51. Bloesch, 106f.

52. Bloesch, 106, 107 (emphasis added). Compare Bloesch's wording in his article in *Evangelical Dictionary of Theology* (1013), where he says that this "spiritual infection is in some mysterious way transmitted through reproduction."

53. Bloesch, 107.

situation is different because there can be no "unconscious faith." Therefore, "there must be some conscious and voluntary decision on our part. Until this is the case, there is only a conditional imputation of guilt."[54] This "conditional imputation" becomes "actual," Erickson concludes, whenever we accept or approve of our corrupt nature. Thus Erickson overcomes the problem by retaining the notion of depravity but by modifying the idea of Original Guilt to the point where the idea of "guilt" becomes virtually meaningless.[55]

While both these theologians who work from a broadly Reformed perspective are grappling seriously with the central issues in an attempt to overcome the traditional difficulties, it cannot be said that they arrive at a fully persuasive solution.[56]

Contemporary Wesleyan Theology

Similarly, another recently published systematic theology, this time from the Wesleyan perspective,[57] can only concede the complexity of the issues and the lack of consistency amongst Arminians. In the end, its author, Charles W. Carter, rejects the Augustinian/Calvinist position for two major reasons. The first reason for rejection is that the idea of original guilt contradicts the idea of guilt as "a culpable act traceable to the unethical conduct of a morally responsible person." The second reason for rejection is that of "the Augustinian tendency to identify sin with physical being [which] leads to a materialistic understanding that attributes a sort of tangibility or 'thingness' to it."[58] Such a tendency subtly transforms the concept of sin.

According to Carter, Arminianism can be defended because it avoids this problem by maintaining that biblical terms such as "flesh" and "the old man" should not be interpreted literally but as "symbols or metaphors to communicate nontangible realities." Consequently, sin is not "an independent metaphysical entity" but a "moral reality that exists only in the distorted relationships between God and fallen humanity."[59] In this way, the dynamic concept of sin and grace is maintained which tends strongly to preserve the sense of personal responsibility on the part of man. Although such a position seems quite distinct from Augustinianism with its strong reifying process, Carter believes that a

---

54. Millard J. Erickson, *Christian Theology*, 3 vols. (Grand Rapids: Baker, 1983), 639.

55. A. H. Strong (596) speaks of a similar qualification.

56. The authors themselves show a certain tentativeness about their own positions. E.g., Erickson (639) refers to "the current form of my understanding. . . ."

57. Charles W. Carter, ed., *A Contemporary Wesleyan Theology: Biblical, Systematic and Practical* (2 vols.) (Grand Rapids: Zondervan, 1983), 7, "Harmartiology." The editor is the author of this chapter. This work is useful as a sample of Wesleyan thinking, but it is neither full nor conclusive and suffers from a lack of clarity of aims and methods.

58. *Contemporary Wesleyan Theology*, 261, 267.

59. *Contemporary Wesleyan Theology*, 261.

better understanding of the structure of Arminian and Calvinist theological systems, especially in regard to the definition of sin, would reduce the differences in line with Wesley's opinion that there was "but a hair's breadth" between them.[60]

Conclusions

The substantial differences of opinion which do remain indicate that stronger measures yet are necessary to overcome the difficulties in formulating this doctrine. As a first step in achieving this, the structure of the traditional evangelical approach needs to be clearly recognized.

The common aim is to produce a systematic statement of the biblical teaching about the universality of sin and to correlate this with the data of human experience and with other areas of theology. The fact of the universality of sin is clearly found in Scripture, but there is much less support for specific teaching about a concept of race-sin, its nature or cause, and its link with Adam's sin, assuming that the history of the Genesis record is to be accepted, at least in a general sense.

However, the desire to provide an explanation for the universality of sin and thus to provide a substantial basis for soteriology leads many theologians to notions of a generic human nature corrupted by the fall of Adam and to theories of imputation to account for the transmission of this corruption and guilt. But it is only possible to hold to such ideas on the basis of particular philosophic presuppositions which do not necessarily find unambiguous support in Scripture.

Consequently, from a biblical point of view, it is possible to adopt other philosophical principles which do not postulate such explanations, but are content simply to speak of the way all mankind does sin and is therefore in need of salvation. The biblical data do not seem to require anything more than this if they are taken quite naturally and within their proper context. Yet at the same time, they exclude the Pelagian error which proposes the avoidability of sin and hence the possibility of salvation apart from grace. Biblical passages referring to Adam are interpreted as either symbolical statements of the existential condition of man, or, more conservatively, as showing how man has sinned ever since the beginning.

Therefore it can be concluded that one major problem with the traditional formulation of the doctrine of original sin is the desire to go beyond Scripture by seeking rational explanations for the causes and mechanisms of sin. One result of this is to distort the biblical witness by placing heavy dependence on extrabiblical philosophical doctrines, rather than putting the emphasis where

60. *Contemporary Wesleyan Theology,* 272.

the Bible does, viz., upon moral relationships which speak of the "confession of our sin" or "the guilt character of all sin."[61]

But once it is recognized that Scripture does not offer an explanation for the universality of sin, many of the traditional difficulties with the exegesis of passages noted above dealing with sin fall away,[62] leaving them to be interpreted in their original pastoral context. There is therefore no inclination to add anything to the doctrine of sin to sharpen its impact, and no need to hedge soteriology around with any protective doctrinal affirmations. This means that there is no need to elaborate theories of imputation and, furthermore, there is no pressure to develop a doctrine of sacramental infant baptism or to move in the direction of the Catholic Marian dogmas of the immaculate conception or of the bodily assumption. It also frees up the idea of the Virgin Birth and enables it to make a more dynamic contribution to Christology.

As well as dealing with the racial aspects of humanity's existence, this doctrine also deals with the "morally vitiated condition in which we find ourselves at birth."[63] The inclusion of the term "sin" in the description of this condition is another major problem facing the doctrine. This is because the word "sin" in theology is usually associated with a strong sense of personal responsibility. But it is used in a special sense in the doctrine of original sin to refer to our moral condition at birth. It is ethically difficult, however, to assign responsibility for a state or condition of existence and one over which the individual has no personal control. Yet, biblical teaching and human experience will not allow the simple Pelagian solution of denying that humankind exists in a morally vitiated condition.

The use of the term "depravity" as an equivalent or alternative to original sin as found in some Arminian theology offers a promising lead for resolving the difficulty. The terms "depravity" or "innate moral corruption" may be used to refer to the fact that, due to the absence of God's gracious presence and power resulting from the fall, humankind exists in a morally deprived condition. He is therefore unable to please God or to prevent himself from falling into sin. By virtue of this condition, he is therefore under the displeasure of God and "by nature a child of wrath" (Eph 2:3). To refer to this as "sin" (as the traditional formulations do) may be correct if the definition of sin is broadened to include the idea of "moral corruption," but it is certainly misleading, and could well be avoided by the use of other terminology which differentiates between sin and the morally vitiated state of mankind.

To speak of "innate moral corruption" instead of "birth sin" not only resolves the ethical problem relating to "sin" and the idea of "inherited guilt," but also has a clarifying effect on the corresponding view of salvation. The new

---

61. Berkouwer, 466ff.; Hendrikus Berkhof, 192.

62. See, e.g., Strong, 553 (d), (e), where there is an overexegesis in regard to the personification of sin.

63. Mascall, 556.

terminology stresses inability, lostness and separation from God and his life-giving presence. The motifs of salvation which correspond to these are recon-ciliation, redemption and liberation. These are prominent in biblical teaching as well as common enough in evangelistic practice. However, they are not always associated with theological statements relating to humankind's need of salvation arising out of original sin, but are instead often overshadowed by the penal substitutionary view of the atonement. This exclusive dependence upon only one of the biblical models of the atonement (which is distinctive of the entire system of evangelical soteriology) can be corrected by the new approach to the doctrine of original sin. The universality of sin and its penal consequences require penal substitution, while "innate moral corruption" calls for reconcil-iation, redemption and liberation.

Thus it can be concluded that the biblical data as they stand speak of the universality of sin and humankind's needy moral condition, both of which require the intervention of divine grace for salvation. The term "original sin," as Griffith Thomas suggests, is "not the most accurate phrase to employ."[64] Happily, it may be set on one side without any fear of either compromising biblical teaching about sin or undermining soteriology. To make the change would be in accord with a more satisfactory methodology for evangelical the-ology and would result in a simpler and therefore stronger doctrine by elimi-nating the causes of most speculation, misunderstanding and controversy. To discard the terminology would be no loss, for it is not biblical in any case, and what we have to do is maintain the "anti-Pelagian motif," not its "formulation in a doctrine of Original Sin" as such.[65]

64. Griffith Thomas, 158.

65. Brunner, 103. A good candidate for simplification by following such a process is to be found in John Murray's re-evaluation of imputation where he does not hesitate to critique previous Reformed theologians and others for making misleading statements or failing to guard against misunderstanding. (See, e.g., his critique of Charles Hodge — Imputation, 78). But in the process, he places so many qualifications on the notion of imputation, as expressed in Romans 5:12-20, that the doctrine is reduced virtually to a plain statement of the factuality of the universality of sin. "Solidarity was constituted by divine institution and the solidarity is of such a nature that the sin of Adam devolves upon all naturally procreated posterity" (Imputation, 41; see also The Epistle to the Romans, 186).

Religions, Cultures, and the Struggle for Justice: Aspects of North-South Dialogue

STANLEY J. SAMARTHA

The relationship between nations in the North and those in the South is usually discussed in terms of trade and commerce, that is, in political and economic terms, while the religious and cultural components of this complex relationship are almost always completely ignored. Quite often, the religious-cultural elements are discussed in such isolation from the economic-political ones that their interconnectedness is seldom recognized. Thus, human life is broken and fragmented almost beyond repair. One of the purposes of this essay is to draw attention to the inner relationship between the struggle for justice on the one hand and the quest for a more positive theology of religions on the other. This is indeed a highly complex relationship, the roots of which are not always clear. However, it is important to affirm that there is a relationship and, if possible, to dig for the roots so that the brokenness of life can be mended and its wholeness be recovered.

That there is *economic* injustice in the trading relationship between the North and the South is obvious. When one looks at the exchange rate between their respective currencies, this fact should be clear to most people, not least to those who travel between North and South. Is there also a *theological* injustice in the relation between Christianity as the religion of the North and the religious traditions of the South? Does this apply to Northern studies of Southern religions as well? At the moment, the Judeo-Christian Western tradition is at least nominally the religion of the rich and powerful North. People who follow other religious traditions in the South are poor and weak, at least in economic,

---

In its original form this was an address prepared for delivery at the North-South Dialogue at the University of Utrecht (Netherlands) during the university's 350th anniversary celebration, on which occasion the author received an honorary D.Th. Published in the *Journal of Ecumenical Studies* 25/3 (Summer 1988): 383-98. Used with permission of the journal.

political, and military terms. However, such religions as Hinduism and Buddhism in India, and Confucianism and Taoism in China, for example, have sustained societies, cultures, and civilizations for several thousand years and are very much alive even today. Is there, then a connection between poverty and religiosity?

The notions of justice and peace are related: There can be no justice without peace and no peace without justice. However, justice is not just a matter of redistribution of economic resources nor peace simply a question of re-arranging power relations between nations of the world. They are much deeper at the roots where they touch each other and broader where they influence relationships between people in society and nations in the world. In every culture, whether in the North or the South, the notions of justice and peace have religious roots, even though in a technological age they are often torn away from their religious moorings. Surely, one should not minimize the secular-humanistic contributions to both the clarification and the practice of these notions. Nevertheless, at a time when interreligious relationships are developing in the world in both pace and depth, perhaps as never before in human history, it should be possible to affirm the religious roots of justice and peace and to recover them, in order that different religious traditions can make a significant contribution to the emergence of a more just global community of nations.

I

To hold together the economic-political and the religious-cultural components of life, one needs a much larger, more comprehensive, and genuinely ecumenical framework that is free from narrow parochial interests. True universality cannot be understood as the extension of one particularity at the cost of others. Therefore, if one particular economic pattern seeks to dominate the world, or if one particular religious tradition strives to conquer other religious traditions, peace would be disturbed and justice destroyed. This is true of political ideologies as well. Therefore, a recognition of plurality as a style of life that helps mutual criticism and mutual enrichment may be a necessary pre-condition of just relations among religions, cultures, and ideologies. The larger framework envisaged could therefore be not so much a conceptual framework of ideas as a network of relationships between people who hold their particular religions and cultures to be precious and who have to live together in a world where economic resources and power relations are, at the moment, unjustly distributed.

Nowhere else is the power of impersonal economic forces over human life more manifest than in the structural imbalances in the global economic system. The Non-Aligned Movement (NAM) and the group of seventy-seven nations (G-77) persistently draw attention to this at every international forum.

It would be a mistake to think that these are merely "economic" forums of poor nations whose function is to "clobber" the North for its real or imaginary exploitation of the people and resources of the South. These groups also have a cultural identity within which religious dimensions play an important part, even though the latter do not come to the fore. The nations of the South are also struggling to establish their cultural identity, a struggle in which their economic poverty weakens their effort, except in the case of recently affluent states in West Asia. Even though they have persistently drawn attention to the injustice in the economic relationships between the North and the South, so far very little has been done to bring about any significant changes in this structure.[1]

"North-South" is not just a geographic concept. It is a spirit, a mood, an attitude on the part of nations that are accustomed to exercise power and enjoy affluence, at least during the past few centuries, toward those in the South that have succumbed to that power and, in their helplessness, have allowed the North to continue to grow rich at their expense. They are up against a system that continues to grow powerful through a combination of economic power, political domination, overwhelming military strength, and an ideological structure in which religions and cultures are either ignored or subtly exploited to serve the powerful and the rich. Academic studies of religions, therefore, have an important part to play here for the sake of justice and peace.

There is also a North-South divide within the nations of the South where — in spite of all goodwill and economic help — the gap between the rich and the poor, the powerful and the weak, the privileged and the marginalized is increasing at an alarming pace.[2] The alliance between the North in the South and the North in the North keeps the exploitative system going, particularly through trans-national corporations. The investment of foreign companies in countries such as India has been growing over the years, making their economy vulnerable to outside fluctuations.[3] Because of this vulnerability, the advice given by financial

1. See, e.g., the Final Communique of the Non-Aligned Movement foreign ministers' meeting in New Delhi, April 16-20, 1986, in the *Deccan Herald* (Bangalore), April 21, 1986, 5; "North-South Dialogue: Retrospect and Prospect," an interview with Gamani Corea, ending his term as Secretary General of UNCTAD in December, 1984, who drew attention to the need for solidarity among G-77, in *Mainstream* (New Delhi), vol. 23, no. 25 (February 16, 1985), 6ff.; and "Following the WB and IMF Line" by "BM," in *Economic and Political Weekly* (New Delhi), vol. 21, no. 8 (February 22, 1986), 327ff.

2. C. T. Kurien, an Indian economist, has noted that although on the eve of the seventh five-year plan (1985) India produced annually 152,000,000 tons of grain compared with only 50,000,000 tons annually in the early 1950s, it has not made any difference to mass poverty because the poor have no purchasing power. From 1984 to 1986, the price of rice went up by 70% and wheat by 61% (Aruna Jnanadason, ed., *The National Situation* [Madras, 1986], 2-3).

3. In 1948, just a year after independence, the total private foreign capital in India amounted to about Rs. 2,650,000,000; by 1986, it had risen to Rs. 15,000,000,000 (Kurien Mathew, "Asian Issues in Perspective," in *Out of Control*, the official report of the Asia Youth Assembly [Delhi: Asia Youth Assembly, 1985]). According to British information Services (release B-246), Britain agreed

institutions of the North to countries in the South is less than helpful. When the president of the World Bank suggested that India, China, and Pakistan needed economic policy changes, V. P. Singh, then finance minister of India, asked how the *same* economic prescription could apply equally to countries so different from each other as India, China, and Pakistan are in political ideology, cultural values, and religious beliefs.[4] When the International Monetary Fund advised Julius Nyerere of Tanzania that he should divert funds from education to "development" projects, meaning cash crops for export, Nyerere replied that he knew no form of development better than the education of a nation's youth.[5] Tragically, even when national leaders of the South know what is good for their people, the exploitative patterns within their own countries and the world economic system make it impossible for them to put it into practice.

It would, however, be wrong to blame the North entirely for the poverty and injustice within the nations of the South. The South cannot escape its own responsibility for this matter. Blaming the North for all the ills of the South is a futile exercise that lacks credibility. Writing immediately after the Sports Aid program, in which more than 20,000,000 people all over the world ran in support of the project "Race against Time" (May, 1986) to raise money for Africa, Professor George Aiyitty of Ghana remarked, "We Africans have made development dependent on foreign exchange, of which we have less and less, and foreign aid whose variables we cannot control."[6] He pointed out that

---

to give Rs. 19,500,000 in aid to finance a pilot project to provide computers to 250 Indian secondary schools and to supply 25,000 secondary schools by 1990. The computer chosen for the program was Acorn. According to M. Nanda (*Indian Express,* August 15, 1984), Acorn was reported to have already netted a profit of Rs. 30,000,000 from the Indian pilot project. According to Chris Miller, British industry benefitted by £46,800,000 in just November and December of 1980, through orders arising out of grants and loans to developing countries (*Community Development Journal,* vol. 18, no. 1 [1983], 42-49; quoted by Krishna Kumar in an article, "Educational Recovery," which shows "the vulnerability of our educational and developmental interests to the interests of foreign corporate capital" (in *Seminar 1985 Annual,* January 1986, New Delhi, 53-59]).

4. A. W. Clausen, in a speech to the German Foreign Policy Association in Bonn (*Deccan Herald,* April 18, 1986, 5). V. P. Singh also said that when the policy of a government fails it has to pay the price at the time of elections, but when the advice of international organizations fails, to whom are they accountable?

5. In an article entitled "Transition" by a "Reporter at Large" on Julius Nyerere, five days after he stepped down from the presidency of Tanzania after twenty-three years. This has some of the most revealing observations on North-South relations by a respected leader in Africa (William E. Smith, in *The New Yorker,* March 3, 1986, 72ff.).

6. George Aiyitty, in an article entitled "To End Hunger Set the Peasants Free," in *The London Times* (London), May 27, 1986, 12. In the U.N. General Assembly's special session on Africa (May 28, 1986), George Schultz of the U.S.A. and George Howe of Britain urged Africa to help itself. In response to the request of African nations to grant $80,000,000,000 as aid over the following four years, only two nations responded: The Netherlands agreed to cancel payments of interest and principal for five years ($80,000,000) and Canada promised sub-Saharan countries a fifteen-year moratorium on repayment of loans ($25,000,000) (*The Guardian* [London], May 29, 1986, 1 and 32). This is true of many nations in Asia as well.

agricultural complexes in Ghana were still not working ten years after completion. In Ghana there are more than seventy different types of tractors in various
stages of disrepair on state farms. African farmers pay the heaviest confiscatory
taxes. The cocoa farmers in Ghana pay seventy per cent of their net produce in
taxes; Gambia's peanut farmers, about eighty per cent. "If these oppressive
policies continue," wrote Aiyitty, "No amount of aid or U.N. conferences can
rescue Africa. . . . It is misplaced blame that keeps Africa in poverty."[7]

To complicate this matter further, new alignments are taking place in the
world economic structure that make the North-South equation slightly out of
date. Professor Yoshi Tsurumi, president of the Pacific Foundation in New York,
points out that the Pacific basin now overshadows the North Atlantic in terms
of gross national product. Whereas in 1982 U.S.-Europe trade amounted to
$115,000,000,000, U.S.-Pacific trade totalled $165,000,000,000, thus ending 350
years of North Atlantic domination of the world economy. The summit meeting
of seven industrialized nations, including Japan, held in Tokyo in May, 1986,
was a pointer in this direction. Even more significant is Tsurumi's claim that
Japan has now succeeded in blending Confucian cultural values with the best
of Judeo-Christian-Western values in the American capitalist system to produce
a more effective blend of economy as the world moves into the twenty-first
century.[8] The consequence of this new alliance is already being felt in the life
of nations in both North and South.

That the economic is one aspect of the total relationship between the
North and the South was accepted by the United Nations as early as 1971, when
it pointed out that in the life of the nations "the political, social and ideological
aspects are inextricably inter-related."[9] There are many thoughtful economists
and political leaders who, in their struggle for just relations in economic matters,
recognize that what is at stake is the well-being of people as a whole. Ajit Singh
pointed out that "the essential purpose of any trading system should not be
trade, or for that matter free trade for its own sake, but trade as a means of
promoting the economic well-being of the people."[10] The late prime minister
of India, Indira Gandhi, speaking of the prosperity of human society as a whole,
said:

7. Aiyitty, "To End Hunger," 12.

8. Yushi Tsurumi, "The Future of American Trade," *New York Times,* January 4, 1984. See
also Barry Bluestone and Bennett Harrison, *The Deindustrialization of America: Plant Closings,
Community Abandonment, and the Dismantling of Basic Industries* (New York: Basic Books, 1982);
and Jerome E. Deal and Allan Kennedy, *The Corporate Cultures* (Reading, MA: Addison Wesley
Publishing Co., 1982). Also see the article by Peter Wilsher, "The New Continents," in the Pacific,
the Islamic world, the Poles, North and South America, and Africa, in the *Sunday Times Magazine*
(London), October 12, 1985, 42ff.

9. Report on "Social Development in Asia: Retrospect and Prospect" (New York: United
Nations, 1971), 1ff.

10. *Economic and Political Weekly,* vol. 20, no. 1 (January 5, 1985), 26.

Justice is the very condition of human survival. Its denial will be an invitation to violence. This is why market economies cannot exist without taking cognizance of social realities. That is why politics has to interfere with economics. We believe that the prime justification for all politics, all economics, and all business is the furtherance of human welfare and the removal of human want and suffering.[11]

This emphasis on the wholeness of life, the well-being of all people in the global community, touches the very core of human existence in a world that today is threatened by violence in the continuing struggle for a just society.

Religions and cultures are mentioned together here as providing resources to strengthen a sense of the wholeness of life. In most countries of the South, particularly those in Africa and Asia, religion and culture are inextricably bound together. There are indeed forms of culture that are torn away from their religious roots, as well as a growing technological culture that is dominated by machines. In spite of this, religion and culture can seldom be discussed separately. Religion is the substance of culture, and culture the form of religion. If religions are responses to the Mystery of Life, cultures are expressions of those responses not only through words and ideas but also through symbol and sound and color. Throughout history and even now oppressed people everywhere express their identity, their joys and sorrows, and their longings for freedom, self-respect, and human dignity through their religions and cultures.

Culture refers to "the whole complex of distinctive spiritual, material, intellectual, and emotional features that characterize a society or a social group. It includes not only arts and letters, but also modes of life, the fundamental rights of human beings, value systems, traditions, and beliefs."[12] The cultures of all people, rich or poor, majorities or minorities, form part of the common heritage of humanity. Every culture represents a unique and irreplaceable body of values through which people assert their identity and demonstrate their presence in the world. Thus, a world economic system that subordinates other people's religions and cultures to considerations of trade and commerce or imposes an alien religion and culture on other people goes against the freedom of the human spirit. To reject or exploit or patronize or dominate other religions and cultures is a form of injustice that needs to be set aright.

The power generated by the economic domination of the South by the North also affects its attitudes toward the religions and cultures of the South. The connection between economic power and an aggressive religious militancy is not always recognized. The economic influence of some Islamic countries contributes to the expansion of Islam today, even as the affluence of the West

---

11. In a speech delivered on December 6, 1976, quoted in *Mainstream*, vol. 24, no. 32 (April 12, 1986), 9.

12. The UNESCO Mexico City Declaration on Cultural Policies, 1983, in *Cultures: Dialogue between Peoples of the World* (Paris), vol. 9, no. 1 (1983), 1.

during the colonial period contributed to the expansion of Christianity. There are many people in North America and Europe who believe that people in the South are poor *because* they follow religions other than Christianity. Thus, it becomes easy for them to take a theologically negative attitude toward other religions and cultures, to patronize them or even take an overtly or covertly contemptuous attitude toward them. The very description of neighbors of other faiths as "non-Christian," that is, in negative terms, is a symptom of this theological oppression of the South by the North, which is nominally but powerfully Christian in some of its ideological assumptions.

This crypto-colonialist theology of religions and cultures that lies hidden in the heart of the North prevents neighbors of other faiths from cooperating with Christians in urgent matters of justice and peace in the world. Christians in the South are often regarded as allies of the North and viewed with suspicion and distrust. Attempts to deal with economic poverty in the South without taking into account its religions and cultures are as one-sided as dealing with their religions and cultures without recognizing that here, too, the issue of justice is involved. Worse still is the serious damage done to just and peaceful relations among different religions through the attitude of regarding *people* of other faiths as mere statistics — the 2,000,000,000 "lost souls" — as numbers without faces, to be counted, sampled, compiled, and stored in computers in order to be recalled at the touch of a key and used in a game of numbers with scant regard for the freedom, self-respect, and human dignity of people.[13]

II

In drawing attention to religions and cultures in the context of North-South dialogue, it is not claimed that religions have answers to the desperate problems of injustice in the world where economic and political solutions have failed. To do so would be unwise and presumptuous. Evidence in the long history of religions is against any such conclusion. Established religions have often divided people and nations and given rise to tensions and conflicts. They have held up scientific progress, resisted social change, supported the rich and the powerful over against the poor and the weak, and often added religious fuel to military conflagrations, making reconciliation more difficult. Of all the wounds human beings inflict on each other, religious wounds are the most difficult to heal. Therefore, organized religions are of little use in the struggle for justice and peace.

13. David Barrett suggested how "instant surveys" could be made of the "unreached two billion," when he wrote: "One would have to resist the temptation to ask sensitive or loaded questions like, 'Are you saved?' or 'What think ye of Christ?'" and to ask instead "guarded questions which do not reveal one's evangelistic objectives" ("Five Statistical Eras of Global Mission: A Thesis and Discussion," *International Bulletin of Mission Studies* 8 (December, 1984): 167.

What is meant here by the term "religions" is not the established institutions of religion or systems of belief of boundaried social groups with their sense of separation from others but, rather, the spiritual resources within religions, the inner experiences of the Spirit, their visions of reality, their responses to the Mystery of Truth, the liberative streams within religions that break through human limitations to reach out to neighbors in the global community.

The connection between vision and reality — between religious experience and religious institutions — is difficult to explain. However, the fact that the relation between the spirit and forms of religion is complex is no reason to dismiss religions altogether as of no consequence for the struggle for justice and quest for peace. Since religions have endured in history much longer than any secular ideology, the possibility that religions might still offer resources to recover the sense of the wholeness of life should at least be explored seriously instead of being rejected rudely as of no consequence. This is urgent for at least three reasons.

First, while it is true that organized religions have often failed to provide answers to the problems of justice, the same judgment is also true in the case of contemporary secular ideologies. In the history of religions, there have indeed been prophetic streams of justice not just in the Judeo-Christian tradition but also in the Hindu, Buddhist, and Islamic traditions. In an unjust situation, justice is more a matter of willingness to share resources than of evolving new economic structures. A lower economic standard need not necessarily mean a lesser quality of life. All religions call for simplicity of life, a change within, a transformation of the human heart, and therefore a change of attitude toward neighbors.

Second, there is today a growing uneasiness about the adequacy of the secular way of life and an increasing sensitivity to the transcendent dimension of life. The speed and the manner in which politicization of religions is taking place in countries in the North and the South bring out the dangers and opportunities in this situation. The separation of life into the sacred and the secular is being questioned today by many people who are deeply aware of the wholeness of all life. Religious insights, particularly those that hold humanity, nature, and God together in a cosmic unity, may be important here.

To these must be added a third factor that has decisively entered into the history of human relations today, namely, the interreligious dialogues that are going on at national, international, and global levels, as perhaps never before. This is being strengthened by increasing travel, particularly by young people in different countries; by rapid means of communication; and, perhaps even more importantly, by communities of people of other faiths living in many of the Christian countries of the North. Through long centuries, religions developed in isolation from each other, often in suspicion and fear. Today, people of different religious persuasions are increasingly being drawn together as they share a common future and face problems of life and death. This should provide a sense of urgency to academic studies on an interreligious basis with greater cooperation between scholars in the North and South.

One of the prerequisites here is to avoid uncritically negative judgments on religions in general or by one particular religious community on the religious traditions of others. Very often, there is great suspicion of the role of religions in society, particularly in such countries as India, where, unfortunately, "religious" riots occur with alarming frequency. There are highly complex factors here, including the economic and political, that get mixed up with religious feelings and lead to serious conflagrations. This is true of Catholic-Protestant relationships in Northern Ireland or Jewish, Muslim, and Christian relationships in Lebanon. One must also note that, in countries or cities in the North where significant numbers of people of other faiths live together with a majority-Christian community, tensions between them do arise. Nevertheless, this should not prevent scholars and leaders of different communities from recovering the peace potentials within different religious traditions. Recent studies in India by sociologists, economists, political scientists, and theologians have brought out the fact that, while religious feelings were indeed involved, they were used cunningly for economic and political purposes. Religion was not the *causative* factor but the *instrumental* factor in such riots, yet it was made to appear to have been causative.[14] Just because religions get involved in such disturbances in one way or another, the resources within religions for peace and justice should not be ignored.

Further, exclusive claims made by any one religious community lead to theologically negative judgments on the validity of other religions. This not only leads to tensions in the larger community, but it also affects the scholarly study of religions. When such exclusive claims are allied with economic, political, and — as has often happened in history — military power, a situation is created where objective studies of religion become difficult if not impossible. The ethical consequences of such heavily negative judgments vitiate all interreligious relationships. Perhaps a careful systematic study of such exclusive claims by an interreligious group of scholars selected from both North and South could be of help in bringing out the issues objectively.

In China, the gentle entry of Buddhism, far from supplanting existing traditions, coexisted with them. It had no alliance with the political powers of the country, and unlike Islam and Christianity in India, had no open or hidden economic interests. To the question of why a Chinese should allow her- or

---

14. In recent years, several thoughtful studies have been made on this complex subject. See Asghar Ali Engineer, ed., *Communal Riots in Post-Independence India* (Hyderabad: Sangam Books, 1984); several case studies are included in this volume. Also see Bipan Chandra, *Communalism in Modern India* (New Delhi: Vikas Publishing House, 1984); Kishan Swarup Thapar, "Genesis of Partition," *Mainstream*, vol. 22, no. 48 (August 18, 1984), 10ff.; Nirmal Srinivasan, "Majority Communalism versus Minority Communalism: Is It a Threat to Indian Secularism?" *Religion and Society* (Bangalore), vol. 30, no. 3-4 (September/December, 1983), 138-46; etc.

himself to be influenced by foreign Indian ways, the Chinese scholar Mou Tzu replied: "Why should I reject the Way of Yao, Shun, the Duke of Chou, and Confucius . . . Gold and jade do not harm each other. You say that another is in error when it is you yourself who err."[15] Wing-Tsit Chan has pointed out that in China people of three traditions — Confucian, Taoist, and Buddhist — mutually influenced each other over the centuries: "Religious doctrines, symbols, ceremonies and even deities have been so intermingled that scholars cannot tell if they are of Confucian, Buddhist, or Taoist origin. It is often said that the average Chinese is one who wears a Confucian crown, so to speak, a Taoist robe, and Buddhist sandals."[16] This may not be the most creative framework to bring out the distinctiveness of each tradition; nevertheless, it did provide for friendlier relationships among the different religions within the nation. In central Asia, for nearly 1,000 years before the sea route to the South was discovered (1497-99) by Vasco de Gama, three major civilizations of West Asia, India, and China intermingled along with three religious traditions — the Buddhist, Chinese, and Islamic — in a critical and enriching relationship without economic or political domination, even though trade was obviously the common purpose that brought them together.[17]

III

Perhaps the time has come to examine more critically some of the assumptions behind the Northern study of Southern religions. Scholars from the North have indeed done a great service in the study of world religions, and continue to do so. The world of scholarship should be grateful to them for drawing attention to the fundamental values within the religions of the South at a time when they were often smothered by racial, political, or missiological considerations, which often went unrecognized even by their own adherents. Such studies also brought out the importance of religions and cultures other than European during a period when the concerns of the nations in the North were more for commerce and profit than for culture and knowledge. It is true that at certain points there were hints of a convergence between colonial interests and academic scholarship. Even today there might be some connection between the research industry

15. Quoted by Theodore de Bary, *Sources of Chinese Tradition*, 3rd printing (New York: Columbia University Press, 1961), 274.

16. Wing-Tsit Chan, "The Historic Chinese Contribution to Religious Pluralism and World Community," in Edward J. Jurji, ed., *Religious Pluralism and World Community: Interfaith and Intercultural Communication,* Studies in the History of Religions 15 (Leiden: E. J. Brill, 1969), 115.

17. Wilfred Cantwell Smith, "Traditions in Contact and Change: Towards a History of Religion in the Singular," in Peter Slater and Donald Weibe, eds., *Selected Proceedings of the XIV Conference of the International Association for the History of Religions* (Waterloo, Ont.: Canadian Corporation for Studies in Religion, 1983), 12ff.

largely based in the North and the neocolonial enterprises in the South. However, rather than being "hurt" by suggestions like this, which need to be critically examined, and instead of developing this into a full-fledged controversy that will deflect scholars from their genuine academic work, what is urgent and important is to seek ways of scholarly cooperation between the North and the South, through which the resources of the religious heritage of humankind may be brought to bear upon the urgent problems facing all people in the world.[18]

The assumptions behind the Northern study of Southern religions are based on developments during a particular period in European history. The difficulties of imposing the term "religion" on Southern *dharmas* are well known, but, in using terms such as "scientific" or "classical," who selects the criteria? Surely, in such a country as India, with its long history of multireligious life, Hindus had to study the heterodox religions of Buddhism and Jainism and, later, Islam and Christianity. Also, within Hinduism itself the relationships between different *sampradāyas* were studied systematically by the great *ācāryas* and their disciples. Most of these studies are in Sanskrit or Pali or another Indian language, so they may be inaccessible to those who cannot use these languages. But can they be so totally ignored when using the terms "scientific" and "classical"? This is not to deny or minimize the significant contributions made by scholars from the South to several anthologies edited by scholars in the North but, rather, to draw attention to the content of such terms as "scientific" and "classical" in relation to these studies.[19]

Frank Whaling is certainly right in asking:

> What is the significance of the fact that religions outside the West have been studied in a western way and, to a lesser extent, that religions outside Christianity have been studied in a Christianity-centered way? To what extent has this pre-1945 attitude of often unconscious superiority been superseded in the contemporary situation? To what extent have western scholars of religion subsumed the whole spiritual creation of mankind under one interpretation of religion and then absolutised it?[20]

18. For a brief discussion of Edward W. Said's *Orientalism* (New York: Pantheon Books, 1978), see Frank Whaling, ed., *Contemporary Approaches to the Study of Religion,* vol. 1, *The Humanities* (Berlin, New York, Amsterdam: Mouton Publishers, 1983), 394-97.

19. Jacques Waardenburg's *Classical Approaches to the Study of Religion: Aims, Methods, and Theories of Research,* vol. 1, *Introduction and Anthology* (The Hague, Paris: Mouton, 1973), begins with F. Max Müller (1823-1900) and ends with Gaston Berger (1896-1960). In the introduction to his 1984 book in the same series, Frank Whaling wrote: "These books are written by an authentically international team and our only *slight* regret is that it has not been possible to include a non-western scholar" (p. 5, italics mine). How can a team be *authentically* international without a single scholar from the South, particularly when the book deals with *contemporary* approaches to the study of religion? Drawing attention to such matters should not be misunderstood as "clobbering" or "lambasting" the North but as a plea for greater collaboration in a common academic task.

20. Whaling, *Contemporary Approaches,* 12.

Scholars from the South, for example, Santosh Chandra Sen Gupta, have pleaded that such a complex religion as Hinduism should not be "misunderstood" by applying to its study criteria derived from an entirely different culture.[21] An earlier volume by K. Satchidananda Murthy included readings in Indian history, politics, and philosophy that are particularly helpful because they draw attention to the conception, interpretation, and methodology of history, a topic alleged to be neglected by India's religions and cultures.[22] Subhas Anand has referred to the place of women in the Hindu view of life and way of life, a topic that is important at a time when it is often alleged that it is difficult to find contributors to discuss this subject.[23]

Recognizing that the historical situation after 1945 has decisively changed in the world, and emphasizing that religions that developed in isolation from each other during the past are now increasingly being drawn closer together, K. L. Seshagiri Rao has called for a new departure in the study of world religions: "The future usefulness of any religious tradition depends on its ability to cooperate with other traditions."[24] The "scientific" approach to the study of religions is, of course, important; there is no call to abandon it. However, when it is applied to the study of religions, it may tend to regard them as "objects" of study rather than people's living faiths.

None of the religions that are being studied "scientifically" in the North and about which Christians theologize originated in Europe, nor were their

21. Santosh Chandra Sen Gupta, "The Misunderstanding of Hinduism," in John Hick, ed., *Truth and Dialogue in World Religions: Conflicting Truth Claims* (Philadelphia: Westminster Press, 1974), 96ff.

22. K. Satchidananda Murthy, ed., *Readings in Indian History, Politics, and Philosophy* (Bombay: Allied Publishers, 1967).

23. Subhas Anand, "Women in Hindu View of Life and Way of Life," in *Jeevadhara* (Kottayam, Kerala), vol. 17, no. 92 (January, 1987), 51-63. There are a number of journals devoted to the question of women in the religions of India and in Indian society today. *Manushi* is a journal about women and society edited by Madhu Kishwar and published in both English and Hindi by Archana Printers, Delhi (U.S. agent: Manushi Distributors America, c/o Esther Jantzen, 5008 Erringer Pl., Philadelphia, PA 19144). Many other journals noted for their intellectual and scholarly quality, such as *Mainstream* (ed. Nikhil Chakravarty; Perspective Publications, New Delhi), have significant articles written by women contributors. *Religion and Society*, published by the Christian Institute for the Study of Religion and Society in Bangalore, from time to time publishes articles and books on women's questions; e.g., vol. 32, no. 2 (June, 1985), is on the theme "Religions and the Women's Status," including articles by such women writers as Ranjana Kumari ("Femaleness: The Hindu Perspective"), Doris Franklin ("Impact of Christianity on the Status of Women"), etc. In vol. 31, no. 1 (March, 1984), on the theme "The Law, the Oppressed and Women," *Religion and Society* has articles by Noorjehan Razah ("Muslims and the Civil Code"), Lotika Sarkar ("Women's Rights"), etc. There are many other Hindu, Muslim, Christian, and Sikh women writing scholarly articles on their concerns that refer critically to their respective religious traditions. The references here are to the Indian situation only because the author is more familiar with it. There are certainly women writers in other countries of the South.

24. K. L. Seshagiri Rao, "Human Community and Religious Pluralism: A Hindu Perspective," in C. D. Jathanna, ed., *Dialogue in Community* (Mangalore: Karnataka Theological Research Institute, 1982), 162.

testimonies written in a European language. Studies in the ontology of language have shown that to depend on any kind of "translation" is a serious limitation, particularly in the matter of "understanding" the religious and cultural life of people other than ourselves.[25] Even the notion of knowledge *(gnosis-jnāna)* — its content, character, and epistemological possibilities — differs in different cultures. J. A. B. van Buitenen noted: "Central to Indian thinking through the ages is a concept of knowledge which . . . is foreign to the modern West. Whereas for us, to put it briefly, knowledge is something to be *discovered,* for the Indian knowledge is something to be *recovered.* . . . at its very origin the absolute truth stands revealed."[26] Further, the kind of religious knowledge that people in the South cherish depends not so much on the written texts as on hearing and seeing the word. *Śruti,* that which is heard, has far greater authority than *Smriti,* that which is remembered and written down. The notion that truth stands concealed behind texts and that, through an exercise of exegesis it will reveal itself, is unknown in Hindu and Buddhist religious traditions.[27] Greater collaboration between scholars in the North and the South may help to complement the concern of each in the methodology, structure, and purpose of academic religious studies.

There is also the intriguing question of why the North feels so compelled to study Southern religions, when people who are being thus studied show little interest in studying the religions of the North. Should one look for reasons in the historic context of a particular period when European nations were discovering other peoples, religions, and cultures? The perceptions of the "discoverers" and the "discovered" cannot be the same. A one-way study-process quite often has inhibiting and sometimes negative effects on those being studied. Does the study of Southern religions contribute to the pool of religious values in the North? Does it change habits of thought, action, and attitude toward people of the South who live by these faiths? Does it significantly influence the self-understanding of the people whose religions are being studied? Is it because in a monoreligious and monocultural context there is greater need for people to know other religions and cultures than for people who for many centuries have been living in open multireligious and multicultural situations? Or, is it because of an inner compulsion to seek new ideas, thus extending the frontiers of human knowledge? Surely, that inner compulsion for *jnāna* is no monopoly of the North but is to be found

25. See Charles H. Craft and Thomas N. Wisely, eds., *Readings in Dynamic Indigeneity* (Pasadena: William Carey Library, 1979), 259-60; Jacques Derrida, *Writing and Difference,* tr. and intro. Alan Bass (Chicago: The University of Chicago Press, 1978), 280ff.; Paul Ricoeur, *Essays on Biblical Interpretation,* ed. Lewis S. Mudge (Philadelphia: Fortress Press, 1980), 4.

26. J. A. B. van Buitenen, "On the Archaism of the *Bhāgavata Purāṇa,*" in Milton Singer, ed., *Krishna: Myths, Rites, and Attitudes* (Honolulu: East-West Center Press, 1966), 35.

27. See Gopinath Kaviraj, *Aspects of Indian Thought* (Burdwan, W. Bengal: University of Burdwan, 1966), 41ff.; C. S. Kashikar, *Preface to Rig Veda Samhita* with the commentary of Sāyaṇā edited by N. S. Sontakke and C. G. Kashikar, vol. 4 (Poona: Vaidika Samshodhana Mandala, 1946).

among people in the South also. These are indeed new questions that need more careful and systematic study in the coming years, through collaboration between the North and the South, in order that uncritical claims are not made nor unwarranted conclusions drawn.

This means that the academic implications of interreligious dialogues on the one hand and the implications of interreligious dialogues for the academic study of religions on the other need far more recognition and acceptance. New steps have to be taken with more hope than caution. If one considers the relationship between religions in the world today in connection with the global struggle for justice, scholars of different religious traditions in the North and the South need to probe more deeply into the implications of interreligious dialogues for more just human relations in the global community. There is no reason to think that such studies will deflect the academic quality of the work or undermine the sense of objectivity necessary for scholarly pursuits. There is probably a threefold task involved here: (1) to bring out, through careful study, the religious roots of the notions of peace and justice in different religious traditions; (2) to examine the inner connection between the two, drawing out its ethical implications for people of different religious persuasions; and (3) to probe more deeply into the relationship between humanity and nature in different religious traditions, so that the question of justice does not remain merely at the level of sharing the resources of nature but also of being at peace with nature and in harmony with the cosmos.

It is not possible — and would be premature — to enter into an elaborate discussion on these matters here. The methodology, structure, and direction of such studies should from the beginning be discussed by the North and the South together if what is envisaged here is to be taken seriously. However, some of the areas of concern may be indicated.

The notion of peace and the practice of justice have religious roots. Though the secular and the humanistic contributions are certainly recognized, often they are torn away from their original religious moorings. Justice and peace are related. Without the experience of peace, there can be no practice of justice. Without the establishment of justice, peace will remain an unending quest and a distant dream. Peace in the sense of inner tranquility and peace in the sense of harmony in its deepest sense both depend on just relations among humanity, nature, and God. However, the content of these two notions and the manner in which they are related to each other are perceived differently in different religious traditions. If this is correct, the perception of exactly what a just community is in a multireligious society will be affected whether in a nation or in the world. Therefore, any romantic notions of harmony between religions should give place to the recovery of the critical distinctiveness of each tradition. Also, the persistence of evil and suffering within the human heart and in the structures of society makes the discussion even more complicated. Scholarly investigations into these matters might help to avoid romantic and uncritical notions about peace and justice as well as to recover critically the distinctiveness of each tradition for mutual criticism and mutual enrichment.[28]

The connection between *Shalom* and *mishpāt* is perhaps more transparently seen in the biblical tradition, both Hebrew and Christian, than is that between *Shānti* and *Dharma* in the Hindu tradition. The connection between power and justice, with power to be exercised by the king, is perhaps more strongly emphasized in Islam than in other traditions. In the shelter and protection provided by the king as "the shadow of God," justice and security are to be found. That the relationship between compassion and justice extends not only to human life but even to animals and nature is perhaps more movingly brought out by the Buddhist tradition than by others. These are indeed generalizations, and they may fail to take into account the intricacies and complexities within each tradition. Nevertheless, they point to insights that need more careful study.

That the fragile gift of peace cannot be taken for granted and that one should work for peace *(Shalom)* was emphasized by Jesus (Mt. 5:9), but he also drew attention to peace as that inner quality which removes fear and enables the heart not to be troubled (Jn. 14:27). To the Jew the Sabbath experience opens the way to *Shalom*. To live sabbatically is to be immersed in sacred time while moving along in chronological time. The restfulness of *Shalom* is rooted in God's love and compassion and leads to righteousness and justice in society.

In both the Hindu and the Buddhist traditions there is a strong emphasis on peace as an inward quality of life that requires discipline to acquire. The *Shānti mantra* is central to Hindu experience. There are indeed many strands within the complexity of Hindu life and practice: therefore, one should be careful not to isolate any particular one at the expense of others. The constant emphasis on the inward dimension of peace may be the real contribution of Hinduism to religious life at a time when *doing* rather than *being* seems to be more in demand as a mark of religious life. The compassion of the Buddha *(mahā karuna citta)* expresses itself in social relationships as well as extending it to just relationships between humanity and nature.

28. Attempts are being made in this direction, some tentative and preliminary, some more ambitious. See, e.g., S. J. Samartha and Lynn de Silva, eds., *Man in Nature — Guest or Engineer: A Preliminary Enquiry by Christians and Buddhists* (Colombo: The Ecumenical Institute for the Study of Dialogue, 1979). A large conference called by the World Council of Churches at the Massachusetts Institute of Technology in 1979 on the theme "Faith and Science in an Unjust World," brought together scientists, theologians, and historians of religions, including Buddhists and Muslims, who produced a statement on this topic: Paul Albrecht, ed., *Faith and Science in an Unjust World*, vol. 2, Reports and Recommendations (Geneva: World Council of Churches, 1980), 36. A more systematic and carefully prepared work is in the *Journal of Dharma*, vol. 11, no. 2 (April-June, 1986), on the theme "Peace-Experience in Religions." This was published in collaboration with Sri Aurobindo Research Academy, Pondicherry, India; the Department of Asian Studies, Seton Hall University, South Orange, NJ, U.S.A.; the Department of Religious Studies, University of Lancaster, U.K.; and the Dharma Research Association, Center for the Study of World Religions, Dharmaram College, Bangalore, India — a good example of Southern initiative and Northern cooperation.

Although the Christian tradition regards creation as good, it seems to be less interested in nature as such than the Hindu and Buddhist are. One must examine this matter far more carefully, but it looks as if biblical tradition places stronger emphasis on the distance between God and nature, whereas the Hindu and Buddhist traditions emphasize the continuity between nature and humanity. Hints about this are to be found not only in the Upanishadic tradition of the forest meditations but also in the theistic traditions, as, for example, that of Rama. Forest becomes the dwelling place of Rama where rivers, mountains, trees, and animals seem to participate in his sufferings and struggles. Monkeys are his allies in the battle against Ravana, and even the little squirrel does its bit by rolling itself in sand and shaking itself to drop particles of sand at the location where the bridge is being built to Lanka.

Neither the notion of peace nor the practice of justice, therefore, can be narrowly defined to touch only human relationships. They need to include nature as well. Human freedom and finiteness are somehow mixed up with the relation among humanity, nature, and God. The ecological problems that bother human life today are partly the result of technology, so they cannot be solved by more refined technology. Vision, values, and a recovery of the original relationships are necessary to pursue a more responsible and less exploitative attitude toward nature. The religious insistence on the stewardship of nature's resources combined with the idea of partnership with nature might help human beings to live together more justly and with peace and harmony in the larger unity of the cosmos.

III.6

Ecology and the Recycling of Christianity

KWOK PUI-LAN

In Asian religious art, the circle is as prevalent as the crucifix in Western Europe. Tibetan Buddhist monks make sand *mandala* to enhance their visualization of the sacred. The serene Buddha or the *bodhisattvas* are portrayed in images of circles and concentric circles to symbolize inner peace, grace and perfection. Hindu mythology and religious art vividly portray the powerful symbol of reincarnation to address human suffering and finitude. People living close to the land have always described the movement of the moon and stars in a cyclical way.

The image of the circle is also important for women in both biological and symbolic ways. Women's bodies follow periodical cycles with significant hormonal and physiological changes. More attuned to the cycles of the seasons, women from time immemorial have performed rituals when the moon waxes and wanes. Today, women cast the circle in spirituality groups, learn to dance Sarah's or Hagar's circle to express their solidarity, and create circles of sisterhood for fellowship.

Since the Enlightenment, Western Christianity has understood time and history in a linear and progressive way. The Prometheus myth was reinforced by developments in science and technology. But Christians with an ecological awareness have begun to question the presuppositions of the Enlightenment and the promises of technology. They have rediscovered "recycling" as a significant ecological and spiritual theme. When asked whether she is a Christian or not, Anne Primavesi, author of *From Apocalypse to Genesis: Ecology, Feminism and Christianity*, answers that she is a "recycled Christian."

Asian people, women all over the world, and conscientious Christians suddenly find a common language when they talk about the sacred and the natural process: circles, cycles and recycling.

Reprinted with permission from the *Ecumenical Review* 44/3 (July 1992): 304-7.

Ecology and Women's Concerns

Our present ecological crisis is a result of the breaking down of the great chain that connects human beings, all sentient things, and nature. The disruption of the eco-balance and interconnectedness has a devastating effect on the most vulnerable segments of the link: women and children in the third world. Deforestation, acid rain, soil erosion, and the indiscriminate use of fertilizers and pesticides lead to the breaking down of the local sustenance economy upon which most women and children are dependent. An increasing number of women migrate to the cities to work as cheap labour in factories, and some of them end up selling their bodies in the flourishing sex industry. Others who cannot find jobs at home seek employment in the Middle East and other newly industrialized countries. Many of these migrant workers are exploited and some are sexually abused.

Third-world women do not benefit from development models based on industrial and technological growth. In fact, they have paid a heavy price for so-called "national development" or "economic miracles." Women's productive and sexual labour are exploited and women's lives are becoming more subject to technological surveillance, and state and corporate control.

Third-world women are also blamed for causing the population explosion, leading to the disequilibrium between human beings and natural resources. Pharmaceutical formulas and new contraceptive devices are tested on third-world women, and sterilization has been forced on great numbers of them. Technological advances such as the ultrasound test have had the unintended effect of selective abortion of the female fetus. Recent demographic studies reveal the stark data that 100 million women are missing in the world, 60 percent of them in Asia.

Technological control, a model of development oriented towards the West, and patriarchy form an "unholy trinity" dominating the lives of marginalized women. At Nairobi in 1992, participants in the meeting of the Ecumenical Association of Third World Theologians condemned patriarchal structures which dehumanize women, the denial of women's rights and economic and political freedom, and all forms of violence done to the female sex. Such oppression is often condoned or reinforced by patriarchal religions, androcentric language and expressions, and male interpretations of the classics and scriptures. Feminist philosopher Mary Daly has argued that women must speak of "gyn/ecology," an environment that is healthy for women's well-being and growth.

The Recycling of Christianity

The ecological crisis and the degradation of women challenge us to reflect on whether Christianity has promoted interrelatedness, mutuality and eco-justice.

Many eco-conscious Christians are aware that an anthropocentric, hierarchical and patriarchal religious system is part of the problem, and not part of the solution. Some of our traditional Christian beliefs need to go through a recycling process so that they can be reappropriated for the contemporary world. The idea of "recycling" is not new in our tradition: its meaning is anticipated by the religious themes of conversion, metanoia, and even resurrection.

From a Hierarchical to an Ecological Model

Feminist theologians have pointed out for a long time that a dualistic, hierarchical understanding of God and the world is the root problem of Western Christianity. A hierarchy of being puts God infinitely above human beings, and human beings above nature; a dualistic worldview separates the mind from the body, the male from the female, and humans from the nonhuman world. The worth of an individual or a natural object depends on its position in the hierarchy, instead of on her or its intrinsic value and dignity. An ecological model does not project God as away from the world and above human beings. God-human beings-nature are interdependent and interrelated, just like the three interconnected arrows of the sign of recycling. A dualistic perception of the world must give way to a correlative and holistic understanding, just as each dot on the circle is related to the center and to the other dots. An ecological model values diversity in the biosphere and respects multiplicity in terms of race, gender and sexual orientation.

From Anthropocentrism to Bio-centrism

Western Christianity places human beings at the centre of the universe. The whole creation was made for the benefit of human beings, who are to have dominion over the fish, the birds, and every living thing upon the earth. Creation was condemned and cursed as a result of human sinfulness. But by the grace of God, human beings are offered the possibility of salvation. They, in turn, can save the planet by assuming responsibility as sons and daughters of God.

By contrast, creation can also be understood by telling the story of the earth and the biospheres. As Thomas Berry has pointed out, planet earth came into being about ten billion years ago, and life on the planet seven billion years later. Plants appeared about six hundred million years ago, and animals arrived a little later. Human consciousness only came about two million years ago. The biosphere existed long before us, and its complexity has just begun to be understood by biologists in the twentieth century. It is arrogant on our part to think that the earth exists solely for our disposal, and that the salvation of the vast and expansive galaxy depends on just five billion human beings.

Western anthropocentrism thinks of God in terms of the image of human beings: God is king, father, judge and warrior. God is the Lord of history, intervening in human events. On the contrary, Oriental people and indigenous people who are tied to the soil imagine the divine, the Tao, as silent and nonintrusive. They speak of the earth with respect and reverence as the mother who is sustaining and life-affirming. A shift from anthropocentrism to biocentrism necessitates a change in our way of thinking and speaking about God.

From a Passive Spirituality to a Passionate Spirituality

The quest for an adequate spirituality has become increasingly urgent in our eco-crisis. In the past, spirituality has been seen as synonymous with asceticism, spiritual discipline, meditation, prayer and other-worldly pursuits. According to a dualistic worldview, the spirit is against the body, the emotion and the appetite. We now need to speak of a holistic, biophilic and embodied spirituality. Instead of being passive and emotionless, this new spirituality must be passionate, erotic and full of fire. It must move us to love with our full capacity, to seek justice in our relationships, and to walk humbly with God and mother earth. It must evoke wonder and awe in us when we see the falling star, the autumn leaves and the morning dew.

This passionate spirituality must enable us to work for peace. Peace is not the absence of war or conflict, but harmony, well-being and blissfulness because of just relationships. Peace is not a passive waiting for politicians and strategists to work out a solution for us, but passionate action in our local communities to empower the powerless, to strengthen the weak, and to restore what has gone wrong.

A New Solidarity in the Nineties

The challenge for the churches in the nineties is to broaden our vision and deepen our commitment to work for the integrity of creation, justice and peace. When the ecumenical movement first took shape, the vision was to promote church unity to carry out the church's witness and mission. In the seventies, people of other faiths were included through religious dialogue as a step towards building a wider human community. In our present age, the ecumenical movement must move from an *ecclesial solidarity* to an *ecological solidarity*.

The word "solidarity" originated in the French legal tradition, and referred to the natural bond of people of the same background. Later, this term was used by the Christian workers movement, and was understood by Marx as the self-organization of the oppressed. Its usage in Europe has implied a strong tradition of justice. However, people in Asia understand "solidarity" rather differently. In Chinese it means gathering together into one and connecting to each other. In Indonesian, it connotes binding one another into a circle. Its usage in Oriental languages awakens the ecological awareness of the interconnectedness of all things.

Ecological solidarity is closely related to the Ecumenical Decade of the Churches in Solidarity with Women (1988-98). The World Council of Churches has urged the churches to pay attention to women's full participation in church and community life, to struggle against racism, sexism and classism, and to give visibility to women's perspectives and actions in the struggle for justice, peace and the integrity of creation. For many decades women of the third world have been active participants in the struggle for justice, human rights, freedom and the integrity of creation. In the first world, women are among the most vocal leaders and visionaries of the peace movements and the Green movement.

Ecological solidarity means assuming mutual responsibility instead of seeking scapegoats and creating new victims. Indigenous peoples have been saying for centuries that the taking of their land robbed them not only of the means of existence, but of the meaning of life. Our world will not be safer if the testing of nuclear explosives, the dumping of radioactive wastes and the storing of nuclear weapons are done far away from Europe and America in the Pacific. Our cities will not be less dangerous if the toxic waste is dumped in the Osage nation in Oklahoma or in the Rosebud Sioux reservation in South Dakota. Our lives will not be enriched if we ask the next generation to pay for our debts and to be responsible for the mess we have created. We are part of each other, and the breaking down of one eco-system affects all the others.

Ecological solidarity is our covenant with the land, the ocean, the forest, the rivers, and the mountains. Without the hills, where else can we lift up our eyes to ask for help (Ps. 121:1)? Without the trees of the field, who will clap their hands when we go out in joy and are led back in peace (Isa. 55:12)? If we poison the Red Sea, even God might not be able to perform mighty miracles. Our covenant with nature is not based on fear and anxiety because nature is seriously polluted and its resources are limited. We need to renew our covenant with planet earth out of joy, celebration and gratitude because we are part of nature and the natural process.

An African Theology of Death:
The Plenitude of Human Life

EVARISTI MAGOTI, W.F.

Introduction

It is not possible to articulate a comprehensive African theology of death within the parameters of a single essay. The subject of death is vast and the issues which can be brought into it are complex. A complete theology of death is normally made up of four major questions: namely, life, dying, death itself, and life after death. Although these questions are in themselves different, they cannot be treated in isolation from each other. They are inseparably linked. What is more, with reference to Africa these questions give rise to another set of specific questions related to African traditional beliefs and philosophy vis-à-vis the teachings of the Bible and the magisterium of the church. In order to formulate a proper and sound theology of death relevant to our life and faith here, these questions too must be treated with care and exactness. For the moment, that is not what I wish to do. I will here limit my discussion to only one aspect of death — namely, the plenitude of life.

Status Questionis and Task

There has always been debate about death, not only what it is, but whether there is a heaven or hell. In the West the debate involves theologians, anthropologists, philosophers and medical doctors. The West's interest in death arises from the fact that it is one of life's most fundamental questions. In the face of death "man

Reprinted from the *Africa Theological Journal* (published under the auspices of the All-African Lutheran Churches, centered in Arusha, Tanzania), 20/3 (1991): 176-88. Used with permission.

is not only tormented by pain and the gradual breaking up of his body, but also, and even more so, by the dread of forever ceasing to be."[1] Because of this, the terms of the debate in the West have constantly been seeking not only to identify, but also to dispel the fear of death and to restore the unity of the person in death. Thus the conviction in Western theology that the person dies but does not really disintegrate. He/she retains in death both his/her physical and metaphysical compositions.

In Africa the situation is a little different. Apart from having the highest mortality rate in the world, the reality of death does not figure prominently in African theological thought. It may be said that the question of death has hardly ever been dealt with explicitly in African theology. But this is not to say that it has been totally neglected. Assertions about death are frequently being made in homilies, at burials and other liturgical ceremonies. However, these are either taken from Scripture or from the teachings of the church, with only an added African content. So, although the reflection there no doubt highlights our awareness of the finite nature of the human person in death, and shows death to be the separation of the soul from the body, an initiation, a change in the state of being, a rite of passage, a rebirth,[2] they do not give sufficient attention to the facts of death and dying from the African perspective.

And even what is proposed in the African context concerning death is not spelled out clearly. For instance, does the "initiation" spoken of take place after or before death? Could it be that this initiation, this passage is an intrinsic factor of death itself? Is this initiation an activity which the dying person actively performs, or is it performed by other factors extrinsic to him/her? All of these questions need to be addressed specifically by an African theology of death.

Death and what comes after it are inseparably linked, and to this extent, what is proposed as taking place during or after death can provide a noteworthy indication for an African theology of death. Since, as we have noted, little theological consideration has been given to the reality of death and dying, it is the task of the African theologian to try to grasp consciously and to formulate expressly a systematic theological content of these moments. What is articulated in the following lines is intended to offer a small contribution towards that end.

---

1. F. Austin, ed., *Vatican Council II, The Conciliar and Post-Conciliar Documents* (New York: Castello Publishing House, 1975), 917.

2. See R. R. de Asua Altuna, *Cultura Tradicional Banto* (Secretariado Arquidicesano de Pastoral Luanda, 1985), 439-40.

Approach to the Subject

One of the methods called for by the task at hand is to begin with an African understanding of the nature of death. This means that one would have to begin by asking: Why is there death? What are its causes here in Africa? Then one would have to listen to the reasons carefully and inquire into their real background. A comparison between these reasons and those offered by Scripture would have to be made. Then we would have to examine the experience of the dying in order to find out how they react to death, how they resist or accept it. After that it would be necessary to listen to the revelation of God, that is to say, to look at the reality of death and dying in the light of faith. Only then would it be possible to draw valuable conclusions which are related to our pastoral concerns for the dying.

Within the space of this essay, we cannot take that route. We are therefore going to adopt a method, in itself problematic but nonetheless not useless, of considering first the African notion of life. The main reason for this is that death is an event of life. It is as much part of life as childhood, youth and man/womanhood. There cannot be any living without dying, and vice versa. As such, one cannot talk about death without talking about life at the same time. This is the methodological principle from which everything here will take its cue. We will therefore begin by examining the African notion of life so as to understand the meaning of death and its practical implications.

I. God as the Foundation of Life

God is the source of life. This statement is simple, valid and correct. It sums up very well the known biblical conviction in God as the one who shapes human beginnings and who brings about the origin of everything that is. The belief is neither new nor strange to African faith and religiosity.

The studies carried out by the students of African culture show that there are many ethnic groups in Africa (e.g., the Masai, Kikuyu, Akamba, Banyarwanda, Bahima) who see God as the foundation of their life.[3] They believe that the first ancestors received life from God in order to communicate it and to protect it. Therefore we may claim this belief as a constitutive element of the African faith in God.

Life is communicated by the ancestors, but it is the origin given to humanity as a gift from God. For this reason, it falls directly under the category of sacred realities.[4] And since this life is sacred by reason of its connection with

---

3. See B. Bujo, "Can Morality be Christian in Africa?" in *CHIEA African Christian Studies*, 4:1 (March 1988): 6.
4. de Asua Altuna, 46. See also Bujo, 7ff.

the divine, the destruction of it is, among the Bantu, a crime against God, an ontological sacrilege. The destruction of life is thus immoral and unjust.[5] The question here is whether this conclusion is not too simplistic. However, simplistic or not, the conclusion makes one point clear: to the African life is sacred. To say, then, that God is the foundation of life is to assert the divine origin of this life on the one hand, and to evaluate this life as something noble and sacred on the other.

A. *Meaning of Life*

In the African language Swahili,[6] for example, the word "life" involves two distinct but interrelated realities of *Uhai* and *Maisha*.[7] The concept of life as Uhai refers mostly to what a person is in his/her physical and metaphysical compositions. As such, it points to him/her simply as an entity present before oneself with all the potential and possibilities of becoming and actualizing oneself. Very often we refer to this aspect of human life simply as bare existence.

But we would not be doing justice to the notion of life in the African sense if we were to conclude that life means simply *Uhai* or mere existence. For, in the African conception, life also means *Maisha*. That is to say, the way in which a person realises and actualises him/herself in the mundane temporality of his/her existence. The concept, therefore, refers to a person's interaction with and experience of the concrete things of his/her world: people, trees, stones, animals and all created reality. Thus the phrase "that is life" can be understood as an exclamation at what a person experiences in and through his/her interaction with the concrete reality around him/her.

It must be emphasised that *Uhai* and *Maisha* are both seen as equal realities of human existence. The two may be distinguished but never separated. If this is so, we can affirm that life, as an African person understands it, is a dialectic unity of *Uhai* and *Maisha*.

This understanding confirms the unity of the essential elements of life. But there is a further question: What does it (i.e., this unity of life's elements) really mean in the concrete experience of our existence? It means several things. First, it affirms that there is more to life than mere existence. Secondly, it implies that life cannot be realised in complete isolation from the family, clan or tribe. Life is not purely an individual project which one must carry on independently of the world around one. Life is realised in community with other men and

---

5. de Asua Altuna, 508.

6. Swahili is a Bantu language spoken mostly in Eastern and Central Africa.

7. The English equivalent of *Uhai* and *Maisha* is simply life. There is no distinction in the sense in which we explain it here.

women. It is the community which is the locus and context in which an African person realises his/her life.

The Sena[8] people of Mozambique, for instance, on coming back from a burial, do not enter the house of the deceased without first having taken a special medicine to protect themselves against the ghost or the spirit which killed the deceased.[9] The point is that by participating in such community rites and by learning the community myths and moral laws, the person is integrated into the community. Very often these integrational values include the promotion of life (procreation), the protection of life, the importance of strength and solidarity, how to maintain law and order in the community, the value of peace, love and justice, the wisdom of the ancestors, respect of the elderly and good health. All of these help the person to know him/herself, who he/she is, what is expected of him/her, what he/she wants him/herself to be in freedom and what in fact life entails for him/her. By thus integrating oneself into the group, one gains fullness of life. For the community is the source of life, or to put it differently, life is a gift from the community.[10]

B. The Plenitude of Life

For many Africans, to live fully is to live a life free from suffering, disgrace and harm. It means living this life in peace, love, justice, joy and cheerfulness. But for this to become true, there must be a genuine mutual respect for each other's differences and uniqueness. That is why Africans emphasise that members of a community must stop crippling each other by mutual hostilities. Further, the desire for the fullness of life obliges one to refrain from idolising one particular way of being and doing things as the norm for what it means to live. It makes the fullness of life to be understood essentially as freedom to be.

But there can be no fullness of being where there is no freedom.[11] In situations where there are constant military interventions and surveillance, arbitrary arrests, tribalism, hunger, corruption and alienation, there is no space to develop the most valuable of human potentials. That is why, in order to live fully as a human being, a person must be free.

These aspirations of freedom find their intensive moments in prayer. Christian ministers in Africa sometimes get very wary when a great number of the prayers of the faithful ask for protection against enemies, disgrace and

---

8. Sena is an ethnic group and a language in the province of Sofala in Mozambique.

9. The rite is very common, especially among non-Christians.

10. See C. Nyamiti, "The Incarnation Viewed from the African Understanding of Person," in *CHIEA African Studies,* 6:1 (March 1990): 9.

11. Freedom is the capacity to be fulfilled by action. It is the possibility for self-achievement and thus for personal becoming. See K. Rahner, "Theology of Freedom," in *Theological Investigations,* vol. 14, 179-86.

suffering. But they would do well to understand this as a deep longing of the people to live this life in its fullness. For this is what everyone hopes and prays for: that if it may be God's will, this life may continue to be lived with relative ease until one sees one's grand- and great-grandchildren. Thus the aspiration for the plenitude of life has both qualitative and quantitative elements: to live this life fairly well and for many years.

Those aspects of life which constitute a person's plenitude of living are gifts of life. This means that aspects of life such as freedom, peace, love, justice, the capacity to have children, the maintenance of relatively good health for many years, and being protected from harm, suffering and enemies are not a consequence of pure human effort. All these things are gifts which one receives from God through the community (of both the living and the dead) as a blessing. Thus God is not only the foundation of a person's life (understood as *Uhai*), but he is also the source and the foundation of his/her fullness of life. Again, the belief in the fullness of life as a blessing from God is so common in Africa that we may well claim it as another constitutive element of the African faith in God.

We have established that life in its essential dimensions is a gift over which the individual has no absolute claim. It is given to him/her gratuitously. But how does this work? What is the procedure of this gift which is given to us freely and without charge?

In this process, God is the giver. He gives himself, his own life, so that humanity may have life in its fullness. The key word here is "may." It leads to the understanding that the attainment of the fullness of life is a possibility but not necessarily a guarantee. To attain the fullness of life, the human person, the receiver, must live those values for which the giver gave his life. That is to say that the achievement of the plenitude of life depends also on the individual's dispositions and response to God's call. God calls each one of us to the fullness of life, not by force, but through a free choice. As such we can refuse the invitation or accept it. Life in its essential dimension is, therefore, a gift which presupposes a person's inner disposition and response.

In most African traditions this process is linked to moral laws and precepts. In most African traditions, in order not to endanger life and so be able to live many happy years, it is forbidden to kill, steal, lie, humiliate others, fornicate and be disobedient to elders. On the contrary, fidelity, generosity, hospitality, truth, justice, peace, love and faithfulness are encouraged.[12] The lesson one gets from this traditional teaching is that the person who lives according to these precepts will be given by God and the community a long and fortunate life. He/she will be blessed with children; he/she will be protected from enemies; evil spirits will not descend against his/her house; he/she will not experience much suffering in his/her life. People generally will like him/her.

---

12. de Asua Altuna, 517.

On the contrary, the person who does not live according to these laws in most cases lives a short and troublesome life. He/she experiences poverty; his/her children die young; he/she will not be very much liked or respected. He/she will generally feel alienated.

According to tradition, then, the faithful person lives a long and fortunate life. The unfaithful person, the sinner, lives a short and troublesome life.

C. The Death of the Blessed

The death of the blessed has a further meaning in the African view. The blessed bring their life to an end in complete harmony with what it has been. Theirs is not a fear-filled death of forever ceasing to be. It is not a regretful end for not having lived long enough to accomplish what life could have. For the faithful or the blessed one, his/her experience of many years has enriched him/her and he/she has grown, to use the Psalmist's language, from foolishness to wisdom. He/she has learnt to accept the realities of life (of which death is a part). The fundamental moral decision made during his/her active life is already, at the point of death, in its maturity and final definitiveness. The blessed cannot become anything else but what he/she has made him/herself out to be during his/her active life. That is why he/she is serene and calm at the moment of death since he/she sees death as the natural conclusion of his/her existence.[13]

It is precisely because the blessed often die at an advanced age that their death is much more calm and tranquil. They are more at peace with themselves and the world. Because for them death is a fulfillment of life well lived, their whole life history is summed up in it and what they have been in the world assumes eternal validity. At the funeral, many Bantu ethnic groups invoke the names of the elderly deceased, sing in gratitude for all they have done to/for the family and clan, and recount and exult their virtues.[14]

Thus also is the life history of the deceased summed up socially. From then on it will remain in the mind of the living in the community or clan. The dead person's will and wishes will be respected. Children will be named after him/her and his/her qualities will be promoted in them. Sacrifices will be offered in his/her name and he/she will be counted among the ancestors. Even though dead, the blessed person continues to live in this way in the memory and deeds of the living.

For the strict empiricist this "memory" may not constitute "existence" at all. Yet it is impossible to deny that in the cosmology of many Africans the presence of the dead in the memory and actions of the living *is* existence. It forms a constitutive dimension of the African understanding of "eternal life."

13. K. Rahner, *The Theology of Death* (London: Burns and Oates), 31.
14. de Asua Altuna, 448.

II. The Paradoxical Expression of Death

The perspective of a long, fulfilled life is only one side of the coin of human reality. Our discussion would be one-sided and therefore false if it did not take into consideration the countless victims of "meaningless" death: by lightning, road accidents, war, floods, epidemics and other diseases which bring about an early or sudden death. Here, life is cut short; it is not allowed to reach its maturity.[15] Everything happens so suddenly that one is given no time to put personal or family affairs in order.[16] There is no time to make some kind of evaluation of how one lived one's life and understood it so as to make some kind of decision on it (the final decision).[17] There is no time to make peace: to call relatives together, see them for the last time, leave them one's wishes and bid farewell to them.

What can we make of this kind of death? How does death really present itself in these cases of "premature" death? If, as we have argued, death for the Bantu is a natural conclusion of a person's life and the attainment of a mature existence, the question arises whether in the case of sudden, early death this maturation is possible.

A. Premature Death

In most Bantu ethnic groups, the death of a child or a young person is shocking. The community feels much wounded by it. For most Bantu, the death of the young is an aberration; it should not happen. Persons are not made to die young.[18] If such deaths occur, there is only one explanation for it: Sin. This belief in premature death as a consequence of sin is expressed in various African myths. In some ethnic groups death is attributed to the sin of the first woman's behaviour against the creator.[19] In Burundi it is the behaviour of the man in rejecting a deformed child that God had created for him that was sinful and brought about death.[20] But in

15. See E. Kübler-Ross, *On Death and Dying* (New York: Macmillan Publishing House, 1970). This is perhaps the best treatment of the psychological aspect of the moment of death and dying.

16. See H. Karlen, *Pastoral Guidance No. 1: Reflections on Death and Dying*, Zimbabwe Catholic Bishops Conference.

17. The main proponent of this theory is Ladislaus Boros. He has maintained that the moment of death provides a situation for a radical decision on the part of the dying person. It is the moment when the person comes to understand most distinctively his/her life both in the past and at present. This happens because the moment of death is, according to Boros, the moment of absolute freedom. As such it is the "moment of truth." See his *The Moment of Truth* (London: Burns & Oates, 1965), 9.

18. de Asua Altuna, 444.

19. Ibid., 434-35.

20. Ibid., 435.

all cases, the presence of death for the original man and woman is a punishment for their sin. Since then humanity lives in expectation of death.

The myths make one point clear: "where the antithesis between God and man comes to light in this way, there sin is also clearly manifested. . . . [The] shallowness and futility of human life . . . [are] the necessary result of a wrong attitude to life and to its divine background. . . ."[21] Human mortality is therefore a moral issue because it has a connection with sin.

We must recall here what we said earlier about the life of the unfaithful, or those who do not live according to the precepts set out by the community. By not living according to these precepts, the unfaithful separate themselves from the source of life. But we have seen that this source of life is God and the community of both the living and the death. Thus, by separating themselves from this source they attempt to gain life and bring it to fulfillment through their own effort. This, however, is not possible. Consequently, the unfaithful, in their separation from God and the community, live miserably and die prematurely.

B. The Paradox

In the past the link between what a person does and the manner of his/her death was accepted universally in Africa almost without question. If somebody died suddenly in an accident or by lightning, it was because he had done something wrong which displeased the ancestors. His death was interpreted as a punishment for his sin(s). No funeral rites were allowed for such a death. The same applied to death in childbirth, by leprosy or heart attack.[22]

Today, the great majority of people find it hard to accept this way of understanding death. People know from experience that not only the unfaithful die prematurely, but also the faithful and blessed. As a matter of fact the evildoers who accumulate wealth for themselves by exploiting others sometimes do live longer and more enjoyably than those who dedicate their entire lives to the service of others. What is more, people find it hard to understand today the presumed link between how a person lives and how he/she dies, for instance in the case of the death of a child. Why should the child die before it is able to make a conscious decision on the pattern of its own life?

All that this leads to is the conclusion that although the attainment of maturity, peace and tranquillity in death at an old age is a serious possibility, it is not a necessity or a given. We all die at a time when we are not ready for it. That is the fact, and it holds true for the young as well as for the old. As such, it is theologically true to say that death is a punishment for sin for both the

---

21. A. Weiser, *The Psalms* (Philadelphia: Westminster Press, 1962), 598-99.
22. de Asua Altuna, 444.

faithful and the unfaithful, the young and the old. In a sense, we have all sinned and all of us die a premature death.

Yet we must, at the same time, maintain the possibility that there are some people who are able to bring their life to an end in total acceptance and therefore in peace and tranquillity. They accept death as a normal aspect of their growth. That is what makes death a paradoxical reality. On the one hand it expresses itself as a meaningless breaking off of one's life — in a sense, a punishment for sin; on the other hand it shows itself as the attainment of a fully mature existence.

This paradox is illustrated, once again, by the activities at funerals of the Bantu. Here death is viewed with both joy and sadness. During funerals, people cry and wail. They mourn and are deeply sorrowful at the passing of one of their own. But they also celebrate. They beat the drums, dance, eat well and discuss and settle issues. The first set of activities shows the negative aspect of death while the second illustrates its positive side, that life has found its fulfillment in death.[23]

C. The Death of Jesus

In Christianity, the death and resurrection of Jesus have salvific value. In traditional theology, this finds classical expression in the doctrine of the "Atonement."[24] According to this teaching, it was through his death and resurrection that Jesus overcame all the powers of evil and thus brought humanity the assurance of liberation and life. Seen from the perspective of God's struggle against the forces of evil that hold humanity captive,[25] the Atonement is the turning point in the struggle. It begins a new and definitive phase of divine victory against evil in the world. Thus, for the Christian, the events of the cross and resurrection are central and fundamental.

If now an effort is made to understand the meaning of the Atonement from the African point of view sketched in the foregoing paragraphs, we have to say that Jesus died the death of both the faithful and the sinner. His death was at one and the same time a fulfillment and a meaningless cutting short of his life. The most significant scriptural texts with regard to this observation are the three predictions of the passion (Mk. 8:31, 9:31 and 10:33-34), the logion about the son of man giving his life as a ransom for many (Mk. 10:45), the parable of the wicked husbandmen (Mk. 12:1-12), and the last supper narratives

23. J.-M. Ela, *My Faith as an African* (Maryknoll, NY: Orbis Books, 1988), 168.

24. See J. Macquarrie, *Principles of Christian Theology* (London: SCM Press, 1981), 318. But perhaps the more detailed study of the doctrine is that of F. W. Dillistone, *The Christian Understanding of the Atonement* (London: SCM Press, 1984). See especially 102-5.

25. Dillistone, 104-5.

in Mt. 6:26-29, Mk. 14:22-25 and Lk. 22:15-20. These comprise the early church's understanding of the meaning of Jesus' death.

What becomes clear from these texts is that death did not take Jesus by surprise. He knew, by the growing opposition around him, that death was inevitable. The celebration of the farewell meal (the Passover) with his disciples indicates clearly that he knew his death was near. It is significant that he did not try to evade it. On the contrary, he went to Jerusalem to face it. The journey to Jerusalem may be taken as a metaphor for Jesus' gradual personal acceptance of his imminent death. It may be understood as a time during which he confirmed the stance or decision of his life before his Father. This confirmation of trust was confirmed by Jesus when he cried out in the words of Psalm 22, "My God, my God, why have you forsaken me?" With the words "It is finished," he brought his life to consummation or fulfillment.

Once we have affirmed that Jesus brought his life to fulfillment, we must also go on to say, equally seriously, that he died the death of a sinner. Let us point out the fact that he died at the age of around thirty. A young man, he must have experienced his death as a meaningless cutting short of his life. To compound this, he died with the knowledge that he had been rejected and betrayed by those who were his own. And he was killed as a common criminal; he did not die naturally in his bed. So Jesus died with a deep sense of abandonment. But due to his trust and commitment to the Father, he was enabled, even in these circumstances, to awaken the fullness of life.

D. Concluding Remarks

Let us now summarise our discussion. We looked at death from the perspective of the "plenitude of human life." The aim in doing so was to avoid the danger, so common in some eschatologies, of looking at death in isolation from life. It was to avoid the impression that death is something which comes from outside of the person, that it is not really present in one's life and that it does not, therefore, concern one here and now. In trying to put death into the perspective of life, the message we wished to get across is that it is not death but the plenitude of life that is the purpose of life. In other words, a person does not live in order to die but rather lives to live life completely and fully. Death is therefore present only as an inner factor (not a determinant) of life.

To live a long, fulfilled life, we noted, is for the African a blessing from God and the community. The death of the aged is a realisation of this blessing. Death in old age seems to be what God and the community intend for every person. Consequently, society and its institutions must create conditions which help each person to live out the limit of our physical life. This is especially true of Africa. They must see it as a moral duty to protect each person from falling victim to injustice, exploitation, poverty, war, violence, disease, famine and so on. Why? Simply because these are realities that diminish life and bring about premature death. So, if society cannot prevent death, it can nevertheless help persons to bring their life to a dignified conclusion. This means that hospitals, for instance, should be environments which are conducive for people to arrive at death in dignity as human persons. The fact that many hospitals in various parts of Africa, due to lack of elementary facilities, cannot do so is a serious ethical problem.

In our discussion, we acknowledge that maturity and fulfillment in death are only a possibility and not a given in all cases. For the fact is that most people die either too young or at a time when they are not ready for death. This is to say that most people, young or old, die prematurely. To the extent that this happens it shows death as a consequence of sin, by which we mean, as we have explained, an attempt to bring life to a fulfilled conclusion apart from God and the community. If we are to die in communion with God and the community, we must learn to renounce selfishness and not to hang on too much to material possessions. The struggle not to give up our physical life peacefully when death comes is indicative of our failure to learn to let go of our selfishness.

One of the tasks of people working with the dying is therefore to help them to hand over their life to God in confidence and dignity. Because the moment of death is also the moment when the dying take the final decision for the orientation of their life, conditions must be created for them to be able to do this. A noisy environment, for instance, does not help the dying person to come unanimously to a final decision.

The death of Jesus is an answer to all death. In taking death upon himself and dying both the death of the blessed and the death of the sinner, Jesus showed that he is present to all those who die. Because he went through the experience of both types of death, through him every death has been taken up and raised to the level of salvation. Thus, the death of Jesus gives hope to all of us, but especially those who are dying. Hope is the only and best thing our faith has to offer to the dying person.

Some Further Contributions to the Discussion

William Amy and James Recob, *Human Nature in the Christian Tradition.* Washington, D.C.: University Press of America, 1982.

G. C. Berkouwer, *Man: The Image of God.* Translated by Dirk Jellema. Grand Rapids, MI: Wm. B. Eerdmans Publishing Co., 1962.

Harry R. Boer, *An Ember Still Glowing: Humankind as the Image of God.* Grand Rapids, MI: Wm. B. Eerdmans Publishing Co., 1990.

Emil Brunner, *Man in Revolt: A Christian Anthropology.* Translated by Olive Wyon. London: Lutterworth, 1939.

José Comblin, *Retrieving the Human: A Christian Anthropology.* Translated by Robert R. Barr. Maryknoll, NY: Orbis Books, 1990.

Janet Crawford and Michael Kinnamon, *In God's Image.* Geneva: World Council of Churches, 1983.

Bruce Epperly, *At the Edge of Life: Holistic Vision of the Human Adventure.* St. Louis, MO: Chalice Press, 1992.

Virginia Fabella, ed., *Asia's Struggle for Full Humanity.* Maryknoll, NY: Orbis Books, 1980.

Langdon Gilkey, *Reaping the Whirlwind: A Christian Interpretation of History.* New York: Seabury Press, 1976.

Douglas John Hall, *Imaging God: Dominion as Stewardship.* Grand Rapids, MI: Wm. B. Eerdmans Publishing Co., 1986.

Philip Hefner, *The Human Factor.* Minneapolis, MN: Augsburg Fortress Press, 1993.

Philip Edgcumbe Hughes, *The True Image: The Origin and Destiny of Man in Christ.* Leicester, England: InterVarsity Press/Grand Rapids, MI: William B. Eerdmans Publishing Co., 1989.

Paul K. Jewett, *Man as Male and Female: A Theological Point of View.* Grand Rapids, MI: Wm. B. Eerdmans Publishing Co., 1975.

Marianne Katoppo, *Compassionate and Free: An Asian Woman's Theology.* Geneva: World Council of Churches, 1979.

Eugene Lauer and Joel Mlecko, eds., *A Christian Understanding of the Human Person*. New York: Paulist Press, 1982.

Vladimir Lossky, *In the Image and Likeness of God*. Translated by A. M. Allchin. London: Mowbrays, 1975.

Martin Luther, *The Bondage of the Will*. Translated by Henry Cole. Grand Rapids, MI: Wm. B. Eerdmans, 1931.

J. Gresham Machen, *The Christian View of Man*. Grand Rapids, MI: Wm. B. Eerdmans, 1937.

John Macquarrie, *In Search of Humanity: A Theological and Philosophical Approach*. London: SCM Press, 1982/New York: Crossroad, 1983.

Marianne H. Micks, *Our Search for Identity: Humanity in the Image of God*. Philadelphia: Fortress Press, 1982.

Minjung Theology. Singapore: Christian Conference of Asia, 1991.

J. P. Moreland and David M. Ciocchi, eds., *Christian Perspectives on Being Human: A Multidisciplinary Approach to Integration*. Grand Rapids, MI: Baker Book House, 1993.

J. N. K. Mugambi, *The African Heritage and Contemporary Christianity*. Nairobi, Kenya: Longman Kenya, 1989.

Emerito P. Nacpil and Douglas J. Elwood, eds., *The Human and the Holy: Asian Perspectives in Christian Theology*. Maryknoll, NY: Orbis Books, 1980.

Reinhold Niebuhr, *The Nature and Destiny of Man: A Christian Interpretation*. New York: Scribner, 1964.

Mercy Amba Oduyoye and Musimbi B. Z. Kanyoro, eds., *The Will to Arise*. Maryknoll, NY: Orbis Books, 1992.

Wolfhart Pannenberg, *Anthropology in Theological Perspective*. Translated by Matthew J. O'Connell, Philadelphia: Westminster Press, 1985.

Winston Persaud, *The Theology of the Cross and Mark's Anthropology: A View from the Caribbean*. New York: Peter Lang, 1991.

Karl Rahner, *Foundations of Christian Faith*. Translated by William V. Dyck. New York: Seabury Press, 1978.

————. *Hearers of the Word*. Translated by Michael Richards. New York: Herder and Herder, 1969.

Paul Ricoeur, *Fallible Man*. Rev. ed.; New York: Fordham University Press, 1986.

E. G. Rupp and P. S. Watson, eds., *Luther and Erasmus: Free Will and Salvation*. Philadelphia: Westminster Press, 1969.

Rosemary R. Ruether, *New Woman, New Earth*. New York: Seabury Press, 1975.

Letty Russell, *Human Liberation in a Feminist Perspective*. Philadelphia: Westminster Press, 1974.

Helmut Thielicke, *Being Human — Becoming Human: An Essay in Christian Anthropology*. Garden City, NY: Doubleday, 1984.

Emilie Townes, ed., *A Troubling in My Soul: Womanist Perspectives on Evil and Suffering*. Maryknoll, NY: Orbis Books, 1993.

Henry Nelson Wieman, *The Source of Human Good.* Chicago: The University of Chicago Press, 1946.

Delores S. Williams, *Sisters in the Wilderness.* Maryknoll, NY: Orbis Books, 1993.

PART IV

The Significance of Jesus Christ

INTRODUCING THE ISSUE

Understanding and Proclaiming Christ as Savior

Jesus' question to his first disciples — "Who do you say I am?" — is addressed also to us. Just as his early followers tried to answer this question in the context of their times (as reflected, e.g., in the titles they used to speak of Jesus: Teacher, Christ, Lord, Savior, etc.), we today must try to give as adequate an answer as possible in the context of our times. How should we speak of Jesus in our conflictive world of the late twentieth century? As God Incarnate? As the Man for Others? As the Forerunner of a New Humanity/Community/Creation?

Every generation and every follower of Christ has to give a response to Jesus' question in the many different contexts in which they find themselves, and a response that is not only from their lips but also with their lives. The church, too, throughout her history has sought to respond to Christ's question in confessions of faith and forms of life. Particularly in the Nicene and Chalcedonian confessions, the church outlined its faith with respect to the full divinity and humanity of Christ's person. But no comparable formulation of soteriology or the doctrine of Christ's redemptive work has gained ecumenical consensus in the church. From the New Testament to the present, a number of theories of the atonement have circulated in the church, some gaining wider recognition than others (see further on this, e.g., H. D. McDonald, *The Atonement of the Death of Christ;* Grand Rapids: Baker, 1985). In more recent christological discussion this division between conceptions of Christ's person and Christ's work has itself been questioned and efforts have been made to develop a more unified Christology focused on the identification and presentation of Jesus in his ministry, culminating in his death and resurrection.

The essays in this section exhibit concern for a more unified understanding of Jesus Christ and attempt to discern his significance not only for eternity but also specifically for today.

In his essay "Recent Trends in Christology," Gerald Bray responds from an evangelical perspective to recent discussion especially in British theology, led by John Hick and others, concerning what they call "the Myth of God Incarnate," and their objections to the exclusivistic claims that are often attached to traditional notions of the incarnation of God in Jesus Christ. Bray reviews the question of the historical Jesus and some modern reconstructions of Christology, pointing out the concern for a closer integration of notions of Christ's person and work, and concludes with a summary of the recent statement of the Vatican's Pontifical Biblical Commission that seeks to set forth a Christology closer to the biblical portraits of Jesus. Bray suggests that this may point the way toward an increasing convergence of Protestant and Catholic christological understanding.

Mark Heim, who has been active in ecumenical relations, approaches the issue from a rather different position, emphasizing the importance of praxis as well as conceptualization in christological understanding, particularly as underscored by feminist and liberation theologies. Heim also explores implications for interreligious dialogue of Christian witness to Christ. Drawing on Paul Knitter's suggestion of a "Theocentric Christology," Heim affirms the need to move beyond both an exclusivistic Christology that would deny truth in other religions and an "inclusivistic Christology" that tends to read Christ into other religious traditions as implicit or hidden in them. But at the same time he is critical of Knitter's view that "theocentrism" is adequate to solve all the problems here, since the concept of God requires some concrete reference point and principle of definition. For Christians this is Christ. But it is also important that Christians realize and make clear in their witness to Christ that Jesus focused attention on God, not primarily on himself (as, e.g., Mark 10:18 makes clear). Yet at the same time his proclamation and life manifested the power and presence of God at work among us. Heim suggests that an initially functional Christology evolves later into an ontological and dogmatic Christology, although there remains some inner tension between these. Nevertheless, Heim argues, the normativeness and decisiveness of Christ do not rest only on ontological claims concerning him; rather, they have to do more with the love, power, truth, and saving and transforming impact of Jesus on those he encountered and who responded to him in faith.

Those who responded to Jesus included women, Ellen Leonard points out. Yet the image of Christ, she says, has for some women become ambiguous or ambivalent: many women continue to find this figure inspiring and redemptive, but an increasing number are concerned that to identify the revelation of God in a male figure lends support to male dominance in church and society. Out of women's experience the author raises the question: Is it possible to develop a Christology that affirms female experience and embodiment? After reviewing recent feminist critiques of Christology, Leonard examines some efforts by feminist theologians to "reinterpret" Christ drawing on the biblical accounts in a way that affirms women. Among these efforts are Julian of Norwich's description of Jesus as "our true Mother," Christ as incarnate Sophia or Wisdom, Jesus as Sophia's prophet heralding a new community of equality and mutuality, and

Christ as this new community ("Christa/Community"), which includes but is not limited to Jesus himself. Leonard concludes by urging the development of an inclusive Christology affirmative of the full humanity of women and men, in which patterns of domination and submission are displaced by new patterns of mutuality and reciprocal service.

But, as Jacquelyn Grant points out, for women of color the movement toward overcoming sexism must involve the overcoming of other forms of discrimination and oppression as well. Jesus was not indifferent to the oppressed of his day but identified with them — indeed, he was one of them. He affirmed their personhood, lifted them to their feet, and set them moving on the road to freedom. Drawing on Black women's experience, Grant sketches a "womanist" (Black feminist) theology of God's solidarity with the suffering and oppressed in which Jesus (in distinction from white feminists' emphasis on Christ or Christa) is the concrete presence of God in identification with the weak and abused. It is from Jesus that women of color find the strength, endurance, and hope to persist in their struggle for recognition and fair treatment. For women of color from slaves to the contemporary struggle for respect in a society that demeans them, Jesus becomes a source of power that lifts them up and enables them to keep on in the struggle for freedom.

That is also a note, though sounded in a different way, made by John Onaiyekan in the contemporary African context. Following a review of some of the main trends in recent African Christology, the author surveys some attempts to relate biblical categories to familiar notions in African cultures and experience. Particularly the notions of the role of the ancestors, kinsmen, the chief, and the healer, but also more distinctive tribal notions such as the master of initiation and the Yoruba's *Orisha* (agent and servant of the Supreme Being), he suggests, may be helpful in christological interpretation. Images of Jesus as liberator, as leader in working for justice and peace and community, and as one who, as in Scripture, affirms faith even beyond his own circle of followers, are emerging as leading themes in current African Christology. But the goal of this quest, says the author, is not just a pleasing picture of Jesus for its own sake but rather an effort to plunge deeper into understanding and service of the one who is being studied.

Australian theologian Denis Edwards explores the cosmic implications of the proclamation of Christ's resurrection. With awareness of current scientific and philosophical views of the formation of the universe, Edwards contends that the resurrection of the body (of Christ) manifests God's concern to redeem the whole of creation, physical as well as spiritual. "God's power to save embraces not just humanity, but all of creation." Yet, Edwards argues, Christian hope for the redemption of creation does not necessarily exclude violence, suffering, or increased entropy; on the contrary, these are part of the evolutionary history of the universe and part of God's promise of the salvation of the cosmos in Christ. Going beyond Karl Rahner's view of the risen Christ as the victory hidden in all cosmic reality, Edwards suggests that the divinity as well as the humanity of Christ links the cosmos with the triune God. Thus "Jesus of Nazareth, risen from the dead, is one with the dynamic power at the heart of cosmic processes."

Such cosmic Christology is brought back to earth, so to speak, in Joyce Hollyday's story of an old priest who seeks to communicate the reality of Christ to the poor of his parish and finds that in walking with them he is also walking with Jesus.

Recent Trends in Christology

GERALD L. BRAY

In the eyes of a British student there can be little doubt that a study of recent trends in Christology ought to begin with the symposium *The Myth of God Incarnate,* which appeared in July 1977.[1] Ten years later the book is still in print, and although it is neither a particularly original nor a particularly profound Christological study, it did manage to create an atmosphere which has provided a talking-point for the subsequent decade. The "myth makers," as the contributors to the symposium were irreverently dubbed, were quickly and almost universally criticized by most scholars working in the field, and a number of studies soon appeared which did their best to demonstrate that they were on the wrong track.[2] Before long there were even secondary symposia dedicated to an examination of the "myth debate," in which proponents and opponents of the original work met each other and agreed to differ, often sharply, from one another.[3]

The *Myth* was criticized for two main reasons. First, the contributors were not agreed about what they meant by the word itself, and this led to some confusion in the minds of readers. Behind the verbal uncertainty lay an uncertain approach to historical facts which revealed itself in the cavalier approach which some of the contributors took to the evidence of the Gospels. On the whole it would probably be fair to say that for most of them, as good post-Bultmannians, the historical Jesus had little or no importance for the development of Christology.

---

1. John Hick, ed., *The Myth of God Incarnate* (London: SCM Press, Ltd., 1977).

2. For discussion of this, see J. A. Ziesler, *The Jesus Question* (London, 1980), 108-19; K. Runia, *The Present-Day Christological Debate* (Leicester, 1984), 78-86.

3. Michael Goulder, ed., *Incarnation and Myth: The Debate Continued* (London: SCM Press Ltd., 1979); A. E. Harvey, ed., *God Incarnate: Story and Belief* (London, 1981).

Reprinted from *Themelios* 12/2 (January 1987) and the *Evangelical Review of Theology* 12 (January 1988): 52-63. Used with permission.

But in this respect the symposiasts were out of step with a large section of scholarly opinion, and they were criticized for naïvely swallowing an approach to the biblical data which was strongly reminiscent of classical (i.e., pre-1914) liberalism and which is now generally regarded as obsolete.[4]

The *Myth*'s influence on Christology had therefore little to do with its actual content. Rather, what the book did was to bring into view the problem of whether and to what extent traditional dogmatic Christology ought to be revised in the light of the findings of biblical scholars and the speculations of modern theologians. Indeed, one might go so far as to say that it was precisely the *Myth*'s failure to handle either of these matters satisfactorily which produced a spate of material endeavouring to correct and supplement its shortcomings. To that extent the book opened up an area which had been too long neglected, and which urgently needed serious attention.

History and the Gospels

The precise relationship of the Gospels to scientific history has long been recognized to lie at the heart of much Christological debate. The authors of the *Myth* were basically complaining that the early church took the biblical texts at face value and out of them constructed a dogmatic structure which, while it was internally coherent, was based on a false assumption. In saying this they were following in the footsteps of Rudolf Bultmann, who had died the previous year, but ignoring the widespread reaction to his ideas which had come to dominate Christological studies in Germany. Käsemann's "new quest" for the historical Jesus, Pannenberg's assertion that the resurrection must be regarded as a scientifically historical event, and Hengel's wide-ranging and generally conservative studies of the New Testament church — all these were simply ignored. This astonishing oversight can perhaps be explained by the fact that German historical and archaeological studies have usually fit comfortably within a liberal theological framework. They have not been designed, as they have been in the English-speaking world, to support the historical truthworthi- ness of the Gospels as the chief prop of classical orthodoxy. The myth makers, coming as they did from an Anglo-Saxon environment, understood that only a radically antihistorical approach could serve as a persuasive basis for their theological reconstruction. Thus they were obliged to overstate their case and ignore developments in Germany which might be interpreted as evidence against it.

But in spite of its lingering attachment to orthodoxy, the main charac- teristic of recent Anglo-Saxon historical study has been its relative detachment from theological questions, and this tradition has reasserted itself in the debates

4. See Alasdair Heron, article review in *Scottish Journal of Theology* 31 (1978): 51-71.

of the past decade, which found many in the conservative camp unprepared to argue on the myth makers' chosen ground. The *Myth* appeared too soon after John Robinson's *Redating the New Testament*[5] for the latter to have exerted any influence upon it, but the contrast between them was soon perceived and commented upon.[6] Robinson was a theological radical schooled in the English tradition of conservative biblical criticism, and in his book he managed to present a case for saying that the entire New Testament canon was in existence by A.D. 70 without ever suggesting what implications that might have for a radical rejection of the Gospels as historical evidence. Robinson subsequently went even further and attempted to demonstrate that the Fourth Gospel was the one closest to the original *kerygma,* although here he was prepared to admit that there may have been a long period in which John was able to meditate on Jesus and develop his Christology before committing it to writing.[7]

From the conservative side came John Wenham's *Easter Enigma,* which was an attempted harmonization of the four Gospels in their accounts of the passion, death and resurrection of Jesus.[8] Wenham was criticized for his forays into speculation, but impartial readers also pointed out that this is inevitable if harmonization is ever to be achieved. What Wenham did was to show that harmonization is not impossible, so that the claim of the Gospels to historicity deserves to be taken more seriously than it has sometimes been. Furthermore, it was generally recognized that Wenham was writing in defence of traditional orthodoxy, though he nowhere attempted to develop this. Even so, this reaction demonstrates the degree to which it is still assumed that the historicity of the Gospels and traditional orthodoxy stand or fall together, and it reminds us why John Robinson failed to carry conviction when he tried to unite a radical theology to a conservative biblical criticism.

Specific attempts to unite a conservative view of the reliability of the Gospels as historical narrative with a fairly traditional theological position which nevertheless was prepared to take the modern debates into account were made by I. H. Marshall[9] and C. F. D. Moule.[10] Marshall's study is more limited in scope, being primarily an examination of Jesus' self-understanding and using the main titles of divinity which are applied to him in the New Testament. He concludes that New Testament Christology makes sense only if we posit the belief that Jesus himself taught that he was the Son of Man, the Son

5. J. A. T. Robinson, *Redating the New Testament* (London: SCM Press Ltd., 1976).

6. See Eric L. Mascall, *Theology and the Gospel of Christ* (London: SPCK, 1977), 111-20.

7. J. A. T. Robinson, *The Priority of John* (London: SCM Press, Ltd., 1985).

8. John Wenham, *Easter Enigma* (Exeter: The Paternoster Press, 1984). A similar approach to this can be found in M. J. Harris, *Easter in Durham* (Exeter: The Paternoster Press, 1985), which is a scholarly rebuttal of the Bishop of Durham's denial of the historical resurrection of Jesus.

9. I. Howard Marshall, *The Origins of New Testament Christology* (Leicester: Universities and Colleges Christian Fellowship, 1976).

10. C. F. D. Moule, *The Origin of Christology* (Cambridge: Cambridge University Press, 1977).

of God, the Messiah-Christ and Lord. Moule endorses the same view, though perhaps somewhat more cautiously, and goes on to develop the idea of the "corporate Christ," in which Jesus ceases to be merely an historical individual and becomes, in the understanding of the New Testament church, a cosmic figure who transcends individual personhood to embrace a new humanity in himself.

It is at this point that Moule deserts orthodox Christology, which says that each believer has a relationship with Christ, who enables him/her to approach the Father in the trinitarian communion which is our inheritance in the Holy Spirit, and opts instead for an all-embracing, essentially eschatological view, according to which Christ is the agent of the transformation of the entire creation — a universalism not at all that distant from the teaching of Gregory of Nyssa and Maximus the Confessor, although Moule acknowledges no specific debt to either of them.

Far more radical than Moule is J. D. G. Dunn,[11] who reduces his Christological understanding of the New Testament to two fundamental presuppositions. First, he argues that the early church worshipped Jesus as Lord, which soon came to mean God, even if this was not necessarily immediately clear at first. Second, Dunn argues for an ontological continuity between the Jesus of history and the Christ of faith; in other words, whatever happened on the first Easter morning, the early Christians believed that the Christ whom they met in the postresurrection appearances was the same person as the Jesus whom they had known before the crucifixion. These two assumptions allow Dunn to claim a kind of minimalist orthodoxy while accepting the main substance of the classical liberal position on the composition of the New Testament writings, the emergence of early Catholicism, and so on. In a sense, therefore, he may be called the diametric opposite of John Robinson, and the perceived incongruity in his position has similarly failed to carry conviction.

Finally, representing an even more radical line, there is J. Mackey,[12] who accepted all the most antihistorical beliefs of the myth makers and endeavoured to give their views a systematic framework rooted in the New Testament. It is Mackey's contention that Jesus was himself a myth maker propounding a highly symbolic "kingdom of God," and that the task of his followers, especially the apostle Paul, was to substitute a myth based on Jesus for the one created by him! Mackey's work is valuable chiefly because it shows us how far it is possible to go in rejecting history when constructing a Christological theory. In purely intellectual terms it represents a considerable achievement, but one which is too weakly grounded to be regarded as a serious contribution to theology.

---

11. J. D. G. Dunn, *Christology in the Making* (London: SCM Press Ltd., 1980).
12. James P. Mackey, *Jesus: The Man and the Myth* (London: SCM Press, Ltd., 1979).

Orthodoxy

Mackey comes from a Roman Catholic background, which may explain why he takes the myth building of the early church far beyond the New Testament. According to him the Pauline myth did not finally become orthodoxy until the defeat of Arius, which thus represents a watershed in Christological development.

The attempted rehabilitation of ancient heretics is a recurring feature of modern Christology, though until recently the figures usually selected for this honour have been either Theodore of Mopsuestia (d. 428), whose case rests on the fact that he was not condemned until 553, and Nestorius who has been shown to have expressed agreement with the *Tome* of Leo, a document which was used at the Council of Chalcedon to reinforce his condemnation at Ephesus in 431. Scholars continue to argue over the merits of Nestorius' case,[13] but it seems as if the main efforts at rehabilitation may have shifted to the famous arch-heretic, Arius. Certainly this was the intention of Robert Gregg and Dennis Groh,[14] who argued that Arianism owed its distinctive Christology to soteriological considerations whose strength was such that the "orthodox" opposition was reduced to a handful of diehards around Athanasius of Alexandria.

The belief that soteriology determined Christology in the Arian controversy represents an ingenious attempt to read a modern situation back into ancient times. Gregg and Groh have taken the "functional" approach to Christology which is common in Germany, where Oscar Cullmann and Ferdinand Hahn have been its leading exponents, and applied it to the fourth-century debate. It is interesting in this connection to note that whereas Cullmann believes that the functional Christology characteristic of the New Testament gave way to a more ontological approach later on, Gregg and Groh seem to be saying that the Arian controversy was the moment when matters came to a head and the "biblical" Christology represented by the functional soteriology of Arius finally succumbed to the ontological approach now associated with orthodoxy.

This view has been seriously challenged by Rowan Williams,[15] who argues that it misrepresents the thrust of Arius' teaching. Arius, says Williams, was primarily concerned to deny the (faulty) ontological assertions of the church of Alexandria, which seemed to him to be raising Christ to such a level of divinity that the person of the Father and his role as *fons deitatis* were being compromised. Instead of this, Arius proposed an alternative ontology which would leave the Father's uniqueness intact and at the center of Christian theology. In general terms, Williams is certainly correct in his assessment of Arius'

---

13. For a full discussion see A. Grillmeier, *Christ in Christian Tradition* I (2nd rev. ed.; London: A. R. Mowbray & Co., Ltd., 1975), 559-68.

14. R. C. Gregg and D. E. Groh, *Early Arianism: A View of Salvation* (Philadelphia: Fortress Press, 1981).

15. R. Williams, "The Logic of Arianism," in *Journal of Theological Studies* 34 (1983): 56-81.

mind, though he may have underestimated the appeal of soteriological factors to some, at least, of his many followers.

One interesting feature of recent discussion is that traditional orthodoxy has come to be associated with the Council of Chalcedon, perhaps because it is the usual stopping place in university courses on early church history, even though that Council has little claim to such a distinction. This has been forcefully pointed out by E. L. Mascall,[16] and two timely, though little known, studies bear him out.[17] More recently, however, there are signs that the neglect of post-Chalcedonian developments is being repaired, at least to some extent. David Calvert[18] extends his rejection of classical Christological terms to the period beyond Chalcedon, and Glenn Chesnut[19] does his best to refashion post-Chalcedonian terminology into distinctively modern concepts. Chesnut is particularly concerned to demonstrate that the exponents of Chalcedon, and in particular Maximus the Confessor, had a theology which can quite easily be transferred into existentialist terms. It is a brave attempt, but apart from the fact that it assumes that existentialism is *the* modern philosophy, it is open to the same kind of objection that Rowan Williams has levelled at Gregg and Groh. Once again we are faced with an attempt to graft a modern way of thinking onto an ancient author whose own perspective was rather different.[20]

Modern Reconstructions

Nevertheless it is fair to say that "Chalcedon" is now widely used as shorthand to represent traditional orthodox Christology, and that recent speculative work in the field can largely be divided according to whether it accepts or rejects this heritage. This in turn involves a preference for either an ontological or a functional approach to the figure of Jesus. In view of the tendency of biblical scholars to opt for the latter, it is scarcely surprising that the majority of recent studies have done the same, but the ontological approach is by no means dead and has recently acquired some notable exponents and defenders.

Among the books devoted to a basically functional approach, we may mention the 1980 Sarum Lectures given by Schubert Ogden,[21] who argues for an understanding of Jesus as the man who has given us the key to achieve

16. Eric L. Mascall, *Whatever Happened to the Human Mind?* (London: SPCK, 1980), 28-53.

17. Jean Meyendorff, *Christ in Eastern Thought* (Washington, D.C.: Corpus Books, 1969); P. T. R. Gray, *The Defense of Chalcedon in the East* (451-553) (Leiden: E. J. Brill, 1979).

18. D. G. A. Calvert, *From Christ to God* (London, 1983).

19. Glenn F. Chesnut, *Images of Christ* (Minneapolis: Augsburg Press, 1984).

20. *Maximus Confessor: Selected Writings* (London: Paulist Press, 1985) gives some idea of his thought. But for a full treatment of the question, see P. Piret, *Le Christ et la Trinté selon Maxime le Confesseur* (Paris: 1983).

21. Schubert M. Ogden, *The Point of Christology* (London: SCM Press Ltd., 1982).

authentic personal freedom. Ogden's approach is reminiscent of the existential-ist morality of the 1960s, and he is clearly sympathetic to the authors of the *Myth*. However, his approach is so firmly tied to the supposed desire of "modern man" for the subjective experience of "freedom" that any reference to the his-torical Jesus is obliged to serve this fundamental point. Because of this it be-comes difficult to know whether Ogden is really presenting a Christology at all, or merely using Jesus-language as a hangover from the past which might still be useful for expressing human emotions today.

Much less radical than this is the work of Anthony Tyrrell Hanson,[22] who rejects the Chalcedonian framework without departing from the Bible or the theological tradition as a whole. Hanson argues that the teaching and experience of Jesus which the early Christians received obliged them to develop a theology which allowed for distinctions within God. In particular, they were forced to develop a Logos, or Word, doctrine, according to which God could communi-cate with humankind through the activities of a particular human being. We appear to be on the road to a modern form of Arianism, though Hanson is careful to reject this. He also rejects the revamped adoptionism of Geoffrey Lampe,[23] though he is broadly sympathetic to the concerns which Lampe raises. In the end, Hanson pictures Jesus as the greatest of the saints, a man in whom God has revealed his Word but who nevertheless remains a finite creature who is not identical with that Word.

Hanson's work is especially notable for the amount of attention it gives to the question of Christ's pre-existence and the problem of the ongoing influ-ence of his sacrifice as a mediatorial propitiation for our sins. Both of these concepts he resolutely denies, though in doing so he opens up the whole field of medieval and Reformation Christology, including the eucharistic controver-sies of the period, which have largely been left to one side in modern debates.

Roman Catholic theologians have also been prominent in advocating various forms of functional Christology, though their dogmatic commitment to Chalcedon has usually prevented them from being quite as radical as their Protestant counter-parts. In general they have been content to stress the implications of Christ's complete humanity, particularly in the realm of his conscious self-awareness. "A humanity completely open to God" is the way Piet Schoonenberg,[24] Karl Rahner,[25] Hans Küng[26] and most profoundly Edward Schillebeeckx[27] have described and developed their approach to Christ. For them the psychological experiences of a

22. A. T. Hanson, *The Image of the Invisible God* (London, 1982).

23. G. H. Lampe, *God as Spirit* (Oxford: Clarendon Press, 1980).

24. Piet Schoonenberg, *The Christ: A Study of the God-Man Relationship in the Whole of Creation and in Jesus Christ* (New York: Herder and Herder, 1971).

25. Karl Rahner, *Theological Writings*, vols. 1, 13, 16, 17 (London: Darton, Longman & Todd Ltd., 1974-81).

26. Hans Küng, *On Being a Christian* (Garden City, NY: Doubleday, 1976).

27. Edward Schillebeeckx, *Jesus* (London: William Collins Sons & Co. Ltd., 1981).

first-century Jew are all-important to our understanding of Christology, and it is the meeting of Jesus' self-consciousness with ours which makes him the model for us to follow in the pursuit of our salvation. To all of these writers, as to Hanson, the traditional ontological approach suffers from being drawn largely from the Fourth Gospel, which they all agree is a late and unreliable source.[28]

In opposition to this tendency there is the wide-ranging and solidly based work of Jean Galot, whose earlier writings were introduced to the English-speaking world by Eric Mascall,[29] and some of whose major work has now appeared in English.[30] Galot tackles the modern Christological debates head-on, and argues that only a return to the ontological categories of Chalcedon, suitably updated to embrace the concerns of modern psychological research, can solve the problems which theologians believe confront them. Galot insists that the biblical witness, taken as a whole, leads inevitably to the ontological definitions of Chalcedon, which he believes are sufficiently open-ended to accommodate modern concerns. He rightly criticizes many modern theologians for having rejected transitional terminology without either understanding it or bothering to investigate its hidden potential. Galot's work is a first-class restatement of traditional orthodoxy in modern terms, and deserves to be more widely known than is the case at present.

Another defender of the traditional ontological approach is Colin Gunton,[31] who argues that to neglect it is to fall back into the dualistic approach to reality which characterized ancient tendencies towards adoptionism and docetism. As Gunton points out, modern reconstructions of Christology often bear more than a passing resemblance to ancient heresies, and he attributes this fact to the rather superficial rejection of the traditional orthodox inheritance on the part of modern theologians. Gunton's book is a fresh and learned philosophical approach to the subject and should be taken more seriously than it has been so far. Gunton does not appear to know Galot, but the two men have a good deal in common and their approaches complement each other in a quite remarkable way.

The Work of Christ

The predominance of a functional, soteriological approach to Christology is a reminder of the importance of the work of Christ within the framework of the doctrine of his person and natures. As Colin Gunton points out, modern

28. Hence the importance of J. A. T. Robinson's *The Priority of John* (London: SCM Press Ltd., 1985).

29. E. L. Mascall, *Theology and the Gospel of Christ,* 151-88.

30. Jean Galot, *Who is Christ? A Theology of the Incarnation* (Chicago: Franciscan Herald Press, 1981).

31. Colin E. Gunton, *Yesterday and Today. A Study of Continuities in Christology* (London: Darton, Longman & Todd Ltd., 1983).

theologians frequently miss the fact that the classical two-natures Christology has a profoundly soteriological purpose in ensuring that Christ was an adequate saviour of mankind and mediator between man and God. But although the soteriological theme has received great prominence, its content has been left remarkably vague. Very often the most that is said is that Christ is our "liberator," a term which is usually understood in terms of individual emotional and psychological experience, though of course it has also been applied to social and political freedom in the context of the liberation theology which has grown up on the frontiers of Christianity and Marxism.[32]

The most serious critique of this from the traditional Roman Catholic perspective is that by Jean Galot,[33] who attempts a systematic application of Chalcedonian Christology to the saving work of Christ on the cross. Galot does not stop with the atonement, however, but extends his treatment to cover the resurrection and ascension of Christ, as well as the sending of the Holy Spirit at Pentecost. Unfortunately, the wholeness of Galot's vision is compromised by a limitation of the substitutionary role of Christ's sacrifice to allow for a human contribution to the work of salvation, and a universalizing of redemption which has no place for the satisfaction of the Father's justice by the payment of the human debt of guilt.

It has been left to Protestant theologians to defend the classical teaching of the Reformation on the atonement, and this has been done in at least three works of substantial importance which have appeared in recent years. In Germany, Martin Hengel[34] has carefully demonstrated the validity of atonement language both within the circle of Jesus' followers and in the wider Graeco-Roman world. As it is often supposed that a concept of substitutionary sacrifice would not have fitted the socio-cultural context of earliest Christianity, this is a contribution of major importance. More strictly biblical in scope is the work of Leon Morris,[35] who shows in great detail just what the range of meaning inherent in Jewish and Christian concepts of atonement actually was. Morris' scholarship is unashamedly conservative, with a wealth of biblical reference and a constant concern to answer the charges levelled against the traditional teaching by scholars of an earlier generation like C. H. Dodd and Vincent Taylor.

Complementing Morris' work is the massive study by H. D. McDonald,[36] who takes us through the traditional doctrine, the evidence of the New Testament for it, and the treatment which atonement has received in history.

---

32. J. Andrew Kirk, *Liberation Theology: An Evangelical View from the Third World* (London: Marshall, Morgan & Scott, 1979).

33. J. Galot, *Jesus, Our Liberator* (Rome, 1982).

34. Martin Hengel, *The Atonement* (London: SCM Press, Ltd., 1979).

35. Leon Morris, *The Atonement: Its Meaning and Significance* (Leicester: Universities and Colleges Christian Fellowship, 1983).

36. H. D. McDonald, *The Atonement of the Death of Christ in Faith, Revelation and History* (Grand Rapids: Baker Book House, 1985).

Complete chapters are devoted to the contributions of Anselm, Abelard, Dale, Forsyth, Aulén and Moberly, and no fewer than 28 theologians are briefly discussed in the last chapter, including Leon Morris (but not C. H. Dodd, for some curious reason). McDonald is a conservative in the Reformation mould, but he is always scrupulously fair to his opponents and his book is likely to become and remain a standard work of reference on its subject.

Other Approaches

One might expect, in an age dominated by Karl Barth, that there would be a steady stream of theological studies relating the doctrine of Christ to the Trinity, but although such studies have appeared from time to time, they have been surprisingly rare. No doubt the strong functional approach to Christology has had a lot to do with this neglect, but it is quite astonishing how far the issue has been left to the defenders of traditional credal positions. Since the appearance of James Dunn's *Jesus and the Spirit* there has been almost nothing of comparable significance, in spite of the widespread growth of charismatic and "renewal" movements in the churches. Ecumenical interests have prompted the World Council of Churches to produce its excellent symposium on the *Filioque* dispute,[37] which has been supplemented more recently by Yves Congar,[38] but the only major work on the place of the Son within the Godhead is that by Louis Bouyer,[39] which has not had the circulation it deserves or will need if it is to make any serious impact on Anglo-Saxon Christology.

On a completely different track is Jaroslav Pelikan's recent work dealing with the place of Jesus in the history of culture.[40] This is an unusual subject which has seldom been studied, and never put together in such comprehensive detail. Pelikan takes eighteen different pictures of Christ which he sees as having dominated at successive periods in the history of the church, and he deals with each in the light of the theology, literature and art of its time. The book is a very useful reminder that Jesus has never belonged to theologians, and it even suggests to us that theology has reacted to the forces of the age in which it has been written more frequently than we have often thought. It is a book which deserves to be read and pondered carefully by all students of Christology, whatever their own particular approach to the subject might be.

Lastly, something should be said about the Statement of the Pontifical Biblical Commission, which appeared in Latin and French in 1984 and has

---

37. L. Vischer, ed., *Spirit of God, Spirit of Christ* (Geneva: World Council of Churches, 1981).

38. Yves Congar, *The World and the Spirit* (London, 1986).

39. L. Bouyer, *The Eternal Son: A Theology of the Word of God and Christology* (Huntingdon, IN: Our Sunday Visitor, 1978).

40. J. Pelikan, *Jesus Through the Centuries: His Place in the History of Culture* (New Haven and London: Yale University Press, 1985).

recently been translated into English with a commentary by J. A. Fitzmyer.[41] The Commission surveys the different trends which have appeared in modern Christology, and criticizes them for a one-sided approach to the Scriptures. Its remedy is a deeper and more comprehensive use of the Bible, including the Old Testament, for establishing a Christology which will have pastoral relevance in the church today. The document betrays no sign of denominational bias, though its comments on particular theologians are necessarily very brief. Here the commentary is a help because it fills in the background to the Commission's thinking as far as this can be done by one who was not a participant in the discussions. The document is valuable not only as a handy reference tool, but also because of the remarkable Part II, which outlines the framework of what the Commission believes is a truly biblical Christology. This turns out to rely heavily on the covenant offices of prophet, priest and king as the key to an Old Testament Christology, and insists that Jesus can be understood only by giving priority to his filial relationship to God. It is this consideration, says the Commission, which ought to be the criterion of investigation into the meaning of Christ for believers today. The Protestant observer can hardly help wondering whether he has stumbled back into the pages of Calvin by mistake, since that is certainly the impression which this Statement gives.

As a call to the church to develop a relevant Christology, the Statement of the Papal Commission makes a fitting conclusion to a survey of the past decade. No one can dispute that much has been said and written during that time, but it remains very much an open question how much of what has appeared will eventually form part of that great tradition which is the witness of God's faithful saints in every age to the reality of his presence with us in the person of Jesus Christ.

41. J. A. Fitzmyer, *Scripture and Christology* (London: 1986).

Thinking about Theocentric Christology

S. MARK HEIM

I

Christology is a particularly yeasty field today. The challenges raised in philosophical and biblical studies continue to be debated. However, despite occasional furors like that over *The Myth of God Incarnate*, these fields no longer seem to generate the greatest interest. The discussion is more prominently focused in two areas. One of these is a *praxis* imperative applied to Christology primarily by feminist and liberation theology: the criteria for contemporary Christology are evolved both from the argued past effects of traditional Christology and the foreseen personal and social effects of new views. The second area of ferment comes out of consideration of Christology in an interfaith perspective. Here the questions of Christology are addressed with interreligious dialogue in mind and a change in Christianity's attitude toward other religions at heart.

In a world of many faiths, Christianity is increasingly exhorted not to evaluate its theology only according to "internal norms." It is also called to consider how its doctrines shape the possibilities of cooperation and community in a pluralistic world, including the attitudes of "Christian" nations toward those not predominantly so. In its continued relation to its parent faith, Judaism, Christianity is faced with the necessity to articulate its belief in Jesus Christ with reference to terms and history that belong rightfully as well to a people who do not share that belief. In the face of the political and social struggles for liberation and identity, Christianity is faced with an increasingly acute *praxis* test for its doctrine: what is the "cash value" of various theological perspectives, and which serves most effectively to further the work of God? In all these areas there are concrete histories which give added point to the concerns: colonialism, Antisemitism, sexism, and oppression.

Originally published in the *Journal of Ecumenical Studies* 24 (Winter 1987): 1-16. Reprinted with permission.

Those who work in these various streams of theological reflection tend to find their concerns converging in Christology. Some, at least, find broad agreement on the direction theological reconstruction in this area ought to take. The term "theocentric Christology" is sometimes used to indicate such agreement. An "exclusive" Christology is one which sees salvation as limited to those in direct and conscious relation to Jesus Christ, while an "inclusive" Christology would say that, by virtue of God's act in Christ, salvation is open to those beyond the arena where the name is named.[1] Obviously, any theology which believes Paul to be correct when he tells us Abraham was saved by faith is to some extent "inclusive." Much recent Christian theology has been broadening and systematizing the character of this inclusivity, along the lines of Karl Rahner's "anonymous" Christianity.

"Theocentric Christology" is not a synonym for inclusive Christology. Indeed, it would criticize inclusive Christologies as halfway houses, still founded on an "exclusivist" view of Christ's role and significance, while spreading the christological "benefits" about in a more universal and inclusive manner. If we might borrow a phrase from economics, inclusive Christianity is faulted because it is a "trickle-down" Christology: God's saving grace to humanity — even though it be supposed to be everywhere available and not necessarily bound to confession of Christ — nevertheless passes decisively, uniquely, and normatively *through* Christ. It is this notion to which theocentric Christology places itself in opposition.

For the purposes of this discussion I will deal specifically with the recent book by Paul Knitter, *No Other Name?*[2] Knitter is not the inventor of the substance or the title of theocentric Christianity, but he provides one of the most careful and thorough presentations of its character. His is a book to be reckoned with by those interested in this discussion. To gain the advantages of specificity and to avoid the dangers of straw persons, I will deal with Knitter's views. He reminds us, however, that these views are largely if not totally congruent with those of a number of other theologians: most notably John Hick, Stanley Samartha, Rosemary Ruether, Tom Driver, and Raimundo Panikkar, to name a few. With them, Knitter sees himself as part of a broad front in theological reformation.

Knitter's book has three parts. The first is a consideration of three popular approaches to the fact of various religious faiths in the world: "They are all relative," "They are all essentially the same," "They all have a common psychological origin." The first three chapters critically examine these pieces of conventional wisdom, taking Troeltsch, Toynbee, and Jung as representative, if

---

1. The categories of exclusivism, inclusivism, and pluralism (Knitter's "theocentrism") are taken from Alan Race, *Christians and Religious Pluralism: Patterns in the Christian Theology of Religions* (Maryknoll, NY: Orbis, 1983).

2. Paul F. Knitter, *No Other Name?* (Maryknoll, NY: Orbis, 1985).

sophisticated, spokespersons for them. The second part of the book treats major models of Christian theological response to the fact of religious pluralism. A chapter each is given to the conservative evangelical, the Roman Catholic, the mainline Protestant, and the developing theocentric models. In the final section of the book, Knitter offers his own version of theocentric Christology and a prospect of the way this Christology would condition interfaith dialogue.

Theocentric Christology represents what Knitter calls a "Copernican revolution" or paradigm shift in Christian understanding of other religions and of Christ. Yet, it is a shift which he sees as part of a long evolutionary process in Christian consciousness. A recent crucial step in this process was a shift from ecclesiocentrism to Christocentrism in theology. The ecumenical movement and the Second Vatican Council moved toward the admission that no single church captured the full reality of Jesus Christ, that even the church universal was not to be identified with the realm of God, and that there was salvation outside the church. Christ, not the church, was the center. Further, Christ might be at work "incognito" outside the church, which meant also within other religions. As this tendency developed in the Christian ecumenical environment, another evolutionary shift began within the context of interfaith relationships. As narrow understandings of the church had been an obstacle to ecumenical dialogue, some began to see that narrow understandings of Christ were barriers to interfaith dialogue. Above all, the insistence upon the finality and normativity of Christ was such a barrier. Thus, the evolution at hand is from Christocentrism to theocentrism.

Those who led in the journey from ecclesiocentrism to Christocentrism performed a great service. But, as is often the case in evolutionary process, it is precisely the norm or lever which they used to move from one stage to the next which must be relativized now in order to go further. As it was well to subordinate the church to Christ, it is logical now that we take seriously the subordination of Christ to God. The various theocentric theologians whom Knitter reviews are, he says, trying to place God and not the church or Christ at the center of things. They advance different types of arguments, some stressing the "myth of the incarnation," some expanding upon a *logos* Christology, some departing from a prior "theology of religions." Knitter does not endorse all of these in equal measure — indeed, some are incompatible — but he is certain that they move in the right direction.

One of the notable aspects of Knitter's own argument is his attempt to meet the objections of theocentric Christology on their own ground. He recognizes that his proposal might appear to violate the New Testament understanding of Christ and to undercut both personal commitment to Christ and a distinctly Christian contribution to the world's pluralism. His intention is to show that this is not the case. In other words, theocentric Christology is not only the key to amicable and fruitful interfaith relations, but it is also authentically Christian and can be validated as such from scripture and tradition. He recognizes that it cannot be a precondition of dialogue that any faith, including Christianity, be required to give up its essential identity. Therefore, it is crucial that theocentric Christology be sustained by reference to Christian norms.

On this point Knitter is commendably clear, and this clarity undergirds his criticism of simplistic conventional solutions to the problem of religious pluralism, as well as his reservations about some aspects of others' theocentric Christology. His book presents theocentric Christology in a careful and nuanced way. It would seem that critical reflection upon it would prove to be of broader application as well. Accordingly, I should like to explore two types of questions which arise from his exposition. The first type has to do with the positive meaning of theocentric Christology, which still remains rather cloudy, given that Knitter deals more extensively with the "why" than the "what" of this view. The second type has to do with the Christian warrants which Knitter adduces for it.

II

The power of Knitter's argument can be summarized in a few sentences. Christ divides, being the unique object of faith of one tradition. God unites, being the supposed common object of worship of all faiths. Given that for Christians Jesus Christ is the Son and Word of *God,* the servant and herald of the reign of *God,* the revealer and image and incarnation of *God,* would it not be both faithful to Christian belief and fruitful in present circumstances to shift the focus from Christ to God? God is inclusive, Christ exclusive. By getting the priorities right — and surely this means putting God first — the inclusiveness comes uppermost. The exclusiveness is seen to be secondary and functional.

For *Christians,* Christ is exclusive. That is, they do not divide their loyalty and love for Christ by apportioning them in graduated measure to other objects of faith, any more than a husband or wife portions out equal measures of commitment to many spouses. However, they simply ought to recognize that this exclusivity is not normative, not founded on objective fact. Or, to add an important nuance in Knitter's presentation, they ought to recognize this *provisionally.* It is just conceivable that Christ is the "norm above all other norms." If this is so, there must be reasons for its being so which are universally and equally available to all people.[3] Only in interfaith dialogue could this be discovered, for only there would universal reasons for Christ's finality become apparent.

Theocentric Christology presents itself as the way to surmount several nasty problems and yet to allow Christians to remain as warmly fervent as ever in their personal devotion to Christ. It has all the marks of an irresistible

3. Ibid., 143.

proposal: no visible drawbacks. Yet, there is some puzzlement about the coherence of the notion itself.

As Knitter expounds the paradigm shift from ecclesiocentrism to Christocentrism to theocentrism, it is assumed that the meaning of theocentrism is made clear as the extension of a long-term process whose character is constant. The meaning is given by analogy: theocentrism is to Christocentrism what Christocentrism was to ecclesiocentrism. This is a definition which obscures more than it reveals. If we cut one foot off a piece of lumber, and then cut off another foot, we are continuing the same process. It is not obvious, however, that we have now made it twice as likely to fit its intended use. We may have passed the point where it can serve at all for that use. In one sense, we have continued in the same direction; in another, we have not.

Christocentrism in theology represents a change of focus, as Knitter says. In this shift, the new focus serves to define the old. The church is seen to exist to serve and to proclaim Christ. Where it fails in this task, Christ is the norm by which it is found wanting and by which forces or groups other than the church may be affirmed. The church exists with Christ as its head, for the sake of the reign of God. The church, with its institutional practices, teachings, and traditions, is not to be the norm for Christ and so for theology. Instead, Christ, known through scripture, Spirit, and experience (all undeniably shaped by the church), is the norm for the church and so for theology. If this was a step in the right direction, Knitter says, theocentrism takes us further in the right direction. This is arithmetic and linear logic, of the sort illustrated in the lumber analogy. The question is whether it is appropriate to the case.

Both ecclesiocentrism and Christocentrism provide norms for theological work. In both cases we have clear resources and standards which we may use in our effort to build a church- or Christ-centered theology. What does Knitter propose as the analogous touchstone by which we may seek to be God-centered? Instead of the church being judged by reference to Christ, Christ is now to be judged by reference to God. If this is so, there must be some firm knowledge about God available somewhere. What is the source of this knowledge about God which must be so much more precise and certain than that claimed by Christians — or indeed by any faith? An answer to this question would seem to be a prerequisite to any meaningful talk of theocentric Christology.

At the risk of belaboring the obvious, Christocentrism is a *form* of theocentrism, not a substitute for it. That is the only rationale for being christocentric. The definitive and normative status attached to Christ reflects a *way* of being theocentric. Quite so, Knitter might respond: *one* way among others. This is true. What is not clear is where, short of the adoption of some other way, a standard would be found to which this one (Christ) could be subordinated. Christians affirm that to know and follow God most adequately one should follow Christ. This may be wrong, radically wrong. If so, there must be another way of being theocentric, of knowing and relating to God, which can serve as a norm and corrective. Where does it come from?

If we intend to be "centric" in any respect, we must locate a center. In ecclesiocentrism or Christocentrism we have some idea of what that location might be. Therefore they seem to be both workable and corrigible — though not necessarily correct — theological norms. In the ecumenical discussion among churches to which Knitter refers there is an ostensible norm which also has practical content: shared scripture and tradition. In the discussion which he proposes as analogous among religions he suggests an ostensible norm (theocentrism) without providing any practical content. Christocentric theology asserts that Christ is its norm for defining and understanding God, the guide for locating the center such that God is there. Theocentric Christology asserts that God is its norm for understanding Christ. The problem is that for there to be a theocentric Christology there must certainly first be a theocentric theology. In it, presumably, *theos* will be the norm for defining . . . *theos*. What does or can this mean?

It may be proposed that meaning can be given to *theos* as a norm if we use and sift *all* religious faiths and data, producing from them an inclusive picture of God. However, unless the data be shamelessly skewed from the start — practicing exclusivism in method and selection rather than in confession — this is surely an impossible project. Knitter asks how it is possible for a Christian theology of religions to use religious data honestly,[4] to which it only remains to add that the same question would seem to carry equal weight for any project which seeks to derive a norm from all religions. We cannot build an inclusive picture of God from the total field of religious data without practicing some selectivity, without excluding, for instance, those options which do not recognize or which reject the idea of *theos* or the idea of "center."

It will be necessary to sift the data with some principle in mind. For those traditions which intend to be "theocentric," each has some norm which guides the effort. For Christians this is Christ. What is the principle which will take that place in theocentric Christology? If it is borrowed from some other tradition, why is that tradition's norm to be accepted as universal? If it is formulated by admixture from many traditions, why is this formulation given a status different from that of the individual norms, many of which also purport to be a kind of admixture? Why is this synthesized norm not simply another one way, among many?

Presumably, there is or ought to be a theocentric understanding of the Qur'an in Islam and of the Torah in Judaism. Neither ought to be considered by its adherents the decisive and normative revelation of God, relevant to all people. If, then, they are to be understood as partial aspects of a true theocentric norm, it would seem that those in these traditions are entitled to know what

4. Ibid., 115.

this inclusive characterization of God is and where it comes from. Knitter adumbrates several possible responses to this question. One answer would be to propose an ethical norm as the key to theocentric theology. Knitter states clearly that he does not want a norm so broad that it would validate *every* kind of religious expression, even if all kinds are the proper field from which to derive the norm.[5] Some standard is required. It is not entirely clear what this standard is to be for Knitter. The closest thing to such a standard appears to be "social betterment" and individual wholeness.[6] This ethical, if somewhat cloudy, principle would become the norm in theocentric theology.

This is certainly intelligible and would be functional, given a quantum improvement in the detailed description of social betterment and individual wholeness. The very vague nature of the universal *"tao"* which is sometimes argued to exist across religions is not very helpful, since the terms in which it is expressed are themselves understood by various groups in heavily religion-dependent ways. In other words, the more general the *"tao,"* as in the notions of social betterment and personal wholeness, the more plausible is its universality. The more concrete its definition, so as to be able to serve in some meaningful way as a norm, the less universal it looks. This will then lead to the question of why an affirmation of a "once for all" revelation of God is presumed to be so problematic and pernicious, while a "once for all" ethical norm of this sort (which certainly is not recognized everywhere) is exempt from such presumption.

There is another possibility latent in Knitter's exposition. Perhaps what I have said so far represents a misunderstanding of his project. It may be that theocentrism has no normative principle and desires none. It is precisely the open-endedness of theocentric Christology which is its virtue. No special separate insight into the nature of God, different from that of individual religious traditions, is presupposed. What is presupposed is that normlessness is, at least provisionally, normative.

We do not have a way of locating God which can serve as a norm above all the various religious faiths. *Theos* remains a center without location. The meaning of theocentrism is that each particular norm for *theos* must be held as nonabsolute. To be theocentric is to be centerless, to refuse to fill the center, out of piety. It is the commandment against idolatry, or the "Protestant principle," on a world religious scale. We should be open to the possibility that to be truly theocentric would be to hold open a center which is at some remove — as yet undefined — from each of the religious norms. To be theocentric would be to refuse to "locate" God definitively as personal and equally to refuse to "locate" God as impersonal, and so on. We do not know that this is the correct course to take, but somehow each of us in our own faith and thinking ought

5. Ibid., 53.
6. Ibid., 70.

to take it into account. *How* ought we to do so? Certainly one of the fundamental ways Knitter has in mind would be to adopt the presuppositions of interfaith dialogue which he proposes. These are three in number. First, dialogue must be based on personal religious experience and firm truth claims. Second, it must be based on recognition of the possible truth in all religions, grounded in the hypothesis of a common ground and goal for all religions. Third, dialogue must be based on openness to genuine change and conversion.[7]

The second proposition is significant. Knitter says that, although religions may have a common interest in the unity of humankind and in warding off world destruction, this goal cannot really be achieved unless their efforts are rooted in a deeper common ground, which allows them to be talking, in different ways, about the same reality. The deepest level of dialogue, he says, *cannot* (emphasis mine) be a matter of "apples and oranges." If we are not talking about the same God, then ultimately humanity itself is apples and oranges. "Division, the fertilizer of discord and destruction, will have the final word."[8] Though it is called a hypothesis, this appears to be a fundamental tenet of theocentrism as Knitter understands it. He speaks of its verification in dialogue, for instance, but not of its possible lack of verification. It would seem, then, that theocentrism cannot simply be a conviction that all religious norms are to be regarded, at least provisionally, as penultimate. It proposes a principle for locating *theos,* and, broad though the principle may be, it would appear that it must be universally normative, or else the theocentric project as Knitter conceives it collapses. The caution of theocentrism is not that some or all religious norms may be imperfect or simply wrong: Quite the contrary! Its caution is that they all must be regarded as true. The real question is: what is that about which they can all be telling the truth?

Theocentrism does not intend to be skeptical but deeply credulous. This would rule out the option which we have just considered — that theocentrism is a principled normative normlessness. God can be located in one absolute sense as that identical reality with which all "phenomenal" religions have to do. This is a positive and normative statement. It is a view favored by many sociologists and some philosophers of religion, but as a universal norm for *theos* it will have to be defended with other arguments than those used in favor of a provisional relativizing of all definitions of God. If it is itself relativized, then the kind of dialogue which Knitter commends is only one among many and has no claim to be *the* form of dialogue.

Perhaps the theocentric norm is to be defended by reference to the ethical norm mentioned above: being the only way to make religion function to overcome the nuclear danger, say, such an approach is necessarily normative for all religions. The cogency of this will rest on two considerations. The first will have

---

7. Ibid., 207-12.
8. Ibid., 209.

to do with the status of the ethical norm, as discussed above. The second and related consideration would be whether or not it is empirically true that the theological conviction advanced by Knitter is the one and only doctrine which would serve the desired ethical end. Are those who believe that the object of their faith is not the same as the object of all other people's faith simply heretics on ethical grounds? Or is it possible that they, too, may have a crucial contribution to make toward securing peace among people who assuredly have and will continue to have different political, social, and personal beliefs?

In Knitter's approach, which he calls "unitive pluralism," pluralism itself is accorded only a curiously superficial reality. Though the distinctions it represents are not to be done away with, it is to be presumed, as the basis of dialogue, that they are distinctions of one basic thing, rooted in common apprehension of a single reality. True polytheists are not welcome in this world of pluralism, yet there is no reason to rule out a further reach of pluralism, in which we find not that under surface differences we have to do with the same thing but that under surface differences we are truly different. This possibility is not in view here, save as a pernicious doctrine to be anathematized. Why this is so — besides a deep conviction that pluralism must serve us as a solution rather than in any way as a problem (we have so many!) — is not plain.

To raise one final question in this area: why ought we to assume that theocentrism is the last term in this series? Is it not necessary to go beyond the imperialism of *theos*, to escape the dangers and sins of "theofascism" as well as of "Christofascism"?[9] Why make normative a theology which is centered on a reality denied or simply ignored by important groups, including some Buddhists and most humanists? Should we not, on Knitter's grounds, look toward a further and yet more adequate paradigm shift which might take us perhaps to a numinocentric theology? John Hick speaks of "one spirit" or "one divine reality" or "one *logos*" and carefully does not use the word "God." Knitter is less cautious, but he does not address the question of whether a more thoroughgoing paradigm shift is mandated by his own logic.

As the ante is upped — church, Christ, God — we would appear to be moving increasingly toward a more transcendent, more universal, and less limited perspective, but at some point in such a progression it may be we begin to do exactly the opposite. When we reach a concept so transcendent that it is said we have *no* comprehensible or tangible criteria for it, we have not attained universality but parochialism. Since there is no common set of reference points for understanding "God," the appeal to God — as in theocentrism — can represent less of a curb on our narrow outlooks, not more. It does not mean that we are necessarily forced to define God in a broader, wider, more universalistic way than that given in an individual tradition (which likely encompasses many centuries and many different cultural settings). It does mean that we are free

9. See ibid., 164.

to define God in line with a limited contemporary cross-section of various traditions and experiences, construed within present dominant modes of thought. Interfaith dialogue is the apparent antidote for this difficulty, in Knitter's view, for it ought to overcome the limitations of any single tradition. What then of the conditions which Knitter wishes to place upon this dialogue, by making theocentrism its norm? Is this not simply a different kind of limitation?

As long as the norm for *theos* is as indistinct as it seems to be in theocentric theology, that norm will be interpreted — in effect supplied — by the predilections of the practitioners. Christians are often criticized by reference to the norms they have themselves professed. These norms seem to be sufficiently concrete for Christians to have them turned against themselves and to acknowledge on occasion the validity of the process. In theocentric theology one would hope this capacity would be heightened, not diminished.

These comments are all simply to indicate that it seems to me that there is some difficulty, even with the assistance of Knitter's impressive exposition, in knowing what theocentric Christology actually means. It seems that such Christology relies heavily upon intuitive "picture" concepts to make its case. It is presented largely as though there were a basic block, "God," upon which some people put a second block, "Christ," while others put instead a block "Qur'an," and so on. Many people readily think in this way, but the fact that they do so is not necessarily the result of wide and deep experience of pluralism. It may be exactly the opposite.

The notion of a common or root concept of God is one that comes readily to those of us who have been immersed within a monotheistic tradition. If some within this cultural context deny the specific particulars of such a tradition (a "Christian" God or a personal God), it may be that they still vehemently affirm as universal a generalized form of that particular (not monotheism, but theocentrism). What we learn of various cultures and faiths, however, brings home to us the manner in which ideas of God (where there are such ideas) are particular, "down to the ground," so to speak. It is not a matter of a simple, common foundation, with many various superstructures. This is why interfaith dialogue is the fascinating and perplexing experience that it is: the other's life and belief cannot be grasped finally in pieces but only all at once. It is this very "all-at-onceness" of the various faiths, which Knitter values and is in one sense the occasion of his work, that makes his theocentric Christology problematic.

III

I have tried to indicate some puzzlements about the *meaning* of theocentric Christology. In conjunction with his exposition of this Christology, Knitter advances several clear arguments for it on the basis of Christian norms. It is to these arguments that I now turn. As I have already indicated, Knitter addresses himself directly to the grounding of theocentric Christology in scripture, using three main arguments. The first is that Jesus was theocentric. The second is that there is a diversity of christological trajectories within the New Testament. The third is that the "one and only" language about Jesus in scripture was a function of the cultural medium, not the true message of Christian faith.

Knitter also stress a fourth point: that Christian christological interpretation itself developed out of dialogue with a pluralism of other religions and cultures. This is a significant observation, and it would seem to conflict with Knitter's earlier statement about pluralism's posing questions which "religious persons of the past, secure in their own isolated religious camps, never had to face."[10] When coming to the New Testament material, Knitter implicitly acknowledges that such a bald statement is indefensible. The early Christians indeed had to face pluralism. Knitter argues in fact that their minority status was one of the things that led them to their "accidental" forms of exclusive language with respect to Christ. He also argues that, because the church's confession was to some extent shaped by encounter with other religions, there is a mandate for us to shape our confession today in response to modern pluralism.

The argument that Jesus was theocentric is surely sound. Knitter's treatment of the New Testament is notable for his familiarity with the broad outlines of recent scholarship. Both implicitly and explicitly he distances himself from Hick's attempt to maintain an unreconstructed unilinear view of christological development. He recognizes that it is not possible to divide the New Testament data into earlier "low" views of Jesus and later "high" views. Instead, we find trajectories, each of which has preferred categories for understanding Jesus, each of which has very early roots, and each of which represents from the beginning its own version of a "high" view of Jesus.

The transition of Jesus from proclaimer to the one proclaimed is an intrinsically valid transition, in that Jesus understood himself in some way as a final eschatological prophet, God's "last word" to humanity. The fact that some or all of the christological titles are applied to Jesus by the church is, Knitter acknowledges, in no way as decisive as earlier liberal scholars had thought or as Hick continues to assume. Thus, for instance, Knitter recognizes that the theory that Christian views of Christ were determined by conformity to a prior gnostic redeemer myth has not proved to be tenable. It is probable that Christian thought influenced the development of such myths themselves, the most that Knitter can add being that such influence was (perhaps) mutual. He also acknowledges that none of the images and titles used for Jesus was a perfect fit for that which Christians experienced in Jesus.

This is notable, for it forecloses the wide and simplistic path to theocentric Christology. Knitter faces it squarely. He summarizes this history, in carefully chosen words, as "an evolution from a predominantly functional, eschatological

10. Ibid., 1.

understanding of Jesus as Son of God to an incarnational, even ontological, proclamation of his divinity."[11] Both Jesus and the church saw Jesus as unique and special in representing God. Much of New Testament language about Jesus is exclusive and/or normative. To close one's eyes to this, says Knitter, is dishonest. When the early Christians used "one and only" language about Jesus they did not understand it as "mythic conditioning" or as "love language" in Krister Stendahl's sense.[12] They meant it. However, if Christology is evolutionary, Knitter wonders whether such "final" language really belongs to the main content of what the church believed and what Jesus actually was, or to the "accident" of the language in which he was described. He argues that the latter was the case.

Given the cultural context in which these experiences took place, it was natural — "even necessary" — that they were described in terms of finality and exclusivity. There was "no other way, no other language" for them to talk about it. Living in a classicist culture that took it for granted that truth was one and certain, when they encountered the overwhelming truth of Jesus, "they would have to describe it as the only or the final truth."[13] Expecting the end of history, they naturally did not even consider the possibility of further revelations.

As the intensive use of imperative and exclusive language on Knitter's part indicates, this is the point where the argument comes to rest. Living, as fish in water, in a culture with a mistaken view of truth, Christians inevitably and helplessly expressed the very real truth of Jesus in a medium — in fact, a whole variety of mediums — which was incidental or actually inimical to it. Now, however, Knitter argues, there has been a genuinely new evolution in the texture of human experience that makes our context different from that of the New Testament. Not to understand Jesus anew in this texture "is to run the risk of confining the past in an idolatrous 'deposit of faith,'"[14] and the way to understand Jesus anew is to see him as indeed universally relevant, but not universally decisive or normative.

Knitter starts out to show that theocentric Christology is in keeping with scripture. His conscientious survey indicates that in fact it is not, if we take that evidence on its own terms. He then argues that it *is* in keeping with scripture if we subtract the "accidental" medium of culture. Since we live in a radically different culture, it is imperative for us to understand Jesus according to our context. Several things may be said about this approach. The first is that it seems to be a peculiarly modern way to attempt to escape the constraints of critical-historical method (which are part of our context for understanding Jesus). Having examined scripture with the question of "what it meant then" in mind, Knitter finds the answer largely uncongenial to the tack he would like to take

11. Ibid., 180.
12. Ibid., 185.
13. Ibid., 183.
14. Ibid., 173.

in terms of "what it means now." Instead of pressing on with this sticky problem of drawing present meaning and past meaning into coherent relation, Knitter appeals instead to the expansion of the interpretive horizon of the text: as "human experience evolves from the tribal to the global, there *must* be new interpretations of the text."[15] Surely there must be. The question is whether the text in its original context exercises any control over the variety and validity of these interpretations.

It does seem to me valid to say that the way a text uses its own sources, its own authorities, can be taken to some extent as authorization for analogous use of that text itself. Thus, Knitter appeals to the fact that reflection on Christology seems to have developed internally in the New Testament out of encounter and dialogue with other religions and cultural forces. He takes this as a scriptural mandate to do christological reflection today in the midst of such dialogue. I think this is sound. However, as he notes, on the different trajectories of this scriptural development the decisiveness and normativeness of Christ are retained, even though categories of expression change. It would seem, then, that here we find a similar internal scriptural norm: that in the interplay of many different cultures and forms of expression the decisiveness of Christ shall continue to be expressed. At this point, however, Knitter turns to the assertion that a common culture, transcending all the religious and cultural pluralism which affected the New Testament, locked in an accidental affirmation of Christ's normativeness.

This aspect of the argument turns largely on Knitter's philosophical view of an ontological or "classicist," as opposed to a "processive-relational," view of reality. In a view which regards creation as a stable and hierarchical order of being, the classicist view of truth is natural. Knitter further suggests that it is from this ontology that the "one and only" or normative view of Christ flows. However, our new context teaches us that reality is instead properly understood more as becoming than as being, more in terms of a nexus of relations than in terms of individual interactions. Knitter does not provide a great deal of explication of this, other than some references to Teilhard, to Darwin, to physicist David Bohm, and (more extensively) to process thought. It appears at the very least questionable whether this distinction can be sustained in the categorically historical way Knitter puts it.

Whitehead, at any rate, was much more hesitant to suggest the "processive" view of reality as a uniquely modern discovery. He suggested the Psalms as being a rich illustration of at least a poetic apprehension not only of the flux of reality but also of the reality of flux.[16] If this new view of reality comes to regard persons much less as atomistic individual existents and more as centers of relation, it would seem that it was to some extent anticipated by Hebrew views,

---

15. Ibid., 172-73.
16. A. N. Whitehead, *Process and Reality* (New York: Macmillan, 1929), 317.

views which were the soil for interpretation by and of Jesus. In short, more argument is required if Knitter intends to enforce this hermetic seal around early thought about Christ, so that, since no notion of relational reality could even come within its horizon, its view of Christ as normative may be discounted. Nor does Knitter address himself to the sticky question of how we might recognize a valid claim to normativeness which might be made within a cultural situation where, apparently, all claims would accidentally be cast in this form.

Even if it were the case that early Christians were victims of a cultural necessity to think that truth is one, certain, and unchanging, it is patently obvious that they were under no such compulsion to think that there could be only one decisive and normative *form* of this one truth. Readily apparent around them were approaches to religious pluralism which took just this tack. That one and the same God should be called by different names or take a slightly different form in different cultures was not only supposed by the educated but also accepted in practice by many ordinary people. On Knitter's assumption — that the normativeness of Christ was no part of the essential Christian message but only of its determined cultural form — we should expect that amidst the variety of christological interpretation in the New Testament there would be some which availed itself of this option, present in the cultural environment. In other words, there would be trajectories which identify Christ with Apollo or with Mithras. Some may argue that such "heterodox" notions existed but were kept out of the New Testament canon. Were this so, however, it would only reinforce the point at issue here: the early church *knew* of such options and rejected them. It may have been wrong, but the church definitely had the *chance* to be at least partially right, in Knitter's terms. Knitter cannot rectify the choice now by maintaining that it never really existed.

When they encountered an overwhelming truth in Jesus, gentile Christians, at least, would find no cultural taboo on supposing this one truth was present under other forms. Indeed, there was significant cultural compulsion for them to go in precisely this direction. These early Christians *did* identify Jesus with some of the greatest figures of Israel's tradition and, at the same time, within the earliest strata, with that tradition's God. In other words, they did say that the one truth known in Jesus was in fact known, at least to some extent, under another "form" — the revelations of Yahweh to Israel. They made this identification within a Jewish context where there was certainly hostility to the extreme (incarnational) of such identification. Yet, in the midst of other cultures, which were in principle much more receptive to such notions, they rejected the idea that Jesus could be identified with existing deities.

This certainly does not forget the way in which the apologists, for example, were willing to argue that philosophy had reached in a parallel and anticipatory way some knowledge of Christian truth. The point is not that early Christians believed Christ to be the exclusive *exhaustive* truth. The point is a more limited one. It has to do with the question of Christ as a singular and decisive norm and of whether the early church was somehow incapacitated, unable even to conceive of any alternative to a "once for all" norm. While the cultural alphabet of the early Christians may have been limited, it appears that it was not so impoverished that it could not spell a rather decided negative on Knitter's hypothesis about the accidental character of Christ's normativeness.

Just as Knitter assumes that ideas of normativeness or finality are necessary accidental attendants of an ontological view of reality, he seems to assume that they are necessary casualties of a "processive-relational" one. This latter point seems, if anything, even more questionable. Knitter seems to presume as a matter of course that the idea of Christ as normative and decisive rests upon incarnational and ontological forms of interpretation of Christ. If the latter are only forms within which the reality is interpreted, then the former is likewise a dispensable interpretive form. Nevertheless, on the basis of his own exposition of the New Testament evidence, this hardly seems to be the case. In other words, Knitter acknowledges that the very earliest strata of Christian witness view Christ in extraordinarily high functional terms. This is so even apart from any use of the ontological language of divine being, yet Knitter goes on to claim that it is interpretation of Christ in terms of a certain "level" of being which itself actually entails the normative claim.

Strictly speaking, normativity is independent of this debate over ontology. In a processive-relational reality there may still be persons, moments, decisions, relations which are decisive and normative, even universally so. Otherwise, Knitter, in arguing for a processive-relational view of reality, would be arguing necessarily for normlessness. He clearly is not doing this. Conversely, even in the "classicist" worldview he paints, to have a certain level of being is not automatically to be exclusively normative, unless one can know in fact that there is no other who shares that level of being. There is no *a priori* reason that Christians could not have viewed Christ as God fully incarnate, the divine bodily present among them, *and* also as not exclusively normative, for this same event could have been thought to take place on other occasions.

The first Christians professed that they had functionally (savingly) encountered in Christ unparalleled normative truth, power, and love. To Knitter's mind, this *means* that, since what they encountered was a relational reality for them, it could not be normative, and their expression could not have been intended as normative. However, the question will not admit of being resolved in such an imperious way. What they encountered might have been transforming in an unparalleled manner for them and not regarded as normative, *or* so transforming and also regarded as normative. The evidence seems to favor the latter case. The "high" early Christology which Knitter acknowledges need not have been "high" only on the believers' end (that is, this is so very important *to us*) simply because it was often expressed in functional terms.

To put it plainly, Knitter seems to think that, if one could move the focus away from incarnation (ontological being) and toward salvation (processive becoming), then Christ would necessarily become less normative. However, as Kenneth Surin has persuasively argued, as long as one wants to keep some contact with the New Testament (as Knitter does), the idea that a focus on salvation obviates Christocentrism is profoundly mistaken.[17] If anything, the opposite is true. Even if we grant Knitter both the philosophical dichotomy of "classicist" and "processive" worldviews and the hard historical periodization which would make the former the blanket reality of the past and the latter the unique discovery of recent modernity, it does not seem that these can decide the question.

IV

I have explored a few questions about the meaning of theocentric Christology and suggested that, despite the urgency with which its necessity is argued, the positive features of such a Christology remain somewhat unclear. This may be a natural stage for a view which, originating as a criticism of traditional approaches to pluralism, is only now beginning to find its own constructive formulation. It may, alternatively, indicate defects in the whole line of approach. I have also argued that the warrants which Knitter advances for theocentric Christology on Christian grounds are not persuasive. This would appear to raise important questions for a theology like Knitter's which is so commendably scrupulous about dealing with religious traditions on their own terms.

I have not been able to deal with all the aspects of Knitter's significant book. In particular, I have not dealt adequately with the form and conditions of interfaith dialogue which Knitter sees as correlative to theocentric Christology. Since Knitter and others suggest that such stated conditions of interfaith dialogue should increasingly become internal norms in the work of Christian theology, this question is one that deserves further attention in its own right. I hope to return to it in a future discussion.

The issues which Knitter has so carefully raised are crucial ones for us all. Those who wish to pursue them can hardly do better than to start with his work. I trust it will not be taken amiss if I hope that they do not stop there.

17. Kenneth Surin, "Revelation, Salvation, the Uniqueness of Christ, and Other Religions," *Religious Studies* 19 (September, 1983): 323-43.

Women and Christ:
Toward Inclusive Christologies

ELLEN LEONARD

Christology claims a universal significance for Christ. Contemporary Christologies struggle with the implications of this claim, raising questions about the inclusivity of Christology from many perspectives, including questions arising from Jewish-Christian dialogue, dialogue with other religions, and most recently ecological concerns. My focus is on the inclusion of women in our understanding of Christology.

The image of Christ is ambiguous for many contemporary women, serving both as a source of life and as the legitimator of oppression. Women have found, and continue to find, comfort, strength, and courage through their faith in Christ, while at the same time the image of Christ can be interpreted as a symbol of male dominance and female submission. As women become aware of the patriarchal and androcentric bias of Christianity, the fact that the central symbol in Christianity is a male saviour raises basic questions about the nature of humanity and divinity. What is the significance of the maleness of Jesus? Does it support the view of the male as normative humanity? Does it reveal God as male? How has the symbol been used in the praxis of the community? Is it possible to develop a Christology which is nonandrocentric, a Christology which is truly inclusive of women and men?

The history of Christian theology is not reassuring in regard to such an inclusive Christology. Christ has generally been presented throughout the ages as the male revealer of a male God whose divine authority supports the patriarchal structures of church and society. Nor does the present praxis of the Christian churches encourage Christian feminists who would like to retrieve the Christ symbol. Fundamentalist groups continue to preach the headship of

Reprinted with permission from the *Toronto Journal of Theology* 6 (Fall 1990): 266-85.

Christ over the church in order to uphold male headship in the family as well as in the church. The Orthodox and Roman Catholic Churches use the maleness of Jesus as a reason for not recognizing the leadership gifts of women. Ordained women in other churches suffer from the patriarchal patterns which endure not only within society but also in their churches. A visit to the art gallery, where we are able to see how succeeding ages have imaged Christ, reinforces the view of the male as dominant, the female as supportive. The young mother is portrayed on her knees before her infant son, while the sorrowful mother stands with other women at the foot of the cross. The message from all sides is that women's role is one of support for men.[1] History, contemporary church praxis, and art all present images of Christ which legitimate the subordination of women. It is not surprising that for some contemporary women there is no place for Christ: Naomi Goldenberg expresses the conviction of these women:

> Jesus Christ cannot symbolize the liberation of women. A culture that maintains a masculine image for its highest divinity cannot allow its women to experience themselves as the equals of its men. In order to develop a theology of women's liberation, feminists have to leave Christ and the Bible behind.[2]

Can women who have experienced Christ as a source of life, and who continue to find in the image of Christ strength and courage in their own struggles for justice, abandon the symbol which has shaped their religious response to life?

In the past it might be argued that women were included within the lower part of male humanity and in this way were included in the incarnation and redemption of Christ. But in our day, the Aristotelian biological basis for the view of the female as a "defective" male cannot be used to support Aquinas' argument that Jesus' maleness was an ontological necessity. Maleness no longer represents universal generic humanity. This fact is acknowledged by many disciplines as the androcentric nature of knowledge itself is recognized and challenged. Philosophy, theology, anthropology, psychology, sociology, history, literature — all have considered the male as normative humanity and the female in relation to the male. As women become active subjects in all these disciplines, this androcentric view of humanity is no longer tenable.

Changes in our understanding of humanity raise questions in theology as well as in other disciplines. What would Christology be like if it were truly inclusive? Perhaps even more important, how might popular devotion image

---

1. Religious images play a powerful role in shaping cultural patterns and social structures. For studies which take gender as a primary category of analysis, see *Immaculate and Powerful: The Female in Sacred Image and Social Reality,* eds. Clarissa Atkinson, Constance Buchanan, and Margaret Miles (Boston: Beacon Press, 1985).

2. Naomi Goldenberg, *The Changing of the Gods: Feminism and the End of Traditional Religions* (Boston: Beacon Press, 1979), 22.

Christ in ways that do not contribute to male domination? Can the central image of Christianity support the full personhood of women?

I speak as a middle-class, white, Anglophone Canadian. I cannot presume to speak for "women," but I have listened to some women's voices as they confront images of Christ and either reject or transform those images. These voices are not only North American but also Asian, African, and Latin American. I am becoming conscious of the strong voices of Afro-American women who are proposing a womanist theology and Christology that is emerging from their experience as black women.[3] I am also conscious of the voices which I have *not* heard, even within my own country, and my own city — voices of Francophone women, native women, immigrant women, poor women.[4] This paper reflects on what I have heard.

Part I will focus on particular areas of women's experience: female embodiment, female oppression, and women's experience of interrelatedness. Part II considers specific problems that the Christ symbol poses if one takes these areas of women's experience seriously. In this section I draw on the work of Mary Daly, who provides the clearest critique of the functioning of christological imagery, and of Rita Nakashima Brock, who raises the problem of the atonement in a particularly graphic way. Criteria are established to assess attempts to rethink the image of Christ in the light of women's experience and critique. Constructive attempts to transform the image of Christ in ways that are inclusive of women are presented in Part III. Part IV explores characteristics that must be found in any Christology if it is to be inclusive of women's experience.

I. Women's Experience

Studies of women's lives show that women's experience is pluralistic and deeply influenced not only by gender but by race, class, and culture. Among the diverse experiences of women, some areas are common and underlie the way women are confronting and transforming Christology. Three areas of experience seem to be particularly formative: the experience of female embodiment, women's experience of oppression, and women's experience of interrelatedness. Women from different situations will experience their embodiment, their oppression, and their interrelatedness differently, but these three areas of women's experi-

3. See Jacquelyn Grant, *White Women's Christ and Black Women's Jesus: Feminist Christology and Womanist Response* (Atlanta: Scholars Press, 1989). Grant argues that feminist Christology reflects the concerns of white, Western women. See also Susan Thistlethwaite, *Sex, Race and God: Christian Feminism in Black and White* (New York: Crossroad, 1989), especially her chapter on "Jesus and Christa," 92-108.

4. For a Francophone presentation of feminist Christology, see Louise Mélançon, "Quelle figure du Christ pour une théologie non-sexiste?" presented to the Société canadienne de théologie in Montreal in October 1989. For stories of native women, see *Enough Is Enough: Aboriginal Women Speak Out,* presented by Janet Silman (Toronto: The Women's Press, 1987).

ence — often ignored, denied, or subsumed under male experience — are being claimed by women today and are thus becoming the ground for new understandings of human life and new insights into the Christian tradition.[5] They raise central questions about the way that Christology has functioned and they point to ways that it must be rethought.

The first of these areas of experience, that of female embodiment, has been viewed within the Christian tradition in a negative way. Western theology has been based on a dualistic worldview which placed history over nature, soul over body, male over female. In this dualistic view, women have been identified with nature and with the body, while men have been identified with spirit. Our bodies were viewed by the "church fathers" as "the gateway to hell," an attitude which continues to be reflected in pornography and is implicit in much of modern advertising. A positive view of female embodiment which does not identify women with the body nor view biology as destiny, but which takes the importance of the female body seriously, is crucial for Christianity. Christianity is an incarnational religion, but it has often been uncomfortable with the body, particularly the female body. Many women, including theologians, are writing from the experience of their own bodies, drawing on images of birth, of nourishment, of women's suffering and joy. For some women, the consciousness of the sacredness of the female body has led to a rejection of the image of Christ. Rita Nakashima Brock articulates the problem as they experience it:

> The doctrine that only a perfect male form can incarnate God fully and be salvific makes our individual lives in female bodies a prison against God and denies our actual, sensual, changing selves as the locus of divine activity.[6]

The question must be addressed: Is it possible to develop a Christology which will affirm female embodiment? In an effort to provide this, some women are searching for new images of Christ and for new approaches to Christology.

Women's experience of oppression is the context in which women confront images of Christ. Women in all parts of the world are becoming aware of the systemic oppression of women in every culture. The ways that this oppression is experienced differ radically throughout the world, but one common question arises from reflection on the experience of oppression. Does the image of Christ encourage a passive acceptance of suffering, or does it provide energy to engage in the struggle against evil?

Voices from the third world offer new insights from the perspective of

5. Feminist historians are studying the experience of women during other historical periods. A fascinating work that explores how religious women in the Middle Ages experienced the body and their relationship to Christ is Caroline Walker Bynum's *Holy Feast and Holy Fast: The Religious Significance of Food to Medieval Women* (Berkeley, Los Angeles, London: University of California Press, 1987).

6. Rita Nakashima Brock, "The Feminist Redemption of God," in *Christian Feminism: Visions of a New Humanity,* ed. Judith L. Weidman (San Francisco: Harper & Row, 1984), 68.

persons who are conscious of their place at the bottom of society. They turn to Christ as one who was despised, who died as a criminal, and who willingly associated with the marginalized, including women. They turn also to his mother, a poor woman, an unwed mother, a refugee, a widow, the mother of a convict. The see themselves not only as standing by the cross, but as on the cross.

It is not only in the third world countries that women are oppressed. Patterns of domination and submission vary, but they are present worldwide. Feminist studies are exploring the structure of oppression in the light of race, class, and gender and are discovering global connections within the web of oppression. Can we find in the symbol of Christ hope in our struggles for justice for ourselves and all women? Christology in the past and present has supported structures of dominance and submission. The headship of Christ over his body, the church, reflected in the headship of the husband over *his* wife, has legitimated male dominance and female submission. The language of Christ as servant has encouraged submissive attitudes, especially among the powerless. Can Christology help women to address structures of domination and submission, or does the image of Christ contribute to the victimization of women? Can Christology be empowering for all women?

The experience of interrelatedness is one which feminist writers ascribe to women.[7] Women have traditionally found identity in relation to others as mothers, wives, sisters, daughters. As women become more aware of themselves as autonomous historical subjects, the values of interrelatedness continue to shape women's consciousness and are reflected in efforts to reshape Christology. In the past, the single male individual could represent all humanity. Today an emphasis on concreteness recognizes the particularity and limitations of each human life while at the same time we are becoming more aware of our interrelatedness — not only to one another in our global home, but to the generations who preceded us and to those who will come after us. This awareness of interrelatedness is extending to all of creation, reaching beyond plant Earth to embrace the cosmos.

As women move from a position of inferiority and domination to one of equality and full personhood, ways of relating to one another in family, society, and church are being challenged. Hierarchical images of domination are being replaced by images which stress interdependence and mutuality. These images refer not only to human relations but to our relationship with nature. The subordination of women and nature is being recognized in all its destructiveness.[8] Our very survival as humans demands new ways of being and of being-

---

7. For example, see Carol Gilligan, *In a Different Voice: Psychological Theory and Women's Development* (Cambridge: Harvard University Press, 1982).

8. Sallie McFague illustrates the urgent need for new ways of thinking about God in a nuclear age. See *Models of God: Theology for an Ecological, Nuclear Age* (Philadelphia: Fortress Press, 1987).

in-relationship with one another and with nature. Can Christology be open to such a future, or does it bind us to the past?

I wish to explore how these three areas of experience — female embodiment, female oppression, and female interrelatedness — challenge our ways of imaging Christ and demand that we transform these images and rethink our Christology. The work has already begun. But before considering some of the constructive attempts to transform Christology in the light of women's experience, it is necessary to look at the problem. What are the critiques which have been raised and which must be considered by all who desire Christianity to be "good news" for women?

II. Feminist Critique of Christology

One of the strongest reactions to the image of Christ is that of Mary Daly, who in her 1973 book *Beyond God the Father* was already calling women to move "beyond Christolatry" to a world without models:

> As a uniquely masculine image and language for divinity loses credibility, so also the idea of a single divine incarnation in a human being of the male sex may give way in the religious consciousness to an increased awareness of the power of Being in all persons.[9]

In response to those who admit that the Christ symbol has been used in ways oppressive for women, but that it need not be so used, Daly replied:

> If the symbol can be "used" that way and in fact has a long history of being "used" that way, isn't this an indication of some inherent deficiency of the symbol itself?[10]

It is not just that the symbol is male, and in Daly's words: "If God is male, then the male is God."[11] It is particularly the image of Jesus as sacrificial victim which Daly sees as destructive for women. She points out that the qualities that Christianity idealizes, especially for women, are those of a victim: sacrificial love, passive acceptance of suffering, humility, meekness, and so forth. Women are not able to measure up to this impossible model, nor are they able, in the Catholic Church, to identify ritually with Christ's sacrifice as priests. "Thus doomed to failure even in emulating the Victim, women are plunged more deeply into victimization."[12] They are encouraged to imitate the sacrificial love

---

9. Mary Daly, *Beyond God the Father: Toward a Philosophy of Women's Liberation* (Boston: Beacon Press, 1985), 71.

10. Daly, 72.

11. Daly, 19.

12. Daly, 77.

of Jesus, but they remain identified with Eve and with evil.[13] Daly's confrontation with images of Christ led her to a definitive rejection of Christianity.
Because Christianity imposed a male model from the past, Daly is convinced
that it prevents women from discovering God, or "New Being," incarnated in
the present in their own lives.

The doctrine of the atonement raises special problems in Christology. We
have considered Mary Daly's critique that Christology has encouraged women
to be victims. Rita Nakashima Brock argues that Christology supports the
patriarchal family by its language of father-son. She refers to God the Father's
acceptance of his son's death as "cosmic child abuse," writing that the "father
allows, or even inflicts, the death of his only perfect son."[14] It is all too easy for
Christology to glorify suffering and to discourage the acceptance of personal
responsibility for one's own life. As women become autonomous subjects of
history, the myths that have encouraged women to be passive victims within
families and society are being shattered. Is Christology such a myth, or can it
offer women the energy, courage, and hope to work for change and, if necessary
and possible, to move out of oppressive situations?

These concerns must be addressed by those who are unwilling to reject
Christianity and its central image. While acknowledging the difficulties, a number of feminist theologians have undertaken the task of transforming images
of Christ in the light of women's experience. The pioneering work of Elisabeth
Schüssler Fiorenza has been particularly helpful in developing a critical hermeneutic that uncovers the oppressive and the liberating aspects of Christianity
for women.[15] Rosemary Radford Ruether was one of the first systematic theologians to undertake the task of "liberating Christology from patriarchy."[16] Rita
Nakashima Brock has attempted "the feminist redemption of Christ."[17] Patricia
Wilson-Kastner even suggests that Christology and feminism can be mutually
enriching.[18]

I will consider some efforts to rethink the central image of Christianity

13. In 1973, Mary Daly suggested that the Antichrist and the Second Coming of women
were synonymous. This Second Coming of women would overcome sex stereotyping and implied
a leap toward psychic androgyny, a concept which Daly has since rejected. There was even a
possibility that the Second Coming of women might release the memory of Jesus from its destructive uses. See Daly's "Original Reintroduction," written in 1985 for *Beyond the Father*, xxiv.

14. Brock, *Journeys by Heart*, 56.

15. See *Bread Not Stone: The Challenge of Feminist Biblical Interpretation* (Boston: Beacon
Press, 1984); *In Memory of Her: A Feminist Theological Reconstruction of Christian Origins* (New
York: Crossroad, 1983).

16. See Rosemary Radford Ruether, "The Liberation of Christology from Patriarchy," *New
Blackfriars* 66 (1985): 324-35. This article also may be found in *Religion and Intellectual Life* 2
(1985): 116-28. Patricia Wilson-Kastner attempts to free Christology from patriarchy in *Faith,
Freedom, and the Christ* (Philadelphia: Fortress Press, 1983).

17. Rita Nakashima Brock, *Journeys by Heart*, especially 50-70; also "The Feminist Redemption of Christ," in *Christian Feminism: Visions of New Humanity*, 55-74.

18. Wilson-Kastner, *Faith, Feminism and the Christ*, 5.

in the light of these concerns, addressing three questions in considering each attempt: Does it affirm female embodiment? Does it reject victimization based on patterns of domination and submission? Does it enable women to move from the past into the present and future?

III. Transforming Images of Christ

To re-image Christ requires courage and creativity. Carter Heyward describes what needs to be done and why it must be done:

> To re-image Jesus is to claim the authority to play freely with both Scripture and subsequent tradition in order to comprehend our own existence. To re-image Jesus may involve letting go of old images, "letting the dead bury the dead" and bringing Jesus to life — that is, to our life together. It is to sketch images of Jesus within, and for the benefit of, our communities — of seminarians, women, gay people, black people, poor people, whoever our people are. Our images do not necessarily reflect Mark's image, or John's, or Augustine's, or Luther's.[19]

To re-image Jesus for the benefit of women demands that women's voices be heard.

The early Christian communities remembered Jesus in many different ways according to their own situation and community needs. No one image was adequate, and so we find many different images and Christologies within the New Testament itself.[20] This pluralism has continued throughout the tradition as succeeding ages transformed images of Christ according to their needs. In our day, Christian women are re-imaging Jesus and beginning to develop Christologies which take women's experience seriously. As women reflect on Christ in the light of their gendered experience, new insights into the meaning of Jesus the Christ for the lives of twentieth-century women and men are emerging. Women's prayers, poems, songs, and stories reflect changing images of Christ and provide a resource for further theological reflection.[21]

19. Isabel Carter Heyward, *The Redemption of God: A Theology of Mutual Relation* (New York: University Press of America, 1980), 30.

20. See Mary Rose D'Angelo. "Re-membering Jesus: Women, Prophecy and Resistance in the Memory of the Early Churches," in *The Future Church: The Global Agenda of Feminist Theology*, eds. Maryann Hedaa and Marc Ellis (San Francisco: Harper and Row, 1990); also James D. G. Dunn, *Unity and Diversity in the New Testament: An Enquiry into the Character of Earliest Christianity* (London: SCM Press, 1977) and *Christology in the Making* (Philadelphia: Westminster Press, 1980).

21. For examples of prayers, poems, songs, and stories which reflect women's transformed consciousness of self and of their relationship to Christ, see "Ecumenical Decade 1988-1998: Churches in Solidarity with Women," a special issue of *Women in a Changing World*, January 1988.

We turn now to some constructive attempts to work out an inclusive Christology. I shall describe five approaches to Christology in contemporary feminist theology. They are:

1. envisioning Christ's humanity in female terms
2. envisioning Christ as the incarnation of female divinity
3. beginning from the Jesus of history as prototype
4. beginning from the Jesus of history as iconoclastic prophet
5. relocating Christology in the community

Woman Christ

The image of Christ as a woman is shocking for some twentieth-century Christians, as was evident both in New York and in Toronto when sculptures of the crucified woman were presented to congregations.[22] Images of the Christa, Christ imaged as female, and particularly as crucified woman, provide strong visual reminders that women are finding creative ways to re-image Christ. The Christa invites the viewer to see Christ in a female body and to recognize that God suffers in the suffering of women.[23]

In spite of the shock many Christians experienced in seeing the image of a female Christ, the image of Christ as woman has a long history in the Christian tradition.[24] There are references to Christ as mother in the writings of Clement, Origen, Irenaeus, John Chrysostom, Ambrose, Augustine, Bernard, Anselm, and numerous other traditional theologians. Christ as woman was particularly popular during the Middle Ages in the writings of both men and women as a way of emphasizing the humanity of Christ. Divinity was associated with maleness, humanity with femaleness. Christ, who had no human father, took his flesh from Mary — a fact that led a number of the mystics to refer to the flesh that Christ put on as in some sense female. Caroline Walker

22. The "Crucified Woman" by Almuth Lutkenhaus was hung in Bloor Street United Church in Toronto in 1979. In 1986 it was presented to Emmanuel College, Toronto, and placed on the grounds. The *Christa* by Edwina Sandys was shown in the Episcopal Cathedral of St. John the Divine in New York in 1984. For details concerning these sculptures and reactions to them, see Doris Dyke, "Crucified Woman: Art and the Experience of Faith," *Toronto Journal of Theology* 5 (Fall 1989): 161-69.

23. For "Reflections on the Christa," see *Journal of Women and Religion* 4 (1985): particularly Edwina Hunter, 22-32.

24. For a history of the use of female imagery for Jesus, see André Cabassut, "Une dévotion médieval peu connue. La dévotion à Jésus notre mère," *Revue d'ascétique et de mystique* 25 (1949): 234-45; Eleanor McLaughlin, " 'Christ My Mother': Feminine Naming and Metaphor in Medieval Spirituality," in *Nashotah Review* 15 (1975): 228-48; Caroline Walker Bynum, "Jesus as Mother and Abbot as Mother: Some Themes in the Twelfth Century Cistercian Writing," in *Jesus as Mother: Studies in the Spirituality of the High Middle Ages* (Berkeley, Los Angeles, London: University of California Press, 1982), 110-69.

Bynum, in her study of medieval writers, shows that both men and women saw the female body as food and female nature as fleshly. Woman was to man as spirit was to flesh. Thus both men and women described Christ's body in its suffering as a mother giving birth and feeding her children from her own body.[25]

Julian of Norwich in the fourteenth century was the theologian who most fully developed the image of mother to describe Jesus' nurturing love for all humanity.

> But our true Mother Jesus, he alone bears us for joy and for endless life, blessed may he be. So he carries us within him in love and travail, until the full time when he wanted to suffer the sharpest thorns and cruel pains that ever were or will be, and at the last he died. And when he had finished, and he had borne us so for bliss, still all this could not satisfy his wonderful love.[26]

She then described how our mother Jesus continues to nourish us through the eucharist.

Our medieval sisters and brothers saw human mothering as a sacrament of divine love. Their view was based on a stereotype of the female or mother as generative and sacrificial, bringing forth her child in pain, and as loving, tender, and nurturing, feeding her child from her own body.[27] From their experience of human mothering, they were able to express the mystery of the Word made flesh, of Christ's sacrificial death, and of the eucharist. In doing so they gave meaning to their own lives, especially to the reality of suffering and of service.

The image of Jesus as mother in the tradition has drawn on the experiences both of being mothers and of mothering. These experiences continue to provide a rich source for reflection by contemporary theologians. From a context of extreme oppression, African theologians Elizabeth Amoah and Mercy Amba Oduyoye reflect on the Christ as woman and African. In a society where childless women are despised, Christ is seen as the one who liberates women from the assumptions of patriarchal societies. "The Christ of the women of Africa upholds not only motherhood, but all who, like Jesus of Nazareth, perform 'mothering' roles of bringing out the best in all around them."[28]

25. Caroline Walker Bynum, *Holy Feast and Holy Fast,* especially 260-76.

26. Julian of Norwich, *Showings,* eds. Edmund Colledge and James Walsh (New York: Paulist Press, 1978): 297-98. Kathryn Johnson reflects on Julian's insights in "Our Precious Mother Jesus," *Dialog* 24 (1985): 64-66.

27. Bynum, in "Jesus as Mother," shows how medieval theories of physiology supported this view of the female. See pp. 131-35.

28. Elizabeth Amoah and Mercy Amba Oduyoye, "The Christ for African Women," in *With Passion and Compassion: Third World Women Doing Theology,* eds. Virginia Fabella and Mercy Amba Oduyoye (Maryknoll, NY: Orbis, 1988), 43-45.

The image of Christ as woman offers an avenue for taking women's embodiment seriously, and recognizes in the experience of giving birth and nursing powerful symbols of Jesus and of his saving work on Calvary and in the church, particularly in the eucharist. This image also arises out of women's experience of oppression, particularly in third world countries where women often bear the total responsibility for children and family. For these women, finding food, and the water and fuel with which to cook it, are exhausting activities. Those who struggle for survival live close to birth and death and to the endless task of providing food. Jesus as mother expresses a strong sense of relatedness — perhaps one of the reasons that our medieval sisters and brothers as well as our third world sisters have found it a helpful image for Christ.

Woman Christ includes the female in the image of Christ's humanity. However, it is androgynous rather than truly inclusive. The inadequacy of androgynous Christologies has been demonstrated by Ruether:

> The very concept of androgyny presupposes a psychic dualism that identifies maleness with one-half of human capacities and femaleness with the other. As long as Christ is still presumed to be, normatively, a male person, androgynous Christologies will carry an androcentrical bias. Men gain their "feminine" side, but women contribute to the whole by specializing in the representation of the "feminine," which means exclusion from the exercise of the roles of power and leadership associated with masculinity.[29]

In an androgynous Christology, Woman Christ gives positive meaning to women's embodiment but does not allow women to represent full human potential, nor does it challenge the structures of submission and domination. It may provide strength in the present, but it does not open up the future. In the search for an inclusive Christology, I turn from one which includes the female in the male humanity of Jesus to a Christology which draws Christ's male humanity into the female image of divinity.

Christ as Incarnate Wisdom

A number of scholars have noted the use of the female image Sophia as an image for Jesus. Elizabeth Johnson provides a careful study of the wisdom tradition as a biblical basis for an inclusive Christology.[30] She shows how the

---

29. Rosemary Radford Ruether, *Sexism and God-Talk: Toward a Feminist Theology* (Boston: Beacon Press, 1983), 130. For her discussion of androgynous Christologies, see 127-30; also *To Change the World: Christology and Cultural Change* (London: SCM Press, 1981), 49-53.

30. Elizabeth A. Johnson, "Jesus, the Wisdom of God," *Ephemerides Theologiae Lovanienses* 61 (1985): 261-94. Joan Chamberlain Engelsman studies the repression of the feminine, and in particular of Sophia, in *The Feminine Dimension of the Divine* (Philadelphia: Westminster Press,

Jewish tradition used personified wisdom or Sophia to describe God's creative and saving involvement with the world. Johnson traces the relationship of Sophia to goddess material and demonstrates how the biblical writers were able to use this material while maintaining their monotheistic faith. The communities of Jewish Christians drew on this Sophia tradition as a way to describe their experience of Jesus of Nazareth. Beginning with Paul and the early christological hymns, Johnson shows that Jesus is identified with divine Sophia.

Whereas the earlier Q material interpreted Jesus as the child of Sophia, Matthew saw Jesus as the embodiment of Sophia. Rather than portraying incarnation as the act by which an invisible and all-powerful male person becomes visible in the world, Johnson argues that the Sophia tradition "reflects the depths of the mystery of God who has approached us in Jesus Christ and points the way to an inclusive interpretation of the humanity of Jesus as in genuine solidarity with the whole human race, women as well as men."[31] John's Gospel continues this identification of Jesus with Sophia, although the prologue replaces the female term "Sophia" with the male term "logos." Johnson suggests that the logos texts in Scripture and in theology can be read through the hermeneutics of wisdom categories.

Wisdom Christology offers an alternative to the view of Jesus as the image of God as male. In addition to categories of Father and Son, the Bible presents Sophia and her child who is Sophia incarnate. We can image Jesus as the embodiment of Sophia, God imaged as female. While recognizing the maleness of Jesus as part of his specificity, the distorted theological use of the maleness of Jesus is challenged by the blend of female and male imagery in Jesus/Sophia. All who are disciples of Jesus/ Sophia can do the works of Sophia. Johnson sees her work as a contribution to "the redesign of Christology in the face of enormous cultural changes in the position of women."[32]

Johnson takes seriously women's experiences of embodiment, oppression, and interrelatedness. In particular she sees the need to develop ways of relating to one another which are nonhierarchical and inclusive, and she recognizes the power of images in addressing structures of dominance and submission. She develops a resource from within the tradition for thinking about Jesus and God in ways that are inclusive.

Christ as incarnate wisdom has possibilities as an inclusive Christology. However, since the Jewish understanding of Sophia and the Christian view of Jesus as Sophia developed within a patriarchal social structure where women were inferior to men, the resulting theology and Christology are not truly inclusive. As Brock notes: "Wisdom, or Sophia, is not currently a feminine

---

1979). Elisabeth Schüssler Fiorenza discusses the influence of the Sophia tradition on the Jesus movement in *In Memory of Her*, 132-40.

31. Johnson, "Jesus, the Wisdom of God," 284.

32. Johnson, "Jesus, the Wisdom of God," 294.

equivalent to Yahweh or logos, though we might work to make her so."[33] The male human incarnation overwhelms the female divine persona of Sophia. Johnson has helped to uncover a resource in the past which may be helpful in redesigning a Christology that is truly inclusive and able to move women into the future.

We have seen how Woman Christ introduces the female into the male image of Christ, while Christ as incarnate Wisdom includes Jesus' male humanity in the female image of the divine. Both are attempts at inclusivity, but in societies where maleness is the norm the results are not inclusive. I turn now to a different approach to the problem. Instead of attempting to include femaleness in Christ, it will consider how Jesus functions within the tradition.

Jesus as Prototype

Elisabeth Schüssler Fiorenza has claimed Jesus and the praxis of the earliest church as prototype rather than as archetype. Thus they become a possible *resource* for women's struggle for liberation rather than an authoritative source.[34] Schüssler Fiorenza has uncovered this resource through her reconstruction of Christian origins using feminist critical hermeneutics. The hermeneutical centre of Schüssler Fiorenza's feminist biblical interpretation is women-church, which she describes as "the movement of self-identified women and women-identified men in biblical religion."[35] The experience of contemporary women struggling for liberation and wholeness is the hermeneutical principle for critically evaluating biblical texts.

Schüssler Fiorenza presents the Jesus movement as a renewal movement within Judaism. She asks what was it like for a woman in Palestine to be involved with Jesus and his movement. Jesus' vision of the *basileia* was one of inclusive wholeness which found expression particularly in his table community with the poor, with sinners, tax collectors, and prostitutes. Jesus is Sophia's prophet who, through his teaching and his healing miracles, calls forth a discipleship of equals. At the heart of his proclamation of the *basileia* of God is liberation from patriarchal structures. Schüssler Fiorenza argues that Jesus' use of "father" as a name for God does not legitimate patriarchal structures but is a critical sub-

---

33. Brock, *Journeys by Heart*, 61.

34. Schüssler Fiorenza's method is carefully laid out in Part I of *In Memory of Her*. See also "Women-Church: The Hermeneutical Center of Feminist Biblical Interpretation," in *Bread Not Stone*, 1-22. For her understanding of archetype and prototype, see *In Memory of Her*, 33-34 and *Bread Not Stone*, 61.

35. *Bread Not Stone*, xiv. For discussion of women-church see the epilogue of *In Memory of Her*, "Toward a Feminist Spirituality: The Ecclesia of Women," 343-35 and "Women-Church: The Hermeneutical Center of Feminist Biblical Interpretation," in *Bread Not Stone*, 1-22.

version of domination.[36] The *basileia* vision of Jesus is a feminist vision which "calls all women to wholeness and selfhood, as well as to solidarity with those women who are the impoverished, the maimed, and the outcasts of society and church."[37] Jesus is described by Schüssler Fiorenza as "the woman-identified man" who called forth a discipleship of equals.[38]

Unfortunately, the church did not live up to the vision of Jesus. Patriarchal structures were soon imposed on the followers of Jesus, even within the period covered by the New Testament writing. Schüssler Fiorenza traces the patriarchalization of the church and ministry, but she also focuses on women as paradigms of true discipleship in the Gospels of Mark and John, seeing in these Gospels indications of the apostolic leadership of women.

Schüssler Fiorenza has reclaimed the New Testament and Jesus for women by showing that women were at the centre of the movement around Jesus of the early Christian communities. She argues that the discipleship of equals or women-church was submerged and often oppressed by ecclesiastical patriarchy, but that it has never ceased to exist. It challenges contemporary patterns of male domination and female submission.

Schüssler Fiorenza takes women's embodiment, oppression, and interrelatedness seriously. The experience of contemporary woman is the hermeneutical base for her interpretation of the Christian story. In this way she points women toward the future. Jesus as prototype invites women to full membership in the discipleship of equals. Over and against later church practice, Jesus' teaching of the *basileia* breaks the politics of subordination and domination.

Jesus as Iconoclastic Prophet

The fact remains that Jesus who is the Christ was male. Rosemary Radford Ruether asked the important soteriological question: "Can a male saviour save women?"[39] Her own answer to this question is focused on the Jesus of the Synoptic Gospels, whom she sees as an iconoclastic prophet speaking on behalf of the marginalized and despised groups of society and challenging the social and religious hierarchical structures of his day. Women in the Gospels often represented the lowly, the last who will be first in the reign of God. One thinks of the Samaritan woman, the Syro-Phoenician woman, the widows and prostitutes. Jesus brought a message of liberation to such persons.

36. *In Memory of Her*, 151.
37. *In Memory of Her*, 153.
38. *In Memory of Her*, 154.
39. Ruether raises the question in *To Change the World: Christology and Cultural Change*; see also *Sexism and God-Talk: Toward a Feminist Theology*, 116-38. For a study of Ruether's Christology see Mary Hembrow Snyder's *The Christology of Rosemary Radford Ruether: A Critical Introduction* (Mystic: Twenty-Third Publications, 1988).

For Ruether, Jesus' maleness has no ultimate theological significance, but it does have a symbolic significance within societies of patriarchal privilege.

> In this sense Jesus as the Christ, the representative of liberated humanity and the liberating Word of God, manifests the *kenosis of patriarchy,* the announcement of the new humanity through a lifestyle that discards hierarchical caste privilege and speaks on behalf of the lowly.[40]

According to Ruether and other liberation theologians, what is most significant about Jesus is his message of good news to the poor. It is this message which needs to be carried on by his followers, for Christ as redemptive person and Word of God is not confined to the historical Jesus. Jesus is seen as paradigm for liberating personhood, but Christ includes all of redemptive humanity. Ruether insists that the image of Christ must take on ever new forms — "as woman, as Black and Brown woman, as impoverished and despised woman of those peoples who are the underside of Christian imperialism."[41]

The iconoclastic prophet speaks to the experience of oppression, challenging us to continue his mission as redeemed humanity and to find him particularly among our sisters who are the oppressed of the oppressed. Ruether insists that "Christians must formulate their faith in Jesus as Christ in terms which are proleptic and anticipatory, rather than final and fulfilled."[42] The future must be kept open.

Both Schüssler Fiorenza and Ruether have found in the Jesus of the Synoptics a figure sympathetic toward women. His life and teachings challenged, and continue to challenge, all structures of dominance and submission. It was a challenge that led ultimately to his death. However, the fact remains that this saving figure is a male figure in the past. By presenting Jesus of Nazareth as prototype or as anticipatory of redeemed humanity, Schüssler Fiorenza and Ruether leave room for future revelations of the divine in our sisters as well as our brothers.

Christa/Community

Rita Nakashima Brock criticizes Ruether's iconoclastic Christ as a unilateral hero and liberator who finds his strength in a private relationship with his Abba.

---

40. *Sexism and God-Talk,* 137; the emphasis is Ruether's. The same point is made by Sandra Schneiders in *Women and the Word: The Gender of God in the New Testament and the Spirituality of Women* (New York: Paulist, 1986): "Because he was a man Jesus' choice of life-style stood out as a contradiction of the current definition of masculinity and thus of humanity as defined by the dominant male culture," 59.

41. Ruether, *Womenguides: Readings Toward a Feminist Theology* (Boston: Beacon Press, 1985): 113.

42. Ruether, *To Change the World,* 42.

Seeing the need for mutuality in relationships, she looks for a Jesus who draws on the community and together "they co-create liberation and healing from brokenheartedness."[43] She relocates Christ in the community of which Jesus is one historical part so that the community generates the erotic power which heals and thus becomes the locus for redemption. She chooses the term "Christa/Community" to describe this. For Brock, Christa/Community is not limited to the historical Jesus even during his lifetime, but always includes the whole community.

Brock rejects understandings of Jesus' death as necessary and divinely willed, claiming that such beliefs mute our ability to be angry about unnecessary suffering. With liberation theologians, she understands Jesus' death as a political act which was the result of the way Jesus chose to live for himself and the people he loved. The disciples did not allow Jesus' death to be the end of their community but rather they remembered his presence and affirmed divine power among them. In Brock's words: "The Christa/Community incarnated and re-incarnates the power which restores heart."[44]

Like Elisabeth Schüssler Fiorenza, Brock recognizes the key role of the unnamed woman at Bethany who anointed Jesus.

> This woman, as a woman, represents the revelatory and healing power of heart. She becomes prophet and healer by her act as representative of the Christa/Community that would survive Jesus' death and witness his resurrection.[45]

Rita Nakashima Brock speaks out of her own experience of embodiment as an Asian American woman of colour who has experienced oppression by both race and gender. Her project is to salvage and transform Christianity, for, as she states: "Christianity has nurtured as well as wounded me."[46] A strong sense of interrelationship underlies her christological enterprise, which locates healing in the erotic power of love flowing between persons.

Brock pointed out that Sophia has not yet achieved wide acceptance as a feminine equivalent to Yahweh. Certainly at the present time Brock's Christa/Community is not recognized as equivalent to Christ/Church. However, the insights that come from hearing the Gospels with different ears" can correct distortions within the tradition and open up the future for those who are oppressed.

---

43. Brock, *Journeys by Heart*, 67. See 63-65 for her summary and critique of Ruether's Christology.
44. Brock, *Journeys by Heart*, 103.
45. Brock, *Journeys by Heart*, 97.
46. Brock, *Journeys by Heart*, xv.

IV. Toward Inclusive Christologies

The approaches we have considered are not complete Christologies, but rather attempts to re-image Jesus who is the Christ in ways that take women's experience seriously. Woman Christ and Christ as Incarnate Wisdom try to make room for the female within the male image. The other attempts consider how Jesus functions in the tradition. Some authors, such as Ruether, emphasize the historical Jesus, distinguishing him from later christological developments. Schüssler Fiorenza and Nakashima Brock de-emphasize the historical Jesus and stress instead the community of his disciples, and particularly his women disciples. Jesus is seen as part of a community rather than as an isolated individual, an approach supported by contemporary Scripture studies which insist that it is impossible to separate Jesus from the communities of faith who remembered him and whose witness is expressed in the writings of the New Testament.[47]

Whether the primary focus is the historical Jesus and his teaching, or the community of faith that gathered around Jesus during his life and continued to live by his spirit after his death and resurrection, the hermeneutical principle for interpretation is the same: the reality of contemporary women moving from a position of inferiority to full personhood. Both the praxis of Jesus and that of the early communities of disciples can support this movement of liberation. Both may be used to promote inclusive communities which image Christ today. Women-church, redeemed humanity, or Christa/Community are different ways of imaging inclusive Christian communities. Schüssler Fiorenza argues that women-church has always existed in some form alongside the patriarchal church. We need to claim our past, but the past does not provide an adequate base for women. The only acceptable basis for rethinking images of Christ is the present reality of contemporary women throughout the world who are engaged in a critical re-evaluation of the Christian tradition, including the central symbol of that tradition.

From the work that has been done, is it possible to suggest criteria for inclusive Christologies? I believe that all contemporary Christologies need to take seriously the half of humanity which has often been silenced and made invisible in theological reflection. No Christology stands alone. It is built upon an anthropology and forms the basis for an ecclesiology. To be inclusive, Christology must be built upon an inclusive anthropology and be reflected in an inclusive ecclesiology.

In considering criteria for inclusive Christologies I return to the areas of experience discussed above: female embodiment, female oppression, and female interrelatedness. In relation to female embodiment, I see the need for an inclu-

---

47. See, e.g., the work of Mary Rose D'Angelo, especially "Re-membering Jesus: Women, Prophecy and Resistance in the Memory of the Early Churches," *The Future Church: The Global Agenda of Feminist Theology.*

sive anthropology which accords full humanity to the female person as embodied spirit and as revelatory of the divine. The experience of female oppression must recognize and name women's suffering, and evoke an active response
which offers hope and energy for change. The experience of interrelatedness
raises issues concerning ecclesiology, the nature and mission of the church, and
our relationship to one another and to our world. Patterns of submission and
domination must be recognized and new ways of relating discovered. Our
Christology influences how we understand humanness, how we cope with
suffering, and how we live with one another and with nature in our world.

The maleness of Jesus need not be an insurmountable problem for an
inclusive anthropology and Christology. The fact that the historical Jesus was
male is seen as a particularity along with the fact that he lived in the first century
and was Jewish. Diane Tennis probably expresses the experience of many women
when she refers to Jesus as "the one utterly reliable man in the lives of many
women." For her, Jesus' maleness has a positive dimension. "It delivers a judgment on patriarchy through the model of self-giving for men, and transcends
patriarchy by legitimizing experimental authority for women."[48] An inclusive
Christology recognizes the maleness of the historical Jesus but does not equate
maleness with humanity.[49]

Images of Christ have often seemed to glorify suffering and have legitimated a passive attitude among those who are powerless. An inclusive Christology must reflect seriously on Jesus' death and resurrection. Christian faith
in the resurrection witnesses to the fact that suffering and death do not have
the last word. A Christology which takes the massive human suffering in our
world seriously must be based on an orthopraxis which struggles to overcome
the injustices which contribute to suffering. The dangerous memory of Jesus'
death and resurrection, as well as memories of the suffering and courage of
Christ's body throughout the centuries, motivate this work of justice. An inclusive Christology must hear the silent cries of women through the ages and from
all parts of the world.

Theology arising out of the experiences of women is discovering that the
image of Christ need not lead to the passive response of a victim, but rather
can provide the energy necessary to work for social change.[50] An example of
the power of a transformed image of Christ to convert meaningless suffering

48. Diane Tennis, "Reflections on the Maleness of Jesus," *Cross Currents* 28 (1978): 137-40:
quote from 140.

49. Schneiders interprets Jesus' personal choice of celibacy as a renunciation of patriarchal
privilege. By not taking possession of a woman, Jesus was free to relate to women as equals. Since
he had no children, he did not have to dominate them. *Women and the Word*, 63.

50. Dorothée Soelle has distinguished three phases that suffering may take: the suffering of
the victim which is mute, passive acceptance; the awareness and articulation of suffering which
refuses to be a victim; and, finally, organization to change the conditions which produce suffering.
Suffering (Philadelphia: Fortress Press, 1975): 71-72.

into a dangerous memory which can lead to change was the gathering around the "Crucified Woman" at Emmanuel College, Toronto, following the killing of fourteen women students in Montreal in December, 1989.

Theories of atonement which seem to glorify suffering or which do not respect personal responsibility must not be perpetuated. The causes of suffering need to be addressed, especially the ideologies which have perpetuated the suffering of certain groups at the hands of the powerful. Inclusive Christologies will build on the dangerous memories of women's suffering and oppression and include a commitment to work for justice for all.[51]

Finally, an inclusive Christology will be based on interdependence and mutuality.[52] It will not take over human responsibility by claiming that we are already saved in Christ, nor will it support an ecclesiology which assigns responsibility to one class of men who can represent Christ, while all other persons are expected to be silent and submissive. Rather, an inclusive Christology will empower all persons to be responsible for one another and for our world. While recognizing the significance of the past, it is not locked into the past but is open to new ways of responding to this moment in human history. An inclusive Christology which is empowering for all women and men must be reflected in the praxis of inclusive Christian communities. Only then will Christ and Christianity be experienced as "good news" for women.

---

51. This attitude toward suffering was expressed in the final document of the Intercontinental Women's Conference in Oaxtepec, Mexico, December 1-6, 1986: "Suffering that is inflicted by the oppressor and is passively accepted does not lead to life; it is destructive and demonic. But suffering that is part of the struggle for the sake of God's reign or that results from uncontrollable and mysterious conditions of humankind is redeeming and is rooted in the Paschal Mystery, evocative of the rhythm of pregnancy, delivery, and birth. This kind of suffering is familiar to women of all times, who participate in the pains of birth and the joys of the new creation." *With Passion and Compassion,* 184-90: quote from 188.

52. Geoffrey R. Lilburne in "Christology: In Dialogue with Feminism," *Horizons* 11 (1984): 7-27, suggests that the Trinity points to patterns of differentiation which do not involve hierarchy and to modalities of relationships which do not entail domination. He proposes that a postpatriarchal Christology should reappropriate a trinitarian understanding of God which models mutuality, equality, freedom, and interdependence.

Womanist Theology: Black Women's Experience as a Source for Doing Theology, with Special Reference to Christology

JACQUELYN GRANT

I. Introduction

This paper is an exploration into the experiences of Black Women for the purpose of providing alternative sources for doing theology.

Black theology and other third world theologies of liberation have shown through their challenge of the methodologies of classical theologies that experience of the dominant culture has been the invisible crucible for theologizing. They have demonstrated that theology is not unrelated to socio-political realities of existence; and that historically it has been used to maintain the social and political advantages of the status quo. The portrayal of the universal God was such that an affirmation of this God meant a simultaneous negation of all others' cultural perceptions of the divinity, as well as a negation of those very cultures. Nowhere was this more clear than in the area of Christian foreign missions, where conversion to Christianity implicitly meant deculturalization and acceptance of the western value system on the part of Asians, Africans, and Latin Americans. Upon conversion, one had to withdraw from indigenous ways of imaging the divine reality, and embrace foreign, western ways which often served to undergird oppressive religious, social and political structures.

This is true not only in the foreign missions field but also in the western world; it is reflected in the ways in which oppressors deal with oppressed people within their own territory. We see this with respect to third world people in the first world context as well as with respect to women.

Reprinted with permission from *The Journal of the Interdenominational Theological Center* 13 (Spring 1986): 195-212. This paper was the Charles B. Copher Annual Faculty Lecture at ITC for 1986.

An illustration emerging out of Black theology and Feminist theology will make the point. Theologians in both these theological camps propose an alternative understanding, for example, of Christian love.

James Cone in an early work makes a distinction between the non-threatening love of many Christians and the radical love of Jesus which demands justice.

> There is no place in Christian theology for sentimental love — love without risk or cost. Love demands all, the whole of one's being. Thus, for the black [person] to believe the Word of God about [God's] love revealed in Christ, he/she must be prepared to meet head-on the sentimental "Christian" love of whites, which would make him/her a nonperson.[1]

Cone insists that one cannot practice Christian love and at the same time practice racism. He argues:

> It seems that whites forget about the necessary interrelatedness of love, justice, and power when they encounter Black people. Love becomes emotional and sentimental. This sentimental, condescending love accounts for their desire to "help" by relieving the physical pains of the suffering blacks so they can satisfy their own religious piety and keep the poor powerless. But the new blacks, redeemed in Christ, must refuse their "help" and demand that blacks be confronted as persons. They must say to whites that authentic love is not "help," not giving Christmas baskets, but working for political, social, and economic justice, which always means a redistribution of power. It is a kind of power which enables the blacks to fight their own battles and thus keep their dignity. "Powerlessness breeds a race of beggars."[2]

Black people do not need a love which functions contrary to the establishment of Black personhood. This understanding of love was just recently affirmed by Black theologians (lay and clergy, professional and nonprofessional) in Southern Africa in their challenge to the church through *The Kairos Document*. They cautioned, "we must also remember that the most loving thing we can do for both the oppressed and for our enemies who are oppressors is to eliminate the oppression, remove the tyrants from power and establish a just government for the common good of all the people."[3] Here, love is not defined in the interest of those who wish to maintain the present status quo. But it is defined from the point of view of those on the underside of history — the victims of the oppressors' power.

1. James H. Cone, *Black Theology and Black Power* (New York: The Seabury Press, 1969), 53-54.

2. Ibid., 54.

3. The Kairos Theologians, *The Kairos Document: Challenge to the Church*, 2d ed. (Braamfontein, South Africa: Skotaville Publishers, 1985; rept. Grand Rapids, MI: Eerdmans Publishing Co., 1986), 24-25.

In a similar vein, feminists challenge traditional understandings of love. Valerie Saiving Goldstein expresses her suspicions of traditional theological works in the following way:

> I am no longer certain as I once was that, when theologians speak of "man," they are using the word in its generic sense. It is, after all, a well-known fact that theology has been written almost exclusively by men. This alone should put us on guard, especially since contemporary theologians constantly remind us that one of man's strongest temptations is to identify his own limited perspective with universal truth.[4]

Lifting up the Christian notion of sin and love, Goldstein suggests that it would be equally unsatisfactory to impose universal understanding on those concepts. The identification of these notions with self-assertion and selflessness respectively, functions differently in masculine experience and feminine experience. She explains further:

> Contemporary theological doctrines of love have, I believe, been constructed primarily upon the basis of masculine experience and thus view the human condition from the male standpoint. Consequently, these doctrines do not provide an adequate interpretation of the situation of women — nor, for that matter, of men, especially in light of certain fundamental changes now taking place in our own society.[5]

Because of their feminine character, for women love takes the form of nurturing, supporting and servicing their families. Consequently, if a woman believes

> the theologians, she will try to strangle other impulses in herself. She will believe that, having chosen marriage and children and thus being face to face with the needs of her family for love, refreshment, and forgiveness, she has no right to ask anything for herself but must submit without qualification to the strictly feminine role.[6]

For women, too, the issue is one of personhood — are women to deny who they are in order to be saved?

Goldstein then argues that when experience in theology is scrutinized, we will discover that because it has been synonymous with masculine experience, it is inadequate to deal with the situation of women.

In other words, Black theologians and Feminist theologians have argued that the universalism which classical theologians attempt to uphold represents

4. Valerie Saiving Goldstein, "The Human Situation of a Feminine," *The Journal of Religion* 40 (April 1960): 100.
    5. Ibid.
    6. Ibid.

merely the particular experiences of the dominant culture. Blacks identify that experience as White experience; and women identify it as male experience. The question then is, if universalism is the criteria for valid theology, how is such a universalism achieved?

What I will be exploring here is how Black women's experiences can provide some insights into this question. In doing so, Black women not only join Blacks and feminists in their challenge of theology but they also provide an internal critique for Black men as well as for White women. In this paper, I will focus primarily upon Black women's experience as related to the development of feminist theology. (In a rather limited way, I have addressed the issue of Black women's experiences and Black theology in an article entitled "Black Theology and the Black Woman."[7] That subject certainly has not been exhausted, and shall be treated in more substantive ways in the future.)

But here I am interested in engaging Feminist theology with reference to its constructive efficacy for Black women given the peculiarities of their experiences. The results will be the beginnings of a theology from a Black woman's perspective with special reference to Christology.

In order to create a common starting point, let's begin with a synopsis of the basic tenets of Feminist theology. First, Feminist theology seeks to develop a *wholistic theology.* Feminist theology rejects the traditional forms of oppressive and one-sided, male-dominated theologies which arise out of patriarchal religion(s).[8] Women have begun to see that their continuous oppression in the church and society has its basis in these patriarchal religion(s). Historically, the theologies of religions have emerged out of the experiences of men, making the theologies representative thereof. Because humanity is comprised of both men and women, Feminist theologians seek to develop a more wholistic perspective in theology.

Second, in seeking to produce a wholistic perspective in theology, Feminist theologians call for the *eradication of social/sexual dualisms* in human existence which are inherent in patriarchy. A patriarchy is characterized by male domination and female submission and subordination. In such a society, men are considered strong, intelligent, rational, and aggressive; women are considered weak, irrational, and docile.

A third function of Feminist theology is to *conceptualize new and positive images of women.* Throughout history, including the history of theology, women have been portrayed in negative ways. They have been sources of evil (snakes),

7. Jacquelyn Grant, "Black Theology and the Black Woman," in *Black Theology: A Documentary History, 1966-1979,* eds. Gayraud S. Wilmore and James H. Cone (New York: Orbis Books, 1979), 418-33.

8. See Sheila D. Collins, *A Different Heaven and Earth: A Feminist Perspective on Religion* (Valley Forge, PA: Judson Press, 1974); Mary Daly, *Beyond God the Father: Toward a Philosophy of Women's Liberation* (Boston: Beacon, 1973); Mary Daly, *The Church and the Second Sex: With a New Feminist Post Christian Introduction by the Author* (New York: Harper and Colophon, 1975).

authors of trickery (witches), and stimulants (therefore causes) for the sexual perversions of men (temptresses and prostitutes). These negative images must be changed to reflect reality.

Finally, Feminist theology must *evaluate male articulated understandings of the Christian faith.* Doctrines developed in a system of patriarchy merely perpetuate patriarchal structures. As the patriarchal theological system is challenged, so are the doctrines of, for example, God, Jesus Christ, the Fall and the Church.

II. Emerging Black Feminist Perspective

It has been argued by many Blacks that the women's liberation movement is a White middle-class movement. Therefore, it is believed to be totally irrelevant to the situation of Black women since the majority of them are not middle-class.

Brenda Eichelberger gives several reasons for Black women's noninvolvement in feminist causes. Among them are such things as class differences, the lack of Black women's knowledge about the real issues involved and the suspicion that the middle-class White women's movement is divisive to the Black community, which claims prior allegiance.[9] In spite of these and other negative responses to the White women's liberation movement, there has been a growing feminist consciousness among many Black women and some Black men. This consciousness is coupled by the increased willingness of Black women to undertake an independent analysis of sexism, thereby creating an emerging Black perspective on feminism. Black feminism grows out of Black women's tri-dimensional reality of race/sex/class. It holds that full human liberation cannot be achieved simply by the elimination of any one form of oppression. Consequently, real liberation must be "broad in the concrete";[10] it must be based upon a multi-dimensional analysis.

Recent writings by secular Black feminists have challenged White feminist analysis and Black race analysis, particularly by introducing data from Black women's experience that has been historically ignored by White feminists and Black male liberationists.

In only a few of them do Black women employ only a gender analysis to treat Black women's reality. Whereas Ntozake Shange focuses chiefly upon sex-

9. Brenda Eichelberger, "Voice of Black Feminism," *Quest: A Feminist Quarterly* 3 (Spring, 1977): 16-23.

10. This phrase is used by Anna Julia Cooper, *A Voice from the South* (Xenia, OH: Aldine Publishing House, 1852; repr. Westport, CN: Negro Universities Press, 1969), cited by Bell Hooks, *Ain't I A Woman: Black Women and Feminism* (Boston: South End Press, 1981), 193-94. I use it here to characterize Black women's experience. To be concerned about Black Women's issues is to be *concrete.* Yet because of their interconnectedness with Black men (racism), White women (sexism) and the poor (classism), it is also to be, at the same time, concerned with broad issues.

ism, Michelle Wallace, like Alice Walker, presumes that White racism has had
an adverse effect upon the Black community in a way that confuses and reinforces the already existing sexism. Sharon Harley, Rosalyn Terborg-Penn, Paula
Giddings and Gloria Wade-Gayles all recognize the inclusiveness of the oppressive reality of Black women as they endure racism, sexism and economic oppression. Barbara Smith, Gloria Hull, Bell Hooks and Angela Davis particularly
explore the implications of this tri-dimensional oppression of Black women. In
so doing, Black women have either articulated Black feminist perspectives or
developed grounds for doing so.[11] These perspectives, however, have not led to
the resolution of tensions between Black women and White women, and they
even have brought to the forefront some tensions between Black women and
Black men.

On the contrary, the possibly irreparable nature of these tensions is implied in Walker's suggestion that the experience of being a Black woman or a
White woman is so different that another word is required to describe the
liberative efforts of Black women. Her suggestion that the word "womanist" is
more appropriate for Black women is derived from the sense of the word as it
is used in Black communities:

> Womanist, from womanish. (Opp. of "girlish," i.e., frivolous, irresponsible,
> not serious). A Black feminist or feminist of color. From the Black folk
> expression of mothers to female children, "You acting womanish," i.e., like a
> woman. Usually referring to outrageous, audacious, courageous or willful
> behavior. Wanting to know more and in greater depth than is considered
> "good" for one. Interest in grown-up doings. Acting grown up. Being grown
> up. Interchangeable with another black folk expression: "You trying to be
> grown." Responsible. In charge. Serious.[12]

Womanists were Sojourner Truth, Jarena Lee, Amanda Berry Smith,
Ida B. Wells, Mary Church Terrell, Mary McCloud Bethune and countless
others not remembered in any historical study. A womanist, then, is a strong
Black woman who has sometimes been mislabeled as domineering, castrating

11. See Ntozake Shange, *For Colored Girls Who Have Considered Suicide When the Rainbow
is Enuf* (New York: Macmillan Publishing Co., Inc., 1975); Michelle Wallace, *Black Macho and the
Myth of the Superwoman* (New York: Dial Press, 1978); Alice Walker, *The Color Purple* (New York:
Harcourt, Brace and Jovanovich Publishers, 1982); and *In Search of Our Mother's Garden* (New
York: Harcourt, Brace and Jovanovich Publishers, 1983); Sharon Harley and Rosalyn Terborg-Penn,
eds., *Afro-American Women* (New York: Kennikat Press, 1978); Paula Giddings, *When and Where
I Enter* (New York: William Morrow and Company, Inc., 1984); Gloria Wade-Grayles, *No Crystal
Stair: Visions of Race and Sex in Black Women's Fiction* (New York: Pilgrim Press, 1984); Bell Hooks,
Feminist Theory: From Margin to Center (Boston: South End Press, 1984); Barbara Smith, Gloria
Hull, and Patricia Scott, *All the Women are White, and All the Blacks are Men, But Some of Us are
Brave* (New York: The Feminist Press, 1982); Angela Y. Davis, *Women, Race and Class* (New York:
Vintage Books, 1981).

12. Walker, *In Search of Our Mother's Garden,* xi.

matriarch. A womanist is one who has developed survival strategies in spite of the oppression of her race and sex in order to save her family and her people. Walker's womanist notation suggests not "the feminist," but the active struggle of Black women that makes them who they are. For some Black women that may involve being feminine as traditionally defined, and for others it involves being masculine as stereotypically defined. In any case, womanist means being and acting out who you are and interpreting the reality for yourself. In other words, Black women speak out for themselves. As Black feminist critic Barbara Christian explains, referring to Audre Lorde's poem about the deadly consequence of silence, Black women must speak up and answer in order to validate their own experience. This is important even if only to ourselves. It is to the womanist tradition that Black women must appeal for the doing of theology.

III. The Beginnings of a Womanist Theology with Special Reference to Christology

Womanist theology begins with the experiences of Black women as its point of departure. This experience includes not only Black women's activities in the larger society but also in the churches, and reveals that Black women have often rejected the oppressive structure in the church as well.

These experiences provide a context which is significant for doing theology. Those experiences had been and continue to be defined by racism, sexism and classism and therefore offer a unique opportunity and a new challenge for developing a relevant perspective in the theological enterprise. This perspective in theology which I am calling womanist theology draws upon the life and experiences of some Black women who have created meaningful interpretations of the Christian faith.

Black women must do theology out of their tri-dimensional experience of racism/sexism/classism. To ignore any aspect of this experience is to deny the holistic and integrated reality of Black womanhood. When Black women say that God is on the side of the oppressed, we mean that God is in solidarity with the struggles of those on the underside of humanity, those whose lives are bent and broken from the many levels of assault perpetrated against them.

In a chapter entitled "Black Women: Shaping Feminist Theory," Hooks elaborates on the interrelationship of the threefold oppressive reality of Black women and shows some of the weaknesses of White feminist theory. Challenging the racist and classist assumptions of White feminism, Hooks writes:

> Racism abounds in the writings of white feminists, reinforcing white supremacy and negating the possibility that women will bond politically across ethnic and racial boundaries. Past feminist refusal to draw attention to and

attack racial hierarchy suppressed the link between race and class. Yet class structure in American society has been shaped by the racial politics of white supremacy.[13]

This means that Black women, because of oppression determined by race and their subjugation as women, make up a disproportionately high percentage of the poor and working classes. However, the fact that Black women are a subjugated group even within the Black community and the White women's community does not mean that they are alone in their oppression within those communities. In the women's community poor White women are discriminated against, and in the Black community, poor Black men are marginalized. This suggests that classism, as well as racism and sexism, has a life of its own. Consequently, simply addressing racism and sexism is inadequate to bring about total liberation. Even though there are dimensions of class which are not directly related to race or sex, classism impacts Black women in a peculiar way which results in the fact that they are most often on the bottom of the social and economic ladder. For Black women doing theology, to ignore classism would mean that their theology is no different from any other bourgeois theology. It would be meaningless to the majority of Black women, who are themselves poor. This means that addressing only issues relevant to middle-class women or Blacks will simply not do. The daily struggles of poor Black women must serve as the gauge for the verification of the claims of womanist theology. Anna Julia Cooper makes a relevant point:

> Women's wrongs are thus indissolubly linked with all undefended woes, and the acquirement of her "rights" will mean the supremacy of triumph of all right over might, the supremacy of the moral forces of reason, and justice, and love in the government of the nations of earth.[14]

Black women's experience must be affirmed as the crucible for doing womanist theology. It is the context in which we must decide theological questions. More specifically, it is within the context of this experience that Black women read the Bible. A (brief) look at Black women's use of the Bible indicates how it is their experiences which determine relevant questions for them.

IV. The Bible in the Womanist Tradition

Theological investigation into the experiences of Christian Black women reveals that Black women considered the Bible to be a major source of religious validation in their lives. Though Black women's relationship with God preceded their intro-

13. Hooks, *Feminist Theory*, 3.
14. Cooper, *A Voice from the South*, 91.

duction to the Bible, this Bible gave some content to their God-consciousness.[15] The source for Black women's understanding of God has been twofold: first, God's revelation directly to them, and, secondly, God's revelation as witnessed in the Bible and as read and heard in the context of their experience. The understanding of God as creator, sustainer, comforter, and liberator took on life as they agonized over their pain and celebrated the hope that, as God delivered the Israelites, they would be delivered as well. The God of the Old and New Testament became real in the consciousness of oppressed Black women. Of the use of the Bible, Fannie Barrier Williams quite aptly said:

> Though the Bible was not an open book to the Negro before emancipation, thousands of the enslaved men and women of the negro race learned more than was taught to them. Thousands of them realized the deeper meanings, the sweeter consolations and the spiritual awakenings that are part of the religious experiences of all Christians.[16]

In other words, though Black people in general and Black women in particular were politically impotent and religiously controlled, they were able to appropriate certain themes of the Bible which spoke to their reality. For example, Jarena Lee, a nineteenth-century Black woman preacher in the African Methodist Episcopal Church, constantly emphasized the theme "Life and Liberty" in her sermons, which were always biblically based. This interplay of Scripture and experience was exercised even more expressly by many other Black women. An ex–slave woman revealed that when her experience negated certain oppressive interpretations of the Bible given by white preachers, she, through engaging the biblical message for herself, rejected them. Consequently, she also dismissed white preachers who distorted the message in order to maintain slavery. Her grandson, Howard Thurman, speaks of her use of the Bible in this way:

> "During the days of slavery," she said, "the master's minister would occasionally hold services for the slaves. Always the white minister used as his text something from Paul. 'Slaves, be obedient to them that are your masters . . . as unto Christ.' Then he would go on to show how, if we were good and happy slaves, God would bless us. I promised my Maker that if I ever learned to read and if freedom ever came, I would not read that part of the Bible.[17]

What we see here is perhaps more than a mere rejection of a White preacher's interpretation of the Bible: it is an exercise in internal critique of the Bible. The

---

15. Cecil Wayne Cone, *Identity Crisis in Black Theology* (Nashville, TN: African Methodist Episcopal Church Press, 1975), passim, especially chapter III.

16. Bert James Lowenberg and Ruth Bogin, eds., *Black Women in Nineteenth-Century American Life: Their Words, Their Thoughts, Their Feelings* (University Park, PA: The Pennsylvania State University Press, 1976), 267.

17. Howard Thurman, *Jesus and the Disinherited* (Nashville: Abingdon Press, 1949), 30-31.

liberating message of the gospel is seen as over against the oppressive elements in the Bible.

The truth which the Bible brought was undeniable, though perception of it was often distorted in order to support the monstrous system of oppression. Sarcastically responding to this tendency, Fannie Barrier Williams admonished, "do not open the Bible too wide." Biblical interpretation, realized Williams, a nontheologically trained person, had at its base the prior agenda of white America. She therefore argued:

> Religion, like every other force in America, was first used as an instrument and servant of slavery. All attempts to Christianize the negro were limited by the important fact that he was property of a valuable and peculiar sort, and that the property value must not be disturbed, even if his soul were lost. If Christianity could make the negro docile, domestic and less an independent and fighting savage, let it be preached to that extent and no further.[18]

Such a false, pernicious, demoralizing gospel could only be preached if the Bible was not opened wide enough, lest one see the liberating message of Jesus as summarized in Luke 4:18. The Bible must be read and interpreted in the light of Black women's own oppression and God's revelation within that context. Womanists must, like Sojourner, "compare the teachings of the Bible with the witness" in them.[19]

To do Womanist theology, then, we must read and hear the Bible and engage it within the context of our own experience. This is the only way that it can make sense to people who are oppressed. Black women of the past did not hesitate to do this, and we must do no less.

V. Jesus in the Womanist Tradition

Having opened the Bible wider than many White people, Black people, in general, and Black women in particular, found a Jesus who they could claim, and whose claim for them was one of affirmation of dignity and self-respect.

In the experience of Black people, Jesus was "all things."[20] Chief among these, however, was the belief in Jesus as the divine co-sufferer, who empowers them in situations of oppression. For Christian Black women in the past, Jesus was the central frame of reference. They identified with Jesus because they believed that Jesus identified with them. As Jesus was persecuted and made to

---

18. Lowenberg and Bogin, *Black Women*, 265.

19. Olive Gilbert, *Sojourner Truth: Narrative and Book of Life* (1850 and 1875; rept. Chicago: Johnson Publishing Co., 1970), 83.

20. Harold A. Carter, *The Prayer Tradition of Black People* (Valley Forge: Judson Press, 1976), 50. Carter, in referring to traditional Black prayer in general, states that Jesus was revealed as one who "was all one needs!"

suffer undeservedly, so were they. His suffering culminated in the crucifixion. Their crucifixion included rapes, and husbands being castrated (literally and metaphorically), babies being sold, and other cruel and often murderous treatments. But Jesus' suffering was not the suffering of a mere human, for Jesus was understood to be God incarnate. As Harold Carter observed of Black prayers in general, there was no difference made between the persons of the Trinity, Jesus, God, or the Holy Spirit. All of these proper names for God were used interchangeably in prayer language. Thus, Jesus was the one who speaks the world into creation. He was the power behind the Church.[21] Black women's affirmation of Jesus as God meant that White people were not God. One old slave woman clearly demonstrates this as she prayed:

> "Dear Massa Jesus, we all uns beg Ooner [you] come make us a call dis yere day. We is nutting but poor Etiopian women and people ain't tink much 'bout we. We ain't trust any of dem great high people for come to we church, but do' you is de one great Massa, great too much dan Massa Linkum, you ain't shame to care for we African people."[22]

Implicit in the description "nothing but poor Black women" and what follows is the awareness of the public devaluation of Black women. But in spite of that Jesus is presented as a confidant who could be trusted while White people could not be trusted. This women affirmed the contribution of Abraham Lincoln to the emancipation of Blacks, but rejected Mr. Lincoln as her real or ultimate master. Quite a contrast to the master's (slave owner's) perception of his/herself.

This slave woman did not hesitate to identify her struggle and pain with those of Jesus. In fact, the common struggle made her know that Jesus would respond to her beck and call.

> Come to we, dear Massa Jesus. De sun, he hot too much, de road am dat long and boggy (sandy) and we ain't got no buggy for send and fetch Ooner. But Massa, you 'member how you walked dat hard walk up Calvary and ain't weary but tink about we all dat way. We know you ain't weary for to come to we. We pick out de torns, de prickles, de brier, de backsliding' and de quarrel and de sin out of you path so dey shan't hurt Ooner pierce feet no more.[23]

The reference to "no buggy" to send for Jesus brings to mind the limited material possessions of pre– and post–Civil War Blacks. In her speech, "Ain't I a Woman," Sojourner Truth distinguished between White women's and Black women's experiences by emphasizing that Black women were not helped into carriages

21. Ibid.
22. Ibid., 49.
23. Ibid.

as were White women.[24] In the prayer, this woman speaks of that reality wherein most Blacks didn't even have carriages or buggies. For had she owned one, certainly she'd send it to fetch Jesus. Here we see the concern for the comfort and the suffering of Jesus. Jesus suffers when we sin — when we backslide or when we quarrel. But still Jesus is identified with her plight. Note that Jesus went to the cross with this Black woman on his mind. He was thinking about her and all others like her. So totally dedicated to the poor, the weak, the downtrodden, and the outcast was Jesus that in this Black woman's faith Jesus would never be too tired to come. As she is truly among the people at the bottom of humanity, she can make things comfortable for Jesus even though she may have nothing to give him — no water, no food — but she can give tears and love. She continues:

> Come to we, dear Massa Jesus. We all uns ain't got no good cool water for give you when you thirsty. You know, Massa, de drought so long, and the well so low, ain't nutting but mud to drink. But we gwine to take de 'munion cup and fill it wid de tear of repentance, and love clean out of we heart. Dat all we hab to gib you, good Massa.[25]

The material or physical deprivation experienced by this woman did not reduce her desire to give Jesus the best. Being a Black woman in the American society meant essentially being poor, with no buggy and no good cool water. Life for Black women was indeed bad, hot and at best muddy. Note that there is no hint that their condition results from some divine intention. Now, whereas I am not prepared to say that the same woman or any others in that church the next day would have been engaged in political praxis by joining such movements as Nat Turner's rebellion or Denmark Vesey's revolt, it is clear that her perspective was such that the social, political and economic orders were believed to be sinful and against the will of the real master, Jesus.

For Black women, the role of Jesus unraveled as they encountered him in their experience as one who empowers the weak. In this vein, Jesus was such a central part of Sojourner Truth's life that all of her sermons made him the starting point. When asked by a preacher if the source of her preaching was the Bible, she responded, "No honey, can't preach from de Bible — can't read a letter."[26] Then she explained, "When I preaches, I has jest one text to preach from, an' I always preaches from this one. My text is, 'When I found Jesus!'"[27] In this sermon Sojourner Truth recounts the events and struggles of life from the time her parents were brought from Africa and sold "up an' down, an' hither

24. Sojourner Truth, "Ain't I A Woman?" in Mariam Schneir, ed., *Feminism: The Essential Historical Writings* (New York: Vintage Books, 1972).

25. Carter, *The Prayer Tradition*, 49.

26. Gilbert, *Book of Life*, 118.

27. Ibid., 119.

an' yon . . ."[28] to the time that she met Jesus within the context of her struggles for dignity of Black people and women. Her encounter with Jesus brought such joy that she became overwhelmed with love and praise:

> Praise, praise, praise to the Lord! An' I begun to feel such a love in my soul as I never felt before — love to all creatures. An' then, all of a sudden, it stopped, an' I said, Dar's de white folks that have abused you, an' beat you, and an' abused your people — think o' them! But then there came another rush of love through my soul, an' I cried out loud — "Lord, I can love even de white folks!"[29]

This love was not a sentimental, passive love. It was a tough, active love that empowered her to fight more fiercely for the freedom of her people. For the rest of her life she continued speaking at abolition and women's rights gatherings, and condemned the horrors of oppression.

VI. The Womanist Traditions and Christological Reflections

More than anyone, Black theologians have captured the essence of the significance of Jesus in the lives of Black people, which to an extent includes Black women. They all hold that the Jesus of history is important for understanding who he was and his significance for us today. By and large they have affirmed that this Jesus is the Christ, that is, God incarnate. They have argued that in the light of our experience, Jesus meant freedom.[30] They have maintained that Jesus means freedom from the sociopsychological, psychocultural, economic and political oppression of Black people. In other words, Jesus is a political messiah.[31] "To free [humans] from bondage was Jesus' own definition of his ministry."[32] This meant that as Jesus identified with the lowly of his day, he now identifies with the lowly of this day, who in the American context are Black people. The identification is so real that Jesus Christ in fact becomes Black. It is important to note that Jesus' blackness is not a result of ideological distortion of a few Black thinkers, but a result of careful Christological investigation. Cone examines the sources of Christology and concludes that Jesus is Black because "Jesus was a Jew." He explains:

> It is on the basis of the soteriological meaning of the particularity of his Jewishness that theology must affirm the christological significance of Jesus'

---

28. Ibid.
29. Ibid.
30. James Deotis Roberts, *A Black Political Theology* (Philadelphia: The Westminster Press, 1974), p. 138. See especially chapter 5. See also Noel Leo Erskine, *Decolonizing Theology: A Caribbean Perspective* (New York: Orbis Books, 1980), 125.
31. Roberts, *A Black Political Theology*, 133.
32. Albert Cleage, *The Black Messiah* (New York: Sheed and Ward, 1969), 92.

present blackness. He *is* black because he was a Jew. The affirmation of the Black Christ can be understood when the significance of his past Jewishness is related dialectically to the significance of his present blackness. On the other hand, the Jewishness of Jesus located him in the context of the Exodus, thereby connecting his appearance in Palestine with God's liberation of oppressed Israelites from Egypt. Unless Jesus were truly from Jewish ancestry, it would make little theological sense to say that he is the fulfillment of God's covenant with Israel. But on the other hand, the blackness of Jesus brings out the soteriological meaning of his Jewishness for our contemporary situation when Jesus' person is understood in the context of the cross and resurrection. Without negating the divine election of Israel, the Cross and resurrection are Yahweh's fulfillment of his original intention for Israel. . . .[33]

The condition of Black people today reflects the cross of Jesus. Yet the resurrection brings the hope that liberation from oppression is imminent. The resurrected Black Christ signifies this hope.

Cone further argues that this christological title, "The Black Christ," is not validated by its universality, but, in fact, by its particularity. Its significance lies in whether or not the christological title "points to God's universal will to liberate particular oppressed people from inhumanity."[34] These particular oppressed peoples to whom Cone refers are characterized in Jesus' parable on the Last Judgment as "the least." "The least in America are literally and symbolically present in Black people."[35] This notion of "the least" is attractive because it descriptively locates the condition of Black women. "The least" are those people who have no water to give, but offer what they have, as the old slave woman cited above says in her prayer. Black women's experience in general is such a reality. Their tri-dimensional reality renders their particular situation a complex one. One could say that not only are they the oppressed of the oppressed, but their situation represents "the particular within the particular."

But is this just another situation that takes us deeper into the abyss of theological relativity? I would argue that it is not, because it is in the context of Black women's experience that the particular connects up with the universal. By this I mean that in each of the three dynamics of oppression, Black women share in the reality of a broader community. They share race suffering with Black men; with White women and other Third World women, they are victims of sexism; and with poor Blacks and Whites, and other Third World peoples, especially women, they are disproportionately poor. To speak of Black women's tri-dimensional reality, therefore, is not to speak of Black

33. James H. Cone, *God of the Oppressed* (New York: Seabury, 1975), 134.
34. Ibid., 135.
35. Ibid., 136.

women exclusively, for there is an implied universality which connects them with others.

Likewise, with Jesus Christ, there was an implied universality which made him identify with others — the poor, the woman, the stranger. To affirm Jesus' solidarity with the "least of the people" is not an exercise in romanticized contentment with one's oppressed status in life. For as the resurrection signified that there is more to life than the cross of Jesus Christ, for Black women it signifies that their tri-dimensional oppressive existence is not the end, but it merely represents the context in which a particular people struggle to experience hope and liberation. Jesus Christ thus represents a threefold significance; first he identifies with the "little people," Blackwomen, where they are; secondly, he affirms the basic humanity of these, "the least"; and thirdly, he inspires active hope in the struggle for resurrected, liberated existence.

To locate the Christ in Black people is a radical and necessary step, but understanding of Black women's reality challenges us to go further. Christ among the least must also mean Christ in the community of Black women. William Eichelberger was able to recognize this as he further particularized the significance of the Blackness of Jesus by locating Christ in Black women's community. He was able to see Christ not only as Black male but also Black female.

> God, in revealing Himself and His attributes from time to time in His crea-
> turely existence, has exercised His freedom to formalize His appearance in a
> variety of ways. . . . God revealed Himself at a point in the past as Jesus the
> Christ a Black male. My reasons for affirming the Blackness of Jesus of
> Nazareth are much different from that of the white apologist. . . . God wanted
> to identify with that segment of mankind which had suffered most, and is
> still suffering. . . . I am constrained to believe that God in our times has
> updated His form of revelation to western society. It is my feeling that God
> is now manifesting Himself, and has been for over 450 years, in the form of
> the Black American Woman as mother, as wife, as nourisher, sustainer and
> preserver of life, the Suffering Servant who is despised and rejected by men,
> a personality of sorrow who is acquainted with grief. The Black Woman has
> borne our griefs and carried our sorrows. She has been wounded because of
> American white society's transgressions and bruised by white iniquities. It
> appears that she may be the instrumentality through whom God will make
> us whole.[36]

Granted, Eichelberger's categories for God and woman are very traditional. Nevertheless, the significance of his thought is that he is able to conceive of the divine reality as other than a Black male messianic figure.

---

36. William Eichelberger, "Reflections on the Person and Personality of the Black Messiah," *The Black Church*, II, 54.

Even though Black women have been able to transcend some of the oppressive tendencies of White male (and Black male) articulated theologies, careful study reveals that some traditional symbols are inadequate for us today. The Christ understood as the stranger, the outcast, the hungry, the weak, and the poor makes the traditional male Christ (Black and White) less significant. Even our sisters of the past had some suspicions about the effects of a male image of the divine, for they did challenge the oppressive use of it in the church's theology. In so doing, they were able to move from a traditional oppressive Christology, with respect to women, to an egalitarian Christology. This kind of equalitarian Christology was operative in Jarena Lee's argument for the right of women to preach. She argued, ". . . the Saviour died for the woman as well as for the man."[37] The crucifixion was for universal salvation, not just for male salvation or, as we may extend the argument to include, not just for white salvation. Because of this, Christ came and died no less for the woman than for the man, no less for Blacks than for Whites. For Lee, this was not an academic issue, but one with practical ramification.

> If the man may preach, because the Savior died for him, why not the woman? Seeing he died for her also. Is he not a whole Saviour, instead of half one? as those who hold it wrong for a woman to preach, would seem to make it appear.[38]

Lee correctly perceives that there is an ontological issue at stake. If Jesus Christ were a Saviour of men, then it is true the maleness of Christ would be paramount.[39] But if Christ is a Saviour of all, then it is the humanity — the wholeness — of Christ which is significant.

Sojourner was aware of the same tendency of some scholars and church leaders to link the maleness of Jesus and the sin of Eve with the status of women, and she challenged this notion in her famed speech "Ain't I A Woman?"

> Then that little man in black there, he says women can't have as much rights as men, 'cause Christ wasn't a woman! Where did your Christ come from? From God and a woman. Man had nothing to do with Him.
>
> If the first woman God ever made was strong enough to turn the world upside down alone, these women together ought to be able to turn it back, and get it right side up again! And now they is asking to do it, the men better let them.[40]

---

37. Jarena Lee, *The Life and Religious Experiences and Journal of Mrs. Jarena Lee: A Colored Lady Giving an Account of Her Call to Preach* (Philadelphia, PA: n.p., 1836), 15-16.

38. Ibid., 16.

39. There is no evidence to suggest that Black women debated the significance of the maleness of Jesus. The fact is that Jesus Christ was a real, crucial figure in their lives. However, recent feminist scholarship has been important in showing the relation between the maleness of Christ and the oppression of women.

40. Truth, "Ain't I A Woman," in *Feminism,* ed. Schneir, 94.

I would argue, as suggested by both Lee and Sojourner, that the significance of Christ is not his maleness, but his humanity. The most significant events of Jesus Christ were the life and ministry, the crucifixion, and the resurrection. The significance of these events, in one sense, is that in them the absolute becomes concrete. God becomes concrete not only in the man Jesus, for he was crucified, but in the lives of those who will accept the challenge of the risen Saviour — the Christ. For Lee, this meant that women could preach; for Sojourner, it meant that women could possibly save the world; for me, it means today, this Christ, found in the experience of Black women, is a Black woman.

VII. Conclusion

I have argued that Black women's tri-dimensional reality provides a fertile context for articulating a theological perspective which is wholistic in scope and liberating in nature. The theology is potentially wholistic because the experience out of which it emerges is totally interconnected with other experiences. It is potentially liberating because it rests not on a single issue which could be considered only a middle-class issue relevant to one group of people, but it is multi-faceted. Thus, the possibility for wholistic theology is more likely. Feminist theology as presently developed is limited by virtue of the experience base for Feminist theology. That is, when feminists say that experience is the crucible for doing [Feminist] theology, they usually mean White women's experience. With few exceptions, feminist thinkers do their analysis primarily, and in some circles exclusively, based on the notion that because sexism is the longest and most universal form of oppression, it should claim priority.[41]

Black women, by and large, have not held this assumption. Many have claimed that because of the pervasiveness of racism, and because of its defining character for black life in general, racism is most important. Though Sojourner Truth never did develop a sophisticated social analysis, she was aware of the fact that she (and her people) was poor because she was black, and perhaps poorer because she was woman. I say "perhaps" simply because in the slave economy one could argue that there was relatively little distinction between the property status of slaves by virtue of gender; women were no less property than men. As property, they were part of the material distributed, rather than participants in the inequitable (system of) material distribution. Thus, as indicated above in the black woman's prayer, material possessions of blacks were limited. In a sense one could say that by virtue of one's race, one was slave and by virtue of that status one was poor.

41. This question is explored further in Jacquelyn Grant, "The Development and Limitation of Feminist Theology: Toward an engagement of black women's religious experience and white women's religious experience" (Ph.D. diss., Union Theological Seminary, New York, 1985).

Still, as we see the issues today, class distinctions which have emerged even in the Black community, and sex differences, which have taken on new forms of institutionalization, must be addressed. For liberation to become a reality, race, sex and class must be deliberately confronted. Interconnected as they are, they all impinge greatly on the lives of black women. Overwhelming as are these realities, black women do not feel defeated. For, as Jarena Lee observed, the hope of the struggle is based on the faith that Jesus died (and was raised) for the woman as well as the man. This realization gave inspiration for the struggle. Black women today inside and outside of the church still bring an optimistic spirit, as reflected in the conclusion of Maya Angelou's poem "Still I Rise":

> Out of the hut of history's shame
> I rise
> Up from a past that's rooted in pain
> I rise
> I'm a Black ocean, leaping and wide,
> Welling and swelling, I bear in the tide
> Leaving behind nights of terror and fear
> I rise
> Into a daybreak that's wondrously clear
> I rise
> Bringing the gifts that my ancestors gave
> I am the dream and the hope of the slave.
> I rise.
> I rise.
> I rise.[42]

42. Maya Angelou, *And Still I Rise* (New York: Random House, 1978), 42.

Christological Trends in Contemporary African Theology

JOHN ONAIYEKAN

Introduction

Perhaps the first attempt at Christology is in the incident mentioned in all the synoptic Gospels and in a most developed form in Matthew's Gospel (Mt. 16:13-20): "But you, who do you say I am?" This is the basic question to which every Christology must address itself. Belief in and commitment to Christ is a response to God's gracious call, which is in itself grace. The formulation of what this faith and commitment means to the Christian does not come naturally. It requires an effort of reflection. As the Gospel story shows, it is relatively easy to report what others are saying about Jesus. It is much more difficult to confess in all honesty what one really believes Him to be. Only Peter ventured an answer, and even that did not come to him through "flesh and blood" (Mt. 16:17).

In this paper, we shall try to give a brief survey of what some of our colleagues in the African Church have published as their attempt to document, analyse and synthesise what our people are saying and thinking about Jesus Christ, whom they have accepted as Lord and God.

Part I: General Characteristics of Christology in Africa

In his contribution to a collection of essays published in 1968[1] Mbiti felt he had to apologize for the title he gave to his essay: "Some African Concepts

---

1. John S. Mbiti, "Some African Concepts of Christology," in George F. Vicedom, ed., *Christ and the Younger Churches* (London, 1972), 51-62.

Reprinted from *The Nigerian Journal of Theology* 1/6 (May 1991): 11-27.

of Christology."[2] The title, he thought, was misleading "because African concepts of Christology do not exist." I do not know what he would say today after over twenty years. Perhaps if one were looking for a long list of heavy books on African Christology, one would almost say that not much has changed since 1968. But if one understands Christology as the effort to express what Christ means, then there were indeed "African concepts of Christology" even in 1968 — as Mbiti's beautiful essay actually went ahead to demonstrate. Since then, progress has been made, and efforts have been made by others after Mbiti to document this progress.[3] To be able to appreciate this progress, one needs to be familiar with some general characteristics of the Christological enterprise in Africa. We shall mention five; there may be more.

0.1 Christ as Centre

If it is true that Christology is at the very heart of all Christian theology,[4] it is particularly true for African Christian theology. It is by now generally agreed by most students of African traditional religions that our peoples have always had a clear idea of and firm belief in the Supreme Being. They have a faith in God which is indigenous and cannot be attributed to foreign influences, whether Christian or Islamic. In this regard, Africa is similar to the Jewish world to which Jesus presented Himself. Although the popular slogan "Jesus is the Answer" may be true in many ways, it is also true to say that "Jesus is *the* question." Kibicho spoke of the "radical continuity . . . of the African conception of God into and through Christianity."[5] If there is a radical discontinuity in the acceptance of the Christian faith, as indeed there must be, this is to be found in the Person of the Lord Jesus.

From the foregoing, we infer that most of what we call "African Theology" really boils down to Christology from an African perspective.

2. Mbiti, in *Christ and the Younger Churches,* 51.

3. For other attempts to survey Christological trends in African theology, see P. Stadler, "Approaches Christologiques en Afrique," in *BTA,* V (1983), 35-49; F. Kabasele, J. Dore, and R. Luneau, eds., *Chemins de la Christologie Africaine* (Paris, 1986), hereafter cited as *Chemins . . .*; R. Moloney, "African Christology," in *TS* 48 (1987): 505-15.

4. G. O'Collins, *What Are They Saying about Jesus?* (New York, 1977), 29.

5. S. G. Kibicho, "The Continuity of the African Concept of God into and through Christianity. A Kikuyu Case Study," in E. Fashole-Luke, et al., eds., *Christianity in Independent Africa* (Ibadan, 1978), 370-88. See p. 371.

0.2 Christological Trends or Christology

As a corollary to the above point, we find that in African theology, we are very often dealing with "Christological trends" and rather rarely with Christology as such. It may be because of our relative youth in the Christian faith and the fact that Christian theology at least in sub-Saharan Africa is still in its beginnings.[6] But it may also be due to the fact that we tend to concern ourselves with life issues considered in a global approach. There is therefore not much concern to respect the compartmentalization which has become characteristic of classical Christian theology. I think here we are closer to the approach of the early Church Fathers, whose theology was generally directed to concrete issues.

0.3 A Richness of Trends

There is a wide variety of trends in African Christology, sometimes even in the same person. This variety is also a richness. The diversity of *cultural background* of the African Christian often results in different ways of understanding and presenting the mystery of God Incarnate. For example, while in Central and East Africa Bantu culture the ancestors seem to play a predominant role in religion, in the Bight of Benin, the Yorubas and related peoples lay much emphasis on the divinities and spirits.

There is a diversity of socio-political climate in Africa, and this is reflected in the different attempts at Christology. Those engrossed in wars of political liberation in Southern Africa often see and present Christ from the point of view of the oppressed looking for a Liberator. Their counterparts in nations where the major preoccupation seems to be to rediscover and promote a lost cultural identity tend to have a more "poetic" portrait of Jesus based on cultural images.

Another source of diversity is the influence of the different Christian traditions through which the African came to know Christ. Thus, Catholics find it easier than evangelical Protestants to make Christian sense out of African rituals and symbolic cult objects like statues, images and amulets. The same goes for the whole area of sacrifice. From this combination of diversities in African cultural background, in socio-political circumstances, and in different Christian traditions, a wide range of trends emerges.

---

6. Here we are not counting the ancient African Church Fathers such as St. Augustine and St. Cyprian.

0.4 Specifically African and Universally Christian

There is the tendency for people to be looking for and demanding from the African Church a Christology that is "specifically African." There is also often the temptation on the part of African theologians to try to meet such expectations, as if we need to prove that "we too have our own theology." The inordinate pursuit of "originality" can be merely the result of an inferiority complex.

We are happy and proud of whatever in our culture is [a] specific contribution to the richness of a constantly growing Christian theology. But what is specifically African in our theology may not necessarily be what is most important in the life of the African Christian. The African Christian is first of all a human being and a member of the one Church of Christ.

It is therefore important to keep in mind that even though we may have some African ways of expressing what Christ means to us, it is still the same Jesus of Nazareth that we are confessing, within the context of the common Christian theological patrimony.

0.5 Professional and Popular Christology

A final general characteristic of Christology in Africa, valid for African Christian theology in general, is its concern to bridge the gap between the speculations of the professional theologians and the popular understanding of the ordinary faithful. It is sometimes said that the intellectual is often a generation or two ahead of his contemporaries.[7] But if the theologian is to fulfill the mission of clarifying and documenting the faith of the community, he cannot afford the luxury of writing for himself and his professional colleagues alone, leaving the people behind, like a locomotive detached from the train.

What the African is saying about Christ is not to be found only in the books and articles published by the few who have the time and facilities for such literary expressions. We must, in characteristic African fashion, listen to the oral expressions of the people: their hymns, sermons, and proverbs.[8] I have heard some of the most profound Christological insights from the mouths of poor illiterates, rich in nothing but their deep faith in Christ. It is my belief that the African theologian must count among his primary tasks the effort to listen to, and speak on behalf of our people as they express their life in Christ in the daily circumstances of their lives.[9]

---

7. Sometimes this is seen as the prophetic role of the intellectual who sees ahead of others.

8. On what I called "silent theology" in Africa, see J. Onaiyekan, "Nigerian Theology: Preliminary Questions," in *The Nigerian Journal of Theology* 1 (1985): 1-20. See p. 7.

9. For an example of such a "Village Christology," see E. J. Penoukou, "Christologie ou Village," in *Chemins*, 69-106.

Part II: Main Trends in African Christology

In his programmatic essay on African concepts of Christology referred to already, Mbiti suggests that the task of Christology must take into account four rich sources of material.

> These are: the Bible, the theology of older Churches, the traditional African concepts, and the living experiences of the Church in Africa.[10]

I have found these "four sources" a convenient framework for outlining the different ways in which African Christians reflect and speak about Jesus. Although the framework is basically methodological, we shall try to use it to bring out not only *how* but also *what* African Christians are saying about their Lord and God.

1. The Bible

In line with the perennial tradition of the Church, the Fathers of the Second Vatican Council stressed the need for Scripture to be the "soul of theology."[11] If Christology is concerned with getting to know who Jesus is, Scripture is an indispensable gate of access to him. In Scripture, especially in the New Testament, we have "the essential data for any Christology."[12] This is true too of African Christology.

The New Testament is more than just raw materials for Christology. It tells a story as well as presenting doctrines about Christ.

1.1 The Story of Christ, especially as told in the Gospels, is received with great fascination. The average African Christian takes the story at its face value. He is quite at home with the stories of unusual events, be these apparitions, visions or miracles. They take it for granted that reality is best described by myths, and therefore would find demythologization a questionable enterprise. They seek for the historical Jesus — and are happy to find him in the Gospel stories.[13] Here was a real man, with a human history, a lineage well-documented in the Gospel genealogies, member of a tribe with illustrious ancestors. The most immediate picture of the Lord Jesus is precisely that of the Gospels, from miraculous conception to glorious ascension.

They are so attached to the historical Jesus that they often reject attempts to depict him as an African in painting or sculpture. They know that Jesus was

---

10. Mbiti, in *Christ and the Younger Churches*, 51.

11. Vatican II, *Dei Verbum* (On Divine Revelation), 24.

12. G. O'Collins, *Interpreting Jesus* (London, 1983), 13.

13. S. O. Abogunrin, "Le recherche moderne du Jesus historique et le Christianisme en Afrique," in *Journal Theologique d'Afrique* 1 (1980): 34.

not a Yoruba or Kikuyu. They know he was a Jew, and have accepted him in spite of that. Pilgrimage to the Holy Land is fascinating because it brings them close to the earthly realities of Jesus.

1.2 Biblical Christology: The New Testament gives us not only a story but also a theology. This is recognised even in the Gospels, as recent studies in redaction criticism have clearly shown. Behind the various titles given to Jesus, there is a Christology with deep roots in Israelite traditions.[14] Most of these titles also speak loudly to our people to the extent that they evoke familiar concepts in our traditional religious culture. Mbiti talks of varying degrees of relevance.[15] Examples of the most relevant ones are as follows:

1.2.1 Son of God: "God so loved the world that He gave His only Son . . ." (Jn 3:16). That God could have a son, and that this son was sent into the world on a mission makes good sense for a culture used to divinities with varying degrees of affinity to the Supreme Being.

1.2.2 Lord: God is recognised as having all authority. Earthly rulers must rule on behalf of God, which is why, in many tribes, the king has a bit of the divine in him. Christ is therefore easily accepted as the greatest of all Lords. Among the people of Kabba, one of the Yoruba tribes, the titular divinity of the Land, the Ebora, is also called "Oluwa," "Lord." Thus, he is invoked as "Oluwa l'oke" — "The Lord on the hills," a reference to the wooded hills on which his cult is celebrated. On accepting Christianity, Christ is invoked in similar circumstances as "Oluwa li sosi" — "The Lord in the Church." The Lord Jesus has replaced the titular divinity: the Lord of the traditional religion.

1.2.3 Saviour: Mbiti claims that "there are no parallels with the title of 'Saviour' in traditional African concepts."[16] This is hardly true of all Africans. The Yorubas do expect the divinities *(Orisha)* of which they are devotees to save them. In a worldview filled with dangers, visible and invisible, the quest for salvation is a primary preoccupation of religion.[17] Many have been converted to Christianity not by hearing the word of preaching but by experiencing salvation in Christ where the gods of the ancestors seem to have failed. And salvation is conceived in concrete terms: deliverance from sickness, rescue from danger, liberation from oppression, etc. The Yoruba word for Saviour is *Olugbala.* It has the connotation of someone who snatches me away to safety and survival. That is what Christ is to the believer.

I would agree with Mbiti, however, that when we consider Christ as Saviour in an eschatological perspective, he represents something new in African

---

14. P. Stadler, *BTA*, V, 43-44. See also Mbiti, in *Christ and the Younger Churches*, 58.

15. Mbiti, 58.

16. Mbiti, 60.

17. C. R. Gaba, "Man's Salvation: Its Nature and Meaning in African Traditional Religion," in Fashole-Luke, et al., eds., *Christianity.* For a detailed study of how this is handled in Independent Churches among the Annang of southeastern Nigeria, see K. Enang, *The African Experience of Salvation* (London).

religious perspective. We have no examples of the expectation of a future saviour who would bring paradise back on earth. But that fact only makes the idea of an eschatological Saviour all the more relevant. "This portrait of Jesus fits into the yearning and longing of our peoples, fulfilling something for which there has been no other known means of fulfillment."[18]

1.2.4 Redeemer: Jesus the Redeemer is welcomed as he who rescues us from the enslavement of the evil forces that surround us, and even from the shackles with which the demands of traditional religion often keep people captives. In Yoruba, the Redeemer is often translated *Oludanda,* "he who breaks the bonds of my captivity."

1.2.5 There are also the titles which strengthen faith by guaranteeing the reality of the earthly Jesus. *Son of David* presents him as descending from great ancestors. Everyone is proud of his or her ancestors, especially if they leave behind them records of greatness. *Jesus of Nazareth* identifies him with his birthplace. As a child, I remember that my aged father, in moments of great crisis, would invoke Jesus of Nazareth, as if to bring home the urgency of his entreaty.

1.2.6 There are other titles which, while being important in the New Testament, have little relevance in the African context. *"Son of Man"* is taken to mean no more than "human being." If it has any profound meaning from its Old Testament connections, this does not say much for the people. The *Messiah,* being a typically Jewish-oriented title, needs to be explained before it can be understood. Although *Christ* is a literal rendering of the Hebrew *Messiah,* "the anointed," it is hardly ever associated with Messiaship or anointment. It is significant that the Hausa do use in the liturgy the expression "Yesu Almasihu" for Jesus Christ.

The title "Almasihu" has the same root as the Hebrew "Messiah." But it is still unlikely that the ordinary Hausa Christian associates the title "Almasihu" with the concept of "the Anointed."

In most other languages, Christ is transliterated in different forms, and people would simply take the word as another name for Jesus. The situation is therefore, as in Latin, where no attempt is made to translate "Christos." This further makes the title theologically inaccessible.

2. The Theological Patrimony of the Church

There is a classical Christology built up as the result of intensive theological reflection, debate and controversies in the early centuries of the Church. It was a long and at times tortuous journey whose milestones are the great christological councils and their pronouncements. By the Council of Chalcedon (451) the main elements of this Christology had been put together.

18. Mbiti, *Christ and the Younger Churches,* 60.

Later theology has tried to make these basic doctrines relevant to the Church in each generation. Even today, the process continues also in the older churches.[19] The question is "What do these traditional formulations have to say to the African Church?"

2.1 The first thing to note is that for us, as for all Christians worldwide, these formulations are still considered valid reference points for our understanding of Jesus the Christ. What is taught in seminaries in the tract on Christology is basically this classical Christology. Our theology manuals are the same as those used in other continents. This is not just because we are too lazy to produce our own Christology; rather, we consider this classical Christology part of the common theological patrimony of the Church, of which we are full-fledged members.

It is not only theology students who are exposed to this "Christologia Communis." It reaches down to the grassroots through Catechetical materials based on these traditional formulations; and above all through the creed that is recited regularly as part of the liturgy. Thus, the ordinary African Christian is as familiar as his European counterpart with formulae like "true God and true Man," "One in Substance with the Father," "One Person [in] two natures," etc. The effort to explain these to the people through catechesis is not totally futile. A measure of success is achieved to break through the cultural barrier of these unfamiliar expressions.

2.2 But we must also admit that the cultural barrier is real. The philosophical background of the Chalcedonian formula is far removed from the world of the contemporary African. Even with the serious effort made to initiate theology students into the world of Greek philosophy, it is always a difficult task for the seminarian to grasp what these formulae are saying about Jesus.

The problem is greater still for the ordinary Christian. In most African languages, to translate the creed is a great problem. In Yoruba, for example, while the Apostles' Creed is easily understood, the Nicene Creed is not so straightforward. Some of its key concepts, such as "person," "substance," "nature," have no direct equivalents in our languages, and the translations have to make do with approximations which can be tragically misleading.

Let us take an example. The "homoousios" of the Nicene Creed comes out in Yoruba as "of the same character with the Father" — "character" in the sense of a person's behaviour or reputation, which is a good deal away from the "ousia" of the Greek Fathers.

2.3 But despite these difficulties, the validity of the traditional formulae is not denied. We see in them a precious link with the rest of the Christian Church today and in the past, while we continue in the effort to reformulate their content in the light of our context of life and culture.

---

19. See, e.g., G. O'Collins, *What Are They Saying about Jesus?* (New York, 1977), 1-12.

3. African Traditional Religious Concepts

The project of an African reformulation of Christology looks in two broad directions:

a. African traditional culture
b. Contemporary African realities.

We have to take both together, otherwise one may fall into one of two extremes: extreme "culturalism" on the one hand, and extreme "economism" on the other.[20] First let us look at the cultural dimension. In this direction, we have seen many tentative efforts made to present Christ to Africans in the light of concepts with which they are already familiar. We must add immediately that none of them claims to have found a comprehensive and perfect portrait of Jesus. They are like symbols and images which tell the story of those who understand the language. As an illustration of what is going on, let us look briefly at a few attempts.

3.1 Ancestor: This is a direction being explored by some African theologians, especially from East and Central Africa. It seems that in these parts, the veneration of ancestors plays a key role in traditional religious life. Christ is therefore presented as the greatest of all ancestors. In 1984, Nyamiti published a dense pamphlet with the significant title "Christ as Our Ancestor: Christology from an African Perspective."[21] According to him, ancestors are believed to acquire supernatural status and are therefore able to act as mediators between men and God. Because of their kinship with their descendants, they are concerned about their welfare. Jesus fulfills all that the Bantu expects of his Ancestors in an eminent degree, and can therefore be considered as an Ancestor, or perhaps more accurately as "our Brother Ancestor."[22] Bujo goes along the same line, from an ethical viewpoint. He describes Christ as "le proto-ancetre."[23] Earlier on, he had published an interesting study on the Bantu concept of ancestors, whom he describes as "these unknown saints" ("ces saints inconnus").[24] Kabaselé adds to the concept of ancestor that of "elder" in his study on the same matter. Milingo, the world-famous healer and former Archbishop of Luska, also has some beautiful things to say about "Jesus the Ancestor." But he is at pains to show that Jesus is the Ancestor of all mankind, and that his

20. The terminologies are from J. Dore, in his introduction to *Chemins,* 12.

21. C. Nyamiti, *Christ As Our Ancestor: Christology from an African Perspective* (Gwero, Zimbabwe, 1984).

22. C. Nyamiti, "The Mass as Divine and Ancestral Encounter between the Living and the Dead," in *African Christian Studies* (A.C.S.) 1 (1985): 25-48. See p. 33.

23. B. Bujo, "Pour une Ethique Africano — Christocentrique," in *BTA,* III (1981): 41-52. See esp. p. 43.

24. B. Bujo, "Nos Ancestres ces Saints Inconnus," in *BTA,* 1 (1979): 165-78.

position is nevertheless not incompatible with maintaining due regard for our family ancestors.

3.2 The Kinsman: Linked with the concept of Ancestor is that of Kinsman. Jesus, is "the firstborn of all creation" (Col. 1:15). We are reborn like him through the spirit. Born "of God Himself" (Jn. 1:13), we too become, like him, "children of God" and thus acquire the status of kinship with Jesus. The African kinship leads to a relationship of strong solidarity not only horizontally among living members, but also vertically with those who have gone before and those who will follow. The implications of this idea on Christian living in community are very demanding. All Christians are my kinsmen through Christ, the great Kinsman. This links up with such classical Christian doctrines as "the Body of Christ," "the Communion of Saints," and life "in Christ."

The roots of the concept of "Kinsman" as a theological image go deep into the Old Testament. Twice in the story of Jacob, in Gen. 31, v. 31 and v. 53, the God of the Patriarchs is called "Pahad Yishaq," a title which is generally translated as "The Fear of Isaac," that is, "the God whom Isaac fears." But Albright and some others after him, for example, the Jerusalem Bible, have suggested with solid reasons that this title could be translated as "the Kinsman of Isaac." If this rendering is accepted, then we have already in the Old Testament an ancient precedent for the use of Kinsman as an African Christological title.

3.3 The Chief: Taking as a point of departure the role of the chief in Bantu culture, Kabasélé has also tried to paint a portrait of "Christ comme Chef."[25] The Christ is a hero, very often son of a great Chief, strong, powerful, generous, and able to make peace within his domain. Christ is Lord, the "Chief of Chiefs," just as he is "King of kings and Lord of lords" (Rev. 19:16).

3.4 The Healer: Sickness and healing play such a great part in African religious feeling that some have suggested that the healing power of Jesus may be a most effective way of presenting him to the African mind. Thus, Kolié speaks of "Jesus Guerisseur."[26] On the one hand, sickness and healing are considered as coming from God or the spirits, among most Africans. On the other hand, the Gospels show Jesus as being constantly busy healing. His healing is also presented as a sign of salvation. To the blind man of Jericho, Jesus said: "Go: your faith has saved you" (Mk. 10:52). Thus, Christ the Healer is Saviour and Redeemer. The healing ministry must be an essential part of the Christian message in Africa. If not, many people will continue to lapse into pagan practices whenever their lives are in danger.

While Catholics and the so-called mainstream churches have a good record of a healing apostolate through hospitals and clinics, the African Pentecostal churches have always emphasized healing by direct intervention of Jesus the

25. F. Kabasélé, "Christ as Chief," in *Faces of Jesus in Africa*, ed. Robert J. Schreiter (Maryknoll, NY: Orbis Books, 1991), 103-15. See also Katende Cyovo, *Violà la nouvelle lune, dansons!*, Ceeba (Bandundu, 1977).

26. C. Kolié, "Jesus as Healer?," in *Faces of Jesus in Africa*, 124-50.

Healer. The recent charismatic renewal in our Church has brought miraculous healing into the forefront of Church attention. What is required now is to recognise the need for both expressions of Christ's power, healing and delivering, and to co-ordinate them in a wholistic approach to health and well-being.

3.5 The Master of Initiation: Bishop Sanon of Boukina Faso has taken us into the sacred groves of Bukinabe initiation ceremonies to make us discover an unusual portrait of Jesus as "Maitre d'Initiation." He shares with us the profound experience of going through a tribal initiation rite, highlighting the key role of the Master of Initiation. He pleads for a niche in the universal gallery of christological portraits for this "etranger tard venu." He explains what it means to say that Jesus is the Master of Initiation:

> It is to recognise in him, in our cultural context, the elder who guides towards perfection those who have been at the initiation rites; that is those who, with him, have taken the road to experience the invisible through what is visible, to meet God through man, to touch eternity through the symbol of the present life.[27]

We meet here African symbolism at its most profound. Bishop Sanon calls his portrait of Jesus as Master of Initiation, "a stranger late arrived." But in fact this portrait, which now seems unfamiliar to us, is neither a stranger nor a late arrival in the gallery of Christological portraits. Some of the Greek Fathers already spoke of Jesus as a "mystagogos," a title which derives from pagan Greek mystery religions and refers to the leader of the initiation rites. Thus, Gregory of Nazianzen calls Christ in his earthly ministry: "ho mystagogos ho anapheron eisepignosin aletheias" (the leader of initiation who leads into the knowledge of the truth). The reference here is clearly to Jn. 16:13.

3.6 Christ, the Great Orisha: May we be permitted to add a sixth and final model, this time from the Yoruba religious milieu. Yoruba traditional religion is almost exclusively concerned with the cult of the divinities called *Orisha*. They are as agents and servants of the Supreme Being *Olorun*, who is rarely a direct object of religious cult, though he is not by any means a remote God. Orisha is so much a characteristic of Yoruba religion that the followers of that religion are called *"Aborisa,"* that is, "worshippers of *Orisha.*" That the Orisha cults are still very much alive in far away South America among descendants of African slaves from the Yoruba cultural zone, especially in the Bahia area of Brazil, shows how deep-rooted and all-pervading the Orisha (heritage) can be.

Yoruba converts from traditional religion to Christianity often speak of giving up the *Orisha* in order to accept Jesus. This way of speaking points to two significant observations. First, it means that the convert perceives faith in

---

27. L. K. Sanon, *Le chant du "Sini": une approache du Projet madare de l'homme* (Abidjan: Institut Catholique de'Afrique de l'Ouest, 1982). See also A. T. Sanon, "Jesus, Master of Initiation," in *Faces of Jesus in Africa*, 85-102.

Jesus as being incompatible with the veneration of the *Orisha*. Second, it means that they see Jesus as taking the place of the *Orisha* in their spiritual lives. There is, however, never a question of conversion to a new God.

It is therefore possible to present Christ as the great and unique *Orisha*, superior to all others, to such an extent that faith in him makes attention to them redundant and useless. In this context, there is special sense in St. Paul's hymn to Christ as one who enjoys preeminence over:

> all things in heaven and on earth, everything visible and everything invisible, Thrones, Dominations, Sovereignties, powers (Col. 1:16).

3.7 Limits of Images: In the foregoing attempts to present Christ in African cultural colours, there is a constant recognition of the limits of our images. Christ is more than an Ancestor. He is our Kinsman; but he is so by choice, we by adoption. He is a Chief, who is also meek and humble of heart. His relationship with the Father is unique and different from that of any *Orisha* with the Supreme Being. Though he is a Healer, his healing miracles are only a sign of his power to restore human beings to perfect wholeness. Our images cannot say it all. But, nevertheless, they do say something which is often a good point of departure for a deeper encounter with Him who has no parallel in any culture.

4. Modern African Situation

One of the most serious criticisms against some attempts at African theology is that they are so concerned with the past cultures of Africa that they become irrelevant to our contemporary African needs and concerns. It is possible to end up in a sort of exotic archaeological theology, which may perhaps fascinate foreigners, but has nothing relevant to say to the day-to-day life of our Christians.

In the search for an African Christology, attention to the socio-political dimension helps to restore whatever balance is needed. Let us examine some lines of research.

4.1 *Jesus the Liberator:* The theme of Jesus as Liberator is not a monopoly of Latin American theologians alone. It has its own African version. But this is to be found mainly among the exponents of the "Black Theology" of Southern Africa. In these zones, the socio-political environment in which the black Christian lives is characterised by racial discrimination and economic oppression. The fact that the oppressor claims to be a Christian only sharpens the anguish and increases the dilemma.

The crying need is for freedom and dignity. It is intolerable to believe in a Jesus who would not be on the side of the struggle for justice and equality. The names in this area include Allan Boesak, Desmond Tutu, both from South Africa, and the Angolan Methodist Bishop De Carvalho. In the midst of the sharp racial confrontations in South Africa, there are still prophetic voices, like that of A. Moyo, who insists we must see Christ not only as a Liberator but also as a Reconciler. This was also the sense of the powerful intervention in the hall of the Roman Synod on the Laity in October 1987, by Bishop Napier, President of the South African Bishops' Conference. He spoke about rejecting the "conflicting agenda of violence and counter-violence."

In the recent new climate of liberation blowing through these zones, especially after the release of Nelson Mandela and the unbanning of the A.N.C., these voices of reconciliation and peace will become even more necessary if all South Africans are to enjoy lasting peace in true freedom.

4.2 Jesus of Justice and Peace: While in South Africa blacks have been living under an oppressive white minority regime, in the rest of Africa there is almost everywhere political independence under black rule. The promised land has, however, turned out *not* to be flowing with milk and honey. There is a serious crisis of leadership characterised by debilitating instability on the one hand and oppressive dictatorship on the other. Many contemporary African rulers, when it suits them, invoke Christian concepts to consolidate their power. We have had Redeemers, Saviours, Messiahs — Christological titles derived from the Christian faith, to which they pay only lip service. An image of Jesus as the King of Justice, peace and love will shed the light needed to expose and denounce all forms of "messianismes usurpe's." If the Latin Americans are pursuing their "Theology of Liberation," in most African nations there is a dire need for a "Theology of Justice and Peace."

We note here, by the way, that not only Christian political leaders manipulate religion for their selfish purposes. Islam, with its virtual identification of religion and politics, lends itself more naturally to such manipulation. In Nigeria, for example, many of those agitating and scheming for the Islamisation of public institutions are not doing so for the love of Allah — as their corrupt and wicked lifestyle clearly shows. Rather, it is part of the political game whereby they seek to acquire or preserve the privileged position which an Islamised state guarantees the Muslim politician. We know, as well as they themselves know, that even in an Islamic state, their lust for domination and exploitation will oppress Muslim masses as much as non-Muslims. This mask too must be exposed.

4.3 Jesus and the Religions: In Africa, Christians are living almost everywhere side by side with peoples of other faiths. These may be those who have retained or returned to the religion of our ancestors, or those who have embraced other non-Christian religions. Islam constitutes a particularly dynamic companion and serious rival. We can no longer hang on to an exclusive Christology developed by those who have not had our type of challenge and opportunity to experience living with people of other faiths. This experience has opened us to the richness of others. For most of us, the pagan is not a savage tribesman lost in some remote jungle. He is my friend, my brother, perhaps my father. The Muslim is not a distant Bedouin in a desert oasis. He is sometimes my sister, my brother-in-law, my next-door neighbour. In such circumstances, we are bound to re-interpret Christianity "away from Greco-European metaphysics . . . into more inclusiveness." Dialogue with others is no longer an option, but a necessity. Therefore, we have somehow to "make Christianity more open to the visions of God of other religions, thus making a fruitful and meaningful dialogue with them possible."

Our Christology must therefore emphasise the universal dimension of the Lordship of Jesus; not only that he is Lord of all, but that he is also the Lord *for all*. Our Christology must carry us beyond our little ghetto of Christianity, as we explore the implications of its dimensions of creation, incarnation and resurrection. Following the indications of Vatican II in *Gaudium et spes*, our present Pope has constantly insisted on the validity of the Christian message for all people, in their present predicament of fear and anxiety for the future. Whatever we do, we can no longer reduce Jesus to the status of a sectional hero, or a tribal titular divinity.

This is why we must reject as untenable the extreme positions of the Christian fundamentalists who condemn everyone but themselves to the realm of Satan. In their desire to affirm the Lord Jesus as their "personal Saviour," they end up reducing him to the level of a sect leader. Christ means more than Christianity. Christology has implications that go beyond the narrow limits of explicit Christianity.

5. Conclusion

In this essay, we have tried to give a general idea of how African Christians are thinking about Jesus. A large number of our peoples have received the gift of the Christian faith. In most cases there is palpable evidence of God's grace at work in the depth and extent of their positive response to Christ.

Christology, as a systematic exposition of how we understand the person of Jesus, is still at the beginning stages. We are familiar with a variety of portraits of Jesus; some from the biblical data, others from our common patrimony of Christian theology. But at the same time other portraits are emerging from our own African experience of culture and daily life in Christ.

If we have really met the Lord, we should be able to tell the world how we see him and what we believe about him. That is the task of an African Christology, in whose emergence the Nigerian theological community must be seen to be very active participants.

But even then, our primary objective is not to produce a beautiful Christological portrait for its own sake, but to be led into an ever more intimate knowledge and love of Jesus of Nazareth, our Lord and God.

The Relationship between the Risen Christ and the Material Universe

DENIS EDWARDS

In recent years a number of scientists have attempted to communicate a new understanding of the universe to the public.[1] One aspect of this new understanding is simply the size of the universe. We now know that our Sun is one of more than a hundred thousand million stars that make up our galaxy, the Milky Way. This galaxy is so wide that light, travelling at three hundred thousand kilometers a second, takes a hundred thousand years to cross it. Our Sun is a star of average size, situated about 30,000 light-years from the centre of the galaxy, near the edge of one of the spiral arms.

We have come to know that there are many galaxies far larger than the Milky Way. It is sobering to remember that it was only in 1924 that the American astronomer Edwin Hubble demonstrated that our galaxy was not the only one in the universe. Astronomers now tell us that the observable universe contains more than a hundred thousand million galaxies.

---

1. A significant example of a modern scientist reaching out to the general public is Stephen Hawking in his *A Brief History of Time: From the Big Bang to Black Holes* (London: Bantam Press, 1988). Another is Ilya Progogine. In their introduction to *Order out of Chaos* (London: Heinemann, 1984) Ilya Progogine and Isabelle Stengers write: "We must open new channels of communication between science and society. It is in this spirit that this book has been written." Paul Davies has written widely and clearly on recent developments in science. See, for example, his *God and the New Physics* (London: Penguin Books, 1983); *Superforce* (London: Heinemann, 1984); *The Cosmic Blueprint* (London: Unwin, 1987).

Reprinted with permission of the journal and the author from *Pacifica: Australian Theological Studies* 4 (1991): 1-14. These reflections are a revised version of a paper delivered at the 1990 meeting of the Australian Catholic Theological Association. The themes presented here have been developed further in the author's recent book *Jesus the Wisdom of God: An Ecological Theology* (Maryknoll, NY: Orbis Books, 1995).

Edwin Hubble also investigated the fact that the spectral lines of the light coming from distant galaxies are shifted to the red. He concluded that the light from these stars is "red-shifted" because they are moving away from us. This meant that the universe could no longer be understood as static. The distance between galaxies is growing all the time. We inhabit an expanding world. Stephen Hawking, a prominent theoretical physicist and the Lucasian Professor of Mathematics at Cambridge University, has said that "the discovery that the universe is expanding was one of the great intellectual revolutions of the twentieth century."[2]

The fact that the universe is expanding suggests that the expansion began from an extremely compressed and dense state. It supports the idea of an initial explosion. According to the most common scientific view, the universe had its beginning between 10,000 and 20,000 million years ago with a primeval explosion, known as the "big bang."

Science understands this explosion to be the origin not only of matter, but of space and time as well. Einstein's general theory of relativity argues that gravity is a distortion of both space and time. Time is inextricably linked to space. As space stretches, so does time. The expanding universe is not seen as matter exploding through space, so much as space-time itself stretching and inflating.

The discovery in 1965 of background microwave radiation throughout the universe has lent further support to the big bang theory over "steady state" and other theories of the universe. It is believed that this microwave radiation survives from the radiation era of the big bang, so that scientists can describe the universe filled with this radiation as "bathed in the afterglow of the big bang."[3]

The long process of formation of galaxies began as the great hydrogen clouds of the exploding universe began to coalesce and fall in upon themselves under the pull of gravitation. As temperatures rose because of gravitational forces, nuclear reactions ignited at the core of the nebulas, fueled by the conversion of hydrogen into helium. The first stars were born. About 5,000 million years ago our solar system had its origins as a huge cloud of swirling particles of dust and gas. Gravitational pressure eventually ignited the thermonuclear action of the Protosun. Rings of matter spun off from the nebula formed in individual units around the Sun, and their own forces of gravitation began to mold them into the spherical planets we know.

According to most scientists, our expanding universe faces a grim future. The most universal law of physics is the second law of thermodynamics, which tells us that within any isolated system disorder is always on the increase. Things moved towards a flat state of equilibrium. Usable energy is depleted. Things run down and wear out. Physicists describe the quantity of disorder in a system

2. Hawking, *A Brief History of Time*, 39.

3. Edward Harrison, *Cosmology: The Science of the Universe* (Cambridge: Cambridge University Press, 1981), 347. See also Robert Wagoner and Donald Goldsmith, *Cosmic Horizons: Understanding the Universe* (San Francisco: W. H. Freeman and Company, 1982); Jayant Narlikar, *The Structure of the Universe* (Oxford: Oxford University Press, 1977).

by the word *entropy*. Experiments show that the total entropy in an isolated system increases, but never decreases.

The consequences of the second law of thermodynamics for the whole universe are obvious enough. If the universe has a limited amount of accessible energy (order), and this is being constantly used up, then the universe will eventually die. This is known as the "heat death" of the universe, and it has been discussed by scientists for over a hundred years.

Modern astronomy can observe the birth and the death of stars. Eventually the fuel which powers the nuclear cycle of a star is used up, and the force of gravity causes it to collapse in upon itself. Some stars first expand into fiery "red giants," and then shrink and cool; they end up as black dwarf stars. Bigger stars, those which have a mass twice that of our Sun, die as spectacular supernovae, blowing themselves up brilliantly. They eventually become small, dense, neutron stars. Some of the truly massive dead stars continue to shrink at an escalating rate, ending up as black holes in space, places where gravity is so extreme that nothing, not even light, can get out.[4]

When we look at the larger system of the whole universe, it is not clear what the future will be. One scenario is that of the "open" universe. In this picture the universe will continue to expand, but it will run down and cool down. Galaxies will continue to move apart, but within themselves they will condense into giant black holes, which, as Stephen Hawking has explained, will eventually decay through radiation. All solid matter will disintegrate.[5]

But there is another possible outcome, that of the "closed" universe. In this scenario the expanding universe will slow down, and then gravity will take over and it will begin to reverse its motion and contract. Galaxies that are now moving apart will begin to move towards each other. The movement will be slow at first, but will accelerate over millions of years, becoming more and more intense, until the whole universe ends up in a "big crunch" which will echo the "big bang" of the beginning. The entire universe then "shrivels into less than the size of an atom whereupon space-time disintegrates."[6] Many physicists believe that this is the end of the physical universe: total annihilation in what is called a "singularity."

Science has not yet reached certainty about whether the universe will keep expanding or begin to contract. There is, at present, a near balance between the

---

4. This statement needs some qualification, since Stephen Hawking has combined general relativity and quantum mechanics to describe the existence of radiation from black holes. See *A Brief History of Time*, 99-113.

5. Paul Davies tells us that all the structures we now know, which are so full of splendour and activity, are destined to pass away. What will remain will be only "cold, dark, expanding, near-empty space, populated at an ever decreasing density by a few isolated neutrinos and photons, and very little else." He comments: "It is a scenario that many scientists find profoundly depressing." See *God and the New Physics*, 204.

6. Davies, *God and the New Physics*, 205.

forces of expansion and the forces of gravitation. It is, of course, precisely this balance which makes our galaxy, our solar system, and life on Earth possible.[7]

Science itself is undergoing enormous change. For three centuries it has been dominated by the Newtonian paradigm of the machine-like universe, and then by the thermodynamic paradigm of the degenerating universe. At present it is in the midst of a paradigm shift.[8] What is emerging has been called "the new paradigm of the creative universe."[9] This paradigm recognises the progressive and innovative capacity of nature. It studies the capacities of nonlinear systems to organise themselves and to break through to new and more complex structures.

The standard thermodynamic paradigm gives us a picture of a universe which begins with an extraordinary amount of order and then degenerates. The new paradigm sees creation as an ongoing process. The universe is capable of self-organisation: "Instead of sliding into featurelessness, it rises out of feature-lessness, growing rather than dying, developing new structures, processes and potentialities all the time, unfolding like a flower."[10]

It is not yet clear how this new work will influence our thinking about the "heat and death" of the universe. At the very least it raises the possibility of new and unforeseen creativity on the part of the cosmos.[11]

---

7. One of the crucial questions which science has yet to resolve is the gravity of the universe, which, of course, depends upon its density. Stephen Hawking says that the present evidence suggests "that the universe will probably expand forever, but all we can really be sure of is that even if the universe is going to recollapse, it won't do so for at least another ten thousand million years, since it has already been expanding for at least that long." Hawking has attempted to combine general relativity and quantum theory in a new working model of the universe. He proposes a model in which space-time is limited, but which has no boundaries. There would be no edge of space or time, no singularities, either at the beginning or the end of the world as we know it. He suggests that we think of the universe as a great globe, like the globe of the Earth. As there is no edge of the Earth at the North Pole, so there is no edge or boundary to the universe either at big bang or the end. In this model, and in all its complex mathematical underpinning, Hawking is attempting to describe the universe completely, including its beginning and its end, in terms of known laws of science. See *A Brief History of Time*, particularly 115-41. Hawking first presented these ideas at a conference on cosmology in the Vatican in 1981. At the very same conference where Hawking was attempting to do away with the necessity for divine intervention in the big bang, Pope John Paul II argued that it was beyond the capacity of science by itself to account for the beginning of the universe.

8. This paradigm shift is described in Ilya Progogine and Isabelle Stengers, *Order out of Chaos*.

9. Davies, *The Cosmic Blueprint*, 2.

10. Davies, *The Cosmic Blueprint*, 200. Arthur Peacocke has suggested that we might imagine entropy as a great stream of disorder. This stream generates within itself very large eddies, and within these eddies there is an increase in order and functional organisation. There would be no eddies without the stream. Perhaps, he suggests, the eddies are the very point to the stream of entropy. Peacock concludes his reflections with these words: "Thus does the apparently decaying, randomising tendency of the universe provide the necessary and essential matrix *(mot juste!)* for the birth of new forms — new life through death and decay of the old." Arthur Peacocke, *God and the New Biology* (London: Dent, 1986), 160.

11. Ilya Progogine and Isabelle Stengers suggest that we simply do not know enough to be sure about what will happen to the universe: "In spite of the important progress made by Hawking

A Theological View of the Material Universe

It must be admitted that according to much of science the long-term prospects of the universe are bleak. This creates a serious question for theology. John Macquarrie has said, "If it were shown that the universe is indeed headed for an all-enveloping death, then this might seem to constitute a state of affairs so wasteful and negative that it might be held to falsify Christian faith, and abolish Christian hope."[12]

I believe that, in fact, the scientific picture does not falsify Christian faith or abolish Christian hope. On the one hand, in scientific terms, we are only just at the very beginning of our understanding of principles of self-organization in small nonlinear systems here on Earth. It is obvious that a system as complex as the universe might yet hold many surprises in store for us.

On the other hand, in theological terms, it is important to note that the foundation of all Christian theology is the conviction that the God of Jesus Christ can and does bring life out of death. John Polkinghorne has suggested that we can see the predicted death of the universe as the cosmic counterpart to the fact that we human beings will certainly die. Just as we believe in the resurrection of the body we can believe in God's fulfillment for the material universe as well. God's power to save embraces not just humanity, but all of creation.[13]

Can we say more than this about our future, and the future of the material universe? Karl Rahner discusses the biblical promise of a "new heaven and a new Earth."[14] What this means, he says, is that the world is directed to a point which is not the end of its existence, but the end of its unfinished and continually developing history.[15]

He asks the question: Who can say how far this end is the very "running-itself-to-death" of the universe? Or is a halt to the expanding universe called by God's creative Word? This, then, raises the further question: To what extent can these two be understood as ultimately the same thing?[16]

What revelation makes clear is that the history of the world will come to an end, and this will not be a simple ending or annihilation, but the participation of the whole universe in the consummation and divinisation of conscious beings.

The material world is not something that becomes superfluous to spiritual beings in their eternal life in God. The human spirit is always a material,

---

and others, our knowledge of large-scale transformations in our universe remains inadequate." See *Order out of Chaos,* 117.

12. John Macquarrie, *Principles of Christian Theology* (London: SCM Press Ltd., 1977), 356.

13. John Polkinghorne, *Science and Creation: The Search for Understanding* (London: SPCK, 1988), 65.

14. "According to his promise we wait for new heavens and a new earth in which righteousness dwells" (2 Peter 3:13). See Isa. 65:17; 66:22; Rev. 21:1-5. See also the theme of the "new creation" (Gal. 6:15; 1 Cor. 7:31; 15:45-49; Rom. 5:15-19; 8:18-23; Col. 3:9; Eph. 2:15; 4:22).

15. See Karl Rahner, "The Resurrection of the Body," *Theological Investigations,* vol. 2 (London: Darton, Longman and Todd, 1963), 211.

16. Rahner, "The Resurrection of the Body," 212.

incarnate, inner-worldly spirit. It is always a spirit of the cosmos. It is always the cosmos come to consciousness. The resurrection of the body involves the consummation of cosmic history.

The end of the world must be understood as a participation of the world in the resurrection of Jesus Christ. His Second Coming takes place at the moment of the perfection of the universe, as the cosmos comes to share the reality which Jesus already possesses. Then the risen Jesus Christ will be revealed as the innermost secret of the world and its history, the victory hidden at the heart of cosmic history.

Christianity rejects any vision of the future which does not include the world of matter. The material world cannot be understood to be like a stage on which the drama of human relationship with the divine is played, so that when the play is over the players leave the stage dead and empty and abandoned.[17] Nor can matter be thought of as simply a "launching pad" which will become unnecessary in a further spiritual state of existence. On the contrary, the material world will still be the expression of human spirit, and will participate in the final glorified state of this spirit.[18]

We cannot imagine the how of this bodily and cosmic transformation. Rahner notes that modern physics presents us with many concepts which are beyond imagination, and suggests that this may help us cope with theological ideas which escape imagination. Even though we cannot imagine it, the cosmos will share in the consummation of the kingdom of God.[19]

Rahner writes that we Christians are "more clearly materialistic than those who call themselves so." In his view we are the "most sublime of materialists" because we cannot think of any ultimate fulfillment of the human spirit without thinking at the same time of matter enduring and reaching its perfection.[20]

Because matter itself is to be taken up into the final consummation of all things in God, Rahner is not prepared to agree with those scientists who would have the whole material world simply disappear into nothingness through a gravitational collapse. Of course, science can rightly consider various possible ways in which the "heat death" of the universe might occur. But science cannot rule on a transformed resurrection life for the dead, nor on the future of the material universe transformed from within by the power of God.

17. Karl Rahner, "Christianity and the 'New Man,' " *Theological Investigations*, vol. 5 (London: Darton, Longman and Todd, 1966), 147.

18. Rahner, "Christianity and the 'New Man,' " 148.

19. In some ways this has already begun, because God is already at work as a dynamic power at the heart of creation. Rahner can say: "It is no mere pious lyricism when Dante regards even the sun and the other planets as being moved by that love which is God himself as he who bestows himself. The innermost principle of this self-movement of the sun and the other planets towards their consummation, which lies concealed in the incomprehensibility of God as the absolute future, is God himself." See Karl Rahner, "Immanent and Transcendent Consummation of the World," *Theological Investigations*, vol. 11 (London: Darton, Longman and Todd, 1974), 289.

20. Karl Rahner, "The Festival of the Future of the World," *Theological Investigations*, vol. 7 (London: Darton, Longman and Todd, 1971), 183.

Christian optimism about the future of matter does not exclude negativity, violence, suffering or increased entropy. All these are already part of our evolutionary history, and they will be part of the future evolution of the universe. In this evolutionary history, we must be prepared to allow for "surprises, defective developments, dead ends," and even for "a total halt to progress as such."[21]

Christian faith claims that these will not be the last words, any more than the apparent failure of Jesus, and his death on the cross, were the end of him and his mission. Christian faith, in the face of all pessimism about the future of matter, affirms that, through God's gracious relationship with bodily human beings, our evolving world can and will arrive at immediacy with God. It affirms that even now it has begun an irreversible stage of its history.

Jesus Christ is God's irrevocable promise of salvation within the evolving cosmos. In the light of Jesus, and God's promise given in him, Christian theology knows that final catastrophe, and a total halt to progress, are not the future of the unfolding universe. The final goal of evolutionary history for free bodily human beings is intimacy with God, and this future is shared by the whole created cosmos.

The Risen Christ and the Cosmos — Taking Rahner a Little Further

What is the relationship between the risen Christ and the expanding universe? It seems to me that, at this critical point, Rahner's theology is not as developed as it might be.[22] He has worked out an evolutionary theology in which God is understood as a dynamic power acting from within creatures, enabling evolutionary change to occur through the process of active self-transcendence. He has developed a Christology in which Jesus of Nazareth is understood as the self-transcendence of the cosmos into God, and as God's definitive self-communication to the cosmos. But in his major systematic works, Rahner leaves the relationship between the risen Christ and the cosmos unexplored.

There are some undeveloped references to this issue in Rahner's writing on the resurrection, and some poetic insights concerning the cosmic role of the risen Christ which appear in unexpected places. It is to two of these that I turn now.

---

21. Karl Rahner, "Natural Science and Reasonable Faith," *Theological Investigations,* vol. 21 (London: Darton, Longman and Todd, 1988), 55.

22. Before Rahner published his evolutionary Christology, Teilhard de Chardin had already developed his synthesis focused on the risen Christ as the Omega Point of cosmic history. Teilhard's work was built upon a complex mixture of scientific argument, extrapolation from the evidence of our evolutionary past to build a picture of a converging future, and Christian revelation. Rahner mentions Teilhard's works a number of times, and acknowledges some similarities, but notes that, unlike Teilhard, he writes only as a theologian, using only the common ground available to all theologians. See Karl Rahner, "Christology Within an Evolutionary View of the World," *Theological Investigations,* vol. 17 (London: Darton, Longman and Todd, 1981), 218; and *Foundations of Christian Faith* (New York: Seabury Press, 1978), 180.

In his book *On the Theology of Death* Rahner reflects on the connection between the death and resurrection of Jesus and the material universe. He writes: "When the vessel of his body was shattered in death, Christ was poured out over the cosmos: he became actually, in his very humanity, what he had always been in his dignity, the very centre of creation."[23] This strikes me as a rich and important theme that needs to be developed. How is the risen Christ, "in his very humanity," the centre of creation?

In this book Rahner writes that Jesus in his death, understood as a culmination of his whole life, becomes open to the whole of cosmic reality. Jesus Christ becomes a permanent ontological determination of the whole of cosmic reality. The risen Christ influences and shapes the very being of the material universe. Rahner comments that this might be a way to understand the meaning of the descent into hell, the lower world of Sheol. The salvific reality of Christ, which is consummated in death, is built into the unity of the universe, so that the world is a radically different place from what it would have been if Christ had not died.[24]

This human being, Jesus of Nazareth, who is truly of the Earth, truly part of the biological evolution of the universe, has become, in his humanity, the very centre of creation. Jesus Christ in his life and death, in his grace-filled human reality, has become a power shaping the whole cosmos.

Another place in which Rahner expresses some of his convictions about the relationship between the risen Christ and cosmic reality is in one of his meditative writings on Holy Saturday. Here the risen Christ is described as the victory hidden in all cosmic reality, at the heart and centre of the Earth, which Rahner calls "our mother":

> Christ is already at the heart and centre of all the poor things of this earth, which we cannot do without because the earth is our mother. He is present in the blind hope of all creatures who, without knowing it, are striving to participate in the glorification of his body. He is present in the history of the earth, whose blind course he steers with unearthly accuracy through all victories and all defeats onwards to the day predestined for it, to the day on which his glory will break out of its own depths to transform all things. He is present in all tears and every death as the hidden joy and the life which conquers by seeming to die. . . . He is there as . . . the most secret law of a movement which still triumphs and imposes its authority even when every kind of order seems to be breaking up. He is there as the light of day and the air are with us, which we do not notice; as the secret law of a movement that we do not comprehend because that part of the movement which we ourselves experience is too brief for us to infer from it the pattern of the movement as a whole. But he is there, the heart of this earthly movement and the secret seal of its eternal validity. He is risen.[25]

23. Karl Rahner, *On the Theology of Death* (New York: Herder and Herder, 1961), 66.
24. Rahner, *On the Theology of Death*, 65.
25. Karl Rahner, "Hidden Victory," *Theological Investigations*, vol. 7, 157-58.

In these extracts Rahner expresses two fundamental theological insights: first, through his death and resurrection, Jesus Christ, in his grace-filled *human* reality, has become a power shaping the cosmos; second, the risen Christ is the victory hidden in all cosmic reality, drawing it towards its consummation. It is these two insights that I will attempt to take a little further.

The Cosmic Role of the Humanity of Jesus

In his writings on the resurrection, Rahner has suggested a line of thought on the enduring role of the humanity of Christ.[26] He recalls the view of Thomas Aquinas that the glorified humanity of Jesus is the "efficient instrumental cause" of our salvation and our resurrection.[27] According to this view our relationship with God, both in this life through grace, and in eternal life through glory, occurs only through the humanity of Jesus.

Rahner notes that this opinion has been the occasion of some controversy. Nevertheless, he believes that a contemporary theology needs to retain and develop the idea that the humanity of Jesus has an enduring role in our relationship with God.

In 1953, Rahner wrote an article, "The Eternal Significance of the Humanity of Jesus for Our Relationship with God."[28] He began this article by asking the broad question: In our relationship with God, are we simply taken up into the blazing abyss of God, so that all creatures, including Mary mother of Jesus and the Saints, and even the humanity of Jesus, become inconsequential?

Rahner's answer is a complete rejection of the idea that in seeking the absolute reality of God we can despise or reject the limited, finite reality of creatures. We are not called to relate to a God without a world. The only God we know is God-with-a-world. Our God is a God of unconditional love of created reality. To love this God we must also love what this God loves. We are called to love this created world as God loves it. This world of creatures is "divinely and religiously significant before God."[29]

This is the context in which Rahner considers the more particular issue of the humanity of Christ. Here God's relationship with creation reaches its climax. Rahner argues that the humanity of Jesus is always and everywhere our way to God. He writes of Jesus: "this created human nature is the indispensable

26. See Rahner's article "Resurrection: D. Theology," in *Sacramentum Mundi: An Encyclopedia of Theology,* vol. 5 (New York: Herder and Herder, 1970), 332-33; and "Dogmatic Questions on Easter," *Theological Investigations,* vol. 4 (London: Darton, Longman and Todd, 1966), 124-26, 132-33.

27. See Thomas Aquinas, *Summa Theologiae,* 3, 56, 1 ad 3.

28. Karl Rahner, "The Eternal Significance of the Humanity of Christ for Our Relationship with God," *Theological Investigations,* vol. 3 (London: Darton, Longman and Todd, 1967), 35-46.

29. Rahner, "The Eternal Significance of the Humanity of Christ," 41.

and permanent gateway through which everything created must pass if it is to
find the perfection of its eternal validity before God."[30] Jesus is "the gate and
the door, the Alpha and the Omega."

Our union with God occurs not through some purely mystical flights into
the absolute, but through Jesus of Nazareth. We meet God in and through "this
finite concrete being, this contingent being, who remains in all eternity."[31] The
human reality of Jesus, continuing to exist forever as the reality of the Word of
God, has eternal significance for salvation. Jesus is now and forever the permanent openness of finite created being to the living God.

God's grace is forever mediated to men and women through the human
reality of Jesus Christ. He is the permanent mediator of salvation. All our
religious acts go through the humanity of Christ to God. Human experience of
God's grace is always experience of the risen Christ. Both our acts of worship
towards God and God's self-giving to us are mediated by the Word made flesh.

In Rahner's writing on the resurrection, there is a suggestion that this
concept might be applied not just to human salvation, but to the cosmos itself.
He writes that the resurrection is "the beginning of the transformation of the
world," and "in this beginning the destiny of the world is already in principle
decided and has already begun."[32]

He holds that there is an intrinsic and ontological connection between
the resurrection of Jesus and the renewal of the world, so that Jesus can be
understood as the "pledge and beginning of the perfect fulfillment of the world,"
and as the "representative of the new cosmos."[33] The world is such a unity,
physically, spiritually and morally, that the death and resurrection of Jesus, who
is a biological part of this material world, must be understood as "the irreversible
and embryonically final beginning of the glorification and divinisation of the
whole reality."[34]

The risen Christ, freed from the limits of bodily existence in this life, is
present to the whole world in a new bodily relationship in and through the
resurrection. Jesus, in his bodily humanity, is a permanent part of this one world
and its evolutionary dynamism. His resurrection is the beginning of the transfiguration of the world.[35]

There are three important principles at work in Rahner's theology which
can be brought together at this point: first, the understanding that our relationship with God is permanently mediated through the humanity of Christ; secondly, the conviction that God's relationship with human beings is always also
a relationship with the whole cosmos in and through human beings, who are

30. Rahner, "The Eternal Significance of the Humanity of Christ," 43.
31. Rahner, "The Eternal Significance of the Humanity of Christ," 44.
32. Rahner, "Resurrection: D. Theology," 333.
33. Rahner, "Resurrection: D. Theology," 333.
34. Rahner, "Dogmatic Questions on Easter," 129.
35. Rahner, "Resurrection: D. Theology," 333.

the cosmos come to self-awareness; thirdly, the concept that the whole cosmos forms a unity with the risen Jesus, so that his resurrection is the beginning of the divinisation of the world.

When these three principles are brought together in this way, they provide the basis for a further theological assertion: the humanity of Jesus is eternally significant, not just for God's relationship with human beings, but for God's action at the heart of cosmic and evolutionary history.

Not only is it true that the humanity of Jesus is eternally significant for our salvation, this same humanity of Jesus is eternally significant for the whole created universe. Jesus, like us a child of the cosmos, is God's instrument in the transformation of the whole cosmos.

The historically limited and particular Jesus, now risen from the dead, has become the means of transfiguration of the universe. The final consummation of matter will take place in and through the concrete and specific humanity of the glorified and risen Jesus. Already our evolving and self-organizing universe is empowered from within by resurrection life, in and through the humanity of the risen Christ.

The Risen Christ as the Dynamism at the Heart of the Cosmos

It is one thing to affirm that cosmic and evolutionary history are linked to the humanity of the risen Christ, it is another to attempt to show more clearly *how* the risen Christ is connected to the expanding universe and the whole world of matter. There is a further systematic link that needs to be made between the risen Christ and evolutionary history.

Rahner does not make this connection explicit, although it is implicit in his system. It can be made through linking together our understanding of the risen Christ with the theology, which Rahner has already developed, of God as the power of self-transcendence at the heart of the cosmos.

The link can be made simply enough. It depends upon the unity in Christ of divine and human natures. The classic Christian doctrine of the two natures in the one person means, of course, that we must understand the risen Jesus Christ as consubstantial with the dynamic, absolute being of God.

But, as Rahner has demonstrated, this dynamic and absolute being of God is the power of self-transcendence at the heart of the universe. It is this very divine nature which empowers the evolutionary movement from within. The divine nature of Jesus Christ is precisely the same divine nature which is creatively at work in all cosmic history, as the power of self-transcendence acting from within creation. The risen Christ is radically and permanently one with the absolute being which empowers the universe. Jesus the Jew, born of Mary, like us forged from stardust, is truly the cosmic Christ.

The mainstream Christian tradition has always taught that creation is the work of the whole Trinity. Thomas Aquinas tells us that creation must be understood as the work of the divine essence, common to all three divine persons.[36] This is consistent with the theological and doctrinal principle concerning God's efficient causality with regard to the world, which states that the three persons of the Trinity form one principle of divine action *ad extra*. The whole Trinity, then, must be understood as involved in the work of creation.[37]

This does not deny that the inner structures of the divine act of creation are trinitarian. Aquinas goes on to point out how each of the Trinity relates to creation distinctively, in accordance with the trinitarian processions. He explains this by way of an example taken from the workplace. As a person engaged in a craft works from an idea in the mind, and from love in the will, so God creates through the Word and through Love. God the Father creates through the Word and in the Spirit. The press of the divine from within creation is trinitarian.

In his evolutionary theology Karl Rahner has transformed the theological understanding of God's creative action. He has shown how it can be understood as the impulse of the divine from within the evolving universe. This divine impulse, this press of God at the heart of the universe, must be understood, then, as the work of the divine essence of God. It is the work of the whole Trinity. It is therefore the work of the Word.

The Second Person of the Trinity, the Wisdom of God, the Word of God, the One in whom all things were created, the One in whom all will be redeemed and made new, is at the heart of the evolutionary movement of the planet, and the story of the expanding universe. The dynamism from within creation occurs in and through the Word.

Jesus Christ, the Word made flesh, is not simply the self-transcendence of the universe into God, and God's self-communication to the world. He is not simply the One in whom all things were created. Nor is this Jesus simply the pledge of God's future for all creation. He is not simply the One who is to come. We can go further and make the assertion: Jesus of Nazareth, risen from the dead, is one with the dynamic power at the heart of cosmic processes. The press of the divine from within creation, which springs from the One who is unbegotten generativity, and occurs in the life-giving Spirit, takes place now and always in and through the risen Christ, the Liberator and Saviour of the material universe.

We are told at the beginning of John's Gospel that the Word was with God at the beginning, and through this Word all things were created (John 1:2-3). The press of the divine being from within creation was always directed towards the Word made flesh. In the event of incarnation, this dynamic creative power

36. Thomas Aquinas, *Summa Theologiae*, 1.45.6.
37. On these issues see Leo Scheffczyk, *Creation and Providence* (New York: Herder and Herder, 1970), 145-53; Michael Schmaus, *God and Creation* (London: Sheed and Ward, 1969), 84-97.

of divine being is radically united with a specific human being, and through this human being with all of creation.

In the resurrection, Jesus of Nazareth becomes the Cosmic Christ. The risen Christ is the power of the divine at the heart of the creation, but this divine power is now mediated through the humanity of Jesus, the firstfruits of the new creation. A sentence of Rahner's which I have already mentioned, perfectly captures these ideas: "When the vessel of his body was shattered in death, Christ was poured out over all the cosmos; he became actually, in his very humanity, what he had always been in his dignity, the innermost centre of creation."[38]

This theology of the cosmic Christ attempts to capture the decisive meaning of Jesus for a new time and a new cosmology. It strives to remain faithful to the insights of the New Testament hymns, which did the same thing for a different time and a different cosmology. They expressed with great power the conviction of the early church that all things were created in Jesus of Nazareth, and that all creation was to be caught up in the resurrection:

> He is the image of the invisible God,
> the first-born of all creation;
> for in him all things were created,
> in heaven and on earth,
> visible and invisible,
> whether thrones or dominions or principalities or authorities —
> all things were created through him and for him.
> He is before all things,
> and in him all things hold together.
> He is the head of the body, the church;
> he is the beginning,
> first-born from the dead,
> that in everything he might be pre-eminent.
> For in him all the fullness of God was pleased to dwell,
> and through him to reconcile to himself all things,
> whether on earth or in heaven,
> making peace by the blood of the cross.[39]

---

38. Rahner, *On the Theology of Death*, 66. Some of the ideas developed in this section can be found expressed in the work of Gustave Martelet, who has been much influenced by Teilhard de Chardin. Martelet has developed the relationship between a cosmic Christology and eucharistic theology. See his *The Risen Christ and the Eucharistic World* (London: Collins, 1976), particularly 160-79. In quite a different way Peter Chirico also treats the relationship between the risen Christ and the cosmos as part of his theological system. See his *Infallibility: The Crossroads of Doctrine* (Wilmington, DE: Michael Glazier, 1983), particularly 66-85, 125-36.

39. Col. 1:15-20; see also 1 Cor. 8:6; Phil. 2:5-11; Eph. 1:3-14; Heb. 1:1-3; John 1:1-18; 1 John 1:1-4.

The Word Become Flesh:
A Short Story for Christmas

JOYCE HOLLYDAY

The old priest thought about the task he faced and sighed, settling into the worn chair behind his desk. He had lost count of the number of winters that had passed since he had come to this neighborhood. Other communities changed, people came and went, the city was bursting at its center and seams with growth. But this neighborhood seemed only to grow poorer.

His church was flanked by families whose ancestors had once lived in the slave quarters of southern plantations, whose parents and grandparents had migrated north at the turn of the century; by Appalachian mountain folk who had fled rural despair in search of promised jobs a generation later; and by Spanish-speaking refugees who had arrived in the last decade with violence at their heels. Some of the older families had lived together for years, generation after generation, their children becoming friends as they had years before. But the mix had grown uneasy, explosive at times, as jobs disappeared and extended families crowded in together and resources never seemed to stretch far enough.

It was about 2 o'clock in the afternoon when the old priest sat down to write, about the time the snow began to fall. The clock in the church's tower rang out the hour in two dull, slow gongs. His life was so full with the demands of his parish that it had become tradition for him to carve out space the day before Christmas to begin his sermon for the next morning. He remembered as a young priest beginning to think of the next week's sermon as soon as he had finished the last, taking the week to pore over commentaries and polish his thoughts. Now even his most important sermon of the year found time only the day before.

Reprinted with permission from *Sojourners* 20 (December 1991): 25-27.

He had no sooner begun to pick up his pen than a knock came at his door. It was a young woman from the parish, the worn lines on her face adding a decade to her appearance. One of her young, dark-haired daughters clung to her right leg, and another grasped her left hand.

"Mama is home with the baby. Baby is sick. We need food." Desperation and the complexities of a strange language had driven her to be direct in her request, each word shrouded in a thick Spanish accent.

The old man went downstairs with her to the church's pantry and took out the last of the donated food from the large bin. He was embarrassed at the meager offering of bread and canned soup. There would be only this for their Christmas dinner — no turkey and dressing, no sweet corn and mashed potatoes; no family gathered around a huge table, praising her as the warm aroma of a feast filled the room. He thought sadly of how long it had been since he had sat, young and wide-eyed, with his sisters and brothers around the old family table, awaiting a festive holiday meal.

His mother was always simple grace, floating in and out of the kitchen, keeping dishes filled; his father, a tall figure at the end of the table sitting straight like a soldier, eyeing with pride his abundant and joyful progeny. A fire always crackled in the fireplace, punctuating their laughter and casting a warm glow over the animated conversation. The family dog lay expectantly under the table — always at his feet — waiting for crumbs to fall, and for that moment when the priest as a boy would drop a naked drumstick its way.

The priest's focus wandered back as he caught the woman's younger daughter longingly eyeing a pink doll lying at the top of a bin marked "Toys." He reached in and gave it to her, then found a similar one for her sister. Their eyes smiled at him. Then he rummaged through the bin and found a stuffed dog, telling the older girl, "Give this to your baby brother." They walked back out into the cold then, the woman clutching the food and her daughters hugging the dolls close to themselves.

The old priest sighed again and began walking back up the narrow stairs to the rectory — his "cell," he called it with affection. He had grown more and more at home in his tiny upper room next to the old clock tower, with a bed, a desk, and a chair his only furnishings. The dark wood within the church's stone walls gave the room a medieval feel, and there were times, when life seemed to press close, that he felt a monk's calling would suit him.

The room's only window allowed him a narrow view of the street below. Its diamond-shaped panes let in a stream of sunlight each day for just an hour in the late afternoon, before the sun edged behind the clock tower.

He returned to his small desk — an old roll-top that had belonged to his grandfather — mahogany. With a slightly arthritic hand, he picked up his pen again, but he did not write. He gazed beyond the tiny window at the snow, which continued to fall — about three inches on the ground now. And he observed to himself what a beautiful hush it had brought to the city.

His mind wandered to visions of the young priest: the enthusiasm, the way he was going to change the world — or at least write his sermons more than one day before he preached them. An ironically sad smile crept over his face and hung there for a moment.

A shout from the street below interrupted his mental meanderings. "Hey, Father!" The voice was that of a man everyone called simply "The General." No one knew his whole story, but there were bits of it that circulated the streets — a once-successful man who had come too close to an enemy grenade during World War II; a piece of something that imbedded itself in his skull and kept him in a coma for months; a family that couldn't bear the strain and left him for good in the hospital.

There was some residual brain damage, and an awkwardness to his movements, leftovers from a paralysis that at one point was believed permanent. A military cadence seemed to march through his head and, when sober, he strutted the streets to beat the band. But today he was not sober. He usually wasn't around holidays.

"Jesus isn't here, preacher!" he shouted agitatedly toward the priest's window, losing his footing on a patch of snow. The priest walked quickly down the narrow stairs and, placing an arm under The General, helped him up. His eyes were bloodshot and vacant, his breath stale with the smell of alcohol. "Jesus is gone," he muttered quietly as the priest helped him, stumbling, into the church.

There was always a warm corner for The General. Some of the parishioners didn't like it, but they didn't complain — at least not too often. His only other home was a steam grate a few blocks away, which belched hot air to envelop him in scant comfort on cold nights. It was his preferred home, but he was terrified of things falling from the sky — including rain and snow. The priest had expected him to show up at the church that day.

"Jesus is gone!" The General shouted once more through an angry stupor, his eyes wide and riveted on the priest, whom he clutched tightly. Then he grew quiet again, and a tear slid down his old face, weathered and outlined in several days' worth of whiskers. Prying loose his grasp as he gently covered him with a blanket on the floor of a Sunday school room, the priest said soothingly, "It's all right, General. Jesus is here. Everything's all right. You get some sleep now."

The clock in the old tower sounded out 4 o'clock as the priest sat back down at his desk. An orange streak of sunlight fell across his blank paper. He gazed at it emptily. He was distracted by the interruptions, unfocused, doubtful that he had anything new to say about the marvel of the incarnation, the miracle of the Word become flesh. It was an old story, one he had told many times.

He put his head into his hands and sat motionless as the sun slipped around the clock tower. As the dark of twilight began to encroach on him, another knock came abruptly on his door — loud and incessant, hammering the stillness.

"They've arrested my son! They've taken him away!" wailed the mother who had lived in this neighborhood since childhood. Her son was 15 now — the age she had been when she gave birth to him. There was a husband once, but he had beaten her one too many times and she left him when their second child was still an infant.

Through her sobs the story came out. Her son had been caught shoplifting — "trying to steal a doll for his little sister for Christmas," she said with a voice tinged with both pride and anguish. She was a woman who lit votive candles often and came to Mass every week — not because she was a Catholic, but because she believed that every avenue to God should be tried. Ten percent of her already scant welfare check went to an unscrupulous TV evangelist, and various form letters of gratitude and prayer cloths "blessed by the preacher himself" and light-in-the-dark Jesus plaques were now fading on her walls.

The local shopkeeper had reported her son and given the police his address. They had come to the house and taken him away in handcuffs. His 11-year-old sister ran out of the house crying.

"It's Christmas Eve," his mother pleaded, shaking with fear for both of her children. "Can't you do something?"

The priest encouraged her to go home and wait for her daughter, while he grabbed his old poncho, threw it over his shoulders, and headed out the door. The snow was deep now, and it crunched under his feet as he walked toward the police station. The poncho smelled musty. It was a relic from another era, when he was a young priest on a mission in Latin America. Those were heady days, when hungry peasants were beginning to see the message of social upheaval in the words of Jesus; when talk was of justice and peaceful revolution; when prayer centered on the demise of governments and the end of exploitation and the flourishing of communities of faith that saw the Bible as their handbook for resistance.

The revolution never came. Only more brutality. He left disillusioned, broken from the weight of shattered hope and the knowledge that the suffering would never end for his friends. He took his option to return home. It was a choice they couldn't make. That truth had haunted him for 30 years.

The wind picked up as the sun sank behind the street's buildings, and he drew the poncho more tightly around himself. He thought about his room. He hoped that he wouldn't be long at the police station. He was anxious to go back, start a fire in the small stone fireplace in the corner, and write his sermon by firelight while the logs crackled comfortably and friendly shadows danced on the walls. The fireplace was one of the things he liked best about his room, and he was sure the coziness of the scene would inspire him, would give him just the right words for his congregation tomorrow.

He was at the police station for hours. The officers on duty, unhappy to be at work on Christmas Eve, were not enamored of a meddling, old priest. They refused even to acknowledge at first that they had arrested the young man he had come for. They left the priest waiting, then sent him to another police station. He waited again, only to be told that the young man he was looking for had already been taken to the jail. No pleading on his part moved the officers to release the boy to him or even to allow him to go see him.

The snow was swirling in the streets as he left the station, the wind slicing through his poncho. He trudged slowly through the deserted neighborhood, his footsteps heavy with defeat, his face to the ground.

As he turned a corner a few blocks from the church, he glanced up and was surprised to see a small figure walking ahead of him, bent over with the weight of something. He approached and called out, not wanting to cause fright. The figure turned, and he saw the young sister of the boy he had been seeking at the police station.

A shiver wracked her body as he walked toward her. In her arms was the large figure of the baby Jesus from the church's Nativity scene, made of heavy oak, crafted by one of the parishioners who at a happier time had been a woodcarver in the Appalachian foothills. The Nativity set, put on display in the church's foyer every Christmas, was the pride of the parish. Wrapped around baby Jesus was the girl's coat.

The priest drew up close to her. "I want to be good, Father," the girl said somberly, rocking Jesus and staring at her right foot as she scuffed it through the snow. Then she looked up into his eyes and whispered, "But I don't know how."

The priest took off his poncho and placed it around her trembling shoulders, noticing how threadbare it was but for the first time in a long time thankful for its warmth.

A lone tear descended the girl's cheek and dropped into the snow. "Mama says I got to be walkin' with Jesus," she said as more tears flowed. "But I lost my way."

The priest's eyes grew moist. "Here, let me help," he said, gently taking Jesus from her arms. He cradled the baby Jesus in one arm and placed the other around the girl. "Let's walk with Jesus together," he said, barely able to voice the words.

As the church came into view, the clock in the old tower chimed 12 times. The priest looked toward the sky and smiled. It was Christmas, and he still hadn't put a word on paper.

Some Further Contributions to the Discussion

Mortimer Arius, *Announcing the Reign of God*. Philadelphia: Fortress Press, 1984.

Athanasius, *On the Incarnation of the Word*.

Gustaf Aulén, *Christus Victor*. Translated by A. G. Herbert. New York: Macmillan, 1951.

Donald M. Baillie, *God Was in Christ: An Essay on the Incarnation and Atonement*. London: Faber and Faber, Ltd., 1948.

Karl Barth, *Church Dogmatics*, Vol. IV. Translated by G. W. Bromiley and T. F. Torrance. Edinburgh: T. & T. Clark, 1956-1969.

G. C. Berkouwer, *The Person of Christ*. Translated by John Vriend. Grand Rapids: Wm. B. Eerdmans Publishing Co., 1954.

————, *The Work of Christ*. Translated by Cornelius Lambregtse. Grand Rapids: Wm. B. Eerdmans Publishing Co., 1965.

Leonardo Boff, *Jesus Christ Liberator: A Critical Christology for Our Times*. Translated by Patrick Hughes. Maryknoll, NY: Orbis Books, 1978.

Dietrich Bonhoeffer, *Christ the Center*. Translated by John Bowden. New York: Harper & Row, 1966.

José Míguez Bonino, ed., *Faces of Jesus: Latin American Christologies*. Translated by Robert R. Barr. Maryknoll, NY: Orbis Books, 1984.

Eugene Borowitz, *Contemporary Christologies: A Jewish Response*. New York: Paulist Press, 1980.

Rita Nakashima Brock, *Journeys by Heart: A Christology of Erotic Power*. New York: Crossroad, 1988.

A. B. Bruce, *The Humiliation of Christ*. 2nd ed. New York: A. C. Armstrong, 1899.

Emil Brunner, *The Mediator*. Translated by Olive Wyon. New York: Macmillan, 1934.

Albert Cleage, *The Black Messiah*. New York: Sheed and Ward, 1968.

Ewert Cousins, *Christ of the 21st Century*. Brisbane, Queensland: Element, 1992.

Donald Dawe, *Jesus: Lord for All Times*. Atlanta: John Knox Press, 1975.

Kelly Brown Douglas, *The Black Christ*. Maryknoll, NY: Orbis Books, 1994.

Millard Erickson, *The Word Became Flesh*. Grand Rapids: Baker Book House, 1991.

Virginia Fabella and Mercy Amba Oduyoye, *With Passion and Compassion*. Maryknoll, NY: Orbis Books, 1988.

Paul Fiddes, *Past Event and Present Salvation: The Christian Idea of Atonement*. Louisville: Westminster/John Knox Press, 1989.

R. S. Franks, *The Work of Christ: A Historical Study*. London: Thomas Nelson, 1962.

Hans W. Frei, *The Identity of Jesus Christ*. Philadelphia: Fortress Press, 1975.

Jacquelyn Grant, *White Women's Christ and Black Women's Jesus*. Atlanta: Scholars Press, 1989.

Mary Grey, *Feminism, Redemption, and the Christian Tradition*. Mystic, CN: Twenty-Third Publications, 1990.

David R. Griffin, *A Process Christology*. Philadelphia: Westminster Press, 1973.

Aloys Grillmeier, *Christ in Christian Tradition*. Translated by John Bowden. 2nd rev. ed. Atlanta: John Knox Press, 1975.

Colin Gunton, *The Actuality of the Atonement*. Grand Rapids: Wm. B. Eerdmans Publishing Co., 1989.

Monica K. Hellwig, *Jesus: The Compassion of God*. Wilmington, DE: Michael Glazier, 1983.

George S. Hendry, *The Gospel of the Incarnation*. Philadelphia: Westminster Press, 1958.

Elizabeth Johnson, *Consider Jesus*. New York: Crossroad, 1990, 1993.

Walter Kasper, *Jesus the Christ*. Translated by V. Green. London: Burns & Oates, 1976.

Leander Keck, *A Future for the Historical Jesus*. Nashville: Abingdon Press, 1971.

Dow Kirkpatrick, ed., *The Finality of Christ*. Nashville: Abingdon Press, 1966.

John Macquarrie, *Jesus Christ in Modern Thought*. London: SCM Press, Philadelphia: Trinity Press International, 1990.

Jean Meyendorff, *Christ in Eastern Christian Thought*. Washington, D.C.: Corpus Books, 1969.

T. A. Mofokeng, *The Crucified among the Crossbearers: Towards a Black Christology*. Kampen, 1983.

Jürgen Moltmann, *The Crucified God*. Translated by R. A. Wilson and John Bowden. New York: Harper & Row, 1974. Minneapolis: Augsburg Fortress Press, 1990, 1993.

————, *The Way of Jesus Christ*. Translated by Margaret Kohl. Minneapolis: Augsburg Fortress Press, 1990, 1993.

Leon Morris, *The Atonement: Its Meaning and Significance*. Downers Grove, IL: InterVarsity Press, 1983.

Charles Nyamiti, *Christ as Our Ancestor: Christology from an African Perspective.* Gwere, Zimbabwe: Mambo Press, 1984.

Gerald O'Collins, *Christology: A Biblical, Historical and Systematic Study of Jesus Christ.* Oxford University Press, 1995.

Thomas Oden, *The Word of Life.* San Francisco: Harper & Row, 1989.

Douglas Ottati, *Jesus Christ and Christian Vision.* Minneapolis: Fortress Press, 1989.

Wolfhart Pannenberg, *Jesus — God and Man.* Translated by Lewis L. Wilkins and Duane A. Priebe. Philadelphia: Westminster Press, 1968.

Jaroslav Pelikan, *Jesus Through the Centuries.* New Haven, Conn.: Yale University Press, 1985.

W. Norman Pittenger, *The Word Incarnate.* N.p.: J. Nisbet, 1959.

———, *Christology Reconsidered.* London: SCM Press, 1970.

Priscilla Pope-Levinson and John R. Levinson, *Jesus in Global Contexts.* Louisville: Westminster/John Knox Press, 1992.

Neal Robinson, *Christ in Islam and Christianity.* Albany, NY: State University of New York (SUNY) Press, 1991.

Jack Rogers et al., *Case Studies in Christ and Salvation.* Philadelphia: Westminster Press, 1977.

Rosemary Radford Ruether, *To Change the World: Christology and Cultural Criticism.* New York: Crossroad, 1981.

Stanley Samartha, *One Christ — Many Religions: Toward a Revised Christology.* Maryknoll, NY: Orbis Books, 1991.

Edward Schillebeeckx, *Christ: The Experience of Jesus as Lord.* Translated by John Bowden. New York: Seabury Press, 1980.

———, *Jesus: An Experiment in Christology.* Translated by Hubert Hoskins. New York: Seabury Press, 1979.

Robert J. Schreiter, ed., *Faces of Jesus in Africa.* Maryknoll, NY: Orbis Books, 1994.

Juan Luis Segundo, *Jesus of Nazareth Yesterday and Today* (3 vols.). Translated by John Drury. Maryknoll, NY: Orbis Books, 1985-1988.

Jon Sobrino, *Christology at the Crossroads: A Latin American Approach.* Translated by John Drury. Maryknoll, NY: Orbis Books, 1978.

———, *Jesus in Latin America.* Maryknoll, NY: Orbis Books, 1987.

C. S. Song, *Jesus: The Crucified People.* New York: Crossroad Publishing Co., 1990.

———, *Jesus and the Reign of God.* Minneapolis: Augsburg Fortress Press, 1993.

John R. W. Stott, *The Cross of Christ.* Downers Grove, IL: InterVarsity Press, 1986.

R. S. Sugirtharajah, ed., *Asian Faces of Jesus.* Maryknoll, NY: Orbis Books, 1993.

T. F. Torrance, *Space, Time and Incarnation.* London: Oxford University Press, 1969.

————, *Space, Time and Resurrection*. Grand Rapids: Wm. B. Eerdmans Publishing Co., 1976.

James Tull, *The Atoning Gospel*. Macon, GA: Mercer University Press, 1982.

Patricia Wilson-Kastner, *Faith, Feminism, and the Christ*. Philadelphia: Fortress Press, 1983.

Arthur Zannoni, *Jews and Christians Speak of Jesus*. Minneapolis: Augsburg Fortress Press, 1994.

PART V

The Church and the Christian Life

INTRODUCING THE ISSUE

Life in the Service of Christ

What is the church? Is it the building on the corner or the meeting place where Christians assemble? Or is it primarily the community of Christians that gathers for worship, study, and witness? Or is the church more clearly manifested where Christians are working with others for justice, peace, and the preservation of creation? Or is the church really an inner, spiritual community/communion of those who truly seek God and experience God's Spirit in their lives? These are only a few of the ways Christians think and speak of the church.

Several years ago Paul Minear made an intensive study of the church in the New Testament and identified some eighty or more different images used by early Christians to speak of the church.[1] Among the chief of these were the church as a people called out by God *(Ekklesia),* the church as the Body of Christ, and the church as a new creation. In more recent discussions still other images have been added to this list, including these: the church as a sign and sacrament of God's coming reign,[2] the church as a manifestation of the movement of the Spirit,[3] the church as a "colony of resident aliens" in the world,[4] the church as a faithful servant of Christ,[5] the church as a community in solidarity with the poor and the oppressed,[6] the church as an "exodus community" pressing on toward God's future,[7] and the church as a community of

1. Paul S. Minear, *Images of the Church in the New Testament* (Philadelphia: Westminster Press, 1960).

2. *Church, Kingdom, World: The Church as Mystery and Prophetic Sign,* ed. Gennadios Limouris, Faith and Order Paper No. 130 (Geneva: World Council of Churches, 1986).

3. See, e.g., William R. Barr and Rena M. Yocom, eds., *The Church in the Movement of the Spirit* (Grand Rapids: Wm. B. Eerdmans Publishing Co., 1994).

4. Stanley Hauerwas and William Willimon, *Resident Aliens: Life in the Christian Colony* (Nashville: Abingdon Press, 1989).

5. Edmund P. Clowney, *The Church* (Downers Grove, IL: InterVarsity Press, 1995).

6. Jon Sobrino, *The True Church and the Poor,* trans. Matthew J. O'Conell (Maryknoll, NY: Orbis Books, 1984).

7. Jürgen Moltmann, *Theology of Hope,* trans. James W. Leitch (Minneapolis: Fortress Press,

equals formed in discipleship to Christ.[8] But even beyond these attempts to form an adequate concept of the church, many Christians are insisting that the church is concretely defined in the way it lives its life in the service of Christ. Perhaps no one definition or lifestyle can be a full expression of the church in our rapidly changing situation. The church would seem to be multifaceted or multidimensional, and Christians have much to learn from one another across denominational and theological perspectives rather than making these causes for further division.

The definition of the church is of course tied closely with the question, How do we recognize the church? In other words, not only must we ask *what* is the church, but we also have to ask *where* is the church, particularly in the face of growing numbers of groups combining elements of Christianity with other views, television evangelism, and dissident groups within the churches. The ancient "marks" of the church mentioned in the Nicene Creed — one, holy, catholic, and apostolic — have often been cited in identifying the church. But today it may be that, important and valid as these criteria are, they have to be supplemented — or more fully explicated in a more specific set of clues for discerning the church amid the confusion and struggle in which the church currently finds itself. What should be these more specific indicators in the context of the late twentieth century?

The essays in this section deal in various ways with this question as well as the larger question concerning the essential nature of the church and the Christian life. In his essay written from the South African context, Thor Halvor Hovland argues that the church should be "the conscience of society." He says that this means that the church should be a community in which all voices can be heard, those of minorities as well as the majority, and where ethical issues relating to politics, economics, medical science, and ecology, among other areas, can be examined in the light of the gospel. Drawing on John Bennett's three-step model of social ethics, Hovland urges the church to eschew being captivated by ideological currents of the day and instead to pursue its God-given task of being a responsible conscience and guide in society.

Reflecting on a number of bilateral dialogues between churches in recent years, especially since the Second Vatican Council, Gennadios Limouris, a Greek Orthodox theologian, points out that these dialogues are bringing to the surface a much larger and deeper understanding of the church as both local and universal, as the visible as well as the invisible community of those of the past and the future whose lives are joined with those in the present. The Orthodox Churches' appeal to Tradition focuses attention on the continuity of the church

---

1967, 1991), chap. 5. See also his *The Church in the Power of the Spirit*, trans. Margaret Kohl (New York: Harper & Row, 1977).

8. Elisabeth Schüssler Fiorenza, *Discipleship of Equals: A Critical Feminist Ekklesia-logy of Liberation* (New York: Crossroad, 1993).

through time and space as empowered and guided by the Holy Spirit. At the same time more recent ecumenical discussion has highlighted the role of the church as "sign, instrument, and first-fruits" of the full coming of God's reign. Yet these dialogues also bring more clearly into focus some of the basic and persistent differences among Christians in understanding and living as the church. Bilateral dialogues do not obscure these differences but rather aim to "bring into harmony the uniqueness of the various historical configurations in which the churches have developed and not to use this as a means of further division." Deeper understanding of Christ and the Spirit leads to deeper understanding of the mystery of the church and its mission. Only via this route, Limouris contends, can the church be led to a more vital and faithful life and witness in the maelstrom of our times. Ecumenical dialogues among churches show that the church is dynamic, "on the move," as it is shaken out of its lethargy by the Spirit and challenged to make a common confession of Christ to the world.

From a Latin American perspective, C. René Padilla contends that it is a mistake for "ecumenicals" and "evangelicals" to oppose each other, for that can only contribute to division in the church and the hampering of its mission. Instead, Padilla argues for a holistic vision and practice of mission in which concern for justice, peace, and preserving creation is part and parcel of evangelical proclamation of the redemptive love of God in Jesus Christ. Ecumenical and evangelical concerns should be complementary and mutually supportive, he argues. But Padilla thinks that the World Council of Churches has lost some of its earlier balance between these dimensions and needs to recover the evangelical urgency of proclaiming the good news of God's redemptive action and call to faith.

Another Latin American voice, that of Julio de Santa Ana, director of the Ecumenical Center for Evangelism and Popular Education in São Paulo, Brazil, expresses concern about the deterioration of the quality of life of the great majority of the world's peoples and the obscuring of this in Western fascination with an "ideology of globalization" that promotes expensive technology, increasingly tying local economies to the world market and increasing demands on the poor for the benefit of the rich. Though the ideology of globalization pretends inclusiveness, it places communication and power in the hands of those who most stand to benefit from integrating ethnic and local groups into the system of the modern free market. In opposition to this, Julio de Santa Ana urges that life in the Spirit, as poured out into the world through Jesus, is a life in community of free women and men in which the excluded are to be welcomed and heard. It is a life in which God's word is *done,* not merely preached on Sunday morning, and in which patriarchal and domineering structures are being replaced by relations of mutuality, concern for the well-being of all, and renewing of the energies of people and of the creation.

Nigel Biggar, chaplain of Oriel College and librarian of Latimer House at the University of Oxford, writes that the conflict between those who back industrial mission and social service of the church and those who believe that the church's mission is principally one of spiritual conversion pointedly raises the question of the essential mission of the church. He examines the arguments on both sides of the question and seeks to clarify the issues involved, noting that salvation is both spiritual and social and that righting social relationships, while crucial, is not in itself sufficient without personal conversion and transformed lives. Yet the gospel requires not only personal holiness and witness but also the living out of God's redemptive work in the whole fabric of our relationships. Thus personal and institutional, immediate and remote relationships are inseparably connected. If the gospel is to be proclaimed in "the text of our lives," says the author, it must also be proclaimed through the life of the Christian community as a whole, through the quality of life, structures, and commitments to justice of the church in its life and witness in the world.

That, of course, is not an easy undertaking, and even such efforts may sometimes mask as well as manifest deep faith in God, Jacques Goulet reminds us. In his essay Goulet explores some of the recent discussions on the nature of faith, particularly in interreligious and ecumenical discussions, and points out the tendency to move beyond thinking of faith as simply acceptance of doctrines or beliefs to an understanding of faith as trusting commitment to ultimate reality in accordance with one's conscience. Such faith is living, growing, and searching, struggles with doubt, and celebrates the gifts of God in the midst of life. It is a firm confidence in the unity of Truth, but it also recognizes that the various churches have only a partial grasp of that Truth, and even that is culturally conditioned and limited. Yet the recognition of the churches' historical finitude need not diminish the confidence of faith but rather can lead to a deeper awareness of what the author calls "the ultimate indiscernibility of faith," the encounter with God as incomprehensible Mystery in the depths of our being.

Yet Aruna Gnanadason, who serves as executive secretary of the All India Council of Women, points out that an authentic Christian spirituality cannot be indifferent to the destruction of others and the environment. Drawing on the songs and insights of village women, the author lifts up a newly emerging sense of inner strength and spiritual power that sustains and guides these women and other oppressed people in their struggle for life. This spirituality is liberating because it gives people the power to resist the dehumanizing effects of modernization and the will to persist in the struggle to overcome the massive poverty and misery in the world. But even more, this emerging spirituality (shakti), says the author, enables women and others to voice their suffering and concerns, to share their stories, and to work together to overcome forms of oppression. As expressed in the Dalit movement, the poorest of the poor of India's masses, such sharing of stories and spiritual renewal gives birth to a new consciousness of identity and determination to endure in their daily struggle.

They perceive that Jesus also identified with the poor of his day, and in this sense "he was a Dalit"; and with joy they receive his blessing and guidance in their struggle. But because their survival is, as for others, so dependent upon natural resources, it is clear that the church's mission must include concerns for the environment as well as for social justice. Such a spirituality, the author suggests, may be better articulated in songs than in theories, for it is a spirituality that is earthy, enacted in dances and art, and capable of being expressed in many different ways in daily life.

The variety of views of the church and its mission articulated in the essays in this section do not yield a unified and complete doctrine of the church, but they do indicate some of the threads that are going into weaving a developing new pattern of the church as it moves toward the twenty-first century.

The Role of the Church in a Pluralist Society

THOR HALVOR HOVLAND

The churches which have tried to follow in Jesus' footsteps have had a difficult time under apartheid rule in South Africa. With the hope of a "new South Africa," many Christians and church leaders look forward to a new era when Christian teaching will permeate the whole nation.

Experience from other countries does not, however, support such an optimistic stance. Let me point to one example. The Church in former East Germany had a spiritual life and an impact on the nation which was in no way matched by the Church in West Germany. The people rallied to the Church for guidance and support in the last months before the collapse of the communist regime. But only a few months later, it seems that the Church has already become obsolete. The same phenomenon may be observed in Poland, although to a lesser degree.

Although the churches in Eastern Europe, as well as those in South Africa, have worked for a new day and freedom for its people, this freedom nevertheless presents the churches with a *greater* — not a lesser — challenge. I do not foresee persecution or harassment, but the churches will be *ignored,* they will be *marginalised* and *privatised.* Both the marginalisation and the privatisation are part and parcel of a broader secularisation. The development of secularisation has in Western societies partly been outside and against the churches, and partly inside the churches. The latter can be seen in the USA, where "civil religion" has penetrated the churches to such an extent that it functions as a hermeneutical key for the understanding of the biblical message. The same phenomenon can be found in the "rule of faith" of the Reformed Churches in South Africa, where apartheid theology has been functioning as the hermeneutical key.[1]

1. See J. A. Loubser, *The Apartheid Bible, A Critical Review of Racial Theology in South Africa* (Cape Town: MM Longman, 1987), 60-69 and 81-82.

Reprinted with permission from the *Journal of Theology for Southern Africa* 80 (September 1992): 65-75.

South Africa will probably follow the American route rather than the European, but the challenge is basically the same: What is the role of the Church in a pluralist society? (I imply that this society is politically democratic.) The question belongs to the field of social ethics, and we will now turn to some basic considerations in social ethics in order to answer our question.

A Three-Step Model

The American ethicist John C. Bennett used a three-step model in his social ethics.[2] The first step in any ethical approach is the underlying motivation, the faith or ideology. The second step is the "middle axioms," a term which Bennett has taken from J. H. Oldham. The term is defined as the "type of behaviour required of Christians at a given period and in given circumstances."[3] The third step is the ultimate decision to choose a particular political solution or party.

Building on this three-step model, one could say that the first step is the fundamental Christian moral teaching. Here the Church may speak with full authority on the basis of God's revelation of his will. The second step is somewhat more problematic, although there are some clear guidelines. Bennett mentions "Land Reform," "Racial Segregation," "Unemployment," and "Self-government" as issues about which there is a great extent of unanimity among Christians. Human rights are also a case in point. In the question of these "middle axioms" the church will also naturally join forces with other groups in society which share the same goals, albeit with a different basis.

The third step can hardly be taken by the Church as such, but has to be the choice of the individual Christian. Here reason and human insight and experiences will play a decisive role, certainly guided by the conclusions of the first and second step. The third step makes clear why Christians with the same moral fundament and with the same goals ("middle axioms") may opt for totally different and indeed opposite political parties.

Such a model does not concern itself with the question of whether politicians, cabinet ministers and members of parliament are themselves professing Christians or not, although Bennett mentions this latter possibility as a matter of indirect Christian influence.

If the Church should be guided in its social-ethical responsibility by the issue of Christian politicians, the impact would soon be minimal. This is partly because Christian politicians are not necessarily the best politicians, and partly because there would normally be only a minority of professing Christians in

2. Cf. *The Christian as Citizen* (London: Lutterworth Press, 1955), 36-47, and *Christian Social Action* (London: Lutterworth Press, 1954), 92-113.

3. See Bennett's books mentioned in the previous note, esp. 39 and 18. The definition is taken from J. O. Oldham and W. A. Visser 't Hooft, *The Church and Its Function in Society* (Allen & Unwin/Willett, Clark, 1937), 210.

any parliament in any country. The Constitution of the USA is regarded by most churches as a constitution in line with Christian principles in spite of the fact that it was mainly written and decided upon by professing non-Christians. On the other hand, from recent American history, the majority of Christians in the USA voted for Reagan against Carter as president, in spite of the fact that Carter obviously was letting his faith determine his politics in a much more direct application of Christian teaching than Reagan.

South Africa may in the future also see a Moslem or atheist win the majority of Christian votes instead of a Christian candidate for the same political office. The three-step model of Christian social ethics explains this phenomenon, but it needs to be undergirded by a Christian teaching of "two kingdoms."

The Teaching of the Two Kingdoms

W. Pannenberg writes: "In the history of Christianity there has always been a more or less marked difference between church and state, between the spiritual and secular spheres of life."[4]

The distinction is to be found in the Eastern as well as the Western churches, the latter deeply influenced by Augustine's *City of God*. The teaching of the two kingdoms has, notwithstanding, been connected particularly to the Lutheran tradition. It has also been denounced as inappropriate and deceitful after the experience of the Lutheran churches in Germany during the Nazi period. But it needs also to be mentioned that it was the very same teaching which enabled the Lutheran churches in Denmark and Norway to resist unanimously and unequivocally the Nazi governments of those countries.[5]

In fact, unless one is satisfied with a totally subjectivistic form of Christian social ethics, reducing the question of the Christian impact in society to the question of getting a professing Christian person into the office of prime minister or president, one has to figure out — in one way or another — a teaching of the two kingdoms.

W. Pannenberg points out that Luther inherited two streams of thinking, which he combined. The one was from Augustine about the contrast of the two realms, the other from Medieval thinking about the two ways in which God rules.[6] Pannenberg holds that the "function of this combination, and its achievement, was that first of all it established the necessity of political authority and

---

4. W. Pannenberg, *Christianity in a Secularized World* (London: SCM Press, 1988), 23.

5. See U. Duchrow, *Global Economy: A Confessional Issue for the Churches* (Geneva: WCC Publications 1987), 4-18 (viz., 14), and E. Berggrav, *Man and State* (Philadelphia: Muhlenberg Press, 1951), 117-26.

6. W. Pannenberg, *Ethics* (Philadelphia: Westminster Press/London Search Press, 1981), 117-26.

at the same time set limits on its claims."[7] The deficiency of Luther's concept is explained thus: "But nowhere in Luther can we find any inspiration to transform political conditions by the powerful vision of the eschatological Lordship of God which already illumines the present world."[8]

Simon S. Maimela has an incisive article about the teaching of the two kingdoms and how it can be used as a sound basis for a Christian critique of a usurping government, namely, the apartheid government.[9] He concludes by saying:

> The church plays a critical role in delineating and distinguishing between temporal and ultimate authority, political truth and eternal truth, secular expediency and everlasting justice. The teaching of the twofold governance and its statement by the church will make clear that God is active in both realms, so that we may avoid confusing God's work in political activity and God's activity in salvation.[10]

But Maimela also underlines that there is a certain reciprocity between the two kingdoms:

> The spiritual governance needs the civil order and peace which the secular kingdom establishes through law and the sword if the spiritual kingdom is to gain a hearing for the preaching which God uses to transform persons. In turn, the proclamation of God's will by the spiritual form cultivates the virtue, good will, and good deeds among people which are needed by the secular side. . . . By preaching the law and its civil use, the church reminds the state that its laws are to protect the underdogs against powerful exploiters, and that the law exists to serve justice, divine goodness, and love.[11]

With these comments from two contemporary (Lutheran) theologians, we should now be able to embark on the various issues facing the Church when it tries to define its role in a pluralist society.

The Fundamental Responsibility of the Church

Central to any Christian teaching on the two kingdoms is a certain independence granted to the two forms of governance. But this does not have to be

---

7. Ibid., 126.

8. Ibid., 130.

9. A. Pero and A. Moyo, *Theology and the Black Experience* (Minneapolis: Augsburg Publishing, 1988), 97-109.

10. Ibid., 109. Cf. also B. Lategan, J. Kinghorn, L. du Plessis, and E. de Villiers, *The Option for Inclusive Democracy* (Stellenbosch: Centre for Contextual Hermeneutics, 1987), 11 and 14ff.

11. Ibid., 99.

understood in the sense that there are two separate spheres, as it has sometimes been explained in the Reformed as well as in the Lutheran tradition.

Gustaf Dalman has made it clear that the Kingdom of God in the New Testament means "the kingly rule of God," "the sovereignty of God," or "his activity in ruling."[12] This is the way it should be understood in the teaching of the two kingdoms: God is the ruler in both kingdoms, although he rules in two different ways.

The apartheid government, as well as any other totalitarian government, such as a series of communist governments and Moslem governments, has tried to make the Church subservient to its own ideological worldview. It is instructive to see how the churches (or part of them) responded to such an attack by the respective Nazi governments in Germany, Norway and Denmark.

The Barmen Declaration stated: "We reject the false doctrine, as though the state, over and beyond its special commission, should and could become the single and totalitarian order of human life, thus fulfilling the Church's vocation as well" (Par. 5).

And the Norwegian confession *The Foundation of the Church* pointed out: "When the power of the state parts with justice, the state will no longer be an instrument of God, but a demonic power."

The Danish declaration *The Church and Justice in the Present Situation* expressed the same idea:

> The Church does not want to invade the area of secular power, but indeed wishes to respect the state's sovereignty as the servant of God (Rom. 13:4). But this does not mean, however, that the Church has nothing to tell the secular authority. In that moment when secular authority threatens to abandon the basis of justice and dissolve itself into the despotism of arbitrariness, then it is the obligation of the Church to stand up for the protection of justice.

I have quoted so extensively from these declarations because they all highlight the one fundamental point: The Church is fighting for its independence from the state not for its own sake, but for the sake of *justice*. There is always an inherent danger in any political authority becoming totalitarian and despotic, and this can only be checked and controlled by a Church which is ultimately obedient to another authority, to God.

Critics may then accuse the Church of being selfish and narrow-minded, because it takes no account of other religions or people without any religion. This is not the point, however. The Church in a pluralist society will by implication also defend the right of other people to have an authority beyond and above the state. But it cannot compromise its own belief, and the church's own

---

12. Cf. N. Perrin, *The Kingdom of God in the Teaching of Jesus* (London: SCM Press, 1963), 24.

defence against any totalitarian ideology will secure justice for all groups in a pluralist society.

Let me indicate some examples: There are several countries in Africa which at times have been ruled by governments calling themselves Marxist. Three of them are Ethiopia, Zimbabwe and Madagascar. The churches in those countries experience quite different situations. Whereas the churches in Ethiopia, and particularly the Evangelical Church — Mekane Yesus, have been persecuted and harassed, the opposite has been the experience for the churches in Madagascar. The Church in Ethiopia has necessarily an obligation to protest, not only and primarily for its own sake, but for the sake of the people who are governed unjustly according to a totalitarian ideology. There have been some incidents where the churches in Zimbabwe also had to protest against some of the measures that the government there has been taking against its opposition. In Madagascar, on the other hand, it seems that the government has been willing to listen to the quest for justice which the churches have expressed, although it should be added that the results have been meager.

The churches in these African countries have in fact heeded the same principle as the European churches, namely the independence of the spiritual governance. One may, of course, discuss whether the churches have done this with enough integrity, but the principle itself of the independence of the Church for the sake of justice should be clear.

We could also mention Moslem governments, finding a vast difference between the governments in Sudan and Algeria, or between Saudi Arabia and Morocco, in spite of the fact that all these governments call themselves Moslem.

The criterion for an evaluation and criticism from the side of the Church will not be what kind of label the governments put on themselves, but whether they accept that people have an authority which goes beyond and above the authority of the state. This must include that they accept the independent basis of evaluation which the churches have, and through this show that they accept to be measured according to an independent norm for justice — in Christian terms, God's norm.

We may also point to the South African government as an example of a government which has used the label "Christian," without doing justice, and which has tried to coerce the churches to be subservient to its own totalitarian ideology. There are also other governments in Africa in the same boat — for example, the Ivory Coast, and previously the Central African Republic.

To sum it all up: the teaching of the two kingdoms makes it plain that *justice* is the fundamental basis for any legitimation of a government. This does not coincide with the label of the government, but with its attitude to an independent spiritual governance with an authority beyond and above the authority of the secular governance.

The Societal Responsibility of the Church

One of the basic societal responsibilities of the Church in South Africa, as elsewhere, is to be the *conscience of society*. The above-mentioned Danish declaration states this in an exemplary manner:

> The Church is the conscience of every secular authority through her passionate concern for justice. The Church has certainly something to tell the people. She shall exhort to obedience towards the proper authorities, and she shall try to counteract the hatred and revenge that poison people's minds. But these exhortations make no sense if the Church is not simultaneously the conscience of the authorities.

This will be necessary even in the best conceivable democracy. I could mention examples from the last decade from Great Britain as well as from all the Scandinavian countries where the bishops and other church leaders have been compelled to act against their government, knowing full well that those governments have had the support of the majority of the people. There will always be minorities in a society who need a voice, and the churches cannot avoid becoming the voice of the voiceless for the sake of justice. One case in point is the liberal law on abortion resolved by most European countries.

The two last books written by Michael Cassidy, *The Passing Summer* and *The Politics of Love*, are also stirring up people, appealing to their conscience.[13] This is an important part of the role of the Church.

The second societal role of the Church is to be a *guide for the society*. The Church must be a guide in all spheres of life. Allow me once more to quote from the Danish declaration: "To say, 'The Church shall stick to preaching the Gospel,' asserts an important truth. This is the case when it is understood that the Gospel itself throws light over all human circumstances and brings peace to all suffering situations of mankind."

The very same point was expressed in the so-called *Mapumulo-Memorandum* from 1967 as a consensus of all the Lutheran churches in South Africa:

> Having reviewed this doctrine of the two Kingdoms biblically and historically, we came to the conclusion that the Church has an active and responsible service to the State and Society: The Church shall protest to the temporal authority when evident injustices have been committed. She is also entrusted with the positive function to interpret and counsel the temporal authorities in terms of the ordinance of creation given for the support and performance of human life.

---

13. M. Cassidy, *The Passing Summer* (London: Hodder & Stoughton, 1989), and *The Politics of Love* (London: Hodder & Stoughton, 1990).

Let me briefly point out some spheres of life where the churches need to make an impact if they shall be true to their calling:

(a) I shall start with the *political sphere,* where most churches today will opt for a democratic dispensation. This point can, however, only be argued indirectly, and the churches have in fact legitimised many nondemocratic governments — and still do. The argument for democracy stems from the previous point of justice as the basis for any legitimate government. In Bennett's three-step model, this point belongs to the first and fundamental step of social-ethical norms; and a democratic dispensation seems to safeguard justice better than any other known political dispensation. But democracy also seems to create the best opportunities for the implementation of "middle axioms." On this level the Church needs broad support from various groups in the society to be able to promote its values and goals in the political sphere.

Many things could be said about the checks and balances which are necessary, and the need to place political power in the right form to the right people. The Old Testament records of the division of power between king, priests and prophets give us an indication of the route to follow.

But in our situation in South Africa, the most urgent task is to bring forth a broad consensus on human rights There is no agreement as to the (eventual) theological basis for human rights, and this failure is reflected in the way the churches are handling this burning issue.

The failure is deep-rooted, because it originates in the theological problems of a Christian anthropology. I cannot go into any details, but will try to sketch a few basic ideas in this regard.

One biblical idea which is important to any Christian anthropology is the idea that God "created man in his image," "male and female he created them" (Gen. 1:27). This idea has partly been understood in such a way that each person has an inherent quality and dignity in the tradition of natural law.[14]

But it has also been understood as pointing to responsibilities and privileges in the relationship which people have with God, in the community with other people, and with the rest of nature.[15] There is a wide spectrum of opinions regarding the basis of this relationship, however. Some will base it on a theology of creation, others on a theology of salvation. Among the latter again, theologians in the Reformed tradition have emphasised the relationship of the covenant(s), whereas Lutherans have emphasised justification by grace as the fundamental basis.

There is, though, in spite of these differences of opinion, a unanimity among Christians that human rights cannot be based on any inherent value in

14. Cf. the encyclical *Pacem in Terris,* 1963.
15. Cf. P. Ramsey, *Basic Christian Ethics* (London: SCM Press, 1950), and W. Huber and H. E. Tödt, *Menschenrechte* (Stuttgart: Kreuz Verlag, 1977).

human beings (contra John Locke, etc.). They can only be based on the conviction that every single human being is a creation of God.

This brings us to the first point where the Church has to give guidelines on this issue: Human rights are always intimately connected to human responsibilities, because they originate in a relationship. W. D. Jonker has described this acutely when he explains the Ten Commandments in the light of human rights. Each of the Commandments is at the same time a protection of the rights of the neighbour.[16]

The second point is to maintain that the formulation of human rights can never be final. The formulations need to be scrutinised continuously in the light of the Word of God. Historically one can observe how the *Universal Declaration of Human Rights* from 1948 already in 1966 was amended and expanded by the United Nations with statements on *Civil and Political Rights* and *Economic, Social and Cultural Rights.*

W. Huber and H. E. Tödt have condensed the various rights into three main issues: firstly, the right to personal freedom; secondly, the right to equal treatment; and thirdly, the right to participation in society.[17]

If we interpret these issues on the basis of the relational understanding of the image of God, bearing in mind the two points mentioned above, we will have a comprehensive — and I think sound — principle for a Christian theological input in the current debate in South Africa.

In fact, the Church should urgently make its own contribution, considering the many inputs which are made from various sides.[18] I think that such a contribution, where individual rights are balanced against social rights, and both evaluated from the view of Christian anthropology, would be most valuable.

Although the Bible tells us nothing about human rights, this is one of those "middle axioms" where I think the Church may speak with great courage.

(b) But the Church ought to be a guide in the *economic sphere* as well. There is a strong tradition to exempt economics from ethics, particularly since Adam Smith wrote *The Wealth of Nations.* Christian ethicists have only recently tried to redress this tradition, and I can here only make some basic comments.[19]

The *Ekonomiese Volkskongres* which convened in 1939 summarised its economic policy with the term *volkskapitalisme,* and the Nationalist rule of the

16. W. D. Jonker, *Christelike geloof en menseregte,* in D. A. du Toit, *Menseregte* (Cape Town: Tafelberg, 1984), 54-55.

17. W. Huber and H. E. Tödt, *Menschenrechte,* 162.

18. See, among others, M. M. Corbett, *Guaranteeing Fundamental Freedoms in a New South Africa* (Johannesburg: SAIRR, 1990), and A. Sachs, *Protecting Human Rights in a New South Africa* (Oxford: Oxford University Press, 1990).

19. See U. Duchrow, *Global Economy,* and L. L. Rasmussen, *Economic Anxiety & Christian Faith* (Minneapolis: Augsburg Publishing, 1981); J. Ph. Wogaman, *Economics and Ethics: A Christian Enquiry* (London: SCM Press, 1986); K. Nürnberger, *Power and Beliefs in South Africa* (Pretoria: University of South Africa, 1988).

last forty years has pursued this policy to such an extent that the economic dispensation of South Africa is most akin to that of the (former) communist Soviet Union or other centrally controlled national economies. South Africa has throughout these years not been governed according to the ideas of a free market system, but in the tradition of a nationalist socialist economy.[20] This form of state capitalism has at the international level ground into the free market trade system. This phenomenon is, of course, not peculiar to South Africa, but is more or less equivalent to many other developing countries. The government has, however, persistently called its economic policy "capitalist" for ideological reasons, thus confusing the terms as they are usually defined, and making any discussions about the future economic dispensation more difficult. But before entering into some points regarding South African economy, I will try to bring out the most basic features of a Christian approach to economical ethics.

Our most basic reference to the Biblical message will be the understanding of work. There is a somewhat ambivalent understanding of work in the Bible. It is, on one hand, divine, and God himself works. God created the universe by working in six days, and all human beings are appointed to be his co-creators and masters of this world. Persons are also called to be God's co-workers in his work of redemption (Gen. 1:28-29; 1 Cor. 3:9; 2 Cor. 5:18-20). But work is, on the other hand, a curse. It is a toil which people have to do because they are chased away from the Garden of Eden and God's blessings. Work is hence intimately connected to the sinful life of the human race (Gen. 3:17-19).

For this reason Christian ethics has to rule out any economic dispensation which is dependent on the good will and/or superhuman insights of a group of people. The communist system with a "central committee" cannot be condoned. But the idea of an "invisible hand" has also to be rejected. This kind of dispensation gives the stronger hand the right to exploit the weaker hand without any moral corrections. The story about Naboth's vineyard exemplifies this point and shows the need for a moral evaluation of economics (1 Kgs. 21:1-29).

The Church in South Africa has to maintain that the new economic dispensation in this country must neither be centrally governed (be it in a communist or national socialist fashion) nor be a laissez-faire free market system. In order to restrain the sinful actions and desires of people in the economic sphere, it has to be ordered and controlled.

Political control is necessary as one way to check and balance economic activity. But there will be a need for built-in check mechanisms within the economic sphere itself as well. The workers' unions are one of the most important check mechanisms in any industrialised society. The local communities

20. See, among others, M. Lipton, *Capitalism and Apartheid, South Africa 1910-1986* (Cape Town: David Philip, 1986), 269, and D. Yudelman, *The Emergence of Modern South Africa* (Cape Town: David Philip, 1983), 283-88.

and the consumers are other partners who should be involved. If the Church maintains that justice is best safeguarded by democracy in the political sphere, it ought to give guidelines for democracy in the economic sphere also. These guidelines cannot be copied directly from the political sphere, as the two spheres have different structures, but a democratisation would help to promote the Christian goal of mutual concern and stewardship in the economic life, and would reduce the non-Christian "survival of the fittest."[21]

Klaus Nürnberger mentions in his book *Power and Beliefs in South Africa* that there are three Biblical paradigms [for] the use of structural power, namely "survival," "justice," and "concern" (agape). There is a connection between them so "that the principle of concern overrides the principle of survival. . . . Where concern rules supreme neither survival nor justice is in danger."[22]

The Church cannot condone the paradigm of survival as the normative factor in the economic sphere in the same way as it cannot condone the use of military power and armed violence as the normative factor in the political sphere.

This means in practical terms that the Church has to formulate ethical guidelines as to how the stock exchange should be ruled, so as to minimise the effects of sin in the struggle for survival. It has also to study carefully the role of monopolies in particular, and transnational companies in general. To twist an American pun, one could say: "What is good for Anglo-American is not necessarily good for South Africa." This is not to indicate that Anglo-American is governed by evil people, but to indicate that any company as close to a virtual monopoly as Anglo-American (with De Beers) is also very close to the non-acceptable extremes of an economic dispensation.

Further, the Church in South Africa has to address the ethical problem of commercial export of arms. The majority of churches will accept the use of military power and military alliances, and consequently condone the production of weapons for this purpose. But the commercial sale of arms to any buyer without any regard for the abuse of these deadly weapons is of profound ethical concern.[23]

The political and economic spheres are, to my understanding, the most crucial issue where the churches in South Africa have to bring their input, neglecting which they are in peril of becoming rapidly obsolete. The churches have no need for a party–political platform and they should not involve themselves in large-scale economic enterprises. The task is to give the "new South Africa" the needed fundamental values. The churches should function like the

---

21. See, e.g., A. Storkey, *A Christian Social Perspective* (Leicester: Inter-Varsity Press, 1979), 314-478; K. Nürnberger, *Power and Beliefs*, 301-19; J. Ph. Wogaman, *Economics and Ethics*, 37; L. L. Rasmussen, *Economic Anxiety*, 80-84.

22. K. Nürnberger, *Power and Beliefs*, 304.

23. Cf. A. Storkey, *Christian Social Perspective*, 375.

warp in a tapestry, where the political and economic actors do the woof, the churches thus setting the proper framework and giving the direction.

There are other spheres which cannot be neglected, because they pose such direct challenges to the value system governing our society.

The Responsibility of the Church in the Cultural Field

The culture of our society is decisively influenced by rapid technological developments, and this situation presents the Church with new challenges. I will mention only a few concerns within medical science and ecology.

Medical science presents the Church with a series of problems among which abortion, euthanasia and genetics are the most urgent. Whereas technology in general is seen to be unrelated to ethics and moral evaluation, it is obvious that technological developments in medicine have an immediate bearing on moral values and our culture in general. One could therefore assume that there would be as broad a consensus on these issues — even in a pluralist society — as we can observe it with respect to human rights. This is, however, not the case. The argument against the Church is that nobody can impose his or her values on others in a pluralist society. Everybody should have the right to stick to his or her own anthropology; thus the slogan that a woman has the right to decide over her own body, and to ask for a voluntary abortion.[24]

Abortion is the easiest problem to solve, viewed from an ethical side. The question is to evaluate life against life, in spite of the fact that the one life in question is not yet born. Medically and ethically, life starts with conception, and any decision to effect an abortion has to be decided in this light. One may still find variations in borderline cases, but the ethical basis should be clear enough. To rule that life starts with the twelfth week after conception — or any other date previous to birth — is totally arbitrary and cannot be defended on any moral grounds, Christian or not.

Euthanasia is, ethically speaking, a more complicated issue. If one assumes only an inherent value in human beings, as it has partly been argued in discussions on human rights, there seems to be no objection to euthanasia. Each person will in this case have the right to evaluate his or her *own* value independently of any other references, and each person will himself or herself be the only arbiter to decide whether or not to terminate his or her life. Only when the value of human beings is based outside the person, in the Creator, will the ethical objection to euthanasia become clear. No person can "devaluate" himself or herself before God.

---

24. D. Cook, *The Moral Maze* (London: SPCK, 1983), gives a good introduction. A comprehensive reader is S. E. Lammers and A. Verhey, *On Moral Medicine* (Grand Rapids: Eerdmans, 1987). A South African book is W. S. Vorster, ed., *The Right to Life* (Pretoria: University of South Africa, 1988).

What the Church has to argue in a pluralist society is that euthanasia —
although it may seem humane in some extreme cases — opens the sluice gates
for a devastatingly inhumane society, where life is valued according to the
absence of pain, the capacity to be productive, etc. Even a pluralist society should
not allow this to happen.

The most complicated issues are found in modern *genetics*. It combines
a variety of medical technical developments, and it is difficult to keep abreast
with every new discovery. The whole field is in urgent need of ethical assessment
and legal regulations. Many conferences have addressed the issues, and many
books have already been written. The Church needs to present this in an intelligible and intelligent way, both to its own members and to the public in general.
It is also necessary to make an effort to influence politicians and the scientists
and practitioners who are involved.

The whole field of medical technology is a gigantic challenge which the
South African churches barely have started to address because of the overwhelming task of terminating apartheid. It will, however, probably be one of
the battle grounds in the new, pluralist, South Africa.

(c) Another issue which is already crippling parts of South Africa concerns
various aspects of *ecology*, particularly with respect to land. How is land going
to be redistributed in the new South Africa? Will it be possible to accommodate
all those who have a justified claim on land, and is it possible to avoid the fact
that land is overexploited, as we can see in Transkei and many other places
already?

The whole question may easily become one of technical legality. The
Church should see to it that legality is not allowed to overrule morality in trying
to find a viable solution to the mess which is the result of the various acts
pertaining to land ownership in South Africa.

In other ecological matters one will have to stand up against a combination
of economic exploitation and technology gone rampant. The looming ecological
disaster shows eminently why there is a need for an independent spiritual
governance in addition to the temporal governance.[25]

It shows how Christian eschatological expectations ought to guide the
approach of the Church. The apostle Paul wrote that the creation waits with
eager longing for the revealing of the sons of God, and the creation itself will
be set free from its bondage to decay and obtain the glorious liberty of the
children of God (Rom. 8:19-21).

The Church has to stress that ecology has to do with the individual's
relationship to other people, with the mutual relationship of people who are
going to occupy this earth in the future, and ultimately with the relationship

---

25. W. S. Vorster, ed., *Are We Killing God's Earth?* (Pretoria: University of South Africa,
1967), particularly K. Nürnberger's article "Ecology and Christian Ethics in a Semi-Industrialised
and Polarised Society," 45-67.

to God. But we are not conserving nature [simply] for nature's sake. To rescue animals from extinction at the expense of people is hence a move that cannot be condoned by the Church. To multiply natural reserves is not automatically the answer to the ecological crisis.

Conclusion

I have used Bennett's model for social ethics, and included the teaching of the two kingdoms in order to focus on some urgent social ethical challenges for the churches in South Africa.

The basic challenge is, as always, to safeguard the independence of the Church within society. The Church is not doing this for its own sake, but for the sake of *justice*. Justice is a fundamental responsibility of the Church at all times and under all circumstances. From this follows the responsibility of the Church to be a conscience and a guide in society — in all spheres of life. I have emphasised the political and economic spheres together with the vast field of ethical concerns, including medical and ecological issues.

There are no easy answers to any of these questions. Moreover, the Church is always in danger of being pushed into giving ideological answers instead of revelational answers. The task of performing spiritual governance has always been hampered by the fact that the Church itself is a sociological structure, organised and led by people, implicating structural as well as personal sin.

This insight should, however, never deter the Church from its God-given task. Until Christ returns in judgment and glory, the Church has to be an *ecclesia militans,* a struggling Church, also as it tries to be God's mouth in societal responsibilities.

The Understanding of the Church Emerging in the Bilateral Dialogues — Coherence or Divergence?

GENNADIOS LIMOURIS

In the nascent theological trialogue between the great historic traditions of Christendom, Orthodoxy has assured its due place. Protestantism and Roman Catholicism — first in confrontation and during these past decades in conversation — have been occupying centre stage. The result of the millennial separation between Eastern and Western Christianity has been a spiritual impoverishment whose crippling effects are only now beginning to be surmised. The Western partners became increasingly aware that they cannot proceed much further without the third partner. It is therefore of momentous significance that the Orthodox churches have in recent years become actively engaged not only in the ecumenical movement at large, but also in the expanding bilateral theological conversations with other churches and confessions.

We will follow a customary definition of the term "bilateral" — as the Orthodox understand and use it — to denote theological conversations sponsored, directly or indirectly, by two churches, traditions or confessional families, with purposes ranging from promoting mutual understanding to achieving full communion in true faith and love, and reconciling hostilities and divisions of the past.

It hardly needs to be emphasized that these dialogues, as they are presented in the ecumenical spectrum, manifest considerable pluralism of discussions, agreements, or disagreements on joint statements on converging issues. This variety, of course, is inevitable due to the fact that each dialogue has its own history, character, thematology, and structure of decision-making, and that the dialogues are at different stages in the ongoing process toward the goal and vision of unity and union among churches. They have also been increasingly led to bear

---

Reprinted from the *Greek Orthodox Theological Review* 36 (1991): 1-20. Used with permission of the journal.

Christian witness, and an atmosphere of mutual appreciation, friendship, and fellowship has already become a reality. But has this development also led to a deeper mutual theological understanding? Have the profound differences between the Orthodox churches and the other churches in bilateral dialogues been theologically clarified? This question is legitimate. At least, at first sight, there is a discrepancy between the degree of theological agreement and the factual fellowship which the different traditions have found in the ecumenical movement.

In this perspective Fr. John Meyendorff, for the second meeting of the Orthodox–Roman Catholic Joint Commission in Munich (1982), has written that ". . . the meeting seems to be an extraordinary event that at a time when the ecumenical movement has become entangled in the ambiguities of secularism and polarization, Orthodox and Roman Catholics had the moral strength to look at the fundamentals of the faith, i.e., the mystery of the Church, the Eucharist and the Holy Trinity, as the only true and real issues of Christian unity. . . ."[1]

Today, on the international level, the Orthodox churches are engaged in six bilateral dialogues: they are in conversations with Anglicans, Old Catholics, Roman Catholics, Oriental Orthodox, Lutherans, and Reformed. The third Pre-Conciliar Pan-Orthodox Conference in 1986 examined and carefully evaluated these dialogues and endorsed their importance, significance, and results towards their pilgrimage on the way to unity in true *faith* and *love:*

> The Orthodox Church . . . is fully conscious of its responsibility with respect to the unity of the Christian world. It recognizes the real existence of all Christian churches and confessions. At the same time, it is convinced that all its relations with these churches and confessions must be based upon the clarification, as quickly as possible, of ecclesiological questions and particularly of the common teaching with respect to the sacraments, grace, priesthood, and apostolic succession. The bilateral theological dialogues currently being conducted by the Orthodox Church are the authoritative expression of this consciousness of Orthodoxy. Of course . . . the Orthodox Church is not unaware of the difficulties attached to such undertakings; it realizes that they are not to be avoided on the road to the common tradition of the early, undivided Church and hopes that the Holy Spirit, who builds the entire body of the Church, will provide for the deficiencies. In this respect . . . the Orthodox Church does not depend only on the human strength of those carrying on the dialogues, but also on the guidance of the Holy Spirit and the grace of the Lord, who prayed "that all may be one" (Jn. 17:21).[2]

1. J. Meyendorff, *A Comment on the Munich Document: "The Mystery of the Church and the Eucharist in the Light of the Mystery of the Holy Trinity,"* Joint Orthodox–Roman Catholic Commission, Munich, June 1982, in *St. Vladimir's Theological Quarterly* 4 (1983): 294-98.

2. Cf. Final Texts and Decisions of the Third Pan-Orthodox Pre-Conciliar Conference (28 October–6 November 1986), Section 3: "The Relation of the Orthodox Church to the Rest of the Christian World," in *Episkepsis* 369 (1986): 9 (in Greek/French); see also the English text in *Diakonia* 1 (1987): 44.

In addition to taking part in these international dialogues, several Orthodox churches are also conducting theological conversations with other churches on the local level or in other countries. Historical and social-political relations in the past as well as theological factors were the main reasons that such talks were undertaken. Many such meetings have already taken place and considerable results have been achieved. Their aim, in the first place, is to remove misconceptions and to promote mutual acquaintance and rapprochement; they further serve as a preparatory stage for later "dialogues in truth" on the world level, exploring possibilities of fuller communion in faith and sacramental life. They should also be considered "co-partners" and "facilitators" to the international dialogues rather than be seen in isolation and without any relation to them. But these efforts are somehow dispersed and lead, therefore, to less visibility and less public recognition than the official dialogues. However, they reflect a serious involvement on both sides, and we must be grateful for their contribution. As we have seen, the dialogues thus represent widely differing stages of developments.

The question which interests us here is therefore "the understanding of the Church emerging from the bilateral dialogues — coherence and divergence"; it has not yet been discussed explicitly in all the six dialogues, but it is only referred to in some of them (e.g., Anglican, Old Catholic, and Roman Catholic). Thus the present dialogical exercise is somewhat limited from the Orthodox point of view. It seems to us that it was preferable and even desirable that our theme should be extended to the other international dialogues in order to identify either common perspectives, coherence, or divergence on the issue, or at least new ways of reflection and substantial developments. This should rather render a service to the ongoing process of the theological conversations, mainly for those which did not yet reach "the mature steps" to deal directly and explicitly with the doctrine of the Church, the nature of the Church, and ecclesiology in particular.

Being in Dialogue — Sharing Truths

God's creation constitutes a single and whole entity. There is no drastic separation between the visible *Ekklesia* or local community, and the invisible *Ekklesia*, the Church triumphant; both constitute the wholeness of God's creation. God's creation is all-encompassing, and the physical is sometimes linked with the metaphysical. It is for this reason that in Orthodox theology the supernatural aspect of the Church is not treated in isolation from the physical or visible Church; and that the saints, the Fathers, the martyrs, and all those who, by the guidance of the Holy Spirit, experienced the illumination, the theosis, are in fact contemporaries. The present incarnates the past and anticipates the future. Their Church is our Church of Jesus Christ, and our

Church is in direct historical continuity with their Church. Therefore, "God's revelation in Jesus Christ is realized and actualized in the Church and through the Church as the body of Christ," as Lutherans and Orthodox state.[3] The past lives in the present and will continue as long as human beings live in this world.

History and revelation are mutually determined and conditioned. It is of their historical conscience that the Orthodox appeal to the authority of the Tradition, the mind of the Fathers, the decisions of the Ecumenical Councils, the holiness and the experience of the past. Thus, "the Holy Tradition is the authentic expression of divine revelation in the living experience of the Church, the body of the Word incarnate."[4]

However, in the dialogues with Anglicans, Lutherans, and Old Catholics common agreement can be found in the dogmatic expression which is given on the nature of the Church in the Nicene-Constantinopolitan Creed (381) and confirmed by the Fourth Ecumenical Council in Chalcedon. In this Creed the confession of faith in the triune God is followed by the confession of faith that the Church is "One, Holy, Catholic and Apostolic." Looking at this affirmation is the Orthodox–Roman Catholic dialogue. It is implicitly stated (Munich, Bari, Valamo), but somehow it appears as a reference to issues related to faith and sacraments.

Several of the advanced dialogues have a common beginning in the ecclesiological debates by describing the mystery of the Church in relation to its essence and nature in Christological and trinitarian perspectives. The mystery of the Church, as Anglicans and Orthodox state, "cannot be defined or fully described. But the steadfast joy of people who discover new life and salvation in Christ through the Church reminds us that the Church itself is a lived experience. The Church is sent into the world as "a *sign, instrument,* and *first-fruits* of the Kingdom of God."[5] Use of the word "mystery" also serves a double purpose: to give the sense of a reality which is greater than anything we might say about it, and to indicate that here is something which is God-given and not just "man-made," something in and through which God is at work and in which human beings are involved.[6] Because of its very nature the Orthodox and the Old Catholics agree that "the Church is intimately related to the mystery of the triune God who reveals himself in Christ and the Holy

3. Cf. Third Lutheran-Orthodox Joint Commission, *Agreed Statement on the Divine Revelation* (Allentown, USA, 24-30 May 1985), in *Episkepsis* 341 (1985): 13 (in Greek/French), original text in English.

4. Cf. Fourth Lutheran-Orthodox Joint Commission, *Agreed Statement on Scripture and Tradition* (Chania, Crete, Greece, 28 May–2 June 1987), in *Episkepsis* 381 (1987): 18-19, par. 3 (Greek/French), original text in English.

5. Anglican-Orthodox Dialogue. *The Dublin Agreed Statement 1984* (henceforth quoted as *Dublin*) (London, 1985), p. 9, par. 3.

6. Cf. C. Davey, "The Doctrine of the Church in International Bilateral Dialogues," in *One in Christ* 2 (1986): 136.

Spirit (cf. Eph. 5:32)."[7] It is, as Saint John Chrysostom confirms, "the treasure house of God's ineffable mysteries."[8]

In the Orthodox–Roman Catholic dialogue some — Orthodox and non-Orthodox — have found it "logically difficult" to follow who claims to be the Church. To be more accurate, the Roman Catholics have declared that "the one true Church of Christ subsists in the Roman Catholic Church,"[9] whereas the Orthodox state that they are "the One, Holy, Catholic and Apostolic Church."[10] Or, in the Dublin Statement, with the Anglicans they say, "It is the one true Church of Christ, which as his body is not and cannot be divided."[11] This clearly proves that from the beginning both sides, Roman Catholics and Orthodox, insisted that their dialogue must take place "on equal terms" — and the consequence of such an insistence for both participants is that for those who are "engaged in the dialogue a change in ecclesiology is required."[12] Encouraging results can be seen in the Munich Statement, which begins from the "actual" rather than the "ideal." "In the New Testament the Church describes a 'local' reality. The Church exists in history as local church . . . in a given place."[13] But it is not just manmade — it is not simply "formed by the persons who come together to establish it. There is 'Jerusalem from [on] high,' which 'comes down from God,' a communion-koinonia which establishes the community itself," so that "the Church comes into being by a free gift, by the act of the new creation."[14]

Here Roman Catholics and Orthodox make the reality "of communion between God and human beings in fellowship" the basic, God-given experience which the language of ecclesiology describes and of which the local Christian community is an "expression." For the Church "which is in a given place," "manifests itself when it is assembled."[15] It is "fully assembled when it celebrates the Eucharist"; moreover, in the local church, as it celebrates the Eucharist, "a new unity is communicated which overcomes divisions and restores communion in the one Body of Christ, a unity which transcends psychological, racial, socio-political, or cultural unity. It is the communion of the Holy Spirit. . . ."[16]

7. Old Catholic–Orthodox Dialogue, *Agreed Statement on Ecclesiology* (Chambésy, Switzerland, 23-30 August 1977), Section 3/1: "The Nature and Marks of the Church"; see English text in *Growth in Agreement*, ed. H. Meyer and L. Vischer (New York/Geneva, 1984), p. 401, par. 1.

8. Cf. St. John Chrysostom, *Homily on the 1st letter to the Corinthians*, 16.3 in PG 61.134.

9. Cf. Vatican II, *Decree de Ecclesia, Lumen Gentium.*

10. Old Catholic–Orthodox Dialogue, p. 402, par. 8.

11. *Dublin*, pp. 10-11, pars. 8-9 and p. 45, par. 100(e).

12. Cf. C. Davey, *The Doctrine*, 138.

13. First Roman Catholic–Orthodox Joint Commission, *Agreed Statement on The Mystery of the Church and the Eucharist in the Light of the Mystery of the Holy Trinity* (Munich, FRG, 30 June–6 July 1982) (from now on: *Munich*) Section 2, par. 1; see English text in *Information Service (IS)* 49 (1982), 109; see also text in Greek/French in *Episkepsis* 177 (1982).

14. Ibid.

15. Ibid.

16. Ibid.

Thus the Church which is the body of Christ is to be one, and therefore to manifest a "new unity" of all people. The role of an ecumenical dialogue is precisely to bring into harmony the uniqueness of the various historical configurations in which the churches have developed and not to use this as a means of further division, but for a more real and deeper understanding of the personal God who reveals himself in *time* and *space* for the salvation of all of humanity.

The Dublin Statement clearly points out that the reality of division between Anglicans and Orthodox does not yet allow them to find themselves to be one: "We are disrupted Christian people seeking to restore our unity. Our divisions do not destroy but damage the basic unity we have in Christ, and our disunity impedes our mission to the world as well as our relationships with each other."[17]

It is important to note the language used above, especially the words "destroy" and "damage." The use of these terms becomes central, especially in the light of how Anglicans are accustomed to see the divisions existing within the Church; "they do not believe that they alone are the one true Church, but they believe that they belong to it."[18] On the other hand, the Orthodox ". . . believe that the Orthodox Church is the one true Church of Christ, which as his body is not and cannot be divided."[19] But at the same time they see the Anglicans "as brothers and sisters who are seeking together with them the union of all Christians in the one Church."[20] And this difference is reconciled in the evaluation section of the epilogue: "But . . . we agree in our fundamental understanding of the church that it is the One, Holy, Catholic and Apostolic."[21]

Another important point can be found in the different accounts given of the sinfulness and division observed in the life of Christian communities. Orthodox say that the human members of the Church on earth are sinful [but] do not believe that sinfulness should be ascribed to the Church as the body of Christ, indwelt by the Holy Spirit.[22] Anglicans follow St. Augustine's doctrine in holding that "immaculate" is a proper epithet of the Church triumphant and of the Church as the body of Christ, but not of the empirical society of believers: "The Church," affirm the Anglicans, "under Christ is the community where God's grace is at work, healing and transforming sinful men and women; and because grace in the church is mediated through those who are themselves undergoing such transformation, the struggle between grace and sin is to be seen as characteristic of, rather than accidental to, the Church on earth."[23]

17. *Dublin*, p. 11, par. 9.
18. Ibid.
19. Ibid.
20. Ibid.
21. Ibid., p. 44, par. 96(a).
22. Ibid., pp. 44-45, par. 96.
23. Ibid., par. 99(d)

The ecclesiological concept of the Church as the household or family of God presupposes that believers accept *love (agape)* or *philanthropia* as a common denominator, freely flowing, expecting nothing in return. It is this type of unmerited philanthropy that made Christianity very attractive among the less fortunate members of the Roman Empire's society. It transformed an anthropocentric and limited humanism into a theocentric and ecumenical philanthropy.

Recognizing its own reality in the light of divine Revelation, the Church very early saw itself above all as that area of Christian humanity within which the Spirit of Christ (cf. Eph. 2:8) is re-creating the communion — koinonia — of humanity with God himself and therefore welding into one *communion* all peoples, races, cultures, social classes and differences between the sexes.[24] The vision which dominates the Epistle to the Ephesians — undoubtedly the first Christian document to be open to all dimensions of the "catholicity" of salvation — is not merely an afterthought to this wakening of the Church to its own true nature (cf. Eph. 2:15-22). On the contrary, it expresses what is its essence: that the unity of the Church "is inseparable from the divine purpose of reuniting humanity — in the blessings of the messianic age — a reunification which is *already* taking shape in the Church."[25] It is easy to see why the Early Church Fathers regarded the eucharistic synaxis — in which men and women of every class, culture and race were henceforth one in the Body of Christ — as both the supreme embodiment of the nature of the Church and the supreme statement of God's design for humanity.

In the Roman Catholic–Orthodox dialogue, this concept of the Church as communion-koinonia[26] was taken up from the beginning, strongly emphasized and further developed in the Munich statement (1982) — as well as in the following statements — which refers to St. Ignatius of Antioch's affirmation: "where Christ is, there is the catholic Church."[27] This also implies that "catholicity or wholeness is a property of each local church."

However, Roman Catholics and Orthodox, wanting to avoid the danger of mere congregationalism, sometimes associate "eucharistic ecclesiology" with a concept of a koinonia-communion between the local churches, as they have indicated in the Munich Statement: "the one and unique Church finds its identity in the koinonia of the churches."[28]

Clearly, at this point, difficulties and potential disagreement might emerge as the discussion proceeds. What are the forms and conditions of the koinonia?

---

24. Cf. J. M. R. Tillard, "Koinonia-Sacrament," in *One in Christ* 2 (1986): 107.

25. Cf. J. M. R. Tillard, "Two Programmes — A Single Task," in *Faith and Renewal, Faith and Order Paper No. 131* (Geneva: World Council of Churches, 1986), 100-110.

26. See the excellent study on the meaning "communio-koinonia" in different traditions, ed. by the Institute for Ecumenical Research, Strausbourg, 1990.

27. Cf. St. Ignatius, *To the Smyrneans* 8.

28. *Munich*, Section 2, p. 111, par. 2.

Is it a eucharistic reality/and experience? If so, asks Fr. Meyendorff, it would also need a eucharistically responsible ministry. And would that be a conciliar institution or a ministry realized in the function (or person) of a universal primate?[29]

The concept of koinonia-communion implies a relationship between local churches that, according to Roman Catholics and Orthodox, "is constitutive of the Church. . . . institutions make it visible and, so to speak, 'historize' it." What is implied here — so it seems — is that the mystery of the Church, while always remaining a mystery, manifests itself in history through institutions that, like all realities of history, are changing.[30]

The basic thesis of a pneumatological Christocentrism is the starting point for overcoming the recent theological neoscholasticism while looking for exact exclusive statements in the form of definitions. The balance of the incarnate Word of God and the eucharistic mystical experience within the one body, the Ekklesia of God, is the focus of the theology of the Church in a dynamic perspective. The title of the Munich Statement itself reveals this truth: "The mystery of the Church and the Eucharist in the light of the mystery of the Holy Trinity." The Pentecostal event is the fullness of the paschal mystery and inaugurates the eschaton of time and history. Through the Spirit the work of Christ continues in history and Church, but ultimately it points beyond history to the full realization of God's design for his creation. "The Church itself in which God's grace is at work is the sacrament par excellence, the anticipated manifestation of the final realities, the foretaste of God's kingdom, of the glory of the God and Father, of the *eschaton* in history," as the Valamo Statement affirms.[31]

This eschatological perspective challenges Anglican, Orthodox, and Roman Catholic as well as Old Catholic and Oriental Orthodox partners — in common mind — to express the understanding of apostolicity, which does not only refer to what has been received from the past; it also points to what is awaited at the last day. The Apostles are not only the authoritative witnesses to Christ's coming in history; they also are companions of the eschatological Christ enthroned for judgment (cf. Mt. 19:28).[32] In this perspective "apostolic succes-

29. Cf. Meyendorff, "A Comment," p. 296.

30. *Munich,* Section 2, p. 111, par. 2.

31. Fifth Roman Catholic–Orthodox Joint Commission, *Agreed Statement on The Sacrament of Order in the Sacramental Structure of the Church, With Particular Reference to Apostolic Succession for the Sanctification and Unity of the People of God* (Valamo, Finland, 19-27 June 1987) (from now on: *Valamo*), Section 2; see English text in *IS* 68 (1988), p. 175, par. 22; see also text in Greek/French in *Episkepsis* 404 (1988): 9-18.

32. Cf. ibid., Section 2, p. 175, par. 19 (English text); cf. also Old Catholic–Orthodox dialogue in *Growth in Agreement,* Section 3/1, pp. 403-4, par. 17: ". . . The apostolicity doctrine preserved by the Church is the inner aspect of its apostolicity. Its other element is the unbroken series and succession of pastors and teachers of the Church, starting from the Apostles, which is the outward mark and also the pledge of the truth of the Church . . ."; cf. *Dublin,* pp. 13-14, par.

sion" means more than a mere historical transmission of power from Christ through the Apostles to bishops in the Church. Ecclesial ministry is apostolic not only "because it is carried out in continuity and in fidelity to what was given by Christ and handed on [in] history by the Apostles,"[33] but also "because the eucharistic assembly at which the minister presides is an anticipation of the final community with Christ."[34]

It is precisely in the Eucharist that history and eschatology meet, that the work of Christ and the Spirit are actualized, that the "Church manifests its fullness,"[35] that "the role of the bishop and of the priest appears in its full light,"[36] and "finds its accomplishment."[37] Coherence and common agreement exist therefore with the above partners in this issue when they strongly empha-size the centrality and importance of the Eucharist for the life of the Church in all its aspects. Here especially we see the convergence of modern Orthodox and Roman Catholic thought. Whether we begin with Orthodox "Eucharistic Ecclesiology" or with Second Vatican's Lumen Gentium, the conclusion is the same: The Eucharist makes the Church what "it is called to be"[38]: it is both source and criterion for all aspects of the Church's life, including its ministry.

Perhaps the most striking issue developed in all dialogues, and its ante-cedents, concerns "the close link between the work of Christ and that of the Holy Spirit."[39] Again and again the statements caution against "seeing the economy of Christ in isolation from the Spirit."[40] With remarkable consistency most of the statements have taken a pneumatologically conditioned Christology as their departure.[41] The Spirit "which eternally proceeds from the Father and reposes on the Son prepared the Christ event and achieved it,"[42] from the incarnation and baptism through the sacrifice of Calvary and glorification.

17: ". . . The apostolicity is manifested in particular through the succession of bishops. This suc-cession is a sign of the unbroken continuity of apostolic tradition and life"; cf. Second Orthodox-Oriental Orthodox Joint Commission, *Second Agreed Statement and Recommendations to the Churches* (Chambésy, Switzerland, 23-28 September 1990), p. 5, par. 9 (mimeographed, not yet published).

33. *Valamo*, Section 2, p. 175, par. 14.

34. Ibid.

35. Ibid., Section 3, p. 176, par. 34.

36. Ibid.

37. Ibid., p. 177, par. 41.

38. *Munich*, Section 1, p. 108, par. 4(b).

39. *Valamo*, "Introduction," p. 174, par. 2.

40. Ibid., par. 3.

41. Cf. J. Erickson, "The International Orthodox–Roman Catholic Commission's Statement on Ordination" (*Valamo, Ecumenical Trends* 18/4 [1989]: 49).

42. *Valamo*, Section 4, p. 177, par. 44; cf. also *Anglican-Orthodox Dialogue, The Moscow Agreed Statement* (from now on: *Moscow*), ed. K. Ware and C. Davey (London: 1977), Section 6, "The Filoque Clause," p. 87, par. 19; *Growth in Agreement*, Section 1/3, "The Holy Trinity," p. 394, par. 14/3; Orthodox–Oriental Orthodox Joint Commission, First Agreed Statement on Christology (Anba Bishoi Monastery, Egypt, 20-24 June 1989), see English text, ed. T. Fitzgerald, in *Ecumenical Trends* 19/3 (1990): 47; see also text in Greek/French in *Episkepsis* 422 (1989): 7-8.

From this Christology springs a pneumatologically conditioned ecclesiology, for the same Spirit which anointed into Christ's Body and the same Spirit which empowered the ministry of Christ ensures that his unique ministry "remains in action in history" within the Church.[43] In a characteristic formulation, Orthodox and Roman Catholics affirm that the newness of the Church's ministry consists in that "Christ, servant of God for humanity, is present through the Spirit in the Church, his body, from which he cannot be separated. For he himself is the first-born among many brothers."[44] Here, as elsewhere, the statement offers a healthy corrective to that one-sided "Christomonism" of which Western Christianity so often — and perhaps rightly so — has been accused. Too often we think of Christ as an isolated individual apart from the humankind which he has come to save. We lose sight of the whole Christ, "caput et corpus," to use the phrase of Saint Augustine. We make a disjunction between Christ and his Church, and as a consequence we tend to make the Church into an autonomous, self-sufficient institution. Here a pneumatological corrective is essential for the Church in what it is because the same Spirit who anointed Christ anoints it.

The Church, as a sacramental organism, is a body continually being formed and built up, not simply as institution "established" or "founded" long ago by Christ and then left to its own devices. So its ministry also is not simply a vocation to holiness, a life lived according to the gospel.[45] It is by necessity charismatic, for without the manifold gifts of the Holy Spirit[46] — and without that personal experience of God which is possible only in the Holy Spirit — the Church with its official ministry would not just become "institution": it would cease to be the Church. As the Munich Statement points out, the Church — and its ministry — "is continually in a state of epiclesis."[47] Therefore, the Eucharist and the Church are the body of the crucified and risen Christ and become the locus of the energies of the Holy Spirit.

This understanding prevents us from seeing the economy of Christ in isolation from the Spirit. The actual presence of Christ in his Church "is also of an eschatological nature since the Spirit constitutes the earnest of the perfect realization of God's design for the world."[48] Orthodox and Roman Catholics affirm that ". . . in this perspective the Church appears as the community of the New Covenant which Christ through the Holy Spirit gathers about himself and

43. *Valamo*, Section 4, p. 177, par. 44.

44. Ibid., Section 1, p. 174, par. 9.

45. Cf. ibid., Section, 1, par. 8, and Section 3, p. 177, pars. 39-40.

46. Fourth Roman Catholic–Orthodox Joint Commission, *Agreed Statement on Faith, Sacraments, and the Unity of the Church*, Bari, Italy, 9-16 June 1987 (from now on: *Bari*); see English text in *Information Service* 64 (1987), Section 3, p. 84, par. 15; see also text in Greek/French in *Episkepsis* 390 (1987): 5-15.

47. *Munich*, Section 1, p. 108, par. 5(c).

48. *Valamo*, Introduction, p. 174, pars. 3-4; cf. also Section 4, p. 177, par. 44.

builds up as his body. Through the Church, Christ is present in history; through it he achieves the salvation of the world."[49] Both sides avoid a merely local limitation to the Eucharist; so they add: "the koinonia is eschatological."[50] And therefore, everything begins in the Eucharist through conversion and reconciliation, with an ultimate presupposition which is always "repentance" and "confession."[51] It is also this koinonia, as the central event within the Church, which is also and on the same basis "kerygmatic,"[52] proclaiming the event of the mystery of God to the assemblies, to the whole world, to the whole community and the whole creation, and "the response of faith is given by all."[53] Thus the Eucharist is "inseparably sacrament and word since in it the incarnate Word sanctifies in the Spirit";[54] and that is why the whole of the liturgy, and not only the reading of the Holy Scriptures, constitutes the proclamation of the Word under the form of doxology and prayer. The Word proclaimed "is made flesh and becomes sacramental."[55]

Old Catholics and Orthodox, who have in principle concluded their theological dialogue and come to an agreement on doctrinal issues, present the concept of the "local church" as "a fellowship of believers united around the bishop and the priests, and as the Body of Christ, each local church *is the manifestation of the whole Christ* in one particular place. It represents the sacramental reality of the whole Church in its own locality. . . . each local church, on the contrary, has that life in its fullness."[56]

Thus, for all the differences in custom and usage, the life of the local church is in essence one and the same: "There is one Body and one Spirit, one Lord, one faith, one baptism, one God and Father of all . . ." (Eph. 4:4-6). There *are not* many bodies, but the one Body of Christ, undivided and whole in each place. This unity of life in the local churches reflects the unity of the Holy Trinity itself. "Since the Church in this present time still awaits deliverance from all evil and must therefore pray God so to deliver it, to make it perfect in his love and bring it together from the ends of the earth into his kingdom,"[57] the local churches must devotedly maintain the essential unity given to them, and constantly "struggle against the forces of sin and division."[58]

However, this eucharistic communion as actual union with Christ for the divided world becomes a foundation stone and a springboard of social interest

49. Ibid., par. 4.

50. *Munich,* Section 2, p. 109, par. 2.

51. Ibid.

52. Ibid.

53. Ibid.

54. Ibid.

55. Ibid.; cf. also *Dublin,* pp. 32-34, pars. 53-65.

56. Old Catholic–Orthodox, *Agreed Statement on Ecclesiology,* Section 3/3, p. 405, pars. 23, 24.

57. Ibid., par. 24; cf. *Didache* 10.5.9,4.

58. Ibid., par. 24.

and welfare preparing for an eternal fellowship (Mt. 26:26-29; Jn. 6:32-59; 1 Cor. 11:20-34). This understanding of the Church was expressed centuries ago by St. John of Damascus, who wrote on Holy Communion as a union because "through the Church we share Christ's flesh and his divinity." "Yes," he wrote, "we have communion and we are united with one another through the Church. For since we partake of one bread, we all become one body of Christ and one blood and members of one another, being one body with Christ."[59]

At this point, rather than say one *is* and one *is not* the true Church of Christ, Orthodox and Roman Catholics begin with a declaration that both can accept: "The Body of Christ is One. There exists only one Church of God."[60] But they continue to affirm with an assertion, which again could be accepted by both, about the local church: "Each Eucharistic assembly is truly the holy church of God, the body of Christ, in communion with the first community of the disciples and with all who throughout the world celebrate and have celebrated the memorial of the Lord."[61]

Meanwhile, there seems to be a cloudiness about what eucharistic communion means when Anglican and Orthodox go on to affirm that the Eucharist is the visible expression of the catholicity of the Church, as evidenced in the following: "The catholicity of particular local churches, each of which, being in eucharistic communion with all the other local churches, manifests in its own place and time the one catholic Church. These local churches, in faithful response to their own particular missionary situation, have developed a wide diversity in their life. As long as their witness to the one faith remains *unimpaired*, such diversity is to be seen not as a deficiency or cause for division, but as a mark of the faithfulness of the one Spirit who distributes to each according to his will (1 Cor. 12:11)."[62] How, specifically, does each church determine whether the witness of the one faith is unimpaired? Does each church assume that this witness is unimpaired in itself, but is impaired in the other church?[63]

In relation to the eucharistic celebration, Roman Catholics and Orthodox agreed that "the entire assembly, each according to his or her status, is 'liturge' of the koinonia, and is so only through the Spirit."[64] ". . . [T]here are varieties of ministries, but the same Lord (. . .). To each is given the manifestation of the Spirit for the common good" (1 Cor. 12:5, 7).[65] The koinonia culminates in the celebration of the Eucharist in which Christian initiation is completed,

---

59. St. John of Damascus, *Exposition of the Orthodox Faith*, PG 94.1153A; see also St. John Chrysostom, *Homily* 46, in PG 160.

60. *Munich*, Section 3, p. 111, par. 1.

61. Ibid.

62. *Dublin*, p. 12, par. 12(c).

63. Cf. P. Baktis, "The Dublin Statement: Investigations and Analysis," *One in Christ* 2 (1989): 171-72.

64. *Valamo*, Section 3, p. 175, par. 24; cf. also *Munich*, Section 2, p. 109, par. 2.

65. *Valamo*, Section 3, p. 175, par. 24.

through which all become one body of Christ. . . . In fact, bearing the variety of gifts of the Spirit, the local Church has at its centre the bishop, whose communion realizes the unity of all and expresses the fullness of the church. "This unity of the local church (in an eucharistic perspective) is inseparable from the universal communion of the churches. . . ."[66]

Using eucharistic imagery, therefore, to validate the use of eucharistic ecclesiology as a principle to be employed in the dialogues on the way to church union, we may see this confirmed in particular in the Moscow Statement, in which Anglicans and Orthodox agree that "the eucharistic teaching and practice of the churches, mutually confessed, constitutes an essential factor for the understanding which can lead to reunion between Orthodox and Anglican churches."[67] This essential requirement is based upon the understanding that "in each local eucharistic celebration the visible unity and catholicity of the Church is fully manifested";[68] and it also allows for other aspects of churches' theologies to add in the process of union, but eucharistic theology is placed as the most essential factor. In the light of this they affirm mutually that "the eucharistic understanding of the Church affirms primarily the presence of Jesus Christ in the Church, which is his body, and in the Eucharist. Through the action of the Holy Spirit, all faithful communicants share in the one body of Christ and become one body with him."[69] Thus the Eucharist actualizes the Church. The Christian community has a basic sacramental character. The Church can be described as a "synaxis" of an "ekklesia" which is — in its essence — a worshipping and eucharistic community. The Church, celebrating "the Eucharist, becomes fully itself, that is, koinonia, fellowship-communion." The Church celebrates the Eucharist as the central act of its existence, in which the ecclesial community, as a living reality confessing its faith, receives its realization. Thus the eucharistic action of the Church is "the Passover from the old to the new; it is the action of the Holy Spirit." When it is articulated, "the *Epiclesis* voices the work of the Spirit with the Father in the consecration of the elements as the body and the blood of Christ."[70]

However, this thesis brings disagreement concerning the issue of communion and intercommunion, particularly with the Anglicans. The Dublin Statement openly affirms that "it is clear that there has been a considerable development in ecumenical and inter-church relations in recent years which has resulted in the Anglicans sharing the Eucharist with members of other churches on special ecumenical occasions, in times of special need, or on a more regular basis."[71] The Anglican tradition "accepts as legitimate, in certain situations, the

---

66. Ibid., par. 26.
67. *Moscow,* p. 88, par. 22.
68. *Dublin,* p. 47, par. 109(b).
69. *Moscow,* p. 88, pars. 22-23; cf. also *Dublin,* ibid.
70. *Moscow,* pp. 88-89, pars. 24, 26, and 27.
71. *Dublin,* p. 14, par. 18(a).

use of intercommunion as a means towards the attainment of full organic unity."
On the other hand, the Orthodox disagree and completely reject the notion of
intercommunion because "there can be communion only between local
churches that have a unity of *faith, ministry* and *sacraments*."[72]

In fact, this results in that for the Orthodox, "communion" involves a
mystical and sanctifying unity created by the body and blood of Christ, which
makes them "one body and one blood *(sessomoi* and *synemoi)* with Christ,"[73]
and therefore they can have "no differences of faith."[74] This eucharistic "uneasiness" with the Anglicans challenges the Orthodox and Roman Catholics, by
repeating the Dublin declaration, to affirm that "because of this reciprocal
recognition that the faith handed down in each local church is one and at the
same time (as are the priesthood and the sacrament) that they recognize each
other as genuine churches of God and that each of the faithful is welcomed by
the churches as a brother or a sister in the faith."[75] Therefore, this "communion
in the sacraments expresses the identity and unicity of the true faith which the
churches share";[76] and Old Catholics will affirm that "where communion is
violated, the Lord's Supper can no longer be celebrated together. Restoration
of eucharistic communion while division in faith continues is a contradiction
in terms since the churches live in separation from one another. . . . eucharistic
communion — so they conclude — is a manifestation of communion of faith
in one Church."[77]

Summarizing

The inheritance from the past expressed in beliefs, practices, values, and even
forms is not an ossified and static relic but a vigorous force augmented and
strengthened by the contributions of succeeding generations of the people of
God through the centuries. Churches and confessions, in their multilateral and
bilateral conversations, today need this kind of listening theologically to each
other's doctrines in order to find the common roots of the Christian Tradition
stated by Jesus Christ himself. Theology should not be considered as monolithic.
There is also a renewed interest in the bilateral dialogues to identify what
churches consider authentic theology — a theology which understands the content of divine revelation and through faith leads to a communion with God

72. Ibid., p. 15, par. 20(b).
73. Ibid.
74. Ibid.
75. *Bari*, Section 5, p. 85, par. 21.
76. Ibid., par. 23.
77. Old Catholic–Orthodox Dialogue, *Agreed Statement on the Sacraments* (Kavala, Greece,
12-19 October 1987); see English text in *The Journal of the Moscow Patriarchate* 8 (1988): 74; see
also text in Greek/French in *Episkepsis* 394 (1988):6.

and fellow human beings. This revelation consists of trinitarian theology, Christology and eschatology, according to God's plan for the salvation of the world. There is also a movement among churches and confessions today towards a biblical theology in the light of patristic exegesis, and the experience of the local church — the Christian community in history.

The emphasis on the centrality of the Eucharist in the Church is hardly unique to Orthodox and Roman Catholic conversations. It is a recurrent theme in many of the recent bilateral and multilateral dialogues. Yet on the basis of their shared understanding of the Eucharist and its implications for church life, Orthodox and Roman Catholics are able to make certain affirmations with which other Christians might have difficulties. Nothing reveals the advanced degree of agreement which already exists between the two theologies which brings the two churches closer. Rather, there has been the slow, patient working out of a principle enunciated even before the dialogue began: Start with what Orthodox and Roman Catholics have in common — above all, the sacraments — and only from within this broader context go to points on which there is disagreement. Of course, there have been many sudden changes of direction, even if some new and painful issues (uniatism, proselytism) have emerged which need to be clarified further.[78]

However, without any doubt, the boundaries of bilateral dialogues are today becoming broad enough in order to allow a certain freedom of movement as well as full expression. Nevertheless, all theological conversations have a common task and goal, namely, to seek unity among churches in the light of true Christian faith and life. Maintaining a balance between historical facts of the early times and of contemporary situations in which churches live and which they experience is absolutely essential and should be kept in the minds of theologians who sometimes are skeptical of reductionism and relativism and who insist on loyalty to the experience of the Church in history, theology and tradition.

Loyalty to the tradition of the Church is not static but rather dynamic, in the sense that it permits dialogue and renewal. The theology of truth is committed to preserve the theology of undivided Christianity and indeed its identity, but also to share its convictions and perceptions within different traditions and religious beliefs.

Where does this dialogical-theological exercise in union negotiations lead from here? How do theologians from different traditions and confessions perceive the future of these bilateral conversations and the goal that should be achieved? Some see them as a vibrant and appealing call to unity; others have expressed high hopes not only for their future, but also because they interrelate

78. Sixth Roman Catholic–Orthodox Joint Commission, *Declaration on Uniatism and Proselytism* (Freising, FRG, 6-15 June 1990); see English text in *Information Service* 73 (1990): 52-53; see also text in Greek/French in *Episkepsis* 443 (1990): 11-13.

this concern with the future of Christianity. Still others fearfully complain that the bilateral dialogues are facing today a chaotic situation emphasized by an individualism and fragmentation; finally, others also admire the fact that a lot of hostilities and difficulties of the past have already been overcome, and considerable common agreements have been formulated on convergent issues.

The more the churches come closer theologically, being in dialogue and agreeing in joint statements, the more they feel the "sacred zeal" to sometimes protect their particularities in defense of Christian faith. Do they really want visible and organic church unity? Are they ready to make sacrifices towards that end? The road to unity is costly and painful. It is grasped and enacted as a process of change and renewal, resulting from their listening in common to the prophetic Word of God and requesting the repentance-answer, a common confession of the one true church of Christ and a conversion of hearts and minds in the light of the contemporary secularized world.

Finally, the impression arising from the different dialogues, when viewed emphatically and analyzed together, is that the ecumenical movement, both East and West, is "on the move" and not static. It is much easier to understand the different nature and goal of each dialogue, the continuous repetitions which are unavoidable within the statements, the various styles and languages, the emphasis on the biblical references or not, their relevance to contemporary theology or not. There can be little doubt about the value of the achievements that have been made. As a consequence, some schemes may have collapsed in their search for the necessary agreement in faith to carry unity schemes, but nevertheless encouraging strides are being made. An appropriate stage has now been reached in the goal towards which churches are moving. Doctrinal agreements *are not* an end in themselves, but sought in order to move the churches into a closer relationship in faith, life and practice.

Therefore, the six dialogues undertaken by the Orthodox Church are continuing with their engagement in order to reach "the day of the Lord," the "full eucharistic communion" in simplicity, sincerity, in oneness of mind (cf. Acts 2:46) and in common faith and reconciliation.

The patient and serious approach to theological dialogue exemplified in the work of the joint commissions offers hope for the eventual restoration of such a communion between churches. While such dialogues will not in themselves bring about the full and perfect unity of the churches, any unity is hard to imagine without God's will and that of human beings, too.

Wholistic Mission:
Evangelical and Ecumenical

C. RENÉ PADILLA

If anything shows how easily we Christians let prejudice condition our attitude towards those who do not move in the same circles as we, it is the way in which we react towards the use of the two theological and ecclesiastical terms "evangelical" and "ecumenical." Neither of the two can be unequivocally defined; both lend themselves to diverse interpretation; they are not always mutually compatible. And yet both have been converted into symbols of opposed positions and of divisions that deeply affect the unity of the body of Christ.

In the letter that the "participants with evangelical concerns" directed from the seventh assembly of the World Council of Churches (WCC) to churches and Christians around the world,[1] reference was made to the institutional expressions of the polarization between "ecumenicals" and "evangelicals" at a world level. The letter indicates that, following the common stereotypes, "the World Council of Churches can only help the churches in matters involving questions of justice and human rights, so much so that one must turn to organizations such as the Lausanne Committee for World Evangelization and the World Evangelical Fellowship in the search for help with evangelization." It could be further added that the churches that maintain contact with these international organizations, looking for their help with the particular specializations mentioned above, are in the minority: the great majority of the churches in Latin America, at least, opt for other alternatives. They either identify with a single outlook (whether "ecumenical" or "evangelical") and link themselves

---

1. See "Evangelical Perspectives from Canberra," in *Signs of the Spirit: Official Report of the Seventh Assembly*, ed. Michael Kinnamon (Geneva: WCC Publications, and Grand Rapids, MI: Wm. B. Eerdmans, 1991), 282-86.

Reprinted with permission from the *International Review of Mission* 81 (July 1992): 381-82.

with the bodies that, in their opinion, articulate this outlook institutionally, or they close themselves within their own denominational structures, or they become islands with no connection whatsoever with other churches, which is even worse.

From the perspective of wholistic mission, there is no place for the polarization between an ecumenical outlook and an evangelical one.

To be an ecumenical Christian is to be a Christian who conceives of the whole *oikoumene* (the inhabited world) as the place of God's transforming action. It is to commit oneself to the construction of a world of justice, peace and integrity of creation. It is to see the church from the perspective of God's purpose, that is to say, as a community of the Spirit, a worldwide missionary community whose unity transcends human division.

To be an evangelical Christian is to be a Christian who conceives of the gospel as good news of the love of God in Jesus Christ, the living Word witnessed to by the Bible, the written word of God. It is to confess and to live out the gospel of Jesus Christ as Lord of the whole of life in the power of the Holy Spirit. It is to work together in the proclamation of the gospel to all the peoples of the earth (without distinction of race, culture, nationality or social class) and in the formation of local Christian congregations that nurture and share the faith.

Thus understood, what is "ecumenical" and what is "evangelical" do not exclude but complement each other. They point to two inseparable realities through which the church is born and lives: the *oikoumene* of men and women for whom Jesus Christ died and rose again, and the gospel, which offers the key to human history. Ecumenism without the gospel is secularism; it is the world of projects of social redemption centered on the human being without reference to God. The gospel without an ecumenical dimension is *logos asarkos*, the doctrine of salvation without incarnation.

The ecumenical movement — "the great new reality of our time," according to the description of the late Bishop William Temple — is not confined to the WCC. However, the immense contribution that this worldwide organization based in Geneva has made to the cause of ecumenism in this second half of the twentieth century is indisputable. Sadly, it is not possible to say the same about its contribution to the proclamation of the gospel, in spite of the fact that it defines itself constitutionally as a "fellowship of churches which confess the Lord Jesus Christ as God and Saviour according to the scriptures and therefore seek to fulfill together their common calling to the glory of the one God, Father, Son and Holy Spirit." Everything seems to indicate that the healthy balance between the ecumenical and evangelical dimensions with which the World Council of Churches was organized in 1948 has gradually been lost and that, at this moment, the most urgent need of the council is to regain the gospel for its ecumenical work. Those who from within this ecumenical organization insist on the need for a "vital and coherent theology" that would relate the programmes initiated by the WCC to its confessional base, are right in doing so.

If the mission of the church is the mission of the reign of God, it must be both evangelical and ecumenical at the same time. Evangelical because it proclaims the good news of the inbreaking of a new reality in history through Jesus Christ, and calls individuals and nations to return from their idols to the true and living God. Ecumenical because it has the "universal" Christian community as its horizon, through which God wishes to demonstrate his love and justice to all the nations. It must be evangelical and ecumenical in faithfulness to Jesus Christ, for the sake of a better world, and to the glory of God.

Spirit of Truth — Set Us Free!

JULIO DE SANTA ANA

The second half of the 1980s has been a period of tremendous acceleration of changes in history. The geo-political order that was established after the second world war has come to an end and now we are being introduced into a very new situation. Something similar is happening at the world economic level: after four decades of "internationalization of [the] economy," which above all meant the internationalization of the economic powers which operate on the level of the world market (TNCs), now we are coming into a period of "globalization" (in French, Spanish = "mondialization") of economy of a clearly oligopolistic nature. The common affirmation is that this process will bring about a new ecumenical situation: the divisions that the world community received as a heritage of the second world war are coming to an end, and those who manage this trend assert that we are at the beginning of a new historical period in which the prevailing differences among peoples and cultures are bound to disappear.

We are experiencing a moment of history which can be considered as a "turning point." It is not surprising that certain words, such as "crisis," are frequently used. Among Christians, the Greek word *kairos* (= a precise point in place, situation or time) has become fashionable. Such words indicate a general awareness of instability and change. The immobility which prevailed during the first part of the 1980s came quickly to an end. Humanity is agonizing to find a way which could diminish as much as possible the costs of this transition.

The Ideology of Globalization

As is generally true about human life, things are not clear and neat. The so-called process of "globalization" is not an inclusive one. Those who take advantage of

---

Reprinted with permission from the *Ecumenical Review* 43 (July 1991): 364-71.

the benefits of the new situation are a minority among the world population. For the vast majority the quality of life is deteriorating — in most of Africa, Latin America, the Caribbean and Asia. And not only in the "periphery"; there is growing insecurity and anguish among a number of people who live in those areas of the world which usually are considered to be affluent. It is not difficult to see that the so-called process of "globalization" creates exclusion and marginalization.

The world order which is emerging is clearly one of imbalance. Consider the volume of investments for scientific research and technology; it is only a minority of nations and interests that have such possibility. Most of the nations of the so-called South cannot enjoy this privilege. We should also consider the fact that such investments are not for development, education or people's health, but for armaments and purposes connected with war. The relations of the powerful North with the weak South are aimed at promoting the self-interest of the former. The exceptions only prove the rule.

Those who advocate the ideology of "globalization" underline that now we see the reality of the worldwide market as indisputable. Economic interests pretend that they can move freely in this enlarged market, which is perceived as one of the most important results of modernity. Nobody can deny the fact that more and more the organization and administration of world markets are in the hands of the private interests of "free enterprises." But, while their concern for raw materials is global, it is not helpful to the poor of the world. People, for the powers of the market, only matter when they have possibilities of high levels of consumption. That is, the "globalization" of economy does not take the poor into consideration. The rationality of the world market, as it is managed by the "free economic interest" which prevails in it, does not aim to include all the people to participate in the benefits that are generated by commercial transactions.

The ideology which pretends to legitimize this trend appeals to the argument that those who operate in the market aiming at the promotion of their self-interest are led by an invisible hand which finally promotes the interests of the whole society. The ideology of the free market can be considered as the theology of a pseudo-religion. The problem is that "the best possible world" marginalizes and excludes. The "invisible hand" is the instrument of an idol greedy for sacrifices. And those who are sacrificed are the poor and the powerless.

The excluding rationality of this ideology is also manifested when we analyze the situation of ethnic groups and cultures which were dominated by the expanding Western interests and cultures. White racism (conscious or unconscious) is still strong. It is true that we can rejoice and thank God because some progress in the combat against racism has been made in Southern Africa during the last fifteen years. However, we must be aware that a lot remains to be done in order to create better and just relations among ethnic groups and cultures. It is at this point that it seems necessary to recognize the value of the cultures and energies of racially oppressed groups. That is, we must recognize that the identity of these groups should be affirmed on their own terms, and not according to the standards of the dominant modern culture. The identity of the excluded involves, in many cases, a relation with land and a particular history. These considerations have been denied by racist powers, with the consequence that land was not only literally stolen from the people, but their history was broken and their being denied. Thus their humanity was impoverished and degraded. Those who impose the dominant culture on others want them to become like them, to be reflected and mirrored by them. It is an expression of the sin that we find in the story of the Tower of Babel: to deny God's creation, which is not of a uniform people, but of diversity and plurality.

The same logic is found in the administration of patriarchal structures which for thousands of years have been used to exclude women from participation on an equal footing with men in the family and in economic, social and political organizations. Today the patriarchal order is crumbling. Women's energies, all over the world, are promoting one of the most important revolutions in all human history. Through their efforts they demonstrate that they should be considered protagonists of history in the same way as men. The human includes male and female, each one with his or her peculiarities. It is the expression of a difficult, even painful tension. However, without this tension there cannot be meaningful human growth. In spite of these advancements there remains a lot to be done in order to countervail the rationality of exclusion at this level, both in society and in the churches.

As implicitly stated above, communication is a major characteristic of human beings. In our time great steps have been taken to improve communications among all the peoples of the earth, especially at the level of technology. However, it is also necessary to recognize the perversion that has taken place at this level of human existence: information has been put in the place of communications. To communicate means a relationship of two different identities; it is a personal exchange, a dialogue between I and thou. When information is taking the place of communications, then the *other* is denied. A clear example is what is happening with the war in the Gulf: the news that we receive is that which interests the powers involved. We are informed of bits and pieces of a tragedy which concerns us all, but we do not know what is going on. We lack communication. Information is under the control of oligopolistic powers, which select the information they think is appropriate for public consumption. This perversion has helped to develop the industry of information, which is clearly managed to serve the requirements of the modern free market. There are some alternative ways and means which are being used by groups aiming at more participation and exchange. Through these an advocacy function of the marginalized and oppressed people is fulfilled. But this is clearly not enough.

The logic of exclusion which prevails today is a manifestation of aggression. In this sense it is not an active force, but a reactive one. It is against the *other*, aiming to suppress the *other*. It is the rationality of the powers of death, the logic of nihilism. . . .

The ideology of "globalization" pretends to be an expression of inclusiveness. It claims that, if unfortunately "defence" or aggressive measures have to be adopted, it is in order to confront the other who hinders the practice of inclusion. For example, if the economy of a country is seriously indebted, it has to be readjusted (e.g., it has to become functional to serve the interests of the lending powers). If ethnic groups look for the affirmation of their own integrity and identity, then they should be better "integrated" into the global order. However, in fact, economic readjustment means more poverty, imposed integration creates more and unnecessary confrontations. The ideology of "globalization," which pretends to be global, ecumenical, is not what it seems to be. In this sense, and in spite of its bewitching aspect, it is a *lie*.

To Live in the Spirit Is to Do the Word

It is at this point that we must relate our reflections to chapter 8 of the Gospel of John. It is a crucial text of the fourth Gospel: the theological reflection that the evangelist develops can be understood in the light of the controversy that took place between Jesus and the Jews, as it is recorded in this chapter. It is important to note that Jesus challenged the Jewish leaders because they were not able to understand that he was the "I am who I am," the one who was sent by the Father (John 8:27-28). "As he was saying this, many came to believe in him" (John 8:30). However, Jesus perceived that such belief was not conversion. Therefore, he continued to challenge the Jews: what was called for was not "to believe in him," but to be true disciples. In the Gospel of John, truth is a question of *Logos,* but the *Logos* is not a saying, but a *being* (Jesus said: "I *am* the way, the *truth* and the *life*" [John 14:6]). That is, the truth that really counts is not so much what we say, but *who we are.* The Jews could say that they believed in Jesus, but they will be his disciples only when they put into practice the message of Jesus. To *do* the Word is to know the truth. This is the way to be truly free.

The Jews pretended to be free because they descended from Abraham. Jesus affirmed that such pretension had no real basis. Actually, they were slaves. They were captives of a system of laws and customs controlled by the constellation of power which had its axis around the temple of Jerusalem, a place which had been converted into a market (John 2:16). The Jews were not able to discern that to become a disciple meant to break with the powers that had distorted the meaning and the function of the temple. The house of prayer had been transformed into the centre of a system of social and economic domination. That is, it became a sacred place, more important than God. If the Jews were true disciples, then they would have been able to understand that it was only by living the truth of Jesus that they could be truly free.

Remaining captives of the powers of the temple, in spite of their affirmation that they believed in Jesus' message, they were *liars*. They claimed that they were free because they were children of Abraham. But they didn't behave like him. Abraham had faith and courage enough to leave his native land, where he and his family were living under the domination of oppressive landowners. Abraham was free; listening to God's calling he became free, moved by hope (Heb. 11:8-9). Unfortunately, the Jews who said they believed in Jesus did not behave like their ancestor.

Keeping their links with the temple, they maintained their attachment to a centre where some people were accepted and many were excluded. Those who participated in the ceremonies of the temple, who could pay for the purification sacrifices prescribed by the ritual system (Ex. 34:23-24), were accepted. But others, like the poor who could not pay, or the Samaritans, or even the women, were considered as unworthy, impure, unclean. Therefore, in one way or another, they were excluded. The Jews were not ready to break their ties with the system of the temple and its order.

Jesus, who lived fully with the Spirit of God (John 1:32-34), embodying the Spirit of truth, was free — and liberator. He was the Messiah, the Christ, chosen by God. And he called men and women of his time and situation to build up a movement of messianic character. The permanent affirmation of the Gospels is that the manifestation of the Messiah is always an expression of the Spirit of God: "all who accept his testimony are attesting the truthfulness of God, since he whom God has sent speaks God's own words: *God gives him the Spirit without reserve*" (John 3:32-34). To be a true disciple is to become a member of that liberating movement, of a community of free men and free women, seeking the justice of the kingdom of God, where the excluded of the system are welcome (John 10:14-16).

After the crucifixion and resurrection of Jesus the community of his disciples received the Holy Spirit. It then started a process which brought the community, *ekklesia*, to break with the temple, that is, to *live in the Spirit*. The awareness of the churches at that time was that the Spirit is the source of freedom. After mentioning the fruits of the Spirit ("love, joy, peace, patience, kindness, goodness, trustfulness, gentleness and self-control"), Paul added: "There can be no law against things like these, of course" (Gal. 5:22-23), meaning that those who live in the Spirit are free from the tyranny of legalism. The law and the order of this world cannot control them. In another place, Paul was even more affirmative; he says that unfortunately the majority of the Jews were unable to understand the messianic role of Jesus. It was as if a veil was put over the eyes of the Jews. He said then that "the veil is over their minds. It will not be removed until they turn to the Lord. Now this Lord is the Spirit, and *where the Spirit of the Lord is, there is freedom*" (2 Cor. 3:15-17).

For Jesus, to live in the Spirit, to be a true disciple, means to do *the word.* When God's presence in our life becomes part of our identity, the nonnegotiable convictions which determine our existence, rooted as they are in the word of God, are like energies which make freedom real in our lives. That was the experience of Jesus when, *led by the Spirit,* he went into the wilderness. The temptations were indeed tempting. To eliminate hunger from the earth, to seduce the hearts of men and women and to bring about with power a new order in the world. Jesus faced these three temptations (the economic, the religious and the political) not only recalling texts of the Old Testament, but above all living according to the word of God. That is what it means for Christians to be free: to sustain the nonnegotiable convictions rooted in the word of God against the threats of the powers that be. This is not the result of our strength, but of the force of the Holy Spirit operating in each of us and in the Christian communities. This is the meaning of Jesus' words: "If you make my word your home, you will indeed be my disciples; you will learn the truth, and the truth will make you free" (John 8:31-32).

It is only by making Jesus' word our home that we can become members of the messianic community. However, those who are part of it, living in the Spirit, affirming freedom and working for liberation, do not belong to the powers of this world. The messianic community is shaped out of powerlessness. The Messiah is not a victorious warrior; he is neither an astute politician nor a clever entrepreneur. The destiny of the Messiah took him to the cross. But it did not finish there; it was followed by the resurrection. But that happened only after death on the cross. To participate in the movement of the people who live in the Spirit, the messianic community, means to share this freedom of action for the sake of justice, this option for self-giving, which is the opposite of the rationality of the market.

When this is affirmed, as it was in Jesus' life and among the faithful of the early Christian community in Jerusalem, the effect is a strong release of the winds of liberation. For us today this means that neither male domination and patriarchal styles of life, nor the financial powers which take advantage of the debt which burdens many third-world countries, nor the infernal machinery of death used by imperialistic forces which invade small and defenseless nations, nor racism and the agents of it, nor the interests that control the market subjecting the poor to injustice, can separate us from the love of God. Pain, suffering, the cross, could well be the experience of the struggles of the messianic communities against the powers that be. But the latter will not have the final say. The Spirit who sets us free, who renews the creation, also renews the energies of people.

Again, the problem is not one of speech, but of *praxis.* Life in the Spirit has to be witnessed in the context of the realities of the world. Liberation through the Spirit is not limited to an internal "spiritual experience." It is more than the temporary relief of tension, a spiritual escape from the harsh contradictions of reality. The Spirit of truth liberates by confronting people with their distorted perceptions of themselves and of the world (John 8:32; 16:8ff.).

But there is more involved here than simply eyes being opened to the truth. For too long, the presence and the operation of the Spirit have been limited to the realm of insight, inspiration and understanding. The New Testament, however, refers to the experience of being liberated through the Spirit as a *new birth, the beginning of new life, as a new act of creation* (John 3:3-5; 2 Cor. 5:17). All of creation receives its vital energy through God's Spirit (cf. Ps. 33:6; 104:29); even more so does the new creation which is the work of God "who gives life to the dead and calls into being things that do not exist" (Rom. 4:17).

The energy of this new creation is the Spirit of God, who has raised Jesus the Messiah from the dead; it is the power of resurrection. "If the Spirit of him who raised Jesus from the dead dwells in you, he who raised Christ Jesus from the dead will give life to your mortal bodies also through his Spirit which dwells in you" (Rom. 8:11). This Spirit, therefore, has been confessed since early times as "the Lord, the giver of life" (Acts 17:25; cf. 1 Cor. 15:45). Life in the Spirit, then, is not simply a particular dimension or quality of life to be cultivated following some spiritual experiences. Rather, it is a new life altogether, life in all its fullness, life in true communion with God, with other humans, and with all of creation.

The Failure of Idols — and the Way Forward

From the beginning till now, *the entire creation, as we know, has been groaning in one great act of giving birth;* and not only creation, but all of us who possess the first-fruits of the Spirit, we too groan inwardly *as we wait for our bodies to be set free.* For we must be content to hope that we shall be saved — our salvation is not in sight, we should not have to be hoping for it if it were — but, as I say, we must hope to be saved since we are not saved yet — it is something we must wait for with patience (Rom. 8:22-25).

The experience of the power of freedom can happen when human beings are yearning for liberation, resisting oppression and injustice. The longing for freedom which still persists in human hearts is confirmed by a new impetus, a new force given to the powerless: there is the movement of the Spirit of God. The groan from the depth of our being, as well as of nature, is taken up by the force of the Spirit; a new thing is introduced in human life, and new trends are developed in history. The action of God does not deny this kind of human aspiration; as a matter of fact, God redeems our life, taking into account who we are, our weakness and feeble energies.

At this point it is necessary to distinguish between energy and power. If it is true that power cannot exist without its basis in the development of human energies, it is also important to indicate that energy is manifested as self-affirmation, especially when life has to be supported or defended. Power, on the other hand, appears as domination or oppression. Energy aims at freedom, looks for the affirmation of life (cf. Krister Stendahl, *Energy for Life*), while when power is built up, it becomes almost unavoidably a threat for those who want to be free.

Modern Western culture has among its main characteristic a great impulse for freedom. This became very clear at the time of the Enlightenment, which was understood as a cultural process towards realizing the autonomy of human beings. Such movement towards "coming of age," human adulthood without limits, was conceived as being inherent in the process of human history. Enlightenment looked for human liberation and therefore criticized religious beliefs without becoming aware that its affirmation of the infinite progress of humanity was also a religious belief. In their search for autonomy, the supporters of Enlightenment were caught in the trap of a new captivity. Energies deployed for freedom became powers of domination and turned into tools of oppression.

The forces of Enlightenment proposed two great historical projects. *On the one hand,* private capitalists wanted "free-market societies." In this case, freedom is not of human beings, but of commodities. The space where this freedom becomes concrete is the market, which has to be preserved by all means from any kind of foreign interference. The "market is free," but human beings should bow before the market's power. The laws of the market, through which works the "invisible hand," should be accepted and obeyed without discussion. To confront them means to be irrational, and becomes a sign of lack of realism. In this process the market is sacralized. It is turned into a modern idol, a contemporary Baal. This perversion of the market is not inherent in it. As a matter of fact, the market is a human place par excellence, as in any small local markets. However, in large modern centres of transaction, human communications are set aside, and what matters is the control of information. The rationality of the modern market does not make room for human relationships, only for aggressive competition. As Max Weber said, the rationality of the market cannot exist among those who want to remain brothers and sisters. It is a rationality which, at the same time that it aims at the freedom of commodities, abolishes the liberty of people. In this sense, this historical project of Enlightenment involves a lie, a deep falsehood.

On the other hand, labour forces which resisted the aggression of private capital powers developed the other great historical project of the Enlightenment: to suppress the reign of need and to inaugurate the kingdom of freedom, which meant the abolition of both the market and the state. It was a very ambitious project, looking for the concretization of the full autonomy of human beings, whose primary condition was understood to be that of workers. Such transition will call for a period when the organized workers' power should be exercised in a dictatorial way: the dictatorship of the proletariat! Three things indicate the weakness of this project. First, freedom cannot be affirmed if it is suppressed. Second, the market, being a very human place, cannot be abolished. What central planned economies never understood is that what is needed is not to suppress the market, but to humanize it. The question is how to be free human beings in the market. Third, the state is necessary for the administration of human life. To administer is to serve, and it implies that more important than the use of power are the expectations and the rights of the people.

Both projects of the Enlightenment have created idols, false gods: the market in the case of the project of private capital, and the one-party state in the case of labour's project (especially as it was formulated by Leninist parties). We cannot deny the contribution of both projects: the first created conditions for managerial efficiency, scientific and technological progress, as well as economic growth; the second was able to lift up the standard of life of the masses in quite a few places. However, the goal of both projects, i.e., to advance freedom, proved elusive.

The problem is a cultural one. It is not possible to support the cause of freedom by suppressing or diminishing it. Or, to say it theologically, the powers that be create orders and laws which are contrary to the movement of the Holy Spirit, the source and force of freedom and liberation, both at the level of personal and social lives. Freedom is for life; it cannot be transferred to objects or structures. When life is free, then it is possible to use our availability for others. Then we are not afraid to share, to join forces, to live together.

The worst thing that can happen when we become aware of the failure of both projects is to fall into the trap of "realism." In the case of the "free market society," the "wealth of nations" is merely the wealth of the few. And in the case of the socialist societies, freedom has not been built up, only suffocated, in most cases. If we give way to "realism," the bewitchment created by the feeling of powerlessness, we lose our energies. We close ourselves against the force of the Spirit and we surrender to the powers that be. This means acquiescing in injustice and oppression. For Christians, this is serious; it indicates that God's design is turned into mockery. In that sense it is blasphemy. To make a mockery of the movement of freedom is part of the political realism of the powers of the world. But it also means blasphemy against the Holy Spirit, to adopt a position against the messianic force which was present in Jesus and now moves in the messianic energies among the people.

Of course, a sense of realism is a must. What is metaphorically called in the Bible "the kingdom of God" is *an eschatological realism,* which helps to introduce seeds of biblical eschatological vision in human behaviour and social reality.

This *utopian reason* is more inclusive indeed than the instrumental reason of the Enlightenment. The latter is moved by its immediate intentionality: its intention is to resolve this particular problem that is placed *now* in front of us. Generally, instrumental reason does not take into consideration its nonintentional effects, and therefore, trying to resolve one problem, very often gives rise to a multiplication of troubles. Utopian reason is not looking for effectiveness, for it is moved by ultimate goals. In this sense, the transcendent dimension of life (which instrumental reason does not take into account) is affirmed. Utopian reason seeks peace, the humanization of the market, the end of racism and sexism, the recognition of human rights, a world where dialogic communication among people and cultures could prevail, substainability of personal, social and natural life. It is part of the movement of freedom, a sign of messianic energy. It is, because of all this, an inclusive rationality. It involves the fruits of the Spirit: love, joy, peace, patience, kindness, goodness, trustfulness, gentleness and self-control — such elements of the Christian character against which there is no law.

The Church's Witness
in Evangelism and Social Praxis

NIGEL BIGGAR

What Is the Church's Mission?

A major focus of conflict in the Church of England was recently highlighted in a report on industrial mission.[1] On the one hand, it observed, there are those engaged in industrial mission who believe that the Church's primary calling is to support communities in their struggle for social justice, regardless of their religious convictions. On the other hand, there are those in the rest of the Church, especially the parishes, who see her mission primarily as that of enabling spiritual conversion.

The report specifies this conflict as one between the practitioners of industrial mission and those responsible for parochial ministry.[2] But it is in fact much broader, running through most reaches of the Church; and it is, of course, confined neither to the Church *of* England nor to the Church *in* England. Still, it is particularly poignant that on the very eve of the Decade of Evangelism

---

1. *Industrial Mission — An Appraisal*, The Report of a working party commissioned by the Industrial and Economic Affairs Committee of the Church of England's Board of Social Responsibility (London: Board of Social Responsibility, 1988). Sadly, the follow-up paper, *Church and Economy: Effective Industrial Mission for the 1990's* (London: Board of Responsibility: 1989), which was intended to develop and stimulate discussion on the issues raised by *Industrial Mission,* is entirely devoted to organisational concerns. Theological issues were supposed to have been reserved for the complementary paper, *Ministry and Mission Examined: Stories and Reflections on Industrial Mission Today* (London: BSR, 1989). This, however lacks all trace of awareness of the fundamental theological conflict identified by *Industrial Mission*. Only *Church and Economy* reached the General Synod for debate.

2. *Industrial Mission,* 43-44.

Reprinted from the *Evangelical Review of Theology* 16 (July 1992): 296-309, originally published in *ANVIL* 8 (1991). Used with permission.

there should be in the Church of England such debilitating disagreement over what the mission of the Christian Church is, over what the Church is for, and over what it is that Christians are called to do.

It is the aim of this essay, first, to identify the concerns that characterise the opposing positions; second, to clarify the controversy by distinguishing the crucial issues from the tangential ones; and finally, by addressing those crucial issues, to offer an account of the Church's mission that pays due attention to both sets of concern.

I. Identifying Opposite Concerns

First, then, what are the concerns? Why is it that some feel driven to identify the Church's mission with social action? And why is it that others find this so objectionable?

Mission as Social Praxis

There seem to be at least three reasons why some see the Church's basic duty as that of promoting just community in society as whole. One is that they have lost confidence in the characteristic truth claims of traditional Christianity. They no longer believe in a God who has acted uniquely and decisively in Jesus Christ to save the world. They see Christianity as one of several culturally conditioned ways to God, and they regard its traditional claims to special status as insupportable, even immoral. Moreover, given the overriding moral imperative of preventing global nuclear holocaust and the strife between human communities that would kindle it, these religious pluralists argue that the "truth" of a religion is to be measured by the extent to which it fosters social praxis; that is, active commitment to the task of building just community. Orthodoxy divides; orthopraxy unites.[3]

A second reason for identifying the Church's mission with social praxis is the belief that religion is virtually reducible to social morality. This was the conviction of the social gospel movement, which was originally a late nineteenth- and early twentieth-century American phenomenon. Unlike contemporary pluralists, the apostles of the Social Gospel did believe in the uniqueness of the Christ-event, albeit on Schleiermacher's terms, and not those of classical orthodoxy.[4] However, they inherited from Kant a strong antipietistic

3. For arguments along these lines see the essays in *The Myth of Christian Uniqueness,* ed. John Hick and Paul Knitter (London: SCM Press, 1987).

4. The Christ-event is unique, according to Schleiermacher, in the sense that the absolute God-consciousness which is communicated through the corporate life of the Christian community was original to Jesus. See his work *The Christian Faith* (Edinburgh: T & T Clark, 1928), Second Part, Second Aspect of the Antithesis: Explication of the Consciousness of Grace, First Section.

inclination to regard the specifically "religious" dimension of Christianity —
the dimension of prayer and worship — as an immoral distraction from the
performance of moral duty which is the substance of genuine religion. Then,
under the influence of Albrecht Ritschl, they specified the building of God's
Kingdom here and now in the form of a more just and democratic society as
the most Christian and most urgent moral duty.[5]

The third reason for making social praxis the main business of the Church
is apologetic. For when faced with human beings suffering injustice, how else can
the Church maintain her integrity except by committing herself to overcome it?
How else can she preserve the credibility of the gospel of God's costly love for the
world? This apologetic concern was a major cause of the genesis of Liberation
Theology.[6] The context of its birth was the long history of economic exploitation
and political oppression in Latin America, in which the leadership of the Church
(i.e., predominantly the Roman Catholic Church) had tended to play a conservative role, virtually sanctioning the unjust status quo. When this conservative stance
was contrasted with the readiness of others, especially Marxists, to risk their lives
in trying to combat injustice, the Church's reputation and the gospel's suffered
grievously. Liberation Theology, then, emerged as an attempt to rescue Christianity's credibility by showing that the Church of Christ cares enough to put itself
at risk in the struggle to overcome oppression and exploitation.

We have now adduced three reasons why some regard social praxis as the
heart of the Church's mission: first, because they believe that it is the main
measure of the truth of its beliefs; second, because they believe that it is the real
point of the Christian religion; and third, because they see it as necessary to the
integrity of the Church and so to the credibility of its witness to the gospel of
Christ. Now we shall turn to the other side of the debate, to those who deny
that social praxis should take first place on the Church's agenda. What are their
driving concerns?

Mission as Spiritual Concern

There are at least three. First, they are concerned to uphold the truth claims of
traditional Christianity. They believe that traditional Christian assertions about

---

5. In one of the classics of the Social Gospel literature, Walter Rauschenbusch's *A Theology
for the Social Gospel* (Nashville: Abingdon, 1945), there is no discussion of the spiritual disciplines
of prayer and worship, and in the chapter on the sacraments, baptism and the Lord's Supper are
given an exclusively social significance. We are told, for example, that baptism was originally "not
a ritual act of individual salvation but an act of dedication to a religious and social movement"
(198); and that in inaugurating the Lord's Supper, Jesus intended to create "an act of loyalty which
would serve to keep memory and fidelity alive" (202).

6. See, e.g., Enrique Dussel, *Ethics and Community,* Liberation and Theology 3 (London:
Burns & Oates, 1988), 220-21, where Liberation Theology is described as a form of "fundamental"
theology, i.e., "self-justifying" or apologetic theological discourse.

the resurrection of Jesus from the dead, the divinity of Christ, his definitive revelation of God's character, and God's act of atonement through him, are true claims and that there are good reasons for believing them. Therefore they deny that the "truth" of Christianity can be measured simply by the criterion of social praxis. It should also be measured by the logical coherence of its metaphysical claims and by their empirical and historical grounds. This brings them into conflict with religious pluralists.

Their second concern is to preserve the distinctive importance of the religious or spiritual dimension. In opposition to the proponents of the Social Gospel, therefore, they deny that the Christian religion finds its real substance simply in morality, whether personal or social.

Their third concern has to do with the meaning of "social praxis." "Social praxis" usually means something more specific than "social responsibility." It means an active commitment to the cause of social justice. Further, it is usually assumed that this commitment involves resistance to the economic, social, and political status quo; and the status quo is usually taken to consist primarily in certain social structures. Further still, resistance is often understood to include the use of violence. So those who object to the identification of the Church's mission with social praxis do so partly because they doubt that the Christian Church should avail itself of violent means to fulfill its social responsibility.

II. Clarifying the Crucial Issues

We turn now from the concerns that fuel the debate over the place of social praxis in the church's mission to the task of distinguishing the crucial issues from the tangential ones. We shall do so in two steps. In the first we distinguish the issue of the missionary role of social praxis from that of the reduction of the Christian religion to social praxis. There are many who believe that social praxis is integral to the Church's mission, but who do not believe that is all that Christianity is about. Many Liberation theologians, for example, are theologically orthodox. They take for granted the classical Christological claims about Christ's divinity, and therefore classical trinitarian theology. They acknowledge that Christianity makes claims about God's redemptive activity as well as about right political behaviour. So the debate over the identity of Christianity between the theologically orthodox on the one hand and religious pluralists on the other, is in principle quite distinct from the debate about the place of social praxis on the Church's agenda. We shall concentrate exclusively on the latter.

In the second step we distinguish the question of the missionary role of social praxis from that of the propriety of the use of violent force. It is perfectly possible consistently to advocate the missionary priority of active commitment to social justice and against unjust structures without endorsing the use of violence. The question of the use of violent force by Christians is in principle a distinct one, which is strictly tangential to the issue which concerns us. Therefore we shall pass it by.

Now that we have sharpened our focus, let us proceed directly to address the issues upon which the matter of the missionary role of social praxis turns. There are (predictably) at least three of them: what is it that God works to save us from? how should the Church bear witness to the gospel of God's saving activity? and what should we understand social justice to mean? We shall take each in turn.

Salvation as Spiritual and Social

First, from what has God acted in Jesus Christ to save us? The traditional answer, of course, is "sin." When we talk of "sin" as distinct from "a sin" we refer, not to a particular wrong act, but to a more basic wrong disposition or orientation. Moreover, we refer to a quite distinct species of wrong disposition, one that is specifically religious. In the first place, "sin" characterises the relationship, not between one human being and another, but between human beings and God. It refers to the human rejection of God either because of proud self-assertion or because of an anxious refusal to trust. On this account, therefore, salvation is primarily about the overcoming of this estrangement of humanity from God. It is about God's reconciliation of humankind to himself. It is about the divine atonement.

Sometimes, however, those who put social praxis at the top of the Church's agenda seem to think of sin only in its secondary, social manifestations. Likewise, they think of salvation only in its secondary sense of the putting right of the distortions which sin introduces into human relationships and institutions. So, for example, some Liberation theologians virtually collapse "sin" into "offense against the neighbour," and "salvation" into "liberation" from economic, social, and political oppression.[7] One of the reasons for this "secularisation" of the concept of salvation is undoubtedly opposition to the pietistic abstraction of the religious relationship from its social context. But it is surely unnecessary, as well as theologically disastrous, to affirm the moral and social significance of salvation by collapsing it into its secondary sense. One can affirm a very intimate connection between spiritual and social salvation without abolishing the distinction. This is what the Christian tradition has done from the beginning in

---

7. E.g., Dussel, *Ethics and Community*, 19 and 26, where we are told that "offence of God is *always and antecedently* an act of domination committed against one's brother or sister" (my emphasis); and that "there is no such thing as a religious sin that is not a political or economic sin." Accordingly, when Dussel discusses the "Reign of God" in the Christian life (7-8), the emphasis lies almost entirely on the social dimension of "being together with others." It is true that this "being together" is described as being "with God," but since no explanation of the significance of this qualification is offered, it is hard to see it as much more than a formality.

arguing that love for God — or, if Luther is preferred to Augustine and Aquinas, faith in God — causes love for the neighbour. Even if one chooses to go further. and specify love for the neighbour in terms of social praxis, there is no logical reason why one could not still retain the priority of faith or *caritas*.

So why do some Liberation theologians decline to settle for this traditional description of the connection between the religious relationship and secular ones? In some cases, the reason is an oddly unqualified subscription to the Marxist doctrine of economic determinism, according to which economic relationships determine all others. The lack of qualification is odd because it is hard to see how anyone can believe in economic determinism and remain confessionally committed to Christian theology. For if economic structures lie at the root of what is wrong with the world, then "salvation" must lie simply in the economic reorganisation of society. The question of the status of one's relationship with God loses all immediate relevance to the problems of temporal life. Therefore insofar as Liberation theologians endorse the doctrine of economic determinism, we can only conclude that their eagerness to stress the power of economic interests to deform human relationships and institutions (including religious ones) has made them theologically careless. We should certainly follow them in acknowledging that love for God or faith in him makes demands upon our economic relationships and structures, as upon our social and political ones. But the moment they imply that sin and salvation refer simply to secular relationships, we should part company. Of course the gospel bears upon our secular relationships, personal and institutional; but in the first place it refers irreducibly to the state of affairs existing between us and God.

III. Declaring the Gospel in Word

So much for what the gospel is about. Now for the question of how to declare it. The initial answer is no less correct for being obvious. We declare the gospel by testifying that God has acted decisively in the life and death of Jesus Christ to remedy our relationship with him; that we believe this to be the case for certain reasons; and that what happened in Christ bears upon us in certain ways. In other words, our declaration of the gospel will take the primary form of an historical claim, a claim about an event and its significance for us here and now. This is what is usually understood by "evangelism."

The Text of Transformed Lives

But evangelism in this sense often faces a major problem that it cannot overcome by itself. And that problem is that there are many people who cannot immediately see why the gospel matters, what difference of importance and for the better it could possibly make to the lives that they lead. Quite apart from the question of the content of the gospel and its truth, there is the question of its meaningfulness. And no amount of persuasive argument about the historical reliability of the New Testament or intelligible explanation of the doctrine of the atonement will suffice to make God's action in Christ interesting to those who are not especially hounded by guilt or weighed down by existential *Angst* and whose lives, busy and rich with more or less decent occupations, seem satisfying enough.

For this reason, at least, declaring the gospel cannot simply take the form of "evangelism" in the sense just given. It also has to take the form of lives governed and transformed by faith and love for God, lives that display the deep integrity of worshipping and obedient humanity, lives whose lively beauty draws the beholder first to itself and then to its divine cause. Karl Barth makes the point well, albeit in his own terms:

> What is to be expected of [Christians] is that this [Word of God] will give their choosing and willing a specific character so that their lives will become a text accessible not only to their fellow Christians but also to their non-Christian fellows. So long as they do not have the vocabulary, grammar and syntax, the latter may not understand it, but it is legible to them as written by a human hand. In the persons of Christians as hearers of God's Word, the Word itself is present to their non-Christian fellows also. In the way that Christians shape their lives as people of the world confronting the same problems as others, their life's task in the midst of others documents the Word, brings it to notice, and draws attention to it. They cannot do more than this and they should not try. It may be that in time they will have to answer questions concerning the reason for the special character of their works, that they will have to comment to others on the text of their lives, that they will have to offer an introduction to the understanding of the text and therefore speak about it. But the first and proper thing that as men of the world they owe other men of the world . . . can only be the 'behaviour without words' which 1 Peter 3:1 commends. . . .[8]

Sometimes we will be called upon to comment on the text of our lives, to explain how they came to be written and what they signify. But our main task is simply to let our lives be texts which refer to the God who has loved us in Jesus Christ, and which are sufficiently attractive to make their referent interesting.

Now it is certainly true that we may signify God in the text of our individual lives. It is these that the gospel of God's love addresses directly, and these that it would govern and transform. Nevertheless, our individual lives have a social dimension. They are social. From conception on they stand in the

---

8. Karl Barth, *The Christian Life: Church Dogmatics*, IV/4, *Lecture Fragments*, 201-2.

context of relationships with others. Who we are, what really makes us tick, is revealed most sharply in the quality of our relationships with other people, in how we treat them and let them treat us. So, if God speaks his word through the text of an individual life, he necessarily speaks it also through the social context in which that life is embedded. He speaks it through the set of relationships, immediate and remote, personal and institutional, with which that life is inextricably bound up. He speaks it through the text of individuals-in-society.

Indeed, it is one of the major themes of the Bible that where God's authority is acknowledged, there mere society becomes true community. There the members of a society treat each other justly and generously, living together in that convivial peace which is itself a mark of God's presence. In the New Testament the role of the Christian community *as a witness to God's Word in it's own right* features prominently. Let us take, for example, the early chapters of the Book of Acts. In the first verse of chapter 6 we are presented with a social problem — or, to be more precise, with an instance of social injustice within the Christian community: "Now in these days when the disciples were increasing in number, the Hellenists murmured against the Hebrews because their widows were neglected in the daily distribution." At the end of chapter 2 we were told that immediately after Pentecost the believers had pooled their capital and were using it to provide for those who had insufficient income (vv. 44-45). This is reiterated at the end of chapter 4 (vv. 32, 34-35). What the first verse of chapter 6 tells us is that the allocation of resources from the common fund, referred to in the text as "the daily distribution of food," had become corrupted by ethnic prejudice. Widows who were culturally Greek (the "Hellenists") were being neglected, presumably because the distribution was in the hands of Aramaic-speakers who were culturally Palestinian ("the Hebrews"). In other words, the unity of the Christian community was being jeopardised by an injustice perpetrated by a partisan abuse of power.

Now, it is possible to interpret the Apostles' response to this problem as implying that the only reason for addressing it was that it threatened to distract them from their real business of proclaiming the resurrection of Jesus from the dead: "And the twelve summoned the body of the disciples and said, 'It is not right that we should give up preaching the word of God to serve tables.'" Their response could be read as suggesting that social harmony in the Church is important only because it provides an undistracting environment for preaching the word of God. In other words, a peaceful community and the social justice that sustains it is significant only because it enables preaching. Community is simply instrumental to the preaching of the word.

But there are at least two good reasons why this interpretation would be mistaken. The first and major one is that the formation of a community where social justice prevails is presented in the early chapters of Acts as one of the primary manifestations of the power of the Holy Spirit. The creation of a common fund to supply the needs to the poor was, according to chapter 2, one of the very first things that the believers did after Peter's speech on the day of Pentecost (2:42, 44). A couple of chapters later this point is repeated and we are told (4:33-34) that "much grace was with them all. There were no needy persons among them." Social justice is an immediate manifestation of the gracious power of the Holy Spirit. It is not, of course, the only manifestation. Two others are mentioned in chapters 3–5: the power to do miraculous works of healing (chapter 3) and the power to preach the resurrection of Jesus boldly (chapter 4). But the point is that the formation of just community is not merely a necessary condition for an efficient preaching ministry, but rather a manifestation of the power of the Spirit in its own right.

Further (and this is the second, minor reason), this equality of status between the building of community and the preaching of the word, insofar as both are manifestations of the Spirit's power, is corroborated in the opening verses of chapter 6. For there the word "distribution" in "the daily distribution of food" and the word "ministry" "in the ministry of the word of God" are both in fact translations of the same Greek word: *diakonia*, or "service." They share the same label. What this means is that the first few verses of Acts 6 treat preaching and the business of maintaining just community as different species of the same thing.

So, the early chapters of Acts do not allow us to regard the building of community and of the social justice it required simply as necessary means to the end of effective preaching. They make it quite clear that both are manifestations of the Spirit's power. They also make it clear that both are effective in bringing about repentance and conversion and so in enlarging the Church. At the end of Peter's address in chapter 2 we read (in v. 41): "Those who accepted his message were baptised, and about three thousand were added to their number that day." But likewise at the end of the passage which follows immediately and is largely devoted to describing the quality of the believers' community, we also read (in v. 47): "And the Lord added to their number daily those who were being saved." *Both* preaching *and* community are effective means of saving grace, which, since both are manifestations of the Spirit's power, should not surprise us, for the power of the Spirit is nothing other than the grace of God at work redeeming the world.

The Quality of Communal Life

So far we have argued that we should declare the gospel, not only through verbal statements of what we believe to be true and why, but also through the text of our lives as individual members of the Body of Christ. In the first instance, what this text says will be a matter of how we treat each other: of our ability to behave respectfully, humbly, openly and generously and of our capacity both to grant forgiveness and to receive it. In the first place, the quality of our communal life will consist in the quality of our personal relationships with others. These relationships may be with family members or friends, but they may also be with political opponents, whether on the worship committee or on the PC or in Synod. In this respect there is no distinction between the private and the public realms.[9]

Integrity in Power Structures

There is, however, a distinction between the personal and the structural dimensions. So, in addition to the question of the quality of our personal relationships in the Christian community, there is also the question of the quality of the public conventions and institutions which order those relationships. There is also the matter of political structures. Every community has political structures. It has sets of conventions which regulate the exercise of power, determining who gets to exercise a certain kind of power under certain conditions. These conventions may be formal and explicit or they may be informal and tacit. More to the point, they may be more or less just. They can give some people or classes of people too much power, and others too little. They can institutionalise the lie that only the skills of a few are important for communal well-being by the custom of refusing others the opportunity to discover and exercise their own. Political structures in the Christian community may or may not be faithful, for example, to Jesus' constant refrain that the power that really counts is the power of the servant (Matt. 20:25-28; Mark 10:42-45; Luke 22:24-27); and they may or may not be true to St. Paul's organic vision of the Christian community as one where the obscure (domestic or parochial) service is recognised to be just as vital to the life of the community as the prestigious (synodical or episcopal) one (Rom. 12:4-6a; 1 Cor. 12:4-31). The gospel bears upon us, not only in the ways we treat each other at home or on the public stage, but also in the ways in which we organise our communal life. It bears upon political structures too.

Hitherto I have spoken only of the Christian community, arguing that the quality of its personal relationships and political structures is a necessary and important dimension of witness to the gospel of Christ. This is the primary form of the Church's social responsibility: to demonstrate in the fabric of its own life the power of God's Spirit to restore human beings to the kind of lives they were created for — of lives where love for God orders all other loves and makes community possible. Through this demonstration the Christian church

---

9. Although Emil Brunner distinguishes between the private and the public spheres as between the personal and the impersonal, he qualifies the distinction when he acknowledges that there are personal spaces present in all social institutions — "not in the actual activity of the institution itself, but 'between the lines'" (*Justice and the Social Order* [New York and London: Harper, 1945], 129).

addresses secular society at once as gospel and judgement. It declares the gospel by displaying proper human life, the kind of social life which we were made to enjoy and for which we all deeply yearn. But by the very same token, it indirectly pronounces judgement, exposing how far sinful society falls short of genuine community by throwing into sharp relief the injustice of its personal dealings and its structures. So simply by being the Church, by reflecting God's Kingdom, by affording glimpses of convivial community under God's authority, the Christian Church fulfils its primary responsibility to secular society.[10] This is the view of the Johannine literature in the New Testament, where the unity of the Church is plainly presented as the main medium of the light of Christ to the world: "By this all men will know that you are my disciples, if you love one another" (John 13:35).[11]

Commitment to a Just Community

Nevertheless, if the Church's responsibility for society begins with the nurturing of its own communal life, it does not end there. It continues in commitment to the cause of just community beyond the circles of confessing Christians. There are (as always) at least three reasons for this. First, if we regard just community as a good at all, then we are bound to care for it wherever we see it, even when it appears beyond the sociological boundaries of the Church. Love for justice is indivisible. Second, to affirm that just community ultimately depends for its fulfilment and its final security upon the right ordering of humankind's relationship with God, is not to deny that just community exists in some form and to some degree outside the Christian Church. There is plenty of empirical evidence, at the very least, that non-Christians retain some sense of the justice requisite for a measure of social peace; and that their self-interest can still be sufficiently rational for them to take steps to meet that requirement. Not even Luther and Calvin, with their heightened sense of the depth and extent of sinful corruption, could avoid acknowledging the persistence of an awareness and practice of justice among pagans.[12] The final reason why the Christian Church should be committed to the cause of social justice in society as a whole is that the boundaries of the true Church are not crystal clear to us. This side of the *eschaton* we cannot be finally sure who belongs and who does not. So when just community appears among non-Christians we cannot dismiss it summarily as a mirage; for it could be the Holy Spirit's work.

10. This is the kind of line taken by Karl Barth, J. H. Yoder, and Stanley Hauerwas.

11. See my discussion of the Johannine understanding of the relationship between the Christian community and social concern in *Theological Politics*, Latimer Study 29/30 (Oxford: Latimer House, 1989), 14-16.

12. See J. T. McNeill, "Natural Law in the Teaching of the Reformers," *Journal of Religion* 26 (1946): 168-87.

In response to the question, "How should the Church bear witness to God's saving activity in Christ?" we have argued that it should obviously declare its belief in the Christ-event and give reasons for it; but that it should also show the significance of that event by nurturing just community, primarily among its own ranks, but secondarily in society as a whole. We now move rapidly to a conclusion by pointing out two respects in which the concept of social justice as we have used it differs from that assumed by many who urge the missionary primacy of social praxis. Here we respond to the last of our three crucial questions.

IV. The Personal and Religious Dimensions of Social Justice

First, as we have conceived it, social justice is not simply a matter of political structures; it is also about personal relationships. We cannot make our *institutions* sufficiently just that *we* can afford not to be. So if we would promote social justice, then we must do it not only by organisational reform, but also by the moral reformation of the individual-in-community. Therefore, secondly, social justice depends ultimately on spiritual conversion. For ultimately whether we treat each other justly depends upon how we regard ourselves, and how we regard ourselves depends on how we regard God. If we see ourselves as autonomous individuals, finally responsible to no one else, then we will try to play god with each other, abusing and manipulating and judging self-righteously. But if, worshipping God the Creator, we accept ourselves as the creatures we are, limited in power and responsibility and naturally lacking in self-sufficiency; and if, accepting the forgiveness of God in Christ, we recognise each other as equal in sin and in debt to grace, then the mutual respect, forbearance and sympathy that are requisite for just community will be forthcoming. Social justice depends ultimately on the kind of people we are; and ultimately the kind of people we are depends on whether we stand with God or against him.

Conclusion

Our conclusion, then, is that evangelism and social praxis are both equally necessary to the mission of the Christian Church. Apart from the witness of just community, evangelism will be unable to demonstrate why the gospel matters, why it should interest real human beings who are individuals-in-community. If it would address the world in such a way as to be heard, the Church must show how what it says promotes the human good, a good which is irreducibly (albeit not merely) social. If the Church proclaims the gospel without simultaneously building just community, then it will speak empty words to ears that are hungry for words of substance.

On the other hand, to engage in social praxis apart from evangelism is to neglect the personal and religious dimensions of just community and to lay its cause wide open to all sorts of utopian illusions and totalitarian self-deceptions. For the promotion of social justice is not simply a matter of enacting new laws and reforming old institutions. At its most substantial it is also a matter of refashioning relationships between persons, together with the tacit codes and conventions and attitudes that govern them. And since our regard for others is decisively shaped by our regard for ourselves, and our self-regard by our regard for God, the cause of social justice itself raises the religious question — and scans the horizon for glad tidings.

The Ultimate Indiscernibility of Faith

JACQUES GOULET

My title seems to advocate subjectivism, that is, to deny any criterion of truth outside the subject, to propagate a radical subjectivity familiar to the post-Kantian idealist tradition developed by Hegel. It also appears to repudiate any criterion of evaluation for the superiority of any faith, and to entirely eliminate the question of the relevancy of Christian tradition, in particular its claim of unique truth and of absolute necessity and its history of dogmas and anathemas.

In the Christian tradition, faith is regularly defined as a surrender of the mind, as a submission of our intelligence, moved by love, to the truth revealed by God. Faith is seen as an obedient acceptance of Church teaching. For too many Christians, new truths are someway added to our intelligence (regarding the Trinity, for instance), truths to which human reason cannot reach, revealed by God and handed down by the Church, which will make sense only in the next world.

Today faith, for more and more Christians, has come to mean some type of handing over of oneself to a Transcendent named God. No longer are many believers quite happy to accept revealed mysteries that made very little sense to them in this world, but they remain open to transcendence, with the hope, too, that it will someway enlighten their human way. Faith in this sense, then, is not only a leap of acceptance, but also the continuous call within one to go beyond oneself, probing what is most human.

The Indian Catholic theologian Raimundo Panikkar understands faith as an openness to the beyond, to transcendence, personal or not; but it is an unlimited capacity for growth, a dynamic constitutive dimension of man who continuously wishes, searches, questions.[1]

---

1. Raimundo Panikkar, *L'homme qui devient Dieu. La foi dimension constitutive de l'homme* (Paris: Aubier, 1969).

Reprinted with permission from *The Journal of the Interdenominational Theological Center* 13 (1985-86): 33-38.

In that perspective, faith is not essentially a doctrine or a moral code, but an essential element of man, grounding man's unlimited ability to grow. Through faith, man may discover his limitation, contingence, indigence, and also his "natural" desire for perfection, his unlimited capacity to know, to love, to live, his unquenchable thirst for more, for better. That possibility of discovery constitutes faith as a central tension: a tension between two axes: my "I" which wants to be autonomous, securely limited, and the Transcendent within me calling me. My being must lose itself first, by acknowledging a second axis, and then by going as far as to acknowledge that the beyond is the true axis.

> The progress of faith means the conflict between these two poles. There are mutual feints, approaches, and withdrawals; alternate tension and relaxation; until finally both poles coincide to form what we call a Christian existence, expressed by the words of St. Paul: "I live, yet not I, but Christ lives in me."[2]

But, as Panikkar explains, faith, having its roots in the Absolute, cannot be bound by a final mode of expression, because that faith must always be expressing the Transcendent. Since man is "viator," faith has to be a "pilgrim" faith.[3] And so the condition of Faithfulness appears as a process whose articulation is radically secondary to the core dynamism of its undefined presence.[4] Moreover, this root subordination of articulation, or creed, to ultimate faith reveals the basis of common opinion regarding good faith.

Someone who is, thinks and acts according to his conscious interior conviction is of good faith. The man of good faith is someone whose conscious commitment is in accordance with reality as he experiences and understands authenticity, honesty, personal integrity. The man of good faith acts according to his conscience understood in its triple dimension or role: as an ontic element of the personality itself, as a judgment formulating general ethical norms, and as an existential act of personal decision in the actual situation.

Good faith is personal: my faith! It belongs to the individual to develop an interior conviction, which must include and integrate as harmoniously as possible all that a person is, all his experiences — neurotic, psychotic, whatever — and all their ramifications. And we can then say that the "will of truth" is the "truth of the will," that is, authenticity of the will.

Such a personal faith as articulated is my limited, relative, continent way

---

2. Romano Guardini, *The Life of Faith*, trans. J. Chapin (London: Newman Press, 1961), 21.

3. Raimundo Panikkar, *L'homme qui devient Dieu*.

4. Catholic theology has been slower than Protestantism in appreciating this distinction. For a recent Catholic expression, see Bernard Lonergan, *Method in Theology* (New York: Herder and Herder, 1972), chapter 4.

of understanding, of living and celebrating. It includes growth, doubt, search, my uniqueness, and therefore change which acknowledges my gradual trans-formation and that of others.

However, there is the ever-prevalent temptation to universalize and abso-lutize as divine Truth and Will insights and values specifically bound and limited to a local temporary culture. Too often the high priests of these various cultures accuse their competitors of infidelity, of deception, of heresy, of superstitions, of atheism.

By contrast, the man of bad faith is one who refuses to live according to what he considers true. The following terms could describe that person, namely: liar, cheater, inauthentic, simulator, deceiver, willfully ignorant, voluntarily self-deluding, unfaithful, sinner.

In contrast to good faith, open to the oddities of subjectivity, true faith is considered to be that of the believer who not only is committed according to his conscience, that is to say, by interior conviction, but whose experience, insight, understanding, judgment, decision and action correspond *de facto* to reality. But what criteria can be applied to demonstrate such a correspondence? None which could definitely establish it as manifest, unveiled. To claim other-wise is to place in the finite subject a luminosity of Intelligibility that denies his historical finitude. Intelligibility is us, and hence efforts at objectifying it or its criteria are irremediably perspectival[5] and opaque. The objectification that is our pronouncement, our ritual, our living, is infinitely remote from the extrinsic infinite intelligibility to which faith threads us. And it is this infinitude of gap that ultimately constitutes faith as indiscernible.

Yet even that indiscernibility is not manifest. Just as the difficulty of the Socratic project, "know thyself," is manifested to the individual only insofar as that individual labours long for self-knowledge, so that opaqueness of the seed of transcendence in history only reveals itself slowly through the toils and labours of religious living and conflict and reflection. So, in our time, it is significant that with the growing realization within the *Geisteswissenschaften* (human sciences) of the remoteness of human meaning there comes forward a renewal of the theology of mystery and the theology of hope, a reaching for "things unseen."

But the basic thesis of the ultimate indiscernibility of faith is not a radical shift in theology: it is a tenet (but, unfortunately, a hidden tenet) of the entire Christian tradition, articulately present even through centuries of religious war grounded in its denial. Let us pass on here to view some aspects of that articu-lated presence. Aspects that we may touch on are long-respected views on the primacy of conscience, on the universality of salvation, and on the fact that propositions cannot be salvific by themselves.

Primacy of conscience as an articulated presence — manifest in words

---

5. See Bernard Lonergan, *Method in Theology,* see Index under "perspective."

even if without perhaps the living presence — is spread through Christianity. Already it is in Saint Paul:

> For instance, pagans who never heard of the Law but are led by reason to do what the Law commands, may not actually 'possess' the Law, but they can be said to 'be' the Law. They can point to the substance of the Law engraved on their hearts — they can call a witness, that is, their own conscience" (Romans 2:14-15).

and it is echoed as recently as the Second Vatican Council:

> Conscience is the most secret core and sanctuary of man. There he is alone with God, whose voice echoes in his depths.

and later in the same document:

> Conscience frequently errs from invincible ignorance without losing its dignity.[6]

What is being articulated here is an aspect of the ultimate indiscernibility of faith, an articulation filled with life even through the historic darkness of departure from the reality it articulates.

Again, there is the ancient tenet of the universality of the salvific reach of God, "who wants all . . . to be saved and to come to the knowledge of the truth" (1 Tim. 2:4). But that tenet in history has been performatively contradicted by the zeal with which the coming to knowledge was required. History succeeds slowly in teaching us that the truth in the core of our meaning is seen but only in a glass darkly — the coming to knowledge is a stumbling of feeble intellect prior to the eschatological dawn.

Thirdly, there is little stress in New Testament writings on the salvific properties of articulate propositions, with a dominant stress on the interpersonal quality of salvation. As Aquinas put it succinctly in the medieval period:

> The act of the believer does not terminate in a proposition, but in a thing.[7]

There is a sense here, as in the example of the other two illustrative tenets, in which history has slowly made manifest the incarnate quality of faith, the shroud of Personal Mystery that hides from us the meaning of divine love.

But there are objections to be met. Is not all this a shift to a basic subjectivism, a relativism? Does it not eliminate even a minimum of certitude

---

6. Pastoral Constitution on the Church in the Modern World, No. 16: *The Documents of Vatican II*, ed. Walter M. Abbott (London: G. Chapman, 1966), 213-14.

7. *Summa Theol.*, IIa IIae, question 1, article 2, objection 2; trans. by the Fathers of the English Dominican Province (New York: Benzinger, 1947), 1170.

and security? Does it not eliminate the possibility of heresy? Let us look at these in turn.

As one contemporary theologian has said, God reaches us "from within outwards," not "from without inwards," that is, from the very core of [the] density of our existence, at the very point where we flow from God's creative hands.[8]

A subjectivist theory of knowledge is obviously not proposed. Of course, God and the world of things exist in themselves, independently of me and of my life. What is said in this paper has nothing to do with Hegel or Kant (who see history as only an idea or ideal), but it has much to do with Blondel's concrete reflections, with Husserl's search for a grounded authentic subjectivity, with Lonergan's position that objectivity is in fact grounded in authentic subjectivity.

The meaningful world in which I find myself, which is seen and lived by me, which gives a meaning to my existence, and to which my existence gives a meaning — my existential world, in other words — does not exist without me; and it exists all the more in that I am and live more intensely.[9]

But, whatever the debates about subjectivity, the proposed indiscernibility surely results in a relativism? So, for example, are not all faiths equally slavific?

The basic issue here is that "all faiths" is a misnomer. There is only one faith, whose discernment is shrouded in mystery. Has it an authentic articulation which stands out from all other articulations as the day from night? One must distinguish finite articulation from ultimate articulation. Authenticity may pertain to finite articulation, however deviant or feeble. But yet, that is an Ultimate Authentic articulation, in light inaccessible. And within history there are shreds of articulation that converge on that ultimacy — but who is to discern the meshing of those shreds as they relate to the living of an authentic life?

What then of the minimum of certitude within that life?

Here one might draw on the distinction made by Lonergan between religious conversion and moral or intellectual conversation, and mesh his discussion of religious conversion with Tillich's view of ultimate concern. Our ground security, our "peace, joy . . . ," etc., is *within* the zone of indiscernible faith, the zone of being taken up by ultimate concern.[10] Outside this zone one is on the tossed insecure waves of a life in personal and cultural perspective.

Finally, there is the question of heresy. What we have said above concerning the shreds of authentic articulation applies also here. But much more pointedly, as Quentin Quesnell remarks in a study of the issue,

> But what is the objective value of holding objective criteria to which each of mutually contradictory parties can appeal, finding in them simultaneously

8. Piet Fransen, *The New Life of Grace* (New York: Desclee, 1969), 130-31.

9. Romano Guardini, *The Life of Faith*, 48, n. 1.

10. Bernard Lonergan, *Method in Theology*, chap. 4, especially p. 106.

their own orthodoxy and their opponent's heresy? . . . How does such an analysis promote the cause of objectivity?[11]

What is of objective value is that broad ecumenism which listens in the Spirit and is willing to share what shreds of light that be, trusting that Ultimate Concern is bringing forth salvation in ways indiscernible.

In closing, I would make my own the words of Piet Fransen:

We do not possess truth in faith; but in faith, truth possesses us.[12]

Indeed, our faith does not encompass the living God who remains Transcendent. God reaches every one of us, touches every one of us, calls us by our name, with an Infinite Call, but in a human way.

11. Quentin Quesnell, *The Foundations of Heresy*, to be published.
12. Piet Fransen, as reported in *The National Catholic Reporter* (November 3, 1972): 9.

V.7

A Spirituality That Sustains Us
in Our Struggles

ARUNA GNANADASON

A fight for truth has begun
At Sinsyaru Khala.
A fight for rights has begun
At Malkot Thano.
Sister, it is a fight to protect
Our mountains and forests.
They give us life.

Embrace the life of the living trees and streams.
Clasp them to your hearts.
Resist the digging of mountains
That brings death to our forests and streams.
A fight for life has begun
At Sinsyaru Khala.[1]

So sing the simple tribal women of the Chipko movement[2] in the Garhwal region of the Himalayas, who have been involved for nearly twenty years in a

---

1. This protest song, composed by Chamundeyi, a tribal woman of the Doon Valley in the Himalayas, was inspired by a Chipko poet, Ghanshyam "Shailani." Quoted by Vandana Shiva, a feminist ecologist, in her book *Staying Alive: Women Ecology and Survival in India* (Delhi: Kali for Women, 1988), 210.
2. The Chipko ("to cling") movement refers to an ecological struggle of nearly two decades in the Utharkhand region of the lower Himalayas, spearheaded largely by tribal women who have carried a relentless crusade to save their forests by clinging to the trees and defying with their bodies the contractor's sword. They have also involved themselves in protecting their mountains from indiscriminate mining, etc.

Reprinted from the *International Review of Mission* 80 (Jan. 1991): 29-41. Used with permission.

struggle to protect their trees, their rivers, their mountains, their way of life. Their songs demonstrate not merely the ecological perceptions of these simple women who initiated and have sustained for two decades a struggle against deforestation and other onslaughts on their environment, but it reflects the deep spiritual commitment and knowledge of women who "work daily in the production of survival."[3]

Itwari Devi, a village woman elder who has guided a Chipko movement in the Doon Valley, of the lower Himalayas, to blockade mining operations there, describes the spiritual energy that sustains their struggles, in these words:

> *Shakti* (strength) comes to us from these forests and grasslands; we watch them grow, year in and year out, through their internal *shakti,* and we derive our strength from it. We watch our streams renew themselves and we drink their clear and sparkling water — that gives us *shakti.* We drink fresh milk, we eat *ghee* (melted butter), we eat food from our own fields — all this gives us not just nutrition of the body, but a moral strength, that we are our own masters, we control and produce our own wealth. That is why "primitive," "backward" women, who do not buy their needs from the market but produce them themselves, are leading Chipko. Our power is nature's power, our *shakti* comes from *prakriti* (nature). Our power against the contractor comes from these inner sources, and is strengthened by his trying to oppress and bully us with his false power of money and muscle. We have offered ourselves, even at the cost of our lives, for a peaceful protest to close this mine, to challenge and oppose the power that the government represents. Each attempt to violate us has strengthened our integrity. They stoned us on March 20 when they returned from the mine. They stoned our children and hit them with iron rods, but they could not destroy our *shakti.*[4]

The newly emerging consciousness of their inner strength, *shakti,* has indeed been the spiritual power that has sustained them and other oppressed groups in their struggles for life.

A Search for a New Spirituality of Liberation

The search for the spiritual source for liberation of oppressed people, and of creation, is becoming stronger in Asia, both in the church and in people's movements. A theology is emerging that is integral to the struggles of the poor relating to the interrelationship between two dominant characteristics of the Asian reality — poverty and religiousness.

3. Shiva, *Staying Alive,* 210.
4. Itwari Devi, a village elder who led the Chipko movement against mining operations in the Doon Valley. Quoted by Vandana Shiva, *Staying Alive,* 208-9.

It cannot be ignored that the visible expressions of religion — its rituals and institutions and the spirituality that is embedded in them — exercise a powerful influence over oppressed identities in Asia, and more specifically in India. But many questions are being raised as to whether these influences are liberating or oppressive:

> In India, with its rich heritage of religion and culture, there is a bewildering variety of spiritualities. What role do they play in the movements for liberation? What forms of spirituality have been and continue to be used to legitimize the dominance of upper castes/classes over the masses? Is there a spirituality that is germane to the life and experience of the poor in our villages and slums? Are there new forms of spirituality that are emerging out of people's movements? In short, in what sense can we speak of a spirituality of liberation in the Indian context?[5]

The church in Asia has to take these questions seriously in a context where the spiritual and moral fibre of an essentially "religious" society is being seriously eroded by increasing poverty, the widening gulf between the rich and the poor, the repeated incidents of social tensions and conflicts caused by caste divisions, the rapid breakdown of tribal values and the tribal way of life due to aggressive "development" and modernization, the strengthening of religious and communal self-interest fed by increasing religious fundamentalism and chauvinism — the list of the many ugly faces of "the beast" is endless and puts the church in an unenviable position. It has to respond with courage and conviction to the challenges before it.

As Dr. Samuel Rayan puts it:

> This quest presents the churches of Asia, small and limited as they are, with challenges and tasks which are immense and complex, and often enough, baffling and painful. . . . Nevertheless we meet the challenges and take up the tasks, even as we agonize over the situation of massive poverty and misery in a world in which nobody indeed need suffer hunger or want. The situation is not something outside us. With its tears and laughter, it struggles and hopes, it is part of ourselves and our history, part of the life of our earth and of humankind. We are beginning to sense the power of a deep-going spiritual-social-historical solidarity which binds the earth together. We know that God holds this tangled mess, instinct with life, close to God's own heart. We know God is always loving it into clarity and freedom and enabling it to walk its own path and carve out its own destiny in partnership with God. God is here, deeply involved in the history we are making, profoundly interested in it,

---

5. *An Indian Search for a Spirituality of Liberation*, report of a discussion of a small group of theologians and others organized by the Indian EATWOT, in Madras, India, in 1989. Unpublished mss. I have quoted extensively from this report as I was a participant in this discussion and was also on the drafting team.

profoundly affected by it. God is here, urging and challenging us to transform our earth into something of God's Kingdom where divine dreams are realized and the divine name is experienced as meaningful.[6]

It is this spiritual quest, this imperative to find new and vital ways of knowing God, that has led to the emergence of new voices — new sources of power. It is drawn out of the organized strength of oppressed groups of people who have been pushed to the periphery for centuries. They are now being drawn into the centre, as their struggle for life and dignity are being recognized as "a spiritual necessity"[7] of our times. Some of these new spiritual movements can be identified as the women's movement, the Dalit movement, the tribal movement and the ecology movement. These relatively new expressions of resistance have brought new dimensions and new insights into the life of the church and society in India. I will speak briefly of these before going further.

The Emerging *Shakti*

Among these voices is the rebirth of *shakti*, which Itwari Devi quoted earlier, described as the "inner source" or spiritual energy that sustains women in their daily struggle for survival. It has also led women into a "hermeneutics of suspicion" of traditional spiritualities, of traditional interpretations of the scriptures and even of traditional understandings and analysis of society. It has led to a critique of models of development and patterns of life. It has therefore liberated Asian women from narrow definitions of what women's freedom and power may mean. It is not individualistic or based on the wresting of small concessions or benefits within existing unjust structures. It has made women conscious of their responsibility to all of humanity — particularly the most oppressed — and to all of creation. It is in this re-emergence of *shakti*, or spiritual energy, that Asian women find God.

It is energy that bursts out of the *han* (accumulated anger, as Korean theologians would call it) of the exploited and powerless women of Asia. In the words of the Korean Minjung theologian Hyung Young-Hak:

> *Han* is a sense of unresolved resentment against injustice suffered, a sense of helplessness because of the overwhelming odds against it, a feeling of total abandonment ("Why hast thou forsaken me?"), a feeling of acute pain, of sorrow in one's guts and bowels making the whole body writhe and wriggle,

---

6. Samuel Rayan, S.J., in "Asia and Justice," in *Liberation in Asia: Theological Perspectives,* ed. S. Arokiasamy, S.J., and G. Gispert-Sauch, S.J. (Gujarat: Delhi and Gujarat Sahitya Prakash, 1987), 3.

7. K. C. Abraham, "A New Spirituality," in *Break Every Yoke* (Abraham Malpan Memorial Lectures; Ecumenical Christian Centre publication, 1983), 60.

and an obstinate urge to take "revenge" and to right the wrong that all these constitute.[8]

Asian feminist methodology has been formed from this experiential base. Women have discovered a new spiritual power in being able to come together and share in each other's everyday experiences of pain or of celebration. From the depths of women's stories of joys and sorrows, triumphs and defeats, we can draw a tapestry of theological exploration that is contextual and based on a community in struggle for humanhood. Asian feminist theology also therefore embodies women's yearning to find theological meaning for their suffering and pain.

> Asian women's theology has emerged from Asian women's cries and screams, from the extreme suffering in their everyday lives. They have shouted from pain when their own and their children's bodies collapsed from starvation, rape and battering. Theological reflection has emerged as a response to women's suffering.[9]

Asian feminist methodology has attempted to place the oppression of women within the system of patriarchy that keeps gender injustice and all other forms of oppression — of class, race, caste, religious and cultural domination — intact. This leads them to a critical study of their historical past in order to discover the liberating possibilities of the feminist paradigm for today, with a view to challenge an economic and social order that has devalued women's labour, sexuality and their dignity as human beings. This has led to a reflection on the "development" paradigm, which is an offshoot of the Industrial Revolution in Europe and which has become the universal, undermining the knowledge and experience of large sections of the nations on the periphery of the "development" worldview. This development mode has been understood by women as

> . . . a patriarchal project, because it has emerged from centres of western capitalist patriarchy, and it reproduces those patriarchal structures within the family, in community and throughout the fabric of Third World societies. Patriarchal prejudice colours the structures of knowledge, as well as structures of production and work, that shape and are in turn shaped by "development" activity. Women's knowledge and work as integrally linked to nature is marginalized or displaced, and in its place are introduced patterns of thought and

8. Hyung Young-Hak, quoted by Chung Hyun Kyung, "Han-pu-ri: Doing Theology from Korean Women's Perspectives," in *We Dare to Dream: Doing Theology as Asian Women*, ed. Virginia Fabella and Sun Ai Lee Park (Asian Women's Resource Centre for Culture and Theology and the EATWOT Women's Commission in Asia, 1989), 138.

9. Chun Huan Kyung from Korea, in her doctoral thesis on Asian Feminist Theology submitted to Union Theological Seminary, New York. To be published.

patterns of work that devalue the worth of women's knowledge and women's activities and fragment both nature and society.[10]

The newly emerging feminist consciousness has therefore strongly criticized this "mastery" of the earth and of marginalized groups (particularly women) by an aggressive science and technology mind-set. They recognize in this appropriation of the earth for profit and human gain, a breaking of the spiritual bond between humanity and creation. Women call for a wholistic eco-spiritual vision based on care and nurture of the earth and of all those people who have been denied the right to personhood and human dignity.

Women have also begun to uncover a new understanding of their biblical and extrabiblical history, so that they can discover the liberative strands in the gospel. This has led them to a critique of church dogmas, doctrines, theology and ecclesiastical practices, liturgies, language and symbols as well as patterns of ministry — all of which have been formulated out of male experiences. Women seek ways by which their spiritual gifts can become an integral part of the life of the church, so as to transform the church into becoming a community of concerned people, able and willing to play a prophetic role in the world today.

The Spiritual Quest of a "No" People to Become a "New" People

The Dalit movement for liberation is the organized voice of fifteen percent of the Indian population who are viewed as "outcastes" in the caste hierarchy, which had been introduced by Aryan/Brahmanical Hinduism into Indian society. This institutionalized system of social gradation has legitimized gross forms of violence and brutality against the Dalits, who have been crushed to dust by dominant caste groups.

The Dalit movement has given birth to the emerging Dalit spirituality, as an effort of Dalits to delve into their past history and heritage, in order to reconstruct it.

> The history of conflict, alienation and cultural subjugation of Dalits by the dominant culture and its agents, is told in the language of myths, stories, hybrid religious symbols and rituals. We have also archeological and linguistic data available to reconstruct the outlines and, in some cases, the details of subjugation.
>
> This process of the Dalits' regaining a new identity is essentially in conflict with not only the material interests of the ruling caste groups but also with their cultural and religious hegemony. Therefore what is required is a spirituality that endures conflict and provides hope for the new.

10. Vandana Shiva, in "Let us Survive. Women, Ecology and Development," in *Sangarsh*, an occasional journal of Vimochana, Bangalore, 1986.

The practitioners of this spirituality are small groups and organizations made up of Dalits and others who have taken upon themselves the task of redeeming Dalit human dignity and who are convinced that they would humanize their opponents in the process.[11]

With this new consciousness of identity and spiritual power, Dalit theology has come into being as an attempt to influence all disciplines of knowledge from the underside of history, informed by the perspective of Dalits. Arvind Nirmal, a leading Dalit theologian in India, writes:

It (Christian Dalit theology) will be based on their own Dalit experiences, their own sufferings, their own aspirations and their own hope. It will narrate the story of their sufferings and their pathos — it will anticipate liberation, which is meaningful to them.[12]

It is in the anticipation of liberation promised to the people in Christ that they would place their hope. Nirmal affirms that "Jesus Christ, whose followers we are, was himself a Dalit."[13] The Dalit who has always played a servant role — housemaid, sweeper, *bhangi* (servant) — can be identified with the Servant God of Isaiah. The servant-language in the Servant Song depicts all the pathos and servanthood role in the life of a "despised, smitten and afflicted Dalit."

It is relevant to point out that Dalit women, who have been described as "the Dalit of the Dalit" or the "dust of the dust," are thrice jeopardized in this context. Increased restrictions on women, particularly on their sexuality and their movement, and on their right to inheritance, are integral parts of a rise in caste hierarchy. M. N. Srinivas, the renowned sociologist, states that "sanskritization results in harshness to women."[14] Since the main threat to the purity of the caste groups comes from female sexuality and in women's capacity to infuse low quality blood into the "pure" upper castes, women had to be guarded and controlled. So *purdah* (veiling) and seclusion become the norm. The Aryans brought with them the patriarchal joint family as an effective means of controlling women. Women came to be viewed as property of males — just as males' fields or property belonged to them. Only sons could inherit property; therefore, the birth of sons became crucial. Women could not participate in certain rituals (due to the impurity associated with their menstruation), and therefore the birth of a son was essential to continue the family name and to perform rituals — particularly to light the funeral pyre of his father, so as to ensure him a better life after death.

Throughout Indian history there has been a stream of spiritual resistance

11. *An Indian Search.*

12. Arvind P. Nirmal, in *NCC Review,* a magazine of the National Council of Churches in India, February 1988, 76.

13. Ibid., 77.

14. M. N. Srinivas, *Caste in Modern India* (London: Asia Publishing House, 1962), 46.

against the ridigity of patriarchal brahmanism. At different times there has been a resurgence of mother goddess cults and fertility worship. The *shakti* cult, representing the female power principle, became strong. The *shakti* cult, a strong non-Aryan southern movement, brought in anti-caste, anti-patriarchy challenges to Hinduism. Matriarchal and populist cultures continued to make their opposition felt, in spite of the consolidated strength of patriarchy. Brahmanism was forced to make some concessions. For example, since the mother goddess cult could not be suppressed, she was finally incorporated into Brahmin ritual by providing "brahmanical" husbands to non-brahmanical mother goddesses.

The spiritual contributions of the Dalit liberation movement, and more specifically of the pre-Aryan, women-centred fertility cults, must be recognized as we seek ways to draw from our spiritual heritage. Such a path of discovery had imbued the struggles of the Dalits with a spiritual dimension that has sustained them against repeated brutal attacks by dominant caste groups to suppress their voices and their vitality.

A Demand for Identity — A Plea for Wholistic Alternatives

The tribal movement in India, along with the ecology movement with its plea for a totally alternative worldview, is a spiritual search for a more wholistic approach to life. They provide a strong critique of the industrial mode of development that India has opted for, and call for an alternative vision that will not affect so adversely the tribal communities and the nature-centred environment in which they live.

> The five year plans and their industrially oriented focus have deeply affected tribal life. Almost all big dams, factories, hydro-electric and nuclear plants and missile testing ranges are constructed on tribal homelands, with scant regard for tribal life and culture. To the tribals, the colonizing of their lands is a continuing characteristic of the so-called "development" efforts of the dominant groups.[15]

The tribals have always had a deep spiritual bond with nature; therefore, they see their struggles for justice, for a right to their homelands and way of life, as a spiritual journey.

This song, sung by Santhal tribals in West Bengal in their struggle against the Damodar Valley Corporation, which built dams on the River Damodar, captures the anti-life force of so-called development projects. It also reflects people's agonizing search for meaning in these deliberate and conscious efforts to take away from the poor their basic human rights, breaking them from their cultural moorings by displacing and impoverishing them further. The tribal

15. *An Indian Search.*

consciousness also repeatedly warns against the damage this will do to the
eco-system. There is indeed a depth of theological and spiritual truth in their
songs:

> Which company came to my land to open a *karkhana?* (factory)
> It awakened its name in the rivers and the ponds
> calling itself the DVC (Damodar Valley Corporation).
> It throws earth, dug by a machine, into the river.
> It has cut the mountain and made a bridge.
> The water runs beneath.
> Roads are coming, they are giving us electricity,
> having opened the *karkhana.*
> The *praja* (people) all question them.
> They ask what this name belongs to.
> When evening falls they give paper notes as pay.
> Where will I keep these paper notes?
> They dissolve in the water.
> In every house there is a well which gives water for *brinjal* and cabbage.
> Every house is bounded by walls, which make it look like a palace.
> This Santhal tongue of ours has been destroyed in the district.
> You came and made this a bloody *burning ghat* (cremation ground),
> calling yourself the DVC (Damodar Valley Corporation).[16]

The tribal movement cautions against these conscious attempts to erode
the tribal way of life which has as its basic component the continuum of
relationship between nature-humanity-spirit. Such a bonding is seen as the vital
criterion for humanity's desire to be human. Egalitarian tribal values of community ownership of land, the use of produce for the good of all, equal participation of all in social life and in decision-making processes, stressing consensus, and a strict moral code on the use of the earth and its resources have
all been submerged under the waters of "development" projects which put India
on the world map as a "developing" nation but which plunge tribal populations
into deeper and deeper poverty, and perhaps, in the long run, to extinction.
The cry of the tribals for a separate autonomous state within the Indian sub-
continent, where they could demonstrate the strength of tribal values, is a
spiritual quest for bringing healing and wholeness to a society, nation and a
fragmented world.

The ecology movement in India has drawn spiritual energy from Indian
cosmology, which has emphasized the connectedness between person and nature *(Purusha-Prakriti).* These are a duality in unity. All creation reflects this

---

16. A protest song sung in the Purulia District of West Bengal by Santhal tribal women in
protest against dams built by the Indian government-sponsored Damodar Valley Corporation.
Quoted by Vandana Shiva in *Staying Alive,* 190.

dialectical unity, and this has been the core of ecological thought and action. Since there are no dualisms ontologically, and because "nature as *Prakriti* sustains life, nature has been treated as integral and inviolable."[17] The onslaught of industrialization and "development," with its deforestation projects, the building of big dams on the rivers, the construction of factories where once there were hills and forests, pollution of the air, land and sea — all these have in fact been aberrations in the traditional Indian way of life.

It is from such a wholistic vision based on our spiritual past that eco-theology, and more specifically the feminist paradigm within it, draws inspiration. It is an alternative vision of hope, perhaps the only hope for the world. These voices, yet muted, are saying that there are other possible categories for structuring the world and our relationships with nature — we need to have only the political and spiritual will to work them out. It provides a critique of the way we have designed our ideological and theological assumptions thus far, and of our overdependence on the western paradigm of development. It is a challenge coming out of the people's lived experiences of not only weeping with nature, for deliverance and freedom; but also out of years of organized resistance against senseless destruction.

A New Song of Hope — A New Spirituality

Spirituality is a constitutive factor of all these movements and struggles.

> Spirituality is intrinsic to action for liberation. All women and men in our country or elsewhere who have striven and continue to strive against exploitation and oppression, and for justice, dignity and life for all are spiritual women and men. Their stories must be told, their memory cherished, and their inspiration carried forward.
>
> The spiritual is not a dimension added to the people's struggles and protests in order to provide motivation and sacrality. When we stand for justice and freedom and for people's rights to life with dignity, we stand for those realities and values in terms of which all faiths image the Mystery of the Divine: That is why, for Jeremiah, to do justice is to "know" God. When we stand with the oppressed we stand with the one who always takes their side and acts for their liberation (Ps. 103:6). The downtrodden people with their history of hope and struggle is the *locus*, the place, of authentic encounter with God. In confronting injustice and working for a new India, a new world, where people are equal and free, and where resources are for all, there exists a profound spirituality even if it is not recognized, made explicit, or named.[18]

17. Ibid., 40.
18. *An Indian Search.*

Some Facets of This Spirituality

1. Such a spirituality of struggle is not an ephemeral, other-worldly, private, esoteric reality. It is earthy, grounded in the grim realities of living and surviving in an inhuman, exploitative world. In fact, it takes the form of a political movement, an alternative worldview, which seeks new ways of looking at and working for the liberation of people and creation. It is a discovery of new ways in which those on the periphery can participate and contribute their visions to the liberative process.

It is based on the lived experience of suffering and pain, of joy and hope of those whose experiences, whose dreams and aspirations, have been for centuries trivialized and ignored. It reveals itself as a bursting message of hope as out of the dailyness of their lives and out of their wisdom, these oppressed identities are able to articulate a political vision of a more just world order. As an Indian group of theologians expressed it:

> Spirituality for us is bound up with life and all that life involves: freedom and food, dignity and equality, community and sharing of resources, creativity and celebration of the God of life and liberation. Spirituality is all that the Spirit of God originates, gives, guides, and accompanies; all that the Spirit can bless, accept and work with. It is all that can contribute to the balance and blossoming, the healing and wholeness of India, of the human race, the earth, the cosmos. It may be described as the Godwardness of life, the experience of seeing God in all things and all things in God; or, as a sustained search for meaning, depth, transcendence and comradeship, overcoming mental and social inertia and determinisms in order to grow in freedom and be able to relate to reality.[19]

2. It is an effort by people without a name in history to go back to their past and to draw from their spiritual heritage, which has been so distorted or even erased by dominant power groups. Much of this new spirituality is therefore without written records and is revealed in the oral tradition. Songs, dances, folklore, poetry, art and drama that emerge out of the movements of people for justice and dignity, provide a wealth of spiritual resources (the protest songs quoted earlier are examples of this). Archaeological evidences and popular religious experiences that are yet untampered with by assimilation efforts of dominant groups (e.g., women-centered cults) provide the scope for a search for the spirituality that has given the stamina for these oppressed groups to survive centuries of repression.

3. It is a celebration of the plurality of experiences. It rejects efforts to impose uniformity by a process of assimilation and integration, and encourages each group to assert its self-identity. It asserts the right to self-identity and

19. Ibid.

autonomous existence. For people who have come to accept their lot as a "no" people, as people who must remain invisible at all costs, the possibility of gaining visibility, of becoming a "new" people who can assert their sense of belonging and can speak out and demand their rightful share of power and resources, as well as of human dignity, is indeed a spiritual journey of some dimension.

They assert their individual identity and autonomous existence, focussing specifically on the oppression each group faces, so as to deal with these specific forms of oppression, which are often ignored in larger transformative processes. History is replete with examples of this. It also augments the possibility of "transforming a pyramid into a rainbow"[20] as the spiritual gifts of each movement flow into the life and witness of the whole community, suffusing it with vibrant colours and strengthening its "Babel-like" existence.

This will enrich the life of the community by challenging it to be even more responsive to the struggles and needs of the "little ones" within it. It will also bring in spiritual diversity in the community's responses, introducing new forms of resistance, new nonviolent forms of protest, new, more caring and nurturing ways of dealing with people and creation, and new and alternative ways of ensuring justice and peace.

The celebration of plurality within community inevitably will touch the life of the church and the local congregation, encouraging the richness of spiritual and theological gifts of those on the periphery. This would include new liturgical experiences that are inclusive in language, imagery and symbols; a cleansing of hierarchical ecclesial structures to make them more responsive to the yearning for participation of marginalized sections; a radical restructuring of traditional theological, doctrinal and faith assumptions; and a relooking at patterns of ministry to make them more inclusive to the groans of creation for liberation.

4. Into this context must be placed one of the most creative possibilities of this emerging spirituality. As indicated earlier, there have been attempts by these oppressed groups to reinterpret traditional understandings of society to make them inclusive of the experiences and longings of those who have been marginalized. Therefore "development priorities" of ruling groups have been challenged, as have been political ideologies which have ignored questions of race, caste, gender, religion and culture. The demand is for a more wholistic worldview that would not only pose a challenge to domination on the basis of class, but will question forms of domination based on gender and other cultural and social forms of control. The new movements would call for a multi-prolonged approach to struggles for justice and human dignity, so that real and genuine transformation will take place.

Theology has also experienced a sea-change with the emerging new ex-

---

20. Stanley Samartha, *Search for a New Hermeneutics in Asian Christian Theology* (Bangalore: Board of Theological Education of the Senate of Serampore College, 1987), 34.

pressions of liberation theology out of the experiences of these groups — Dalit theology, Asian feminist theology, tribal theology and an eco-spirituality centred theology.

If I may focus specifically on the contribution of Asian feminist theologians: their struggle is complex, as it begins with a critique of traditional theologies and interpretative principles that have grown out of a patriarchal, western, colonial theological ethos. Out of such a critique is emerging a new theology that speaks a word of hope to Asian women as it respects their experiences and responses and provides them with the spiritual energy they need to face questions of survival as Asian women. They seek meaning for the meaningless sacrifices they are called to bear — worst hit by poverty and caste gradation; a cheap source of labour in the capitalist marketplace; sold into prostitution and institutionalized violence in the form of prostitution tourism, and in the rest-and-recreation industry where defence personnel are placed; bartered in the marriage market for pieces of gold and silk; battered and humiliated within the domestic sphere; raped and assaulted either in their workplaces *or* when a lesson must be taught to their men. Are these sacrifices of any value, they seem to ask, as they unearth sources of hope in their scriptures and in their faith heritage.

This has led to a new consciousness of the women-centred spirituality of ancient Indian and other Asian societies as women reinterpret the positive strands from their scriptural past and expose the androcentric biases in their texts and in translation and interpretation.

> Evidence of feminine ultimacy is widely prevalent in India, whether venerated as Nature or the Life-force, as Mother or Virgin, as Great Goddess, or as the Ultimate Reality. As well as the goddess figurines discovered at the various archaeological sites, such as Harappa and Mohenjo-daro, the Atharva Veda, which mirrors the way of life and thought of the indigenous peoples, shows that pre-Vedic, non-Aryan religion and belief were to a great extent female-oriented.[21]

Folk religiosity has also been affirmed as contributing to this new consciousness, as it not only gives a vision of a new community but also emphasizes the restoration of the soil and its nourishment, establishing the principle of humanity's close affinity with and responsibility to the earth and to the feeding of all on the earth.

Such an appropriation process takes place in all these newly awakening groups, empowering them with spirituality and energy for their struggles.

5. Finally, it is a spirituality that stresses unity as the unfinished dream. This points to a wholistic vision of a world turned upside-down, to include the deepest aspirations and longings of all those on the underside. It is a unity that is not to be narrowly defined but rather a unity of the whole inhabited earth

---

21. Ajit Mookerji, *Kali, the Feminine Force* (London: Thames and Hudson Ltd., 1988), 16.

and of all creation. To participate in a transformative process so as to achieve this goal of unity is the spiritual vision of these new voices. It is therefore rooted in participation in larger struggles for a just world order, but with a critical edge. It is not an unquestioning surrender to the analysis and methodology of larger struggles for justice and liberation; it is not an attempt at uniformity. The oppressed identities within the existing political formations and movements participate by emphasizing their own perspective, their own methodologies and their own visions.

Conclusion

The Indian theologians quoted earlier describe succinctly this new vision of a spirituality for struggle:

> The vision grows in clarity and significance as we strive together to embody it in our history and our day-to-day life. We know that the vision is counter-cultural and subversive. It seeks to open prisons, to remove blinds from eyes and let people see reality; to break down divisive walls and set the downtrodden free. It speaks of a community of women and men, equal and free, and celebrant with an unfragmented and wholesome earth and the God of the earth. It is sure, therefore, to clash with principalities and powers and their class systems which need prisons and which can only survive through oppression and fraud.
>
> The vision thus implies a spirituality of conflict. It calls for a spirituality for combat. One that is to mature into a spirituality of "poetry," of untrammelled, joyful creativity. To use Christian imagery, we are for a spirituality of the Cross unfolding into a spirituality of the Resurrection.[22]

A spirituality of new life, of hope and a future where justice and peace will reign — a spirituality wherein the Holy Spirit will empower those ground to the dust to rise up and dance the dance of freedom and liberation — it is this spirituality that sustains us in our struggles.

22. *An Indian Search.*

Some Further Contributions to the Discussion

Baptism, Eucharist, and Ministry. Faith and Order Paper No. 111. Geneva: World Council of Churches, 1982.

Donald Bloesch, *The Crisis of Piety: Essays Toward a Theology of the Christian Life.* Grand Rapids: Wm. B. Eerdmans Publishing Co., 1968.

Leonard Boff, *Church: Charism and Power: Liberation Theology and the Institutional Church.* Trans. John W. Diercksmeier. New York: Crossroad, 1985.

———, *Ecclesiogenesis.* Translated by Robert R. Barr. Maryknoll, NY: Orbis Books, 1986.

Dietrich Bonhoeffer, *The Communion of Saints.* Translated from the German. New York: Harper & Row, 1963.

———, *The Cost of Discipleship.* Translated from the German by R. H. Fuller. New York: Macmillan, 1959, 1963.

Emil Brunner, *The Misunderstanding of the Church.* Translated from the German by Harold Knight. London: Lutterworth Press, 1952.

Walbert Bühlmann, *The Coming of the Third Church.* Maryknoll, NY: Orbis Books, 1976.

James H. Cone, *For My People: Black Theology and the Black Church.* Maryknoll, NY: Orbis Books, 1984.

Harriet Crabtree, *The Christian Life.* Minneapolis: Fortress Press, 1991.

W. E. B. DuBois, *The Souls of Black Folk.* New York: Knopf, 1903.

Avery Dulles, *Models of the Church.* New York: Image Books, 1974, expanded ed. 1987.

Virginia Fabella and Sun Ai Lee Park, *We Dare to Dream.* Maryknoll, NY: Obis Books, 1991.

Georges Florovsky, *Bible, Church, Tradition: An Eastern Orthodox View.* Belmont, MA: Norland, 1972.

Colin E. Gunton and Daniel W. Hardy, eds., *On Being the Church.* Edinburgh: T. & T. Clark, 1989.

Peter C. Hodgson, *Revisioning the Church.* Philadelphia: Fortress Press, 1988.

Fr. Thomas Hopko, *Ministry and the Unity of the Church Liturgy*, Vol. 34. Crestwood, NY: St. Vladimir's Seminary Press, 1990.

James Jones, *Filled with New Wine: The Charismatic Renewal of the Church*. New York: Harper & Row, 1974.

Hans Küng, *The Church*. Translated from the German by Ray and Rosaleen Ockenden. London: Burns & Oates, 1967.

Bernard Lee, *The Becoming of the Church*. New York: Paulist Press, 1974.

C. Eric Lincoln, *The Black Church in the African-American Experience*. Durham, NC: Duke University Press, 1990.

James William McClendon, Jr., *Systematic Theology: Doctrine*. Nashville: Abingdon Press, 1994.

Lewis S. Mudge, *The Sense of a People: Toward a Church for the Human Future*. Philadelphia: Trinity Press International, 1992.

J. Robert Nelson, *The Realm of Redemption*. London: Epworth Press, 1951.

Wolfhart Pannenberg, *The Church*. Translated from the German by Keith Crim. Philadelphia: Westminster Press, 1983.

Marjorie Proctor-Smith, *In Her Own Rite*. Nashville: Abingdon Press, 1990.

Rosemary Radford Ruether, *Women-Church*. San Francisco: Harper & Row, 1985.

Letty Russell, *Church in the Round*. Louisville: Westminster/John Knox Press, 1993.

Edward Schillebeeckx, *Church: The Human Story of God*. Translated by John Drury. Maryknoll, N.Y.: Orbis Books, 1973.

Alexander Schmemann, *Church, World, Mission: Reflections on Orthodoxy in the West*. Crestwood, NY: St. Vladimir's Seminary Press, 1979.

Juan Luis Segundo, *The Community Called Church*. Translated by John Drury. Maryknoll, NY: Orbis Books, 1973.

Jon Sobrino, *The True Church and the Poor*. Translated by Matthew J. O'Connell. Maryknoll, NY: Orbis Books, 1984.

John C. B. and Ellen Low Webster, *The Church and Women in the Third World*. Philadelphia: Westminster Press, 1985.

Claude Welch, *The Reality of the Church*. New York: Scribner, 1958.

Katherine Zappone, *The Hope for Wholeness*. Mystic, CT: Twenty-Third Publications, 1991.

PART VI

Christian Hope

INTRODUCING THE ISSUE

Energizing Hope

In a world in which hopes and dreams are so easily shattered, is there a hope that can sustain and guide us? Christians profess that there is such a hope, but it is a hope grounded not on projections based on current trends nor merely on fantasies about what could or should be, but rather on what God has done, is doing, and will do through Christ. The theological explication of this hope is often called eschatology, the doctrine of the last things or the consummation of God's work. This doctrine aims to explicate not only biblical references to the future but even more inclusively God's promise of redemption and fullness of life. This hope does not shield Christians from disappointments and hardships, nor does it provide neat solutions to the world's problems; but it does give courage, energy, and confidence to persist in the struggle for life and God's transformation of creation.

It is indeed an all-encompassing hope not only for eternal life for the individual but also for a "new heaven and a new earth" or a radical transformation and renewal of creation (both views are intertwined in Scripture; cf., e.g., Isa. 2 and 11 and Rev. 21). Yet such hope is not only future and otherworldly; it becomes an active force in the present as the power of God's coming glory already begins to be manifested in our midst in the transformation of lives, in the struggles of peoples for freedom and fullness of life, in the breaking down of walls of division, and in the healing of creation. Essentially, Christian hope is hope for redemption and fullness of life, both personally and communally, as presented in Christ and implemented through the power and work of the Holy Spirit.

These and other aspects of Christian hope are explored in the essays in this section. Paula M. Cooey emphasizes that this hope transforms not only us but also our understanding of power and exercise of it. Such power is not the power of domination and control but the power of cooperation and empowerment of people to participate creatively in shaping their life together for good, not evil. It involves "conversion," a *metanoia*, a turning around, not only of persons but also of societies. As women have found, such conversion, says Cooey, effects a "re-centering" of life that includes fuller participation in community as well as personal empowerment. It also involves a new sense of identity and a new "heart," which, drawing on Jonathan Edwards, the author interprets as a "full related selfhood." Such conversion is revolutionary, for it exercises a power that can reform and transform lives and relationships within each of our communities as well as in the interconnectedness of these communities around the world.

That theme is focused in another way by the Japanese theologian Kosuke Koyama, who points out that the hope that is defined in Christ is a hope that knows no limits. "No one is beyond the point of periphery at which Christ was crucified." Thus, in Christ a new reality is opened for all persons and for all of creation. No longer is hope to be understood as expectation of the triumph of one group over another, nor of humans "mastering" creation for the sake of their own desires, but it is rather a vision of God's purpose in Christ to redeem the whole of creation, to make it a welcome and supportive home for all. Here concerns for social justice and redemption are joined. But such hope is not without struggle and suffering. It shares in the suffering of Christ, but precisely because it does so it is a hope that cannot be crushed but is continually rekindled by the Spirit in those who share in it.

Greek Orthodox theologian and patriarch Ignatios IV emphasizes in his contribution that such hope also includes attention to the breaking in of the new in the midst of our present conflictive and endangered world. Just as in the midst of the Exile God raised up prophets who proclaimed the coming of deliverance and encouraged the people, so through Christ already in our midst God is working deliverance and transformation. But, as the writer points out, this involves a struggle with "the prince of this world," with the power and powers of evil that continue to enslave and oppress people and that damage and destroy creation, as, for example, in the destruction of species and the using up of irreplaceable resources. Yet in Christian perspective this struggle is not one in which evil will triumph. For God in Christ has acted to overcome evil and has set underway a "new thing," a new direction, eternal life. Yet such hope is not only past-oriented; it is also future-oriented. It envisions God coming to and into the world, ahead of the world, "calling it, telling it to move along," making it "larger and freer." Christ's resurrection is "the inauguration of the Parousia/God's coming final redemption" that is already, albeit only partially and perhaps ambiguously, breaking into the present in the life-giving energy of the Holy Spirit.

But does this mean that ultimately all will be saved (universal salvation)? John R. Sachs traces the history of this notion, showing its rootage in ancient Persian and Stoic philosophies and its entrance into Christian theology via Origen and a few more recent proponents. However, the mainstream of the church rejected the view both because of scriptural passages that seem to indicate a double destiny and because it seemed to undercut the urgency of the gospel and faith (if all are ultimately going to be saved, why is faith now important and urgent?). But God takes our response seriously, and how we respond to the gospel does affect our destiny. "The gospel of God's universal, saving love," says the author, "may not be watered down into a drug-like assurance that, regardless of what we do, 'in the end God will make everything all right,' any more than it may be distorted into the perverse announcement that God will condemn most of the world to hell." Rather, according to Sachs, Christian hope steers between and beyond these alternatives, following God's aim, as clearly indicated in Scripture, to seek and save the lost, God's will to save all who repent. That does not mean, however, that persons are compelled to salvation against their will; they may resist and even reject God's gift. But this means, says Sachs, that hell is "what the one who rejects God chooses for himself or herself," not something that God wills.

But William Crockett asks, in effect, whether such a view takes seriously biblical teaching concerning the eternal wrath *(orgē)* of God. He differentiates between this and God's "sternness," which may lead persons to faith. The question then arises whether God's wrath, in Paul's representation of it, is for the sake of punishment, or for reform. It might seem that punishment, endless punishment, is incompatible with God's love and mercy, or that God chastens only in order to reform, much as a parent might punish a child for the purpose of leading the child to change. But, says Crockett, Paul speaks of God's wrath toward unbelievers not as leading the wicked to repentance but with respect to those who continue in disobedience or rejection of God as final and eternal. God's wrath is thus distinct from and parallel with God's love, Crockett argues, not part of it. God's love as revealed in Christ delivers those who receive it in faith from the wrath to come. The author admits that Paul nowhere says explicitly that God's wrath is eternal, but he thinks Paul implies as much in his statements concerning God's deliverance of the faithful in Christ. Yet obviously this essay is part of an ongoing discussion among Christians and within the church over this issue. It raises in a pointed way a number of matters connected with Christian hope: the nature of God's love and aim, the significance of human response, and how we should envision the fulfillment of God's work in Christ. Social and cosmic ramifications as well as questions of personal destiny are interconnected here.

These essays continue the discussion in the Christian community as it seeks a clearer understanding of the "living hope" (1 Pet. 1:3) of Christian faith, the hope it offers all who are concerned for the future of humanity and creation in this world and beyond it.

The Power of Transformation and the Transformation of Power

PAULA M. COOEY

In "The Coming of Lilith," Judith Plaskow observes the following with reference to a women's working group in theology.

> Throughout our discussion of the women's movement, we found ourselves both repeatedly seeing our experiences in the movement as religious experiences and repeatedly questioning the value of doing so. . . . While the words *grace, illumination, mission,* and *conversion* kept cropping up in our conversation, we recognized that women who do not think in religious categories, who would in fact reject them, share the experiences we expressed in this language. We did not wish imperialistically to insist that their experiences too are "really" religious despite their refusal to recognize the fact. Moreover, if we asked what we added to the "root" experiences by calling them *religious,* there was nothing specific we could identify. On the other hand, we did feel this was a valid way of looking at our experiences in the women's movement, a way that could enrich our understanding of both these experiences and of religious experience itself.[1]

The most striking feature of this passage is the ambivalence of the group toward the use of religious language to describe their experience as participants in the women's movement. The passage raises several important questions regarding the nature of religious experience: What does it mean that there was nothing specifically identifiable to be added to the experiences by calling them

---

1. Judith Plaskow, "The Coming of Lilith: Toward a Feminist Theology," in *Womanspirit Rising,* ed. Carol P. Christ and Judith Plaskow (New York: Harper & Row, 1979), 202.

Reprinted with permission of the author and the journal from the *Journal of Feminist Studies in Religion* 1 (Spring 1985): 23-36.

"religious"? Why was it nevertheless regarded as "valid" for the group members to use religious language to describe these experiences? Specifically, how does calling these experiences "religious" enrich an understanding both of these experiences and of religious experiences in general? It is clear that the inclinations and commitments of the women in the group were religious in some sense prior to the group's gathering. The reluctance to be imperialistic further makes it clear that the women's movement is not in the strictest sense a new "religion." What then is the connection between the "root" experiences in the context of the women's movement and religious experience in general?

Gender analysis as a method for analyzing religious institutions, doctrines, practices, sacred texts, rituals, and theologies has become as familiar as race and class analysis for purposes of academic research. To date, however, the application of gender analysis to prevailing conceptions of the formal structures of religious experience, particularly religious transformation, has remained largely implicit. Scholars who employ gender analysis, particularly feminist theologians, have argued that experience is authoritative for both critique of and constructive alternatives to prevailing theological doctrines of sin and grace. These arguments include attention to the role of embodiment in experience.[2] They also stress the differences between life as it is actually lived by women and the cultural expectations placed upon women as factors that distinguish women's experience from men's.[3] In addition, they include, perhaps most importantly, vivid descriptions of the transforming power of women bonding with one another as sisters.[4] What remains to be done, however, is an explicit rendering of how these experiences seriously call into question previous sympathetic and antipathetic formulations of the structures of religious experience, especially transformation.

Using *conversion* as an example, I shall argue that women's ambivalent, but persistent, use of religious language to describe or interpret experience — for example, the experience of consciousness-raising — indicates the need to reconceive the structure and dynamics of religious experience. Feminist analysis of both sympathetic and antipathetic theories of religion and religious experience suggests that, otherwise drastic differences notwithstanding, advocates and detractors of religion alike share a common failure to take seriously the relationship between human transformation and human empowerment. This failure is due in part to the inadequacy of previous conceptions of power held by the theorists, whether sympathetic to religion (for example, Schleiermacher,

---

2. Penelope Washbourn, *Becoming Woman: The Quest for Wholeness in Female Experience* (San Francisco: Harper & Row, 1977).

3. Judith Plaskow, *Sex, Sin, and Grace: Women's Experience and the Theologies of Reinhold Niebuhr and Paul Tillich* (Washington, D.C.: University Press of America, 1980), 29-34.

4. See, e.g., Mary Daly's *Gyn/Ecology: The Metaethics of Radical Feminism* (Boston: Beacon Press, 1978), chap. 9, "Sparking: The Fire of Female Friendship," 354-84; Elisabeth Schüssler Fiorenza, *In Memory of Her: A Feminist Theological Reconstruction of Christian Origins* (New York: Crossroad, 1983), "Epilogue," 343-51.

James, and Otto), or antipathetic (Marx, Freud, and Barth). On a more constructive side, this argument suggests that *power* itself is ambiguous in meaning and plays a crucial, positive role in the structure and dynamics of religious experience, particularly conversion. Indeed, not only is *power* polysemous, but *conversion* as a concept covers a range of experiences, distinguishable from one another in terms of the kind of power involved in religious transformation. In addition, women's ambivalence toward interpreting experience in religious language not only reflects the ambiguity of power, but also operates theologically as a critical principle in evaluating the significance of power.

An analysis of feminist literature describing participation in the movement in religious language calls into question prevailing conceptions of religious experience insofar as these conceptions have focused almost exclusively on a loss of ego and the "inner life" of individual human beings.[5] Concern with human passivity and surrender as these are ingredient to ego-loss has reinforced sexual stereotypes and has led to a lack of sufficient attention to religious experience as a source of personal empowerment and social bonding to form active communities. Perhaps the most pernicious effects of an almost exclusive focus on passivity and ego-loss in particular individuals have been their possibly indirect contributions to the privatization of experience, the reification of deity, and the illusion that such experience provides an alternative to, by way of escape from, daily struggle in our ordinary lives. In short, the use of religious language to describe participation in the women's movement *and* the ambivalence on the part of women toward using such language provide a key to understanding both the traditional proponents of religious experience and their critics, largely male in both cases. Together they suggest a wider understanding of the character of religious life. Conceptions of conversion as a paradigmatic instance of transformation serve as a case in point.

Conversion

The much-debated issue of religious conversion, as it has classically been described, entails both a psychology of individual transformation and a sociology of community formation or bonding. Thus, as a religious phenomenon it has captured the interest of psychologists and sociologists, as well as historians and theologians. For the psychologist of religion, conversion is a matter of interest insofar as it contributes to an understanding of the development of human personality.[6] For the sociologist, the convert constitutes a social type, the ex-

---

5. See, for classic examples, William James's *Varieties of Religious Experience* and Rudolf Otto's *The Idea of the Holy*. See also Friedrich Schleiermacher's *Speeches on Religion, Against Its Cultured Despisers*, especially the second speech.

6. James suggests in the *Varieties* that conversion occurs most often during adolescence. Erik Erikson discusses the possibility that conversion during adolescence or even the twenties facilitates healthy physical maturation (see his *Young Man Luther* and *Identity: Youth and Crisis*).

amination of which fosters a better understanding of how groups form or interact.[7] Conversion is of interest to the historian of religions in part for the purpose of distinguishing whether a major tradition develops predominantly by proselytizing or through familial and national ties. For theologians, conversion is a matter of concern for a variety of reasons. As a religious phenomenon it may contribute to the particular identity of a particular confession. It further precipitates in theological doctrines of sin and redemption. It also may be regarded as an instance of enthusiasm or fanaticism that requires tempering or rejection on theological grounds.

Stated simply, *conversion* is an alteration, a turning around. In a religious context it is associated with the Hebrew *shuv* and the Greek *metanoia,* both of which refer to repentance. The Latin *convertio* further includes connotations of a change of will. *Conversion* thus signifies a form of spiritual transformation. From the convert's perspective, conversion is not self-generated; rather, forces beyond the immediate control of the subject effect the transformation, for example, the reference to grace in a Christian context. The transformation itself involves a recentering of personal identity that marks for the convert a shift from being in some form of bondage to being in a state of liberation. This shift marks the end of an old, negative condition and the beginning of a new, positive one. The subject's first awareness of this shift constitutes a "moment" of illumination. The subject tends to be most keenly aware of the substantive discontinuities between the two conditions, although there are formal continuities as well. To use more theological language borrowed from the Puritans, the convert becomes a "saint" in contrast to having been a "sinner"; nevertheless, what distinguishes "saints" from "sinners" is a newly found energy with which to struggle confidently in the hope of triumph over "sin," rather than the absence of sin altogether in the convert's new life.[8]

Conversion is social as well as psychological in its implications. It may or may not include a turning from the secular order to a particular religious tradition or from one religious tradition to another. For many converts, conversion marks a reconciliation, based on a change in perception, between the subject and the tradition in which he or she grew up. For example, Jesus' invitation to repent and prepare for the coming of the *basileia tou Theou* ("Kingdom of God") was a call to conversion within an existing tradition, Judaism. Augustine's dramatic conversion to Christianity, as analyzed by Nock, is another case in point.[9] In any case, however, conversion marks a transformation of social identity insofar as it includes an invitation to a new vision

7. David A. Snow and Richard Machalek, "The Convert as Social Type" (unpublished MS); and Eugene V. Gallagher, "Missionary Functions of Conversion Stories" (unpublished MS) and "The Social World of Saint Paul" (unpublished MS).

8. Jonathan Edwards, *A Treatise Concerning Religious Affections* (New Haven, CT: Yale University Press, 1959), "Author's Preface," 85.

9. Arthur Darby Nock, *Conversion* (London: Oxford University Press, 1961), 265-66.

of what constitutes community as well as a transformation of the subject's personal life.[10]

Conversion is furthermore social when participation in a community involves a commitment to transforming existing conditions in the world at large, a sense of mission. Whether the community expresses this commitment through individual proselytizing or through directly addressing existing conditions viewed as problematic, conversion in this context presupposes some vision of how society ought to be in contrast to how it actually is.[11]

Conversion, understood as a recentering of personal, social identity due to forces or power beyond one's immediate control, describes very appropriately many of the experiences that have brought and continue to bring women into the women's movement. From a feminist perspective conversion is an appropriate concept, however, only insofar as it includes explicit attention to the issue of the empowerment of the women converted.

For many women consciousness-raising has meant a recentering of identity. Women have turned from a struggle to fulfill destructive cultural expectations, defined according to gender, and turned to a positive sense of what it means to be a woman. Cultural expectations that define women almost exclusively in terms of affiliations with men and male-dominated institutions, and thereby deny women worth as persons in their own right, have isolated women from one another and have fostered what Valerie Saiving has called "the temptations of women as women." These temptations include "triviality, distractibility, and diffuseness; lack of an organizing center or focus; dependence on others for one's own self-definition; tolerance at the expense of standards of excellence; inability to respect the boundaries of privacy; sentimentality, gossipy sociability, and mistrust of reason — in short, underdevelopment or negation of self."[12]

Saiving adds that each of these "temptations" is actually an important character trait gone amuck, so to speak.

> . . . the fact that a female's whole growth toward womanhood has the character of an inevitable process of bodily maturation rather than that of a challenge and a task may lead her to dissipate herself in activities which are merely trivial. Yet it is the same lack of creative drive which may make it possible for her to perform cheerfully the thousand-and-one routine tasks — the women's work which is never done — which someone must do if life is to go on. Her capacity for surrendering her individual concerns in order to

10. Josiah Royce, *The Problem of Christianity,* vol. 1, *The Moral Burden of the Individual* (Chicago: Regnery, 1968), 109-59.

11. H. Richard Niebuhr, "Christ the Transformer of Culture," in *Christ and Culture* (New York: Harper & Row, 1951), 190-229.

12. Valerie Saiving, "The Human Situation: A Feminine View," in *Womanspirit Rising,* ed., Carol P. Christ and Judith Plaskow (New York: Harper & Row, 1979), 37.

serve the immediate needs of others — a quality which is so essential to the maternal role — can, on the other hand, induce a diffuseness of purpose, a tendency toward being easily distracted, a failure to discriminate the more and the less important, and an inability to focus in a sustained manner on the pursuit of any single goal. Her receptivity to the moods and feelings of others and her tendency to merge her selfhood in the joys, sorrows, hopes, and problems of those around her are the positive expressions of an aspect of the feminine character which may also take the negative forms of gossipy sociability, dependence on others (such as husband or children) for the definition of her values, or a refusal to respect another's right to privacy. And her capacity for forgiving love, for cherishing all her children equally without regard to beauty, merit, or intelligence, can also express itself in a kind of indiscriminate tolerance which suspects or rejects all objective criteria of excellence.[13]

A basic presupposition, common to the running amuck of each and all of these actual strengths Saiving cites and to the ensuing periodic guilt, depression, and self-hatred that characterize so many women's lives, is that women's primary identity and source of worth as women have come from affiliations with men and shared children. Living out this presupposition has reinforced subjugation to men — if not to particular men, to male-dominated institutions.[14] What began in the late sixties and early seventies as the consciousness-raising group, and continues today as the support group, includes in part a recognition of the "sin" of male-derived identity and self-negation that is analogous to repentance.

Recognizing one's coparticipation in this situation as a mark of one's own sinful condition reflects a shift in what centers consciousness, similar to William James's analysis of conversion as a reorientation of identity and worth. However, the content of this shift lies 180 degrees away from a surrendering of an autonomous ego, as implied in James's analysis.[15] By contrast, it is an acknowledgment of one's role in abdicating a kind of responsibility normally associated with some degree of autonomy.

This recognition further reflects a simultaneous glimpse of an alternative vision, which Plaskow describes as follows:

We saw the stages of consciousness-raising as analogous to the stages of a religious journey, culminating in the experience of full, *related*, selfhood.

13. Ibid., 38.

14. The movement of women into the public sphere, particularly entry into jobs previously held by men, is, in itself, not a solution to the subordination of women. Unless women transform the public, patriarchal institutions of which they become a part, and until we redefine the meaning of "public" and "private" in nonpatriarchal terms, the social order will remain patriarchal.

15. William James, *The Varieties of Religious Experience* (New York: New American Library, 1958), Lectures IX and X, 157-206.

Again and again we came back to the word *graceful* to describe certain of our experiences with other women. At moments I can never plan or program, I am given to myself in a way I cannot account for by studying the organic progression of my past. Listening to another woman tell her story, I *concentrate* on words spoken and experienced as if our lives depended on them, and indeed they do. And yet I could not say what enables me to be really there, hearing, in a way that makes me feel that I had never really heard before — or been listened to as I am now. Nor could I say why precisely at this moment I become aware of myself as whole, free, fully human. . . . In this moment . . . I feel sharply the limits of myself and my capabilities.

This is where the experience of grace can also become the experience of conversion. Seeing myself in a new way, I am *called* to the transformation of myself. I must become the possibilities I already am in my moment of vision, for I am really not yet those possibilities. The call necessitates a decision, a response.[16]

The references to "religious journey," "grace," "conversion," and "call" and the emphasis on "hearing" and "seeing" formally mirror Jonathan Edwards's account of conversion as a new sense of the heart.[17] Note in addition, however, the frequent use of the words *we* and *our*, the continual reference to *shared* experience, the positive worth placed on being a woman, and the refusal to disassociate one's own identity from or subordinate it to responsibility to others. A positive sense of worth emerges as a gift bestowed through listening to other women, through dialogue with other women. Both extremes, self-negation and egocentricity, are absent. A decision is a response. Consciousness-raising culminates in "the experience of full *related* selfhood."

"Full *related* selfhood" suggests that "conversion" in this context marks a turning toward a sense of balance in which relationships to others no longer stand in opposition to individual identity. Traditional conceptions of conversion have focused on the conflict between one's identity as a unique, individual human being and one's relationships with others in terms of the individual subject's resistance to these relationships.[18] Transformation in these accounts marks a positive acknowledgment of a fundamental dependence beyond individual control and an affirmation of a relationship to a wider community of being. For many women whose identities have been defined negatively in terms of relationships to others, chiefly by dependence on men, the condition prior to transformation is reversed to some extent. Whereas conversion does involve turning toward a wider community of being for women in this context, the

16. Plaskow, "Coming of Lilith," p. 203. See also Rosemary Radford Ruether, "The Consciousness of Evil: The Journeys of Conversion," in *Sexism and God Talk* (Boston: Beacon Press, 1983), 159-92.

17. Jonathan Edwards, *Miscellany*, no. 782, in *The Philosophy of Jonathan Edwards*, ed. Harvey G. Townsend (Westport, CT: Greenwood Press, 1955), 112-26.

18. Josiah Royce is a notable exception here.

vision of this community, characterized in terms of *inter*dependence, includes placing positive value on women as individual women and thus provides an alternative to relationships of subordination and domination along gender lines.

One further significant implication of interdependence is that this conversion is not a turning from heteronomy to autonomy, or from other-directedness to egocentricity. Conversion reflects a shift in power. It does so as a transformation from an identity based on dependence on others, such that positive worth is derivative at best, to an identity based on interdependence that allows for a positive sense of worth associated simply with being a woman and a person. This shift in power is both conceptual and actual. Conversion as a turning toward "full related selfhood" is the first genuine test of what it means to be a person equal to other persons, a full participant in a wider community of being. This taste or sense of freedom calls into question conceptions of power as control in the possession of particular persons or groups precisely because the transformation itself is viewed as gift that widens personal and social identity.

Conversion, to the extent that it includes not only a transformation of individual persons but an invitation to participate in a wider community of being, carries with it a charge to share the vision that actualizes power as it is newly apprehended. Conversion thus becomes a force for social revolution. In the words of Rosemary Radford Ruether:

> To seek the liberation of women without losing this sense of communal personhood is the great challenge and secret power of the women's revolution. Its only proper end must be the total abolition of the social pattern of domination and subjugation and the erection of a new communal social ethic. We need to build a new cooperative social order out beyond the principles of hierarchy, rule, and competitiveness. Starting in the grass roots local units of human society where psychosocial polarization first began, we must create a living pattern of mutuality between men and women, between parents and children, among people in their social, economic, and political relationships and, finally, between humankind and the organic harmonies of nature.[19]

If power is understood in a broad sense as vitalizing energy rather than in a more narrow sense as internal and external control exerted by a person or group, then empowerment characterizes this process of conversion. Power in this broader sense is both personal and social. It is personal in that this energy, viewed as absent prior to conversion, centers individual identity and serves as a source of personal worth and creativity. It is social in that this power relates the members of a community to one another, and the community to the rest of the temporal order, though the latter relationship involves varying degrees of discontinuity as well as continuity. Conversion becomes revolution.

---

19. Rosemary Radford Ruether, "Motherearth and the Megamachine," in *Womanspirit Rising*, ed. Carol P. Christ and Judith Plaskow (New York: Harper & Row, 1979), 51-52.

The chief characteristic that distinguishes religious conversion in its personal and social dynamics from other forms of personal and social transformation (for example, strictly political movements, self-help groups, or psychotherapy) may well be the conviction that the power that transforms individual subjects' relations to themselves, their subsequent relations to the communities in which they begin to participate, and the communities' relations to the rest of the world, is not their own. As Plaskow put it: "I am given to myself in a way I cannot account for by studying the organic progression of my past. . . . I could not say what enables me to be really there, hearing . . . or listened to." However such power is conceived or imagined, and even though it is experienced as present within individual members and the community as a whole, such power exceeds the temporal and spatial confines and control of member and group alike. From a religious convert's perspective, power of this kind is in part analogous to electrical current. The convert is an instrument, vehicle, or occasion for this transforming energy. Thus, power possesses the subject of conversion rather than being in the subject's possession. It is in part for this reason that theologians and scholars have so often emphasized passivity, receptivity, and surrender as chief characteristics of religious experience.[20]

An almost exclusive focus on passivity, receptivity, and surrender also arises, however, from a failure to distinguish among converts in terms of the *kinds* of power or lack of power that characterize conditions prior to conversion. It is one thing to suggest that conversion marks a giving up of control associated with surrender and ego-loss if in fact control and a strongly individuated ego characterize a subject's condition prior to conversion. It is quite another matter to generalize this account of conversion as applicable to all converts.[21] Accounts of religion as grounded in a feeling of absolute dependence and of conversion as an occasion of loss of ego that marks this dependence fail to take adequately into consideration why it is so often the case that powerlessness and identity fragmentation characterize a convert's prior condition.[22] Women who have regarded consciousness-raising as in some sense religious transformation have most often described this transformation as a movement from helplessness and fragmentation to integrity. This integrity is characterized by an energy that is simultaneously redemptive regarding the past and creative regarding the present and the anticipated future.

Women's use of the language of conversion to describe consciousness-raising thus presents scholars with the intriguing possibility that "conversion" may refer to a *range* of transforming experiences. These experiences may differ

---

20. See, e.g., James's lectures on conversion in *Varieties of Religious Experience*.

21. This failure to distinguish may be what led Schleiermacher to suggest in *The Christmas Eve Dialogues* that women did not require conversion.

22. E.g., scholars from Engels to Fiorenza have pointed out that the early converts to the Jesus movement and subsequent Christianity emerged primarily from groups on the margins of power.

not only according to the various institutions, creeds, and practices from which and to which the conversion marks the transition. The experiences may differ not only regarding individual psychological conditions. As important as these may be, the range of differences in *how* the convert experiences and interprets power is at least as significant. Its significance lies in the potential insight regarding the equivocal character of power itself that may be gained by an examination of the differences.

Negative Critiques of Religion

Just as women's use of religious language provides a basis for a critique of existing theory sympathetic to religious experience, so it provides a means by which to assess the strengths and weaknesses of theory antipathetic toward religious experience. Because the language is marked by ambivalence, it points simultaneously to the positive value and the limitations of systematic attacks upon religion. The use of religious language by participants in the women's movement to describe experiences of participation, *conversion* being only one example, reflects an important insight into what Plaskow calls "root experiences." Root experiences such as consciousness-raising include an experience of transformation involving power that is not limited either to the individual participant or to the community of participants. Ambivalence toward the use of this religious language reflects an ambivalence toward the equivocal character of power itself and, therefore, has a critical and creative role to play, as appropriate as the use of religious language itself.

Ambivalence arises not only because of a reluctance to be imperialistic, and not only because of certain inadequacies of traditional conceptualizations of key images like *conversion*, as I have tried to demonstrate. Ambivalence also reflects the extent to which negative critiques of religion and religious life are valid. It further indicates an awareness of the role played by religious traditions and institutions in keeping women in particular at the margins of power as we normally understand it. It suggests, most importantly of all, a willingness, on the part of those who are ambivalent, to be self-critical.

Although literature regarding religious life has largely been generated by figures sympathetic to religious concerns, the so-called modern period has produced an increased willingness to regard religion in a negative light. Representative figures here include David Hume, Karl Marx and Friedrich Engels, Sigmund Freud, and Karl Barth. However these thinkers may differ from one another, they share a common tendency to regard religion in a negative light that emerges out of very practical concerns. Their arguments against religion involve fairly specific concepts of human well-being and include concepts of deity as an object of attack.

Hume, for example, wrote *The Natural History of Religion* and *The Dialogues*

Concerning Religion in the midst of religious persecution. His natural history focuses primarily on the origin of religion in human fear due to an inability to understand and control nature.[23] The dialogues, which he felt necessary to have published after his death, include a rejection of the proof for God's existence from design in nature and thereby sounded the death knell to Deist concepts of God.[24] Both works share an antipathy toward religion due to the intolerance of its various adherents and the view that philosophical pursuits, while perhaps less consoling, offer a positive alternative that avoids the pitfalls of such intolerance.

Marx and Engels's rejection of religion arises in response to the use of religious authority as a means for justifying economic oppression. This rejection involves the perception of religious institutions as forces fostering alienation and includes the rejection of deity as a socially constructed reification of strictly human authority, used for economic and political exploitation by the ruling classes. For reification to be successful, it must include the privatization and mystification of human experience, concomitants of an ideology of individualism. Religion, focused on a reification and divinization of human authority and practiced in an individualistic manner, is thus determined by, cooperates with, and further reinforces an economy based on money and private property.[25]

Freud, who developed the concept of religion as illusion motivated by wish-fulfillment, saw himself standing within an already well-established tradition of critics like Marx and Engels, who rejected religion, its institutions, practices, and beliefs.[26] Quick to anticipate his own critics' responses, he wrote, "I have said nothing which other and better men have not said before me in a much more complete, forcible and impressive manner. . . . All I have done — is to add some psychological foundation to the criticism of my great predecessors."[27] Whether one agrees or disagrees with Freud, it is important to acknowledge that his practical concern to examine the role of religion in precipitating or reinforcing debilitating individual and social neuroses provides both the context and the impetus for his writings on the subject. Like his predecessors, he focuses almost restrictedly, and therefore narrowly, on a conception of deity as monotheistic, parental, and patriarchal. His judgment that such a conception is an illusion based on self-deception, while not as universalizable as he presumed, accounts, nevertheless, in no small way for what has often been claimed to be religious.

It is ironic that, from the perspective of those consciously religious, the

23. David Hume, *The Natural History of Religion*, ed. H. E. Root (Stanford: Stanford University Press, 1956). Hume locates the origin of religion in the feelings of hope and fear but focuses his analysis predominantly on fear.

24. David Hume, *The Dialogues Concerning Religion*, ed. Norman Kemp Smith (Indianapolis: Bobbs-Merrill, 1947).

25. Karl Marx, Introduction to *Contribution to the Critique of Hegel's Philosophy of Right* in *Marx and Engels on Religion*, ed. Reinhold Niebuhr (New York: Schocken, 1964), 41-58.

26. Sigmund Freud, *The Future of an Illusion*, trans. and ed. James Strachey (New York: Norton, 1961), 31.

27. Ibid., p. 35.

most serious assault against religion came perhaps from "within." The charges that Barth, in *The Epistle to the Romans,* leveled against religion as the ultimate expression of human pride sent liberal Protestantism into a disarray from which it has yet to recover fully.[28] His later rejection of *analogia entis* as a vehicle for knowing God further worked, from his perspective, to render specious all human concepts and images of deity and, thereby, human claims to experiencing relationship with deity.[29]

There is much truth in the charges leveled against religion, namely, that it arises from fear and promotes intolerance, that it justifies economic exploitation, and that it promotes escapism, irresponsibility, idolatry, and false pride. As Zora Neal Hurston so succinctly put it:

> People need religion because the great masses fear life and its consequences. Its responsibilities weigh heavy. Feeling a weakness in the face of great forces, men seek an alliance with omnipotence to bolster up their feeling of weakness, even though the omnipotence they rely upon is a creature of their own minds. It gives them a feeling of security. . . . It seems to me that organized creeds are collections of words around wish.[30]

In short, religion not only can, but does, produce any of a variety of forms of false consciousness. Religion's role in human history, so far as this history is characterized by intolerance, economic exploitation, escapism based on illusion, idolatry, and egregious pride, should at the very least make one hesitate to interpret experience in religious language. Furthermore, gender analysis not only supports the charges leveled by critics of religion but also makes vivid the extent to which women of all races and classes have been among the chief victims.[31] Nevertheless, women have historically been, and continue to be, as reluctant to turn religion over to men as women have been ambivalent toward perceiving and interpreting experience as religious in a uniformly positive way.

This reluctance is not simply reducible to false consciousness and wish-fulfillment based on fear and need. Gender analysis in reclaiming women's history has also shown that religious life has served and continues to serve as a creative source for women's personal and social struggle for freedom.[32] The

28. Karl Barth, *The Epistle to the Romans,* trans. Edwyn C. Hoskyns (London: Oxford University Press, 1933), 229-70, 330-61.

29. Karl Barth, *Church Dogmatics* (Edinburgh: T. & T. Clark, 1936), vol. I, pt. 1, 383-99; vol. II, pt. 1, 86ff.

30. Zora Neal Hurston, *Dust Tracks on a Road* (Philadelphia: Lippincott, 1942), 286-87.

31. See, for just one of many examples, Mary Daly's *Gyn/Ecology,* "The Second Passage."

32. See, e.g., Fiorenza's "Women in the Early Christian Movement"; McLaughlin's "The Christian Past: Does It Hold a Future for Women?"; Plaskow's "The Coming of Lilith"; Daly's "Why Speak About God?"; and Christ's "Why Women Need the Goddess: Phenomenological, Psychological and Political Reflections" — all in *Womanspirit Rising.* For more recent examples, see Fiorenza's *In Memory of Her* and Ruether's *Sexism and God-Talk.*

history of this struggle points to the limitations of the critics' arguments against religion by calling into question the extent to which these evaluations are made from a position of Anglo-European male privilege and based upon an assumption held in common with many who are sympathetic to religion that all religious experience is in some sense ultimately identical.[33]

Contemporary women, whether Jewish, Christian, or Neopagan, who apprehend participation in the women's movement as religious, belong to a long-standing tradition of women that cuts across specific religious confessions, race and class, a tradition that is bound by a common resistance to subordination in relation to men and a transcendence of this subordination, rooted in religious experience, various in its particular manifestations and interpretations. While there is good reason for ambivalence toward religion, particularly as it is manifest in the male-centeredness of many of these same confessions, there is little, if any, reason to trust secular institutions and exclusively secular solutions.

Secular institutions are as male-dominated as their religious counterparts and their role in history equally oppressive to women. As examples of false consciousness, the reification of the worker and the classless society are as problematic as the reification of deity. Pursuit of the goal to be rid of illusions, particularly religious illusions, can become yet another form of escapism based on self-deception. The conviction that all meaning is solely human in its origin has easily lent itself in the past to gross androcentrism and admits of no criterion by which to call into question human abuses of power. Barth's *analogia relationis* is no less immune to idolatry than *analogia entis*.[34]

Ambivalence toward Power

Power that transforms persons and bonds them with one another in communities calls into question prevailing conceptions of power as an exercise of control, particularly political, social, and economic control. Experience of this power is profoundly religious; insight into its implications plays a theologically critical role in calling into question androcentric institutions and movements. Nevertheless, the line between power apprehended as shared energy transcending any specific person or group and power conceived as an internal and external exertion of control is a fine one that renders power of any kind ambiguous at best.

This ambiguity dramatically exhibits itself in the contrast between experiencing oppression as powerlessness and experiencing liberation as personal and social transformation. Ambivalence is an important, and indeed logical,

---

33. Friedrich Engels is an exception here. See "On the History of Early Christianity" and *The Origin and History of the Family, Private Property and the State.*

34. Barth, *Church Dogmatics,* vol. III, pt. 2, 220f., 323f.

response to this ambiguity and marks an openness to self-critique. It is precisely the *contrast* between the two modes of power, as expressed in ambivalence toward power in general, that provides a theological critical principle.

Ambivalence in the face of this ambiguity thus plays a positive critical role in relation to power itself. Dynamic tension between an experience of transformation as empowering, on the one hand, and feelings of ambivalence toward power in general, on the other hand, provides the possibility for critical affirmation and continued creativity within individual participants, within the women's communities represented by the women's movement, and in relations between the movement and the world it seeks to transform.[35] Ambivalence toward power, rather than avoided or denied, needs to be regarded as necessary, useful, and a source for self-reflection — in short, as a means by which to detect, analyze, and assess different modes of power.

The experience of transformation as empowering is not in itself new, not new even to women. Making the implications for women as women explicit marks, however, an extension of this insight beyond its previous boundaries. For the various purposes of the study of religion and theological studies, this insight enriches conceptions of *religion* and *religious experience* as well. For the women who share the insight, it widens the horizons of the "root experiences" women have undergone as participants in the struggle for women's liberation. What is unusual and, in the long run, as theologically significant as the insight itself, is the willingness on the part of the women involved to assume the burden of ambivalence along with the joy of insight.

35. For an example of the critical role played by this tension within the women's movement, see the questions Plaskow raises in the conclusion of "The Coming of Lilith."

VI.2

Jesus Christ, Who Has Gone
to the Utter Periphery

KOSUKE KOYAMA

I. Personal Prologue

The Martin Luther King, Jr. Bridge is on the boulevard approaching the capitol building of the state of Rhode Island in the city of Providence. A plaque on the post of the bridge reads: "The forces of both history and providence are on the side of freedom." — Martin Luther King, Jr.

We experience history. But since the experience and appreciation of it differ greatly from person to person, from community to community, from nation to nation, culture to culture, and religion to religion, we cannot say universally what history is. The black minister Rev. Al Sharpton of New York City and his followers staged a demonstration at the foot of the Statue of Liberty in New York harbour. They were demanding that the name of Liberty Island be changed to Martin Luther King, Jr. Island.[1] Without a great deal of knowledge and appreciation of the suffering of black people in the history of the United States, a white person would have difficulty understanding the inner reason and dynamics of that demonstration. Black people's understanding of American history is radically different from that of white people: the book *White Women's Christ and Black Women's Jesus* by Jacquelyn Grant is illuminating in this regard. We experience history, but "history" is an ambiguous concept.

We may experience providence. Providence is, obviously, a theological and confessional concept. Is providence a principle of interpretation of history for believers? Was the assassination of Martin Luther King, Jr. at the height of his

1. *New York Times*, 29 August 1990.

Reprinted with permission from *The Ecumenical Review* 43 (January 1991): 100-106.

ministry of liberation "providential"? Was the nuclear bombing of the inhabited cities of Hiroshima and Nagasaki "providential"?

For "Semitic" believers (Jews, Christians, and Muslims), is there anything which is not providential? Is there a place for free will in the theology of providence? The Hindu/Buddhist teaching of the karma (action/reaction, retribution) may be easier for us to understand than providence. To be religious we accept the workings of providence, but it is an ambiguous concept.

What is freedom? This is clear for those who are oppressed. For Martin Luther King, Jr. what freedom meant was clear. He saw it concretely as freedom from racial oppression (racism). But freedom is not a clear concept for the oppressors (racists). The line between the oppressed and the oppressor is clear to the oppressed, but it is not necessarily clear to the oppressors. To further complicate our discussion, we must see that often a person or community can be simultaneously the oppressed and the oppressor.

Is not freedom fundamentally a spiritual reality? We may feel its preciousness, but we cannot quite understand it. Though our understanding of it remains vague, is it not true that our sense of the value of freedom is what makes us genuinely human? Freedom is a depth reality inside of our souls. The question of freedom, then, is a depth question that we may ask about ourselves. Freedom is a mystery. "Thank God Almighty, I am free at last!"

I am intrigued by these three weighty words: history, providence, and freedom. I humbly and firmly concur with Martin Luther King, Jr. that history and providence are on the side of freedom, even while the complexity of historical realities overwhelms me.

What I am driving home with this short personal reflection is that my dream and vision have their focus in freedom. Freedom is not a secret, it is a mystery. No amount of explanation can demystify mystery. I belong to the believing community which confesses that freedom is one of the most precious gifts to humanity from the Holy Triune God. I share the commitment of the World Council of Churches to the dream and vision of freedom. From the spirit of Christ who has gone to the utter periphery we receive our freedom (1 Cor. 12:3). This is the heart of the theology of the cross.

II. The Theology of the Cross and the World Council of Churches

The theology of the World Council of Churches is a theology of the cross. "Jesus Christ and him crucified" (1 Cor. 2:2) stands at the centre of its theological life.

> For you know the grace of our Lord Jesus Christ, that though he was rich, yet for your sake he became poor, so that by his poverty you might become rich (2 Cor. 8:9).

This Christ embodies the saving truth of the Triune God. Christ illumines and judges the work of the World Council of Churches. The Christ who has gone to the utter periphery is the very centre of the ecumenical movement (Phil. 2:6-8).

The ecumenical movement is a theological movement. Theology is God-word, God-understanding, and God-talk. The concept of theology contains necessarily some kind of "understanding" of God. What kind of understanding? Is it understanding through reasoning, or intuition, or spiritual devotion, or emotion, or mystical or practical experience? Or all of them combined? Yes. "God-devotion," "God-silence," "God-act," "God-word," and "God-mystery" are all contained in "theology." The living principle by which these are included is the spirit of Christ. Christ can contain and examine all these because he has gone, in the name of the Triune God, to the utter periphery. No one is beyond the point of periphery at which Christ was crucified (cf. Ps. 139:7-12). Luther's words come to me: "Not reading books or speculating, but living, dying and being damned make a theologian." "Going to the periphery" as Christ did — "Mission in Christ's Way" — makes a person a theologian.

In *imitatio Christi* Paul goes to the periphery. What an impassioned life! (Ex. 20:5 speaks also of an "impassioned God"). Paul says,

> To the present hour we hunger and thirst, we are ill-clad and buffeted and homeless, and we labour, working with our own hands. When reviled, we bless; when persecuted, we endure; when slandered, we try to conciliate; we have become, and are now, as the refuse of the world, the offscouring of all things (1 Cor. 4:11-13).

The apostolic life is the peripherized life. The periphery is without honour and prestige. In it ecumenical movement originates. The apostolic life is "homeless" (unsettling, *astateō*). The authenticity of the theology of the World Council of Churches must be examined in the light of this apostolic tradition of the unsettling homelessness because of its devotion to the impassioned God of steadfast love (Hos. 6:6; Mark 10:21, *hesed/agapē*). Without this quality, the ecumenical movement will become something other than an apostolic movement. An impassioned ecumenical movement is an expression of an impassioned apostolic life. An "unsettling" theology is the theology of the cross.

In the utter periphery where Jesus Christ is, a new possibility for all creation is created. In the words of the African theologian Manas Buthelezi: "Through the cross God transformed the instrument of violence, vengeance and death into a vehicle of divine love and restoration to new life. . . ."[2]

This cosmic event took place at the utter periphery. How? We cannot know! The *hesed/agapē* of God achieved the transformation (2 Cor. 5:19). Here

---

2. Thomas F. Best, ed., *Faith and Renewal: Commission on Faith and Order, Stavanger* (Geneva: WCC, 1985), 181.

we must feel the heartbeat of Christian theology: love transforms history. Love transforms our knowledge. No genuine transformation is possible apart from love. This is what the theology of the cross affirms.

What does the gospel of Jesus Christ who has gone to the utter periphery say to the faith community of the World Council of Churches?

A. A Vision of Eco-ecumenism

1. "House" (*oikos*) is the common image shared by ecology and ecumenism. Jesus Christ who has gone to the utter periphery has love-knowledge of two houses: the cosmos (ecology — he is "the first-born of all creation") and the church (ecumenism — he is "the first-born from the dead"). I understand the meaning of "the first-born" in the light of the theology of the cross. Christ was "the first-born" as the expression of God's *hesed/agapē* in his humiliation and suffering.

> For in him all the fullness of God was pleased to dwell, and through him to reconcile to himself all things, whether on earth or in heaven, making peace by the blood of his cross (vid. Col. 1:15-20).

It is through the cross — the utter periphery — that the renewal of both the ecumenical (redemption) and ecological (creation) households takes place (cf. Lam. 3:22-23; Rev. 21:5). It is inspiring to think how in the utter periphery, where Jesus Christ has been, creation and redemption are firmly united. The time/space related to creation (cosmology) and the time and space related to redemption (eschatology) have entered into a Christ-centred dialogue because Christ has gone to the utter periphery of both creation and redemption. This dialogue is moving towards the renewal of all things. I understand this to be the meaning of Vatican II, "Baptism, Eucharist and Ministry, 1982," "Stavanger 1985," and "San Antonio 1989." I believe, therefore, that history and providence are on the side of freedom. Freedom originates when the renewal of all creation, including the souls of humanity, takes place (Jer. 31:31-34).

A mutual in-presence of creation and redemption — that is, creation is in redemption, and redemption is in creation — is emerging as an ecumenical vision. This vision is prompted by the actual ecological crisis of our own planet. For the construction of this "oikos-theology," Christians in Asia, Africa and the Pacific have special contributions to make. They prefer, due to their cultures, to look at redemption through creation. They are aware of the painful fact that the planetary ecological crisis has been largely caused by Western Christian civilization. Eschatology confronts. Cosmology embraces. They are anticipating the possibility of an eschatology that embraces.

2. Both history and providence must be seen in the light of the eschatology

that embraces (Luke 15:20). This is eco-ecumenism's eschatology. It is an eschatology that "does not insist on its own way" (1 Cor. 13:5). Yet it is firm because it is rooted in the theology of the cross.

B. A Vision of Christ's Authority Established in the Periphery

1. Jesus Christ established his authority in the periphery (Luke 2:7; Phil. 2:8-9). A nameless Roman imperial centurion who stood at the cross was struck by the glory of this authority. He made the first ecumenical confession of the faith: "Truly this man was the Son of God" (Mark 15:39). The church perceived that the authority of Christ was inseparable from his death on the cross. The cross is the ultimate expression of God's *hesed/agapē*. And Christ's authority *(exousia)* is none other than the power of *hesed/agapē*.

The Gospel of Mark tells us that for Christ "your sins are forgiven" and "Rise, take up your pallet and walk" are interchangeable (2:9-10). For him who has gone to the utter periphery they are interchangeable. For us this may be a possibility only when we partake of Christ's authority by saying from our souls and minds: "kyrie eleison." A theological "either/or" between humanization and evangelism is artificial. The call of Jesus: "Rise, take up your pallet and walk" is usually not recognized as gospel by those who think they can walk (John 9:41; Mark 2:17).

2. Why did Christ go to the utter periphery? The only answer that can be given is that he embodies the *hesed/agapē* of God. Does he not leave the ninety-nine in the wilderness, and go after the one which is lost, until he finds it (Luke 15:4)?

Christians may see themselves as the one for whom Christ came searching. But when they think of people of other religious traditions, they are more likely to think otherwise. They are the "ninety-nine righteous persons" and they see the people of other religious traditions as the lost ones. But this is the way Jesus concludes his parable: "I tell you, there will be more joy in heaven over one sinner who repents than over ninety-nine persons who need no repentance" (v. 7).

This verse transcends the divisions of religions, such as Christianity, Buddhism, Islam and so on, with which we conveniently protect our own spiritual security. The verse is addressed to all human beings irrespective of religious identity. We do not ourselves go to the periphery. We declare our judgment upon the people of other religious traditions from our centres. But all religions, including Christianity, are illumined and judged by the Christ who is radically self-denying and self-giving. "This is the body which is given to you," Tissa Balasuriya writes: "Why is it that in spite of hundreds of thousands of eucharistic celebrations, Christians continue [to be] as selfish as before? Why have 'Christian' peoples been the most cruel colonizers of human history?"[3]

---

3. T. Balasuriya, *The Eucharist and Human Liberation* (Maryknoll, NY: Orbis Books, 1979), xi.

According to the theology of the cross, there is only one way for the Christian faith to affirm itself. That is the way of self-denial and self-giving. Christ affirmed his centrality by going to the periphery. Christ affirmed his lordship by being crucified. "A cloud of witnesses," including Dietrich Bonhoeffer, Martin Luther King, Jr. and Mother Teresa, followed the way of Christ (Heb. 12:1).

A discussion on the plurality of religious truths is important for Christian theology. I see this issue in the light of Christ's authority understood through the theology of the cross. The message of the other great world religions must be approached with "a broken and contrite heart" on our side (Ps. 51:17). It is the eucharistic self-giving Christ who understands the depth of these religious messages. Deep knowledge comes from intense love. Superficial knowledge comes from superficial love.

What would Jesus Christ of the holy communion — the one who has gone to the utter periphery — say about the soteriology of the Buddha or Muhammad? This is the question that faces us. We cannot answer this until we concretely, in our life, go to the periphery. ". . . let him deny himself and take up his cross and follow me" (Matt. 16:24). Only in the periphery may one have something to say about the plurality of truths. Or, in the periphery we may find that our way of formulating the question of "plurality of truths" may not, after all, be important. ". . . being damned makes a theologian." None of our theology is free from idolatry. In theology inevitably we make some kind of "graven images" of God (Ex. 20:4). Our attitude towards people of other faiths derives more from our graven images of God than from the God who came to us in Jesus Christ who has gone to the utter periphery.

(a) In the utter periphery where "the instrument of violence" is transformed into a "vehicle of divine love" by the *hesed/agapē* of God, the meaning of the word "other" in "other religions" must carry a different meaning than we customarily give it. Is there any "other" than the one who has gone to the utter periphery? Is there any "other" for the one who is completely free from idolatry? In the one who has gone to the utter periphery for the sake of others, there is no idolatry. Paul Tillich writes: "And therefore the decisive story is the story in which he accepts the title 'Christ' when Peter offers it to him. He accepts it under the one condition that he has to go to Jerusalem to suffer and to die, which means to deny the idolatrous tendency even with respect to himself. This is at the same time the criterion of all other symbols, and it is the criterion to which every Christian church should subject itself."[4]

It takes "a broken and contrite heart" to reflect upon the relationship between the gospel of Christ and other religious messages. Therefore, a meditation upon a few lines from the writings of Martin Luther King, Jr. has important spiritual bearing on the question of the plurality of religious truths:

4. P. Tillich, *Theology of Culture* (New York: Oxford University Press, 1964), 67.

". . . when you have to concoct an answer for a five-year-old son asking in agonizing pathos: 'Daddy, why do white people treat coloured people so mean?' "[5] We must be able to respond to this agonizing question before we compare the truth of Buddhist nirvana with Christian thought on the reign of God.

(b) A depth encounter among the religions is bound to be rare. Who among us will dare to represent Christianity if we have not been to the periphery? "Let him take up his cross and follow me!" How does the message of the Buddha or the religious spirituality of Hindus come to us when we mediate on the homeless Jesus Christ: ". . . wrapped in swaddling cloths, and laid in a manger, because there was no place for them in the inn"? "Foxes have holes, and birds of the air have nests; but the Son of man has nowhere to lay his head" (Luke 9:58).

C. Christian Ethics of the Utter Periphery

Are the "ill-clad and buffeted and homeless" not the oppressed minorities? Are they not the victims of racism, sexism, and classism? Do we not find thousands of them in lower Manhattan? Under the Brooklyn Bridge? In the Port Authority bus terminal?[6] Do they share the same apostolic sign (sēmeion) of homelessness? The apostolic sign of "ill-clad and buffeted and homeless" stands against the demonic power that makes millions of people "ill-clad and buffeted and homeless." Two passages come to me: "What does the Lord require of you but to do justice, and to love kindness, and to walk humbly with your God" (Micah 6:8). "Behold the Lamb of God, who takes away the sin of the world!" (John 1:29).

Jesus Christ, who has been to the utter periphery, has united the "walking" of Micah (social justice) with the "beholding" of John (redemption). The form (morphē, Gal. 4:19) of this unity is that of the apostolic and Christic "ill-clad and buffeted and homeless." How do you come to the people "ill-clad and buffeted and homeless" unless you share that form too ("the form of a servant," Phil. 2:7)?

The theology of the cross sees God in the humiliation and suffering of Christ (Mark 15:39). One cannot criticize various expressions of liberation theology hastily because it draws its life basically from the theology of the cross. It is written about the black evangelist and reformer Sojourner Truth (1797-1883):

> When asked by a preacher if the source of her preaching was the Bible, she responded: "No, honey, can't preach from de Bible — can't read a letter." Then

---

5. Martin Luther King, Jr., "The Letter from the Birmingham City Jail," 1963.
6. See André Jacques, *The Stranger Within Your Gates: Uprooted People in the World Today* (Geneva: WCC, 1986).

she explained: "When I preaches, I has jest one text to preach from, and I always preaches from this one. My text is, 'When I found Jesus!'"[7]

"When I found Jesus" — Jesus who is as humiliated as black slaves were — I came to know God. Out of this theology of the cross came a stupendous doxology:

Praise, praise, praise to the Lord! An' I begun to feel such a love in my soul as I never felt before — love to all creatures. An' then, all of a sudden, it stopped, an' I said, Dar's de white folks that have abused you, an' beat you, an' abused your people — think o' them! But then there came another rush of love through my soul, an' I cried out loud — "Lord, I can love even de white folks!"[8]

"There came another rush of love!" — What is the ecumenical movement apart from this power of the Holy Spirit (Acts 2:2)?

*   *   *

The Holy Spirit generates within us the spirit of *hesed/agapē*. "Love is patient and kind . . ." (1 Cor. 13:4-7). This steadfast love is constantly engaged in the world.

She [the church] is not neutral in the struggle between freedom and slavery, justice and lawlessness, order and chaos, civil rights and tyranny. And yet, the church has a peculiar mission: to go down, to the very abyss, where men as miserable sinners stand before their Lord, and where men commit clumsy blunders and make inescapable personal and political decisions.[9]

This is the way Hromádka in 1948 expressed his theology of the cross. We "as miserable sinners stand before [our] Lord" who has gone to the utter periphery.

Freedom is realized only in the breath of the Holy Spirit of Christ who has gone to the utter periphery. The World Council of Churches confesses this faith of the theology of the cross. Christ is the centre, in his very going to the periphery. Both history and providence receive their illumination from the truth of Christ, who has been to the utter periphery. In Christ, who has gone to the utter periphery, hope is created for all creation. This is my dream and vision for the future [. . .].

7. Quoted in Jacquelyn Grant, *White Women's Christ and Black Women's Jesus* (Atlanta: Scholar's Press, n.d.), p. 214.

8. Ibid.

9. See Joseph L. Hromádka, "Our Responsibility in the Post-War World," in *The Church and the International Disorder* (London: SCM Press Ltd., 1948), 115-17.

VI.3

"Behold, I Make All Things New"

IGNATIOS IV

The Breaking In of the New

The breaking in of the New is he who comes not from the world of cause and effect nor from the will of man, but from God and from him alone. It is a remarkable fact that this phrase "Behold, I make all things new" is the only one in the Book of Revelation that is pronounced by "him who sits upon the throne." All the other revelations in this book are transmitted to John by an angel, "A fellow servant with you" (Rev. 22:8-9), or are proclaimed by the Lord Jesus (Rev. 1:1ff. and 22:16). If we look in the New Testament for the "moments" when the Father himself speaks, we find only three: the "moment" of Jesus' baptism, the "moment" of the Transfiguration, the supreme "moment," or rather "the hour," when all things were renewed — Easter.

It was for us also that Jesus "sent his angel with this testimony for the churches" (Rev. 22:16) — this revelation which is the source of all the others, "Behold, I make all things new." The Apocalypse unveils for us the meaning of history. It is the Lamb alone who can take the book of history from the hand of him who sits upon the throne, and can open the seven seals (Rev. 5:7-9). The final revelation of the creative word illumines all that went before and reveals its meaning. Peter, one of those who witnessed the Transfiguration, also regarded Christ as "a lamb without blemish or spot . . . destined before the foundation of the world and made manifest at the end of the times for your sake" (1 Pet. 1:19-20).

In order to remind ourselves (if that were necessary) that this Event "upholds the universe" (Heb. 1:3) and "unites all things" (Eph. 1:10), three biblical passages might help to renew us, in the light of Revelation 21:5:

Reprinted with permission from *The Ecumenical Review* 42 (April 1990): 122-30.

A. Genesis 1:1

"In the beginning God created the heavens and the earth." Here again it is God who acts *(epoiēsen)*, and his action affects "all things" ("the heavens and the earth"); there is the same revelation of something new ("in the beginning," "Behold" *(idou)*, a biblical word frequently used to express a new action undertaken by God). The Thora is not an account of religious archaeology; it is the normative revelation of the meaning of every event. Today, in the same way as for the priest who wrote the first chapter of Genesis, the Living God creates all things "in the beginning." He is quite different from the First Cause from which all things flow; that level of reality is old. He is the creative force within everything that is constantly renewing all things. He maintains all things by his powerful Word. "He is before all things, and in him all things hold together" (Col. 1:17).

The New Life, then, does not consist in making something new out of what already exists, nor changing what is outdated in order to bring it up to date. It consists in the fact that someone acts and speaks, he who is the source of "the river of the water of life, bright as crystal, flowing from the throne of God and of the Lamb" (Rev. 22:1). We shall never attain to what is New until we live in what may be called "the dialogue-structure of the cosmos." It is the Living God who speaks and acts: *dabār Yahve, Logos tou Kyriou,* the Word and the Act are inseparable. What exists exists for us because it is "addressed to us" by him. If we live merely on the level of phenomena and causes, we shall remain cut off from this dialogue, this relation between the Logos and ourselves. This is to live in death — the only form of decay mentioned in the Bible.

B. Isaiah 43:19

This passage from Second Isaiah describes the new revelation. It was written during the Exile — that terrible experience of death, which contradicted all the promises of life contained in the Word of God.

We are always in this Exile. Our consciousness is fixed down on the ground, at the level of phenomena; it no longer even perceives the tragic irony of the world of objects. Since everything is "objectivated," the object is the exile of the person. Consumers or revolutionaries, technocrats or underdeveloped peoples, we are tempted to reduce everything to the status of an object — even the depths of the human soul. We seek the object and we find the absurd. Then everything is radically dead — the world and humanity and God. Everything is old, everything is cut off from its roots, from its source of personal renewal. "They have forsaken me, the fountain of living waters . . ." (Jer. 2:13).

It is in the midst of this Exile that God proclaims his renewal. "Remember not the former things, nor consider the things of old. Behold, I am doing a new thing; now it springs forth, do you not perceive it?" (Isa. 43:18-19). In this passage we again find the same action undertaken by God *(poieō)* and the same springing forth *(idou)* of renewal as in Genesis 1:1 and Rev. 21:5. What is special in this passage in Isaiah is the fact that the past is transcended and a new future is announced. This promise was fulfilled in the return from exile in the middle of the sixth century.

For us the prophetic value of this passage is always applicable, in its accomplishment. The "new thing" which has at last appeared is the Christ, and the real return from exile is his resurrection. But what is not changed is our state of exile. The fulfillment of the promise in the Risen Christ shows up even more clearly the apocalyptic struggle in which we are engaged. And we are still living under the regime of the promise. In addition to the return from exile, Isaiah foretold the coming of Christ the Servant; in the same way the Spirit of the promise which lives in us proclaims today the second coming of Christ the Lord. The time of waiting is not over. It is rather painfully revealed all the more strikingly because the Christ is already in our midst.

Today the Prince of Life confronts the prince of this world. In Christ death has been vanquished; but in men and women death has still to be overcome (Rev. 12:17). Thus the structure of this world is not only that of a dialogue animated by the gift of the Logos; it is also demonological, traversed by the devil. If we fail to bear this in mind, our answer to God's Word will either be ecclesial trumphalism or else pathological repentance. In other words, the advent of "the new thing" in history "appears" as a combat against death. This new thing can only be a Paschal drama.

C. 2 Corinthians 5:17

This brings us to the third passage which forms the background for Revelation 21:5: "if anyone is in Christ, he is a new creation; the old has passed away, behold, the new has come." Here the word "to make" is replaced by a word denoting action, "creation" *(ktisis);* the whole thing is personalized (it refers to a certain person — Christ). The expression of Newness is stressed by the word "behold" *(idou)* and by the antithesis with the past *(ta archaia).* But positively Paul tells us that "all this is from God" (v. 18), and in order to try to express this mystery of "something New" he uses the word "birth" *(gegonen)* in the sense of accomplishment, implied by the Greek perfect tense; "a new event is there." This rejoins the variant given in certain manuscripts "all is new," which would bring us close to the passage in Revelation.

It should be noted that in these two passages the promise given in Isaiah 43:19 is fulfilled: the past is forgotten, the old things have passed away, "the former things have passed away" (Rev. 21:4). But the special point about 2 Corinthians 5:17 is that it reveals to us the why and how of this passage, this change. Christ had died to the old world; his resurrection inaugurates the new one by reconciling all with his Father (2 Cor. 5:14-21). *The Easter of Jesus is the Event which has wrought the change.*

In the light of these passages can we enter more deeply into this Event: "Behold, I make all things new"?

1. Firstly, these passages give fresh meaning and value to this "new thing" in history. The facts which co-exist today could be summarized as follows: for us who live in "the last days" the Event of "the new thing," the creative energy of the Logos, The Pantocrator (a word which often recurs in the Book of Revelation), acts "at the beginning" of everything. The structure of the cosmos is *dialogic*, in the proper theological sense of the Logos.

The "new thing" comes in the darkness; it is opposed, it struggles, for the structure of this world is also *diabolic*, in the proper theological sense of the word.

This "new thing" is accomplished once and for all time in the death and resurrection of the incarnate Logos. From that time on the structure of history is *Paschal*, in the proper theological sense of the "passage" from this world to a new creation.

Lastly, this "new thing," as revealed in the words of Revelation 21:5, is coming into this world incessantly and increasingly, so that — for those who perceive Christ in faith — its consummation is a certainty, and it will be definite and total. Thus, the present structure of history is already a *parousia*-structure, in the proper theological sense of the Presence *(parousia)* of God-with-people.

2. Another fact which emerges from this biblical view of history is that the new creative thing is not explained by the past but *by the future*. It is obvious that the action of the Living God is bound to be creative. But the wonderful thing about the God who revealed himself to Abraham, Isaac and Jacob is that his creative act comes from the future. It is prophetic. This God "comes" into the world, as if to meet it. He goes before the world calling it, telling it to move along; he makes it larger and freer. Any other God is a false god, an idol, a dead god, and it is high time that we buried him. This god in many forms inhabits the "old" consciousness of man, is in fact *behind* man as a cause; he commands, he organizes, he pulls man back and alienates man from his true nature. There is nothing prophetic about this old god; on the contrary, he always comes afterwards as a reason for what is inexplicable, or as a last resort for people who are irresponsible. This false god is as old as death, he is an idol made by human hands, and men and women are jealous of him (Gen. 3). He is the project of diabolic falsehood — not the expression of the true Logos. This old god is dead, in actual fact; but he will not be dead in history until all things are new. There is no theology of that god. No, the New Creation enters the world with the word. It does not invent itself, nor prove its own existence; it *reveals* itself. One may either welcome it or reject it, but it comes as an Event. That is why the last words of the Bible were bound to be apocalyptic, a "revelation." The main theme

of the Book of Revelation, the key to history, the meaning of what is truly new and creative, is "He is and He is coming."

3. The New Creation is the Living God — but he enters our world in Christ, his incarnate Logos, who has vanquished death. Irenaeus of Lyons said: "He has given us all things new by giving us himself, he who had been announced; a new principle was to come which would renew and quicken mankind" (*Adversus Haereses* 4.34.1). In the same way, Maxim the Confessor writes: "In the Mystery of the incarnate Word lie the power of the enigmas and symbols of Scripture, as well as the knowledge of sensitive and intelligible creatures. He who knows the mystery of the cross and the tomb understands the *raison d'être* of these creatures. But he who has been initiated in the hidden power of the Resurrection perceives the final foundation upon which God, in his design, is building all things."

"The hidden power of the resurrection" — in these last times, this is the coming of what is New. In this connection we should reread all that St. Paul has written on the *energy* of the resurrection, which has been working upon the world and changing it ever since through the gospel. This means for us that the incarnate Word, the new world, is entering our world of death. This invasion by the Living God is bursting the chains by which people are enslaved — the demons, sin, death, the law, "the flesh" (in the Pauline sense). The cross was the moment when this New Thing — the eschaton, the age to come — broke into our own aeon and destroyed all our tombs. That death on the cross is our own resurrection. "Through the cross joy is spread all over the world" (Byzantine Office at Easter, 6th ode). The most urgent thing for us today is perhaps to rediscover "the immeasurable greatness of his power in us who believe, according to the working of his great might which he accomplished in Christ when he raised him from the dead" (Eph. 1:19-20).

The resurrection is the inauguration of the Parousia in our own aeon. That is why we can wait, with certainty and impatience, for its accomplishment announced by him who sits upon the throne (Rev. 21:5). That is why "we await a Saviour, the Lord Jesus Christ, who will change our lowly body to be like his glorious body, by the power which enables him even to subject all things to himself" (Phil. 3:20-21).

4. How does the Paschal Event, which happened once and for all time, become our own today? Through him who was its artisan from the beginning and will always be so: the Holy Spirit. He himself is this New Thing at work in the world. He is the Presence of God-with-us "bearing witness with our spirit" (Rom. 8:16). Without him God is far away. Christ belongs to the past, and the gospel is a dead letter, the church is merely an organization, authority is domination, mission is propaganda, worship is an evocation, and Christian action is a slave-morality.

But in him, in an indissoluble synergy, the universe is lifted up and groans and travails to bring forth the kingdom, the human being is struggling against "the flesh," the risen Christ is here, the gospel is a life-giving force, the church means communion with the Trinity, authority is a liberating service, mission is like Pentecost, the liturgy is both a commemoration and an anticipation, and human action becomes more godlike.

The Holy Spirit brings the Parousia in a sacramental epiclesis which is mystically realistic; it creates new things, it speaks by the prophets, it concludes all things in the dialogue, it establishes communion by diffusing itself, it draws all things towards the Second Coming. "He is Lord and he is the Giver of life" (Symbol of Nicea-Constantinople). It is through him that the church and the world pray with their whole heart, "Come, Lord Jesus!" (Rev. 22:17-20).

5. This life-giving energy of the Holy Spirit instills a *new dynamism* into our world — a dynamism which is different from our world and yet inherent in it. This is extremely important in order to understand the Event of which the Book of Revelation speaks, but especially in order to live out in the present times what points forward to that Event. The Apocalypse, and the human drama which it unveils, is moving onward on two levels — the level of phenomena and the level of Mystery. There is the level of the world that is bound by the laws of cause and effect, in which the alchemy of civilization and economy can never do more than transform one kind of death into another kind. There is also the level of Mystery on which (ever since Daniel) the seers of the Son of Man have discerned the creative act which comes to save men and women from death.

These two levels are not superimposed, they are interpenetrated. That is the principle of the prophetic interpretation of history, yesterday and today. The second part of the Book of Revelation (chapters 4 to 22) consists of five books, each with seven parts. The proclamation of renewal is taken from the fifth book, which consists of seven visions, each introduced by the words "Then I saw. . . ." It is part of the seventh vision. The literary principle of the Book is based on depth of vision — not on a chronological succession. So the amazing phrase: "Behold, I will make all things new" must not be relegated to a future which transcends history; it reveals the new world which is already breaking into the present aeon.

The dramatic tension in which we live is therefore not a tension between a conceptual transcendence and a phenomenal immanence; it is a struggle between two aeons — the present aeon *(ho aiōn houto)*, which is that of dialogue admittedly, but is also diabolical, and the new aeon, which is that of the Parousia and which makes the present time "Paschal." The tension is engendered by the Holy Spirit. It is more than a permanent revolution; it is a palingenesis *(palingenesia;* cf. Matt. 19:28 and Titus 3:5), a re-creation.

In former times it was believed that the transcendence of God could be safeguarded by identifying it with what is external. Today a reaction has set in: the desire is now to save inwardness by identifying it with immanence. We must reject this disastrous alternative, which is not Christian. The New Event is inherent in history itself, just because it transcends history. Just because God is God, God became man in Christ; and just because God comes in man, a human being cannot be truly human unless he or she becomes more like God. The incarnation of God and the consummation of the human are the same Event — that which is making all things new.

6. There is another aspect which our present crises are sometimes in danger of distorting, or even forgetting completely: *The New Event is seen in the church.* In this seventh vision (described in chapters 21 and 22 of the Book of Revelation) the central reality is the New Jerusalem. Without recourse to the hypothesis of two separate books (held by certain exegetes) one can simply regard the two passages (Rev. 21:1-8 and Rev. 21:9-22) as two different approaches, as was habitual among apocalyptic prophets and writers. One approach describes the immediate future, the other describes the more distant future; the two levels are not superimposed but are integrally merged. The first vision of Jerusalem is no more celestial than the second, and the second one is no more messianic than the first. Jerusalem is a New Jerusalem just because its transcendence is inherent within it. This new time has come with the Easter of our Lord. The church is the symbol and sign of the kingdom of God, because the kingdom is beginning to take form, working like leaven in the church and in the present time.

In what way is this church contemplated in faith, and this kingdom mysteriously and humbly inaugurated, the place where the New Event radiates its light? The answer is found in verses 3 and 4, which immediately precede our text, provided that we read them within the context of the rest of the Bible, especially Ezekiel 37:26, 27 and Isaiah 7:14: "Behold, the dwelling of God is with men. He will dwell with them, and they shall be his people, and God himself will be with them." It is the Mystery of the Temple and the Covenant which Jesus-Emmanuel has accomplished in his own person, and which transfigures Jerusalem. Thus the New Event is the Event of the Covenant. Yahweh is among his people; the spirit is there, in the heart of the Bride. The blood of the Lamb has sealed this Covenant which nothing can break, not even the infidelities of the Bride mentioned in the Song of Solomon. He has given himself, he no longer belongs to himself but to his church. The church does not belong to itself; it exists only because it belongs to its Lord. The New Event is that Love triumphs over Death.

It is this New Covenant which constitutes the church and which is the church's *raison d'être*. The eschatological meaning of our baptism is perhaps too much neglected by Christians today. This sacrament renews us and enables us to enter the new creation, just because it brings us into the communion of the church. That would lead us, in interchurch relations, to recentre everything upon the church as a great sacrament, and to endeavor at a deeper level and to tackle at a deeper level the divergences which exist still in our communion of faith. That would also lead us to live more sharply and more truly the tension between the two aeons, which we mentioned above. The renewal of Christian asceticism depends to a great extent on this eschatological perception of baptism. The renewal of our solidarity with the whole of humankind depends on it also, firstly because the newness of the church would be better lived as transcendent and inherent in the world, and then because the mysterious reality of which the church is the sign — the *agape*, the divine *koinonia* — would be meaningful and active in the life of our contemporaries in all the purity and power of the gospel.

It depends on us whether the breaking in of the New is hidden and remains insignificant, or whether it makes us more godlike and transfigures the world. That is the whole meaning of our responsibility in the present renewal.

Renewal Today

To what forms of renewal does the Spirit call the churches today?

1. A first aspect concerns the very meaning of theology today. Every Christian is a theologian if he "loves the appearing" of Christ (2 Tim. 4:8). The new, creative Life (as we said) manifests itself not in the past but in the future — in what is "to come." Consequently, genuine theology is polarized by the Parousia.

But too often so-called "theological" research consists merely of comments on the past. We are not advocating a fiction-theology, we simply want a *prophetic* theology which is able to discern the coming of the Lord in history. Christians are often criticized for lagging behind in the evolution of the modern world. This situation will not be improved if our churches take a refresher course in sociology or anthropology; what they need is a genuine theological renewal. Instead of interpreting events "afterwards" in the light of the Bible, we have to live them, perceiving in them him who is coming, and promoting his coming through them. Does not the Holy Spirit impel us to hasten the coming of the creative Word, of the saving Christ who "will guide us into all the Truth . . . for he will declare the things that are to come" (John 16:13)?

For the church, everything began, and always will begin, with the Resurrection of its Lord. It was when the church realized that he is "alive for evermore" (Rev. 1:17-18) that it became the church. The church is the new human race which has been granted to know the Father here and now, and through which the Spirit brings to life in the world the *kenosis* of the Lord of history. The *kenosis* (Phil. 2:7) is the eschatological condition of the kingdom, that is, of theology, which is the life of the church. Theology springs from this perception: that Christ is risen indeed, piercing the veil of the first creation. Unless our renewal is theological it will merely be a readaption, which will at once become out of date. Renewal in the church can take place only if the church is rooted more deeply in the Mystery, that second level of history which is inherent in the level of phenomena, and without which the phenomena lead to death.

Evidence of God in faith — that is theology as its source. Evidence of the world in its drama (dialogic, diabolic, paschal and parousiac) — that is the constant renewal of theology.

2. Without yielding to fashion, we must recognize that the New Life is in urgent need of "anthropological integration." If we often suffer from a lack of this, it is partly owing to the false dichotomy (described above) between the conceptual transcendent and the phenomenal immanent, whereas the tension is eschatological. This does not mean that the church must transform itself into a concern for studying anthropology, sociology, or socio-economic development. The theological evidence does not destroy nor neglect the psyche in the human person, but traces it to its source and liberates it. The Holy Spirit is not a super-psychology; it is the Life of the whole person. Similarly, theological evidence does not mean that we need not know the structures in every order of human experience; but it promotes and transfigures the values which are in interaction with the structures. The evidence of the Mystery, "The love of the Parousia" which the Spirit engenders in the hearts of baptized Christians, cannot be dismissed as mere "religious experience" nor explained away psychologically, sociologically or structurally. It is the New Life which enters all these different spheres in order to save them from death, and to lead them towards the new heaven and the new earth.

This evidence is a revelation. If we are not a revelation for our brethren, astonishing or irritating them, it is because we have forsaken the original evidence. In that case we are merely theists, and why should we be surprised if we have secreted atheism? Moreover, the first question in the world today is closely connected with our first Christian evidence. It is not "Does God exist?" It is no longer "What is the human person?" It is "How can the human person conquer death?" which means "Did Christ really rise from the dead?"

3. Appeals of this kind call us to carry out a radical renewal in our churches. We have often transformed the house in which God dwells with people into a robber's den. We want to purify it. But the church cannot be re-formed: the breaking in of the New does not spring from us. The church is given; it comes from God. But what are we doing with this gift? That is the real question. As divine communion given to people in Christ and spread by the Spirit, the church exists in order to serve the agape. Everything else comes from the old letter of the law.

One of the most urgent forms of renewal needed, in my view, is in connection with the charismata in the church, as they are related to the central agape. The *charismata are the organs for the newness of the Spirit*, its manifestation, parousia, for the common good (1 Cor. 12:7). If we carefully reread what Paul said at the end of 1 Corinthians 12 (verses 27-28), we can revise the priorities which exist today. "First, apostles": the apostolic churches live by the sacramental character of this charism. "Second, prophets": what position do prophets occupy in any of our churches today? "Third, teachers . . .": there is undoubtedly an oversupply of these. And one could go on, noting that the charism of administration comes right at the end, just before the gift of languages; here again, what is the position in our churches today?

Paul does not claim to give an exhaustive list of the charismata, either in this epistle or elsewhere. What forms could the gifts of the Spirit take today, in order to interpret and to serve the New Life that is breaking into our world? One of the most urgent seems to be the charism of *reconciliation*. The charism of *dialogue* in disinterested, fraternal service is still difficult to carry out in some areas of the world. There is also the parousiac charism which Paul and the early fathers called virginity, and which we call "the monastic life," for lack of a better term. Its meaning is fully given by the Parousia, which has begun here and now. Are our churches taking these charismata seriously?

4. In face of the situation today in the sphere of personal, cultural and social life, we need to have more discernment. We cannot give way either to pragmatism or to irrealism. But first of all we have to exercise our eschatological sense in order to see in what ways these contemporary situations are "new" in the Christian sense. Their theological solution will then be directed towards genuine Christian theology.

5. In interchurch relations this same eschatological meaning could give new vigor to the dialogue. Would not the best way of solving the doctrinal or pastoral dispute which is still preventing full communion be to turn together towards the coming Lord? There is no pragmatic sentimentalism in this, but rather that same evidence of faith which would enable us to recentre everything in the heart of the Mystery. The dialogue between the churches has perhaps remained at the stage of the time before Isaiah 43:18, when one still considered "the things of old." But it is certain that the Lord is "doing a new thing; now it springs forth, do you not perceive it?"

We should also be led to distinguish better in the church between the *structures* and the *organization*. Ultimately there is no structure in the church except the sacramental one, that is, what the Holy Spirit sets up as a sign of the Lord's coming. The church is essentially sacramental because the Lord is not outside this world nor beyond it; he comes into this world. Organization, on the other hand, comes from ourselves; it is undoubtedly necessary, in the service of the agape, but it is historically conditioned. Organization in itself is not the New Life. The church is not an objective order under the jurisdiction of sociology; it is a power of creation, an organ of the Holy Spirit. It is at this level that the church is structured.

6. The relation between the church and the world is too often seen exclusively at the level of organization, as if they were two systems which can either be reconciled, or else repel one another. But this relation should be lived out in the meeting between communion with God (furthered in the church through

the structures of the sacraments) and the structures of this world, which are inspired by certain values. It is on the level of values that we have to live out the drama of Easter and of the Parousia, in order to restore to life what is enchained by death. It is there that the real New Life can blossom.

The church's mission in the organization of the world today is not to supply techniques. The New Life of the Parousia does not introduce original structures in the world. The mission of certain churches can and must be mutual aid, that agape "in deed and in truth" (1 John 3:18). But the mission of all the churches, rich or poor, according to this world, is to be the *living, prophetic conscience* of the drama of the present time. "The creation is groaning and travailing" (Rom. 8:22); do we know this, as St. Paul supposes? Do we live it out? How do we translate it into the experience of work, of money, of matter, of the cosmos?

7. It seems as if it is in this full eschatological sense that we have to understand our work on ethical problems and liturgical renewal. To put it briefly, the cultural revolution in which these two questions are integrated demands of us a radical renewal, not only at the level of the forms which are in themselves contingent, but especially on the level of the Spirit. Culture, in the light of Parousia, is the true iconography; it is the work of the Holy Spirit which fashions Christ, the new universe out of the first creation.

"Behold, I make all things new." It is not a *deus ex machina* who is speaking, sweeping away the whole scene of the cosmos; it is the breakthrough of the sacramental Liturgy into the eternal Liturgy. What will disappear is not this world, this marvel of the Creative Word; it is death. The labour of generation after generation of men will not be wiped out; it will be transfigured once and for all.

Current Eschatology: Universal Salvation and the Problem of Hell

JOHN R. SACHS, S.J.

The purpose of this article is to take a fresh look at the ancient and much misunderstood theme of apocatastasis [universal salvation]. Increasing contemporary use of the apocalyptic language of hell, hand in hand with the alarming appeal and growth of fundamentalism, sectarianism, and integralism, suggests the urgency of this endeavor. After first surveying the checkered history of this theme from biblical times to the present, I will, second, state and describe the central points of current Catholic theology on these issues. It manifests a remarkable degree of consensus. Third, I shall turn more closely to the highly original thought of Hans Urs von Balthasar, whose approach seems most challenging. Fourth, I shall raise a question concerning the ability of human freedom to reject God definitively. Finally, my conclusion will stress how a properly understood Christian universalism is not only consonant with several central strands of Christian belief, but is also profoundly relevant to the religious and cultural developments of the present age.

The Doctrine of Apocatastasis

The doctrine of apocatastasis, commonly attributed to Origen, maintained that the entire creation, including sinners, the damned, and the devil, would finally be restored to a condition of eternal happiness and salvation. This was an important theme in early Christian eschatology.[1] Even before the Christian era,

1. See, for example, Brian E. Daley, "Patristiche Eschatologie," in *Handbuch der Dogmengeschichte IV/7a: Eschatologie. In der Schrift und Patristik* (Freiburg: Herder 1986), 84-248, as well

---

Reprinted with permission from the journal *Theological Studies* 52 (1991): 227-54.

of course, the idea of an *apokatastasis pantōn* was well known in ancient religion and philosophy. In Eastern thought especially, one finds a predominantly cyclical conception of time and history according to which the end always involves a return to the perfection of the beginning.[2] The idea of a final and definitive obliteration of evil and a corresponding beatification of all creatures is found in Parsiism. Over the course of several hundred years, the rigid dualism between good and evil, for which this religious tradition was known, gave way to the notion in ancient Persian philosophy of a final victory of the good and a fiery process of renewal in which the whole world would be perfected and made eternal.[3] In Stoic philosophy, too, we find forms of this idea. After the present world is destroyed in a cosmic conflagration, a new world would appear, perfecting the former in even the smallest details. Origen's works evidence great familiarity with these ideas.[4] Cicero hoped that ultimately all men and women would live eternally in the Milky Way in their true, divine identity.[5] In Gnostic thought, one finds the basically cyclic pattern of an original spiritual fullness of all being, a subsequent "fall" (resulting in the creation of the material world), and the appearance of a redeemer figure from the spiritual realm who leads the fallen creation back into its original and true divine fullness.[6] The notion that all things, especially the human soul, emanate from the divine One until they eventually reach a turning point for final return is characteristic of Neo-Platonism.[7]

Turning to the Scriptures, we find that language about final restoration is notably scarce. This is not surprising, for the biblical conception of time and history is markedly linear. History is established by virtue of God's action and promise, primarily in the covenant. By virtue of God's promise, a real future is established precisely as fulfillment of the covenant promise (creation, covenant,

---

as an expanded English version recently published under the title *The Hope of the Early Church: A Handbook of Patristic Eschatology* (Cambridge: Cambridge University Press, 1991). J. W. Hanson, *Universalism, the Prevailing Doctrine of the Christian Church during its First Five Hundred Years* (Boston and Chicago: Universalist Publishing House, 1899), is still useful. For general background on the term and its history, see A. Oepke, "Apokathistēmi, apokatastasis," in *Theological Dictionary of the New Testament* 1.387-93; Chr. Lenz, "Apokatastasis," in *Reallexikon für Antike und Christentum* 1.510-16; F. Mussner and J. Loosen, "Apokatastasis," in *Lexikon für Theologie und Kirche* 1.708-12.

2. See Henrich Gross, *Die Idee des ewigen und allgemeinen Weltfriedens im alten Orient und im Alten Testament* (Trier: Paulinus, 1956).

3. G. Müller, "Origenes und die Apokatastasis," *Theologische Zeitschrift* 14 (1958): 175f.; *TDNT* 1.392.

4. For references, see Müller, "Origenes," 176.

5. Brian Daley, "Apokatastasis and 'Honorable Silence' in the Eschatology of Maximus the Confessor," in *Maximus Confessor*, ed. Felix Heinzer and Christoph Schönborn (Fribourg: Editiones Universitaires, 1982), 309-39, esp. 309.

6. Hans Urs von Balthasar, "Apokatastasis," in *Dare We Hope "That All Men Be Saved?"* (San Francisco: Ignatius, 1988), 223-54, esp. 230.

7. Ibid., 226.

David and the prophets, Jesus, Church, end time). It is true that beginning with the prophets, we find a belief that God would reestablish the integrity of the covenant and restore Israel politically; this, however, is not simply a return to an initial state of harmony and perfection but a new future which God has promised to establish.[8] This is surely the background of the disciples' question in Acts 1:6 and the sense of Peter's sermon in the temple to the Jews (Acts 3:21), where we find the only instance of the term *apocatastasis* in the New Testament. There *apokatastasis pantōn* refers to the fulfillment of God's covenant promise to Israel, of "all that God spoke by the mouth of his holy prophets from of old."

While the fulfillment of God's promise is not simply a return to a primordial state of perfection,[9] it is the accomplishment of God's eternal plan from the very beginning.[10] Moreover, the preaching and actions of Jesus suggest that the fulfillment of the covenant with Israel involves all of humanity and the world as a whole. God intends and accomplishes this salvation in Christ for all men and women. Thus, while neither the term nor the concept of apocatastasis plays a significant role in the Bible, there are many texts in the New Testament which speak about universal salvation, at least in the sense of the universal scope of God's saving action in Christ and its effective power.[11]

On the other hand, the Scriptures make it quite clear that every individual person will finally stand accountable to the judgment of God for what he or she has done in life, and for that receive eternal reward or eternal punishment.[12] Paradoxically, it would seem that both the universality of salvation and the inescapable threat of damnation seem to have been a part of Jesus' own preaching.

Belief in human freedom and the conviction that human beings, finally accountable before God, will be rewarded or punished according to their deeds

8. Ibid., 227f. In the Old Testament, the verbal form *(apokathistēmi)* became a technical term for the restoration of Israel to its own land by God (*TNDT* 1.388). As is clear from the later prophets, this restoration is not understood as the perfection and fulfillment of Israel alone. God's eschatological kingdom was to be universal in scope; through Israel all the nations would be called to enter into it. The reappearance of Elijah would signal the coming of the Messiah and the dawn of the end time, which would bring final peace and harmony.

9. See F. Mussner, "Die Idee der Apokatastasis in der Apostelgeschichte," in *Lex Tua Veritas: Festschrift für Hubert Junker* (Trier: Paulinus, 1961), 293-306.

10. See Eph. 1:3-10, esp. v. 4: ". . . even as he chose us in him before the foundation of the world"; Col. 1:15-20; 1 Pet. 1:19f.; and Rev. 13:8, which Balthasar takes to refer to the "Lamb slain before the foundation of the world" *(Mysterium Paschale)* [Edinburgh: T. & T. Clark, 1990], 34f.).

11. "Universalist" texts frequently cited include: Rom. 5:12-21; 11:32; Eph. 1:10; Phil. 2:10f.; Col. 1:20; 1 Tim. 2:4f.; 4:10; Tit. 2:11; Heb. 9:27f.; 2 Pet. 3:9; John 6:37-39; 12:32; 16:33; 17:2.

12. Among the many parables, perhaps the best example, and certainly the one which through art and architecture has had the greatest influence upon Christian piety, is the judgment scene of Matt. 25:31-46. See also Matt. 13:24-30, 36-43; 13:47-50; 18:23-25; 22:1-14; 25:1-13; Luke 16:19-31. Compare Rom. 2:2-11; 1 Cor. 3:11-15; 2 Cor. 5:10; 2 Thess. 1:5-10, as well as the numerous references to Gehenna (Matt. 3:12; 5:22; 18:9), "eternal fire" (Matt. 18:8), "furnace of fire" (Matt. 13:42, 50), and "outer darkness" (Matt. 8:12; 22:13).

in this life, is not unique to Christianity. As we have seen, the notion of a final state of perfect and universal peace, reconciliation, and happiness is also known in many other religions and worldviews. Christianity, however, may be the only faith which seems to profess both. Both the reality of human freedom and the absolutely sovereign and universal saving act of God in Christ are central to the Christian faith. Neither may be denied; one may not be played off against the other. The history of theology shows how difficult it has been to understand the relationship between the two.

From the very beginning, the notion that God's eternal plan for the world and its salvation could fail — that, in sin, human freedom was capable of finally and eternally resisting God's grace — was difficult for many to accept. What would that make of the gospel itself, the proclamation of Christ's victory over sin and death? Origen, the first truly great Christian theologian, wrestled with this problem, wondering which was greater, human freedom (and its ability to reject God) or God's love for sinners. Without trying to force his different opinions into a rigidly systematic position, we find a clear and eloquent expression of hope and confidence in the final efficaciousness of God's universal saving will.[13] Thought by some to have taught the eventual conversion and salvation even of the demons, Origen's school of thought was condemned by the Provincial Council of Constantinople in 543.[14] Nonetheless, several other important patristic authors, such as Clement of Alexandria and Gregory of Nyssa, argued for some form of apocatastasis and were not explicitly condemned. Subsequently, Christian theology seems to have placed most stress on human freedom, divine judgment, and eternal reward or punishment. By the fifth century, the threat of eternal punishment is explicitly mentioned in various symbols of the faith.[15]

The hope that God's universal saving will would in fact be accomplished, that all individual persons would be saved, became nothing more than the slimmest of theoretical possibilities. The pessimistic views of Tertullian and Augustine,[16] who saw the vast mass of humanity as on the road to perdition, struck deep roots. Indeed, it would seem that since the Middle Ages, the threat

---

13. So Henri Crouzel, *Origen* (San Francisco: Harper and Row, 1989), 257-66; "L'Apocatastase chez Origène," in *Origeniana Quarta: Die Referate des 4. Internationalen Origeneskongresses, Innsbruck, 2-6, September 1985*, ed. Lothar Lies (Innsbruck-Wien: Tyrolia, 1987), 282-90; "L'Hadès et la Géhenne selon Origène," *Gregorianum* 59 (1978): 291-329.

14. Müller, "Origenes," 189, makes the interesting suggestion that it was Origen's apparent notion of recurring world-periods (an idea directly contradictory to the biblical understanding of salvation history) that led to his condemnation, rather than this teachings concerning an apocatastasis.

15. See the so-called "Faith of Damascus," often falsely attributed to the fourth-century Bishop of Rome or to Jerome, and the "Quicumque vult," the late fifth-century symbol of faith, falsely attributed to Athanasius.

16. See especially *The City of God* 21.17-27, where Augustine defends the eternity of eschatological punishment at great length.

of eternal punishment has played a more dominant role in Christian preaching and popular piety than the good news of the world's salvation in Christ! By the time of the great scholastic theologians, elaborate justifications for hell and its torments, usually based on the requirements of divine justice, appear as an answer to questions concerning their relationship to God's loving mercy and the final beatitude of the saved.[17]

Throughout history, however, we find a continued interest in the doctrine of apocatastasis, itself a sign that an important truth has been in danger of being lost, a truth every bit as important as that which early church condemnations were trying to defend.[18] Despite the enormous influence of Luther and Calvin, various forms appear even in Protestant theology since the seventeenth century, notably in the work of Jakob Böhme, Friedrich Schleiermacher, and, in our own century, Karl Barth. As is to be expected, Catholic representatives are few, the nineteenth-century German theologian Hermann Schell being an exception.

Turning to recent Catholic eschatology, one finds that the theme of apocatastasis continues to merit reflection. Not surprisingly, theologians follow official church teaching concerning hell. In presenting and explaining the Church's doctrine, however, current theology tries to address two significant pastoral realities. First, for many centuries, the doctrine of hell has had an exaggerated place in the theology and preaching of the Church. For many Christians, the "good news" of the kingdom became the "bad news" about judgment and punishment. Then, in reaction to the excessively judicial and often monstrous images of God which had been prelevant for so long, it has become common to ignore the topic of hell altogether or to deny its existence outright as incompatible with God's love and mercy. Some would suggest that the excessive pessimism about salvation which often characterized the Church since Augustine has been replaced by a naive optimism about salvation which trivializes human freedom and ultimately undermines moral responsibility. The challenge, therefore, has been to identify the true meaning and the proper place of hell in the proclamation of the gospel about the world's salvation in Christ. Among Catholic writers, Hans Urs von Balthasar is prominent as one who, in

---

17. Thomas justifies the eternity of divine punishment in terms of God's mercy and justice. See especially *ST* 3, Suppl., qq. 97-99. In Question 94, he even raises the question concerning the sense of eternal punishment from the perspective of the blessed and suggests that their happiness is all the greater when they behold the suffering which they have escaped! Compare *Sent.* 4, d. 47, qq. 1 and 2; 4, d. 50, qq. 1 and 2.

18. See Esteban Deak, "Apokatastasis: The Problem of Universal Salvation in Twentieth-Century Theology" (Ph.D. diss., Toronto: University of St. Michael's College, 1979). Also Richard J. Bauckham, "Universalism: A Historical Survey," *Themelios* 4/2 (January 1979): 48-54; Wilhelm Breuning, "Zur Lehre von der Apokatastasis," *International katholische Zeitschrift* 10 (1981): 19-31; and Gotthold Müller, "Ungeheuerliche Ontologie: Erwägungen zur christlichen Lehr über Hölle und Allversöhnung," *Evangelische Theologie* 34 (1974): 256-75. For an extensive bibliography, see G. Müller, *Apokatastasis pantōn: A Bibliography* (Basel: Missionsbuchhandlung, 1969).

several recent books and articles,[19] has considered this problem and offered penetrating reflections on the nature of Christian hope. After examining the Scripture and the Church's liturgical, doctrinal and theological tradition, Balthasar concludes that while we may not claim to know the final outcome of human decision and divine judgment with certainty, we may hope that all will be saved. Indeed, it is our duty to do so. Only thus can the disciple truly express the loving solidarity of Christ, who died for all. As we shall see, his is a pointed, but not extreme, position, quite consonant with Church teaching and the thought of most other major Catholic theologians. This makes the negative criticism which his writing has evoked from some Catholic quarters all the more alarming.[20]

Appealing to Scripture, his opponents have claimed that we may not hope for universal salvation, because it is certain that some will in fact be damned. Such a view is usually based on a false, literalist interpretation of biblical texts and is clearly incompatible with official church teaching, but it is not uncommon. Moreover, once one is certain that there will in fact be a hell, one usually finds little difficulty in imagining just who will be among its inhabitants. There are the saved and the damned, the insiders and the outsiders. Such an attitude seems inimical to the "exceedingly abundant hope" with which believers are blessed by God in the Spirit (Rom. 15:13) and often produces a self-righteousness that has little to do with the love for sinners so evident in the life of Jesus. This makes it all the more important to consider anew the ancient theme of apocatastasis and the problem of hell.

Current Catholic Eschatology

The position held by virtually all Catholic theologians who have recently written on these themes may be summarized under five propositions.[21]

---

19. *Was dürfen wir hoffen?* (Einsiedeln: Johannes, 1986); *Kleiner Diskurs über die Hölle* (Ostfildern: Schwabenverlag, 1987); "Apokatastasis," *Trierer theologische Zeitschrift* 97/3 (1988): 169-82 (Collected, ET: *Dare We Hope "That All Men be Saved?"* with *A Short Discourse on Hell and Apokatastasis: Universal Reconciliation* [San Francisco: Ignatius, 1988]); *Theodramatik IV: Das Endspiel* (Einsiedeln: Johannes, 1983), esp. 243-93. Balthasar's interest in eschatology and in this question in particular was already strong several decades ago. See "Christlicher Universalismus" and "Umrisse der Eschatologie," in *Verbum Caro: Skizzen zur Theologie I* (Einsiedeln; Johannes, 1960), 260-75, 276-300 (ET: "Christian Universalism" and "Some Points of Eschatology," in *Word and Redemption* [New York: Herder and Herder, 1965], 127-45, 147-75); "Abstieg zur Hölle" and "Eschatologie im Umriss," in *Pneuma und Institution* (Einsiedeln: Johannes, 1974), 387-400, 410-55.

20. See *Dare We Hope*, 13-19, 163.

21. Important recent works on eschatology include: Gisbert Greshake, *Gottes Heil — Glück des Menschen* (Freiburg: Herder, 1983); Zachary Hayes, O.F.M., *Visions of a Future: A Study of Christian Eschatology* (Wilmington, DE: Glazier, 1989); Medhard Kehl, *Eschatologie* (Würzburg: Echter, 1986); Joseph Ratzinger, *Eschatology: Tod und ewiges Leben* (Regensburg: Pustet, 1977) (ET:

1. *Because human beings are free, they are able to reject God. Therefore hell is a real possibility.* Fundamental to the biblical vision, G. Greshake reminds us, is the belief that all human beings without exception are created and called by God into a personal relationship of love with God. God's free gift of self in love is the final peace, happiness, fulfillment, and salvation of humanity. Human beings find grace and final salvation, therefore, only by freely accepting God's gift of self in such a relationship of love and living out its implications in the concrete events of their lives.[22] Because they are free, they can also turn away from God by rejecting such a relationship and refusing to live according to the promise and demands of God's justice.[23] This is the essence of sin and the reason why hell is a real possibility, for hell is nothing more than the final state of one who has definitively refused to live his or her life with and in God.

God wishes nothing except to be the final salvation of the creature God has made, but precisely because salvation consists in a personal relationship of love, it cannot be forced upon anyone. Love can exist only when it is freely given *and* freely received. God's absolute, eternal love, especially for the sinner, even for the sinner who radically refuses to acknowledge and embrace that love, cannot change or grow weak. But neither can it force the one it loves to love in return. Force is the very opposite of love. "God never by-passes human freedom in order to release people from the results of their free decisions."[24] Thus, one cannot play off God's justice and mercy in order to secure a "happy ending" by suggesting that with infinite love, God must "overlook" the hateful choice of the sinner. God's justice is God's merciful love, but, precisely as love, it must do justice to the free choice of the other.[25] God has created human beings as free creatures and respects human freedom unconditionally.[26]

Even though human beings often attempt to evade responsibility and therefore avoid being taken seriously, God cannot not take creatures seriously. Because human beings are free, Christianity recognizes a godlike dignity in them. No other ideology takes human beings this seriously. In this sense, the Church's teaching about hell says: "You count. You have ultimate significance. What you do in your life is not meaningless; it has final worth."[27] Seen from

---

Eschatology: Death and Eternal Life [Washington, D.C.: Catholic University of America Press, 1988]); Herbert Vorgrimler, *Hoffnung auf Vollendung: Aufriss der Eschatologie* (Freiburg: Herder, 1980). See also Wilhelm Breuning, "Systematische Entfaltung der eschatologischen Aussagen," in *Mysterium Salutis* 5.779-890. Albert Gerhards, ed., *Die grössere Hoffnung der Christen: Eschatologische Vorstellungen im Wandel* (Freiburg: Herder, 1990), while not a systematic treatise on eschatology, is a good collection of essays which treat a number of important issues from exegetical, dogmatic, philosophical, liturgical, and pastoral theological perspectives.

22. Gisbert Greshake, *Gottes Heil*, 249-51.

23. Breuning, "Systematische Entfaltung," 851.

24. Hayes, *Visions*, 187.

25. See Balthasar's treatment of the unity of divine mercy and justice in *Dare We Hope*, 148-57.

26. Ratzinger, *Eschatology*, 216.

27. A. Keller, *Zeit–Tod–Ewigkeit* (Innsbruck, 1981), 126f., quoted by Greshake, *Gottes Heil*, 271.

this perspective, "the possibility of hell is the most radical theological statement about the nature of human freedom."[28] Whether or not human beings are capable of persisting in such radical rejection of God is a question which we shall consider below.

Most theologians point out that such considerations are not designed to resurrect a religion of fear; instead, they may be seen as an effort, from the perspective of Christian faith, to call attention to the ultimate sense and seriousness of human freedom. The gospel of God's universal saving love may not be watered down into a drug-like assurance that, regardless of what we do, "in the end God will make everything all right," any more than it may be distorted into the perverse announcement that God will condemn most of the world to hell.

2. *Hell is, therefore, the self-chosen state of alienation from God and not an additional punishment inflicted by God upon the sinner.* We have seen how the seriousness of human freedom and responsibility before God is clearly expressed in the biblical descriptions of the final judgment which leads either to eternal reward or to eternal punishment. Responding to the problem of how divine punishment, especially eternal punishment, can be consonant with God's loving mercy, contemporary theologians, like many patristic authors, suggest that punishment for sins is not simply an additional, extrinsic act by God. Unlike punishment in the secular, juridicial sphere, which is imposed from without by another (the judge), and consists in a penalty which has no intrinsic connection with the particular crime committed (paying a fine or serving time in a prison), the divine punishment of sin may be viewed as "a connatural consequence of guilt flowing from the proper nature of guilt and need not be specially added by God."[29] God does not torture the sinner in order to avenge Godself or seek retribution from the sinner through punishment. Rather, punishment is the suffering which is immanent to sin itself, something which the sinner brings

---

28. Hayes, *Visions*, 182. In *Foundations of Christian Faith* (New York: Seabury, 1978), Rahner emphasizes that the real freedom given to the human creature, and therefore its capacity radically to refuse God, in no way limits the sovereignty of God, since this is not something that merely "happens" to God, but is something made possible by God's free decision. Nonetheless, he makes the interesting observation that "in his absolute sovereignty and without contradiction at least from our perspective, God can establish freedom as good or as evil freedom without thereby destroying this very freedom. The fact that as subjects of a freedom still coming to be we do not know whether or not God has so established all freedom that it will reach a good decision, at last finally and ultimately, is something to be accepted in obedience as a fact we know from experience, just as we have to accept our very existence in obedience" (105). His formulation is unusual and cautious. He usually insists that human freedom is "the freedom to say 'yes' or 'no' to God" (100). In other words, if freedom could not say a final "no" to God, it would not be freedom. But here he seems to leave another possibility open. All human freedom could be established by God in such a way that it will reach a good decision. This would evidently be a conception of freedom which did not entail the possibility of a final "no" to God.

29. Karl Rahner, "Guilt — Responsibility — Punishment within the View of Catholic Theology," in *Theological Investigations* 6 (New York: Seabury, 1974), 197-217, esp. 215.

upon himself or herself, the inevitable consequence of turning away from God.[30] Even the final punishment of hell which awaits the sinner who refuses to repent is not so much a sentence imposed by God, as it is something which the sinner creates for himself or herself by determining to live apart from God.[31] To turn away finally and completely from God, who alone can give peace and life, inevitably means eternal suffering and death. "If sin is fundamentally the failure to love, then hell can be seen as the final fixation in that state."[32]

Thus, one should not say that God has created hell. If anything, hell is the creation, or better, the "anticreation" of the sinner, who obstinately refuses God's divine will and eternal purpose in creating.[33] Hell is something of the sinner's own doing; it is freely chosen, radical self-isolation and, therefore, quite literally, the sinner's undoing. Salvation, or heaven, is to be with God, or to be "in Christ," and so with all those who are in Christ. Hell is not, by some kind of logical symmetry, being with Satan, the demons, and the other damned. Hell is being with no one at all. In this sense, one should not conceive hell as a place or condition, already possibly inhabited, which exists before one's decision vis-à-vis God and into which one might possibly be consigned. Hell is what I might become personally, not something which we may objectify and "ponder on how many perish in this hell and how many escape it."[34]

According to Rahner, God may be called the punisher of sin to the extent that God has created the objective structures of the human world according to which human beings find salvation only in relationship with God, and perdition when such a relationship is rejected.[35] Greshake sees this not as a merely mechanical, automatic process but as an expression of God's ongoing personal providence. When the Bible pictures God as personally punishing sin, as full of wrath for sinners, it tells us that God does not remain uninvolved in or indifferent to the sinful state of humanity. God wills the life and well-being of the sinner absolutely and unconditionally. Therefore, God providentially wills the suffering or punishment intrinsic to sin as something which can bring sinners to their senses and deter them from sin in the future, much in the same way that pain prevents or at least warns us from putting our hand in a fire.[36] Like many patristic authors,[37] modern theologians view the suffering brought about by sin to have a remedial and therapeutic dimension. The threat of eternal

30. Greshake, *Gottes Heil*, 254.

31. Kehl, *Eschatologie*, 294.

32. Hays, *Visions*, 182, following Michael Schmaus, *Dogma 6: Justification and the Last Things* (Kansas City/London: Sheed and Ward, 1977), 254.

33. Balthasar, *Dare We Hope*, 53-55; compare Johann Auer, *"Siehe, ich mache alles neu": Der Glaube an die Vollendung der Welt* (Regensburg: Pustet, 1984), 98.

34. Balthasar, *Dare We Hope*, 190.

35. Rahner, "Guilt," 215; also Greshake, *Gottes Heil*, 255.

36. Greshake, *Gottes Heil*, 256.

37. For examples, see Daley, "Patristische Eschatologie," 122 (Clement of Alexandria), 131f. (Origen), 152 (Gregory Nazianzus), 156 (Gregory of Nyssa).

punishment as the intrinsic consequence of a radical rejection of God ought to have a deterring force.

Thus, God is not the giver of salvation *and* damnation. God wills only the salvation of all men and women. Heaven is what God chooses for humanity and what humanity must choose to receive. Hell is not something which God can choose for anyone; it is what one who rejects God chooses for himself or herself. Thus heaven and hell may not be viewed as equally possible alternatives from God for human beings at the end of their lies. Speaking of final judgment, Ratzinger insists: "Christ inflicts pure perdition on no one. In himself he is sheer salvation. . . . Perdition is not imposed by him, but comes to be wherever a person distances himself from Christ."[38] God has only one thing to bestow, namely, God's own self as the world's salvation. The basis for a "negative finality," as opposed to "positive fulfillment," at the end of life can only lie in the human sinner, not in God.[39] Still, it is clear that the "theodicy" question remains: How could a loving God create a world in which human freedom has the capacity to damn itself eternally? Would not the (self-)annihilation of the sinner be both a more just and more merciful fate.[40]

3. *Though final damnation remains a possibility with which every individual must reckon, neither Scripture nor church teaching claims that anyone in fact has been or will be finally lost.* First, a few remarks regarding Scripture. Many scholars have pointed out the particular hermeneutical problems involved in the interpretation of those biblical texts which speak of the "last things." In a highly

38. Ratzinger, *Eschatology,* 205f.
39. Kehl, *Eschatologie,* 294.
40. Already suggested by patristic writers, this idea has been presented again recently by Edward Schillebeeckx, *Church: The Human Story of God* (New York: Crossroad, 1990). For entirely understandable reasons, he voices reservations about "superficial" theories concerning universal salvation inasmuch as they "trivialize the drama of the real course of events between oppressed and oppressors, between the good and the evil in our human history" (136). Instead, he suggests that those who are evil "not so much through theoretical denial of God as through a life-style which radically contradicts solidarity with fellow human beings and precisely in that way rejects God" will simply cease to exist at death. That, and not everlasting torture, is hell. Such persons, together with all memory of them, will be totally obliterated, for there is absolutely nothing in them which can have a future in God. "God does not take vengeance; he leaves evil to its own, limited logic" (138). There can be no kingdom of hell; in the end, there is only the one kingdom of God. "The 'eschaton' or the ultimate is exclusively positive. There is no negative eschaton" (139). In his earlier works, Schillebeeckx already suggested that only what is of love is capable of being raised from the dead by God. Still, he does have his doubts about whether such a "fundamental, definitive sinner" actually exists (137), and I think this is an important point. Is it really possible to imagine a human being utterly devoid of good, so completely evil that there is absolutely nothing for God to heal and fulfill in the resurrection? One could not even speak of a truly human person unless there had been at least some minimal, mutual experience of love. And if this were so, despite all the ways it may have been denied or deformed subsequently, how could its reality, if only in the memory of others, be obliterated? For a counterargument based on God's fidelity to creation, see Kehl, *Eschatologie,* 294-96.

important essay[41] Rahner pointed out that eschatological statements have a form and dynamic of their own and must be interpreted accordingly. He distinguished between genuine eschatological statements, which speak about the futurity of the present situation of judgment and salvation in Christ, and (false) apocalyptic statements, which claim to report or predict some additional, completely new event concerning the future end of the world, in a way that attributes even now a kind of a- or supra-historical reality to it. In this terminology, an apocalyptic understanding is either phantasy or gnosticism and has nothing to do with the truth of Scripture.[42] The correct direction of interpretation is always from the present to the genuine future of that present reality, not from a future event pointing back into the present. Thus, biblical texts which speak of the future, like those which speak of origins, are etiological. They attempt to speak of the future (or past) on the basis of what is experienced in the present. The Bible always speaks about the end of the world and its history only insofar as it speaks of what has taken place in the Christ event and the future implications of this event.

Eschatological texts of the Bible are not anticipatory reports of what will happen at the end of the world. They cannot give us information about future events, at least in the sense that they disclose facts about free actions in the future, either God's or ours, as if they were already directly seen and decreed by God, and therefore somehow already existent.[43] It is difficult to see how such a state of affairs would be compatible with either divine or human freedom.

Matthew 25, for example, does not give us information about an eternal hell after death, as if we could conclude that it has already been determined that a certain number will in fact be damned (the goats). Texts like this have a parenetic function which impresses upon the hearers the critical urgency of their own situation as a situation of judgment.[44]

Jesus' parables do not contain a threat that in fact some are going to be damned, but they do confront the hearer with the real possibility that if he or she does not repent and embrace the gospel, he or she will be lost.[45] They do not predict what is in any case certain to happen, but what will happen if one spurns Christ. Such stories issue a clear warning: Don't let this happen to you.[46] Thus, eschatological descriptions concerning final judgment are best understood as ways in which the Bible speaks about human freedom and responsibility before God.[47] Properly understood, therefore, such biblical texts offer no

41. "The Hermeneutics of Eschatological Assertions," in *Theological Investigations* 4 (Baltimore: Helicon, 1966), 323-46.

42. Ibid., 336f.

43. Ibid., 334.

44. See Karl Rahner, "Hell," in *Sacramentum Mundi* 3 (New York: Herder, 1969), 7.

45. Greshake, *Gottes Heil*, 272.

46. Balthasar, *Dare We Hope*, 32f.

47. Hayes, *Visions*, 181.

proof whatsoever that anyone will in fact be damned. The preaching of the gospel, on the lips of Jesus and in the ministry of the Church, is an "open situation."

Church teaching confirms this by insisting that the free response of human beings is not predetermined and by condemning theories of double predestination. A review of the rather modest pronouncements by the magisterium concerning hell[48] shows that the Church teaches the "reality" of hell only in the sense that those who die in the state of moral sin enter into eternal punishment immediately upon death. At the same time the Church has refused to assert that anyone in fact has died or will die in such a state.

One final observation. Precisely because eschatological texts speak about the real possible future of present reality and experience, they must speak of the possibility of final damnation.[49] The reality of sin makes it quite clear that human beings can and do reject God. The possibility of hell is anchored in our present experience of sin. It is nothing more than the possibility that the sinner might choose finally and definitively to persist in such rejection.[50]

4. *The real possibility of hell must be understood in terms of the gospel of God's universal saving will, which is revealed and effected in Jesus Christ. Thus heaven and hell are not to be considered equally possible outcomes, either for humanity as a whole or for individual human beings.* The real possibility of damnation about which Scripture and church teaching speak must be understood in the context of the gospel as a whole. The gospel, however, is not simply a parallel prolongation of the Jewish doctrine of the two ways, the affirmation of a final judgment before God leading either to eternal reward or punishment. Christian faith is not distinctive because it believes that human beings are morally responsible and accountable but because it believes that God has overcome human sin and reconciled the world to Godself.[51] Therefore, according to Rahner, "the eschatology of salvation and of loss are not on the

---

48. According to the Provincial Council of Constantinople (543) the punishment of the demons and impious will have no end (DS 411). Lateran IV (1215) states that the dead will rise and receive, according to their works, eternal reward with Christ or eternal punishment with the devil (DS 801). Lyons II (1274) states that those who die in mortal sin or with original sin only go down immediately *(mox)* to hell *(in infernum)* but suffer different punishments (DS 858). In *Benedictus Deus* (1336) Benedict XII said that the souls of those who die in actual mortal sin go down immediately to hell (DS 1002). Florence (1439) reaffirmed Lyons II (DS 1306). The Congregation for the Doctrine of the Faith (1979) has recently affirmed an "eternal punishment for the sinner, who will be deprived of the sight of God, and that this punishment will have a repercussion on the whole being of the sinner."

49. Rahner, "Hermeneutics," 338, 340.

50. Hayes, *Visions,* 181f.

51. Karl Rahner and Karl-Heinz Weber, *Our Christian Faith: Answers for the Future* (New York: Crossroad, 1981), 122.

same plane."[52] As Hayes puts it, the "possibility of hell stands in sharp contrast with the affirmation of the *reality* of heaven."[53]

For Rahner, this is true in two senses. First, "we know in our Christian faith and in our unshakable hope that, in spite of the drama and the ambiguity of the freedom of individual persons, the history of salvation as a whole will reach a positive conclusion for the human race through God's own powerful grace."[54] Secondly, since grace is not "merely the offer of the bare *possibility* of salutary acts, but must be acclaimed as triumphant, because rendered efficacious by God," it can and must proclaim that some who have died in Christ have attained salvation; but it may not make an assertion about the actual damnation of any individual.[55]

Thus, Christian eschatology speaks in principle of "only *one* predestination" and has but one central affirmation, "the victory of grace in redemption consummated." It speaks of possible damnation only insofar as the "sure triumph of grace" cannot provide the human person with "already fixed and acquired points in his estimation of an existence which is still to be lived out in the boldness of freedom."[56]

In a similar way, Balthasar speaks of a "change of the ages" *(Äonenwende)* in Christ which supersedes the "symmetrical" Old Testament doctrine concerning final reward and punishment and establishes a fundamental "asymmetry" between the reality and possibilities of human sin and the ever-greater grace of God, which always already encompasses it.[57] The cross and resurrection of Christ are (already) God's final judgment upon, and victory over, sin and death and the revelation of the "reward" of eternity. Therefore, the "symmetrical" concept of retribution in the Old Testament (the "two ways" of judgment) collapses. A "fundamental *asymmetry*" now exists, since anything which follows upon it can only be the working out of what is already contained in the cross and resurrection of Christ.[58]

As Balthasar points out, many "universalist" texts in the New Testament express such an "asymmetry." None reflects upon it better than Romans 5, which stresses both the surpassing power and the universal scope of God's saving grace.[59] Moreover, because Jesus himself is God's judgment, he is the

---

52. "Hermeneutics," 338.

53. Zachary Hayes, "Hell," in *The New Dictionary of Theology,* ed. Joseph A. Komonchak, Mary Collins, and Dermot A. Lane (Wilmington, DE: Glazier, 1987), 459.

54. *Foundations,* 435. Compare 444: "Rather the existence of the possibility that freedom will end in eternal loss stands alongside the doctrine that the world and the history of the world will *in fact* enter into eternal life with God."

55. "Hermeneutics," 340.

56. Ibid.

57. *Theodramatik,* 4.246-53.

58. Ibid., 251.

59. *Dare We Hope,* 183-86. Compare Greshake, *Gottes Heil,* 271f. On Romans 5 and related texts, see M. Eugene Boring, "The Language of Universal Salvation in Paul," *Journal of Biblical*

one who will come at the end as judge. In this "the Old Testament image of judgment — which, with few exceptions, is strictly two-sided — may well have become clearer (the Judge is the Savior of all), and . . . as a result hope outweighs fear."[60]

From the perspective of human freedom, too, there is reason to stress the asymmetrical relationship between final salvation and damnation. In the analysis of Karl Rahner, human freedom is not simply the neutral capacity to choose among options, in particular either to accept or reject God. For, "God has not created freedom as the possibility of the creative positing by a subject of what is good and evil but as the possibility of creatively positing what is good."[61] Strictly speaking, human freedom is the capacity to choose God. Its (super)natural end is loving union with God; any other possibility must be understood as inherently against its inner nature, and therefore an inner contradiction. Freedom fails to attain itself in "bad freedom" and, in view of the fact that God has already "freely decided on the victory of love and salvation," is therefore "subject to a peculiar powerlessness which makes it once more impossible to regard the evil decision as an equal realisation of freedom and responsibility on the same plane as the free decision for good."[62]

Following Rahner, Greshake concludes that because the human person is innerly equipped and oriented to choose God and finds his or her appropriate "place" only in heaven, "hell is not only that which should not be, but also, so to speak, that which is much 'more difficult' to attain."[63] I shall return to these suggestions at the end of this essay.

5. *Certain knowledge about the final outcome of judgment for individuals is impossible, but because of Christ's victory over sin and death, we may and must hope that all men and women will in fact be saved.* As we have seen, Catholic theologians follow the official teaching of the Church in maintaining that the human creature can definitely reject God and therefore be eternally lost. Most note that the doctrine of apocatastasis is to be rejected because it trivalizes

---

Literature 105/2 (1986): 269-92. For a less sympathetic judgment: N. T. Wright, "Towards a Biblical View of Universalism," *Themelios* 4/2 (January 1979): 54-58.

60. Balthasar, *Dare We Hope*, 44; on the "asymmetry of grace" and the "symmetry between promise and threat" in the Old Testament, see *Theodramatik*, 4.247f. One should not draw too sharp a contrast between the Old and New Testament here. As Medard Kehl points out, especially in the time before the fall of the Southern kingdom and the beginning of the exile, the prophets, using traditional material, emphasize that God's coming judgment is not the last word. Israel's future is assured in the blessing of the remnant, through whom the whole people, and finally the entire world, will be blessed. It is "not conceived simply as an open alternative between curse and blessing, according to the behavior of the people, but as the sure and lasting appearance of blessing after curse" (*Eschatologie*, 110).

61. "Guilt," 210.

62. Ibid.

63. *Gottes Heil*, 272.

human freedom. If there is anything new or significant about the manner in which traditional teaching is now presented (aside from the fact that all forms of Augustinian double predestination and Jansenist exclusivism are clearly and strongly rejected), it is the distinctly Christological perspective which dominates. While affirming the anthropological truth regarding human freedom and responsibility, contemporary theology stresses the fact that, because of God's action in Christ, human freedom exists concretely in the realm of grace, which undergirds and carries it. Thus Rahner suggests that it would be wrong to view human freedom as "so autonomous that it cannot be seen as embraced by God's more powerful freedom and his mercy."[64] While it is impossible to know the final fate of individuals, Christian faith, professing the death and the resurrection of Jesus Christ as history's *eschaton,* nonetheless proclaims that "the history of salvation as a whole will reach a positive conclusion for the human race through God's own powerful grace."[65] Such a conviction in faith is the ground for the hope that all men and women individually will in fact be saved.

Thus Rahner, like virtually every other contemporary Catholic theologian, explicitly rejects a "positive, theoretical doctrine about an apocatastasis" but at the same time argues for an "unshakable hope" that in the end all men and women will in fact enjoy eternal life.[66] Even as they consider the real possibility of hell, Christians may hope — not know — that as a result of the exercise of their freedom in God's grace, "which dwarfs and also redeems all evil," in fact "hell will not in the end exist." This is a hope which they may have "first for others and therefore also for themselves."[67]

---

64. *Our Christian Faith,* 121.

65. *Foundations,* 435.

66. *Foundations,* 435. Compare Balthasar, *Theodramatik,* 4: *Das Endspiel,* 292f.; Bruening, "Systematische Entfaltung," 850, 860f.; Greshake, *Gottes Heil,* 273; Hayes, *Visions,* 188; Kehl, *Eschatologie,* 297; Ratzinger, *Eschatologie,* 217f.; Vorgrimler, *Hoffnung,* 161. Leo Scheffczyk, "Apokatastasis: Faszination und Aporie," *Internationale katholische Zeitschrift* 14 (1985): 34-46, is an exception. Arguing against current attempts to revive this ancient doctrine in new forms, he seems to reject the sort of "asymmetry" of which these theologians speak in relationship to the two possible outcomes of the final judgment. Moreover, he finds approaches which argue for the hope of salvation for all (despite the real possibility of hell) problematic, because they seem to be based upon an imprecise understanding of the supernatural virtue of hope, which must rest on the "foundation of divine faith." Since "faith does not contain the promise of the non-existence of hell, it cannot give rise to supernatural hope. Hope for beatitude is possible only for the believer herself (and for the other who is bound with her in supernatural love) . . ." (44). Balthasar provides the best critique of such a narrow notion of hope. Surely the hope that believers may have that all will be saved does not necessarily depend upon the promise that this will be so. For such (supernatural) hope, it is sufficient that faith "knows" that God loves all creatures and wills that they be saved and "knows" nothing which positively excludes that this might happen.

67. Rahner, *Our Christian Faith,* 120f.

Hans Urs von Balthasar

No one has argued more forcefully for the possibility and the necessity of such hope than Hans Urs von Balthasar, who notes that even the prayers of the Church's liturgy express the universal scope of Christian hope quite explicitly.[68] Following Kierkegaard, Balthasar emphasizes that damnation is something which each person, strictly speaking, must consider as a real possibility for himself or herself alone, not for others, since hell, in essence, *is* the sinner utterly alone, as one who has rejected God.[69] Here, of course, it is one's life as a whole which is at stake, not merely the state one is in at one's last breath. Judgment does not involve a quantitative weighing of good against bad, but is rather a manifestation of what one's basic decision has been. Even where there seems to have been a "pre-dominantly negative basic decision," Balthasar suggests that, in judging, Christ will search to see if anywhere at all there is something which has been or could be receptive to his divine love, even a "small grain of love" as a response to God's love.[70] Thus, it would seem there is always hope, for is it really possible to imagine a human life which is and has been utterly and completely devoid of love?[71]

But if the cross and resurrection of Christ give me any reason to hope for my own salvation, it is only because there the saving love of God for all men and women is revealed. Thus, despite the long tradition in the West since the condemnation of Origenism, which seemed to reckon quite naturally with the final damnation of some (or most), Balthasar maintains that to hope for one's own salvation and not for the salvation of all would be utterly un-Christian, since Christ died for all men and women.[72] It is Christ's solidarity with all sinners that requires Christian hope to be universal in scope. "We and They," the saved and the damned, are not and cannot be categories into which faith and hope, if they are truly Christian, divide humanity.[73] Thus, according to Balthasar, not only may we hope for the salvation of all, it is our duty to do so;

68. For examples, see *Dare We Hope*, 35-38.

69. *Dare We Hope*, 85-96.

70. *Theodramatik*, 4.269f., citing Adrienne von Speyr.

71. See *Dare We Hope*, 57, where Balthasar relates Dostoevsky's parable of the onion from *The Brothers Karamazov* to illustrate the bare necessity of love. An angel is sent to pull up a selfish old woman from the fire of hell by the onion she once gave to a beggar, the single loving deed of her life. But when others around her tried to hold on as well, she kicked them away, screaming that the onion was hers and hers alone. At that moment the onion broke, sending the woman plunging back into the fire.

72. Aquinas grounded the hope for the salvation of others in the Christian love which binds all together: he therefore represents an advance upon Augustine, who tended to understand theological hope as pertaining solely to the individual's own salvation. Still, for Aquinas, there is nothing like a hope for the salvation of *all* men and women. See Balthasar, *Theodramatik*, 4.289f.

73. Balthasar quotes Marcel: "For there can be no particularism of hope; hope loses all sense and all force if it does not imply the statement of an 'all of us' or an 'all together' . . ." (*Dare We Hope*, 81).

otherwise we are not loving unreservedly and are usually tempted to leave the others to their fate. Hope of "heaven for all" is not an "inducement to laziness in our ethical commitment but rather the heaviest demand upon all of us that one can imagine: the decision for a patience that absolutely never gives up but is prepared to wait infinitely long for the other."[74]

The Mystery of Holy Saturday

For Balthasar, the true depth of Christ's solidarity with sinners is revealed in the mystery of Holy Saturday, which in a unique way brings to expression the Christian understanding of universal salvation.[75] In essence, he challenges the traditional understanding of Christ's descent among the dead, according to which he triumphantly preaches the good news of redemption to the just souls awaiting redemption, destroys the power of death, and throws open the gates of heaven. Holy Saturday, Balthasar suggests, is not Christ's victorious entrance into the underworld, but his utterly dead solidarity with sinners. Obedient to the Father as the expression of God's utterly gracious love for sinners, Christ has identified himself completely with them and their sin. Knowing only that the Father wishes this of him as an expression of God's boundless love for the world, Christ dies as one of them, a sinner, abandoned by God. As God's Son, he experiences the "hell" of the Father's absence in a way impossible for any other person. At the same time, as the one who "descends into hell," Jesus is the expression of the radical unwillingness of God to abandon sinners, even where by definition God cannot be, insofar as hell means the utter and obstinate rejection of God.[76]

> And exactly in that way he disturbs the absolute loneliness striven for by the sinner: the sinner, who wants to be "damned" apart from God, finds God again in his loneliness, but God in the absolute weakness of love who unfathomably in the period of nontime enters into solidarity with those damning themselves. The words of the Psalm, "If I make my bed in the netherworld, thou art there" (Ps. 139:8), thereby take on a totally new meaning.[77]

On Holy Saturday, God erects the cross in hell and shows us the unimaginable depths of God's love and fidelity. In this way, Balthasar suggests, "the

---

74. *Dare We Hope,* 212, quoting Hans-Jürgen Verweyen.

75. See "Abstieg zur Hölle," in *Pneuma und Institution,* 400; *Mysterium Paschale,* 148-88; *Theodramatik,* 4.243-93.

76. Here I have not considered an extremely unusual theory suggested at least once by Balthasar, that hell is ultimately the place not for sinners but for the "unusable remainder" of *sin itself,* separated from sinners by the power of the cross, thus making hell a "gift of divine grace." See *Theodramatik,* 4.287f., 293.

77. *The Von Balthasar Reader,* ed. Medard Kehl and Werner Loser (New York: Crossroad, 1982), 153 (translated excerpt from "Abstieg zur Hölle").

one who has timelessly closed himself off is opened up through the inescapable presence of another, who is just as timelessly near him and calls his presumptuous, seeming unapproachability into question."[78]

Balthasar draws out the consequence of this for the believer in a meditation or suggestion rather than in a theory. Perhaps the vision of the crucified, who is willing to pay any price to be with the sinner, the one who would completely reject him — perhaps this vision of love, greater than which cannot be conceived, is capable of melting the heart of even the hardened sinner.[79] Thus, suggests Balthasar, God, in the visage of the crucified Son, may have ways of moving even the most obdurate human will, not in a way which would deny or overrun human freedom by force, but could in weakness persuade and compel "in his solidarity from within with those who reject all solidarity."[80] For Balthasar this is possible because human freedom is not absolutely autonomous but relative: it is founded upon, and exists within, the mystery of Christ's freedom, in particular, his free self-identification with sinners.[81] Thus what seems for finite freedom to be a definitive rejection of God need not be evaluated by God as definitive. Such a decision cannot be simply overturned or overpowered from the outside but in such a way that God "accompanies the human person to the most extreme situation of this (negative) choice. This is what happens in the passion of Jesus."[82]

What is happening here is not a "theoretical" judgment about two truths: finite human freedom (and its ability to say "no" to God) vs. infinite divine freedom (which, having no such ability to reject the creature, has offered itself in forgiving love as the world's salvation). On the theoretical plane, there would seem to be two truths, neither of which may be sacrificed.[83] The issue which

---

78. *Theodramatik*, 4.286.

79. In literature, Balthasar finds an example of such power to persuade in the final "conversion" of Raskolnikoff through the presence of Sonja in Dostoyevsky's *Crime and Punishment*. See *Theodramatik*, 4.285f.

80. *Reader*, 153. For this reason, Balthasar calls hell a "christological place" where the sinner realizes that "this (like me) God-forsaken one is so for my sake. In this situation one can no longer speak of any overpowering if, to the one who has chosen (maybe one should say: thinks he has chosen) the complete loneliness of being-only-for-oneself, God himself enters into his very loneliness as someone who is even more lonely" (422).

81. Citing Adrienne von Speyr, Balthasar suggests that human beings are not infinitely free: "they are free within the greater freedom of God" (*Theodramatik*, 4.258).

82. *Reader*, 152f.

83. Balthasar makes no effort to resolve this tension. He stresses the fact that human freedom is finite and relative with respect to God's infinite freedom but also the fact that it is real: God "does not overrule, pressure, or coerce with the omnipotence of his absolute freedom the precarious freedom of the creature" (*Reader*, 422). Presuming that this is more than just rhetoric, two words are important here: omnipotence and precarious. It would seem that, for Balthasar, part of the "precarious" nature of human freedom is the questionableness of its ability to definitively reject God, not because of divine "brute force" but because of the far greater compelling "power" of God's loving self-surrender in powerlessness.

presents itself for "practical" judgment is concrete in the cross of Christ, more specifically in the mystery of Holy Saturday. There, suggests Balthasar, divine love shows a power which would seem irresistible. Or to put it more carefully: it seems infinitely more probable that the love which reveals itself so radically in the mystery of Holy Saturday has a compelling power (in weakness!) to change the heart of any sinner.[84]

At the end of *A Short Discourse on Hell*, Balthasar tells us that his position is more exactly expressed by Edith Stein, who also will not in principle dismiss the possibility that the free human will can remain perpetually closed to the divine love. However, because of the nature of this love, she argues, "[i]n reality it can become infinitely improbable" for this to occur. Her argument is based on the efficacy of prevenient grace. Grace, she points out, can and does enter the human heart unsought; it must be already present in order to prepare human freedom even to do the good. Thus, it can steal into the heart of the sinner as well, winning ground and repelling the effects of sin. "And to this process of displacement there are, in principle, no limits. . . . Human freedom can be neither broken nor neutralized by divine freedom, but it may well be, so to speak, outwitted. The descent of grace to the human soul is a free act of divine love. And there are *no limits* to how far it may extend."[85]

Precisely because Balthasar repeatedly and explicitly states that he does not espouse or present a theory of apocatastasis, he goes no further and can go no further than this. Thus, he clearly wishes to push a theology of Christian hope to its very limits, a hope which is universal, free from every form of particularism and elitism, a hope which, Paul assures us, "does not disappoint" (Rom. 5:5).[86]

A Question about Human Freedom

As we have seen, contemporary Catholic theologians, following official Church teaching, hold that hell is a real possibility which each person must take seriously, even while emphasizing the hope that we may and must have for the salvation of all men and women. This is because human freedom is viewed as capable of rejecting God finally and irrevocably. Still, as far as I can determine, this view of freedom, while clearly presupposed by doctrinal pronouncements concerning universal salvation and the existence of hell, has itself not been the object of dogmatic definition. Most contemporary Catholic theologians have cautiously begun to raise questions about the nature of human freedom and about some of

---

84. Compare *Dare We Hope*, 210.

85. Cited by Balthasar, *Dare We Hope*, 219-21.

86. *Theodramatik*, 4.293. For Balthasar, such hope does not simply dispose of the real fear that the sinner must have of judgment, since in every life there has been sin, and sin is something worthy of damnation.

the traditional presuppositions regarding it. Both Balthasar and Rahner, for example, have insisted that the human "yes" and "no" to God are not on the same level. As a conclusion to this study, I would like to focus on human freedom and push these insights further by asking whether or not there are reasons for doubting that human freedom can truly reach final, that is, eternal definitiveness in the state of rejecting God. I believe that there are. And if there are good reasons to question the presuppositions concerning human freedom which lie behind the Church's doctrinal pronouncements regarding the existence of hell, it may be possible to speak to the issue of apocatastasis in a new and positive way.[87]

The place to begin is with Rahner's own insistence that human freedom's "no" to God cannot be simply a parallel alternative to a "yes" to God. This seems to imply that freedom is not merely a neutral capacity for definitiveness and finality (in either a yet unspecified "yes" or "no" to God). We may recall that for Rahner, the human person is "the event of a free, unmerited and forgiving, and absolute self-communication of God."[88] This means that human beings are created expressly as the ones upon whom God freely bestows God's own self in love. Therefore, it would seem to be more accurate to say that human freedom is simply and most radically the capacity for God, not the capacity for *either* God *or* something else. Human freedom is created for one end alone: God. Only God finally "defines" the human person. Therefore, it would seem that human freedom can attain real finality only when it reaches the definitiveness for which it is specifically created. I am suggesting that the definitiveness and finality about which Rahner and others speak is not merely a "formal" characteristic of human freedom but, more importantly, is, in a certain sense, the "matter" or "content" of freedom's divinely willed end. Human freedom is the "capacity for the eternal"[89] not simply as a neutral *capacity* of choice which can become finalized, as opposed to remaining forever revisable. It is quite specifically a *capacity for* the eternity who is God. Human freedom becomes finally and irrevocably definitive only in God, because only in God can it really enter into eternity. As long as human freedom freely rejects God, it would fail to attain that definitiveness and finality for which it was destined.[90]

87. In an interview a few years before his death, Rahner himself remarked that he "would still like to have written something about such a teaching on apocatastasis that would be orthodox and acceptable." See Leo J. O'Donovan, S.J., "Living into Mystery. Karl Rahner's Reflections at 75," *America* (March 10, 1979): 179.

88. *Foundations*, 116.

89. "Theology of Freedom," in *Theological Investigations* 6 (New York: Seabury, 1974), 178-96, esp. 186.

90. In describing the "bad act of freedom," Rahner notes that "God has not created freedom as the possibility of the creative positing by a subject of what is good and evil but as the possibility of creatively positing what is good." The bad act of freedom, therefore, "fails to attain the most proper and innermost nature of freedom itself" ("Guilt," 210). Is there not reason to suppose that final definitiveness belongs to the "proper and innermost nature of freedom," which bad freedom precisely fails to attain?

One could imagine that freedom could persist in such a decision *indefinitely* without for that reason attributing eternal definitiveness to it: it would persist, quite literally, *nondefinitely*. In this sense, one could say that the human person can "decide against God forever,"[91] but that would be something like a state of lasting indefiniteness or nondefinitiveness, not an eternally fixed negative. Moreover, its persistence in a stance of rejection would have to be something which at every moment was an active "effort" against the power of God's inviting, forgiving love, something quite different from the final "rest" of human freedom which freely and finally surrenders to the power of that love.[92]

The fact that during their lives human beings can and do reject God in sin cannot be denied. Because this is so, Rahner is correct to insist that during our lifetime, freedom in the theological sense is always a freedom to say "yes" or "no" to God.[93] However, I do not see that it follows that human beings can finally and definitively — eternally — say "no" to God simply because they can say "no" to God in particular actions or because they can finally and definitively say "yes" to God. This is where I think we must hold a basic "asymmetry." Once human freedom wholeheartedly chooses God, it becomes finally definitive by sharing in God's own eternity. It is the "yes" to God, and this "yes" alone, which makes human freedom eternally definitive in the strict sense. It cannot then not choose God.

It seems to me that the real "point" of Christian doctrine and hope concerning the end is precisely the eternity of salvation: that the blessed really do, finally and irrevocably, reach life and fulfillment in God, beyond every power

91. *Foundations*, 435, here in a sense different, of course, from Rahner's.

92. Several theologians, including Rahner and Balthasar, argue that hell cannot be called "eternal" in the same sense that heaven is eternal, although not in the way that I am suggesting. Balthasar, for example, speaks of hell as everlasting, never-ending duration, "complete withdrawal to the point of shriveling into a disconsolate immovable now," which is utterly absent of opportunity, future, and desire. Heaven, on the other hand, implies the "highest-possible development" within the "absolute vitality of God" (*Dare We Hope*, 133). Of course, Origen, like the Apologists before him, had already argued that human beings can only become "eternal" in God (Christ), since apart from God nothing is eternal (see Müller, "Origenes," 185). It seems possible to me to conceive of human freedom remaining unfixed and therefore subject to change and conversion so long as it does not rest fully in God. One need not think of another life-"time" *after* death in which human freedom has another opportunity to think of a "moment" of encounter which cannot be quantified, not yet eternal, but a transition, a "time" which involves some kind of duration, though not like the time of this world. Compare Ratzinger, *Eschatology*, 230.

The event of death itself could be conceived of as such a process, the entrance of the "time" of a person's whole life into eternity. In this sense, the person would remain somehow in that process of death until that "time" when he or she fully embraced God. It seems conceivable that a person could freely persist in such a state, a very "shadowy" world to be sure, and yet would all the while be capable of turning to the Lord and finally embracing the divine love. This suggestion calls into question not the possibility of rejecting God completely, but the possibility of rejecting God irrevocably and definitively. On the closely related problem of purgatory, see Rahner's unusual suggestions in "Purgatory," in *Theological Investigations* 19 (New York: Crossroad, 1983), 181-93.

93. *Foundations*, 99f.

of sin and death. The definitiveness and finality of salvation must be the point and center of Christian eschatology in a way which the nature of "damnation" should not be. The definitiveness and finality of salvation do not logically or factually depend upon or imply the definitiveness and finality of its opposite.

Another consideration which leads me to question the "eternity" of hell, closely connected with what has just been said, has to do with the significance of final judgment in the process by which human freedom reaches definitiveness and finality. The finality which human freedom is ultimately directed toward, like the very possibility of freedom itself, is a gift from God and something which, in the end, is not achieved but received.

It is just in this line of thought that Rahner presents his theology of judgment. There are two important points which manifest its dialectic nature. (1) Human freedom necessarily involves a process of self-definition and self-judgment precisely as the actualization of a fundamental and final stance for or against God. God's judgment (together with "reward" or "punishment") is not merely an additional, extrinsic act of God in relation to such self-judgment. (2) Nonetheless, because human freedom is created and utterly dependent upon God as its source and goal, no human being is capable of making an absolute and final self-judgment. That belongs to God's judgment alone. Therefore, human freedom is created for and called to a finality for which it is truly responsible but which it cannot achieve by itself. It must, in the end, be received in God's final judgment.

With respect to the first point, Rahner points out that throughout life, in all the particular concrete decisions which we make in freedom, we are always taking a stand for or against God and our own truest selves. This, the Scriptures remind us with particular force, is true especially in terms of the way we treat our neighbor, especially the least of the brothers and sisters. In the most fundamental sense, God has already judged the world and the human race. The Christ event is God's judgment of love and mercy in the face of the world's desperate slavery to sin and death. The place where judgment is yet to occur is in our own actions. By what we do, we judge ourselves, in the sense that we are adopting a stance vis-à-vis the God who has already revealed a final word of love to us.

No single choice or action, nor the sum of them all, can constitute a final decision before God, since each decision we make is in principle revisable. According to Rahner and others, a "fundamental option" is something which takes shape in and through the individual, concrete decisions made during the course of a lifetime as a whole and becomes definitive and finally manifest in the process of death.[94] But the critical question is precisely whether or not such a final option has final, lasting significance. If it does, how does it attain such significance? The decisive meaning of death for the Christian lies fundamentally

94. See "Guilt," 203ff.; "Freedom," 186.

in the conviction that, in Christ, death is not only the end or whole of a life but the transition to final transformation and fulfillment of life.[95] The fact that the whole of a (past) human lifetime manifests a fundamental decision does not of itself imply that such a decision has a real future. This is precisely why Christian faith speaks of judgment (which must be seen in inner unity with the resurrection of the dead) as God's action.

This brings us to the second point. Human freedom, though it tends towards a definitive and final stance vis-à-vis God as the form of its own personhood (its very being or not), cannot attain this finality on its own. This is, of course, evident during life, when human decisions are in principle neither completely self-evident nor irreversible. According to Rahner, no one can "adequately reflect objectively and with absolute certainty on his free decisions" and for that reason Catholic doctrine has always insisted that one cannot make a certain judgment about one's state before God, even though it is true that one does "come ever closer" to one's finality in freedom and as a conscious subject.[96] Such a judgment belongs to God alone: "The total decision in which man finally disposes of the whole of his reality, i.e., posits this totality itself in its freely determined finality, is according to revelation subject to the sole judgment of God."[97]

The point Rahner wishes to make seems to be that while we do make real choices vis-à-vis God in our concrete actions, we cannot know with absolute certitude the real depth and implication of anything we do. This does not relieve us of responsibility for our actions, nor can one avoid making practical judgments about what one has done and, consequently, about what direction one's life is taking. But such judgments about oneself and others are at best provisional.

Nothing makes this clearer than human mortality itself. It is not simply a question of the degree of our knowledge about our decisions. It is finally a question of our mortality. Precisely because of death, the human person does not and cannot come to finality by virtue of a radically (one-sided) autonomous decision but only by virtue of God's final act of judgment.[98] It is only because God comes to us and receives us in death that there can be any talk of finality and finally fulfilled identity. This is where the biblical doctrine of resurrection is an important corrective to the notion of a "natural" and "neutral" immortality of the soul.[99]

But what is the nature of God's judgment? If there were nothing more to final judgment than the finalizing of our own "fundamental option," if that

---

95. Rahner, "Purgatory," 187; Kehl, *Eschatologie,* 262.
96. "Freedom," 191.
97. "Guilt," 204.
98. "Freedom," 191. Compare Breuning, "Zur Lehre," 31.
99. In another context Rahner notes that the "eschatological idea of Christianity" sees "survival from God . . . and not as emerging from history" ("Purgatory," 189).

event were nothing more than the divine declaration that what we have freely made of our life will be so for eternity, if the process of Christian dying were nothing more than a "freezing" of what we have already accomplished (or failed to accomplish!), then the gospel would hardly be good news and we should approach death and judgment with horror. But strictly speaking, God's final judgment can only be the final future fullness of God's forgiving, life-giving judgment in the cross and resurrection of Christ. It cannot be merely a neutral "taking stock"; it is an expression of God's real victory over sin and death, in which anything and everything which has been done in love is saved and perfected by God. Thus, God's final act is a *life-giving* judgment which forgives, heals, purifies, and bestows fullness, and, *therefore*, finality upon human life, that final identity for which it was created and toward which it is directed.[100] Human freedom is able to say "yes" to God finally and definitively only because of God's grace, finally at work in the transforming, perfecting act of judgment. In a way similar to the "quasi-formal causality" which, according to Rahner, already characterizes the operation of grace throughout life, the final, gracious act of judgment on God's part is truly creative of the finality for which human life longs. It does not create it out of nothing, but it fashions it from the "material" of a free history which has been lived by the creature, the unity in difference of its individual free actions and its fundamental option for God.[101] It makes no sense to think of God's final action as bringing a person's freely chosen "no" to God to some kind of fullness and final definitiveness. Sin is a horrible reality, but God does not "raise it up" and "save" it for eternity. And it makes little sense to imagine God as simply abandoning the sinner to his or her "no" — just as it makes no sense to imagine that "the saved" are merely confirmed in the state of their imperfect "yes" to God. It makes more sense to suppose that God can bring only a freely chosen human "yes" — only that which is of love, however small, tentative, and fragile — to fullness and, therefore, to definitiveness and finality. In a certain sense, therefore, grace alone is finally definitive and finalizing of the human person and for the human person.

Perhaps one should be content to speak of the indefinite (and so, nondefinite!) persistence or endurance of a free "no" to God, but not of its finality or eternity. As long as human freedom tries to refuse God, it fails to reach the finality for which it is created, for this finality comes not from human freedom in itself, but from and in God. Until human freedom has chosen God, it has not found its way to finality, and therefore cannot be said to be in a definitive,

---

100. See Rahner, "Purgatory," 187: The believer submits to death in the hope that "he falls then into the hands of an infinite, loving God who brings everything to perfection, even though (as far as our experience goes) we surrender ourselves to him as imperfect beings." Compare Kehl, *Eschatologie*, 283ff., who understands the final event of consummation, in its different aspects of judgment, purgatory, and heaven, as a single process of finally coming to one's true identity through God's action. Compare Breuning, "Systematische Entfaltung," 860.

101. See Rahner, "Guilt," 204.

absolutely irrevocable stance against God. Perhaps it can be said that it is yet bound in the realm and process of death.

Conclusion

We have seen that there is a clear consensus among Catholic theologians today in their treatment of the notion of apocatastasis and the problem of hell. Christian faith proclaims the reality of the universal salvation revealed and accomplished by God in the death and the resurrection of Christ. The real possibility of hell is understood by most to be an expression of the Christian belief in the ultimate seriousness and responsibility of the freedom with which God has endowed humanity. God's offer must be freely accepted; no one can be saved against his or her will.

A properly Christian universalism emphasizes that God wills salvation for all men and women and somehow effectively offers it to them, even where there is no explicit knowledge of Christ or belief in God. It may not be said that only a preordained number will be saved, and certainly not that some are preordained to be damned. Likewise, it may not be said that even one person is already or will in fact be damned. All that may and must be believed is that the salvation of the world is a reality already begun and established in Christ. Such a faith expresses itself most consistently in the hope that because of the gracious love of God, whose power far surpasses human sin, all men and women will in fact freely and finally surrender to God in love and be saved.

When Balthasar speaks of the duty to hope for the salvation of all, he is articulating the broad consensus of current theologians and the best of the Catholic tradition. Like other theologians, notably Rahner,[102] he intentionally pushes his position to the limit, insisting that such a hope is not merely possible but well founded. There is a fundamental "asymmetry" between God's grace and human sin, between a human "yes" to God and a possible "no" to God. While completely convinced that God's gracious self-offer must be accepted in freedom if saving grace is to be efficacious, and that human freedom is indeed capable of such a response,[103] I have tried to show that the presumption that human freedom entails a capacity to reject God definitively and eternally seems questionable. And, although this presumption enjoys the weight of the authority of Scripture and tradition, it would seem incorrect to consider this possibility

---

102. See M. Carmel McEnroy, "A Rahnerian Contribution Towards an Orthodox Theology of Apokatastasis" (Ph.D. diss., Toronto: University of St. Michael's College, 1984). Of special interest is a letter from Rahner on the subject (Appendix A, 438f.).

103. Rahner once pointed out that the salvation of the human person "never takes place without the involvement of this person and the involvement of his freedom," for a "salvation not achieved in freedom cannot be salvation." See *Foundations*, 147. I am not questioning the necessary role of human freedom in salvation, but raising a question concerning its nature and scope.

as an object of faith in the same sense that the ability of human freedom in grace to choose God is an object of faith.

It is often objected that a doctrine of universal salvation undermines Christian faith in individual human freedom and final accountability; it doesn't matter what one does in the end since God will make everything right. If one views human freedom according to the suggestions I have made above, I believe that the final responsibility and accountability of human persons is affirmed, not denied. But, in any case, it seems to me that current stress in theology on the hope for universal salvation can counteract the individualistic and juridical conceptions of freedom, accountability, and judgment of previous ages and help us to view human freedom and its salvation in fundamentally communal terms. As *Lumen gentium* reminds us, Christian faith and hope look for the "restoration of all things," when the "human race as well as the entire world . . . will be perfectly re-established in Christ," and not merely the salvation of individual souls.[104] In a real sense, none of us reaches that perfect destiny for which God has created us until all of us enter into God's Kingdom.

A properly understood teaching about the hope that we must have for the salvation of all is needed today, especially in view of the growing fundamentalism, sectarianism, and integralism both within and without the Christian churches. Unfortunately, history shows all too well that once one preaches the existence of hell with the same force as the existence of heaven, one is all too ready to populate it with those whom one condemns and then gives up on. After Judas, Hitler, and Stalin, why not other groups one may find reprehensible: terrorists, abortionists, atheists, or gays. As Hans-Jürgan Verweyen writes: "Whoever reckons with the possibility of even only *one* person's being lost besides himself is hardly able to love unreservedly. . . . Just the slightest nagging thought of a final hell for others tempts us, in moments in which human togetherness becomes especially difficult, to leave the other to himself."[105]

Finally, a doctrine concerning the obligation to hope for the salvation of all has an important ethical imperative: we must truly live what we hope for. Thus the hope about which we have been speaking is not merely a hope that all will be restored at some final point, but that already here and now, all men and women are being saved. This hope, then, demands a certain posture not only with respect to future fulfillment, but also to present life. Do I live here and now as one who hopes that all are being saved? Hope for the salvation of all requires that radical love and solidarity in our relations with others which Christians recognize on the cross of Christ. It expresses itself in active discipleship which labors for the universal communion of love and justice which God has always intended for the world.

104. *Lumen gentium*, 48.
105. Quoted in Balthasar, *Dare We Hope*, 211.

Wrath That Endures Forever

WILLIAM V. CROCKETT

Universalists commonly talk about the love of God that endures forever. They often argue that since God is love he will eventually draw all humanity to himself. Further, they cite Paul's letters as evidence that even the apostle assumed God loves all his creation, wicked and righteous, with an everlasting love. Whatever the merits of the philosophical argument — that God to be God must always love his creation — this article challenges the latter assumption that Paul believed God always loves. Rather, it will be argued that the apostle assumed that once the wicked portion of humanity was under eschatological wrath, God would withdraw his love from the wicked.[1]

I. The Wrath of God

Paul uses many words to denote God's anger. The most serious is *orgē* ("wrath") because in Pauline theology, as we shall see, it expresses the utter hopelessness of the wicked in the face of an angry God.

Other Pauline words such as *apobolē* ("rejection"), *apotomia* ("sternness"), *ekkathairō* ("cleanse"), *epitimia* ("punishment") and *echthros* ("enemy") indi-

1. Usually particularism is tied to the concept of an eternal, conscious hell. Particularism, however, can be expressed in other ways. Annihilation of the wicked at or some time after death, for example, might be a preferable belief to a particularist than endless punishment in hell. Annihilation has been espoused by C. Pinnock, "Fire, Then Nothing," *Christianity Today* 31 (1987): 40-41; E. W. Fudge, *The Fire that Consumes: A Biblical and Historical Study of Final Punishment* (Fallbrook: Verdict, 1982). But just as there are distinctions within the scope of particularism, there is one common agreement: The wicked are excluded from salvation. This article argues that Paul was a particularist and that in the end the wicked will be separated eternally from the righteous.

Reprinted with permission of the author of the article and the editor of the *Journal of the Evangelical Theological Society* 34 (June 1991): 195-202.

cate anger but have more breadth. Unlike *orgē*, these words are often used by Paul in a way that suggests that salvation still lies within the grasp of the unrepentant even though God is angry with their behavior.

For example, in Rom. 11:15 Paul talks about God's plan to save the world. He says of Israel, "For if their rejection *(apobolē)* is the reconciliation of the world, what will their acceptance be but life from the dead?" Here Paul hints that those rejected might eventually be accepted. In 11:22-23 Paul's use of *apotomia* in relation to the unbelieving allows for hope even though God is said to be a stern Father: "Consider therefore the kindness and sternness *(apotomia)* of God: sternness to those who fell, but kindness to you, provided that you continue in his kindness. Otherwise, you also will be cut off. And if they do not persist in unbelief, they will be grafted in." Here again hope surfaces for eventual salvation.

These terms for anger differ significantly from Paul's use of "wrath" *(orgē)*. When he applies eschatological *orgē* to unbelievers he intends it to be final, but when he uses parallel terms for *orgē*, such as "rejection" or "sternness," his terms are more flexible. Sometimes they are final, yet often they allow for hope even in the face of unbelief. So "sternness" in Rom. 11:22-23 allows for the reversal of faith: Those who enjoy kindness might in the end receive sternness, and those under sternness, perhaps kindness.[2]

The point is that while parallel terms allow for hope, *orgē* does not. When Paul wishes to stress the fierce anger of God and the utter hopelessness of the wicked he uses *orgē*. He chooses this term to underscore the fact that in the *eschaton* rebellious sinners have no hope of salvation. They will be taken from the presence of God and the righteous and placed, in effect, beyond the pale of God's love. The righteous go the way of life, the wicked the way of death.

In Paul's letters *orgē* is used in two ways: (1) He talks about wrath already at work in the present age (Rom. 1:18-32; Eph. 4:17-19; 1 Thess. 2:16); (2) he specifies an eschatological wrath to fall on the wicked in the age to come (Rom. 2:5, 8; 1 Thess. 1:10; 5:9).[3] In the present age God pours out *orgē* on rebellious men and women who continually reject his ways. God "gives them over" to their sinful desires (Rom. 1:24, 26, 28). "Those who do such things," says Paul, "deserve death" (1:32). In the age to come the outpouring of *orgē* takes place

---

2. Much the same may be said about parallel words such as *ekkathairō* ("clean out," 1 Cor. 5:10), *epitimia* ("punishment," 2 Cor. 2:6), *echthros* ("enemy," Rom. 5:10; 11:28). Other negative terms for wrath seem less hopeful because of their contexts: *adokimos* ("worthless," Rom. 1:28); *anathema* ("cursed," Gal. 1:8-9; cf. Rom. 9:3); *dikē* ("punishment," 2 Thess. 1:9); *thlipsis* ("suffering," 2 Thess. 1:6-7); *katakrinō* ("condemn," 1 Cor. 11:32).

3. Paul's other references to *orgē* are ambiguous. We cannot tell whether they refer to present or final wrath (Rom. 3:5; 4:15; 5:9; 9:22; 12:19; Eph. 2:3; 5:6; Col. 3:6). Also, Paul uses another word *(thymos)* for divine wrath, but only in Rom. 2:8, and there it is coupled with *orgē*. Elsewhere in Paul *thymos* refers to human anger (2 Cor. 12:20; Gal. 5:20; Eph. 4:31; Col. 3:8).

at the end during the complex of events known as the "day of wrath" (Rom. 2:5, 8), commencing, it appears, with the wrath of the Parousia (1 Thess. 1:10; 5:9).

II. Punishment and Reformation

To establish whether Paul allows for hope in his use of *orgē* we must decide whether he thinks eschatological *orgē* punishes or reforms. If it punishes, then wrath is final and there is no appeal for the wicked; they are cut off from God's love. If it reforms, then wrath functions as a part of his love. God loves his creation, and while his anger may endure for a time and seem like punishment, it is always constructive, ultimately producing good for his creation.

Naturally it is difficult to discuss punishment and reformation in Pauline theology without some reference to the wider issues generally raised in this kind of discussion. Always in the background the practical questions of fairness arise. To say that God exacts retribution from the wicked following death seems unworthy of a God of love. Conceivably Paul was struck by the same thought. H. H. Farmer, for example, thinks it madness to suggest that the divine love will dispatch vast numbers of persons to everlasting damnation. He wonders how God's love should be viewed were some of his creation to fall irretrievably into hell, or were they to be annihilated. For Farmer, such a fate might be considered a victory of sorts if the God under consideration were a God primarily of justice, but for a God "who is primarily love it could only be the most absolute form of defeat."[4] In effect, it becomes a first-class Pyrrhic victory: A part of God's creation is destroyed, their destruction diminishes the joy of the redeemed, and the divine love appears to suffer a grievous defeat.

If eschatological wrath operates retributively,[5] it offers no recourse for the wicked in hell. It only punishes, and this would seem to diminish God as a God of love. Endless retributive wrath — whether it be annihilation or hell — seems incompatible with a loving God. Wrath is therefore said not to be retributive at all, but God's chastening response to disobedience. Simply put, wrath is not the opposite of God's love; it is an element of his love. So perhaps even in Paul's theology wrath should be viewed as an aspect of divine love designed to lead rebellious ones to repentance, not as a fixed, unalterable condition. Postmortem punishment, then, would be a painful process, but one that would correct, leading to the betterment and purification of souls.[6]

4. H. H. Farmer, *The World and God: A Study of Prayer, Providence and Miracle in Christian Experience* (London, 1935), 255; *God and Men* (New York: Abingdon-Cokesbury, 1947), 169.

5. By retribution, I mean punishment, whether in the form of annihilation or an eternal conscious hell.

6. Origen, *Against Celsus* 5.15; 6.25; Gregory of Nyssa, *Dialog on the Soul and Resurrection; The Catechetical Oration* 8.26, 35; John Scotus Erigena, *On the Division of Nature* 5.31-32.

If we wanted an example of how reformative wrath might work, we could cite the seventeenth-century Cambridge Platonists Peter Sterry and Jeremiah White. They described God's wrath as a consuming love, a raging fire that "burns upon sin and opposition" until the impurities of the soul evaporate in the flames of love. To evangelicals this might sound like a candy-coated dilution of Paul's theology, but Sterry and White insisted that in reality God's wrath is none other than simple reforming love. Direct contact with this kind of love would not be easy for the wicked. Divine love would produce bliss in the saved, but for the rebellious it would produce unspeakable agony — until ultimately salvation was achieved.[7]

All will acknowledge, I think, that a doctrine of reformative wrath is attractive; it has the advantage of making God's wrath seem purposeful. God is not a cosmic maniac gleefully extracting retribution from the fallen part of creation for no purpose at all, except perhaps for revenge. God is above mindless anger. His wrath is good and just, designed to reform and reclaim. Certainly he is angry with sin and rebellion, and severe judgment will indeed fall on unrepentant sinners. But unbridled anger is not his way. He loves all his creation — even in his anger.

Yet when we examine *orgē* in Paul we find no reason to assume that it has reformative elements. For example, Paul begins and concludes his first letter to the Thessalonians with words of encouragement about the eternal hope believers have in Jesus (1 Thess. 1:4-10; 4:13–5:11). He also gravely warns of the coming wrath that will engulf unbelievers. But there is no thought of reformation for the wicked. They receive only wrath (1:10; 5:9). In 5:1-11 Paul makes a sharp distinction between the fates of the wicked, calling one the sons of light and the other the sons of darkness. Those of the day will have eternal peace, but those of the night will be destroyed by the wrath *(orgē)* of God (5:3, 9). If a universalist argues that wrath is chastening anger in Paul, then he needs to show why *orgē* should be understood as reformation — especially since there is no occasion when the apostle uses *orgē* in a reformative sense.[8] *Orgē* appears to be unrelenting anger without any connotation of reformative love.

If Paul understands God's *orgē* not as a chastening, reforming love that eventually leads to salvation but as unrelenting punishment, then it makes little sense to say that God still loves the wicked after they have been annihilated or while they burn in everlasting hell. (At least, our use of the word "love" in this context would differ radically from any ordinary understanding of the word.) If Paul thinks hell is eternal punishment, then it seems reasonable to say that once the wicked are under eschatological wrath God is finished with them. They are cut off from his love.

7. D. P. Walker, *The Decline of Hell: Seventeenth-Century Discussions of Eternal Torment* (London, 1964), 105-15; E. H. Plumptre, *The Spirits in Prison and Other Studies on the Life after Death* (London: Isbister, 1884), 192-93.

8. See n. 13 below.

III. Divine Wrath: The Opposite of Love

The challenge facing particularists is to show why eschatological wrath should be understood as eternal punishment, whether it be annihilation or an everlasting hell. If there is no reason to assume that eschatological wrath extends eternally, then perhaps universalists are right: God loves his creation infinitely, and — after an appropriate duration of punishment for certain wicked ones — he will restore all humanity to himself.

Equally, the challenge facing universalists is to show why *orgē* should be understood in any other way than the common meaning of the word. If in Paul *orgē* is said to have the additional meaning of "wrath that reforms," then some basis for this interpretation must be provided. Short of appealing to the cosmic reconciliation texts, there seems to be little reason to think that *orgē* reforms the wicked in the afterlife.

Of course, the reformation interpretation is advanced by the fact that God is love. Did Paul think God loves — now and forever — all the people he created, and would he ever act contrary to the ultimate welfare of his creatures? Some say that God will always love his creatures, that his love is sovereign. To them, divine love should not be limited by divine wrath, nor should it be considered parallel to wrath, justice or man's freedom. Wrath and justice are not on the same level as God's love; they are manifestations of that love. J. A. T. Robinson writes: "[Wrath and justice] are but ways in which such love must show itself to be in the face of its denial."[9] So when faced with rebellious children, God chastens in order to reform — just the way a parent might punish a child he (or she) loves. God's love is eternal and sovereign, and his love for every human being, rebellious or not, is incontrovertible. In the end, says Robinson, "God is the eternal 'Yea.' "[10]

Robinson's point is well founded, at least, in preexilic OT writings. Not always opposites, love and wrath are at times inseparable. W. Eichrodt calls this "love concealed in wrath."[11] Prior to the exile God's people are most often the recipients of his wrath.[12] But after the exile God's wrath "increasingly centered on the heathen and unfaithful in the community."[13] The wrath of God prior to the exile was largely intended to reform God's people. Afterwards it still retained a sense of reformation, but more and more it operated retributively (punishing rather than reforming). The focus of God's anger shifted, therefore, from chasten-

9. J. A. T. Robinson, *In the End God* (New York: Harper, 1968), 115.

10. J. A. T. Robinson, "Universalism — Is It Heretical?" *Scottish Journal of Theology* 2 (1949): 145.

11. W. Eichrodt, *Theology of the Old Testament* (OTL; Philadelphia: Westminster, 1961), 1.288.

12. Ibid., 464-67; J. Fichtner, *TDNT* 5.397-409.

13. C. J. Roetzel, *Judgement in the Community: A Study of the Relationship Between Eschatology and Eccesiology in Paul* (Leiden: Brill, 1972), following Eichrodt, *Theology*, 1.268-69.

ing Israel in the hope of bringing about repentance to punishing Israel's enemies — both the heathen outside the camp and unfaithful Jews within.

Paul understands God's wrath in a similar postexilic manner. He believes that at the close of the age divine *orgē* will fall only on unbelievers. Believers have been rescued from the *orgē* of God (Rom. 5:9; 1 Thess. 1:10). To be sure, judgment begins at the house of God, and believers who sin may sometimes endure trials in their earthly life (1 Cor. 5:5; 11:27-32). But in Paul's theology the "wrath of God" (*orgē theou*) is reserved for unbelievers. It is far more serious than any chastenings believers might endure. Chastenings reform, but wrath destroys.

Moreover, *orgē* in Paul excludes any notion of divine love. When he speaks of wrath, and especially eschatological wrath, he never hints that it is a manifestation of God's love leading to improvement or repentance. In fact, divine wrath appears to be the opposite of God's love. It does not have that preexilic function of being the austere curtain that conceals God's love. One looks in vain for a remedial use of *orgē*. Paul never suggests that God's *orgē* leads the wicked to repentance, as if it were a chastening anger designed for the good of the recipient.

But it would be a mistake to assume that Paul's use of *orgē* is always final. An exception can be found in Eph. 2:3: "We were by nature objects of wrath" (cf. 5:6). Here "God, who is rich in mercy" (2:4), loves those who were once "objects of wrath." Note that "wrath" in the expression "objects of wrath" is not final, and hence we cannot say that Paul chooses the word *orgē* only when he wants to designate those forever beyond God's love.

This text, however, does not suggest that God's wrath reforms sinners by inducing repentance. Nor does it imply that wrath conceals God's love, as if wrath ultimately brought good to the recipients, or as if it were an instrument designed to draw erring ones back to himself. *Orgē* here, as elsewhere in Paul, is true anger that does not include nuances of love. Indeed, it is the opposite of love.

The point is that the objects of wrath once lived like the rest of mankind, but no longer. Now "because of his great love for [them]" (2:4) they have been "saved, through faith" (2:8). In this text wrath is not the way God demonstrates his love in the face of rebellion, as Robinson thinks (at least when he thinks generally about the nature of God). Wrath does not function as part of God's love. Rather, it runs parallel to his love. God still loves those with whom he is angry, and when his grace is met with faith, objects of wrath receive the gift of God: salvation. Those under wrath who have no faith but continue in disobedience eventually find themselves under God's eschatological wrath, which in Paul is always final.[14]

---

14. In Rom. 13:4-5 Paul uses the word *orgē* specifically for believers. But, as with Eph. 2:3, the wrath forms no part of God's love and has no sense of remediation. Another text, Rom. 3:5, asks whether "God is unjust in bringing his wrath on us." Here "wrath" probably does have eschatological elements since it mentions God's judgment of the world (3:6). But far from indicting believers, Paul uses wrath in 3:5 anthropologically to indict the world (or perhaps more specifically Israel, 3:1), which is "under sin" (3:9). In any case there is no hint of hidden love or remediation within God's wrath.

In order for biblical universalism to work, eschatological wrath must be an aspect of God's love. Wrath in the *eschaton* must have a remedial sense; it must seek to reform. Otherwise it remains undiluted anger. But as we have seen, Paul never hints that eschatological wrath reforms or functions as a part of God's love. He never says, for instance, that the wicked will suffer *orgē* in order to bring them to repentance. Rather, one gets the impression that those who fall under eschatological wrath are forever cut off from God's love.

True, 1 Cor. 13:8 says that "love never fails." This might suggest that God's love for mankind — all mankind — is eternal. But this misunderstands chap. 13. Paul is not talking about the enduring love of God that guarantees salvation for all. He is addressing Corinthian believers who consider their spiritual gifts unexcelled, not wicked individuals under God's wrath. Paul attempts to convince his readers that spiritual gifts will pass away, but love will endure forever. To extrapolate from this that God's love abides forever on the wicked and righteous alike is unwarranted.

There is no reason to assume, therefore, that Paul thought that God's love applied to all people at all times.[15] The universalist is mistaken in thinking that God always loves, even in his wrath. Eschatological *orgē* is not a correcting anger that tutors the wicked after death, eventually leading them to repentance. It is genuine anger devoid of love. In Paul's theology, eschatological wrath means that after death God no longer loves the wicked, nor is he prepared to act on behalf of the wicked.

But what does it mean to say that God no longer loves the wicked? Normally when we speak of God's love for his creation we list the ways God has shown his love for humanity. In the OT, for example, the God who loves is the God who delivers his people from the hand of Pharaoh, who supplies a promised land, gives the Torah, protects from enemies, forgives wrongs, and so on.[16] For Paul, as in the OT, God shows his love through his acts in history. His love is revealed in the Christ-event, the Son's selfless act on the cross, his resurrection in power (e.g., Rom. 5:8; 8:35). God's love elects the beloved (1:7-8; 9:13, 25; Col. 3:12), watches over them (e.g., Rom. 8:28, 35; 2 Cor. 5:14; 13:11) and delivers them from the wrath to come (1 Thess. 1:10).

When we speak of God's love, therefore, we mean his merciful acts in history. His love implies action rather than indefinable feelings divorced from deeds. God is prepared to act on behalf of the nation or individual whom he loves. But as we have seen, when Paul talks about eschatological wrath he never hints that God's anger reforms sinners or purges sins. God does not act on behalf of the wicked. Rather, he separates the righteous from the wicked. There

15. A full discussion would have to account for the so-called reconciliation texts (Rom. 8:19-23; 11:26, 32; 1 Cor. 15:22; Eph. 1:10, 23; Phil. 2:6-11; Col. 1:20).

16. Cf. G. E. Wright, *God Who Acts: Biblical Theology as Recital* (SBT; London: SCM, 1952), passim.

is no meaningful way to say that God loves the wicked after death. When God's wrath finally falls on the wicked, love is not concealed in his wrath.

IV. Conclusion

If it is true that (1) *orgē* does not reform and that (2) God's love is positive action on behalf of others, then eschatological wrath for Paul would mean that at the final judgment God no longer is willing to operate on behalf of the wicked. Love would not be concealed in wrath. There would be nothing but wrath for the wicked. To put it another way, God would no longer "love" them. His wrath at the end would be final.

Paul never says explicitly that God's wrath is eternal, but it is clear that he intends it nonetheless. Sometimes wrath is poured out in the present, sometimes at the close of the age. Once under eschatological wrath, however, the plight of the wicked appears to be hopeless. God no longer acts on their behalf but has withdrawn his love from them. His wrath is permanent and eternal.

Universalists will argue that wrath does not function in this way. It is reformative or purgative, not retributive. God loves his creation, they say, and while it may be necessary for him to punish those who persist in wickedness, he does so out of love, with the intent to restore.

But in eschatological wrath, at least, Paul never suggests that *orgē* conceals God's love. To the contrary, in the age to come it excludes love or hope. At times God's anger does bring sinners to repentance, but in these cases Paul chooses words less definitive than *orgē* (e.g., *echthros, apobolē, apotomia*). These and other terms allow for hope; *orgē* does not. Paul reserves the word *orgē* to stress the utter hopelessness of the wicked who are forever lost. Never does he suggest that eschatological *orgē* is remedial or purgative, and never does he hint that love is hidden in the *orgē*, working out a better fate for the wicked. For Paul, *orgē* is the opposite of love, and once life is over, God's wrath is final.

Some Further Contributions to the Discussion

Nikolas Berdyaev, *The Beginning and the End*. Translated by R. M. French. London: Geoffrey Bles, 1952.

G. C. Berkouwer, *The Return of Christ*. Trans. James Van Oosterom. Grand Rapids, MI: Wm. B. Eerdmans Publishing Co., 1972.

James Montgomery Boice, *God of History*. Downers Grove, IL: InterVarsity Press, 1981.

Ladislaus Boros, *Living in Hope*. New York: Herder, 1969.

Carl E. Braaten, *The Future of God*. New York: Harper & Row, 1969.

Emil Brunner, *Eternal Hope*. Trans. Harold Knight. London: Lutterworth, 1954.

Robert G. Clouse, ed., *The Meaning of the Millennium: Four Views*. Downers Grove, IL: InterVarsity Press, 1977.

A. J. Conyers, *The End: What the Gospels Really Say about the Last Things*. Downers Grove, IL: InterVarsity Press, 1995.

Ewert Cousins, ed., *Hope and the Future of Man*. Philadelphia: Fortress Press, 1972.

Jacques Ellul, *Hope in Time of Abandonment*. New York: Seabury Press, 1973.

Millard Erickson, *Contemporary Options in Eschatology*. Grand Rapids, MI: Baker Book House, 1970.

Jean Galot, *The Mystery of Christian Hope*. New York: Alba House, 1977.

Brian Hebblethwaite, *The Christian Hope*. Grand Rapids, MI: Wm. B. Eerdmans Publishing Co., 1984.

Major J. Jones, *Black Awareness: A Theology of Hope*. Nashville: Abingdon Press, 1991.

Hans Küng, *Eternal Life?* Trans. Edward Quinn. Garden City: Doubleday, 1984.

George Ladd, *The Presence of the Future*. Grand Rapids, MI: Wm. B. Eerdmans Publishing Co., 1974.

John Macquarrie, *Christian Hope*. London: SCM Press, Ltd., 1975.

John S. Mbiti, *New Testament Eschatology in an African Background*. London: Oxford University Press, 1971.

Jürgen Moltmann, *Theology of Hope*. Trans. James W. Leitch. London: SCM Press, Ltd./New York: Harper & Row, 1967; 1st Fortress Press edn., Minneapolis: Fortress Press, 1993, c. 1991.

Wolfhart Pannenberg, *Theology and the Kingdom of God*. Philadelphia: Westminster Press, 1969.

Ted Peters, *Futures, Human and Divine*. Atlanta: John Knox Press, 1978.

John A. T. Robinson, *In the End, God*. London: James Clarke, 1950.

Rosemary Radford Ruether, *New Woman, New Earth*. New York: A Crossroad Book, Seabury Press, 1975.

Letty Russell, *The Future of Partnership*. Philadelphia: Westminster Press, 1979.

Hans Schwarz, *On the Way to the Future*. Minneapolis: Augsburg Publishing House, 1972.

Krister Stendahl, ed., *Immortality and Resurrection*. New York: Macmillan, 1965.

Marjorie Suchocki, *The End of Evil: Process Eschatology in Historical Context*. Albany, NY: SUNY/State University of New York Press, 1988.

Geoffrey Wainwright, *Eucharist and Eschatology*. London: Epworth Press, 1971.

Gayraud Wilmore, *Last Things First*. Philadelphia: Westminster Press, 1982.

Alois Winklhofer, *The Coming of His Kingdom*. Trans. A. V. Littledale. New York: Herder and Herder, 1963.

Index of Names and Subjects

547

Index of Biblical References